The Prehistoric
Archaeology of Ireland

The Prehistoric Archaeology of Ireland

John Waddell

TO JANE

First published 1998 by Galway University Press Ltd

This edition 2000 by Wordwell Ltd, Bray, Co. Wicklow

British Library Cataloguing-in-Publication Data.
A catalogue record for this book is available from the British Library.

Printed in Ireland by ColourBooks Ltd, Dublin

ISBN 1 869857 39 9

Cover and title-page motif: a solar boat based on motifs on the 'Petrie crown'; drawing by Angela Gallagher

Contents

Preface

This work is intended as an elementary introduction to the archaeology of prehistoric Ireland and is an attempt to gather together a wide range of material scattered in articles in journals, in books and in monographs. It is first and foremost a book of evidence. Inevitably a process of selection has had to be employed and in some cases various excavations or studies have been chosen and described with the specific intention of illustrating some particular aspect of archaeological methodology or interpretation.

No work of synthesis of this sort is ever complete. Even though this is an attempt to summarize the results of the work of over 150 years in Irish prehistoric archaeology, the dynamic nature of the discipline in Ireland today is clearly demonstrated by the fact that almost a half of the publications cited in the bibliography have appeared in the last decade. Omissions and errors undoubtedly exist and it would be greatly appreciated if these were gently drawn to the author's attention. It is hoped that the summary accounts and numerous illustrations of this large body of evidence will provide students of the subject with the basis for a more detailed thematic and generalized approach to its further study and that the comprehensive bibliography will prove to be a useful reference work for others as well.

The use of the terms Mesolithic, Neolithic, Bronze Age and Iron Age has been abandoned by a number of writers in recent years for a variety of good reasons. However, they still serve as a useful framework particularly where precise chronologies or some other acceptable terminology are still awaited. In Ireland, a detailed radiocarbon chronology is steadily emerging and these terms are dispensed with in this synthesis wherever possible in favour of absolute dates. Apart from some very early dates cited as years BP (before the present – 1950), all dates in the text are given in calibrated calendar years BC or AD and are for the most part based on radiocarbon determinations; the convention of using cal. BC or cal. AD is dispensed with. The corresponding radiocarbon dates are given in the accompanying end-notes with laboratory reference numbers and cited as years BP. The calibrated dates given and simply cited BC should be considered general approximations: some of these date ranges are presented as calculated by the authors cited but most have been calculated using the Groningen Radiocarbon Calibration Programme CAL 10 (at two sigma).

Preface to the 2nd edition

The text of this second edition is the same as that of the first but the opportunity has been taken to correct a number of minor typographical and other errors. The last few years have seen several important studies on various aspects of Irish prehistoric archaeology, and these and other contributions are documented in the *British and Irish Archaeological Bibliography*. The pace of other developments, such as rescue excavation, has increased considerably. Over 600 archaeological investigations are recorded in *Excavations Bulletin, Excavations 1997* (edited by Isabel Bennett, 1998) and over 700 in *Excavations 1998,* published in 2000. The capability to date cremated bone, as reported by J. Lanting and A. L. Brindley in *The Journal of Irish Archaeology* 9 (1998), will have a major impact on the dating of many aspects of Irish archaeology. Important publications include P. C. Woodman, E. Anderson and L. Finlay's *Excavations at Ferriter's Cove, 1983–95: last foragers, first farmers in the Dingle Peninsula* (1999), which contains two significantly early radiocarbon dates for cattle with calibrated date ranges of 4892–4580 BC and 4495–4165 BC, a further contribution to the debate on the origins of insular agriculture as summarized by I. J. Thorpe in his 1996 *The Origins of Agriculture in Europe.* The world of these early farming communities has been further illuminated by G. Cooney and S. Mandal's *The Irish Stone Axe Project, Monograph I* (1998) and by G. Cooney's *Landscapes of Neolithic Ireland* (2000). A later landscape is the subject of W. O'Brien's *Sacred Ground, Megalithic Tombs in Coastal South-west Ireland* (1999), and some megalith-related matters are also examined by C. Ruggles in his *Astronomy in Prehistoric Britain and Ireland* (1999). The debate about ancient Celts and Celticity continues, and it is interesting to compare B. Cunliffe's *The Ancient Celts* (1997) and H. Birkhan's *Celts, Images of their Culture* (1999) with S. James's *The Atlantic Celts, Ancient People or Modern Invention?* (1999). The latter, however, is unaware of the debate in Ireland on such matters since the early 1980s and is not concerned with the linguistic aspects of the issue addressed, for instance, by P. Sims-Williams in 'Celtomania and Celtoscepticism', *Cambrian Medieval Celtic Studies* 36 (1998).

Acknowledgements

I am very grateful to many people for their support and encouragement in the preparation of this work. It would not have been possible without the skills and assistance of Angela Gallagher and of the ever-helpful staff of the Hardiman Library, National University of Ireland, Galway. I am also particularly indebted to my colleagues, Dr William O'Brien, Conor Newman, and Professor Michael O'Connell, all of whom commented on various sections and none of whom, of course, bear responsibility for what eventually transpired. Many others kindly provided information of one sort or another, or facilitated the provision of illustrations, in which regard I am especially grateful to Professor George Eogan, Professor Barry Raftery, the Royal Society of Antiquaries of Ireland, the Ulster Archaeological Society and the Royal Irish Academy.

The sources of the various figures are as follows and this list offers a good indication of the measure of my debt to the work of many friends and colleagues in the field of Irish prehistoric archaeology: Fig. 1 after Mitchell and de G. Sieveking 1972. 2 after Woodman 1978 and 1985 (Crown copyright. Reproduced with the permission of the Controller of Her Majesty's Stationery Office). 3 and 4 after Woodman 1978a. 5 after Clark 1975. 6 after Woodman 1978. 7 from Movius 1940. 8 after Mitchell 1947. 9 after Movius 1953, Woodman 1977 and 1978a, and Woodman and O'Brien 1993. 10 after Anderson 1993. 11 after O'Connell 1994. 12 from Glob Ard og Plov 1951. 13 after ApSimon 1969a, and Gowen 1988 (reconstruction by Eoin Grogan). 14 after Ó Nualláin 1972, and Simpson 1995 and 1996. 15 after Ó Ríordáin 1954. 16 after Grogan and Eogan 1987. 17 after Caulfield 1992. 18 after Bengtsson and Bergh 1984. 19 from Case 1961, after Kilbride-Jones 1939, and Eogan 1984.

Fig. 20 after Lucas 1967. 21 and 22 after Sheridan *et al.* 1992. 23 after Knowles 1886 and 1909. 24 after Lucas 1964a, Eogan 1963, Collins and Seaby 1960, and Collins 1966. 25 after Raftery 1970, and Lucas 1966. 26 after Ó Nualláin 1989, Herity 1974, and Burenhult 1980. 27 after Twohig 1981 by permission of Oxford University Press. 28 after C. O'Kelly 1971. 29 after O'Kelly 1982. 30 after Eogan 1986. 31 after Eogan and Richardson 1982. 32-34 after Twohig 1981 by permission of Oxford University Press. 35 after Eogan 1986, and Bergh 1995. 36 after Herity 1974. 37 after Twohig 1981 by permission of Oxford University Press. 38 after Ó Nualláin 1989, and Waterman 1978. 39 after Waterman 1965, and Ó Nualláin 1972 and 1976.

Fig. 40 after De Valera 1960 and 1965. 41 after Ó Nualláin 1989, and Topp 1962. 42 after Ó Nualláin 1989, Walsh 1995, Herring and May 1937, and Davies 1939a. 43 after O'Kelly 1958. 44 after J. Raftery 1973. 45 after Case 1973, and Lynn 1988 (Crown copyright. Reproduced with the permission of the Controller of Her Majesty's Stationery Office). 46 after Collins 1957a (Crown copyright. Reproduced with the permission of the Controller of Her Majesty's Stationery Office), and Hartwell 1994. 47 after O'Kelly *et al.* 1983, Sweetman 1987, Brennan *et al.* 1978, Earwood 1992, and various authors redrawn by Case 1995. 48 after Harbison 1976 and 1978, Flanagan 1970, Lucas 1971, and Rynne 1972a. 49 after Harbison 1968, and O'Kelly 1970.

Fig. 50 after Harbison 1968, Lucas 1966, and Rynne 1963. 51 after Harbison 1969a, Raftery

1951, Ramsey *et al.* 1992, Lucas 1970, Coghlan and Raftery 1961, and Coffey 1894. 52 after Armstrong 1933, and Butler 1963 after Paton. 53 after Coffey 1909, Harding 1993, and Eogan 1994. 54 after O'Brien 1994. 55 after Ó Ríordáin and Waddell 1993. 56 after Mount 1995, and Ó Ríordáin and Waddell 1993. 57 after Ó Ríordáin and Waddell 1993, and O'Kelly from Waddell 1990. 58 after O'Kelly and Shee 1974. 59 after Kavanagh 1976, Ó Ríordáin 1967, and Williams *et al.* 1992.

Fig. 60 after Rynne 1964a, Ryan 1975, and Longworth 1984. 61 after Hartnett, Waterman 1968, and Grogan 1990. 62 after Hencken 1935, Brindley and Lanting 1992a, and Hencken and Movius 1934. 63 after Coffey 1911, and O'Sullivan and Sheehan 1996. 64 after Fahy 1959, and Pilcher 1969. 65 after O'Kelly 1954. 66 after Coghlan and Raftery 1961. 67 after Evans and Mitchell 1954. 68 after Ramsey 1995. 69 after Burgess 1974, and Burgess and Gerloff 1981.

Fig. 70 after Armstrong 1917, and Eogan 1983. 71 after Burgess 1974. 72-73 after Eogan 1983. 74 after Eogan 1994. 75 after Eogan 1994, and Armstrong 1933. 76-81 from Eogan 1983. 82 after Eogan 1965, and Colquhoun and Burgess 1988. 83-84 after Doody 1987. 85 after Cleary 1995. 86 after O'Kelly 1989. 87-88 after Moloney 1993. 89 after Mallory 1995. 90-91 after Cotter 1993, 1995 and 1996. 92 after Eogan 1983. 93 after Patay 1990, Evans 1881, and Corcoran 1965. 94-95 after Briggs 1987, and Gerloff 1986. 96 after Lucas 1968, and Briggs 1987. 97 after Raftery 1983. 98 after Eogan 1964. 99 after Coles 1963. 100 after Eogan 1964, and Lucas 1961. 101 after Eogan 1983. 102 after Coffey 1913, and Coles 1971a. 103 after Coles 1962, and Almagro 1966. 104 after Raftery 1982. 105 after Ryan 1983, Coles 1962, and Raftery 1982. 106 from Armstrong 1933. 107 after Eogan 1983, and Raftery 1967. 108 from Armstrong 1933. 109 from Hawkes and Clarke 1963.

Figs 110-111 from Eogan 1994. 112 from Eogan 1994, and from Wilde 1862. 113 after Armstrong 1933, and Eogan 1983. 114 after Eogan 1983. 115 after Eogan 1994. 116 after Herity and Eogan 1977. 117 after Eogan 1983. 118 from Wilde 1862, and after Gerloff 1995. 119 after Raftery 1971. 120 after Eogan 1974a. 121 after Eogan 1983. 122 after Fox 1939, Eogan 1983, Eogan 1964, and Burgess 1982. 123 after Eogan 1964, Pryor 1980, and Harding 1976. 124 after Collins and Seaby 1960, and Williams 1978. 125 after Hencken 1942, and

Newman. 126 after Raftery 1942. 127 after Grogan 1993. 128-129 after Raftery 1976, 1975 and 1987, and after Raftery from O'Kelly 1989.

Fig. 130 after Lucas 1972, Smith 1920, Rynne 1962, and Lucas 1968. 131 after Eogan 1965, Coffey 1906, and Lucas 1960. 132 after Eogan 1965, and Colquhoun and Burgess 1988. 133 after Jope 1962, and Eogan 1983. 134 after Scott 1974, and Raftery 1983. 135 after Scott 1974, and Raftery 1983. 136 after Scott 1977, and Raftery 1983. 137 after Scott 1990. 138-139 after Raftery 1983. 140 after Eogan 1983a. 141 after Raftery 1983, and Warner 1982. 142 after Haworth 1971, and Raftery 1983. 143-145 after Raftery 1983. 146 after Raftery 1983, and Pryor 1980. 147 after Raftery 1983. 148 after Raftery 1983, and Raftery 1984 after Duval. 149 after Raftery 1983.

Fig. 150 after Raftery 1983, and Bourke 1993. 151-153 after Raftery 1983. 154 after Raftery 1983, and Sprockhoff 1955. 155 after Raftery 1983. 156 after Caulfield 1977, and Raftery 1994. 157 after Earwood 1989, and Raftery 1983. 158 after Newman 1993. 159 after Newman 1995, and Bhreathnach and Newman 1995. 160 from Bhreathnach and Newman 1995. 161 from Bhreathnach and Newman 1995, and Raftery 1994. 162 after Newman 1993. 163 from Warner 1994. 164 from Lynn 1997 (Crown copyright. Reproduced with the permission of the Controller of Her Majesty's Stationery Office), and Mallory 1985. 165 after Lynn 1986. 166 from Mallory 1985. 167 from Lynn 1986. 168 from Lynn 1986, and Mallory 1985. 169 after Raftery 1987.

Figs 170-171 after Wailes 1990. 172 from Lynn 1991. 173 from Wailes 1990, and Lynn 1991 and 1992. 178 after Condit *et al.* 1991, Raftery 1968, Raftery 1994, and Condit 1992. 179 after Lynn 1989. 180 from the Ordnance Survey Memoranda, courtesy of the Royal Irish Academy, after a photograph from the National Museum of Ireland, after Rynne 1972, and after a photograph from the Ulster Museum. 181 after Duignan 1976, and Raftery 1983. 182 after Lacy 1983, Cuppage 1986, and Raftery 1981. 183 after Warner 1991. 184 after Bourke 1989, and Ó hEailidhe 1992.

Illustrations and Tables

timber circle.

Introduction

A Short History of Prehistoric Archaeology in Ireland

The systematic study of Irish archaeology began in the 1830s with the work of the Ordnance Survey of Ireland which included a methodical programme of recording field monuments and architectural remains. Far from being the blunt colonial instrument depicted in Brian Friel's play *Translations,* the Survey diligently and sympathetically documented the cultural landscape. It included a famous company of scholars, George Petrie (1789-1866), John O'Donovan (1806-1861) and Eugene O'Curry (1796-1862) who combined archaeological evidence, topographical information and the study of early Irish manuscript sources. Their work would eventually completely marginalize an older tradition of antiquarian speculation. At the same time, the Royal Irish Academy began to play an important role in the development of scientific scholarship and to pursue an active policy of acquiring ancient manuscripts and artefacts, the latter eventually to form the nucleus of the archaeological collections of the National Museum of Ireland opened in 1890.

W. F. Wakeman (1822-1900) was a pupil of Petrie's who produced many illustrations for the Ordnance Survey and became an artist, teacher and antiquarian. He published a small book entitled *A Hand-Book of Irish Antiquities* in 1848. About a third of this work is a summary account of the weapons, ornaments, megalithic tombs, burial mounds, stone circles and other monuments of pre-Christian Ireland. For Wakeman, in this pioneering synthesis, these were the relics of a generalized pagan Celtic past and he did not adopt the new archaeological concept of a sequence of 'Three Ages' of Stone,

Bronze and Iron. Revised and expanded editions of this work were published in 1891 and (by J. Cooke) in 1903.

Although the idea of remote ages of stone, bronze or iron was familiar to some Greek, Roman and Renaissance writers, it was not until the 19th century that the concept was applied in a practical way to a body of archaeological material. The archaeological principle of a Three Age system of a Stone Age, a Bronze Age and an Iron Age was first employed in 1819 by C. J. Thomsen in the National Museum of Denmark when the collections were rearranged and exhibited in three separate cases reflecting these three consecutive ages. This famous and influential hypothesis, simple, effective and radical, was published by Thomsen in Danish and German in the 1830s and in English in 1848. The idea was developed by J. J. A. Worsaae, another celebrated Danish archaeologist, who visited Ireland and addressed the Royal Irish Academy on two occasions in 1846 and firmly placed Irish megalithic tombs, for instance, those 'stone structures called *Cromlechs, Druidical altars, etc.*', in the Stone Period. Both of his contributions were promptly published in the *Proceedings of the Royal Irish Academy* in 1847, and in the 1849 English translation of his book, *The Primeval Antiquities of Denmark*, various Irish stone, bronze and iron finds were allocated to their respective periods. This evolutionary model of successive ages offered a new framework for studying the material remains of the past, one that provided chronological depth and enshrined the principle of the progressive typological development of tools and weapons.[1]

'RELICS OF VERY DIFFERENT AND DISTINCT PERIODS ...'

Despite its potential, the Three Age model found only limited application in Irish scholarly circles in the 19th century. The apparently contemporaneous use of stone, copper and bronze was one reason for scepticism. Thus when drainage operations on the River Shannon at Keelogue, near Portumna, Co. Galway, in the early 1840s, were said to have uncovered a number of stone axes stratified some 30cm below a layer of gravel containing bronze weapons, the claim for the discovery of stone and bronze 'relics of very different and distinct periods' prompted considerable controversy. It was dismissed by Eugene O'Curry in his lectures in 1860 on weapons and warfare; he had been appointed Professor of Irish History and Archaeology in 1854 in the newly founded Catholic University of Ireland. Nonetheless, the very claim is interesting because here we find an early instance of the use of the stratigraphic method, still the basis of archaeological excavation, and an early appreciation of its significance.[2]

William Wilde (1815-1876), eminent medical doctor and amateur archaeologist, was, of course, aware of the Three Age system and around 1850 did assign stone tombs to a stone age which was followed by a bronze age and iron age. However, he did not adopt this model when commissioned to compile a catalogue of the large collection of antiquities in the museum of the Royal Irish Academy even though this was probably the preference of the organising committee chaired by Petrie. Perhaps because of the scale and urgency of the undertaking, Wilde organized the artefacts according to material and use and the first of three volumes, entitled *Catalogue of the Antiquities of Stone, Earthen and Vegetable Materials in the Museum of the Royal Irish Academy*, was published in 1857. Volumes on animal materials and bronze, and on gold, followed in 1861 and 1862. This detailed and illustrated account of over 10,000 objects was a remarkable achievement, the first general classification of Irish archaeological material and one of the first comprehensive museum catalogues.[3]

Various reasons contributed to the disinclination to make full use of the Three Age system. The absence of incontrovertible stratigraphical evidence was evidently one but what O'Curry called 'reasons drawn from a history not yet overthrown, nor likely to be' was another significant inhibiting factor.

O'Curry, Wilde, and others of this generation were greatly influenced by early Irish history and legend. This period witnessed an extraordinary amount of publication of early literary texts, and more often than not archaeological inquiry and the historical study of a Celtic past became inextricably intertwined. That the combination of physical evidence with native manuscript sources was an acceptable methodology is well illustrated in O'Curry's attempts to equate various prehistoric implements and weapons with objects mentioned in early Irish literature and in Petrie's pioneering and more judicious studies of the antiquities on the hill of Tara and of round towers published in 1839 and 1845 respectively. As one 19th century writer put it 'the monument verifies the history and the history identifies the monument, and both become mutually illustrative'.[4]

The chronological implications of a pattern of successive prehistoric ages and the adoption and refinement of the system in Britain and in Europe were not ignored however, and the concept was used with increasing frequency in the latter part of the 19th century. W. G. Wood-Martin (1847-1917) noted it and the attendant chronological uncertainties in his *The Lake Dwellings of Ireland* published in 1886. In 1888, in his *Rude Stone Monuments of Ireland*, a compendium of his studies of the megalithic tombs of Sligo and Achill, he remarked that the Stone Age was now subdivided into two eras, the Palaeolithic or old stone age characterized by chipped stone implements and the Neolithic or new stone age in which implements were sometimes polished with 'distinct traces of an advance in the art of fabrication'. The terms Palaeolithic and Neolithic were first used in Britain by Sir John Lubbock in his *Prehistoric Times* in 1865. Wood-Martin's *Pagan Ireland*, published in 1895, like the third edition of Wakeman's *Handbook* which appeared eight years later, was a synthesis with lengthy accounts of the artefacts and monuments of prehistoric Ireland and a recognition that this island shared in many of the prehistoric developments detected in Britain and on the Continent. Although it was also recognized that much of this material could be assigned in a general way to a Neolithic period, a Bronze Age or an Iron Age, this conceptual arrangement consistently failed to provide a clear sequential pattern in what Wood-Martin described as 'the huge mass of undigested matter now accumulated in the pages of learned societies'.

Ireland's role in a wider European context was one of the themes of W. C. Borlase's three-volume *Dolmens of Ireland*, published in 1897, the first study of the megalithic tombs of the country as a whole. He described over 890 monuments in this remarkable work and compared various Irish tombs to examples in Britain, Continental Europe and the Mediterranean world. This wider context was the principal theme of George Coffey's papers on the origins of prehistoric ornament in Ireland published in the *Journal of the Royal Society of Antiquaries of Ireland* from 1894 to 1897. Here and in his 1912 study of *New Grange (Brugh na Boinne) and other incised tumuli in Ireland*, he, like others at the time, ultimately derived the spiral design from the eastern Mediterranean around 1600 BC. Coffey (1857-1916), who in various publications demonstrates a breadth of scholarship and an appreciation of the significance of typological evolution and of the chronological importance of associated finds, was appointed keeper of antiquities in the National Museum of Ireland at the turn of the century where he transformed the collections. He deserves to be remembered as Ireland's first archaeologist of international stature. The elements of a more explicit linear narrative were to appear in the early decades of the new century in his work and in the publications of E. C. R. Armstrong and R. A. S. Macalister in particular.

The absolute dating of the Stone and Bronze Ages still remained uncertain, though it was now appreciated that they spanned several thousands of years before the Christian era. It was the Swedish archaeologist, Oscar Montelius (1843-1921) who first offered a considered calendrical chronology based on cross-dating. The discovery of objects in direct association, in a grave or a hoard for example, may indicate their contemporaneity, and if an example of a particular artefact type could be correlated with the historical chronologies of the Near East then absolute dates could be extrapolated. Similarities between European and eastern Mediterranean material and actual imports were the two significant elements in this process which though imprecise was the only mechanism for chronological estimation before the discovery of chronometric dating methods such as radiocarbon dating. Many complex relative and absolute chronological schemes were formulated on this basis in the late 19th and in the first half of the 20th century in various parts of Europe and there was an

understandable fixation with the question of direct and indirect Mediterranean connections. The rich civilizations of the Near East were often seen as the inspiration for major developments in European prehistory such as stone tomb building and metalworking. This diffusionist model explained such innovations in terms of trade or the migration of people. In 1885, Montelius divided the northern Bronze Age into five consecutive numbered periods and in 1895 he divided the Neolithic into four. In 1909, in a prescient paper in the journal *Archaeologia*, he extended his Bronze Age scheme to Britain and Ireland and presented a relative chronology of five successive periods to which he gave absolute dates based on Continental evidence; his Period I was a Copper Age commencing about 2500 BC, his final Period V ending about 800 BC. Although he followed the subdivisions proposed by Montelius, Coffey was more cautious and in his book *The Bronze Age in Ireland*, published in 1913, he dated an Irish copper period from 2000 to 1800 BC, with the ensuing Bronze Age extending from 1800 to about 350 BC.

E. C. R. Armstrong (1879-1923) was Coffey's successor in the National Museum and continued this tradition of scholarship with a major catalogue of the prehistoric gold collections, the first edition of which appeared in 1920. Two important papers, one published in 1923, the other a posthumous publication in 1924, were the first detailed accounts of the two phases of the Iron Age, which, following Continental practice, were called the Hallstatt Period and the La Tène Period. In the 1920s, though he had promulgated the term Mesolithic for a middle stone age period between the Palaeolithic and the Neolithic in his 1921 *Text-Book of European Archaeology*, R. A. S. Macalister was reluctant to adopt the term for Ireland. Nonetheless, just over a century after Thomsen had rearranged the archaeological collections in Copenhagen, and after much modification of his basic Three Age system, it is fair to say that a broad chronological framework for Irish prehistory – divided into Stone, Bronze and Iron Ages – was in place. This framework has been further modified since then and is still widely used (Table 1). R. A. S. Macalister (1871-1950) was appointed Professor of Celtic Archaeology in University College, Dublin, in 1909 and was a dominant figure in Irish archaeology for several decades. A prolific contributor to learned journals and author of many books on a variety of topics, he

Traditional phases in Irish prehistory	Approximate dates
Early Mesolithic	7000-5500 BC
Later Mesolithic	5500-4000 BC
Neolithic	4000-2400 BC
Copper Age	2400-2200 BC
Early Bronze Age	2200-1500 BC
Middle Bronze Age	1500-1000 BC
Late Bronze Age	1000-600 BC
Iron Age	600 BC-400 AD

Table 1. Traditional periodization.

also produced a number of important syntheses of Irish prehistoric archaeology. His *Ireland in Pre-Celtic Times* was published in 1921, *The Archaeology of Ireland* in 1928 with a second edition in 1949 and *Ancient Ireland* appeared in 1935.[5]

A NEW ERA

A new era in prehistoric studies began in the 1930s and was marked by a series of field surveys and a number of significant excavations to a modern standard. Estyn Evans (1905-1989) and Oliver Davies (1905-1986) initiated a series of excavations of megalithic tombs with their examination of a tomb at Goward, Co. Down, in 1932. Many of the subsequent excavations in the north of Ireland were published in the *Ulster Journal of Archaeology* which today continues the tradition of publishing important excavation reports. The same year saw the first of a programme of major excavations by the Harvard Archaeological Mission. Hugh Hencken and Hallam Movius excavated a prehistoric burial mound at Knockast, near Moate, in Co. Westmeath, this was followed by a crannog with late prehistoric levels at Ballinderry, Co. Offaly, in 1933, a cairn at Poulawack, in the Burren, Co. Clare, and at coastal sites at Cushendun and Glenarm, Co. Antrim, in 1934, and the Creevykeel megalithic tomb, near Cliffony, Co. Sligo, and at Curran Point, Co. Antrim, in 1935. The excavation of an early Historic crannog at Ballinderry, Co. Westmeath, prompted an early dendrochronological experiment using ash wood which was not successful. A Government Special Employment Scheme initiated in 1934 provided significant amounts of state monies for excavation and no less than 26 were undertaken in the following four years alone.

With the support of the Royal Irish Academy and of Adolf Mahr, Director of the National Museum of Ireland, a Quaternary Research Committee was established; Knud Jessen of Copenhagen was invited to undertake a programme of pollen analysis in Irish bogs and this effectively marked the commencement of the study of the island's vegetation history. The first report on this work appeared in the *Irish Naturalists' Journal* in 1934 and Jessen's work was published in the *Proceedings of the Royal Irish Academy* in 1949.[6] The first detailed review of the physical anthropology of the prehistoric population was attempted in 1935 by C. P. Martin in his *Prehistoric Man in Ireland*. The first comprehensive survey of field monuments commenced in Northern Ireland in 1935 and included an aerial photographic survey of the linear earthwork known as the Black Pig's Dyke; a preliminary inventory was published in 1940. Many of the developments of the 1930s were summarized by Mahr in his Presidential Address to the Prehistoric Society in 1937. Not surprisingly, this pace of development did not continue in the 1940s. Nevertheless in 1942 Hallam Movius published *The Irish Stone Age* and in the same year Seán P. Ó Ríordáin (1905-1957), then Professor of Archaeology in University College, Cork, published the first of several editions of his *Antiquities of the Irish Countryside*, an account of the major categories of field monument. A synthesis by Joseph Raftery (1913-1992) entitled *Prehistoric Ireland* and written in the early years of the war, was published in 1951. The work of the war years was reviewed by Ó Ríordáin in 1946.

The preoccupation with chronological sequences which marked archaeological studies in the late 19th and early 20th century was in time modified by the influential concept of archaeological cultures. Borrowed from German prehistorians of the later 19th century, this new classificatory device was defined in English by Gordon Childe in his 1929 *The Danube in Prehistory*. He defined an archaeological culture as a recurring archaeological assemblage which was the material expression of a particular group of people: 'pot, implements, ornaments, burial rites, house forms – constantly recurring together'. This concept was an important stimulus in combining chronological and spatial analysis and in the recognition of discrete social units. Now it became possible to view prehistory not just in terms of an evolutionary progression of periods, in a sort of vertical stratigraphical sequence, but also in horizontal, spatial or geographical terms as well. It became possible to envisage an ancient Europe composed of an intricate mosaic of definable prehistoric groups changing through time, the 'Beaker Folk' of the later third millennium BC being one classic example. In Ireland, over the years, though the principle of temporal and spatial analysis was firmly established, this model found expression in the identification of a number of loosely defined (and sometimes relatively short-lived) concepts such as the Larnian Culture, the Riverford Culture, the Clyde-Carlingford Culture, and the Boyne Culture, terms all used in either Movius' *The Irish Stone Age* or in Childe's *Prehistoric Communities of the British Isles* in 1940.[7]

The appointment of Martyn Jope (1915-1996) to the Department of Archaeology in Queen's University, Belfast, in 1949, along with the arrival of Dudley Waterman (1918-1979) and A. E. P. Collins (who died in 1991) to work in the newly established Archaeological Survey of Northern Ireland gave further impetus to archaeological research in the north of Ireland. Much of their work was published in the *Ulster Journal of Archaeology* and included major excavation reports and important artefact studies. Waterman began a major excavation at Navan, Co. Armagh, in 1961. The work of the Archaeological Survey in Co. Down was published in a monumental volume in 1966. Excavation and field survey proceeded elsewhere too. Ó Ríordáin, who became Professor of Archaeology in University College, Dublin, in 1943, published many excavation reports in the 1950s including some of the results of his investigations at Lough Gur, Co. Limerick. In 1952 he turned his attention to Tara. His death in 1957 meant that work there had to be completed by his successor in University College, Dublin, Ruaidhrí de Valera, but sad to say, forty years on, the Tara excavations were still unpublished. When in the Ordnance Survey of Ireland, De Valera and his colleague Seán Ó Nualláin had begun a survey of megalithic tombs in 1949; an account of the monuments of Achill was published in the *Journal of the Royal Society of Antiquaries of Ireland* in 1950, several large monographs followed and the work continues to the present day. A general survey of archaeological monuments began in the Republic in 1963 but progress was painfully slow and effective results

were not achieved until the early 1980s.[8] M. J. O'Kelly (1915-1982), Professor of Archaeology in University College, Cork, was also active in the field of prehistoric archaeology; among his excavations was the first modern study and experimental assessment of burnt mounds believed to be ancient cooking places. He was instrumental in obtaining the first radiocarbon dates in Irish archaeology for two of these sites at Killeens, Co. Cork, which he excavated in 1953.[9] He commenced a major programme of excavation and conservation at Newgrange, Co. Meath, in 1962 and George Eogan began excavations in the complex of monuments at nearby Knowth in the same year. These activities and the researches of many others in the following decades are recounted in the following pages. Since the mid-1960s there has been an impressive amount of excavation, systematic field survey and artefact studies in metalwork and pottery in particular, and a significant increase in the application of scientific techniques. Palynological studies have produced an increasingly detailed picture of vegetation history and of the human impact on the landscape. Radiocarbon dating has provided a more refined chronological picture and major advances in dendrochronological studies in Queen's University, Belfast, have been of enormous significance.

The principal methodological or theoretical approaches have been empirical (the practical collection and analysis of data) and cultural-historical. The cultural-historical approach was concerned with the identification of discrete archaeological entities which might correlate with distinct population groups or specific peoples in time or in space. Since archaeologists, like many other specialists, are sometimes in error but rarely in doubt, disputes and debates did occur, focusing on topics such as the origins of various tomb-builders or on the thorny question of the manner and date of the coming of the Celts. Until the 1970s a fairly mechanistic interpretative model of cultural development prevailed, for the most part prehistoric Ireland was considered to have comprised a varying kaleidoscope of successive peoples, Mesolithic hunters were followed by Neolithic farmers, Early Bronze Age Beaker folk, Food vessel people, Urn folk, Iron Age Celts, and so on. Changes in the archaeological record were considered to be the result of isolated factors such as invasion or migration or the diffusion of technological innovation. This is the essential framework, for example, of Michael Herity and George Eogan's *Ireland in Prehistory*, published in 1977.

THE MODERN ERA

The modern phase of theoretical debate began in the 1960s which witnessed a growing dissatisfaction with the traditional concept of archaeological cultures and the diffusionist explanations employed; this decade saw the emergence of what came to be called the 'new archaeology' which, among its concerns, included scientific method and explicit theory, and the objective not merely to describe but also to explain the processes involved in cultural change. Following systems theory, culture was seen as a system with various component subsystems such as social organization, environment, economy, technology and religion. Change initiated in one component element could promote change in one or more other elements of the system and this approach offered the possibility of explaining change in terms of internal rather than external factors. In the 1970s the 'new archaeology' became known as processual archaeology because of its focus on explanation and the process of change. Rather than offering a historical explanation, processual archaeology seeks to explain matters in terms of cultural process involving the study of the interrelationships between the social, economic, environmental and other components in a cultural system. Research has focused on such factors as trade and exchange, the analysis of settlement patterns, social organization, and on what has been called peer polity interaction – the relationship between societies with similar patterns of development and internal change. Processual archaeology with its positivist emphasis on social and economic explanation is now a major school of archaeological theory. However, early practitioners were criticized for their mechanistic or functionalist approach which was preoccupied with economic explanation and with attempts to formulate general laws of human behaviour. A cognitive-processual approach seeks to combine some aspects of processual archaeology with some more recent developments since the mid-1980s.

The term post-processual is often applied to a diverse series of reactions to processual archaeology – though some of its proponents would consider it an archaeological philosophy in its own right. Post-processualists, prompted by developments in post-modernist social and literary theory, believe that the significance of individual behaviour, aspects of cognition such as belief systems and perception and symbolic behaviour have been underestimated or suppressed in processual archaeology. Inspired by structuralism or deconstructionism, some seek to discover patterns reflecting conceptual structures, others argue that material culture, rather than being an objective record of the past, should be considered as text to be read and interpreted in different ways, all interpretations being of equal validity. Processual archaeology, or more precisely cognitive-processualism, now accepts the value of studying belief systems and the significance of ideology and the role of individual creativity but rejects the more extreme relativist aspects of post-processualism.

So brief a sketch of the broad development of archaeological theory, from cultural-historical to processual to post-processual archaeology, might give the impression of a simple linear development, but this would be entirely misleading. The European experience has been extraordinarily diverse, very often with a selective adoption of processualist and post-processualist ideas.[10] This approach has been the Irish experience and the main influences of processual archaeology are probably to be seen in a more rigorous approach to data and the emphasis placed on scientific method, and in a rejection of simple diffusionist models. The pragmatic identification and description of archaeological entities such as metalworking phases or ceramic traditions and the determination of patterns of social interaction and cultural affinity continue to be the norm. There have, of course, been a number of studies since the late 1970s prompted by developments in processual and post-processualist archaeology but the only sustained analysis has been Gabriel Cooney and Eoin Grogan's recent *Irish prehistory: a social perspective* published in 1994.[11]

It is evident that the study of Irish prehistoric archaeology has made enormous progress in a century and a half and, without doubt, new discoveries will continue to illuminate the prehistoric past and new theoretical approaches will demand the reappraisal of old ideas once considered sound and sensible. Prehistoric archaeology will continue to show how communities on this island constantly transformed themselves and will still provide an important long perspective to the island story. There are, needless to say, many facets to this story and some of them are very visible in the archaeological record. Ritual and symbolism, and monuments and artefacts associated with cult, ceremony and display are conspicuous. This is not surprising, in pre-industrial societies the supernatural and natural worlds were not the segregated entities they are today. In the prehistoric past the world and much in it was richly charged with magical and superstitious meaning. A persistent preoccupation with ritual – which, apart from agriculture, has left a greater mark on the Irish archaeological landscape than any other activity – is inevitably a significant theme in the following pages. Less perceptible is evidence for subsistence and agriculture, yet the food quest and the daily round of the farming year were the pre-eminent preoccupations of the majority of the population, millennium after millennium. There is more discernible evidence for social and economic interaction, including trade and exchange, and the products of various technologies – notably stone, pottery, bronze and iron – attest to this. Here again there is bias in the surviving record, wood and leather were probably more important products in various spheres yet are preserved only in exceptional circumstances. Interaction between communities was another constant on both a regional and a wider scale and a recurring theme is the importance of riverine and coastal traffic and the abiding importance of the Irish Sea as a perennial means of contact with various parts of England, Wales and Scotland.

NOTES

1 Brief histories of Irish archaeology: Mitchell 1985; Herity and Eogan 1977, 4. O'Donovan: Boyne 1987. Petrie: Stokes 1868; J. Raftery 1972. Wakeman: de hÓir 1990. Worsaae in Ireland: Henry 1995. For the term 'prehistory': Chippendale 1988; Clermont and Smith 1990.

2 Keelogue: Griffiths 1843; the claim was retracted in 1858 according to O'Curry 1873, 267, also p. ccccvii.

3 William Wilde: Kavanagh 1992; Wilson 1942. Wilde 1850, 223, ascribes cromlechs and kistvaens, some stone weapons and other objects to a stone age and accepts the Three Age concept in broad outline and with some reservations in 1857 and 1861.

4 The quotation is from Stokes' biography of Petrie (1868, 95). For the controversies surrounding Petrie's work: Leerssen 1996, 100.

5 Coffey, Armstrong and Macalister: Mitchell 1985. Bibliography of Macalister's published works: Brennan 1973 with additions in de hÓir 1993.

6 Quaternary Research Committee: Mitchell 1990, 11.

7 Archaeological cultures: Meinander 1981.

8 Archaeological survey: Power 1993; Haworth 1975.

9 These archaeological samples were dated by Willard Libby at the University of Chicago (C-877 and C-878); the first Irish materials to be radiocarbon dated were palynological samples (C-355, C-356 and C-358) submitted by G. F. Mitchell (information from Anna Brindley). The first radiocarbon dating facility was established in the Physics Department, Trinity College, Dublin, in 1959: *Radiocarbon* 3, 26.

10 General works on archaeological theory include Trigger 1989; Hodder 1991; Dark 1995; Ucko 1995; Renfrew and Bahn 1996, 36, 369, 441, 461. Severe cases of post-processual *angst* should read Bradley 1993.

11 Archaeological theory in Ireland: Cooney 1993a and 1995b. There is a growing understanding of the role of political ideologies in the formation of archaeological opinion: Woodman 1995; Cooney 1996; Stout 1996 (for a confessedly partial assessment of some of the work of Estyn Evans).

1

Postglacial Ireland
The First Colonists

he Ice Ages of the remote past, which have left such an indelible impression on the Irish landscape, are a dramatic prologue to the human story on this island. Our knowledge of the Ice Ages in Ireland is largely limited to the events of the last 300,000 years or so. The greater part of Ireland was covered, at least twice, by extensive ice sheets of considerable thickness. The movement of these masses of ice scoured the surface of the land and numerous geomorphological features testify to their passing. Periods of milder temperatures varied in degree and duration and several warm phases have been identified. The present, relatively warm, climatic period, which we happily call 'postglacial' may, in the distant future, prove to be yet another interglacial phase. The suggested dates for these cold and warm phases, particularly the earlier ones, are very tentative indeed. Two great glaciations are well known, the Munsterian (about 200,000-130,000 BP) and the Midlandian (115,000-10,000 BP).

The Munsterian glaciation engulfed the whole of Ireland at one time or another with the possible exception of some mountainous areas in the south-west. The last or Midlandian glaciation covered the northern and central parts of the island with local icecaps in the Cork-Kerry and Wicklow mountains. Many drumlins such as those in Leitrim, Cavan, Monaghan, the Clew Bay area, and north of Ennis in Co. Clare, and the long esker ridges which are such a prominent feature of the midlands, were a product of the dissolution of these ice sheets around 17,000 BP. At the height of this ice age, at about 25,000 BP, the southern part of Ireland probably experienced peri-glacial conditions with an extremely cold climate. However, during the long timespan of this glaciation there were several cold (stadial) and warmer (interstadial) phases when the larger fauna recorded included woolly mammoth, brown bear, giant Irish deer, reindeer, wolf, horse, red deer and arctic fox. A programme of radiocarbon dating of animal bone samples from Irish caves has shown that these animals were present in Ireland before the maximum advance of the last, Midlandian, ice sheet some 25,000 years ago. While there are traces of human occupation in south-eastern England from as early as a half a million years ago, no such evidence has as yet been found in Ireland.[1]

Various claims for the presence of such Palaeolithic or 'Old Stone Age' people are now discounted. What were thought to be primitive stone implements from north-eastern Ireland and from Co. Sligo are now known to be flakes of natural origin. A hand-axe found in a limestone crevice in Dún Aonghasa, Aran, is a genuine example but the date and circumstances of its loss or deposition there are uncertain. Human bones, found in Kilgreany cave, north-west of Dungarvan, Co. Waterford, were associated with the remains of giant deer but deposits in the cave were greatly disturbed by a fluctuating water table and radiocarbon dating of some of the human bones has indicated that these are of more recent, fourth millennium BC, date. However, a small but relatively thick flint flake, measuring 85mm in maximum length, found in Mell townland, near Drogheda, Co. Louth (Fig. 1) apparently came from a deposit of glacial gravel of Munsterian age; a broad striking platform and prominent bulb of percussion

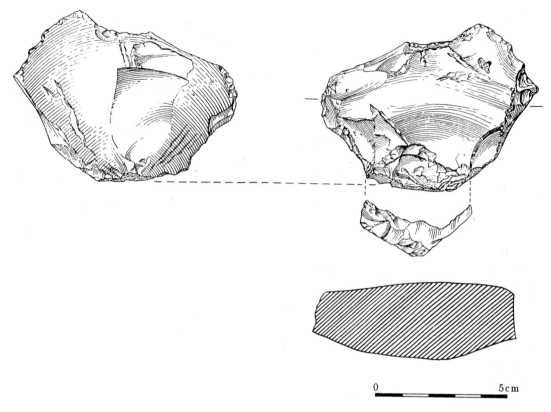

Fig. 1. Struck flint flake of Munsterian age found near Drogheda, Co. Louth.

indicate that it was struck from its parent core by direct percussion with a hard hammer, a technique found in the Clactonian and Acheulian stone industries of southern England. The Drogheda flake is merely a piece of flint worker's waste and it is slightly rolled or blunted by water action so it may have been collected somewhere in the Irish Sea area, along with other debris, by the advancing ice of the Munsterian glaciation. As G. F. Mitchell has remarked, this flake does not demonstrate very early human activity in Ireland, but it does suggest that such hunting and foraging groups may have travelled westwards as far as what was later to become the basin of the Irish Sea. At present, the earliest evidence for a human presence in Ireland is of postglacial date.[2]

A rise in temperature around 13,000 BP marks the commencement of the well-defined Woodgrange interstadial of the late glacial period and heralds the end of the last Ice Age. An arctic or sub-arctic grassy tundra had been gradually established and species of dock (*Rumex*) were prominent. Such a Gramineae-*Rumex* pollen zone is clearly identifiable in a pollen record from Woodgrange, Co. Down, and elsewhere and is followed, as temperatures continued to rise, by the appearance and strong expansion of juniper and some birch (*Betula*) copses in suitably sheltered areas. The improvement in climate did not continue uninterrupted, there was a climatic deterioration around 12,000 BP and juniper and birch were largely replaced by grasslands which provided rich grazing for great herds of reindeer and giant Irish deer. It is conceivable that, as elsewhere in western Europe, these herds of herbivores could have attracted the attention of Palaeolithic hunting groups, but, as already mentioned, no evidence has yet been found.

Severe arctic conditions were to make a brief return: a cold spell known as the Nahanagan stadial, named after Lough Nahanagan, in Co. Wicklow, where it was first recognized, lasted for almost 1000 years and came to an end about 10,000 BP. The grasslands of the Woodgrange interstadial and the giant Irish deer did not survive this icy interlude which immediately preceded the postglacial period. As the ice finally retreated and the climate improved, various plants and animals again colonized the country. At this time there may have been temporary land-bridges with Britain, for, with a considerable body of water locked in ice further to the north, the sea was perhaps 10m-16m below its present level *c.* 9000 BP. However, the continued melting of the ice resulted in a rise in sea-level, a phenomenon termed eustasy, which eventually severed the two islands. This is one of the reasons given for Ireland's considerably more limited range of plant and animal types than Britain. Ireland has only about fourteen native species of mammal and four of these, wild boar, wild cat, brown bear and wolf, are now extinct. Rising sea levels may have combined with other factors, both climatic and geographical, to contribute to a floral and faunal impoverishment which left a smaller variety of mammals for the earliest settlers to hunt. The postglacial mammalian fauna included, in addition to the four extinct species mentioned, wild pig, badger, otter, fox, hare, stoat, red squirrel, pygmy shrew, woodmouse and pinemarten. Whether red deer was present at this time is uncertain.[3]

The rise in temperature in postglacial times continued until the fourth millennium BC and from about 6000 BC there was a climatic optimum which lasted for several thousand years. This was a period of increased summer and winter warmth, the mean annual temperature being one or two degrees centigrade higher than that of today. The changing climate had, of course, a considerable effect on the composition of the vegetation. In general, extensive birch woods were eventually supplanted by forests of pine and hazel, and these in turn were replaced to varying degrees by oak and elm. There was considerable variation in Britain and Ireland, and, not surprisingly, local variations occurred too. Pine, for example, continued to be of considerable importance in parts of the west of Ireland including the Burren in Co. Clare and parts of Connemara and Mayo. Broad generalizations are possible and several authorities have divided the history of vegetational development in late and postglacial times into various phases. A sequence proposed for Scandinavia at the turn of the century has been modified for Ireland by several writers, including G. F. Mitchell (Table 2). Pollen analyses and radiocarbon determinations are now giving us

Approximate dates	Northern Europe	Britain	Ireland (Mitchell 1956)	Major developments in vegetation
			X Modern	Partial reafforestation from 1700AD
AD BC 1200 BC	Sub-Atlantic	VIII	IX Christian VIIIb Pagan	Final Tudor clearances Renewed farming activity and forest clearances following woodland regeneration Climatic deterioration Oak, ash
2500 BC	Sub-Boreal	VIIb	VIIIa	Oak, elm, hazel. Blanket bog in west. Forest clearance and regeneration. Pine declines
3800 BC				Elm decline
	Atlantic	VIIa	VII	Alder, oak, elm. Dense deciduous woodland. Birch and pine on uplands
5800 BC				Appearance of alder
	Boreal	VI V	VI Boreal V	Pine, oak, elm, hazel on limestone, birch. Raised bogs form in midlands. Hazel, birch
9000 BC				
	Pre-Boreal	IV	IV	Birch, willow, juniper
10000 BC	Late glacial			

Table 2. Simplified outline of the vegetation history of Ireland

an increasingly detailed picture of the changing environment in Ireland in the last 10,000 years.

The postglacial vegetation sequence commences with Zone IV in which climatic amelioration and a rapid rise in temperature saw juniper and willow (*Salix*) quickly overshadowed by the expansion of birch (*Betula*) woodlands. With increasing temperatures hazel (*Corylus*) quickly expanded to form the dominant woodland cover throughout the country in Zone V. This early dominance of hazel is characteristic of early vegetation development throughout Europe but was particularly marked in Ireland. Hazel had soon to compete with tall canopy trees and the first of these was Scots pine (*Pinus sylvestris*) and then elm (*Ulmus*) and oak (*Quercus*) which eventually expand rapidly at the expense of birch in Zone VI. The boundary between Zone VI (Boreal) and VII (Atlantic) is marked by the appearance and expansion of alder (*Alnus*).

This brief sketch, of course, obscures the fact that there was considerable regional variation in this forested landscape. Oak and elm dominated the midlands with pine probably confined to the margins of the developing raised bogs. Hazel was probably the main tall shrub in most areas. Pine remained important in the north and in the west, even in the Burren, and continued to be significant in woodlands and on peat until about 2000 BC after which it declined rapidly and was extinct in most areas by the end of the last millennium BC.

It is possible that early hunters and foragers interfered with the forest cover from the seventh millennium BC but, if this happened, it seems never to have been extensive: the fluctuations that occur in the pollen record could be due to natural causes. In general, there seems to have been little human interference with the great primeval forest cover until it was assailed by early farmers around 4000 BC.[4]

The improved postglacial climate and the woodland cover favoured wild fauna such as pig, wolf, fox and bear. Wild pig and a variety of birds and fish were to become the main prey of groups of hunters and food-gatherers moving westwards from Britain, though how these early colonists came is unclear. The eustatic rise in sea-level may have completely severed Ireland and Britain some time around 8000 BP but the history of land and sea relationships at this time is a complex one, still imperfectly understood. Late and postglacial changes in the Irish coastline occurred at different times in different places and for various reasons. The story is not simply one of continuous eustatic inundation, isostatic changes (namely changes in the level of the land in relation to the sea) also took place. With the disappearance of the great weight of Midlandian ice, which had covered the north of Ireland in particular, the land rose and its rise, in some areas, exceeded the eustatic rise in sea level. Some of the submerged peat deposits and forests around the Irish coast, and indeed some drowned archaeological sites, are testimony of the latter phenomenon. Some old submerged forests near Bray, Co. Wicklow, and at Roddansport, Co. Down, were presumably drowned by the sea as it rose to its maximum. Other drowned peaty deposits and trees may be of more recent, prehistoric, date. In Boreal and Atlantic times the rising sea also deposited marine clays in sheltered lagoons in parts of the north-east of Ireland and elsewhere. At Cushendun, Co. Antrim, for example, the rising waves deposited several metres of silts and gravels on a layer of freshwater peat, and the flint implements of hunting and foraging groups were incorporated in these deposits as the sites of their camps were washed away by the slowly rising sea.

The maximum marine transgression, when the sea had risen to as much as 4m above present level, occurred around 4000 BC in many coastal parts, but in the northern half of Ireland, as in parts of Scotland, the isostatic rise of the land continued or resumed. It raised shore lines above the level of the high tide mark producing postglacial raised beaches. These are deposits of shingle or wave-cut platforms, several metres above present sea level, which are to be seen today from Donegal to Drogheda. These ancient shorelines were seasonally frequented by hunters and foragers.

EARLY HUNTERS AND FORAGERS: 7000–5500 BC

An early settlement at Mount Sandel (Upper), Co. Derry, was situated south of Coleraine on a bluff overlooking the valley of the River Bann. Excavation by Peter Woodman from 1973 to 1977 explored a relatively large area of almost 700 square metres and while traces of activity, such as pits and hearths, were scattered over the site, the most significant discovery was an occupation area measuring about 10m by 7m containing the remains of huts. Though the site had been eroded and had been disturbed by post-Medieval agriculture, a charcoal-flecked occupation soil with a maximum depth of 10cm, and pits, hearths and other features did survive in places. A small, artificially enlarged hollow in the ground contained a large number of post-holes and stake-holes some of which could be identified as the remains of several circular huts. These had been constructed, as some sloping post-holes (placed in the ground at an angle of 60°) suggested, with saplings bent over and tied together to produce a more-or-less circular tent-like structure presumably roofed with hides or other materials which left no trace (Fig. 2). They were fairly substantial structures, the saplings were up to 20cm in diameter. Some hearths cut through the remains of post-holes and several arcs of these holes interrupted another arc of stake- and post-holes constructed with its edge around the rim of the hollow. Four slightly egg-shaped huts could be identified, each was about 6m across and had a hearth near the centre. These represent a series of re-occupations of the site and the larger mass of post-holes might represent as many as ten huts altogether. Assuming one hut per occupation, it was estimated that at any one time the Mount Sandel site would have been occupied by fewer than ten people. The hearths were broad and shallow, about 1m across, cut into the compact subsoil and several had a line of burnt earth around their edges; two were re-cut.

Numerous pits of various sizes, some presumably storage pits, also occurred in the hollow and both these features and the hearths were filled with dark occupation soil, rich in organic material, some also containing layers with burnt hazel nut shells and sometimes layers of soil containing fragments of burnt bone. Erosion and later disturbance made analysis of the site organization difficult but specific activity areas were identified. The distribution of some flint artefacts in the hut area suggested that hut entrances may have been on the south-west and, judging from a small concentration of flakes, there may have been a chipping area, perhaps for axe manufacturing, just north of the hearth. Several large pits, some distance from the huts, may have been for rubbish disposal and a number of small pits filled with burnt stones represented another activity on the margins of the site, perhaps hot stones were used to heat liquids in leather containers. To the west of the huts there was a second area of occupation soil, with no pits or post-holes, but which contained large quantities of waste flint material, the result of extensive flint working or knapping on site, water rolled nodules of flint being brought to the site for this purpose.

The faunal remains consisted entirely of burnt bone fragments and judging from the surviving evidence wild pig and fish were the principal sources of food. Of the identifiable remains 15% were from mammals, 4% from birds and 81% from fish. However, pig bones represented 98% of the mammal remains recovered and analysis revealed substantial numbers of young pig; bones of hare also occurred. One bone of a wolf or a dog was found and since the domesticated dog is known elsewhere in Europe at this time, it is not impossible that it was present here. Bird bones included wood-pigeon, woodcock, capercaillie, and grouse as well as ducks and divers such as mallard, teal, wigeon and the red-throated diver. Fish bones, which were common, included salmon, trout and eel as well as some seabass and flounder.[5]

Summer occupation was indicated by the large quantity of salmon bones while winter occupation was demonstrated by certain features of the pig bones recovered: the pattern of bone fusion implied young animals less than two years old, probably butchered in late winter. Winter occupation was also suggested by the presence of foetal pig bones (sows bear their young in April or May). The presence of quantities of hazel nut shells among the charred plant remains denoted at least autumnal occupation (though they could have been collected at this time and stored for consumption later). These nuts and the recovery of water-lily seeds as well as seeds of wild pear or crab apple are a reminder that the foraging of wild edible plants played a significant role in the subsistence economy and this is also the sort of evidence that survives only in exceptional circumstances. Hazel nuts are high in protein and have the advantage that they can be easily stored, and as a concentrated dietary resource they may have been particularly important. There was no evidence to show that the water-lily seeds were processed but they could have been boiled as a soup or even fried in fat to make a sort of popcorn.

The site evidently served as a winter camp but the salmon remains also suggest spring and summer occupation while eel would probably have been fished in autumn when eel migration took place in the River Bann. Mount Sandel was probably occupied throughout much of the year but the

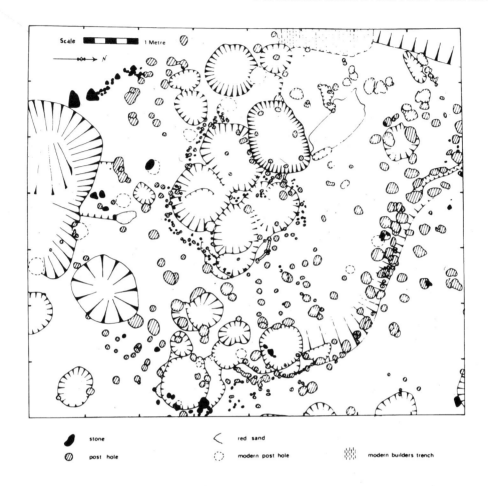

stone

post hole

red sand

modern post hole

modern builders trench

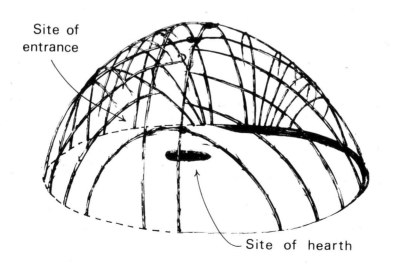

Site of
entrance

Site of hearth

Fig. 2. Plan of Mount Sandel hut sites with illustration of method of hut construction.

number of hunters and food gatherers present may well have varied from time to time and they may have been part of a larger community who occupied several sites in the wider region of the Bann estuary. Mount Sandel may have been a base camp, its inhabitants exploiting a range of resources within a 10km radius or two hours walking distance; in addition to large tracts of Boreal hazel forest, attractive for wild pig, this catchment area would have included coast, estuary and river.

Several radiocarbon dates were obtained from samples of charcoal and hazel nut shells and, even though they lie beyond the limits of high-precision calibration, they suggest that occupation may have occurred around 7000 BC and may well have spanned several centuries.[6]

The flint industry at Mount Sandel included cores and a large number of small narrow blades or microliths on average about 4cm long. Some flint blades of smaller than average size may have been used, without re-working, as parts of composite implements; larger blades may have been struck to provide microliths. The principal types of microlith were scalene triangles, rods and points; flake axes and core axes were also found. The main features of this early flint industry are summarized below.

Drainage of the modern Lough Boora, near Birr, Co. Offaly, resulted in the discovery of another important site broadly contemporary with Mount Sandel. The Lough Boora camp-site was situated on a gravel ridge on the shore of a large lake and was, in time, sealed by peat and subsequently inundated by the modern lake. Excavation revealed several hearths but no traces of structures were found. Burned bone recovered from these hearths provided the only faunal data: the remains were those of mammals (23%), birds (8%) and fish (68%). The mammal bones were mainly wild pig (98%) and a few other smaller animals such as wolf or dog and wild cat. The absence of red deer here and at Mount Sandel is noteworthy given how common this animal was in Britain and on the Continent at this time and it has been suggested that these deer were later immigrants to Ireland. Wood pigeon was common among the bird bones, with jay, teal, mallard, and grouse also present. The large quantity of fish remains comprised bones of brown trout and eel. Hazel nuts suggest autumnal use of the site and the eel bones here probably imply fishing in the lake in the summer months. The stone assemblage comprised chert microliths including rods, points,

and some scalene triangles, as well as cores and three complete axes of partly polished stone and fragments of others.

Charcoal from hearths provided several radiocarbon dates indicating contemporaneity with Mount Sandel and pollen analysis and further radiocarbon dates from peat samples indicate that the peat, which sealed the habitation site, had begun to form there quite rapidly shortly before 6000 BC.[7]

Mount Sandel and Lough Boora have produced a stone assemblage which is a narrow blade industry and these flint and chert types and their technique of manufacture are characteristic of the period 7000-5500 BC.

STONE ASSEMBLAGE

Cores (Fig. 3, 1-2): flint or chert cores with a single striking platform for the production of narrow blades are most common, though dual-platformed and multi-platformed cores also occur. The small size of the striking platforms of the blades struck from these cores suggests that controlled indirect percussion, with a hammer and punch, was used to produce the required blades which are usually considerably less than 7cm in length, often with a striking platform less than 2mm deep indicating that the punch was placed at the very edge of the core.

Microliths (Fig. 3, 3-14): a microlith is a retouched piece of flint or chert, usually a fragment of a blade, and is, in itself, not an implement; microliths served as part of a composite tool or weapon of bone or wood, such as arrow-tips, barbs in an arrowshaft, or as the cutting edges of a knife. The retouching is usually abrupt and, with the exception of points, is confined to the edges. The principal types of microliths found in Ireland include points, scalene triangles and rods. Points or 'needle-points' (Fig. 3, 3-4) are narrow blades trimmed to a sharp point with the usual abrupt retouch; some surface retouching occurs, usually at tip and butt. Some of the narrowest examples are 4mm or less in width. The scalene triangle (Fig. 3, 5) is a microlith which approximates, as its name implies, to an unequal-sided triangle of narrow, elongated form; the amount of retouch varies. Rods (Fig. 3, 6-9) are small blades which are heavily trimmed down one edge only; they are usually 1cm or less in width though a small number of slightly larger blades occur. Other microlith forms include small obliquely-trimmed types (Fig. 3, 10-13) and

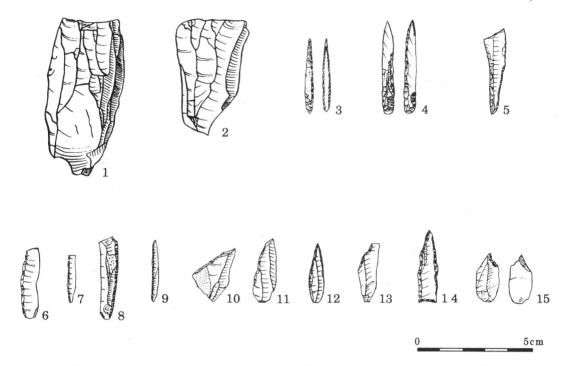

Fig. 3. Early flint assemblage. 1-2. Cores for the production of small blades or microliths. 3-4. Points or 'needle-points'.
5. Scalene triangle. 6-9. Rods. 10-13. Obliquely trimmed. 14. Hollow based point. 15. 'Micro-burin'. All are from Mount
Sandel except no. 5 from Coney Island, Lough Neagh, and no. 12 from Glynn, Co. Antrim.

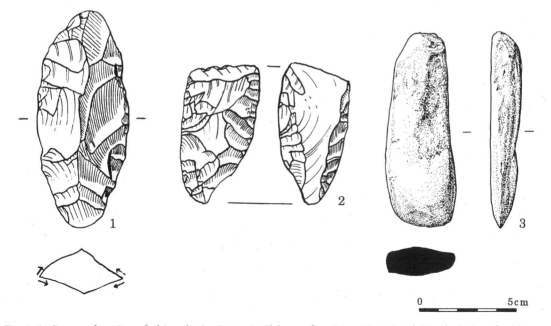

Fig. 4. 1. Core axe from Strangford Lough, Co. Down. 2. Flake axe from River Main, Lough Neagh. 3. Axe of partly
polished stone from Mount Sandel.

hollow-based points (Fig. 3, 14). The so-called 'micro-burins' (Fig. 3, 15) are waste pieces produced in the manufacture of microliths.

Axes (Fig. 4): several types of flint and chert axes are recorded. Core axes are fashioned from a flint nodule, they vary in size and shape and usually have

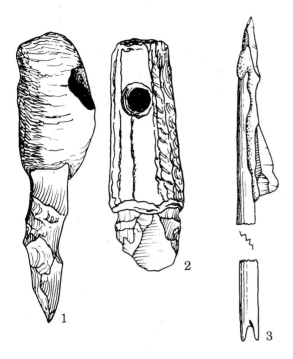

Fig. 5. 1-2. Adzes mounted in antler sleeves. 3. Microliths mounted as arrow tip and barb from Scandinavia.

a diamond or lozenge-shaped cross-section. Sometimes called 'tranchet axes', these implements have a comparatively narrow cutting-edge, produced by a transverse blow, and are sometimes trimmed to an almost pointed butt. In some instances the butt is so carefully pointed as to suggest that it too may have been functional. Flake axes were struck from a prepared core, their cutting edge being an unretouched edge of the primary flake, the rest of the flake was trimmed to a triangular or almost parallel-sided shape up to about 10cm in length. Axes of partly polished stone from the Lough Boora site were sealed beneath the peat which covered the site and suggest that similar implements from less certainly dated contexts at Mount Sandel (Fig. 4, 3) should also be assigned to the seventh millennium.

Other implement types include trimmed bladelets, burins and scrapers. While artefacts such as blades and scrapers were presumably used for a variety of cutting and scraping tasks including the preparation of edible plants and roots, of animal hides, and dismembering carcasses, there is still little evidence in Ireland as to the function and method of use of these various flint and chert types. A study of the microscopic traces of wear on some of the

Mount Sandel material revealed polish on various tool types which could be due to use on wood, bone and hides. There is evidence from Britain and Scandinavia to show that microliths were sometimes used as arrow-heads and barbs in arrowshafts; for example an arrow of pine wood from Scania in Sweden (Fig. 5, 3) has a microlithic tip held, presumably in a notch in the wood, by a resinous substance and a microlithic barb is similarly glued into the shaft; a resin or pitch obtained from birch bark was probably used. Scrapers and blades may have been mounted in various ways in wooden or bone hafts and objects such as flint points may have been used as awls or drills. Core and flake axes may, like their north European counterparts, have been mounted in bone or antler sleeves which, in turn were mounted on a wooden haft or perhaps just hand-held. Indeed, the flake axes may have been mounted in adze-fashion at right angles to the haft (as in Fig. 5, 2) and used as a planing rather than a chopping implement.[8]

LATER HUNTERS AND FORAGERS: 5500-4000 BC

There is an intriguing difference between the stone industry of what has been called the 'earlier Mesolithic' and the 'later Mesolithic'. The earlier controlled knapping technique of the seventh and early sixth millennia which produced narrow blades was replaced about 5500 BC by an industry characterized by heavy blades produced by direct percussion, a development without parallel in Britain or western Europe.

The development of this later broad blade tradition is to be seen at one of several sites at Newferry, in the flood plains of the River Bann just north of Lough Beg; the site in question is Site 3 on the eastern side of the river in Co. Antrim. Here, several occupation levels, evidence of a long history of intermittent habitation on the site, were found in deposits of sand, gravel, silt and diatomite laid down by fluctuations of the river over a period of some two thousand years. The rising of the level of the river had, of course, considerably disturbed the archaeological material; only a few burnt fragments of fish bones (of eel and salmon or trout) were found and in some cases the washed-out remains of hearths were detected spread over an area about 5m across; some flints were slightly rolled, their edges smoothed by water action. A series of radiocarbon dates, mainly from charcoal, confirmed the general

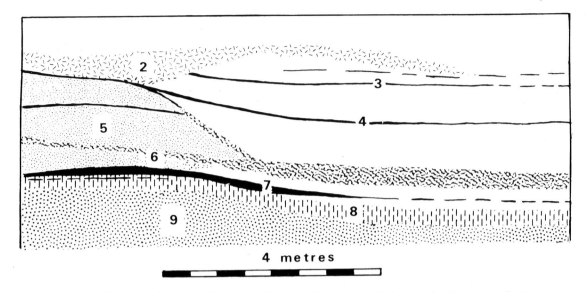

Fig. 6. Simplified illustration of sequence of deposits at Newferry, Co. Antrim, with the vertical scale exaggerated x2.

validity of the vertical stratigraphy which revealed the developments in the stone industry over a long period of time. Woodman divided the complex sequence of deposits into nine zones each containing one or more layers (Fig. 6).

The basal deposit at Newferry (Zone 9) was a sandbank with a couple of flint flakes indicating a little human activity. This was overlain by Zone 8, a layer of peat and layers of microscopic shells of diatoms deposited by the rising river; a small scatter of flint and stone was found. Zone 7 comprised several layers of occupation debris, silt and sand, covered in part by a layer of diatomite also containing some traces of occupation. The only substantial traces of human activity survived in this zone where stones and pieces of wood were thrown down to stabilize the edge of the sandbank. Zone 6 was a layer of silt and diatomite which produced some flint and stonework. The superimposed Zone 5 was a complex series of deposits: at one end of the area excavated it consisted of a sandbank containing several occupation layers and with traces of activity on its surface, at the other end the sandbank gradually tailed off into a layer of silt which merged with the silt of Zone 6. Large quantities of flint and fragments of three bone points were recovered. Zones 4 and 3 consisted of deposits of diatomite containing a certain amount of stone and flint. Zone 2 comprised coarse silts and gravel and represented a phase of erosion and redeposition when a stream of water ran across the site; some flint and stone, and fragments of Neolithic pottery

were found. Above this was a layer of diatomite (Zone 1) and topsoil.

The range of flint implements found at Newferry is very different to that uncovered at Mount Sandel. In addition to flint cores and waste material, Zone 8 and the main levels of Zone 7 at Newferry produced a variety of blades and flakes; only one microlith and a micro-awl were found and small fine blades were absent. Blades were fairly elongated; a quarter of the complete examples were over 7.5cm in length and some were slightly trimmed at the butt. Flint cores and waste material were noticeably rarer from upper Zone 7 onwards suggesting that after Zone 7 the bulk of flint work was manufactured elsewhere and brought to the site. Thereafter, too, there was a general tendency towards the production of a shorter broader type of flint flake, though elongated narrower forms continued to be used. Radiocarbon dates suggested a timespan from 5500 BC for Zone 8 to about the middle of the fifth millennium for Zone 3. Aside from various forms of butt-trimmed flakes, other flint implements from various levels included backed knives, distally trimmed blades, blade points and bar forms; other flint types are rare and include spokeshaves, borers and a few scrapers and burins.

Polished stone axes of schist and mudstone were more common, and polishing stones of sandstone also occurred. Except for polished stone axes, these and other implements characteristic of this later stone industry are known from a considerable number of sites in various parts of the country.

Much of this late assemblage comes from surface collections or old explorations of coastal sandhills and raised beaches. Of those sites which have been scientifically excavated many have produced stone and flintwork in secondary position, they having been, in varying degrees, disturbed by the action of river or sea with a consequent loss of archaeological information and the destruction of faunal and other organic remains.[9]

At Cushendun, Co. Antrim, excavations in 1934 in the raised beach on the western bank of the River Dun revealed that freshwater peat of Boreal age was covered with estuarine silt when the eustatic rise in sea-level overtook the isostatic rise of the land (Fig. 7). The rising waves continued to deposit gravels and silts up to a thickness of about 5m and flint implements were incorporated in various deposits. The lower silt (Horizon 1) was dated to the later sixth millennium BC and along with the lower gravel (Horizon 2) produced flint flakes and blades, both rolled by wave action and undamaged; this was a mixed collection of blades of various sizes possibly from several sites of differing

dates and included elongated blades as in the basal levels at Newferry. The upper gravel or raised beach (Horizon 3) contained a few rolled flints, and later scrapers and a hearth were found in the surface accumulation on this beach (Horizon 4).

Raised beach gravels at Larne, Co. Antrim, are prolific in flint implements, and for many years the term 'Larnian Culture' was applied to this material. However, the term Larnian is now confined to the characteristic stone assemblage of the period 5500–4000 BC. Excavations at Curran Point, near Larne, in a pebbly storm beach overlying beds of gravel and sand, produced some late material and an abundance of rolled flint, most of it waste. Excavations undertaken in raised beaches in different parts of the north of Ireland have also produced typical later flint assemblages: Glenarm, Co. Antrim, Dunaff, Co. Donegal, Ringneill, Co. Down, and Rough Island, Co. Down. Two chipping floors were found at Bay Farm, near Carnlough, Co. Antrim, and quantities of flint cores, flakes, unretouched blades and quartzite hammerstones were excavated.

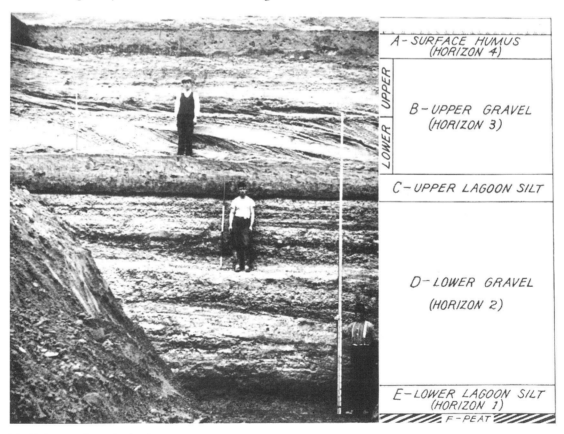

Fig. 7. Stratigraphy at Cushendun, Co. Antrim.

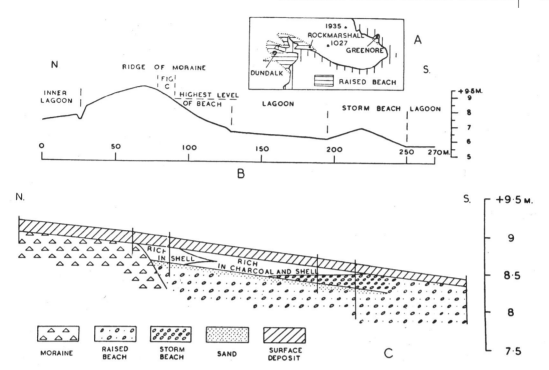

Fig. 8. Rockmarshall, Co. Louth. A. Location map. B. Section to show relation to raised beach. C. Section through midden.

Shell middens of various dates are known around much of the Irish coast and several of these deposits of molluscs and occupation debris are of similar date. A midden at Sutton, Co. Dublin, measured some 100m in length but had a general depth of only 30cm. It had been formed at a time when Howth was an island and the shell layer proper was composed of over twenty varieties of shellfish including limpets, whelks, cockles, scallops, periwinkles, oysters and mussels; it rested on a mixture of clay and shell which overlay glacial deposits. Excavations in 1949 and 1970 produced artefacts of flint, chert and stone, including cores, mainly single-platformed, butt-trimmed flakes, two fragmentary axes of polished schist and several round and elongated hammer-stones. Bone was scanty but the remains of wild pig, hare, wolf and fish were identified. Radiocarbon dates for the wild pig and another animal bone suggest a sixth millennium date; a later hearth in the midden is dated to 4340-3810 BC.[10]

Two middens at the western end of Dalkey Island, Co. Dublin, seem to have accumulated over a long period of time. A sample of shells from one (Site V) was analysed and revealed a very limited range of types, limpet accounting for 70%, periwinkle for 20%. Flint cores and flakes were found as well as hammer stones, polished stone axes and (from Site II) sherds of pottery. Animal bones from both middens included domestic ox, sheep or goat, wild pig, brown bear, grey seal, bones of various seabirds and remains of tope, mullet and possibly cod. Charcoal from Site V was radiocarbon dated to 4480-3710 BC but dates for a range of wild and domesticated animal bones suggest hunting and foraging occupation in the sixth millennium and later activity with domesticates in the fourth millennium.

At Rockmarshall, Co. Louth, two middens (I and II) were situated on a morainic ridge on the southern side of the Cooley peninsula, a third midden occurred higher up on the ridge above the other two. Midden I (Fig. 8) was situated on the highest point of the raised beach and was rich in charcoal and shells, notably oyster, periwinkle, limpet, whelk, mussel and cockle; claws of crab and fishbones were common. Middens II and III contained a similar mixture of shell and charcoal. Flints were few from the three sites: mainly blades and flakes and a number of cores. Some charcoal from midden III provided a radiocarbon date of 4570-4040 BC and a human femur from the same midden was dated to 4774-4366 BC.[11]

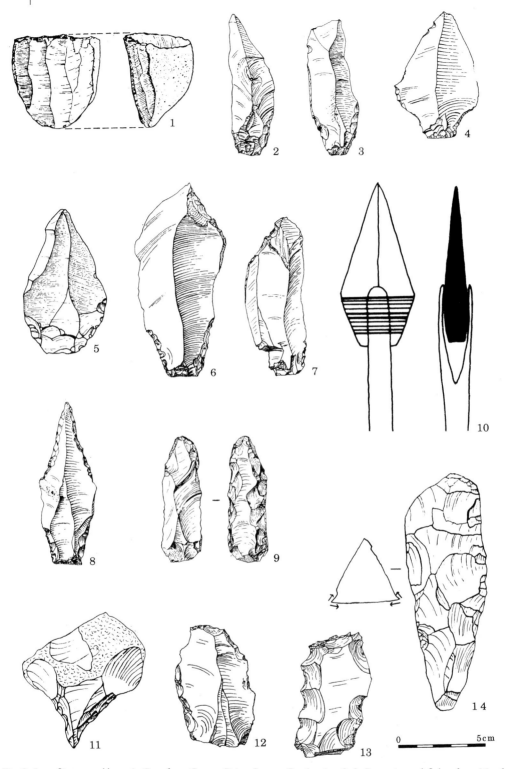

Fig. 9. Late flint assemblage. 1. Core from Curran Point, Larne, Co. Antrim. 2-3. Butt trimmed flakes from Newferry, Co. Antrim. 4. Bann flake from Newferry. 5. Bann flake from Ferriter's Cove, Co. Kerry. 6-7. Distally trimmed flakes from Newferry. 8. Point from Newferry. 9. Bar-form from Newferry. 10. Sketch of a hafted flake. 11. Borer. 12. Heavy flake from Newferry. 13. 'Spokeshave' from Newferry. 14. Pick from Coleraine, Co. Derry.

STONE ASSEMBLAGE

The flintwork of the period 5500–4000 BC differs from that of the earlier period in both the range of implement types and the method of production:

Cores (Fig. 9, 1): the majority of cores are single-platformed, although dual and multi-platformed examples are known. The single-platformed cores differ from their earlier counterparts in the extent to which they were worked; earlier examples were worked in a circular fashion (Fig. 3, 1-2) sometimes right around the striking platform but most later cores were worked to a roughly flat surface with at least half their surface still covered by cortex. The use of this type of core could have contributed to the increased production of shorter, broader blades and would have been suitable for use with a flint knapping technique of direct percussion. This technique, in which a hammerstone might be used directly onto the core's striking platform, would also contribute to the production of blades of greater size with larger striking platforms. In the later industries striking platforms range in depth from 2mm to over 12mm with a mean depth of 7mm to 8mm; depths of less than 2mm are very rare.

Flakes and blades (Fig. 9, 2-7): various types of flakes and blades are particularly frequent ranging from elongated narrow to short broad forms. Smooth striking platforms, well-defined bulbs of percussion and lengths 6cm to 8cm are common. Several forms have been identified. Butt trimmed flakes (Fig. 9, 2-3) are approximately parallel-sided flakes more than 4cm in length trimmed at the butt along at least one lateral edge for about 1.5cm, they have a thin and pointed distal end; on the classic form retouch should occur on both proximal lateral edges; tanged forms also occur. Bann flakes (Fig. 9, 4-5) are flakes 4cm or more in width with light retouch on the proximal (butt) end. In the past, the term 'Bann Flake' has been more loosely used of any leaf-shaped flake. Both tanged flakes and Bann flakes were apparently contemporary in Zone 5 at Newferry, where tanged forms are also earlier.[12] Distally trimmed flakes (Fig. 9, 6-7) are trimmed at the distal end for less than half the length; trimming may or may not occur on the proximal (butt) end. Backed flakes have a steep retouch for more than half the length producing a straight back. Points (Fig. 9, 8) are flakes and blades trimmed to a definite point with the retouch often confined to the distal end, butts are occasionally trimmed. The term bar-form (Fig. 9, 9) is applied to narrow flakes trimmed along both edges and with a rough point.

The function of these various types of flakes is uncertain. It has been suggested that Bann flakes and similar forms were mounted in wooden shafts as the prongs of fish-spears but the thick butts of many examples make this an unlikely hypothesis. These different forms may have served a variety of purposes and even morphologically similar flakes may have had various uses, some could conceivably have been used as projectile tips (Fig. 9, 10), others may have been mounted in wooden or bone sleeves and used as knives and scrapers and some may have been used as woodworking tools.

Heavy flakes or so-called 'spokeshaves' are large, crude, notched flakes (Fig. 9, 13); some heavy, thick flakes with rough retouch, occasionally on bulbar and dorsal surfaces (Fig. 9, 12) are similar. Picks (Fig. 9, 14) are elongated implements with a rounded butt and a narrow point or a working end which is sometimes formed by a transverse blow producing an edge less than 1cm wide. Borers (Fig. 9, 11) are crude, irregularly-shaped implements worked to a point. Flake axes were not used to any extent and core axes are rare. Polished stone axes are more common but are known mainly from Newferry where examples of schist were predominant up to Zone 5 with mudstone more common thereafter.

Other implement types include a few scrapers and burins, and a series of pebbles showing signs of wear: some may have been used as polishing and grinding tools, others as light hammers. Some elongated pebbles from Rockmarshall and Dalkey Island have slightly bevelled ends and may have been used for the removal of limpets from rocks.

It is probable that much of the hunting, fishing and foraging equipment was of organic material. Fragments of three simple bone points were found in Zone 5 at Newferry and serve as a reminder that a wide range of implements of bone and wood were used but survive only in exceptional circumstances. Fragments of bone, trimmed and ground to a slender point, could have been used for a variety of purposes, some perhaps as fish spears. Similar bone points found in the Cutts area of the River Bann are of uncertain date, such simple artefacts could have been used over long periods of time. Several fragments of worked wood were found associated with a hearth at Toome Bay, in the north-west corner of Lough Neagh, these included a small flat piece of hazel wood with three rough holes pierced in it and three narrow pieces of pine wood showing signs of working.[13]

No burials or ritual sites have been found and the rarity of settlement sites with organic remains makes it very difficult to assess the economic patterns of these early hunters and foragers or to gauge the relative importance of hunting, fishing and food-gathering. Only a small number of sites have produced faunal remains (about 13 out of more than 180). The range of stone implements which survives provides few clues and the investigated coastal middens are mostly imprecisely dated, and some, such as Ferriter's Cove, Co. Kerry, are contemporary with communities who practised cereal cultivation and animal husbandry. The remains from the three inland sites which have produced faunal evidence, Mount Sandel, Lough Boora and Newferry, are, therefore, of great interest. Wild pig was evidently an important source of meat. Other animals seem to have been of less consequence: wild cat, hare and dog or wolf have been identified. However, some animals may just have been hunted for their hides and pelts, their carcasses rarely finding their way to the camp-site. While in some cases archaeological evidence is lacking, it is possible that animals such as fox, squirrel, badger, otter, pinemarten, brown bear, and lynx were all hunted or trapped. The absence of red deer on early sites is surprising: the earliest securely dated examples come from fourth millennium contexts. The scarcity of burins (with small chisel-like edges) and scrapers suitable for working deer carcasses, and the apparent absence of early upland sites, might suggest that red deer is a genuine absentee in the Boreal period.[14]

Camp-sites situated close to river or lake would allow not only the exploitation of the fauna of the surrounding forests but would also offer the opportunity for fowling and fishing The fish remains from Mount Sandel and Lough Boora indicate the importance of this food source and dug-out canoes, fish spears, bone hooks, wooden fish traps and nets may all have been used in this pursuit. Part of a dug-out logboat of poplar has been found at Carrigdirty, Co. Limerick, on the tidal foreshore in the upper Shannon estuary, and radiocarbon dated to 4788-4590 BC. Irish evidence is lacking but Boreal fisherfolk on the Continent used simple bone hooks, barbed bone and antler points, as well as logboats; the remains of conical fish traps of twisted willow rods and of a seine-net of double-threaded cord made from the fibrous bark of the willow have

all been found. Intensive fishing was possibly a seasonal occupation when migratory shoals of fish such as salmon, eel or bream were available. It is difficult at present to estimate the extent to which birds may have contributed to the diet and the same is true of edible plants and roots. The occasional discovery of hazel-nuts has been noted, these are an easily stored and valuable source of fat, protein and other elements. In general, the evidence for the exploitation of plant food and nuts, roots and fungi is exceptionally meagre, yet these food sources may have been as important or even more important than meat or fish. Certainly substantial quantities of potential plant foods were available at any time of the year and these could actually have been supplemented by fungi, fish, molluscs and animals. Equally significantly, the evidence from modern foraging societies suggests that women may have been the principal providers since their food-gathering could have produced up to 60-70% of the diet by weight. Thus their status in prehistoric hunting and foraging groups may have been rather better than in later agricultural communities.[15]

The evidence from the coastal middens indicates that a variety of shellfish were gathered and the accumulation of island middens implies the use of logboats or skin boats. Again, the occupation of these sites was very likely limited and seasonal; it has been calculated, for example, that one Scottish midden site at Morton, Fife, was probably visited by a party of about a dozen people for an average of thirteen days a year.

Hunting and foraging communities probably had a shifting, seasonal pattern of settlement and subsistence, some or all of a group exploiting different resources at different times of the year, one site perhaps serving as a base camp for more prolonged settlement. However, so little is known about the settlements of this period, it is still difficult to determine with any degree of confidence the possible migratory cycle of a hunting and gathering group. The evidence from Lough Boora not only demonstrates that the midlands had been penetrated by about 7000 BC but suggests that other early sites may await discovery beneath the raised bogs of the region. Typical broad-bladed chert implements of late date are also known from this area, for example from Lough Kinale and from Lough Derravaragh, Co. Westmeath. Similar material has been found at Moynagh Lough, near Nobber, Co. Meath. Western

Fig. 10. General distribution of Irish Mesolithic material as known at present.

finds, also of late date, include large quantities of worked chert, including Bann flakes, from Lough Gara, Co. Sligo, and a distally trimmed flake and other flakes from the western shores of Lough Corrib, near Oughterard, Co. Galway. A number of finds of flint artefacts, including some microliths, have been found in Munster, mainly in the valley of the River Blackwater, and later activity has been recognized at Guileen and at Dunpower Head on the east Cork coast, and at Ferriter's Cove on the Dingle peninsula. Careful field survey in the south-east has also recovered later stone implements in the Waterford area and in the Barrow valley. The relative scarcity of material from mid-Ulster and much of the southern half of the country (Fig. 10) is still difficult to explain but the large quantity of finds from the north-east may be attributed in part to the activities of a number of assiduous collectors of flint implements. To complicate matters, an absence of diagnostic stone artefacts may not indicate an absence of settlement: a brushwood platform at Mitchelstowndown East, Co. Limerick, and a stone platform on Valencia Island, Co. Kerry, produced no finds but were radiocarbon dated to about 4900 BC and to the sixth millennium BC respectively.[16]

The identification of further settlements is clearly one of the important tasks of the future. Their investigation would not only increase our understanding of subsistence strategies but also possibly explain the difference between the early and later stone industries and clarify the relationship between these industries and those of Britain. The material from Mount Sandel differs in several respects from contemporary British industries notably in the occurrence of flake axes and needle points. Such regional features suggest that an earlier Irish industry may await discovery.[17] However, flint implements such as core axes, micro-awls and the remainder of the microlith types are found in northern England whence the first hunting and foraging communities presumably came. In contrast, the later Irish material finds no parallels across the Irish Sea and, apart for some evidence from the Isle of Man, there is little indication of cross-channel contact. That striking change in character between the early and late stone assemblages is not easily explained. A shift in procurement strategies may be part of the explanation. At sites like Mount Sandel flint nodules were collected on the coast several kilometres away. This collection process may have been an integrated strategy, part and parcel of the normal round of excursions to the coast for fish or other purposes. Judging from the evidence in the north-east of the country, at least, where some large caches of flint blades have been found, the heavy bladed later assemblage may reflect a more organized strategy involving the scheduled procurement of flint by small and specific groups of people. The evidence is inconclusive and whether this change is part of a broader shift in subsistence strategies from expedient hunting and foraging to more intensive resource exploitation remains to be seen.[18]

NOTES

1 Ice Ages: Coxon 1993; Mitchell and Ryan 1997, 35. An Irish Palaeolithic?: Woodman 1986; 1996.

2 Dún Aonghasa hand-axe: Murphy 1977. Kilgreany, Co. Waterford: Tratman 1928; Movius 1935; Molleson 1986: radiocarbon dates for human bone, 4580 ± 150 BP (3650–2920 BC, BM-135) and 4820 ± 60 BP (3776–3382 BC, Pta-2644); reindeer, 10,700 ± 110 BP (Pta-2378). Mell, Co. Louth: Mitchell and de G. Sieveking 1972.

3 Land-bridges (which may have been 'low, soggy, possibly shifting and partially discontinuous linkages'): Devoy 1984 and 1985 who favours a land-bridge from

Inishowen to Islay and Jura in western Scotland; other references in Woodman *et al.* 1997. Early fauna: Woodman *et al.* 1997 with radiocarbon dates in Hedges *et al.* 1997; Woodman and Monaghan 1993; Savage 1966; van Wijngaarden-Bakker 1986, Mitchell and Ryan 1997, 111.

4 Early vegetation: Mitchell 1956 and Mitchell and Ryan 1997, 113. Clearances: Smith 1984; Preece *et al.* 1986; Edwards 1985, 145.

5 Mount Sandel, Co. Derry: Woodman 1985. Dog: the fragmentary nature of the bones means that it is difficult to be certain; it has been claimed that the first indisputable evidence for dog in Ireland comes from Dalkey Island, Co. Dublin (McCormick 1991) but it is now evident the midden there accumulated over a long period of time.

6 Mount Sandel radiocarbon dates include 8960 ± 70 BP (UB-952), 8795 ± 135 BP (UB-2007), 8790 ± 185 BP (UB-951), 8725 ± 115 BP (UB-912), 8555 ± 70 BP (UB-913), 8440 ± 65 BP (UB-2008): Woodman 1985, 148.

7 Lough Boora, Co. Offaly: Ryan 1980; pollen analysis: O'Connell 1980; radiocarbon dates: 8980 ± 360 BP (UB-2268), 8475 ± 75 BP (UB-2199), 8450 ± 70 BP (UB-2267), 8350 ± 70 BP (UB-2200); further radiocarbon dates from peat samples: 8115 ± 80 BP (UB-2269) and 8070 ± 65 BP (UB-2270); faunal remains: van Wijngaarden-Bakker 1985.

8 Stone technology: Woodman 1978, 1978a; Peterson 1990; Anderson and Johnson 1995; Woodman and Johnson 1996.

9 Newferry, Co. Antrim: Woodman 1977; radiocarbon dates ranged from 7630 ± 195 BP (UB-461) for Zone 8 to 5415 ± 90 BP (4458-4040 BC, UB-489) and 5705 ± 90 BP (4778-4364 BC, UB-630) for Zone 3.

10 Cushendun, Co. Antrim: Movius 1940; radiocarbon dates: the basal peat has been dated to 8410 ± 140 BP (I-5135), Mitchell 1971; Horizon 1 produced dates of 7670 ± 140 BP (I-5134) and 7395 ± 65 BP (UB-689). Larne, Co. Antrim: Movius 1942. Curran Point, Larne, Co. Antrim: Movius 1953. Glenarm, Co. Antrim: Movius 1937. Dunaff, Co. Donegal: Addyman and Vernon 1966. Ringneill, Co. Down: Stephens and Collins 1960. Rough Island, Co. Down: Movius 1940a. Bay Farm, Co. Antrim: Woodman and Johnson 1996; radiocarbon dates from charcoal: 5810 ± 100 BP (4940-4460 BC, UB-2603), 5470 ± 95 BP (4510-4044 BC, UB-2604) and 5595 ± 100 BP (4720-4240 BC, UB-2506). Sutton, Co. Dublin: Mitchell 1956a, 1972; radiocarbon dates from animal bone (? bear): 6660 ± 80 BP (OxA-3691) and 6560 ± 75 BP (OxA-3960); wild pig: 7140 ± 100 BP (OxA-4449), see Woodman *et al.* 1997; from charcoal: 5250 ± 110 BP (4340-3810 BC, I-5067); red deer and domesticated cattle bone identifications are uncertain: Woodman *et al.* 1997.

11 Dalkey Island, Co. Dublin: Liversage 1968; Woodman *et al.* 1997; Site V radiocarbon date from charcoal: 5300 ± 170 BP (4480-3710 BC, D-38); dates from animal bone include cattle: 4820 ± 75 BP (3780-3378 BC, OxA-4571); seal: 6410 ± 110 BP (OxA-4572); Site II: sheep: 5050 ± 90 BP (4038-3650 BC, OxA-4566); cattle: 3050 ± 70 BP (1506-1096 BC, OxA-4567); pig: 6870 ± 90 BP (OxA-4568). Rockmarshall, Co. Louth: Mitchell 1947, 1949, 1971; radiocarbon date from charcoal: 5470 ± 110 BP (4570-4040 BC, I-5323); human femur: 5705 ± 75 BP (4774-4366 BC, OxA-4604), Woodman *et al.* 1997.

12 Woodman and Anderson 1990. Stone technology and Bann flakes: Woodman and Johnson 1996; Anderson and Johnson 1993 and 1995.

13 River Bann: Whelan 1952. Toome Bay, Co. Derry: Mitchell 1955; charcoal provided a radiocarbon date of 7680 ± 110 BP (Y-95).

14 Red deer: Woodman *et al.* 1997; McCormick 1986.

15 Carrigdirty, Co. Limerick: O'Sullivan 1996; Lanting and Brindley 1996; radiocarbon date 5820 ± 40 BP (4788-4590 BC, GrN-21936). Mesolithic in northern Europe: G. Clark 1975. Plant foods: D. Clarke 1976; Zvelebil 1994; MacLean 1993. Women foragers: Ehrenberg 1989a, 50.

16 Morton, Fife: Coles 1971. Lough Kinale, Co. Westmeath: Mitchell 1970. Lough Derravaragh, Co. Westmeath: Mitchell 1972a. Moynagh Lough, Co. Meath: J. Bradley 1991. Lough Gara, Co. Sligo: Cross 1953. Oughterard, Co. Galway: Higgins 1978; 1986. Guileen, Co. Cork, and Dunpower Head, Co. Cork: Anderson 1993. Ferriter's Cove, Co. Kerry: Woodman and O'Brien 1993. Waterford area: Zvelebil *et al.* 1987; Zvelebil and Green 1992; Green and Zvelebil 1990 and 1993. Barrow valley: Zvelebil *et al.* 1996. Munster: Woodman 1985a. Mitchelstowndown East, Co. Limerick: Gowen 1988, 180, 197; date from oak charcoal of 6000 BP (*c.* 4900 BC) cited by Woodman 1990. Valencia Island, Clynacartan Bog: date from adjacent peat of 6560 ± 120 BP: Mitchell 1989, 78.

17 An intriguingly early date of 9440 ± 100 BP (Lu-1809) from charcoal from a test pit at Woodpark, on the northern shore of Ballysadare Bay, Co. Sligo (Burenhult 1984, 64) remains unexplained; the charcoal could have a natural origin.

18 Flint caches: Woodman 1978a, 72. Flint procurement: Woodman 1987; socio-economic complexity: Cross 1996; Woodman 1985c.

2

Farmers of the Fourth Millennium

There was a decisive change in the economy of prehistoric Ireland shortly after 4000 BC, a change which traditionally has been considered one of the characteristic features of the Neolithic period. The transition from a hunting and foraging life-style to an economy based on stock raising and cereal cultivation was a radical development with major social consequences. Agriculture would become the fundamental economic activity in pre-industrial society and a crucial factor in shaping the physical and mental landscape. With the advent of domesticated animals and grain cultivation, the fourth millennium saw significant forest clearance, more permanent settlement, a greater concern with territoriality and the construction of large communal ritual monuments. Since the wild ancestors of cereals like wheat and barley and animals such as cattle and sheep did not exist in postglacial Ireland, they had to be introduced. It is commonly believed that these changes were initiated by the arrival of pioneering farming communities who brought with them not just the new domesticated plant and animal species but new artefact types and ritual practices such as stone tomb building as well. It has also been thought that this transition from hunting and foraging to farming was relatively sudden but it now seems that this process may have been more complicated and even quite prolonged with tentative beginnings centuries earlier in the fifth millennium BC. Archaeological and other evidence in this important transitional phase from a hunting and foraging economy to an agricultural one is scarce and what precisely happened is still quite unclear.

There may be some evidence, both archaeological and palynological, for a pioneering phase of early agricultural activity in Ireland in the fifth millennium BC but this evidence is tenuous and ambiguous and the subject of debate. At Ballynagilly, north-west of Cookstown, Co. Tyrone, a number of radiocarbon determinations suggest the possibility of an early date for the presence of stone-using farmers with their characteristic pottery. Here, an occupation area with post and stake-holes and a hearth yielded flint artefacts and sherds of pottery and charcoal which produced a radiocarbon date with a range of 4770-4490 BC and pits containing pottery and charcoal provided dates with ranges of 4670-4360 BC. These early dates have been questioned and it may be that the samples dated are from old wood and thus several centuries earlier than the associated archaeological material. However, they are not impossible and if they do date the typical pottery and some typical flints, then these occupants were farmers who left only scanty traces of their passing. Pollen sampling in an adjacent bog has shown that wide-spread clearance of the primeval forest of birch, pine, oak, elm and hazel did not occur there for several centuries but this very early activity, if it only involved the clearance of a hectare or so of woodland, would leave little or no trace in the pollen record.[1]

Some early dates associated with a number of megalithic tombs in Co. Sligo are also debated. Charcoal from a post-hole found dug into the natural surface below a tomb at Carrowmore, Co. Sligo (no. 7) provided a radiocarbon date of 4330-3820 BC and probably relates to some pre-tomb structure. Charcoal from beneath and between the stones of the lowest level of stone packing around another tomb at Carrowmore (no. 27) has also provided a series of early radiocarbon dates ranging from 3980-3530 BC. This charcoal could indicate an early date for the construction of this tomb but it has also been suggested that the burnt material could be derived from earlier settlement in the locality though whether by foragers or farmers is unknown. Two early dates of 5640-5490 BC and 4675-4460 BC have also been obtained from charcoal associated with cremated bones from a small sub-rectangular megalithic tomb in a cairn on the summit of Croghaun Mountain, south of Ballysadare Bay, in Co. Sligo, and may lend support to the claim that hunters and foragers constructed simple megalithic monuments.[2]

Palynological evidence for agricultural activity of possibly early date has been found in Cashelkeelty, near Lauragh, Co. Kerry. Cereal pollen grains (two of wheat and one of barley) have been identified near the base of a 3m peat core (at a depth of 276cm to 291cm) and at the same level a noteworthy drop in tree pollen was observed. A peat sample (from a depth of 291cm to 294cm in the core) provided a radiocarbon date of 4950-4470 BC. One wheat pollen grain was found at 291cm and associated with a first clearance phase which may have lasted for some 400 years. Given the moist nature of the core at these depths, it is conceivable that some downward displacement of cereal pollen had occurred, but since this initial clearance of pine and birch wood coincided with the appearance of weed pollen, a phase of both clearance and cereal cultivation is possible. One wheat and one barley grain at a depth of 276cm may be associated with a second bout of clearance and agricultural activity of 300-400 years.[3]

Early clearance has also been detected in a pollen diagram from a raised bog at Ballyscullion, Co. Antrim, and dated to sometime in the fifth millennium BC and possibly contemporary with the supposed primary activity at Ballynagilly. While the Ballyscullion land clearance could be the work of early farmers, in the absence of any clear indication of cereal cultivation, the possibility that hunter-foragers may have indulged in a certain amount of interference with the forest cover cannot be excluded. After all some small-scale clearance might encourage game to come and browse on regenerating woodland. It is even possible at a site such as Cashelkeelty that a hunting and foraging community undertook some forest clearance and even supplemented their diet with some cereal growing in spring and summer. But why it may have been necessary to supplement the hunting and food gathering diet in this way is far from clear. Unless there was some scarcity of resources, agriculture – which demands a higher labour input – was not necessarily an attractive option for a hunting community. That said, an agricultural economy would offer greater potential for economic, technological and population expansion and the arrival of even a small number of farming groups from elsewhere with innovations such as pottery and novel stone implements would quickly demonstrate this to the indigenous hunting and foraging inhabitants. The existence of a pioneering early farming phase in the fifth millennium BC and the role, if any, of indigenous hunters and foragers in the adoption of agriculture are questions which are still unresolved.[4]

There is unambiguous evidence for early farming in the fourth millennium BC, from shortly after 4000 BC. The pollen diagram from Ballynagilly shows a noticeable decline in the pollen of elm and pine with a corresponding increase in grass pollen with some cereal and plantain pollen at about 3900 BC. These fluctuations in the pollen record and the presence of charcoal reflect more extensive human interference on the forest vegetation and indicate the creation of open ground by the clearing with fire of a mixed forest of elm, pine and some oak. Some cereal pollen was encountered at this clearance stage suggesting some arable farming but its relative scarcity thereafter prompted the suggestion that pastoral farming may have become predominant.[5]

A marked decline in elm in the pollen record is a widespread phenomenon shortly before and shortly after 3800 BC. In Ireland this elm decline is well dated but the reasons for it are debated. The term *landnam* – a Danish word for 'land winning' – has been applied to this phenomenon where a diminution of tree pollen such as elm is often accompanied by the appearance of pollen of plants which even today are recognized as weeds of cultivation such as ribwort plantain, dock and nettle. The drop in elm pollen occurs so consistently, not only in Ireland, but in Britain and parts of western Europe that it is considered to mark the Zone VII – Zone VIII (Atlantic–Sub-

Boreal) transition in the pollen record. Various explanations have been offered for this remarkably widespread and apparently synchronous decline and these include factors such as climatic change, disease and human interference. The latter anthropogenic explanation has been generally favoured in the past particularly because, as already mentioned, the elm decline at several sites appears to coincide not only with an increase in the pollen of grasses and weeds of cultivation but, occasionally, with the appearance of cereal pollen as well. It is possible that a reduction in elm pollen could be due to the utilization of elm leaves for cattle fodder by early farmers without any necessary reduction in the number of trees but it has also been suggested that in Ireland elm was concentrated in pure stands on patches of light soils, and since such soils are more easily cultivated, early farmers would be quick to appreciate their value. It has also been argued that freely ranging cattle may have been encouraged to winter in woodland when herbage becomes scarce and where elm bark could be readily stripped and eaten. This too could have been a significant contributory factor in the decline of elm but since elm also declines in various localities where it was clearly a minor component in the wooded landscape, and was thus unlikely to be targeted by farmers or their cattle, it is also likely – as we shall see – that an elm disease was introduced at this time.[6]

At Fallahogy, near Kilrea, Co. Derry, detailed pollen analysis combined with radiocarbon dating has provided a general picture of the impact of early farmers on the Atlantic (Zone VII) oak, elder, hazel and elm forest. About 3800 BC in this area, a sharp decline in elm and a slight decline in hazel coincides with an abrupt rise in grass pollen, which represents a clearance stage. This was followed by a rise in weeds of cultivation and bracken denoting a farming stage. After a period of agriculture which presumably drew to a close as the natural fertility of the cleared patches of soil was reduced, the abandoned land was recolonized first by hazel, then by other trees which gradually repressed the grasses and weeds. After a period of secondary woodland during which the soil regained much of its lost fertility, further clearance and farming took place around 3100 BC. No cereal pollen was encountered at Fallahogy but was found, for example, at Beaghmore, Co. Tyrone, where three stages of land clearance and management were also recognized commencing around 3800 BC. A period of land

clearance and some cereal cultivation, which lasted for several centuries and probably included at least a hundred years of continual clearing of new ground, was followed by a phase of possible pastoral activity. This was a shorter phase in which cereal pollen was absent but which did produce grass and plantain pollen, often considered as evidence of pastoralism; a sharp rise in hazel pollen (noted too at Fallahogy) would also be consistent with grazing since cattle find the leaves of this tree unpalatable thus increasing its representation in the pollen diagram. The third phase was marked by regeneration of the woodland. The scarcity of cereal pollen is not surprising because it has poor dispersal qualities and is invariably under-represented in the pollen record. Caution is necessary, therefore, but it may be that grazing and cattle raising were the more important part of the economy.

While well-dated evidence for such land clearance comes from the northern half of the country, it was clearly widespread. A marked decline in elm has been recorded at the beginning of the Sub-Boreal phase at Dolan, near Roundstone in western Connemara, where it is now difficult to imagine that today's dramatically bare landscape was once heavily forested and, from about 7500 BC, was dominated by a dense cover of oak on the better soils of north Connemara and Scots pine on the poorer soils in the south. From about 6000 BC a rise in alder may reflect the wetter and warmer climatic conditions of the Atlantic period.[7]

Lough Sheeauns, near Cleggan in north Connemara, has provided detailed palynological evidence of the changes wrought by early farmers on this landscape. A core from a small lake revealed the existence here in the fifth millennium BC of an adjacent forest dominated by oak, hazel, and alder with only a little elm and birch (Fig. 11). A rise in holly pollen, the appearance of plantain with no corresponding decrease in the pollen of oak and hazel and the occurrence of some wheat pollen demonstrate the creation of limited openings in the forest cover for cereal cultivation shortly after 4000 BC. Though there was some reduction in the number of trees, tree pollen actually increased because the clearings provided greater light which stimulated pollen production. In general, however, these first agriculturalists made little impact on the natural environment. Even though elm may not have been present in any quantity, the classic elm decline is recorded at

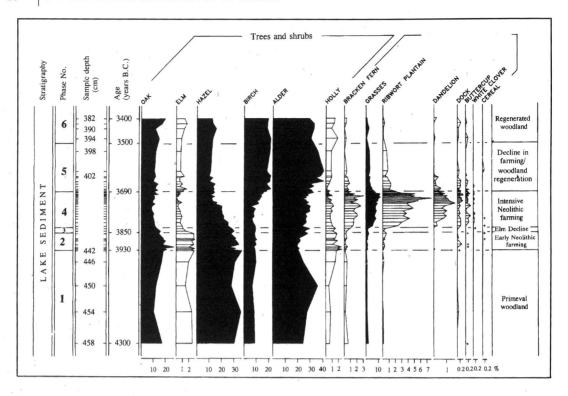

Fig. 11. Part of a pollen diagram from lake sediment at Lough Sheeauns, Connemara, Co. Galway, showing the vegetation history over one millennium and the changes in percentage pollen when farming was introduced shortly after 4000 BC.

about 3800 BC but obviously does not coincide with the appearance of pioneering farmers who had arrived a century before, or with a decrease in other tree pollens or indeed with an increase in herbaceous pollen, all lending some support to the argument that a fungal disease may have been the cause. The occurrence of pre-elm decline cereal is significant and suggests that the occasional discovery of large grass pollen grains of possible cereal type in similar pre-elm decline contexts elsewhere may also denote small scale early farming episodes.[8] The elm decline at Lough Sheeauns is followed immediately by major woodland clearances which involved the more or less complete disappearance of oak and the creation of pasture as demonstrated not only by an increase in grass and plantain pollen but by a rise in pollen of species such as dandelion, buttercup and chickweed as well. Only the occasional cereal pollen occurs and the emphasis seems to have been on pastoral farming. This intensive agricultural phase around Lough Sheeauns lasted for about 150 years and was followed by a phase of diminishing farming activity of about the same duration which was accompanied by a regeneration of woodland.

At Redbog, Co. Louth, elm initially declined around 3800 BC from 18% to 3%, oak also declined with a corresponding rise in grasses and plantain all suggesting land clearance. A single pollen grain was identified possibly implying a low level of arable agriculture. At Céide, Co. Mayo, where pine was probably the dominant species on the relatively poorer mineral soils of the region, the elm decline is recorded about 3800 BC and precedes almost 500 years of pastoral farming with a small arable element; an extensive field system was probably built in the period of most intensive pastoral activity from about 3700 to 3200 BC. In Scragh Bog, near Mullingar, Co. Westmeath, a significant reduction in elm (from about 30% of the total pollen to 3%) was accompanied by a rise in grass and plantain pollen. Cereal pollen occurred here at the beginning of the elm decline before the expansion of grasses and this may suggest that arable farming was important at first. This phase of cereal growing was followed by a period of pastoral activity suggested by substantial increases in grass and plantain pollen (and further forest clearance including that of oak is indicated). Thereafter the land was abandoned and recolonized by woodland. Prior to the *landnam* at Scragh Bog, fluctuations in elm and hazel pollen there, if anthropogenic, might be due to the activities of pioneering farmers.[9]

It has often been claimed that early agriculturalists elsewhere in Europe cleared the land of trees with axe and fire – the 'slash-and-burn' method, and in Denmark the presence of charcoal at the clearance horizon was considered an indication of this practice.[10] At present there is little, if any, evidence for the use of this method in Britain or Ireland. Charcoal in pre-elm decline levels at Redbog was considered to represent natural, non-anthropogenic fires on a relatively dry bogland and abundant charcoal found pre-dating the *landnam* at the Céide Fields, Co. Mayo, may be due to burning quite unconnected with the early farmers there. Charcoal occurred in the later Cashelkeelty record *c.* 3700 BC and at Ballynagilly abundant charcoal in the old soil suggested the possibility of some local clearance in this fashion but other methods may have been used and more often than not trees may have been ring-barked to kill them.

Today's landscape with its large tracts of pasture, bog and tree-less mountain land presents an utterly different picture to that which confronted early farming groups. In the fourth millennium BC, for instance, much of the lowland landscape would have consisted of extensive virgin forest and secondary woodland in various stages of regeneration, the tree cover being broken by occasional tillage patches and areas of rough pasture which might be abandoned when the fertility of the soil was exhausted. There was probably some regional and chronological variation in this general picture of shifting agriculture with varying emphasis on arable and pastoral farming and there were some areas which were more or less permanently cleared of woodland and, as in the Céide Fields in Co. Mayo, enclosed by field systems.

It is also worth remembering that the Atlantic period probably witnessed climatic amelioration with an increase in both summer and winter temperatures, an average improvement on present temperatures in this and the following Sub-Boreal period of $1.0°$ to $2.0°C$ is thought possible. This climatic improvement would also permit a tree-line 200m to 300m higher than that of the present day and means that uplands which are marginal today, like Ballynagilly and Beaghmore, at about 200m or more above OD, were suitable for agriculture. There is even slight evidence for agricultural activity at higher altitudes including possible cereal pollen grains (found in blanket peat dated to the second half of the fourth millennium) at about 450m OD on Slieve Croob, Co. Down, and a saddle quern found on top of Baltinglass Hill, Co. Wicklow, associated with a passage tomb cairn at 384m OD.[11]

As in the rest of north-western Europe, early farming in Ireland was in all probability mixed, being based both on the cultivation of cereals and on animal husbandry. Although the limited evidence is not easy to evaluate it does seem that a pastoral economy may have been predominant with cereal cultivation playing a minor role. Wheat (emmer with some einkorn – both sturdy primitive types) and barley were the principal cereal crops, but information is still limited. As we have seen wheat pollen has been identified from time to time in palynological studies of various lake sediment or bog samples. It has also been recorded in a layer of turves beneath the great cairn at Newgrange, Co. Meath. Cereal grains are preserved in exceptional circumstances: carbonized wheat grains were found beneath that passage tomb cairn on Baltinglass Hill, Co. Wicklow, beneath the mound of a satellite tomb at Knowth, Co. Meath, and on a small habitation site at Townleyhall, Co. Louth, and on settlements at Ballygalley, Co. Antrim, and Tankardstown South, Co. Limerick. Charred barley is reported from a tumulus at Drimnagh, Co. Dublin, and from settlements at Ballygalley, Lyles Hill and Donegore, Co. Antrim. Cereal impressions are also occasionally preserved on pottery surfaces and occur when a grain accidentally sticks to the clay when it is being worked; the grain disintegrates on firing but often leaves a detailed impression. It is now recognized that such accidental inclusions in a confined domestic context are not a reliable guide to the wider picture of crop cultivation. Impressions of grains of both wheat and barley have been recognized on pottery sherds from various localities.[12]

Cereals, ground with rubbing stones on saddle querns, were possibly used for both bread and gruel, and maybe even for fermented drinks. While simple agricultural implements such as wooden hoes, spades and digging sticks were probably used by these early cultivators, evidence from Britain, where plough marks have been found beneath a long barrow at South Street, Wiltshire, indicates the use of a light plough by at least the fourth millennium BC. Plough marks of possibly early date have been found at the Céide Fields. A simple ard-type plough may have

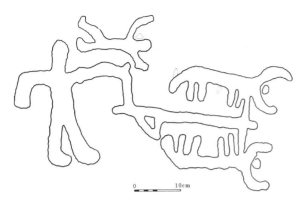

Fig. 12. A rock engraving of a prehistoric crook-ard at Finntorp, southern Sweden.

been used just to break the soil; the simplest form of ard, the crook-ard (Fig. 12) basically consists of a forked branch, one short prong of which acts as a share, the other as a beam. More complicated types of ard had their various wooden elements mortised together or had stone shares. Such ploughs could have been pulled by manpower but the use of oxen for traction is also a possibility.[13]

Information about animal husbandry is quite meagre, indeed the only major faunal assemblage from Newgrange, Co. Meath, is of later third millennium BC date. Relatively few settlements are known and, unfortunately, soil conditions, as at Ballynagilly and Townleyhall, are sometimes inimical to the preservation of bone. Animal bones also come from burial contexts, where they are sometimes considered to be the remains of funeral feasts, but such samples may be biased – possibly reflecting ritual imperatives rather than the animal population as a whole.

Early domesticated animals were cattle, pig, sheep or goat and dog. The introduction of cattle and sheep was undoubtedly an event with significant repercussions, and Peter Woodman has pointed out their appearance effectively doubled the number of types of large mammals in Ireland. As already mentioned, it has been suggested that cattle may have been an important component in the farming economy at an early date but, at present, no firm conclusions can be drawn about the relative importance of cattle and pig, for instance, in the general economy of the fourth millennium BC. The domesticated faunal remains from later settlement sites of the third millennium seem to indicate a significant reliance on cattle: at Lough Gur, Co. Limerick (where the figures may be unreliable) 95% to 99% of

the bones were of cattle and the slaughtering of mainly cattle and pig in an approximate proportion of 3:2 was recorded at Newgrange, Co. Meath. Evidence from a number of sites indicates that wild animals were hunted, these included red deer, brown bear, wild cat, hare, and a variety of birds, but their contribution to the economy seems to have been minimal. Fishing and food gathering were probably quite important but the scarcity of evidence means the general significance of these resources is still impossible to assess.[14]

SETTLEMENTS

A small number of fourth millennium settlements have been archaeologically excavated and a few have revealed traces of substantial timber houses indicating a degree of permanent settlement and shedding some limited light on domestic activities. Food preparation, including grinding grain and cooking, food storage and possibly spinning and weaving may have occurred in or near the house while pottery making and stone tool manufacture may have been undertaken nearby. Though the evidence is limited, at present the generally accepted pattern is that of single farmsteads with associated tillage plots and grazing land. Both rectangular houses and circular houses occur. The burnt remains of a rectangular timber house were revealed beneath blanket bog at Ballynagilly, Co. Tyrone, on a low hill about 200m above OD about 8km north-west of Cookstown. The house measured 39 square metres in area, being 6.5m in length and almost 6m in width; the side walls on the north and south were constructed of oak planks 45cm to 50cm wide vertically set in a narrow trench up to 30cm deep (Fig. 13). Post-holes found on the west and east may indicate end-walls though these were not clearly defined. If these were the end walls of the house the posts presumably supported panels of wickerwork or wattle and daub but it is also possible that the ground plan is incomplete and what survives is just a central room. Two posts in the middle of the house were probably roof supports. A roughly circular hearth and an area of burnt clay, possibly the site of an oven, were found within the house, as were a shallow pit containing sherds of pottery and several leaf-shaped flint arrowheads. Charcoal from the northern wall-trench provided two radiocarbon determinations with date ranges of 4340-3790 BC and 4222-3814 BC which suggest that the construction of the house was

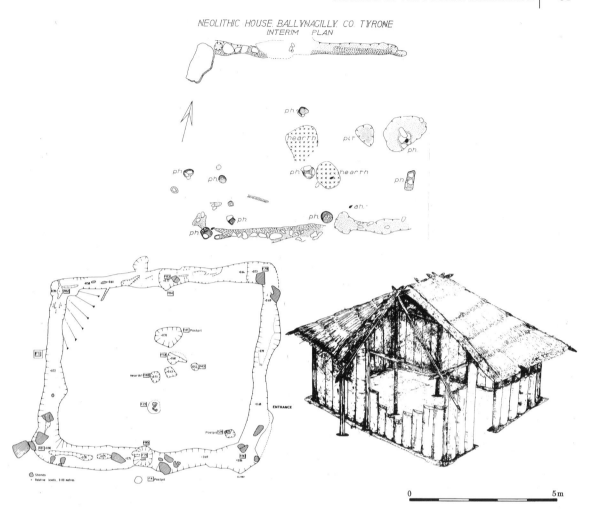

Fig. 13. Above. Plan of house at Ballynagilly, Co. Tyrone, showing postholes (ph), positions of flint arrowheads (ah) and foundation trenches for plank walling. Below. Plan and one possible reconstruction of House 1 at Tankardstown, Co. Limerick.

contemporary with the forest clearance indicated in the nearby pollen record. Two other pits in the vicinity with similar date ranges probably belong to this phase of activity. Later occupation may be attested by a hearth and two pits with dates ranging from about 3900 to about 3400 BC and this may coincide with a phase of possible pastoral activity suggested by pollen analysis.

Finds included narrow flint flakes with secondary trimming of the edges, leaf-shaped flint arrowheads (including three from the house and three more found just outside it), and fragments of polished stone axes; fragments of pottery represented plain, round-bottom shouldered vessels, an early pottery style called Lyles Hill ware. Because the soil was not conducive to the preservation of unburnt bone, only a few small fragments of burnt animal bone survived as did some burnt hazel nut shells.[15]

A similar house was discovered and excavated during construction work on a natural gas pipeline at Tankardstown, Co. Limerick. This (House 1) was one of two houses excavated on this site; rectangular in plan with an area of 47.3 square metres, it measured 7.4m by 6.4m and was also built of split oak planks set in foundation trenches up to 69cm deep (Fig. 13). In contrast to Ballynagilly however, this example was built entirely of oak planking with corner posts, a post in the centre of each of the longer sides, two internal and two external posts, all giving added support to the roof and walls. Concentrated deposits of burnt animal bone were found in the fill of the foundation trench usually near the bases of the packing stones for the posts, and may indicate some ritual practice in the course of construction. No occupation floor survived, ploughing had effectively destroyed everything except those features dug into the subsoil. There was no clear indication of a doorway but, since the house had been destroyed by fire, the absence of burning in a section of the foundation trench on the north-east side may denote the position of a door. An area of oxidized clay with an adjacent post-hole just north of centre may be the site of a hearth. Finds included pottery sherds and a leaf-shaped flint arrowhead. Charred cereal grains of wheat (emmer) were identified and radiocarbon dated to 3938–3378 BC and fragments of hazel nuts and seeds of crab apple were also found, a reminder that food gathering had some role in the economy. A second house, truncated by ploughing, was found 20m to the north-west; of different plan with maximum dimensions of about 15.2m by 7.4m, it had a large central room, 9.2m long, apparently flanked by smaller 2m wide rooms or annexes at either end with a total area of about 112.5 square metres. It too had been destroyed by fire. These gas pipeline investigations also revealed traces of another burnt structure at Pepperhill, near Buttevant, Co. Cork, but only limited excavation was undertaken. Both Tankardstown and Pepperhill were located on south-west facing slopes.

Cereal grains have also been found at Ballygalley, Co. Antrim, associated with the remains of a sub-rectangular house. This house was 13m long and 4.5m wide with a foundation trench for the external walls and three pairs of internal posts; there was a possible entrance on the south-west and an extension or annex (with a shallower foundation trench) at the other north-eastern end (Fig. 14). No traces of timber walling survived and it was assumed that the house may have been dismantled. A saddle quern was found in the annex and six others were also recovered on the site. A considerable quantity of carbonized cereal grains was found (mostly einkorn) and clearly cereal cultivation was probably important but the soil conditions did not favour the preservation of unburnt bone though a few cattle teeth and a little burnt bone were recovered nearby. Large amounts of pot sherds, flints and stone axes were recovered including axe roughouts made of Tievebulliagh and Rathlin porcellanite. A quantity of Arran pitchstone was imported from Scotland and other imported material included two stone axes from Great Langdale, Cumbria, and an axe of possible Cornish greenstone. Situated some 500m inland from Ballygalley Bay, north of Larne, this settlement may have been a redistribution centre of

some importance for local and imported material. The foundation trench of what seems to have been a second rectangular house was partly exposed just over 30m to the south.[16]

Another large house with an annex at one end was revealed beneath part of a megalithic tomb at Ballyglass, Co. Mayo. This structure was rectangular, 75.9 square metres in area and measuring about 13m by 6m, and its remains consisted of surprisingly shallow foundation trenches about 20cm deep and a number of stout post-holes up to 70cm in depth (Figs 14 and 39). The entrance was possibly at the north-western end where the excavator thought that three post-holes and a short foundation trench might represent some sort of porch and entrance passage. There was a narrow compartment or annex at the south-eastern end and while part of its wall was, like most of the house, probably built of timbers which were embedded in a foundation trench, the south-eastern corner was represented by only a shallow depression in the sub-soil and was, it seems, of less substantial construction. Two internal lines of post-holes may have been load-bearing and denote divisions of the house interior. Both the end compartment and the main part of the house contained areas of fire-reddened clay; these possible hearths and the wall trenches and post-holes contained sherds of pottery akin to that from Ballynagilly. Flint implements were few but some leaf-shaped arrowheads and concave scrapers may be associated with this occupation. Charcoal from the wall trenches of the house produced a series of radiocarbon determinations indicating occupation in the second half of the fourth millennium but the nature of this activity is debated and the structure could have had a ritual purpose.

Part of a long rectangular house with a clearly defined internal dividing wall, and measuring at least 10m in length and 6.9m in width, has been found at Newtown, Co. Meath, during construction work on a natural gas pipeline. Situated on the northern side of a gently sloping hill, this house had a row of three posts on its central long axis and a gap in the internal wall has been plausibly interpreted as a doorway; an external entrance probably existed at the north-east corner. Radiocarbon determinations indicate a probable date in the first half of the fourth millennium BC.[17]

Evidence of habitation of various dates has been found on Knockadoon, a rocky peninsula in Lough Gur, Co. Limerick, a majority of house sites being

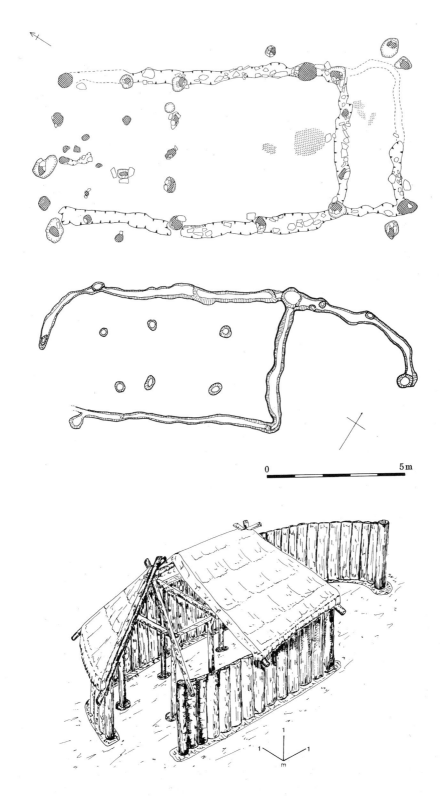

Fig. 14. Above. Plan of house at Ballyglass, Co. Mayo, with annex. Below. Simplified plan of house with annex at Ballygalley, Co. Antrim, and reconstruction.

located on south and south-west facing slopes, a tendency noted elsewhere as well. Site A there was excavated in 1939 and it is interesting to note that this site, the first early prehistoric house to be investigated in Ireland, was visible before excavation with the tops of the stones which marked the position of the walls protruding above the turf; all the others we have considered were accidentally revealed in the course of other work. This proved to be a large rectangular structure, its remains consisted of six rows of post-holes, the outer pair forming the walls which had an irregular stone foundation (Fig. 15), two internal rows supporting the roof. It measured about 10m by 5m internally. Part of the clay floor of the house was paved with stones, there was a central hearth and a gap in the stony wall foundation on the south-west was believed to be the entrance. A considerable amount of charcoal in the soil, particularly in the area of the wall and traces of burning (as at the north-west corner) suggested that the house had been burnt down. It has been proposed that the pairs of wall posts may have retained a wall about 1m thick with an organic fill, perhaps of sods, brushwood or rushes, standing on the stone footing which would have acted as a damp-proof course, a form of cavity wall construction so far found only at Lough Gur. The posts could themselves have supported rafters but they may have been attached to horizontal timbers, wall-plates, which would have allowed greater freedom in the positioning of roof timbers. The roof was probably thatched. Sherds of pottery were found, along with several flint and chert implements including a leaf-shaped arrowhead, several scrapers, a polished stone axe and a fragment of what may have been a slate spear-head. About a thousand fragments of cattle bones may attest to the importance of stock-rearing in the economy.

Round houses were also constructed and Site C at Lough Gur yielded the remains of three small, approximately circular houses possibly of third millennium BC date but not certainly contemporary; their average diameter was about 6m (Fig. 15). Two were built of a double ring of posts, as at Site A, and also possibly had an organic fill retained by facings supported on the timber uprights; an irregular scatter of posts within supported the roof; each contained a hearth and one or more pits perhaps for rubbish or storage. The third structure apparently consisted of a single circle of posts which may have supported a wattle-and-

daub wall. Circular houses are also reported from Slieve Breagh, Co. Meath: two were apparently excavated from 1960 to 1962 but no report has been published. A sequence of sub-rectangular structures may have been built at Site B at Lough Gur but no complete plans were recoverable while Site E may have been no more than an approximately rectangular temporary structure built against a rock face.

Though there is some uncertainty about their precise dates, some settlements were enclosed. At Sites K and L a sequence of occupation was also uncovered and at one stage at Site K an irregularly rectangular house was surrounded by a low enclosing wall. The enclosure had an average diameter of about 25m and consisted of a double ring of low boulders with a fill of earth and rubble between them; four post-holes at an entrance passage on the south-east suggested a double wooden gate (Fig. 16). Finds included leaf-shaped flint arrowheads, scrapers and plain round-bottomed pottery, coarse ware and some Beaker pottery, much of the latter apparently associated with a later phase of activity. The remains of a similar enclosure at Site L surrounded an irregular oval structure. These circular enclosures would have provided some protection for the occupants and perhaps for some of their animals but are too slight to be truly defensive; they and the elaborate entrance at Site K may, however, denote a house of special status and the greater number of beads found on these sites might be supportive evidence of this.[18]

Various structures of uncertain purpose have been found elsewhere: the foundation trench of a small roughly oval timber hut measuring about 4m by 2m was found a short distance to the west of the large tomb at Newgrange, Co. Meath; there was no evidence of domestic activity. Another larger structure has been revealed on the west of the great mound at Knowth, Co. Meath, where a sub-rectangular trench delimited an area 10.7m by 9.1m; post-holes were found only in the eastern trench and none occurred inside, pottery and flints were found but the nature of the structure and its function are indeterminate. Numerous arcs or circles of stake-holes with associated hearths, pits and decorated pottery sherds discovered both under and beside the great mound on the north-east and east are also of uncertain function.[19]

An oval enclosure in Glenulra townland, near Ballycastle, Co. Mayo, may possibly be of late fourth

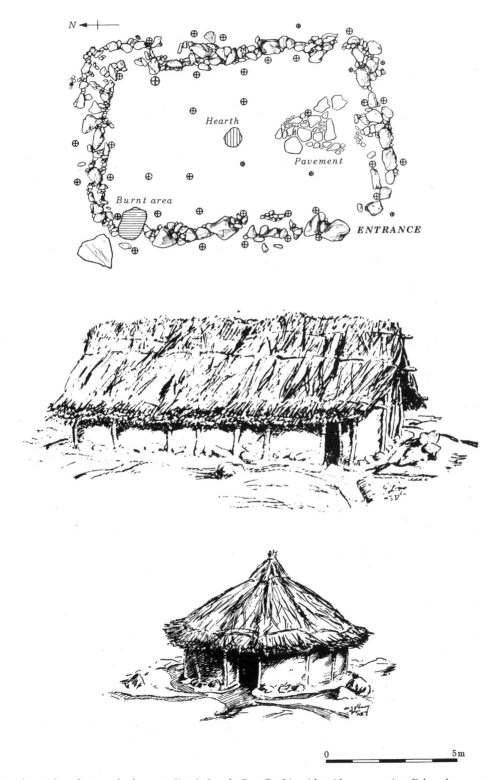

Fig. 15. Above. Plan of rectangular house at Site A, Lough Gur, Co. Limerick, with reconstruction. Below. A reconstruction of one of the circular houses at Site C.

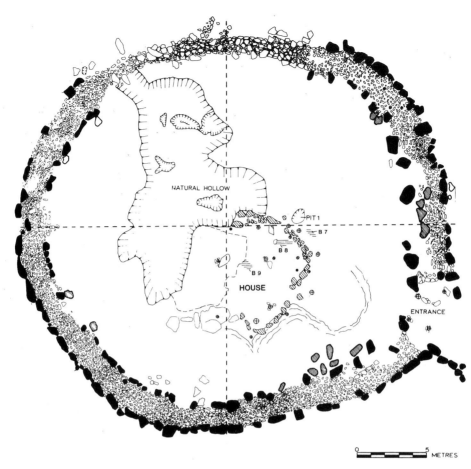

Fig. 16. Simplified plan of enclosed house site (Site K) at Lough Gur, Co. Limerick.

millennium date. It was formed by a low, poorly built stone wall delimiting an oval area 25m by 22m. Stake-holes perhaps representing some sort of structure, pottery sherds, a few chert and flint implements, and the stone tip or share of a primitive plough were found. It is one of several enclosures and megalithic tombs associated with an extensive field system extending over several townlands and now known as the Céide Fields.

The Céide Fields, a complex system of contemporary fields in Glenulra, Behy, and neighbouring townlands, demonstrates that early farmers, in this region at least, did not operate a pattern of shifting agriculture with small tillage plots but had an integrated agricultural system on a considerable scale. Long parallel stone walls, some up to 2km in length and 150m to 200m apart, form long rectangles which are divided by cross walls into large rectangular fields up to 7 hectares in area. The field system, preserved beneath blanket bog up to 4m in depth, has been traced by probing over an

area of over 1000 hectares (Fig. 17).[20] The surviving walls are surprisingly low, usually 50cm to 70cm high, rarely exceeding 80cm. In Seamas Caulfield's opinion the large fields were designed for stock raising rather than tillage though some smaller ones may have been used for growing wheat and barley, a picture supported by pollen analysis. This sort of coaxial field system, possibly planned and certainly laid out with one dominant axis, contrasts with the commoner aggregate field system where an irregular pattern has developed by piecemeal land enclosure.[21] Whether the whole complex was planned and laid out by one or more farming communities to allow easier management of stock and grassland is not certain. Caulfield believes the clearance of this large area of its forest cover and the division of the landscape into stone-walled fields demanded the cooperative effort of a very sizeable settled community and the presence of a dozen megalithic tombs in the general area might give weight to this suggestion. Communal effort is very

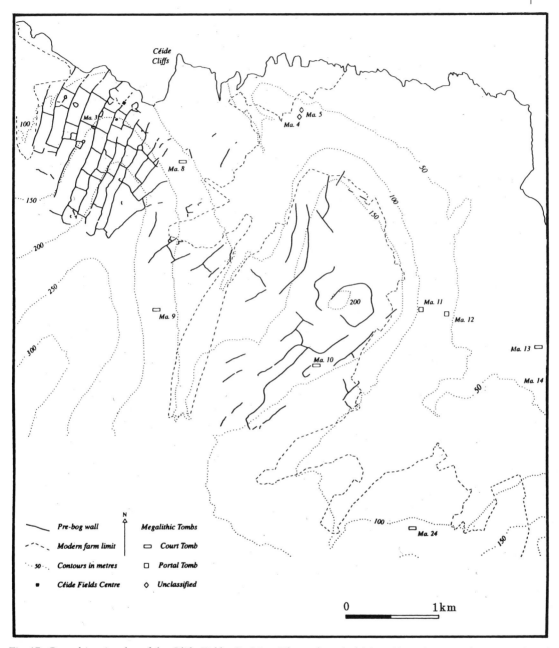

Fig. 17. General interim plan of the Céide Fields, Co. Mayo. The tomb marked Mayo 13 on the east is the court tomb and house at Ballyglass.

probable but the numbers involved are difficult to estimate. Both tomb construction and the development of the field complex may have spanned several centuries. What prompted wall construction and the coaxial rectilinear plan is also obscure; it may be that the long rectangles represent some piecemeal land clearance in long rectangular swathes and the low stone walls were a means of resolving the problem of disposing of cleared stones

and even provided the foundation for some form of fencing. It is also possible that these fields were a social statement asserting ownership and control, the construction of field systems like the building of houses and tombs is a way of laying claim to place. Pollen analysis indicates that the period of intensive farming here spanned some 500 years from about 3700 to 3200 BC and was at its most intensive for about 250 years. The spread of the blanket bog, which was to envelope the field system, was underway by 2700 BC.

A much smaller group of pre-bog stone walls forming small irregular fields has been identified just 7km to the west of the Céide Fields in the townland of Belderg Beg. A series of radiocarbon dates from pine and oak trees growing on a thin layer of peat formed just as the blanket bog commenced to grow suggests that this aggregate field system dates to some time before the early third millennium BC, a date supported by the discovery of some pottery, flints and a polished stone axe. Other evidence of early pre-bog settlement, including field systems, houses sites and megalithic tombs, has been found at Rathlackan, east of Ballycastle.[22]

Limited excavation on the low ridge known as Feltrim Hill, near Malahide, Co. Dublin, produced considerable settlement evidence, including pottery, stone and flint implements, axes, and much waste material demonstrating flint working on the site, but no house traces. Later occupation on the hill in early Historic times may well have contributed to the destruction of the earlier remains. An extensive scatter of flints on Paddy's Hill, in Robswalls townland, 4km to the east, testified to occupation there but excavation just revealed two pits and prolonged agricultural activity on the site may have been responsible for the lack of structural evidence. The picture at Lyles Hill, Co. Antrim, was also complicated by later activity. Excavations by Estyn Evans at various times from 1937 to 1951 on this conspicuous 250m high hill north-west of Belfast concentrated on a low cairn near the summit which proved to be a burial monument of the second millennium BC. It overlay a hearth and occupation area measuring over 4m by 2m which produced numerous flints and hundreds of fragments of characteristic pottery soon to be widely known as Lyles Hill pottery. This material was assumed to be a ritual accumulation derived from nearby settlement; no house foundations were found but the excavator suggested that the quantity of pottery argued for more than brief occupation in the vicinity. Similar pottery was found in an earthen bank which surrounded the hilltop and enclosed an area about 380m by 210m or some 6.25 hectares. It was tentatively suggested that occupation and large enclosure were contemporary but such an early date for a hill-top enclosure was disputed. Further limited excavation in 1987 and 1988 demonstrated

than the enclosing bank was indeed a later feature but also revealed two approximately parallel stone-packed palisade trenches set 3m to 6m apart which were traced for at least 25m around the contours of the hill. A hearth produced some carbonized barley and was radiocarbon dated to the fourth millennium BC. The palisade trenches yielded typical Lyles Hill pottery and charcoal from both indicated dates in the third millennium. It seems likely that the hilltop was enclosed by two timber palisades rather than an earthwork at this time; the inner palisade dated to about 3000 BC, the other to about 2800-2300 BC.[23]

Evidence of extensive hilltop occupation has been found on Donegore Hill, Co. Antrim, 8km to the north of Lyles Hill. Field survey recovered large quantities of pottery and flints in a ploughed field on the summit of this 234m hill. Excavation demonstrated that ploughing had destroyed all but the last traces of various structures but some pits did contain pot sherds, charcoal and carbonized hazel nut shells and many thousands of pottery sherds were found. Waste flint material indicated flint working on site. Aerial photography after a particularly dry spell of weather revealed that the hilltop had been partly enclosed by a parallel pair of ditches which delimited an area about 200m by 150m. Further excavation showed that the ditches were rock cut being dug through the glacial till into the basalt below; they were about 1m to 2m deep and 3m wide and produced more pottery. There were gaps in both at several places recalling the similar interrupted (segmented) ditches of enclosures in England and on the Continent where discontinuous stretches of ditches seem to be a means of symbolically defining areas of special significance. An inner palisade trench is also reported. A series of radiocarbon dates indicates prolonged occupation from about 4000 to 2700 BC. A possible palisaded enclosure has been identified on the Hill of Tara dating to some time before 3000 BC and traces of other palisade trenches have been found at Knowth.[24]

Substantial houses such as Ballyglass and others have been generally interpreted as a reflection of small, individual, farming communities and, as already mentioned, it is generally believed that scattered, self-sufficient farmsteads, rather than villages or hamlets, were the norm in prehistoric Ireland. But this particular bucolic picture is probably due to limited investigation. Given the need for cooperative labour and the various problems posed by early agriculture, settlement clusters may have been common enough. The correlation of some megalithic tombs and good soils suggests a keen awareness of the agricultural potential of certain areas and must have influenced settlement location in a significant way. The general pattern may have been one of scattered clusters of farmsteads and in some areas settlement may have been even more concentrated, as at Lough Gur, at the extensive field systems at Céide, Co. Mayo, and, as Gabriel Cooney has argued, in the Boyne Valley, Co. Meath. While relatively temporary, flimsy and easily replaceable dwellings may have been the norm for a section of some communities and some 'social units may have been fluid and shifting from season to season' as Julian Thomas has claimed, the construction of megalithic tombs would seem to imply a keen territorial awareness on the part of a sizeable population and substantial houses and field systems indicate a settled one as well.[25]

Some settlements were enclosed and, in certain instances, as at Donegore and Lyles Hill, the enclosing palisades may have been expressions of higher status, but such measures may well have been defensive too and indicative of some warlike activity. There is some rather tenuous evidence for violent skirmishing at least: the flint arrowheads found in and near the burnt house at Ballynagilly may indicate a violent end to that homestead and the discovery, in a megalithic tomb at Poulnabrone, Co. Clare, of an adult male with the tip of a flint or chert arrowhead embedded in a hip bone shows how lethal such weapons might be; this could have been an accidental injury, of course, but it would be unwise to assume that warfare was not an occasional early prehistoric pastime.

As already mentioned, some communities may have been less sedentary than others, the practice of transhumance, the movement of livestock to summer hill-pastures, may have involved the construction of flimsy huts, as may seasonal visits to the coast for fishing, shellfish collecting or perhaps salt production. Coastal settlement is certainly attested in marshland at Bay Farm II, near Carnlough, Co. Antrim, and coastal activity of some description by numerous finds of pottery and flints in sand dunes notably in north-eastern Ireland such as Whitepark Bay, Co. Antrim, Portstewart, Co. Derry, and Dundrum, Co. Down. Artefacts from these northern sandhills range in date from the fourth millennium BC to the Medieval era, shells and bones have been found and dark layers in the dunes are interpreted as old land surfaces and deposits of organic refuse. Hearths represented by concentrations of charcoal and burnt stones have been noted from time to time. Few of these sandhills sites have been scientifically excavated but it is clear that because of wind erosion, for example, and for other reasons, material of widely different dates may sometimes occur in association. In the White Rocks sandhills, near Portrush, Co. Antrim, part of a polished stone axe, various flints, a late prehistoric brooch, pottery of the early Historic period and a Medieval coin were all found in or on the same old land surface. Several sites on the Murlough peninsula at Dundrum, Co. Down, have been excavated and have produced evidence of activity in prehistoric and early Historic times. Fourth millennium finds comprised pottery sherds and crude flints and in one area (Site 6) traces of fires were found in the form of charcoal and burnt stones, a rough semi-circle of five stake-holes may have been the remains of a shelter or wind-break and a pair of post-holes some metres away may also have supported a flimsy structure of some sort. Charcoal from a pebble-floored hearth at Site 12 associated with plain, shouldered pottery and some flint-work has provided radiocarbon dates with ranges spanning the fourth millennium. If the reasons for the brief and possibly seasonal visits to Dundrum are obscure, it is evident that the collecting of shellfish was of importance elsewhere. At Culleenamore, Co. Sligo, a shell-midden contained a hearth which produced a fourth millennium radiocarbon date; shells were mainly oyster with some cockles, mussels, periwinkle, scallop and limpet and it has been suggested that this and other coastal middens in the area were one of a series of food sources seasonally exploited by the builders of the nearby megalithic tombs on Knocknarea and at Carrowmore.[26]

A different type of seasonal activity may have taken place on Geroid Island in Lough Gur. Limited excavations there revealed a third millennium occupation layer: charcoal, burnt stones, animal bones, pottery sherds and flints were found and pollen analysis suggested that the island supported oak trees at this time. The small number of animal bones recovered were mainly of cattle and pig but, in contrast to nearby Knockadoon where cattle was predominant, almost 50% of the island bones were those of pig. Since pig is a woodland animal, this small wooded island may have provided seasonal grazing for both pig and cattle.[27]

Not surprisingly both the identification and the explanation of temporary occupation sites present problems. That house found beneath a megalithic tomb at Ballyglass, Co. Mayo, was evidently a substantial structure even if its purpose is uncertain but hearths, spreads of charcoal, pottery sherds and stone implements found beneath other tombs such as Ballybriest, Co. Derry, Ballymarlagh, Co. Antrim, and Baltinglass, Co. Wicklow, are sometimes equally difficult to interpret. While these finds may be the remains of some temporary habitation on the site prior to the construction of the monument, it is also possible that they could represent ritual activity. At Knockiveagh, Co. Down, a layer of black earth beneath a hilltop cairn was up to 10cm thick and contained charcoal, pottery sherds, and carbonized hazel-nuts; this was considered to be an artificial accumulation scraped up from an area of occupation and intentionally dumped on the site; charcoal provided a radiocarbon determination suggesting a fourth millennium date. Occupation found beneath one of the small mounds at Newgrange, Co. Meath (Site L) was clearly earlier than the superimposed monument. A few small pits, a hollow containing broken pottery, a few small areas of burning, and some flint scrapers and waste flakes were all that remained and no traces of structures were found. The hollow containing pottery had silted up and a thin grass line had formed before the mound was built suggesting some period of time between the two phases of activity. A possible hearth and a few scattered post-holes were found beneath Site Z and indicate pre-tomb activity there. Traces of considerable pre-tomb activity, which George Eogan considers probably domestic, has also been found in the vicinity of or beneath several sites at Knowth and include the large rectangular and stake-built structures already mentioned as well as palisade trenches, pits, hearths and areas of pebbling. A little animal bone, pottery, flints and stretches of foundation trenches dating to about 4000 BC and shortly thereafter discovered beneath part of the great mound and just to the east of it constitute the earliest activity there.

Evidence of temporary occupation was also found beneath a megalithic tomb at Townleyhall, Co. Louth, where an occupation layer had a maximum thickness of 15cm and extended over a roughly oval area about 15m by 11m. A scatter of over 140 small stakeholes (with no coherent plan) and nine hearths were revealed. Since some stake-holes were found beneath hearths and one hearth was superimposed on another, it seems likely that the site was occupied on several occasions. Finds included numerous pottery fragments and flint scrapers, as well as carbonized grains of wheat and charred hazel-nut shells. The fact that the bulk of the flints were either concave scrapers or convex scrapers suggests that some specialized activity occasioned this intermittent occupation which, judging from a radiocarbon date obtained from charcoal, dates to the third millennium BC.

Another site at Townleyhall, called Townleyhall I and situated 1.8km to the east, may have been similar. It consisted of a mound which covered a large scatter of over 90 stake-holes again associated with convex and concave flint scrapers; this occupation area was partly enclosed by a low penannular bank with external ditch.[28]

Similar specialized activity seems to have occurred at two sites on Knocknarea, Co. Sligo. Located on the eastern slopes of the mountain at a height of about 275m above sea level and 300m north-east of the great cairn and smaller tombs on its summit, they are part of a small cluster of roughly circular or semi-circular embanked sites 5m to 10m in diameter. The site named Hut Site 1 consisted of an oval penannular stony bank enclosing an area some 7m by 4m (Fig. 18). An external ditch had been dug to provide drainage and a series of 79 dark spots which contained wood remains in most instances were interpreted as former post-holes. The majority of these posts were inclined and set in the low bank and were considered to represent a succession of three light-weight timber-built huts possibly covered with hides or thatch. No hearth was found but some sherds of pottery and hundreds of flint and chert implements were recovered and included an exceptionally large number of concave scrapers. Hut Site 2, about 70m to the west, was similar and burnt limestone slabs in the centre were believed to represent a hearth; it too produced a large quantity of concave scrapers mostly of chert, some showing signs of considerable use. The concave scrapers represented 39.5% and 25.8% of the total number of artefacts at these respective sites and clearly denote some specialized form of work, though exactly what is unknown. The upland location might indicate seasonal hunting or grazing

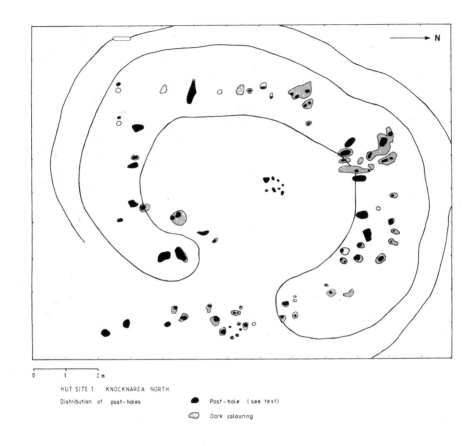

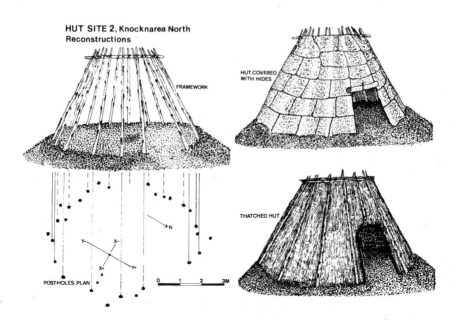

Fig. 18. Above. Plan of Hut Site 1 with low bank and external ditch at Knocknarea, Co. Sligo; the black or hatched spots indicate the position of certain or possible timbers. Below. Reconstruction of the similarly built Hut Site 2.

combined with some cutting or paring activity – and possibly connected with rituals at the nearby tombs as well. Perhaps these sites and the middens at Culleenamore were all part of a spectrum of exploitation of different resources in the fourth and third millennia BC. A scatter of flints, including concave scrapers, and some pottery were found at Windy Ridge, near Carnlough, Co. Antrim, at an altitude of about 300m. Here it is possible that some maintenance and repair activities were carried out perhaps as 'boredom reduction strategies' in the hunting season. A large quantity of worked flint was found on Nappan Mountain, about 9km to the north-east at a slightly lower elevation of 250m, but the presence of hearths and pottery and a significant number of convex scrapers suggested more substantial settlement and a wider or different range of activities. Extensive traces of flint working were found at Goodland, in north-east Antrim, about 240m above sea-level. Some circular structures with occasional rectangular hearths found at an altitude of about 360m at Piperstown in the Dublin mountains may also reflect some particular upland activity.[29]

Temporary camps such as Townleyhall and Knocknarea emphasize how meagre our knowledge is about the diversity of settlement types and about the wider range of subsistence strategies in the fourth and third millennia. It is likely that there was a greater degree of seasonal mobility than is generally believed. The relative importance of such activity in the economy as whole is impossible to assess at present but it does seem likely that some members of some settled communities exploited a range of resources and occupied seasonal camps, both coastal and inland, for purposes as varied as the procuring of the raw materials for the manufacture of stone axes and flint implements, pottery vessels, wooden artefacts and basketry work on the one hand and for activities which included food gathering, fishing, hunting and even tomb building on the other.

POTTERY

Because of its durability, pottery is one of the commonest artefacts to survive on a settlement site or in a tomb. It is assumed to be a characteristic feature of early farming communities but, of course, its manufacture does not prove the existence of a farming economy. Nonetheless, in Ireland as in much of Europe, its first appearance is indeed associated with early agriculturalists. Several different types of hand-made pottery have been recognized in fourth millennium Ireland and several general classifications have been proposed. The fragmentary nature of the evidence is, of course, a problem and considerable variety in form and decoration makes concise description difficult but following the work of Humphrey Case and Alison Sheridan in particular, it is possible, with some modification of their preferred terminologies, to outline the principal types (Fig. 19).

The Carinated Bowl style is the earliest pottery found in Ireland and has close parallels with pottery found in eastern and northern England, Scotland and Wales. This is a well-made, hard, thin, often leathery-looking ware with smoothed or burnished surfaces usually of reddish brown to dark brown in colour, but sometimes virtually black. Pots are round-bottomed with distinctive shoulders or carinations, concave necks and simple pointed or slightly rounded rims. Almost all are open bowls with a mouth diameter as great or greater than the shoulder diameter. Some simple hemispherical bowls or cups also occur. Apart from some finger-tip rippling or fluting executed in the wet clay before firing, decoration is usually absent and wall thickness may be no more than 5-6mm. Perforations, probably for the attachment of cords for suspension, occur on occasion but protruding lugs are rare. This style has a wide Irish distribution and has been found in reasonably securely dated contexts at sites such as Ballynagilly, Co. Tyrone, Ballygalley, Co. Antrim, Newtown, Co. Meath, Tankardstown, Co. Limerick, and Pepperhill, Co. Cork. On present evidence (and discounting the earlier dates from Ballynagilly) this style appears about 4000 BC and is a feature of the first half of the fourth millennium, after which modified regional or local pottery styles appear. These developed styles include Lyles Hill style, Limerick style and Decorated Bowl style pottery which emerge in the middle of the fourth millennium. There is evidence that both they and the Carinated Bowl style were in contemporaneous use for a number of centuries thereafter.

Lyles Hill style pottery, a term coined over 40 years ago and once synonymous with the generic 'Western Neolithic' pottery of some writers which included the fine carinated pottery just mentioned, is now applied to a developed pottery style with a markedly angular shoulder and a straight or almost

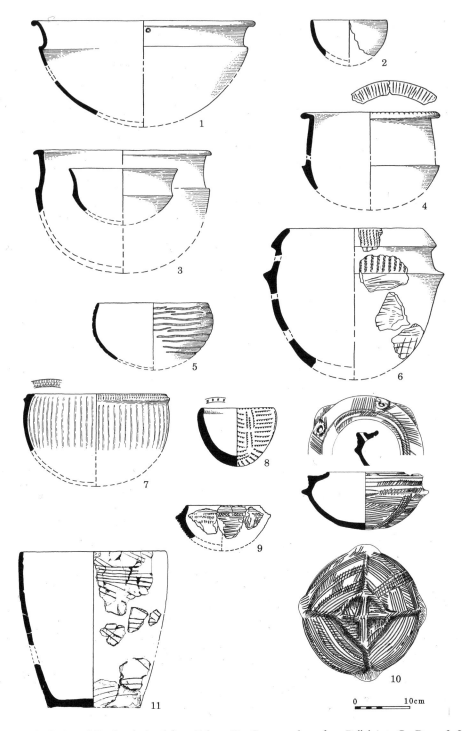

Fig. 19. Pottery. 1-2. Carinated Bowl style: bowl from Cohaw, Co. Cavan, and cup from Ballybriest, Co. Derry. 3. Lyles Hill style bowls from Lyles Hill, Co. Antrim. 4. Limerick style bowl with incised decoration on the rim from Lough Gur, Co. Limerick. 5-8. Decorated Bowl style: 5. Goodland bowl with impressed whipped cord decoration from Lyles Hill, Co. Antrim. 6. Bowl with collared rim from Island MacHugh, Co. Tyrone, with impressed twisted cord and incised ornament. 7. Newferry, Co. Antrim, with incised decoration. 8. Carrowkeel bowl with stabbed decoration from Lislea, Co. Monaghan. 9-10. Bipartite Bowl style: 9. Ballynamona, Co. Waterford. 10. Drimnagh, Co. Dublin. 11. Grooved Ware from Knowth, Co. Meath.

straight neck; rims may still be simple but more often than not are flat, angular or even T-shaped and wall thicknesses are greater, often 6mm-10mm or more. Open bowls are common; closed forms in which the mouth is notably narrower than the shoulder diameter are rarer. Decoration is virtually absent: finger-tip rippling sometimes occurs on neck and rim and some sherds from Lyles Hill itself and a few other sites have simple decoration usually in the form of one or more rows of impressions on or inside the rim. Suspension holes occur. Limerick style pottery is a related regional pottery style, known from various sites in and around the Lough Gur area, this is the Class I pottery of Ó Ríordáin, the Limerick style of Case, and is noteworthy for the occasional occurrence of simple incised decoration mainly on out-turned rims and sometimes near the shoulder. Rim forms are usually simple or flat and out-turned. Mouth diameters are often much the same as that of the shoulder which is often angular.

The Decorated Bowl style is a term used here to embrace a range of decorated round-bottomed bowls of various forms and fabrics given different names by different writers; some are of simple semi-globular form with rare shoulders which, when they occur, are usually poorly defined. This semi-globular form includes pots with rounded or bevelled rims which are often simple but may also be accentuated in several ways – including out-turned, in-turned, T-shaped, and thickened or collared examples. Decoration is frequent, short incised lines or jabs often ornament the rims and the upper part of the vessel or the whole of the exterior may bear incised or cord ornament often made by a twisted cord impressed in the wet clay before firing; simple patterns of parallel horizontal or vertical lines are common and filled triangles and rectangular panels occur. This category includes a group called Goodland bowls, named after a site in Co. Antrim, which have an inturned profile, simple rims and cord-impressed decoration; examples with characteristic basalt grit are more or less confined to east Ulster.[30] Other prominent bowl types include examples with thickened, heavy, collared or flat rims, occasional lugs and cord impressed, grooved or incised ornament, well known on northern sandhills and other sites. These latter types need further study but have been variously called 'Sandhills Western pottery', 'Dundrum bowls', 'Murlough bowls', 'Broad-rimmed vessels', etc. The

Decorated Bowl style also includes Carrowkeel ware, a distinctive, profusely decorated, round-bottomed bowl with simple rim. The fabric is usually hard and invariably relatively thick and coarse with large grits of crushed pebble or shell. The all-over decoration is impressed or incised or both; impressions are executed with a sharp or blunted implement – perhaps a piece of wood or bone, or even occasionally a bird-bone or a shell-edge. A characteristic decorative technique, unhappily termed 'stab-and-drag' ornament, consists of a line made by a pointed implement applied with intermittent pressure producing an indented groove. Impressions are sometimes haphazard, linear ornament (including indented grooves) sometimes occurs in irregular zones or panels and occasionally parallel lines form shallow arcs; one or two horizontal lines just below the rim is a frequent feature.

A Bipartite Bowl style consists of a series of finely made and finely decorated bowls with a sharp shoulder and inturned upper body producing pots with an acute bipartite profile and mouths noticeably narrower than the greatest diameter. Some have been called Ballyalton bowls and are well-made, shouldered, narrow-mouthed, round-bottomed bowls with distinctive decoration. The diameter of the rim is invariably less than that of the shoulder, sometimes very markedly so. The inbent neck of these vessels may vary from slightly concave, as in the Carinated Bowl style and some Lyles Hill pottery, to straight with a quite acute shoulder angle; a variety of rims, including rounded, out-turned and inturned examples, occur. Decoration both above and below the shoulder seems to be the norm: parallel grooved lines are common, impressed lines executed with lengths of twisted cord or whipped cord (that is thin cord or sinew wrapped around a stamp or another piece of cord) are also fairly frequent. Lugs and raised ribs are found on a few vessels and the criss-crossing ribs on the bowl from Drimnagh, Co. Dublin, are a reminder that while some vessels were used as cooking pots others may have been suspended in rope containers and perhaps used for storage purposes. This Co. Dublin example and a significant number of others have been found in burials (Linkardstown Graves, Chapter 3) and some of these very finely decorated Bipartite Bowls may have had special symbolic significance. Some Bipartite Bowls have parallels in Scotland and the type may have been inspired by Scottish ceramic fashions. Decorated Bowl and Bipartite Bowl pottery was used throughout the later fourth and earlier third millennium BC eventually being replaced by new ceramic fashions such as Grooved Ware, as well as fine and coarse Beaker pottery which will be considered in Chapter 4.

The appearance of Grooved Ware, possibly early in the third millennium BC, demonstrates that flat-bottomed tub-shaped pots, some with decoration formed by parallel grooved lines, were also part of the ceramic repertoire at this time. Sherds have been found at Knowth and Newgrange. The date of a series of relatively coarse, flat-bottomed, undecorated tub-shaped pots is uncertain. It is now known that much of this sort of plain coarse pottery at Lough Gur, the Class II ware of Ó Ríordáin and the Knockadoon style of Case, dates to the second or first millennium BC. However, some plain coarse pottery comes from early contexts, sherds from Poulnabrone, Co. Clare, date to the fourth millennium and some sherds of flat-bottomed pottery from Geroid Island in Lough Gur apparently date to the third.

STONE IMPLEMENTS

Though flint and mudstone axes were part of the tool kit of early hunters and foragers and the stone axe continued in use into the third millennium and possibly even much later, the polished stone axe is considered a particularly characteristic implement of the early farming communities of the fourth and third millennia in which it was, no doubt, an important instrument in forest clearance. It could have been used for either ring-barking or felling; experiments have shown that substantial trees, particularly soft woods, can be relatively quickly felled by one person. It has been determined that a young birch tree 15cm in diameter can be felled in as little as 15 minutes; larger trees were probably felled for planking which was presumably radially cleft from split trunks with the aid of wooden wedges. Stone axes were effectively used in the construction of wooden trackways in Corlea and Cloonbony, Co. Longford, in the fourth and third millennia BC. Polishing the edge of an axe can improve its cutting capability but the laborious polishing of the entire surface must also indicate a growing concern with the decorative elaboration of such artefacts.

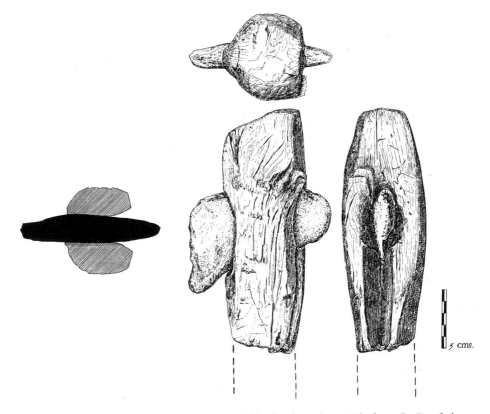

5 cms.

Fig. 20. Polished stone axehead and the remains of its haft of alder found in a bog at Edercloon, Co. Longford.

A small number of stone axes from Britain and Ireland have been found with their perforated wooden hafts and a variety of woods were used. In Ireland, the remains of a haft of alder still retaining its stone axe (Fig. 20) was found at a depth of some 2.4m in a bog south of Roosky, in Edercloon townland, Co. Longford; another fragment of a perforated alder haft and an axe came from the lower levels of a bog at Carrowntreila, south of Ballina, Co. Mayo; a haft of pine was found in Co. Monaghan and an example of apple wood comes from Maguire's Bridge, Co. Fermanagh. Other hafts are reported from Lissard, Co. Longford, and Carrickfergus, Co. Antrim. The axes were inserted into perforated pieces of wood and it is possible that bindings of leather thongs or resin were used to secure them though ethnographic evidence and experimental work suggest that these are not essential. The majority of axes are 8cm to 16cm in length and it is assumed they were used for woodworking, the larger for tree felling, the smaller for lighter work such as coppicing or for more specialized carpentry tasks; small examples may have been mounted in sleeves of antler. Not all axes were necessarily woodworking implements, some examples were probably used as weapons and others – including some very small and some very large ones – may have had a ceremonial and symbolic role.[31]

Different forms of stone axes have been recognized but detailed classifications have yet to be devised. The principal shapes, based on the plan or 'face shape' of the axe, comprise symmetrical oval

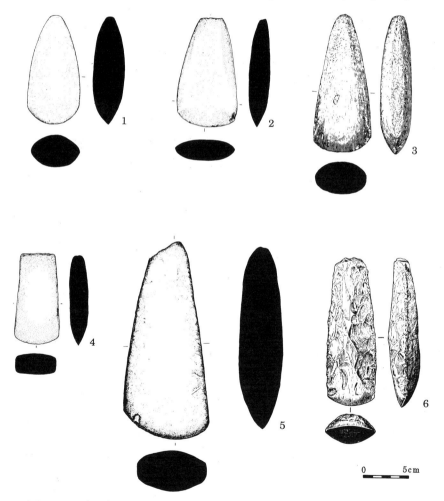

Fig. 21. Stone axes. 1. Symmetrical oval axehead from Co. Limerick. 2. Asymmetrical axehead with one convex side from Loughantarve, Co. Louth. 3. Straight-sided axehead from Mullacrew, Co. Louth. 4. Parallel-sided axehead from Dunbin, Co. Louth. 5. Axehead with diagonal butt from Ballynakill, Co. Meath. 6. Flint axehead with polished cutting edge from Killarida, Co. Kerry.

axes, asymmetrical axes with one convex side, splaying straight-sided axes, parallel-sided axes, axes with diagonal butts, and a large miscellaneous category of other shapes. Flint axes were also used but are rare; both unpolished or partly polished axes of flint are known, mainly from the flint bearing north-east, and some may have had specialized uses as adzes or chisels (Fig. 21).[32]

Axes have a wide distribution with a major concentration in the north-east of the country but other areas of relatively high density occur and include the Lough Gur region, part of the area around inner Galway Bay, and the Shannon at Killaloe. Some regional concentrations probably reflect the energies of local collectors to a certain extent. The great majority of these axes are stray finds, casual discoveries with no apparent archaeological context but, as already mentioned, examples have been found on various settlement sites, such as Ballynagilly, Ballygalley and Lough Gur, and significant numbers have been found in bogs and large numbers have been recovered from rivers, notably from the Bann, the Shannon, the Erne and the Barrow. Over 300 have been found in the River Bann particularly at Portglenone and Toome Bridge and over 700 are recorded from the River Shannon at Killaloe. While some of these were probably accidentally lost and some river finds may derive from riverside settlements, others may represent deliberate ritual offerings, a practice which becomes particularly noteworthy in later prehistory with the formal deposition of metalwork in watery contexts. That deliberate stone axe deposition was an occasional practice is demonstrated by a number of possible hoards. The most notable of these is a group of about 16 fine porcellanite axes found in glacial sand at Danesfort, on the Malone Road, Belfast. The discovery was made about 1872 near a trackway which had been constructed on the side of a hill and the objects were found within a small area 'each standing on its end in the sand with its edge turned upwards'. Some are exceptionally large and highly polished examples and they show no signs of use; they ranged from about 22cm to about 33cm in length. A number have that diagonal butt already mentioned which may be a mark of a prestigious item and the manner of their deposition, with cutting edge upwards, suggests ritual deposition. Three highly polished and unused stone axes, 20cm to 26cm in length, found together in a bog in Canrawer townland, near Oughterard, Co. Galway,

and a collection of two flint axes, 39 flint flakes, a nodule and two other flint implements discovered at the base of one of the stones of a megalithic tomb at Ballyalton, Co. Down, may be similar deposits. Whether a cache of a dozen stone axes found in the 19th century in a small copper mine on Ballyrisode Hill, near Goleen, Co. Cork, should be considered ritual or not is uncertain. A number of complete or fragmentary stone axes have been associated with megalithic tombs and other sites.[33]

A major research undertaking, the Irish Stone Axe Project, has demonstrated that these objects were particularly common in Ireland. Over 18,000 have been recorded, compared with an estimated 4000 in Scotland. Petrological analysis, which attempts to identify the rock types used and the sources of this raw material, can in some cases provide important information about the distribution of specific axe types and about the extent of early prehistoric contacts. A systematic programme of such analyses, a major component of this project, has shown that a wide variety of rock types were used and not surprisingly locally-available materials were often exploited. A hard, blue-grey porcellanite, which outcrops on the slopes of Tievebulliagh, near Cushendall, Co. Antrim, and at Brockley at the western end of Rathlin Island, was particularly popular. This rock type has long been known as a major source of material for axe manufacture but one of the significant results of this study was the recognition that these Antrim sources accounted for 53.8% of Irish stone axe production. Porcellanite axes are widely distributed throughout the country but are particularly common in the north. Fine grained sedimentary rocks such as mudstone and shale are the next most common rocks used (9.6% and 13.6% respectively) but in contrast to porcellanite could have many possible sources including glacial tills and alluvial and beach deposits. They commonly occur in the west, midlands and south. Among the other rock types exploited were sandstone (3.7%), schist (3.4%) and various coarse igneous types. A few other extraction sites have been identified. Naturally formed flat shale pebbles at Fisherstreet, near Doolin, Co. Clare, would have required very little modification to make them into axes with a sharp cutting edge and a dark green porphyry was quarried on Lambay Island, Co. Dublin, for some limited axe production. Coarse grained igneous rocks such as porphyry and dolerite are commonest on the east coast.

Antrim porcellanite was extensively worked at Tievebulliagh and Brockley and these extraction sites have been termed 'axe factories' because numerous waste flakes and axe rough-outs have been found there, the latter roughly shaped lumps of stone being normally transported elsewhere for polishing and sharpening. However, because both the scale and the duration of the quarrying and chipping work are difficult to quantify, the term extraction site is preferable because centralized and large-scale specialized 'factory' production may not have been the case, rather the process may have been episodic and on a modest scale but over a long period of time. To complicate the picture some porcellanite was probably derived from glacial erratics. A number of flaked axe rough-outs have been found in Co. Antrim in particular, including many from the valleys near Tievebulliagh. Sandstone

polishers were used to smooth the rough-outs, sandstone with coarse quartz grains being particularly effective. At Loughaveema, just over 9km from Tievebulliagh, a site has been discovered where considerable trimming and polishing of porcellanite rough-outs seems to have been undertaken: a rough-out and fragments of polished axes were found. Although porcellanite axes did not occur on the Ballynagilly settlement, where the axes were made from the local igneous rock, evidence from Ballygalley and other sites indicates that this rock type was exploited from the earlier fourth millennium. It continued to be widely used throughout the third millennium and a number of porcellanite implements come from early second millennium BC contexts as well.[34]

Petrological analysis indicates that axes of Antrim porcellanite had a wide distribution (Fig. 22). While

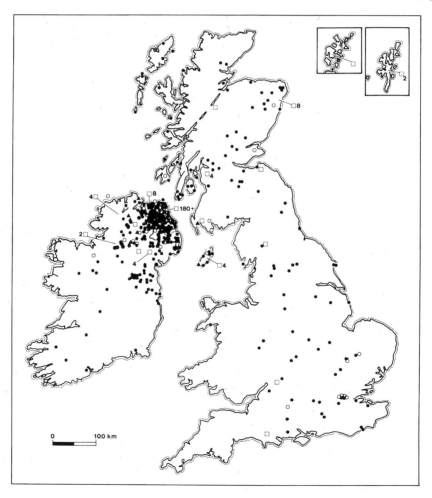

Fig. 22. Distribution of porcellanite axes and other artefacts in Ireland and Britain. Open symbols indicate imprecise or uncertain provenance and numbers denote multiple examples.

the majority occur in north-eastern Ireland, notably in Co. Antrim and in the eastern part of Co. Derry, axes of this rock type have also been found in various other parts of Ireland and as far away as the south of England and in Scotland with distinct concentrations in the Clyde region and in the north-east in Aberdeenshire. Island finds include examples from the Isle of Man, and various islands off the west coast of Scotland including the Hebrides as well as Orkney and Shetland. The apparent scarcity or absence of these axes in some localities, such as Wales, might be explained by the abundance of locally-available axes in these areas. While finished axes were normally exported, a small number of rough-outs have been found in south-west Scotland.

How axes were traded or exchanged has been considered by various writers, most recently by Alison Sheridan who notes that part of the area of densest distribution in Antrim and Derry (and adjacent coastal regions in Scotland and elsewhere) might have constituted a supply zone in which people may have gone straight to the sources and extracted the raw material themselves. Beyond this there also may have been a contact zone in which finished objects or rough-outs were obtained directly from communities in the supply zone. In this contact zone and further afield various forms of exchange seem the most likely distribution mechanism in which communities passed on various supplies, including stone artefacts, to each other through a network of contacts. Exceptionally well-made axes may have had a powerful symbolic value and may have been prestigious elements in ceremonial exchanges. Indeed 'the gift of stones' may have been a complex process perhaps undertaken as part of marriage or initiation rites and the manipulation of such exchanges may have been the prerogative of community leaders, or even a factor in their emergence and in the development of greater social ranking. It is also possible the axes involved may have circulated over a prolonged period of time.[35]

A striking example of an exotic ceremonial axehead type is a series of jadeite axes from Britain and Ireland. Jadeite is an extremely hard greenish rock, almost 100 have been found in Britain and seven in Ireland. Its source is uncertain and is possibly Continental, perhaps from a Piedmont (Alpine) locality. The Irish examples, like their British counterparts, were probably highly-prized possessions perhaps received as special gifts, never used for wood-working and maybe never even hafted. A significant number of axeheads which were imports from Britain have also been identified and include axes of a volcanic tuff from the Great Langdale region, Cumbria, found at Ballygalley, several axes of Cornish gabbro, and examples of preselite from south-west Wales found on Lambay Island, Co. Dublin, and in Co. Antrim. A few flint axes were also imported.[36]

OTHER STONE IMPLEMENTS

Flint and chert were widely used to manufacture a range of implements. The extent to which raw flint or flint implements themselves were traded in prehistoric Ireland is not clear but may have been considerable. A major source of material was the good quality flint which occurs in the basalt-covered chalk in north-eastern Ireland. The flint-bearing chalk is exposed on many parts of the Antrim coast and at several inland outcrops. Open-cast mining has been identified at Black Mountain, near Belfast, and on the southern side of Ballygalley Hill, near Larne in Co. Antrim, where a series of bands of flint nodules in the chalk were mined by flint-workers and numerous waste flakes and cores indicate that knapping took place nearby. Sherds of undecorated pottery and flint implements, found a short distance away on the summit, are from an occupation site possibly contemporary with the industrial activity. Flint found in deposits of glacial drift, river gravels and on beaches elsewhere in the country was another significant source of raw material.[37]

A variety of arrowheads, scrapers and knives of flint and chert were in common use and pressure retouch is a recurrent feature. Small and approximately leaf-shaped or lozenge-shaped arrowheads are particularly characteristic of the fourth and third millennia: manufactured from thin flakes they are usually carefully pressure-flaked on both faces and worked to a sharp point. They were presumably glued with some resinous substance into wooden shafts and in a few cases differential staining on the surface indicates the former presence of the shaft (Fig. 23). A leaf-shaped flint arrowhead was found at a depth of about 3m in a bog, south of Port Laoise, at Clonaddadoran, Co. Laois, with part of a birch shaft attached. Such arrowheads are not an uncommon find in megalithic tombs, particularly court tombs, and on habitation sites and their relative number is presumably a reflection of the importance of archery in both hunting and fighting.

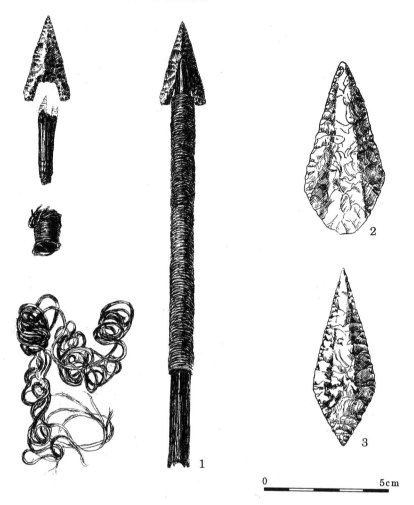

Fig. 23. Flint arrowheads. 1. Concave-based flint arrowhead found in Kanestown Bog, Co. Antrim, still attached to its wooden shaft with some sort of adhesive and with a binding of animal sinew. 2. Leaf-shaped flint arrowhead found in a bog near Glarryford, Co. Antrim. 3. Lozenge-shaped flint arrowhead found in a bog at Teeshan, near Ballymena, Co. Antrim.

A fragment of a bow of yew wood was found in the last century at a depth of about 6m in a bog at Drumwhinny, Kesh, Co. Fermanagh, and has been radiocarbon dated to 1680–1326 BC. Yew was probably favoured for bow manufacture because it is a dense but pliable wood. Other arrowhead types were occasionally used particularly in the third millennium and later. The concave-based arrowhead, a roughly triangular arrowhead with a hollow or concave base, is rarer but examples have been found at sites such as Lyles Hill, Co. Antrim, Newgrange, Co. Meath, and in a late third millennium Beaker context at Ross Island, Killarney, Co. Kerry. One undated concave-based arrowhead recovered from Kanestown Bog, south of Glenarm, Co. Antrim, was found still attached to its wooden shaft with some sort of adhesive; the upper part of the shaft, probably ash, was bound with animal sinew to prevent it splitting (Fig. 23).[38]

A large leaf or lozenge-shaped flint point was perhaps used as a projectile head and is commonly called a javelin head; a polished lozenge-shaped variety is a peculiarly Irish type (Fig. 24). They are occasionally very finely made and one example has a maximum length of about 25cm. Regular pressure flaking may completely cover one or both faces and often part of the faces is carefully polished, sometimes before flaking, sometimes afterwards. While many are merely stray finds, several examples have been found in court tombs and passage tombs and some, like the finer axes, may not have been utilitarian objects. However, that tip of a small arrowhead found embedded in a male hip bone at Poulnabrone, Co. Clare, and a stone axehead found

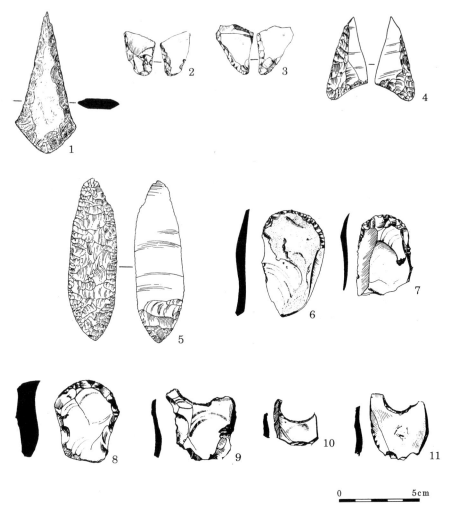

Fig. 24. Flint artefacts. 1. Javelin head found in a bog at Killeelaun, near Tuam, Co. Galway. 2-3. Transverse arrowheads from Townleyhall II, Co. Louth. 4. Petit tranchet derivative from Lough Eskragh, Co. Tyrone. 5. Plano-convex knife from Barnes Lower, Co. Tyrone. 6-11. Convex (6-8) and concave (9-11) scrapers from Townleyhall II, Co. Louth.

with a male burial (with several old skull fractures) at Linkardstown, Co. Carlow, may be painful reminders that some axes and arrowheads were male possessions sometimes used to lethal effect. A series of flint implements of uncertain purpose occasionally found in third millennium contexts have been called 'petit tranchet derivative arrowheads' because, in Britain, they were thought to derive from a symmetrical trapezoidal form of transverse arrowhead with a sharp primary edge at right angles to the long axis of the flake (that is to the pressure rings on the bulbar surface); they may also have steep retouching on both sides. Irish transverse examples with chisel-like cutting edges are not particularly common: they have been found, for example, on the Townleyhall II

settlement and in the Dundrum sandhills. So-called derivative forms of this 'chisel-ended' arrowhead vary in shape and in extent of retouching. A pointed asymmetrical form is better known with a sharp primary flake edge at an angle to a retouched edge and it is thought by some that the sharp edge could have been mounted obliquely in an arrow shaft, the longer retouched edge being set into the wood. It is a measure of how little is known about the use of these implements that they have also been considered to be knives rather than arrowheads. Examples have been found at Newgrange and in the Grange stone circle at Lough Gur, Co. Limerick, and associated with a ring ditch and standing stone at Carrownacaw, Co. Down.[39]

While a variety of worked and unworked flints and pieces of chert probably served as knives, a series of plano-convex flint implements are readily recognisable as such (Fig. 24), they are double-edged implements with the non-bulbar, convex surface wholly or partially pressure-flaked. Several examples have been found in court tombs and on other contemporary sites but finds of similar knives in second millennium graves indicate the type was a long-lived one. Some small thin sharp flint flakes are thought to be sickle inserts; a number of these may

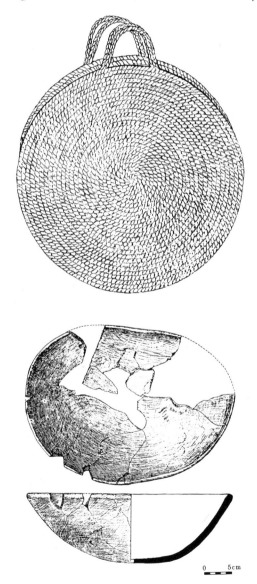

Fig. 25. Above. Reconstruction of a basketry bag from a bog at Twyford, Co. Westmeath. Below. Wooden bowl found in a bog at Timoney, Co. Tipperary.

have been set into hafts of bone or wood which were then used as reaping knives. Various flint shapes served as scrapers. Convex scrapers and concave scrapers are particularly common types. Convex scrapers are blades or flakes with a retouched convex scraping end and could have been used in many ways including the preparation of animal hides. Concave scrapers are broad, thin flakes with a concave or 'hollow' worked edge usually at the distal end of the flake. It has been suggested that these seemingly quite specialized tools were used to prepare wooden rods for such purposes as arrow-shafts, to manufacture bone pins, or that they were used as small saws or even sickles. A hoard of over twenty flint implements, mainly concave scrapers and convex scrapers, found in the valley of the River Braid, at Kilnacolpagh, Co. Antrim, has been interpreted as a workman's tool-kit. Another hoard, probably from the mid-Antrim area, comprised several flint flakes, a polished mudstone axehead, a half-dozen convex scrapers and over sixty unfinished concave scrapers; this may have been a manufacturer's or trader's hoard. As already mentioned, the discovery of numbers of concave scrapers at upland sites such Knocknarea, Co. Sligo, and Windy Ridge, Co. Antrim, also suggests some specialized purpose.[40]

ORGANIC MATERIALS

Very little is known about the bone, leather, wood, basketry and textile work of this period. A variety of bone pins and beads were made and wooden pins, ladles and bowls were also probably widely used and it is likely that leather and wooden containers were even more common than pottery vessels. A finely made round-bottomed bowl carved from a single piece of oak and found at a depth of 3m in a bog at Timoney, near Roscrea, Co. Tipperary (Fig. 25), is believed to be of early date; it was found with the remnants of several basketry bags and the find illustrates just some of the range of organic materials which were probably very widely used. A discovery in Twyford townland, north-east of Athlone, Co. Westmeath, shows what these basketry bags looked like; this was a small, handled bag about 40cm in diameter, found at a depth of over 3m in a bog, each side was made by coiling thin wooden rods into a flat spiral and binding them together with strips of some woody plant. The Twyford bag is undated but the depth at which it was discovered suggests the possibility of an early prehistoric date. Another bag from Aghintemple, near Ardagh, Co. Longford, seems to have been similarly made and this example may well be of fourth or third millennium date for it was found at a depth of almost 4m and contained a miniature axehead of polished limestone only 8.6cm in length. Leather clothing and textiles of vegetal matter such as flax were probably worn but Irish evidence is all but absent. The earliest Irish evidence for flax occurs in a pollen diagram from Essexford Lough, Co. Louth, shortly before 2000 BC and early sheep, being hairy rather than wooly, were probably raised for food rather than fleece at least until the second millennium BC. However, a weighted stick is all that is required to spin flax or wool fibre into thread and such sticks or spindles are commonly weighted with a perforated circular spindle whorl of stone or baked clay. But perforated stones may have various uses and the one possible spindle whorl from an Irish fourth millennium context, a flat, circular, stone 37mm in diameter with a central perforation, from a court tomb at Ballyalton, Co. Down, is equally likely to be a stone bead. Primitive looms consisting basically of two timber cross beams and pegs would leave no archaeological trace in normal circumstances.[41]

NOTES

1 Ballynagilly, Co. Tyrone: ApSimon 1969a; 1976. For comments on the radiocarbon dates see E. Williams 1989 and *Radiocarbon* 12, 288, 294; 13, 105; 15, 218, 599. Early dates include 5745 ± 90 BP (4838-4368 BC, UB-305, charcoal from a hearth in an occupation area with stake-holes, pottery and flints); 5640 ± 90 BP (4716-4350 BC, UB-307, charcoal from a pit containing pottery and flints); 5625 ± 50 BP (4656-4358 BC, UB-197) and 5500 ± 85 BP (4572-4048 BC, UB-559, charcoal from a pit containing pottery and flints); 5370 ± 85 BP (4358-4000 BC, UB-304, charcoal from a pit); 5290 ± 50 BP (4240-3998 BC, UB-551, charcoal from a cooking place). Scepticism about these early dates has been expressed by Thomas 1988, 61, Kinnes 1988, 6, and disbelief by Baillie 1992, 18.

2 Carrowmore, Co. Sligo: Tomb no. 7: 5240 ± 80 BP (4330-3820 BC, Lu-1441); Tomb no. 27: 5040 ± 60 BP (3980-3706 BC, Lu-1698); 5000 ± 65 BP (3970-3694 BC, Lu-1808); 4940 ± 85 BP (3962-3530 BC, Lu-1818); for comment on dates see ApSimon 1986. Croghaun, Co. Sligo: 6680 ± 100 BP (5640-5490 BC, Ua-713), 5685 ± 85 BP (4675-4460 BC, St-10453) both from pine charcoal associated with cremated deposits: Bergh 1995, 104, 225; these early dates are defended by Burenhult 1995.

3 Cashelkeelty, Co. Kerry: Lynch 1981; 5845 ± 100 BP (4950-4470 BC, UB-2413); see Monk 1993 for comments.

4 Various models: Whittle 1990. E. Williams 1989 has argued that the radiocarbon evidence indicates a considerable chronological overlap between hunting and agrarian groups but confesses that the duration is difficult to estimate because of the imprecision of the calibration curve. Baillie 1992 points out that an alternative reading of the radiocarbon evidence suggests little or no overlap; some evidence cited by Williams may now be discounted: Woodman *et al.* 1997. Green and Zvelebil 1990 have argued for a period of coexistence and interaction between hunter-foragers and early farmers; see also Peterson 1990a. Cooney and Grogan 1994, 26-33, review the evidence and conclude that the balance of probability favours the arrival of some early agriculturalists. Thomas 1988.

5 Ballyscullion, Co. Antrim: Smith 1975; radiocarbon dates: 5815 ± 90 BC (4900-4472 BC, UB-296) and 5530 ± 60 BC (4508-4244 BC, UB-116). Ballynagilly, Co. Tyrone: Pilcher and Smith 1979.

6 Elm decline: Mitchell 1956; Smith 1975; Molloy and O'Connell 1987.

7 Fallahogy, Co. Derry: Smith and Willis 1962. Beaghmore, Co. Tyrone: Pilcher 1969. Dolan, Roundstone, Co. Galway: Teunissen *et al.* 1980. Connemara: O'Connell 1994. The nuclei of the later blanket bogs had appeared by late Atlantic times in Connemara but at a considerably later date in north Mayo, for example, and therefore local factors rather than general climatic change may have initiated these developments: O'Connell 1990.

8 The term 'cereal-type pollen' implies a resemblance to cereal pollen but indicates the possibility of pollen of non-cultivated grasses. Pre-elm decline cereal-type pollen: O'Connell 1987; Cashelkeelty, Co. Kerry, Ballynagilly, Co. Tyrone, Newferry, Co. Antrim, Weir's Lough, Co. Tyrone, and elsewhere: Edwards 1985, 196; Edwards and Hirons 1984; Groenman-van Waateringe 1983. Lough Sheeauns, Co. Galway: Molloy and O'Connell 1991. The argument for elm disease at this time is summarized by Molloy and O'Connell 1987; the fossil remains of the beetle which spreads modern Dutch elm disease have been identified in pre-elm decline contexts in England; human activity could have precipitated either the introduction or spread or both of such a disease: Hirons and Edwards 1986.

9 Redbog, Co. Louth: Weir 1995; Céide, Co. Mayo: Molloy and O'Connell 1995; Scragh Bog, Co. Westmeath: O'Connell 1980.

10 Slash-and-burn was an unlikely clearance method according to Rowley-Conwy 1984.

11 Slieve Croob, Co. Down: 4685 ± 85 BC (3690-3136 BC, UB-833), Kirk 1974; Baltinglass Hill, Co. Wicklow: Cooney 1981; see Cooney 1983; the Baltinglass saddle quern could of course have been used for grinding substances other than cereals.

12 Newgrange, Co. Meath: O'Kelly 1982, 219. The macroscopic evidence has been summarized by Monk 1986; Baltinglass Hill, Co. Wicklow: Walshe 1941; Knowth, Co. Meath: Eogan 1984, 327; Townleyhall, Co.

Louth: Eogan 1963; Tankardstown South, Co. Limerick: Gowen 1988, 26, 185; Drimnagh, Co. Dublin: Kilbride-Jones 1939; Ballygalley, Co. Antrim: Simpson *et al.* 1990; Simpson 1995. Monk 1986 also notes grain impressions on pottery; an impression of wheat, possibly emmer, occurs on a sherd from Knockiveagh, Co. Down: Jope *et al.* 1966, xxii. Cooney and Grogan 1994, 35, review the evidence and rightly point out that the role of cereals may be underestimated.

13 Saddle querns: Connolly 1994. South Street, Wiltshire: Fowler 1983, 8. Ard marks at the Céide Fields are of uncertain date but may be early: Molloy and O'Connell 1995. The earliest Irish ards are of late prehistoric date: Raftery 1996a, 266.

14 The high cattle bone percentages from Ó Ríordáin's excavations at Lough Gur are probably exaggerated; the faunal assemblage may include material of different dates and given the excavation methods of the time it is possible that only larger bones were retained: Woodman 1985b, 261. The 'sheep or goat' is a well known entity in faunal analyses because it is often difficult to distinguish between the bones of these two animals. The settlement evidence has been summarized by Van Wijngaarden-Bakker 1974 and 1986, the animal remains from burial contexts by McCormick 1986.

15 For a comprehensive review of the evidence for rectangular and circular houses: Grogan 1996a. Ballynagilly, Co. Tyrone: ApSimon 1969a, 1976; radiocarbon dates include 5230 ± 125 BP (4340-3790 BC, UB-199) and 5265 ± 50 BP (4222-3814 BC, UB-201) from the house wall timbers and from two other pits in the vicinity with dates of 5290 ± 50 BP (4240-3998 BC, UB-551) and 5370 ± 85 BP (4358-4000 BC, UB-304); later activity indicated by 4880 ± 110 BP (3950-3380 BC, UB-306) from a hearth and 4950 ± 90 BC (3952-3388 BC, UB-301) and 4835 ± 55 BP (3776-3388 BC, UB-625) from two pits.

16 Tankardstown, Co. Limerick: Gowen 1988; Gowen and Tarbett 1988; 1990; radiocarbon dates: House 1 from charcoal from foundation trench: 5105 ± 45 BP (3996-3788 BC, GrN), 5005 ± 25 BP (3938-3708 BC, GrN) and 4880 ± 110 BP (3950-3380 BC, GrN); from charred grain: 4890 ± 80 BP (3938-3388 BC, OxA-1476) and 4840 ± 80 BP (3894-3378 BC, OxA-1477); House 2: from charred timber from eastern wall slot of central area: 4995 ± 20 BP (3927-3708 BC, GrN-16557) and 5070 ± 20 BP (3962-3789 BC, GrN-16558). Pepperhill, Co. Cork: Gowen 1988, 44. Ballygalley, Co. Antrim: Simpson 1995 and 1996; radiocarbon dates include 4830 ± 117 BP from charcoal from the house (3776-3386 BC, UB-3491) and several broadly similar early fourth millennium BC dates from charcoal from pits.

17 Ballyglass, Co. Mayo: Ó Nualláin 1972; radiocarbon dates (Ó Nualláin 1976): 4680 ± 95 BP (SI-1450), 4480 ± 90 BP (SI-1452), 4575 ± 90 BP (3612-2938 BC, SI-1451), 4575 ± 105 BP (3620-2930 BC, SI-1454), 4530 ± 95 BP (3506-2926 BC, SI-1453); timber structures interpreted as workshops rather than domestic dwellings were found under a second megalithic tomb in Ballyglass: Ó Nualláin 1972a; for the possible ritual use of the large Ballyglass house see Topping 1996, 168, and Thomas 1996, 5, who note the ambiguity of the archaeological evidence here and at some other sites. Newtown, Co. Meath: Halpin 1995; Gowen and Halpin 1992; radiocarbon dates as cited by Halpin 1992: from charcoal from the foundation trench: 5033 ± 42 BP (3971-3706 BC) and 4978 ± 32 BP (3936-3697 BC).

18 Lough Gur, Co. Limerick: Ó Ríordáin 1954; Grogan and Eogan 1987; Woodman and Scannell 1993. The Site L radiocarbon dates are from charcoal and have large standard deviations: 4410 ± 240 BP (3690-2470 BC, D-40) and 4690 ± 240 BP (3990-2790 BC, D-41). Site J at Lough Gur was probably a third enclosed habitation site of this general date but the later use of the enclosure as a cemetery in late prehistoric or in early Historic times destroyed much of the occupation evidence. Slieve Breagh, Co. Meath: unpublished excavation in Creewood townland by P. Danaher, M. P. Ó hEochaidhe and M. Herity; noted in Lucas 1964, 8; Herity and Eogan 1977, 49; illustrations in de Paor 1967, 55, and Grogan 1996a, fig. 4.3.

19 Newgrange, Co. Meath: O'Kelly 1982, 77; Knowth, Co. Meath: Eogan 1986, 199; Eogan and Roche 1997a, 51; another smaller rectangular structure has been found beneath the great mound: Eogan and Roche 1997.

20 Céide Fields: unpublished; preliminary accounts in Caulfield 1978; 1983; 1988; 1992; Molloy and O'Connell 1995. Charcoal from a hearth in the Glenulra enclosure provided a radiocarbon date of 4460 ± 115 BP (3500-2890 BC, SI-1464).

21 Fleming 1987; 1989.

22 Belderg Beg, Co. Mayo: Caulfield 1978; a circular house and traces of spade-dug ridge and furrow cultivation were also found and may belong to a later phase of activity in the second millennium BC. Some plough marks found beneath the ridges could belong to the earlier phase. Rathlackan, Co. Mayo: Byrne 1991; 1994.

23 Feltrim Hill, Co. Dublin: Hartnett and Eogan 1964. Paddy's Hill, Robswalls, Co. Dublin: Keeling and Keeley 1994. Lyles Hill, Co. Antrim: Evans 1953; enclosure date rejected by O'Kelly 1956; the term Lyles Hill ware was coined by Piggott 1954, 167; Gibson and Simpson 1987; Simpson and Gibson 1989; radiocarbon dates: barley 4755 ± 125 BP (3900-3100 BC); inner palisade: 4433 ± 40 BP (3324-2926 BC); outer palisade: 3974 ± 50 BP (2852-2346 BC).

24 Donegore, Co. Antrim, preliminary reports: Mallory and Hartwell 1984; Mallory 1986, 11; Mallory and McNeill 1991, 35, 78. Tara, Co. Meath: Newman 1997. Knowth, Co. Meath: Eogan 1984, 219. Traces of a large ditch which may have enclosed a low hill are reported at Tullywiggan, Co. Tyrone: Bamford 1971.

25 Grogan 1991; Cooney 1991; Thomas 1996, 5. Settlement, tombs and soils: Cooney 1979, 1983; Henry 1992; Mount 1996a.

26 Bay Farm II, Co. Antrim: Mallory 1992b. Much of the material from northern sandhills was collected in the 19th and early 20th century and has been summarized along with other discoveries by Movius 1942, 252; further finds have been published by Hewson 1938 and May and Batty 1948. White Rocks, Co. Antrim: Collins

1977. Dundrum, Co. Down: Collins 1952, 1959; radiocarbon dates of 4775 ± 140 BP (3940-3100 BC, UB-412) and 4565 ± 135 BP (3630-2920 BC, UB-413) from a hearth at Site 12; 4810 ± 140 BP (3960-3140 BC, D-51) from an occupation horizon: *Radiocarbon* 3, 34; 13, 451. Culleenamore, Co. Sligo: Burenhult 1980a, 41; 1984, 131, 329; radiocarbon date: 4710 ± 100 BP (3770-3110 BC, St-7624) and later dates; Bergh 1995, 56.

27 Geroid Island, Lough Gur, Co. Limerick: Liversage 1958; 4090 ± 140 BP (3030-2210 BC, D-39) from charcoal and 3680 ± 140 BP (2470-1700 BC, D-34) from a later oak timber overlying the habitation layer.

28 Ballybriest, Co. Derry: Evans 1939. Ballymarlagh, Co. Antrim: Davies 1949. Baltinglass, Co. Wicklow: Walshe 1941. Knockiveagh, Co. Down: Collins 1957; radiocarbon date 5120 ± 170 BP (4340-3630/3570-3540 BC, D-37). Newgrange, Co. Meath: O'Kelly *et al.* 1978. Knowth, Co. Meath: Eogan 1984, 211; 1986, 196; Roche 1989; Eogan and Roche 1997 and 1997a. Townleyhall II, Co. Louth: Eogan 1963; radiocarbon date: 4680 ± 150 BP (3780-2930 BC, BM-170). Townleyhall I: Liversage 1960.

29 Knocknarea, Co. Sligo: Bengtsson and Bergh 1984; radiocarbon dates: Hut Site 1: 4250 ± 75 BP (c. 3036-2616 BC, Lu-1947) from charcoal; Hut Site 2: 4440 ± 140 BP (3600-2700 BC, St-9030) from charcoal. Bergh 1995, 58, would see the hut sites as intimately connected with the tombs on the summit. Windy Ridge, Co. Antrim: Woodman *et al.* 1992; Woodman 1983. Nappan, Co. Antrim: Sheridan 1987. Goodland, Co. Antrim: Case 1973. Piperstown, Co. Dublin: Rynne and Ó hÉailidhe 1965.

30 Pottery: Herne 1988; Case 1961; Herity 1982; Sheridan 1989, 1995. Goodland bowls: Mallory 1992b.

31 Tree felling experiments and techniques: Jope 1952, 41, who records that asymmetrical axes were best for tree felling; Coles 1979, 101; Harding and Young 1979; O'Sullivan 1996a, 294 (Corlea 9 and 10 and Cloonbony, Co. Longford). Wooden hafts: Green 1978; Coles *et al.* 1978; Edercloon, Co. Longford: Lucas 1967; Carrowntreila, Co. Mayo: Lucas 1970; Co. Monaghan: Wilde 1857, 46, fig. 53; Maguire's Bridge, Co. Fermanagh: Raftery 1951, 82, fig. 85; Carrickfergus, Co. Antrim: Flanagan 1970, fig. 6. Irish stone axes in general: Sheridan *et al.* 1992; Cooney *et al.* 1995; Mandal 1996. Local studies: Cooney 1985 and Cooney *et al.* 1990 (Louth); Cooney 1989 (north Leinster); Cooney *et al.* 1990 (Tipperary).

32 Stone axeheads: Cooney *et al.* 1995, stone axe 'face shape' categories FS 01 to FS 06 respectively. Flint axeheads: Woodman 1992.

33 Axe distribution: Grogan and Cooney 1990. The role of local collectors on the River Bann: Simpson 1993. Hoards and caches of stone axes (and finds from funerary contexts): Sheridan *et al.* 1992. Danesfort, Malone Road, Belfast: Gray 1873; Armstrong 1918, fig. 2. Canrawer, Co. Galway: Armstrong 1918, fig. 3. Ballyalton, Co. Down: Evans and Davies 1934, fig. IV. Ballyrisode, Co. Cork: O'Brien 1994, 7. A bog deposit found at Lislea, near Clones, Co. Monaghan, comprised a Carrowkeel

bowl and two polished stone axeheads possibly associated with a hearth: Herity 1974, figs 110-111. Two stone axeheads, two hammerstones and a possible hone were found beneath a large stone at Crovraghan, Co. Clare: Mandal *et al.* 1992. Flint hoards include a cache of concave scrapers and other implements found in a field at Kilnacolpagh, Co. Antrim (Flanagan 1966), a similar hoard found in a wooden box in a bog at 'Killybeg', possibly in mid-Antrim (Woodman 1967) and a collection of unfinished flakes found at the base of a kerb stone of the large mound at Knowth, Co. Meath (Eogan 1984, 24). Caches of flint are 'not uncommon' in the north of Ireland: Yates 1985; Woodman 1992, 88. A small hoard of five axeheads of pelite (a fine grained metamorphosed mudstone) was discovered at Ferriter's Cove, Co. Kerry (Woodman and O'Brien 1993, fig. 4.4).

34 Fisherstreet, Co. Clare: Mahr 1937, 300, fig. 11; Cooney 1995. Lambay Island, Co. Dublin: Cooney 1993 and 1995a. Tievebulliagh and Brockley, Co. Antrim: Jope 1952; Sheridan 1986a; Briggs 1988; Meighan *et al.* 1993; Mallory 1990.

35 Edmonds 1995, 50; Bradley and Edmonds 1993, 157.

36 Imported axeheads: Great Langdale (Group VI) and south-west Wales (Group XIII): Sheridan *et al.* 1992, 411; Cooney *et al.* 1995, 32; Mandal and Cooney 1996. Jadeite axes: Murray 1979; Jones *et al.* 1977, list three of the Irish finds – from Raymoghy, Co. Donegal, Paslickstown, Co. Westmeath, and a possible example from Tristia, Co. Mayo.

37 Ballygalley Hill, Co. Antrim: Collins 1978. Flint sources: Woodman 1987; Woodman and Griffiths 1988.

38 Flint arrowheads from Ireland are briefly considered in Green 1980, 89, 100, 141. Clonaddadoran, Co. Laois: Green 1980, 417, fig. 60. Bow fragment from Drumwhinny, Co. Fermanagh: radiocarbon dated to 3220 ± 70 BP (1680-1326 BC, OxA-2426), Hedges *et al.* 1991; Glover 1979. Use of yew wood: Coles *et al.* 1978. Kanestown, Co. Antrim: Knowles 1886. Ross Island, Co. Kerry: O'Brien 1996, pl. 24.

39 Javelin heads: Collins 1981; Green 1980, 75; Herity 1987, 135, where a minimum length of 9cm is suggested. Petit tranchet derivatives (abbreviated to PTD): Flanagan 1970a; Green 1980, 100; O'Kelly *et al.* 1983; Woodman and Scannell 1993, table 6.5; Carrownacaw, Co. Down: Collins 1957b.

40 Plano-convex flint knives: Collins 1966. Sickle inserts: Herity 1987, 144. Convex scrapers (end or 'rounded' scrapers): Herity 1987, 141. Concave scrapers: Flanagan 1965; Herity 1987, 135; hoard from Kilnacolpagh, Co. Antrim: Flanagan 1966; the 'Killybeg' hoard from mid-Antrim: Woodman 1967.

41 Wooden bowl (and basketry bags) from Timoney, Co. Tipperary: Lucas 1966; Earwood 1993, 38. Basketry bags from Twyford, Co. Westmeath, and Aghintemple, Co. Longford: J. Raftery 1970. Flax pollen from Essexford Lough, Co. Louth: Weir 1995, 93. Ballyalton, Co. Down, spindle whorl (?): Evans and Davies 1934, fig. V; Herity 1987, fig. 37; Henshall 1950; for similar beads from Lough Gur (Site L): Grogan and Eogan 1987, fig. 37, 1926, etc. Some evidence for early textiles exists in Britain: Jørgensen 1992.

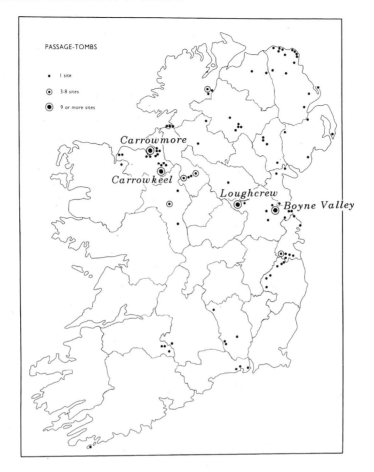

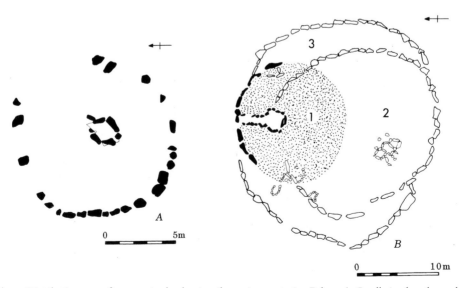

Fig. 26. Above. Distribution map of passage tombs showing the major cemeteries. Below. A. Small simple polygonal passage tomb, the Druid Stone, Ballintoy, Co. Antrim. B. Simple polygonal passage tomb in primary cairn (1) with later additions (2-3) at Baltinglass Hill, Co. Wicklow.

3

The Cult of
the Dead

The most prominent remains of the early prehistoric period are the megalithic tombs (from the Greek *megas*: great, *lithos*: stone), the majority of which were constructed in the fourth and third millennia BC (4000-2000 BC). These are the cromlech and dolmen of earlier writers and the giant's grave, druid's altar and 'Leaba Dhiarmada agus Ghráinne' of popular folklore. Most of these monuments are now assigned to four major classes, each named after an important distinguishing feature: Passage Tombs, Court Tombs, Portal Tombs and Wedge Tombs.[1]

Minor categories such as Linkardstown Graves and Boulder-monuments also exist, as do a number of simple chambered tombs identified in Connemara and elsewhere which cannot be readily assigned to the traditional categories. Systematic field survey has now recorded over 1500 megalithic tombs and the approximate percentages and numbers for each category are: Passage Tombs 15% (about 230), Court Tombs 26% (about 394), Portal Tombs 12% (about 174), Wedge Tombs 33% (about 505) and Unclassified tombs 14% (about 200).

A goodly number of excavations has meant that these monuments are comparatively well documented but many tombs have suffered considerable damage over the millennia, often the covering mound or cairn of stones has been removed and perhaps only a few of the stones of the tomb may survive. Such destruction naturally makes classification a difficult task.

PASSAGE TOMBS

Some of the finest and most spectacular of the surviving Irish megalithic tombs are assigned to the Passage Tomb class and the largest of these monuments, in the Boyne Valley in Co. Meath, have been described as the greatest architectural achievements of those tomb builders in western Europe. However, many small tombs occur among the 230 or so probable examples and there is considerable variation not merely in size but also in tomb plan.

A typical Irish passage tomb consists of a chamber approached by a passage, both covered by a characteristic circular mound. The mounds may be built of earth or stones or a mixture of both and they usually have a kerb or retaining wall of large, contiguous stones around their base (Fig. 26). The diameter of the mound may vary from just over 10m (the 'Druid Stone', Ballintoy, Co. Antrim) or even less, to as much as 85m (as at Newgrange, Co. Meath: Fig. 28) but a majority of mounds range in diameter from about 10m to 25m. Mounds usually, but by no means invariably, contain just one chamber which is centrally placed. Carved ornament on the stones of some tombs is a noteworthy feature.

The distribution and situation of these tombs is remarkable in several respects (Fig. 26). Unlike many other megalithic tombs, they are sometimes prominently sited on high ground, on occasion occupying commanding hilltop positions. Though the latter tombs are often the most spectacular, a majority (about 58%) are situated below 150m and at no great distance from areas of potential settlement. They may occur in groups or cemeteries with one large focal monument often surrounded by a number of smaller satellite tombs. Most passage tombs are to be found in the northern and eastern parts of the country, isolated examples occur in Counties Limerick and Waterford and as far south as Co. Kerry, and a possible site is recorded on Cape Clear island, Co. Cork. There are four major cemeteries variously containing from about 12 to about 60 tombs: the Boyne Valley and Loughcrew (Slieve na Caillighe) in Co. Meath, and Carrowmore and Carrowkeel in Co. Sligo. A few smaller groups of from two to five tombs are found, for example, in Counties Armagh, Donegal, Dublin, Leitrim and Roscommon. None are known in Galway, Mayo or Clare. The identification of passage tombs is, in many cases, not difficult when a cairn has been robbed of some of its material and the tomb exposed. Naturally, identification is impossible if the cairn is intact and many unopened hilltop cairns may prove to contain tombs of this class and only rarely can this be assumed with a reasonable degree of certainty. For instance, on the prominent summit of Knocknarea, just west of Sligo town, the great cairn, Miosgán Meabha, where according to popular belief 'passionate Maeve is stony still', is a conspicuous monument on the skyline. This huge cairn, 10m high and about 60m in average diameter with traces of a kerb, very probably covers a passage tomb; there are the remains of four or five smaller examples in the vicinity and the great cairn was evidently the focal point of a small cemetery and overlooks the larger Carrowmore cemetery to the east.[2]

Passage tombs are usually constructed of large quarried slabs or boulders, the boulders are sometimes split. Passages are narrow and built of upright slabs (orthostats) and roofed in whole or in part with flat slabs (lintels); on occasion passages are divided into segments by one or more low transverse slabs set on edge in the floor (sill stones). Passage lengths vary from as little as 1m to over 40m at Knowth. Chambers are often simple: circular or polygonal, sub-rectangular or trapezoidal. These simple forms are commonest but more complex plans – with one or more additional cells – are well known. Internally chamber diameters may vary from about 1.2m to 6.4m as at Fourknocks I, Co. Meath (Fig. 32). They may be roofed with one or more flat slabs or boulders (capstones) or corbel-roofed with horizontally-laid courses of slabs, each successive course oversailing the one below until it is possible to close the vault with a capstone. The tomb known as the 'Druid Stone', near Ballintoy, Co. Antrim, has a simple polygonal chamber of five stones covered with a large capstone, the short 'passage' seemingly consisted of only two stones (Fig. 26). Tomb no. 7 in the Carrowmore, Co. Sligo, cemetery is of similar plan (Fig. 35). One of three tombs in a cairn on Baltinglass Hill, Co. Wicklow, also had a polygonal chamber, approached in this instance by a 4m long passage (Fig. 26). Carnanmore, Co. Antrim, is a tomb with a corbel-roofed, rectangular chamber and a dry-masonry passage. Some tombs of sub-rectangular or trapezoidal plan have chambers which are difficult to distinguish from the passage itself. Sometimes the chamber is slightly higher or of more massive construction than the rest of the tomb and sometimes a sill stone demarcates the chamber area. Excavated examples of these 'undifferentiated' passage tombs include a number at Knowth, and others at Townleyhall, Co. Louth, Carriglong, Co. Waterford, and Harristown, Co. Waterford.[3]

A cruciform tomb with three cells (a terminal cell and two lateral cells) is a well-known type. Such cruciform tomb plans are well represented among the Boyne Valley monuments. One of the tombs in the great mound at Dowth, Co. Meath, is circular with a single lateral cell, and complex plans with several additional cells are frequent. A tomb in the Loughcrew cemetery (Cairn I) has a large chamber divided into seven cells (Fig. 34). There is considerable variation in tomb orientation: some face east and like Newgrange may be aligned on the midwinter solstice. Occasional patterns are discernible, at Knowth the entrances of many of the undifferentiated tombs face the great mound and at Carrowmore there was a measure of internal focus as well with a number of tombs orientated towards the centre of the cemetery. The range of tomb types and orientation, and the popularity of the cruciform plan is apparent in the major cemeteries.

THE BOYNE CEMETERY

The celebrated cemetery in the Boyne Valley is situated in a loop of that river in Co. Meath between Slane and Drogheda (Fig. 27). The great mounds at Newgrange and Knowth each with nearby smaller satellite tombs, are, along with the mound at Dowth, the largest passage tomb mounds in Ireland. Although not situated on a hilltop like some other tombs of this class, these three exceptional monuments nonetheless occupy commanding positions.

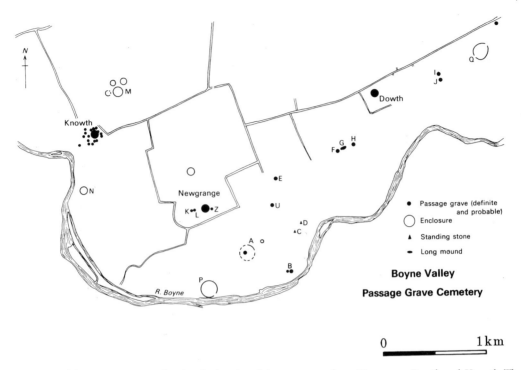

Fig. 27. Map of the Boyne cemetery showing the location of the passage tombs at Newgrange, Dowth and Knowth. The embanked enclosure at Dowth (Q) is shown to the east.

NEWGRANGE

The Newgrange mound was built on the highest point of a low ridge some 61m above sea level overlooking the Boyne.[4] This approximately circular mound (Fig. 28) measures 85m in maximum diameter and about 11m in height; it covers almost 0.4 hectare (one acre) and is composed mainly of water-rolled stones. The mound is surrounded by a continuous line of 97 kerbstones, many of which bear decoration. The entrance to the passage is on the south-east behind a richly decorated kerbstone (Fig. 29) and this entrance was originally closed by a large rectangular slab. A short vertical line in the middle of the decorative composition of the kerbstone is aligned on the entrance. The orthostatic passage is roofed with large slabs; near the entrance these slabs rest directly on the orthostats but elsewhere they rest on corbels (courses of slabs, the upper oversailing the one below). The upper surfaces of some of these roof slabs have grooves or channels picked in them (with a hammer and flint point) to carry off rain water percolating through the cairn. In addition the roof joints were caulked with sea sand and burnt soil. The height of the passage roof increases towards the chamber and the combined length of passage and

chamber is just over 24m. Many of the orthostats and some roof-stones are decorated and this decoration is particularly frequent in the inner parts of the passage and in the chamber.

The chamber with its two lateral cells and one terminal cell is of the common cruciform plan. It would seem that the eastern cell was the more important, it is larger than the others and contains the most decoration. The cruciform chamber is roofed with a very fine 6m high corbelled vault. Four large and slightly hollowed 'basin stones' occur in the chamber, such stones occur in other passage tombs and they may once have contained the burnt or unburnt bones of the dead.

Excavation revealed that a considerable amount of material has collapsed from the mound, a layer of cairn stones 8m to 10m wide lies outside the kerb, and this led M. J. O'Kelly to suggest that a sloping wall of stones, almost 3m high, had rested on top of the kerb stones and that the original mound may have been steep-sided and flat-topped. On the south-east, a lot of angular pieces of quartz were found at the base of the collapse and it seems that the mound, in the area of the entrance at least, was faced in greater part with sparkling white quartz. A similar quartz facing has been found at Knockroe

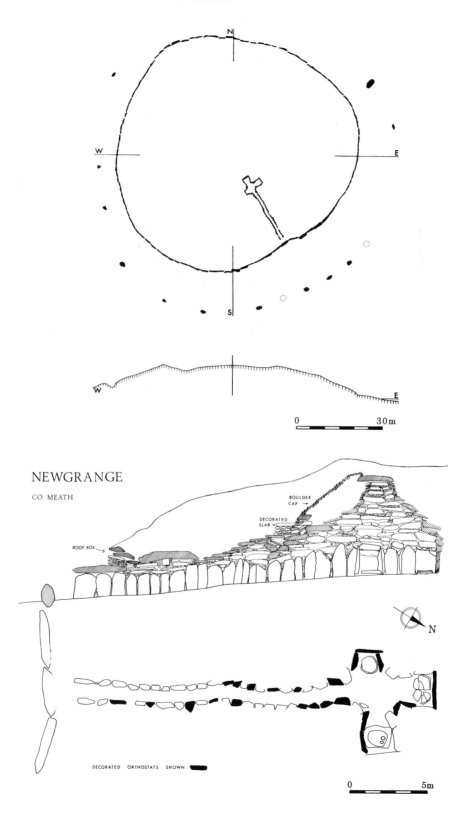

Fig. 28. Plan and section of Newgrange passage tomb.

Fig. 29. The decorated entrance stone at Newgrange.

passage tomb, Co. Kilkenny. The discovery of what has been called the 'roof-box' above the entrance to the passage indicates that the quartz wall very likely turned inwards at the entrance to permit access to this box. This stone-built feature was constructed beneath a decorated lintel and over a gap between the first two roof-slabs of the passage. At dawn on the midwinter solstice, the shortest day of the year, the rays of the rising sun shine through the roof-box and briefly illuminate the chamber. The spectacle occurs for about a week before and after the solstice and lasts for a little over a quarter of an hour but only on the solstice itself does the beam extend to the end cell; indeed it has been calculated that at the time the tomb was built 5000 years ago, the beam of sunlight would have bisected the chamber and illuminated a triple spiral carved on the rear orthostat of the end recess.[5] Clearly the orientation of the tomb was of great importance to its builders and solar phenomena had a very important place in their magico-religious beliefs and practices.

Because the tomb has been open since at least the late 17th century, little has survived of the original contents. Excavation in the chamber recovered some cremated bone (of four or five people) and the position of these bone fragments suggested that the burial deposits may have been placed in the basin stones in the end and side cells. Objects found with the bones, presumably grave goods placed with the remains, are typical of Irish passage tombs and include stone beads and pendants, fragments of bone pins and some small balls of polished stone (including a conjoined pair).

The decoration on the stones of Newgrange was generally picked out, probably with a hammer and a flint point; motifs usually consist of closely-set small pock-marks executed in this fashion and chevrons, zig-zags, lozenges, triangles, spirals, and circles are common. The decoration varies from the haphazard to the formal, from apparently casually and poorly carved designs to the superbly executed and aesthetically pleasing composition of spirals, arcs and lozenges on the celebrated entrance stone (Fig. 29). It is obvious that the designs on the entrance stone and on stones such as the tomb orthostats were meant to be clearly seen, but many, particularly the more casually picked ones, occur on the backs of stones and were lost to sight when these stones were put in place. Presumably the designs had some significance for their carvers and the hidden motifs suggest, in some instances at least, that the very act of carving a particular design may have been more important than its display.

Only a fraction of the huge mound has been excavated and it is possible that it may, like Knowth or Dowth, cover a second tomb. While layers of turves occur now and then in the Newgrange cairn, limited excavation on the northern side of the mound revealed that the kerbstones there had not been set into or upon the old ground surface but were placed in sockets cut into a layer of turves which increased in thickness the further it extended inward under the cairn. This turf mound may cover some pre-cairn structure and it may be significant that the great mound bulges outwards at this point.

Palynological analysis of some turves revealed they contained wheat pollen and they had evidently been stripped from fields in which cereals had grown. Open pasture was also indicated and turves containing pollen of wet-loving plants probably came from the river valley. The stripping of this topsoil alone must have been a large undertaking but the cairn, it has been estimated, contains about 200,000 tons of material, much of it transported from the bed of the River Boyne about 1km away. Some of the rounded stones, such as examples of granite, may have been deliberately selected many kilometres to the north and transported south.[6] When it is remembered that the monument also contains at least 450 large slabs, some over five tons in weight, it would seem likely that it was the work of a substantial and wealthy population with considerable social organization and engineering skill.

Indeed the scale of monuments like Newgrange raises important questions about size and density of population, craft specialization and social structure. Newgrange was built towards the end of the fourth millennium BC. The burnt soil, used to caulk the roof joints of the tomb, contained charcoal fragments which provided radiocarbon date ranges of 3316-2922 BC and 3304-2922 BC which probably date the construction of the monument.[7] Twelve large standing stones survive of what is sometimes assumed to have been a complete stone circle surrounding but not concentric with the mound. However, the original plan of this feature is not known with certainty, if ever complete it may have comprised 35 to 38 stones. While excavations have revealed the sockets of several missing stones on the south of the mound, results elsewhere have been inconclusive. It is possible that the circle was never completed. O'Kelly claimed that cairn material had apparently collected around some of the stones thus indicating that these were in position when the mound commenced to decay but more recent excavations suggest that they postdate a circle of pits and were erected in the later third millennium BC. It is also possible that the collapse of cairn material and of the quartz facing

may have been a deliberate act at this time, marking the formal enclosure of the great mound in much the same way as one of the satellite tombs (Z) was encircled by a later series of pits.[8]

There are three small ruined satellite tombs in the immediate vicinity of the great mound, sites K and L to the west and Z to the south-east. Site K is a small undifferentiated tomb: the chamber area is slightly wider than the passage and the two are separated by a sill stone 60cm in maximum height. Excavation revealed at least two phases of activity: the primary monument comprised the chamber with short passage covered with an earthen mound retained by a kerb of boulders. A penannular ditch (with its entrance aligned on the tomb entrance) surrounded the mound. Some time later the passage was lengthened, the mound enlarged and a new kerb 20m in diameter built, this kerb turned inwards towards the tomb entrance. While the primary tomb was disturbed, it had contained cremated human bone. The extension to the passage contained a homogenous deposit of brown soil and cremated human bone, fragments of bone pins, small chalk balls and a pendant possibly of pottery. This mixture of soil and bone was apparently placed in the tomb as one deposit. Site L was a cruciform tomb and traces of an earlier habitation site, a few pits, areas of burning, some pottery and flint were found beneath the mound. Site Z had been thoroughly destroyed: only the stump of one of the structural stones of the tomb survived but the sockets of the others were located and it was thus possible to reconstruct the plan. Like Site K, this was an undifferentiated tomb with a sill stone demarcating the chamber area in which there was an irregularly shaped basin stone bearing some decoration. An unusual feature was a small cell opening off the inner end of the eastern side of the passage just before it joined the chamber. Fragments of both burnt and unburnt human bone were recovered. Decorated stones were found in each of these three satellite tombs.[9]

KNOWTH

Excavations at the great mound at Knowth, about 1km north-west of Newgrange, have revealed 18 satellite tombs around a huge mound (Fig. 30) which itself contains two fine passage tombs.[10] The large mound was modified in early Historic times and souterrains and other features indicate extensive habitation on the site. The mound is approximately

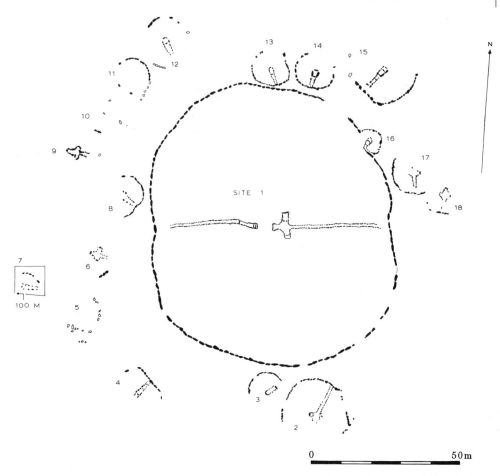

Fig. 30. Plan showing the great mound at Knowth with its two passage tombs (one cruciform, one undifferentiated) surrounded by smaller satellite tombs.

circular and comparable to Newgrange being about 85m in average diameter, about 9.9m in height and surrounded by a contiguous series of 127 kerb stones. Unlike the Newgrange mound, it was constructed of alternate layers of earth and stones. The tombs are placed almost back to back, the entrance of one facing west, the other east. The first few metres of each passage were destroyed when a large ditch was dug around the mound in the earlier first millennium AD and later still the outer parts of the passages were modified for use as souterrains and used for storage or refuge and the interior of each tomb was apparently disturbed.

The kerb curves in slightly at the entrance to the western tomb which lies behind a remarkable decorated kerb-stone on which a design of concentric sub-rectangles is bisected by a vertical line more or less aligned on the centre of the passage entrance. The tomb was originally about 34m in length and has an almost square chamber

divided in two by a low sill stone and separated from the passage by a higher one. Both the chamber and the passage are constructed of orthostats and roofed with capstones which rested on the side stones. The height and width of the passage increases near the chamber and there is a marked curve to the south in the line of the passage about 6m from the chamber. Just before this bend there is a displaced basin stone and just beyond it a sill stone. Like many of the kerb stones, several orthostats and capstones are decorated notably in the area of the chamber.

The eastern tomb is slightly longer (over 40m) and has a more or less straight passage and a fine corbel-vaulted cruciform chamber 5.9m high. As in Newgrange, the right-hand (northern) cell of the cruciform chamber is the largest of the three and has a pair of portal stones at its entrance. Within is a richly decorated basin stone which must have been put in place before the portal stones and the passage

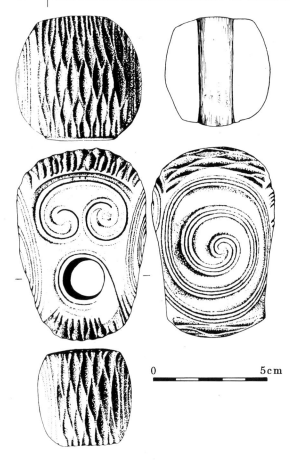

0   5cm

Fig. 31. Carved flint mace head from Knowth.

were built. The burial deposits had suffered some disturbance. For the most part they were confined to the cells and consisted mainly of burnt bone. A few unburnt bones were noted. Several deposits of cremated bone were recorded in the left hand (southern) cell and a stone basin had been disturbed and upturned on top of them. The northern cell also contained a number of cremations around (but not in) the decorated basin stone. Finds included stone beads and pendants, antler pins, and a remarkable decorated flint macehead (Fig. 31) found in the right hand cell. Again, the majority of decorated stones occur in or near the chamber.

The eastern tomb may have been orientated towards the rising sun of the spring and autumn equinoxes (21st March and 21st September) and the setting sun could also have shone into the western tomb at the same times. Like the midwinter solstice so important at Newgrange, the spring and autumn equinoxes, when day and night have equal lengths, would have been significant points in the calendar of a farming community. It is possible that burial or

other rituals may have been timed to coincide with these events. The great mound at Knowth may have been completed, like Newgrange, towards the end of the fourth millennium BC. Charcoal believed to be contemporary with the commencement of construction has provided dates of 3358-2932 BC and 3292-2922 BC.[11]

Excavation has revealed the remains of at least 18 satellite tombs of considerably smaller size in the immediate vicinity of the large mound: most of these sites are situated close by though one (Site 7) is 145m away. All had suffered damage, in some cases so extensive that only a few stones or sockets of stones survived. In most instances it was still possible to recover the tomb plan, at least ten were small undifferentiated tombs and five had cruciform chambers. The small mounds varied from just under 10m to about 20m in diameter. The passage entrances of the undifferentiated tombs were usually orientated towards the large mound. In contrast, all but two of the cruciform examples faced east and the entrances of all five appeared to focus on an area to the south-east of the large mound. However, excavation here produced no explanation for this.

Decoration occurs on some stones of kerb or tomb, or both, in the majority of these satellite sites. Several tombs had traces of cremated burials and a little unburnt human bone was found. For example, in addition to some cremated human bone, of several individuals, and some burnt animal bone, Site 6, a cruciform tomb, produced a fragment of a small pottery bead and a bone pendant. Site 3 consisted of a rectangular chamber 3.5m in length set within the remains of a mound with kerb, presumably originally circular. Because of disturbance, a doubt remains as to whether or not this chamber ever had a passage. If not, this monument would bear some resemblance to a monument with passage tomb affinities at Millin Bay, Co. Down, where an oval mound was found to contain a long, narrow chamber, and is a reminder that passage tomb builders may have constructed other types of monument as well. A little cremated bone was found in the Site 3 tomb along with a large pin or rod of antler or bone decorated with grooving; a sherd of Carrowkeel ware was found near the chamber. Site 4 had suffered considerable damage but was clearly an undifferentiated passage tomb; it is of particular interest because of a series of arcs of small stones found on either side of the passage, placed on the old ground surface and covered by the mound. The purpose of these stone settings is unknown but a complex of arcs and radial lines of stones was associated with an undifferentiated passage tomb at Townleyhall, Co. Louth, not far away. A small circular area roughly paved with quartz pebbles occurred just outside the entrance to the Site 4 tomb, it presumably served some ritual purpose (similar features have been found near the entrances of the two tombs in the large mound and near the entrance of the main Newgrange tomb). Site 2, a disturbed cruciform tomb, contained a stone basin in its surviving western recess, a fragment of Carrowkeel ware was also found. A charcoal spread in the mound of this monument produced a radiocarbon date of 3090-2400 BC. Site 16, an undifferentiated tomb, yielded a date of 3334-2910 BC from a similar context. Both determinations may approximate to the construction dates of the two sites. A cremation in Site 9 dates to 3316-2920 BC.[12]

While Site 2, and other satellite tombs as well, postdate the completion of the large mound, the relationship of all the various monuments to one another is still not clear. The small tombs at Site 13 and Site 16 are probably of earlier date; parts of the kerbs of both were removed to allow the completion of the large mound. It is possible that the large mound was built in several stages. The range of radiocarbon dates suggests that tombs of different types were built at much the same time and indeed that the period of construction of the cemetery as a whole may have spanned a comparatively short period of time.

DOWTH

The large mound at Dowth is the third of the great passage tombs in the Boyne cemetery. It is comparable in size to those of Newgrange and Knowth and was considerably damaged in the course of 19th century excavations. These revealed two tombs both opening onto the western side of the mound. The more northerly of the two is a small cruciform tomb with its passage interrupted by three sill stones and it has a small L-shaped annex extending from the right hand recess of the chamber. A souterrain has been added to the passage of this tomb. The southern tomb has a circular chamber with one lateral cell. Of two small ruined mounds some distance to the east of Dowth, one, at least, contains a passage tomb.[13]

FOURKNOCKS I, CO. MEATH

The Fourknocks tomb (Fourknocks I) near Naul, Co. Meath, is some 15km south of the Boyne cemetery and excavation revealed a cruciform monument covered by a circular mound of turves delimited by a very low dry-stone kerb, too slight to be a retaining wall and of a ritual rather than a functional nature. On the north-north-east the kerb curved in towards but did not connect with an orthostatic and unroofed passage which gave access to the chamber. The approximately oval chamber was unusually large, measuring 6.4m by 5.5m (Fig. 32). Its roof was partly corbelled but the quantity of collapsed stone found in the chamber was not sufficient to provide a complete roof. In the

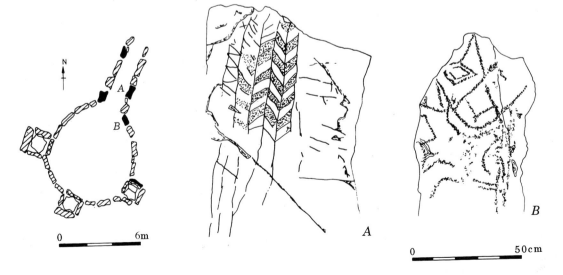

0   6m

A

0   50cm

B

Fig. 32. Fourknocks I, Co. Meath. Plan of tomb and two of the decorated orthostats.

excavator's opinion the roof was originally completed in timber and the discovery of a large post-hole in the centre of the chamber indicated that a timber post may have supported such a structure. A low sill stone separated each of the three slab-roofed cells from the chamber. There were no burials in the chamber, they were confined to the cells and the passage. The primary burial deposits in the cells comprised a homogenous mass, 15cm to 25cm thick, of burnt bone (with some fragments of unburnt bone) covered and sealed by a thin paving of stone flags.[14]

Grave goods were few and included stone and bone pendants and beads and bone pins, some of which showed clear traces of burning. These were mixed through the mass of human remains. Several small chalk balls, also burnt, were found. One 19cm long antler object, burnt and in fragments, was decorated with incised chevron ornament (Fig. 36, 1); it came from the terminal cell. No pottery was found in the tomb, though two sherds of Carrowkeel ware came from the mound.

Burials were found in the passage, mainly nearer the entrance; these consisted of a mixture of cremated and unburnt bone, the latter mostly in the upper levels of the layer of clay and stones which contained the human remains and which was sealed with stones and some clay right to the tops of the passage orthostats. The occurrence of a chalk ball and two bone pins with these burials, and a belief that the passage never had a roof, convinced the excavator that the passage deposits were primary and contemporary with the burials in the cells. However, a single collective burial, in which human remains were accumulated elsewhere over a period and then all deposited at the one time is by no means a certainty. It may be that the cremations were the primary deposit and the unburnt remains which came mainly from the passage were later insertions. The bones from the tomb represented the remains of a minimum of 52 individuals (both adults and children). It was not possible to determine accurately the number of individuals represented: a minimum of 24 persons (adults and

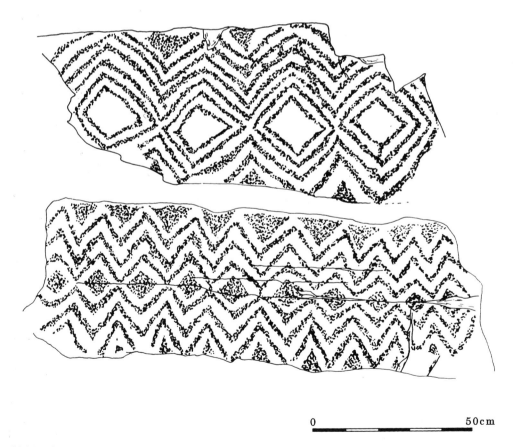

0   50cm

Fig. 33. Two decorated stones from Fourknocks I, Co. Meath.

children) were recognized among the bones from the chamber cells and a minimum of 28 from the passage. The unburnt bones comprised mainly skulls and disarticulated long bones.

Fourknocks I is one of a small number of burial monuments which display interesting evidence of ritual patterning in the funerary deposits. There appears to be a distinction between the way the remains of adults and children were treated and some parts of the body seem to have been accorded special treatment. Cremated adults were normally assigned to the cells while the unburnt bones of children formed a high proportion of the mix of burnt and unburnt bones in the passage. In the passage too there was the occasional deliberate deposition of unburnt adult skulls and long bones. The terminal cell was the most important location: it contained the most bones, the decorated antler rod and was roofed with a finely decorated lintel. Gabriel Cooney suggests that there was a pattern of activity in which children, peripheral location and unburnt burial may be compared with adults, cremation, central position (in the formal burial areas of the tomb) and the provision of accompanying artefacts.[15]

Some animal bones were found, a few mixed through the human bones in the cells and the passage, and some on the floor of the chamber; they were mainly unburnt but a few showed signs of scorching. They included cattle, sheep and pig and were considered evidence of funeral feasting. Even though many questions remain about the Fourknocks burial ritual, it was clearly a most complex process.

Ritual found further expression in the art which occurs on a total of eleven stones of the tomb. Picked zigzag, triangle and lozenge motifs are commonest and they are often arranged to form coherent geometric designs on either the whole surface or on part of the stone (Fig. 33) In this the art is comparable to the formal art at Newgrange. Fourknocks is one of the very few sites where motifs have been claimed to be anthropomorphic, a composition on one of the orthostats of the chamber bears a crescent-shaped motif, believed to be a mouth, with lozenges above suggestive of a nose and one eye (Fig. 32B) but caution is necessary and such assertions should be accepted as no more and no less than subjective guesswork.

A nearby mound (Fourknocks II), surrounded by a penannular ditch, was found to cover a small round cairn as well as a trench and passage thought by the excavator to be a crematorium The latter feature consisted of a short megalithic passage placed within the gap in the ditch, the passage was roofed and contained burials. It terminated in a deep transverse trench, the bottom and sides of which showed considerable evidence of intense heat and which contained charcoal and several deposits of cremated bone. While some burning took place in the trench, it was not certainly a crematorium but the finding of bone or antler pins with the burials and some Carrowkeel ware from the mound indicate that this puzzling monument was the work of passage tomb builders. Here too differences in burial ritual have been detected: cremation was mainly an adult rite and adults were found in both the trench and passage while children were mainly unburnt and disarticulated and deposited in the megalithic passage.[16]

Both of these mounds at Fourknocks were re-used as burial places towards the end of the third millennium and in the second millennium BC as was the Mound of Hostages at Tara, Co. Meath. At the latter site, as at Fourknocks I, the original cairn of a passage tomb was enlarged to take the later graves. The Tara tomb was a small undifferentiated passage tomb with entrance on the east, about 4m in length and divided into three by two sill stones. One of the orthostats has typical passage tomb art. Several crouched burials accompanied by bowls were placed in the tomb greatly disturbing the earlier cremated remains which had been deposited with the usual objects such as pendants of stone and bone, stone and chalk balls, pins of bone and antler and some fragments of Carrowkeel ware. Two complete Carrowkeel pots were found, along with cremated bones, just beside the tomb where they had been placed before the covering mound was built. Part of what may have been a trench for a timber palisade was found beneath the cairn and produced a radiocarbon date of 3355-2465 BC. Another date for pre-tomb activity came from burnt vegetation and has a date range of 3035-2465 BC, and a date for a hearth on the old ground surface in front of the tomb has an even longer calibrated date range of 2875-1945 BC. These suggest the possibility that the tomb was built around 3000 BC. On the one orthostat of the tomb which bears decoration, the principal motif is a cupmark (a small circular depression) surrounded by six concentric circles. A number of unburnt burials and bowls had been intruded into the inner and outermost compartments of the tomb late in the 3rd millennium BC and a mantle of clay was added to the tomb's covering cairn in the second millennium to contain an extensive cemetery. There were several exceptional burials among the forty or so graves (Chapter 4).[17]

THE LOUGHCREW (SLIEVE NA CAILLIGHE) CEMETERY

Loughcrew (Slieve na Caillighe), Co. Meath, is a name applied to a series of hills which, over an area of some 3km, are crowned by an extensive cemetery of at least twenty-five passage tombs. The majority of these tombs are grouped into two major clusters (Fig. 34). The most westerly group is on Carnbane Hill where the huge and disturbed Cairn D is partly surrounded by the remains of some eight sites (A1-3, B, C, E, F and G) of which F is a small cruciform tomb with a number of decorated stones. About 150m north-east of D, a second large cairn (L) is partly surrounded by four smaller cairns (H, I, J and K). Cairn H is a small cruciform tomb and Cairn L has a chamber divided into one terminal and seven lateral cells; both of these monuments and Cairns I, J and K contain decorated stones. Cairn I with its chamber with terminal cell and six lateral cells is similar in some respects to L and the decoration of U motifs, serpentiform motifs, radial motifs, as well as dot and circle and concentric circle motifs are particularly common at Loughcrew. Most of these monuments were excavated in the 19th century after the fashion of the time, and several yielded fragmentary human bones and the occasional bone pin, bead or pendant, and fragment of pottery. Although extensive digging took place in Cairn D in 1865 and 1868, no tomb was found. Cairn H, also investigated in these years, was re-examined in 1943 and both typical passage tomb material and a considerable quantity of later prehistoric material recovered.[18]

The second major group of tombs is situated on the hill known as Slieve na Caillighe or Loughcrew where Cairn T on the summit is partly surrounded by half a dozen smaller tombs (R, R1, S, U, V, W). Cairn T is a cruciform tomb with a cairn 35m in diameter; its entrance faces east and at the equinoxes the rising sun illuminates some of the decorated stones in the interior. Cairn S has a polygonal chamber with a single cell, U is a tomb which appears to be a variation of the cruciform type and V and W are of uncertain plan. Investigation of these monuments also produced burnt bone, Carrowkeel ware and other finds. Many of the stones, particularly in Cairn T, bear decoration. Four other tombs occur on Patrickstown, the next hill to the east.

THE CARROWKEEL CEMETERY

One of the two major passage tomb cemeteries in Co. Sligo is to be found on the Bricklieve Mountains overlooking Lough Arrow. This cemetery, Carrowkeel, is named after one of a number of townlands in which several high limestone ridges bear over a dozen round cairns, some of which contain passage tombs. Fourteen cairns were partly and unscientifically investigated in 1911. Several were found to contain cruciform or related passage tombs which produced mainly cremated bone and typical finds such as fragments of Carrowkeel pottery, bone pins, beads and pendants and stone balls. All but one of the cairns were circular: Cairn E is a long trapezoidal cairn with traces of a straight kerb, what seems to be an unusual orthostatic court occurs at the broader end but has no adjacent chamber; and a cruciform tomb occurs at the narrower end. Some fragments of bones, two bone pins and a boar's tusk were found. It has been suggested that a cluster of some 40 circular hut sites on Mullaghfarna, below Cairn O, may have been the dwelling places of the tomb builders but, in the absence of excavation, this remains speculation.[19]

THE CARROWMORE CEMETERY

The cemetery of tombs at Carrowmore, Co. Sligo, is dominated by the great cairn, traditionally known as Miosgán Meabha ('Maeve's heap'), on the summit of Knocknarea near Sligo town (Fig. 35). This huge unopened cairn very probably contains a passage tomb and in the vicinity are the remains of four or five satellite monuments, one of which is a cruciform tomb. The Carrowmore cemetery proper lies below and to the east of Knocknarea and the surviving monuments are only a fraction of the original number. Some sixty monuments once existed but only about thirty survive in various stages of dilapidation today. Most lie within an area measuring about 1000m by 500m and are situated on a series of low morainic hills; few are conspicuously sited. The majority are boulder

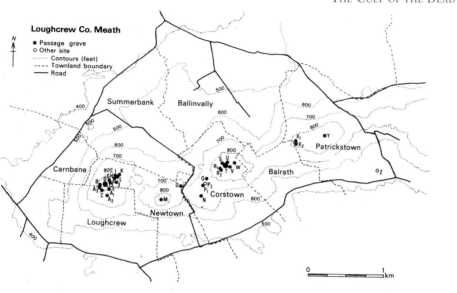

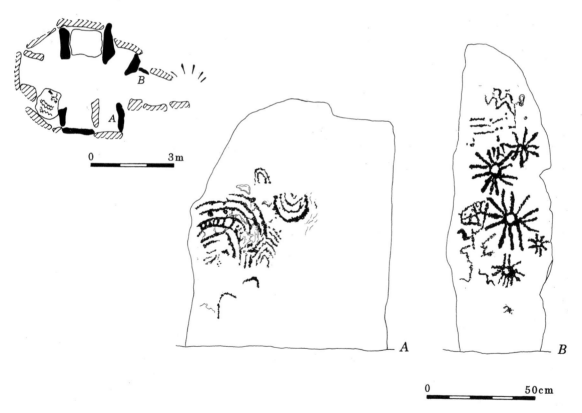

Fig. 34. Map of passage tomb cemetery at Loughcrew, Co. Meath, with plan of tomb in Cairn I and two decorated stones.

circles, consisting of circles or parts of circles of stones which probably once contained centrally-placed stone structures of some description; of the 25 remaining monuments, 24 have or had a central feature. For the most part, diameters range from 10m to 17m. Megalithic tombs survive within the circles in 17 instances and most are monuments with polygonal chambers, some with short passages; they are built of boulders and the capstones are split boulders with a characteristic almost conical shape.

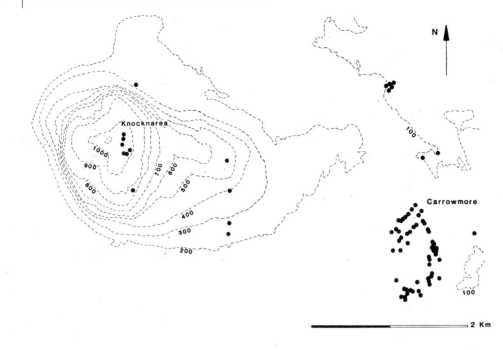

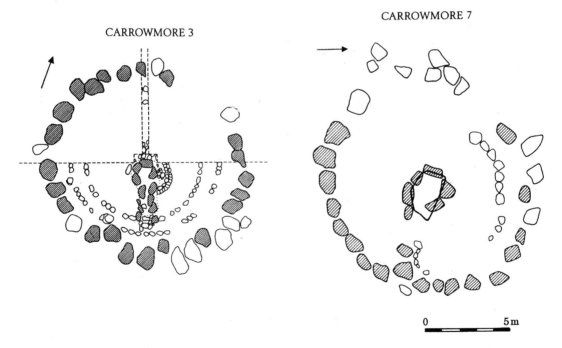

Fig. 35. Map of the Carrowmore and Knocknarea passage tomb cemeteries in Co. Sligo and plans of tombs Carrowmore 3 and 7.

There is also one cruciform tomb (Carrowmore 27) and several rectangular or sub-rectangular monuments. Many of the Carrowmore tombs were investigated in the 19th century and some produced typical finds such as Carrowkeel ware and bone or antler pins.

The largest tomb is Carrowmore 51 ('Listoghil'), more or less in the centre of the cemetery, a cairn about 35m in diameter has the remains of a boulder kerb and a sub-rectangular orthostatic chamber roofed with a single large capstone is visible. A series of picked arcs and a pair of concentric circles with a central dot have been identified on the edge of the limestone roofstone above the present entrance gap to the chamber.[20] The only other art recorded occurs on a number of stones in an anomalous megalithic monument (Carrowmore 30A) in Cloverhill to the east of the cemetery.

Excavation in 1977-78 by Göran Burenhult has demonstrated that Carrowmore no. 7 is a small tomb set within a circle of boulders 12.5m in diameter, the boulders were supported by an internal packing of small stones (Fig. 35). Like so many of the other sites in the cemetery, it had been examined in the 19th century. The chamber was of polygonal plan, constructed of five stones and roofed with a large cap-stone. Excavation revealed traces of a very short passage but no evidence of a covering cairn. Despite the former disturbance, several intact deposits of cremated bone, burnt sea-shells and charcoal were recovered; in one deposit fragments of an antler pin were found, but no pottery. The burnt sea-shells, which included unopened mussels and oysters, were interpreted as funerary offerings. A post-hole, found in the chamber, was believed by to mark the centre of the circle of stones and to be the point about which the monument was built. Charcoal from this post-hole provided an early radiocarbon date with a range of 4330-3820 BC. However, this was just one of four or five post-holes dug into the natural surface below the monument and thus the date probably relates to some structure somewhat older than the tomb for which it provides a terminal date.[21]

Carrowmore no. 26 is a boulder circle with a diameter of 17m and it lies in the eastern part of the cemetery. The boulders were supported by an internal stone packing and the circle had a paved entrance on the south-east. Cremated bone and a fragment of a mushroom-headed antler pin were found at the centre. The circle was re-used in the first millennium BC as a ritual site but the nature of the construction of the stone circle and the antler pin and cremation relate these particular features to the passage tomb monuments of the cemetery; there may once have been a central chamber.

Carrowmore no. 27 is a relatively large monument: a boulder circle with a maximum overall diameter of 23m and a centrally placed cruciform tomb. Excavation showed that the large boulders were partly surrounded by stone packing which also occurred within the line of the circle; the tomb too was surrounded by stone packing delimited by an inner boulder circle 13.7m in

diameter. There was no true passage but two stones flanked the entrance to the chamber which was also marked by a sill stone. All parts of the chamber had been extensively disturbed and much cremated bone found outside had clearly been dug out in the past; antler pins, chalk balls and three sherds of Carrowkeel ware were recovered. The stone packing around the chamber was up to 40cm thick and served as a support for the stones of the tomb. No trace of a more substantial cairn was found and, in the excavator's opinion, the tomb was never covered in this fashion. Charcoal from beneath and between the stones of the lowest level of the stone packing has provided a series of early fourth millennium radiocarbon dates. This charcoal could indicate an early construction date for this tomb but there is also the possibility that the material could be derived from earlier settlement in the locality.

The small monument, Carrowmore no. 3, consisted of a circle of boulders with a diameter of 13m.[22] Like nos 7, 26 and 27, the inner edge of the circle was supported by a packing of small stones. At the centre was a small, more or less polygonal stone chamber measuring only 80cm by 100cm internally and roofed with a small boulder (Fig. 35). Four limestone slabs and several small boulders formed a narrow passage too small to permit access to the chamber; no roof stones were found. Both chamber and passage were constructed in a shallow pit about 30cm deep and surrounded by a packing of stones delimited by a circle of small stones. A second circle of small stones and two small cist graves were located between this circle and the circle of boulders at the edge of the monument. The central chamber and the passage had been greatly disturbed but a considerable quantity of burnt human and animal bone was recovered along with fragments of antler pins. Both of the small cists contained cremated human bone, one also contained a stone ball, the other a stone bead and fragments of antler pins. Charcoal from the base of one of the stones of the chamber produced a radiocarbon date with a range of 4838-4400 BC but a charcoal sample associated with an arc of small stones east of the chamber, apparently part of the stone packing, has given a determination of 3306-2666 BC. According to Burenhult, these dates indicate at least two distinct phases in the history of the tomb, the former representing the construction of the chamber, the latter the much later addition of a half circle of stones east of the chamber. He also believes that the two cists and their associated circle of stones, and possibly an outer part of the passage, represent an addition, in the early phase, to the primary monument. But Arthur ApSimon has suggested that the early date from the foundation pit for one of the chamber orthostats probably relates to earlier activity on the site a millennium before the tomb was built. The second date, from high up in the cairn, may not be very reliable since the sample was small but may give a terminal date for the building of the cairn.

For the excavator the evidence from the Carrowmore excavations implied that small and relatively simple passage tombs were being built as early as the late fifth millennium BC. These supposedly early tombs may not have been completely covered by cairns and had rudimentary passages which did not run all the way from chamber to kerb. Because of the early radiocarbon dates, notably the determination for no. 3, and because of the quantity of sea-shells recovered and the scarcity of pottery, Burenhult has speculated that the Carrowmore megaliths were initiated by a community with an essentially hunting and foraging economy. He suggested that the cemetery was the focus of a hunter-gatherer group with a subsistence pattern which included the seasonal exploitation of coastal shellfish and the fauna of the adjacent countryside. Excavations by Stefan Bergh on the summit of Croaghaun Mountain, south of Ballysadare Bay, Co. Sligo, revealed that a small oval cairn (which had suffered some disturbance) contained a small sub-rectangular megalithic tomb; a number of small deposits of cremated bone, one with an antler pin fragment and some sherds of coarse pottery, were found. Charcoal from this deposit produced a radiocarbon date of 5640-5490 BC and another date of 4675-4460 BC was obtained from another similar sample. For Burenhult, these early dates offer support to his claim that hunters and foragers constructed simple megalithic monuments. However, the absence of diagnostic artefacts of these pre-farming folk is puzzling and most commentators have preferred to see the Sligo tombs in general as a phenomenon of the fourth millennium, their builders combining an agricultural economy with coastal fishing and shellfish gathering.[23]

BURIAL RITUAL AND GRAVE GOODS

Many aspects of the burial ritual of the passage tomb builders are not understood but it is clear that these tombs usually contain remains representing several individuals, frequently cremated but sometimes unburnt. Because cremation was so frequent and because so many of the excavated tombs have been disturbed in the past, reliable details of the numbers buried are often unavailable. But in spite of damage and disturbance, it seems fair to say that cremation was the predominant rite. This was the case at Carrowmore and Knowth, for example, but unburnt bones are frequently reported. Animal bones may be evidence of funeral feasts and the discovery of shells at some sites has prompted the suggestion that shellfish may have been consumed too.

In some tombs it is possible that the human remains were all collectively deposited in a single ceremony: since the burials in the terminal and lateral cells at Fourknocks I, Co. Meath, formed a fairly compact homogenous deposit the excavator was of the opinion that each cell contained a single collective deposit which represented the cremation of a number of corpses accumulated over a period of time. Certainly the presence of some unburnt bones could be said to support this theory for these were clearly fleshless and disarticulated when placed in the tomb and suggested that some corpses at least had been stored for a time elsewhere until they were defleshed. Since smaller unburnt bones such as vertebrae were absent, some selection process clearly took place and, as we have seen, distinctions were made between adults and children and various bone deposits were deliberately placed in certain areas. All the evidence indicates a complex ritual both outside and inside the tomb.

Discrete burial deposits were found in several locations in the Knowth cemetery: all were cremations. In site 15, for instance, an undifferentiated tomb with three sill stones, one segment contained some burnt bones of a child covered by four flat stones. A second larger deposit representing at least one child and two adults lay on top of the slabs but the length of time, if any, between the two deposits could not be ascertained. In site 16, a similar undifferentiated tomb, five separate cremation deposits of at least 16 individuals were identified in both chamber area and passage. Three stratified deposits occurred in the chamber and two in the inner passage, each separated by one or more slabs. Here, as elsewhere, the interval between these burials is unknown but there is no evidence for large scale and prolonged use.

It is not clear what role stone basins may have played in the burial ritual. Some may have once contained deposits of cremated bone but most of those recorded to date come from disturbed monuments. Several Boyne tombs and a number at Loughcrew have produced these enigmatic objects and examples have occasionally been found elsewhere, at Baltinglass, Co. Wicklow and Slieve Gullion, Co. Armagh, for instance.[24]

A limited range of other artefacts occurs fairly consistently with passage tomb burials but their restricted character presents an intriguingly specialized and perplexing assemblage. Beads and pendants, bone and antler pins, stone balls and fragments of Carrowkeel pottery are characteristic finds (Fig. 36; Fig. 19, 8). The small perforated pendants, made of stones such as steatite, limestone or occasionally semi-precious stones such as carnelian and jasper, are often of miniature pestle or

hammer shape. Many bear traces of burning: cracking and heat-crazing indicating some time in the funeral pyre. A few bone or antler examples have been found too. Simple cylindrical and flat circular beads of similar types of stone (and the occasional bone or baked clay example) are known. It is possible that some of the pendants are miniature versions of stone maceheads. Two of these maceheads or hammers have been found at Knowth: half of a perforated macehead of finely polished stone comes from the western undifferentiated tomb in the great mound there and a complete decorated example was found in the cruciform eastern tomb. The latter is an extraordinary object (Fig. 31). Made of pale grey flint and 7.9cm long, it is cylindrically perforated and polished and decorated on all six faces. The principal decorative motifs are extremely finely carved spirals composed of three parallel lines in

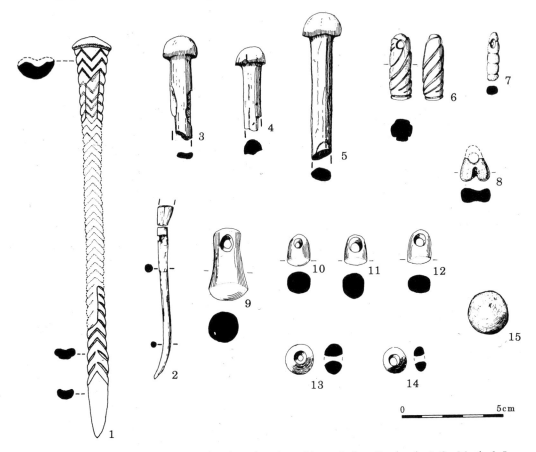

Fig. 36. Finds from passage tombs. 1-2. Decorated antler rod or pin and bone pin from Fourknocks I, Co. Meath. 3-5. Fragments of mushroom-headed pins from Loughcrew, Co. Meath. 6-8. Pendants from the Mound of the Hostages, Tara, Co. Meath. 9-12. Pendants from Carrowkeel, Co. Sligo. 13-14. Beads from the Mound of the Hostages, Tara, Co. Meath. 15. Stone ball from Fourknocks I, Co. Meath.

relief and hollowed lozenges which decorate either end. The polishing, perforating and decorating of this hard flint was a work of exceptional craftsmanship and the object may well have been a prestigious symbol of religious or political authority. Both maceheads are types well known in northern Scotland particularly in Orkney.[25]

The commonest type of bone or antler pin has a rounded mushroom-shaped head. Simpler skewer pins also occur. Many are fragmentary but were probably 10cm to 20cm long and most show traces of burning. Their significance is unknown but a calcined decorated antler example found in the Fourknocks I tomb was considered to be a cult object (Fig. 36, 1). It was decorated with incised chevrons and had, it seems, a shallow groove running for most of its length on one side. A somewhat similar antler or bone object was found in one of the Knowth satellite tombs (Site 3) and a slender 25cm long grooved and conical sandstone object was found near the entrance to the western tomb. This object indicates that at least some of the decorated bone and antler rods were more than mere pins and had some symbolic significance.

Equally enigmatic is a series of carefully made balls of stone and other materials from passage tombs. Eleven of these so-called 'marbles' were found in Fourknocks I, for example; two were made from calcite pebbles, the others were of a chalky material identified as calcium carbonate. They ranged in size from 11mm to 25mm in diameter and some showed traces of burning. Small chalk balls from the main tomb at Newgrange may have been made of material from Antrim and two examples, possibly of serpentine, were also discovered there. Larger, highly polished balls 7cm-8cm in diameter are also known: examples in marble and ironstone are known from Loughcrew. A large limestone ball comes from Fourknocks I. It has been pointed out that some balls fit neatly into some circular pits or cup marks on the stones at Loughcrew and may have been used in ritual performances of some sort.[26] Pairs of small conjoined balls have been found at Newgrange and Tara. Needless to say, the significance of these latter objects is unknown but, not surprisingly, there have been suggestions that both they and the antler pins are expressions of some fertility belief.

Stone implements, such as flint scrapers, are rarely found in the burial deposits. A flint convex scraper from Site K at Newgrange is one of the few identifiably primary finds from such contexts: most of the flints from passage tombs come from the mound or its vicinity or represent some activity on the site prior to or during the construction of the tomb. Fragments of pottery are fairly consistently associated with burials and invariably these are of Carrowkeel ware with characteristic profuse, impressed and incised decoration, hemispherical form and coarse friable fabric. The frequent occurrence of sherds of just parts of pots rather than fragments of complete vessels would seem to suggest that funerary custom often demanded no more than token deposits of pottery perhaps ritually broken elsewhere. Indeed it is possible that some of these pots were specifically made for the burial ceremony. Complete Carrowkeel pots from tombs are rare: one is preserved from Donegore, Co. Antrim, and was found in a possible tomb, a 'subterraneous cavern'; and two were found beneath the Mound of the Hostages at Tara but outside the tomb there: one small bowl was placed in a deposit of cremated bone, the larger bowl contained a cremation, a bone pin and beads.

PASSAGE TOMB ART

Carved decoration on the stones of some tombs is a remarkable feature of this category of megalithic monument and, in Ireland, decoration of this sort is virtually confined to passage tombs. Not all of these tombs contain decorated stones however; the decorated examples, about 50 in number, are found in the north and east of the country and the greatest concentration occurs in Co. Meath in the great cemeteries at Loughcrew and in the Boyne Valley. Decorated tombs, or decorated stones probably from tombs, are also known from Counties Antrim, Armagh, Fermanagh, Sligo, Tyrone, Kilkenny, Louth, Wicklow and Cork.[27]

Ornament has been found on kerbstones, roofstones and orthostats; in some instances it is clear that it was carved after the stones had been put in place, in other cases carved designs were hidden or inaccessible and must have been done prior to placing the stone in position. The designs were executed in two main ways: lightly incised and deeply incised lines are occasionally used but most of the decoration was done by picking with a sharply pointed implement. A flint point or chisel was probably hammered with a wooden mallet to produce a line formed of a series of closely-set 'pick marks'. Sometimes lines such as this were deepened

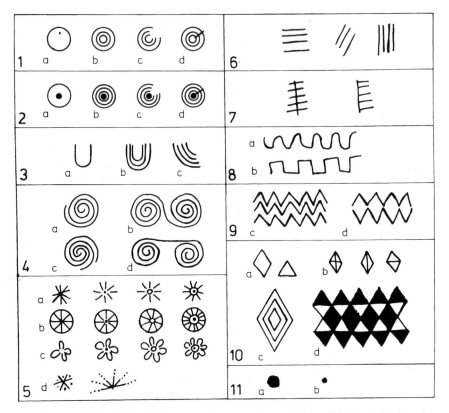

Fig. 37. Passage tomb art motifs. 1. Circles: single, concentric, penannular and with radial line. 2. Circle with central dot. 3. U motif and boxed U motif (b), arcs (c). 4. Spiral motifs. 5. Radial motifs. 6. Parallel lines. 7. Offset motifs. 8. Serpentiform motifs. 9. Zigzag. 10. Lozenge. 11. Cupmark and dot.

by rubbing with a pebble to produce an even groove. Some stones bear designs where broadly picked lines form a pattern which emphasizes the unpicked or reserved areas. Area picking also occurs, particularly in the Boyne Valley: in such designs the picking extends over the whole surface of a motif, a triangle or lozenge, for example; in some cases it may cover large parts of the surface of a stone. No evidence of painting has ever been found in an Irish tomb (though this technique is known in megalithic tombs in the Iberian peninsula). The art varies from the quite haphazard to the remarkably formal. Although some of the more careless and haphazard designs cannot be readily classified, it is still possible to group most of the motifs employed into some 11 general categories (Fig. 37).[28] A full assessment of the components of this art style must await the study of the large amount of material revealed in the Knowth excavations where over 300 decorated stones have been found in the great mound alone.

Single and concentric circles are the commonest motif; they are sometimes penannular as on the kerbstones of the great mound at Knowth. Similar circles with central dots also occur and are particularly frequent at Loughcrew. U-shaped motifs and 'boxed U's' (U motifs set within other U motifs) are also common and are noteworthy in the latter cemetery where in fact they are the commonest motif. They are one of several superbly executed motifs decorating the entrance kerb stone at the main tomb at Newgrange. This stone also illustrates the fact that some of the finest art in this tomb incorporates the spiral motif. Simple clockwise or anticlockwise spirals, double spirals of two parallel lines and linked spirals occur and many have a central circle or dot. They are a notable feature of the repertoire of the Boyne Valley carvers.

Radial motifs, in contrast, are common at Loughcrew but are rarely found elsewhere though good examples do occur at Knowth. The name serpentiform is used to describe an undulating linear motif, though there is no suggestion that the motif represents a serpent. It is widely used and, when rather angular, is sometimes difficult to differentiate from a zigzag (or chevron) motif. The latter motif is sometimes used to form a panel of ornament, as are lozenges and triangles. Other simple motifs include parallel lines and offset motifs in which a series of lines usually project at right angles to a base line, the whole motif being sometimes enclosed in an oval or D-shaped frame. Dots and so-called cupmarks occur frequently; it is not always possible to differentiate between them but cupmarks are usually considered to be more than 2cm in diameter though it is sometimes difficult to distinguish between natural hollows and picked cupmarks.

The listing of individual motifs is a convenient way of summarizing the different elements in this megalithic art but, of course, overlooks the significance of compositional groups and of their location within and without the monuments. The decorative motifs are used in varying combinations and individual tombs seem to have their own distinct style. At Newgrange and on some stones at Knowth, motifs are integrated to form a coherent overall design but sometimes there appears to be no attempt to achieve an overall composition and many stones have just one or two motifs apparently placed at random. Concentric circles, dot and circle motifs, U motifs and serpentiforms are common. The visitor to Newgrange might well assume that spirals, zigzags and lozenges are the principal motifs but, in fact, circles and serpentiforms are well represented. They occur mainly on the upper surfaces of the roof stones of the tomb and on the backs of some of the kerbstones. Some of this hidden ornament may be no more than casual doodling by some of the carvers of the water-grooves, for example, but the use of different motifs to those of the formal art is difficult to explain. Muiris O'Sullivan has identified a depictive or standard style and a plastic style. The former consists of combinations of basic individual motifs such as spirals, circles, chevrons or lozenges; these usually appear haphazard without any obvious attempt to create a coherent pattern though neat two-dimensional compositions may occur occasionally. This style includes the hidden art. In contrast the plastic art is never hidden. It retains elements of the standard art using motifs such as spirals, circles, lozenges, etc. but these are now boldly displayed in visually impressive patterns which take the general shape of the stone into account. There may be a shift in emphasis from individual decorative elements to the structural stone itself. This art seems

rarely to extend to the bottom 30cm of a stone, implying that it was often executed when kerbstone or orthostat had been placed in position. The famous entrance stone at Newgrange is a classic example (Fig. 29). The plastic style may occur on the same surface as the standard style but when this happens it is usually superimposed, cutting through or even partly obliterating the latter.

Various explanations have been offered for individual motifs in this geometric art style. Solar and anthropomorphic explanations have been popular: radial motifs, for instance, have been seen as sun symbols and pairs of spirals have been considered to be stylized human eyes or faces ultimately inspired by vaguely anthropomorphic Iberian plaques and idols. Several Irish carvings have been declared to be stylized representations of human figures, among them the design on one of the Fourknocks orthostats where lozenges and arcs form what the excavator thought to be the head and upper part of a body (Fig. 32B). It has been suggested that this may be evidence that 'an anthropomorphic god and goddess were worshipped in a religion which emphasized ... the principle of fertility in the house of the dead'. This is not impossible but it is a belief which rests on a subjective interpretation of evidence at best described as ambiguous.[29] A face-like design has been seen in a combination of spirals and lozenge on one of the Newgrange orthostats, for example, and on the decorated macehead from Knowth (Fig. 31). Since anthropomorphic designs and human faces are recorded in passage tomb contexts on the Continent, in Brittany and, as already mentioned, in Iberia, stylized representations of this sort are not an impossibility, but clearly interpretation is difficult.

The study of compositional groups and the study of the locational patterns of these compositions may advance our understanding of this enigmatic phenomenon. It is clear that some stones and their art mark significant areas where specific rituals may have taken place: the decorated stone above the Newgrange roofbox is an obvious example, as are the highly decorated kerbstones at tomb entrances. The decorated kerbstones around the great mound at Knowth, like some adjacent settings of stones revealed by excavation, may denote important points on a processional circuit around the site. It is also an interesting possibility that the origin of some motifs may be entoptic (from the Greek *entos*: within, *optikos*: vision), sensory visual images produced in states of altered consciousness induced by hallucinatory drugs, by sensory deprivation or by some other means. Ethnographic evidence and laboratory experimentation suggest that abstract motifs such as U shapes, arcs, spirals, zig-zags and serpentiform motifs, and compositions of triangles or lozenges could have been inspired in this way.[30]

ORIGINS

Megalithic tombs were built in various parts of western Europe from as early as the fifth millennium BC. Passage tombs or related monuments are a widespread phenomenon found mainly in southern Scandinavia, western France, Iberia, Ireland and Britain. In Ireland the majority of examples at least seem to date from the second half of the fourth to the first half of the third millennium BC. The nature of their relationship to the Continental tombs has been the subject of some debate and inconclusive discussion. Various writers have assumed a Breton origin and it has been argued that the first Irish tombs were built by a group of people, several hundred strong, who sailed from the Gulf of Morbihan in southern Brittany to the mouth of the Boyne and then spread westward to Loughcrew and Sligo. Thus the simple monuments in the Carrowmore cemetery would be the ultimate derivatives of the great eastern tombs.[31] Others would disagree and there are various indications that the picture was somewhat more complex. There are also intriguing parallels with aspects of the passage tomb phenomenon in the Iberian peninsula.

Burenhult has argued that simpler monuments such as those at Carrowmore should lie at the beginnings of the passage tomb series which culminates in the great tombs of the Boyne Valley. There is such evidence from Knowth where small tombs pre-dated the great mound and there are indications that other monuments may be of multi-period construction. The final form of such monuments perhaps differing greatly from the primary structure: this seems to have been the case at the passage tomb on Baltinglass, Co. Wicklow (where the small primary tomb was modified at least twice) and at Cairn H in the Carrowkeel cemetery. This tomb seems to have had its passage lengthened at some time and the same may have occurred in the western tomb in the great mound at Knowth.

Alison Sheridan has proposed a developmental sequence of five stages beginning with simple tombs like the 'Druid Stone', Ballintoy, Co. Antrim, and culminating with the large monuments of the Boyne Valley. But even though the evidence from Carrowmore and Croaghaun Mountain is intriguing, unambiguously early dates for simple tombs, have yet to be clearly demonstrated. A small polygonal example at Craigs, Co. Antrim, produced no dating evidence for its construction. Three radiocarbon determinations thought to date the construction of the cairn of a polygonal-chambered tomb (with one terminal cell) at Slieve Gullion, Co. Armagh, might indicate a date range of about 3500 to 2900 BC. The idea that there was a general typological progression from simple to complex plans seems plausible but has yet to be demonstrated and it does not follow that all simple monuments are necessarily early.[32]

Whatever the nature of the typological development of Irish passage tombs, they are generally recognized as one megalithic tomb type with clear Continental parallels. It is also recognized, however, that the resemblances are of a generalized nature as far as tomb morphology is concerned. Thus a majority of the northern and western Iberian passage tombs have round mounds covering corbelled or capstone-roofed chambers of circular or polygonal plan and usually of orthostatic but sometimes of dry-masonry construction. The same is true of the great majority of Breton examples where cairns are generally circular. Sometimes two or more tombs occur beneath the same cairn and rectangular and trapezoidal mounds covering a number of passage tombs placed side by side are also known. A small number of passage tombs have opposed pairs of side chambers or transepts. Details such as these as well as the more generalized resemblances in tomb plan between some Irish and Breton examples form the basis for the belief in a French origin. But significant differences, particularly in date, tomb content and in art styles, have been one factor in the formulation of suggestions of separate regional origins for these and other megalithic tomb types.[33]

In addition to such hypotheses of diffusion or local evolution older notions of the spread of a megalithic cult are still current. M. J. O'Kelly saw the passage tombs (and the other megalithic tombs of western Europe) as various regional manifestations of a cult of the dead which spread among early agricultural communities, no large scale movements of peoples being involved.[34] Of course small scale movements may have taken place and may be quite undetectable in the archaeological record. The suggestion that megalithic tomb building was a practice which spread among communities through normal external contacts has at least the merit of being a persuasive and possibly testable hypothesis. The farming communities of the time did not exist in a social and economic vacuum but were no doubt part of an intricate network of such interrelationships which involved the continuing movement of individuals and the exchange of goods and materials such as axes of polished stone. The reasons why megalithic tombs were built and why different tomb types were apparently in contemporary use are imperfectly understood. These will be considered below.

COURT TOMBS

As the name court tomb suggests, a forecourt of some description is one of the characteristic features of these megalithic monuments. In contrast to passage tombs with their circular mounds, court tombs have long cairns. Essentially a court tomb consists of a long cairn of approximately rectangular or trapezoidal shape with an orthostatically defined, unroofed, court giving access to a longitudinally placed gallery of one or more chambers. Cairn lengths vary but dimensions of between 25m and 35m seem to be common and rare examples from about 40m to 60m in length are known. The maximum width is usually about half the length. Over 390 examples have been recorded and they display considerable variation in shape of court, tomb plan, etc. The distribution of these tombs is mainly a northern one, north of the central plain. Very few examples occur south of a line from Galway to Dundalk: a few examples are recorded in Co. Clare, and one each in Counties Kilkenny, Limerick, Tipperary and Waterford for instance. A significant concentration (about 34% of the total) is to be found in the Mayo-Sligo area. Regional preferences for different types of court tomb are evident: simple tombs with open, crescent-shaped, courts are found mainly in the north-east while elaborate monuments with more complex courts occur mainly in the north-west. Many of these tombs have suffered considerable disturbance and shape of court, number of chambers and other features are sometimes not discernible without excavation.[35]

Several varieties of court tomb have been identified including open court tombs, full court tombs, dual court tombs, and transeptal court tombs. In some of these varieties the number of chambers in the burial gallery may vary but two-chambered galleries are most common. Approximately 70% of tombs with a known number of chambers have just two. Those monuments with a two-chambered gallery and with an open court appear to be the basic court tomb type, most of the other varieties being more complicated variations on this plan. A court tomb at Tully, near Derrygonnelly, Co. Fermanagh, is a good illustration of this two-chambered form with open court and an indication of how excavation can sometimes recover the original plan of even a badly damaged monument. Many of its structural stones had been removed but their sockets or bedding trenches survived. The original trapezoidal shape of the cairn, which would have covered the two-chambered gallery, was also apparent (Fig. 38).

The cairns of court tombs are generally retained by an orthostatic revetment (for example, Ballyglass, Co. Mayo, and Annaghmare, Co. Armagh: Fig. 39), retaining walls of dry-masonry also occur now and then as at Tully where the surviving eastern side of the long cairn had a functional revetment of large stones (with a second non-functional revetment set 45cm to 90cm in front of it). Evidence of the original heights of cairns is scanty: at Carrowreagh, Co. Sligo, a long cairn almost entirely covered by peat is 3m to 4m high at the chamber and slopes to a height of about 1m towards the rear of the monument. Several cairns show such a decrease in height from front of chamber to rear of monument.

Courts are usually defined by orthostats and occasionally dry-walling fills gaps between these stones. Courts of dry-walling alone are rare. As the name suggests open courts are concave: often one-half or perhaps two-thirds of a circle, sometimes slightly U-shaped as at Tully. The court gives access to the burial gallery, the entrance to which is sometimes flanked by two of the tallest stones of the facade of the court, usually a matching pair, which narrow the entry and form a sort of portal suitable for a lintel stone.

As already mentioned, galleries often comprise two chambers but three and four-chambered examples are known. Chambers are rectangular, occasionally sub-rectangular perhaps with slightly concave sides (as at Annaghmare). Galleries are segmented or divided into chambers by pairs of

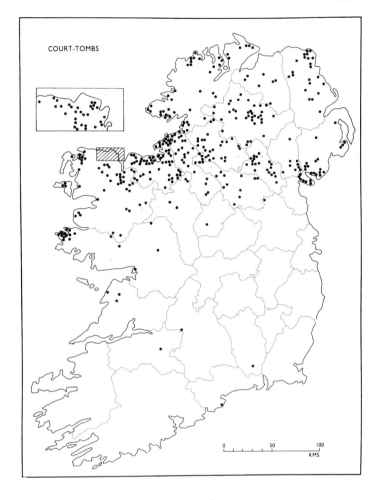

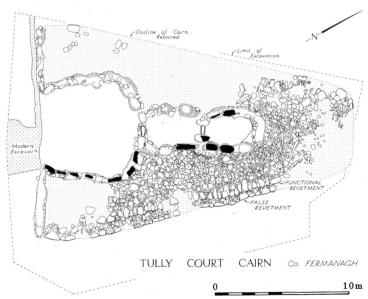

Fig. 38. Above. Distribution of court tombs. Below. Court tomb with open court and two-chambered gallery at Tully, Co. Fermanagh.

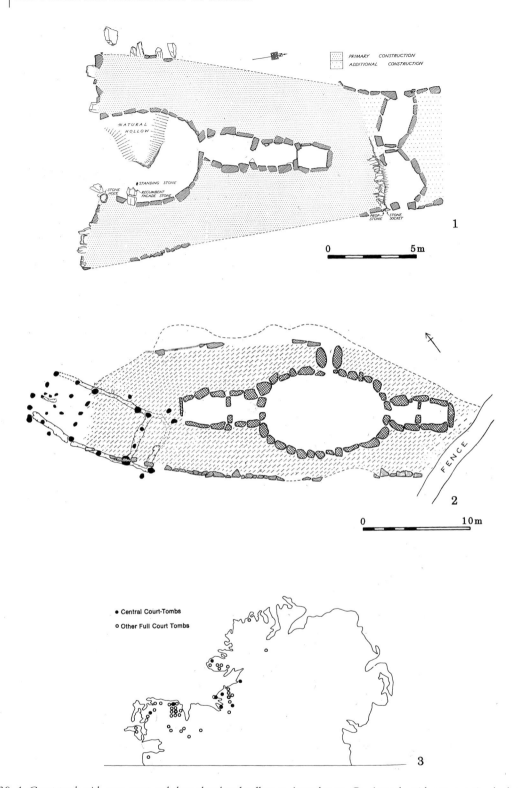

Fig. 39. 1. Court tomb with open court and three-chambered gallery at Annaghmare, Co. Armagh, with segmentation by both a pair of jamb stones and by jamb stones and sill stone. 2. Central court tomb at Ballyglass, Co. Mayo, with the pre-tomb structure visible on the west. 3. Distribution of central and full court tombs.

jamb stones or a combination or jamb stones and sill stone. Jamb stones are upright stones, usually a matched pair, and they may be set against or inset into the side walls. Sill stones, those low transverse slabs set on edge in the floor, are sometimes placed between the jamb stones. Evidence for corbel-roofing of the chambers is fairly common – several oversailing corbels survived at Ballyglass, Co. Mayo, and at Audleystown, Co. Down, for example. Back stones of galleries are occasionally pointed to a gable shape quite suitable for supporting corbelling. Use of corbels in this fashion would probably have demanded a substantial covering cairn to hold them and the roofstones in place.

A number of open and full court tombs have subsidiary chambers at right angles to the long axis of the cairn and opening onto the sides of the monument (such as Annaghmare – Fig. 39). They are normally of simple rectilinear plan sometimes narrowing towards the rear; a pair of jamb stones (sometimes with long axes parallel to the long axis of the chamber) form a portal at the entrance and in some examples a sill stone is placed between the jambs. Little evidence for the form of roofing of these subsidiary chambers has survived but at Annaghmare one was corbel-roofed and several courses of corbelling were noted.

Single court tombs, whether with full or open courts, show a definite preference in orientation. In a clear majority of cases the broader court end faces in a general eastward direction mostly between north-north-east and south-east. This possibly represents an alignment on the rising sun which in these latitudes would give a splay of some 80° between summer and winter positions.

Elaboration of the basic open court plan may have produced the full court tomb in which the court is of more or less oval plan with a narrow entry terminally placed opposite the entrance to the gallery. At Creevykeel, near Cliffony, Co. Sligo (Fig. 40A) a narrow orthostatic passage 4.5m long connects the large court (14m by 9m) with the frontal facade and it is possible that this passage may once have been roofed. Here too a difference in the size of the orthostats of the court clearly differentiates the concave section at the tomb entrance from the rest. A few tombs of this type have a frontal concave forecourt as well.

A rare variant, the central court tomb, combines at least two tombs with a full centrally-placed court with lateral entry. Ballyglass, Co. Mayo (Fig. 39) is a well known example with a large pair of out-turned stones forming an entrance to the court which is just over 11m long and has a two-chambered gallery at both its western and eastern ends. A dry-stone revetment delimited the long cairn which enclosed the court and probably once covered the tombs.

Dual court tombs appear to be another elaboration of the basic tomb plan (the two-chambered monument with open court) in which two galleries are placed back to back. Two-chambered galleries are normal but a few dual court tombs with pairs of three or four-chambered galleries are known. Cohaw, near Cootehill, Co. Cavan (Fig. 40C) consists of a pair of two-chambered galleries (each segmented by jambs and sills) and separated one from the other by a closed chamber. Sometimes the galleries share a common back stone and sometimes they are simply separated by a large or small gap. Audleystown, Co. Down (Fig. 40B), unusual in having a pair of four-chambered galleries, has an intervening gap of just over 2m.

Regional preferences are discernible for different features of the court tomb series: the elaborate full court tombs and the central court variant (both consistently having two-chambered galleries) are to be found in the north-west, mostly in Mayo, Sligo and Donegal (Fig. 39). Open courts predominate elsewhere. Dual court tombs are mainly found in central and southern Ulster: a few examples are recorded in the Mayo-Sligo area and in eastern Ulster but the majority occur in a broad region embracing the counties of Leitrim, Cavan, Monaghan, Fermanagh and Tyrone. A small number of court tombs in the Mayo-Sligo area have the unusual feature of one or two side chambers opening like transepts from the main gallery. These transeptal court tombs mainly have full courts of orthostatic construction. One tomb, at least, has an unusual dry-stone court. At Behy, Co. Mayo (Fig. 40E), excavation has revealed a long sub-rectangular cairn with an oval full court of dry-walling leading through a lintelled entrance into a gallery divided into two by a pair of jambs and a high sill stone. An opposed pair of transeptal chambers open off the inner part of the gallery.

Some regional bias in orientation is also apparent: the eastern rule for single court tombs is fairly constant in the west of the court tomb province but adherence to this custom is less marked in the east notably in Co. Armagh.

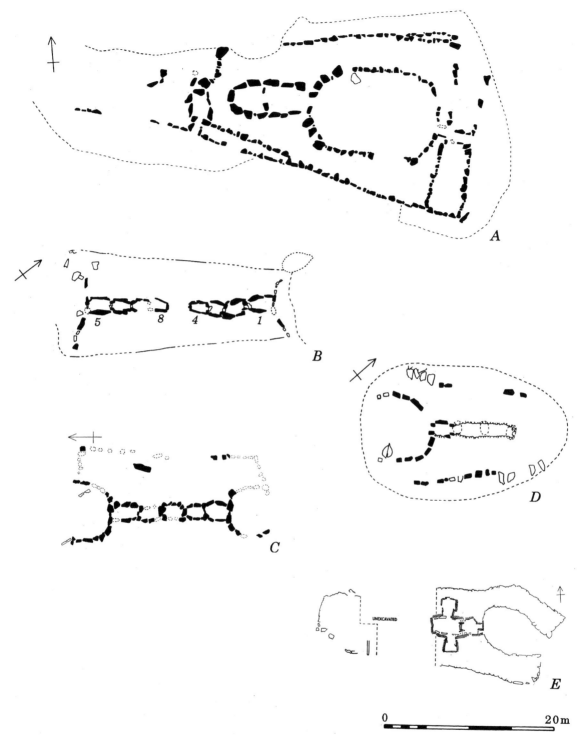

Fig. 40. Court tomb plans. A. Full court tomb at Creevykeel, Co. Sligo. B. Dual court tomb (with two four-chambered galleries) at Audleystown, Co. Down: the chambers in the north-eastern gallery are numbered 1-4, those in the south-western gallery 5-8. C. Dual court tomb at Cohaw, Co. Cavan: post-holes in courts not shown. D. Open court tomb with a single chamber at Ballymacaldrack, Co. Antrim, and pits of mortuary structure north-east of the chamber. E. Transeptal court tomb at Behy, Co. Mayo.

BURIAL RITUAL, GRAVE GOODS AND OTHER FINDS

In spite of damage and disturbance to many tombs, excavation has produced some interesting and puzzling evidence for burial and other ritual practices. A number of sites bear witness to collective burial but some have yielded little or no burial evidence. Browndod, Co. Antrim, Goward, Co. Down, Kilnagarns Lower, Co. Leitrim, and Bavan, Co. Donegal, for example, have yielded no trace of bone – but with the possible exception of Goward, all were extensively disturbed. In contrast, the much damaged tomb at Tully, Co. Fermanagh, still contained the sparse remains of four individuals, all cremated, in the two-chambered gallery. It is possible, if burials were not destroyed by disturbance, that unburnt bones may have simply decayed without trace in certain circumstances. In the relatively well preserved open court tomb at Ballymacdermot, Co. Armagh, for instance, the innermost two of the three chambers of the gallery were used for burial but only a few very small fragments of burnt bone survived and here the acid soil conditions of the area would have been inimical to the preservation of unburnt bone. Phosphate analysis within and without the gallery demonstrated a significantly high concentration in the inner chamber and, while this could be due to the deposition of material from a phosphate-rich context such as a settlement area, enrichment could be caused by the decay of skeletal material, a conclusion favoured by the excavators. Charcoal samples from the burial gallery produced radiocarbon determinations suggesting a date towards the middle of the fourth millennium BC.[36]

Unburnt bones have been found on a few occasions: for instance, at Ballyalton, Co. Down, the very fragmentary bones of at least six individuals were recovered, numerous unburnt bones were found at Audleystown, Co. Down (below), and some teeth and a fragmentary skull of one or two individuals came from Cohaw, Co. Cavan. Cremated remains were also found at the latter two sites. Cremation is recorded from a majority of the excavated court tombs to yield human bone. Five or six individuals were represented at Ballymacaldrack, Co. Antrim, a minimum of two at Clady Halliday, Co. Tyrone; at Cohaw aside from the unburnt bone just mentioned the burnt bones of a child were found, possibly two or more individuals at Barnes Lower, Co. Tyrone, four at Tully, Co. Fermanagh, and

a few fragments of the bones of two children were all that was recovered from the large dual court tomb at Aghanaglack, Co. Fermanagh. Creggandevesky, Co. Tyrone, produced cremated bone representing 21 individuals and the bone was so fragmentary it may have been deliberately crushed after burning; here again acid soil may have destroyed unburnt bones. Given the fragmentary nature of most of this evidence and the difficulties involved in the ageing and sexing of cremated bone most if not all of these figures for court tombs are possibly minimal ones.[37]

Particularly interesting funerary and ritual information comes from a small number of excavations. The dual court tomb at Audleystown on the shore of Strangford Lough in Co. Down had a trapezoidal cairn (Fig. 40B) retained by a dry-stone revetment. Shallow courts and four-chambered galleries faced north-east and south-west respectively. Traces of at least partial corbel-roofing of the galleries were found: it was not possible to ascertain whether corbelling alone completed the roof or whether a combination of corbelling and lintelling was employed.[38] Each gallery was about 10m in length, 1.2m in width, and, when empty, about 1.2m to 1.5m in height; the space between jamb stones varied from 30cm to 60cm. The two inner chambers, nos 3 and 4, of the north-eastern gallery were empty except for the remains of a fire in no. 3. Burial deposits were found in the other six chambers though in nos 5 and 7 in the south-western gallery they had suffered some disturbance. Only cremated bone had survived in no. 5 but in the other chambers there was a 15cm to 30cm thick and compact deposit of earth, or earth and stones, and cremated and unburnt human bone. Numerous fragments of pottery and some flint implements were mixed through these deposits which were packed down and sealed with stones. A few animal bones – including cattle, horse, sheep or goat and pig – were also found.

The human remains from the tomb were unburnt, partially burnt and fully cremated and represented approximately 34 individuals. A majority of these (21 or 22) were represented by unburnt bones which had been placed in a defleshed condition, sometimes in small neatly arranged groups, at all levels in the burial deposits (which contained burnt bone throughout). The remains were those of adults, both male and female, and children. The pottery found was all fragmentary and comprised plain and decorated round-bottomed pots of both Lyles Hill style and Decorated Bowl style (including Goodland bowl and Carrowkeel ware). Flint implements included scrapers, leaf and lozenge-shaped arrowheads, plano-convex knives and a lozenge-shaped javelin head. While the number of persons in Audleystown was large enough to suggest successive burials in the tomb over a period of time, details such as the disarticulated nature of the bones, implying storage elsewhere, and the difficulties involved in re-entering the galleries, led the excavator, A. E. P. Collins, to conclude that a single collective burial was the more likely possibility. A complex sequence of events of unknown duration is certainly indicated: there was possible evidence for the burning of the site before the tomb was built, burning within some of the chambers, deposition of the burial deposits, and then placing of packing stones on top of this. There seems to have been a tendency for a greater number of children and adult females to have been deposited in an unburnt condition.

Annaghmare, near Crossmaglen, Co. Armagh (Fig. 39) is a single court tomb with open court and three-chambered gallery. It also had a pair of subsidiary chambers placed back to back near the rear of a trapezoidal cairn which was just 20m in length, 11.5m wide at the southern end, and 6.5m wide at the northern rear end. The 5.5m deep forecourt was well preserved and was constructed of orthostats with dry-stonework between them – in the so-called post-and-panel technique of building. A matching pair of 1.28m tall orthostats flanked the entrance to the gallery which, as excavation revealed, had been deliberately blocked with horizontally-laid flagstones; these filled much of the court, sloping away from the portal. The blocking extended into the gallery for at least a metre or so; its full extent was not ascertainable because the outer chamber had been disturbed and a pot sherd, a flint scraper and a few scraps of burnt bone were all that remained of its original contents.

In the inner chamber (approximately 1.65m by 1.28m) the burial deposit consisted of a 38cm thick homogenous filling of stones, soil, fragments of burnt human bone, a few scraps of animal bone, sherds of three decorated round-bottomed pots, six flint concave scrapers and charcoal. In the middle chamber (measuring approximately 2.4m by 1.2m) the filling consisted almost entirely of stones with

just a little dark soil. Small fragments of burnt bone were mixed through this filling and a few further sherds of two of the pots discovered in the inner chamber were also found along with a flint javelin head, several concave scrapers and a convex scraper. On this stone filling lay a few unburnt bones of a child and a femur of an adult; these were the only unburnt remains found in the gallery. The burnt bone may represent one child and at least one adult but certainty was not possible. Examination of the subsidiary chambers at the northern end revealed that the eastern one had been dug out in recent times and all but one of the stones on one side removed. The western chamber, with orthostatic concave sides and portal stones narrowing the entrance, had been corbel-roofed. No traces of burials were found and phosphate values were normal.

In attempting to discover the sockets of the missing side stones of the eastern subsidiary chamber, the excavation exposed a dry-stone revetment surviving to a maximum height of 90cm. This wall seems to have been the back of the cairn as first planned and built, and the monument was evidently extended at some later time to accommodate the additional subsidiary chambers. This evidence for multi-period construction at Annaghmare is interesting and suggests continuing interest in and activity at the tomb over a period of time. One radiocarbon date of 3308-2914 BC obtained from charcoal behind the court blocking gives no hint, of course, of the possible duration of this activity. Both the position of several stones in the court blocking and the size of the gallery suggested to the excavator that re-entry was theoretically possible even with the burial deposits in place. Thus intermittent accumulation of these deposits over a period of time could have occurred and the presence of sherds of the same pot in different chambers could be explained by the disturbance and relocation of the tomb contents. However, since the sherds of one pot in the inner chamber were found from top to bottom of the filling, the excavator, Dudley Waterman, concluded that the deposit was introduced in a single act, remaining undisturbed and unaugmented; in other words the mixture of stone, earth, burnt bone, potsherds and charcoal were collected elsewhere and placed in the tomb as a unitary deposit.[39]

Aside from the question of a single or collective deposit, the very nature of the Annaghmare deposit is intriguing. In an analysis of some fifteen court tomb fillings which were seemingly undisturbed, including Annaghmare, Humphrey Case noted the consistent occurrence of earth often containing bone, charcoal, stones and fragments of incomplete pots. Pottery was evidently deliberately deposited as sherds and the absence of complete burials, either unburnt skeletons or entire cremations, raises the possibility that these monuments were not merely, or even primarily, sepulchral and they may have been exercises in sympathetic magic. He suggested that the earth and pottery fragments may represent settlement debris buried as part of some magic rites for the needs of the living and possibly connected with fertility. He was struck by the resemblances between the contents of some court tombs and the contents of pits at a ritual site at Goodland, Co. Antrim (Chapter 4). Rather than being settlement refuse, it is even possible this material may be sacred soil from some other ritual site.[40]

It is not difficult to see court tombs as both tombs and shrines of some description. As tombs, the cult of the dead may have never involved the full and formal burial of all members of the community. As cult places, various rituals may have taken place not just within but also outside the monument. It is generally assumed, for instance, that the unroofed courts had some ceremonial purpose. Traces of fires, fragments of pottery and evidence of blocking from some sites have all been generally considered indications of ritual practice. A few pits of uncertain purpose have been found. A small standing stone in the forecourt at Ballymarlagh, Co. Antrim, a larger one in the court of Browndod, Co. Antrim, and another small example set in the blocking material at Annaghmare, may have some ritual significance. At Creggandevesky, Co. Tyrone, cremated human bone was found in front of the tomb's entrance and what was thought to be the remains of a fire had been placed in the middle of the forecourt. A fallen pair of tall slender stones were thought to have once stood in the northern court at Cohaw, Co. Cavan, where excavation also revealed a series of post-holes, mostly just over 30cm in depth, placed at intervals across the fronts of both courts; their purpose may well have been to screen or close the courts and exclude some people. A tomb with quite a narrow paved court at Shanballyedmond, Co. Tipperary, had its cairn delimited by a series of thirty-four spaced timber posts which for the most part had diameters of

25cm to 30cm. These posts had, it seems, no functional purpose and a ritual explanation is likely; totem poles of some description is not an impossibility. A fire had been burnt for some hours in the outermost of the two chambers of the gallery; in the inner chamber a large pit in the floor also had a fire burnt in it, the ashes removed and some cremated bone of a young male then placed therein.[41]

The creation of the full court at Creevykeel and the extension of the Annaghmare cairn to incorporate subsidiary chambers presumably reflect different secondary ritual requirements. Possible multi-period construction was also inferred in the much disturbed court tomb at Barnes Lower, near Plumbridge, Co. Tyrone, where a two-chambered gallery (with traces of a slightly convex facade) may have been extended to form a four-chambered gallery with a flat facade. The trapezoidal cairn contained four, perhaps five, subsidiary chambers. Unusual ritual evidence comes from excavations in 1935 and 1975 at Ballymacaldrack, near Dunloy, Co. Antrim. This tomb had a semi-circular court and a single-chambered gallery (Fig. 40D). Occasional fragments of pottery were found scattered throughout a blocking of stones in the forecourt. Two polished stone axes were also found in this sealing material. The chamber contained a 90cm deep deposit of earth and stones and finds included pot sherds, two lozenge-shaped flint arrowheads and a bead of serpentine. A few fragmentary animal teeth were found but no human remains. A paved and stone-lined trench was found behind the chamber aligned on the same axis; this trench measured 6.5m in length, some 90cm in depth and 1m to 1.3m in width. Three roughly oval pits occurred in the floor of the trench: one in the middle and one at either end. These pits may have contained timber posts but possible traces of one or two posts were detected only in the westernmost pit though all three contained stones which could have served as packing stones. The trench contained a large amount of charcoal, fire-cracked stones, pottery fragments, a calcined leaf-shaped flint arrowhead, and cremated human bone representing five or six adult individuals. Charcoal from the trench has given radiocarbon dates of 3930-3640 BC and 4226-3708 BC.

Axial pits containing traces of large timber posts have been found in some contemporary British burial mounds and these and other features are considered to be the remains of mortuary structures of wood and other materials, built as a temporary protection for the human remains. In Scotland and in northern England these were sometimes burnt and, while the Ballymacaldrack evidence admits of no clear explanation, some sort of structure or structures may have been burnt here and human remains may even have been cremated in place. A further puzzling feature at Ballymacaldrack is the collapse of at least one of the court orthostats early in the history of the tomb and prior to the deposition of the blocking. This and other evidence of early collapse at Ballymacdermot and Audleystown seem to suggest some lack of interest in cairn maintenance on the part of these tomb builders. In some cases the more important act may just have been the construction of the monument.[42]

In contrast to passage tombs, art is very rarely found in court tombs: a lozenge was carved on a loose stone found on the surface of the cairn at Goward, Co. Down, and two orthostats of a fine court tomb at Malin More, Co. Donegal, are also decorated with motifs including arcs, a lozenge and curving lines.[43]

A range of pottery and flint types occurs. Some or all may have been intended as funerary offerings but in the light of the suggestion that some tombs may have settlement or other debris incorporated in their contents, it is worth bearing in mind that the term 'grave goods' may not be the most appropriate. The pottery comprises both plain and decorated wares, invariably represented by sherds of incomplete vessels; the Carinated Bowl, Decorated Bowl and Bipartite Bowl styles are all represented and a majority of the excavated examples have yielded sherds of decorated pottery The range of pottery types found has led to suggestions that these tombs were in use over a period of several centuries but, as we have seen, the contents of their chambers often present interpretative problems and stratigraphical evidence, when present, is rarely conclusive.

Various flint types occur and they occasionally show signs of burning; flint arrowheads, scrapers and knives are the commonest items found. The arrowheads are of the characteristic lozenge or leaf-shaped forms. Larger javelin heads are known from over a dozen sites and for the most part these are of lozenge shape. Several are leaf-shaped, however, and one of these finely-worked flints from Creevykeel, Co. Sligo, is an oval specimen 13cm in length. Broad oval examples such as this one could have served as projectile heads but use as a knife is a possibility. Double-edged flint knives, sometimes of fine workmanship, have been found in a number of court tombs: two complete finely made plano-convex flint knives (and the fire-damaged tips of two others) were found in Barnes Lower, Co. Tyrone (Fig. 24, 5) and one comes from Ballybriest, Co. Derry. Less well finished knives have also been found as at Audleystown, Co. Down.

Quite a number of the excavated tombs have produced flint scrapers of both the concave scraper and convex scraper varieties. No less than fourteen concave scrapers (four of them burnt) were found in Annaghmare, Co. Armagh, all but one from the burial gallery. This tomb also produced one convex scraper. A few monuments have yielded stone axes: two small and rather poorly chipped axes of flint, found with a hoard of other flints, come from Ballyalton, Co. Down, and among the several examples of polished stone are two of Antrim porcellanite from Ballymarlagh, Co. Antrim, and two from Ballymacaldrack, Co. Antrim; the latter were found in the blocking material at the entrance and were possibly ceremonial offerings: the excavator suggested they were 'the magic guardians of the tomb'. An axe of polished diorite was also found in the forecourt at Creevykeel, Co. Sligo. Among the other artefacts occasionally found are various form of beads: usually of simple disc shape as from Ballymacaldrack and Creevykeel. Two almost spherical beads of polished schist and a larger almost lozenge-shaped bead of similar material were found in the chamber at Bavan, Co. Donegal. The lozenge-shaped stone bead, with a length of 5.8cm has a 5mm wide longitudinal perforation. Another similarly perforated schist bead from Tully, Co. Fermanagh, has a length of 8cm and Waterman suggested that the narrow cylindrical perforation was probably pierced through a larger mass of rock which was then reduced to the requisite size and shape. The drilling demanded considerable stone-working ability. Similar beads were found in a portal tomb at Ballyrenan, Co. Tyrone.[44] A necklace of 112 stone beads is reported from Creggandevesky, Co. Tyrone.

ORIGINS AND DATE

Radiocarbon dates from a small number of court tombs suggest that these monuments, like some passage tombs, are a feature of the fourth millennium BC. Few of these dates come from samples that are certainly coeval with the period of construction and primary use but it is clear that the two tomb types were at least partly contemporary. The burning of the mortuary structure at Ballymacaldrack could have occurred around 4000 BC and the blocking of the megalithic tomb was possibly placed in position (or at least interfered with) some centuries later. The late fourth millennium BC date for the blocking at Annaghmare, Co. Armagh, provides a terminal date for the tomb and a series of dates for the house which pre-dated Ballyglass, Co. Mayo, may indicate a date in the early third millennium BC for that monument. Dates from pre-cairn samples from the dual court tomb of Ballybriest, Co. Derry, imply a construction date sometime in the fourth millennium BC for at least the eastern part of this monument. The radiocarbon evidence indicates that Ballymacdermot, Co. Armagh, was in use towards the middle of the fourth millennium BC. Dates from the chamber and forecourt at Tully, Co. Fermanagh, and from Shanballyedmond, Co. Tipperary, imply the same.[45]

A relationship between court tombs and similar megalithic tombs in England and Wales (Cotswold-Severn tombs) and in Scotland (Clyde tombs) has been recognized for many years and the derivation of the Irish tombs from the latter south-western Scottish monuments was generally assumed. Given that the knowledge of animal husbandry and cereal cultivation did spread westwards across Europe, the concomitant diffusion of certain tomb types, built by these early farmers, was a reasonable belief. Terms such as the Clyde-Carlingford culture or group emphasized the relationship of the Scottish and Irish monuments but with the realization that the bulk of the Irish examples were to be found not in the north-east but in the north-west, Ruaidhrí De Valera proposed a controversial alternative theory. The density of the north-western distribution and the occurrence there of complex full and central court tombs were some of the factors which led him to suggest that these tombs were introduced along with the landfall of early farming communities on the shores of Mayo and Sligo. From this supposed primary focus court tomb builders were thought to have spread eastwards and the transeptal tombs suggested that their origins should be sought in north-western France where a small number of transeptal passage tombs are to be found. Variations in tomb morphology were considered to represent a typological devolution from complex tombs in the west to simpler monuments in the east reflecting a corresponding movement of early farming groups. The presence of fragments of plain shouldered round-bottomed pottery in many tombs seemed to support the notion that these megaliths were built by pioneering farming colonists.[46]

This suggestion, though widely promulgated, never found general acceptance.[47] The absence of suitable prototypes in north-western France for Irish forecourts, for example, as well as differences in pottery styles and flint work, and the implausibility of sea-borne landings in a very restricted area of the Atlantic coast of western Ireland were just some of the reasons for its rejection.[48] Allowing for the fact that general similarities in tomb plan, pottery and flint work, point – as has long been recognized – to some relationship with Scotland and England, the theory of a French connection seems, as A. E. P. Collins once said, 'sadly deficient in economy of hypothesis'.

With the knowledge in recent years that early farming communities were widely scattered throughout the country some time before court tombs were constructed, the diffusion or adoption of these tombs need no longer be associated with the arrival or spread of pioneering agriculturalists. Their origins may be more complex and various suggestions have been offered. They may, for instance, be elaborate translations into stone of the idea of a timber mortuary structure and thus, it has been argued, early megalithic tombs in Scotland may have been relatively simple quadrangular structures, with forecourts, long cairns and further chambers being later and more elaborate additions. The provision of a pair of prominent portal stones at one end of such a simple megalith would produce a monument akin to a portal tomb (below) and, indeed, it suggested that in Ireland such a monument may have evolved into the court tomb.[49] Much more excavation is needed before suggestions such as these can be proved or disproved but they illustrate the lack of unanimity on the question of court tomb origins and development. As far as the problem of origins is concerned, it is possible that no single explanation may suffice.

Suggestions of separate constructional phases in the history of particular monuments (as at Annaghmare, Ballymacaldrack, and Barnes Lower) indicate just how varied and complicated the story of any one court tomb's development may be. The various features of long mound and tomb which together characterize these megaliths are found singly or in differing combinations in a variety of funerary monuments from southern England to northern Scotland. Behind the parallels and distinctions which can be recognized there must lie complicated tales of kinship and regional contacts as well as of parallel evolution and divergence in both islands.

PORTAL TOMBS

Although the portal tomb is invariably a structure of simple plan, some of these monuments are remarkable examples of megalithic engineering. A majority of this type of monument have a single sub-rectangular chamber with an entrance flanked by a pair of tall portal stones (Fig. 41). The tomb is usually covered by a single capstone, sometimes of massive proportions, and, as far as can be judged from rather limited evidence, cairns are of elongated perhaps sub-rectangular form, but short oval and round cairns also exist.[50]

Only a very few of the 174 or so Irish portal tombs have been scientifically excavated and because so many tombs of this class have been denuded of cairn material, the original form of the great majority of cairns is unknown. Indeed, even in the few excavated examples either partial excavation or poor preservation has meant that the original cairn shape could not be accurately ascertained: but long mounds, longer than necessary just to cover the tomb, are reliably attested at about one-sixth of the sites. Ballykeel, Co. Armagh, for example, had the remains of a long sub-rectangular cairn some 28m in length with the tomb situated at the southern end. Normally just one tomb is terminally placed in this fashion but in a few cases there is more than one. Two portal tombs, both facing in the same direction, occurred one behind the other in a 13.7m long cairn at Ballyrenan, Co. Tyrone. An intriguing complex at Malin More, Co. Donegal, comprises two large portal tombs set about 90m apart both facing east; between them are the remains of four small chambers and it is possible that all six may once have been incorporated in the one long cairn. Subsidiary chambers have been noted in some cairns. Excavations at a destroyed tomb at Melkagh, Co. Longford, revealed that the cairn may have been retained by a low dry-stone wall.

Chambers are usually sub-rectangular in plan, narrowing towards the rear but a few tombs

broaden towards the rear. Both sides and ends are often formed of single orthostats and end stones are occasionally gabled as in court tombs. At the entrance a pair of massive portal stones are set inside the line of the side stones; these portal stones are usually the tallest and most imposing orthostats in the structure. In some tombs the space between the portals is closed with a large slab (as with stone 5 at Drumanone, near Boyle, Co. Roscommon: Fig. 41), occasionally a sill stone about half the height of the portals is present and lower sills also occur. In many cases no evidence of closure, either partial or full, survives.

A large single capstone is often used to roof the tomb, resting on portals and end stone. When one end of the capstone is larger than the other, the more massive end is usually poised on the portals, no doubt to give further emphasis to the front of the tomb. Capstones of extraordinary size and weighing many tons were sometimes used. The largest is said to be that at Kernanstown, Brownshill, Co. Carlow, estimated to weigh 100 tons. Some denuded tombs, such as Proleek, Co. Louth, where all that survives is a huge capstone of 30 to 40 tons perched on two portals and a back stone are imposing reminders of their builder's skill. It is not known how such impressive stones were transported and raised but it is assumed that they were pulled by men and perhaps oxen, ropes and timber sleds or rollers being used. While ropes and levers may all have been used to raise large orthostats like some of the portal stones, the larger capstones must have presented considerable engineering problems. These large stones may have been hauled up ramps of earth or stone (and some long cairns may have been thus employed) or they may have been lifted in stages by means of levers and timber platforms or cribs raised gradually to the required height.

The side stones of the chamber do not normally reach the capstone and it has been suggested that these spaces may have been filled by corbelling. As already mentioned, one capstone is the norm but occasionally a small second capstone occurs below the larger one as at Greengraves, Co. Down. In a few instances, as in one of the tombs at Ballyrenan, Co. Tyrone, divided in two by a large slab, two-chambered tombs have been recorded. Another very rare feature, perhaps reminiscent of the courts of court tombs, is the presence of some stones flanking the portals. A small crescent of low stones

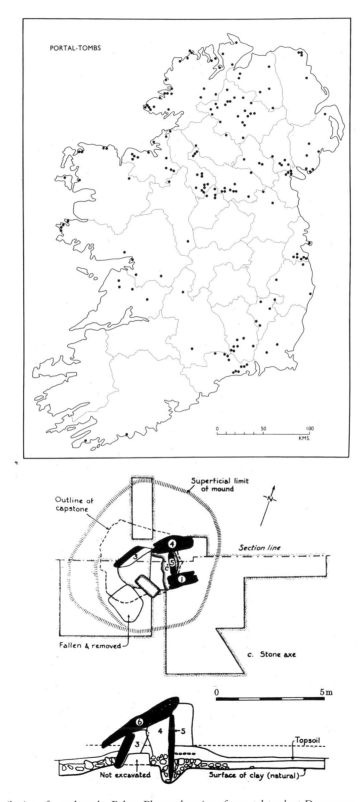

Fig. 41. Above. Distribution of portal tombs. Below. Plan and section of a portal tomb at Drumanone, Co. Roscommon, with the front of the large capstone resting on the portal stones.

has been noted at Ticloy, Co. Antrim, for example, and a pair of low orthostats flank the portals at Aghaglaslin, Co. Cork.[51]

The orientation of portal tombs seems to be fairly variable though a number face in a general eastern direction, sometimes uphill. Some are located in valleys, often near streams as at Aghaglaslin and Ballykeel. The siting of some tombs in sheltered valleys has provoked the suggestion that certain tomb builders were exploiting some more heavily wooded lowland sites. A majority of portal tombs are found in the northern half of the country: a thin scatter of examples lies in the north-west, an area also favoured by court tomb builders. A significant number of portal tombs occurs in Donegal, Tyrone and Derry and the type is represented in Cavan and Monaghan and eastwards to Down and Louth. A few are known in Mayo, Galway and Clare where many are quite close to the coast, and a major group occurs well outside the court tomb province in Leinster and Waterford. Portal tombs are also known in Wales and Cornwall.

Finds are recorded from a small number of these monuments but few have been scientifically excavated in recent years. The examination of Ballykeel, near Camlough, Co. Armagh, yielded some interesting results. Here a long cairn measuring about 28m long and 9m in average width contained a tomb at its southern end. The cairn had been damaged in places but survived to a height of some 75cm. Several cuttings revealed that it was more than an amorphous dump of stones: leaning pairs of stones propped together formed a sort of spine along the central long axis and parallel to this were two symmetrical pairs of lines of stones which in places formed a flimsy wall three courses high. The inner stone rows were clearly buried features, their purpose unknown, but the outer two, in the excavator's opinion, originally may have delimited the cairn. The tomb survived as a large capstone resting on twin portals (averaging 2m in height) and on a back stone which had collapsed inwards. A large slab in front of the portals had once closed the entrance. There were no side stones and excavation revealed no suggestion that there ever were any. (However, if like the back stone they had been placed in a shallow bedding of stones indistinguishable from the cairn material itself, their former presence would have been virtually undetectable.) It is also possible that some light timber work might have served as side walling for

the distribution of finds within the chamber area did suggest some sort of containment. Hundreds of sherds of pottery were recovered and three flints but no bone either burnt or unburnt. Acidic soil conditions may well have destroyed unburnt bones. Phosphate analysis did reveal extremely high concentrations in the chamber area compared to nearby fields but the likelihood of localized rabbit activity contributing to the inflated phosphate values was recognized.

A small amount of plain shouldered, round-bottomed pottery was found inside and outside the chamber: it may be a relic of pre-tomb activity on the site but it is also conceivable that an attempt to clear out the contents of the tomb was made on some occasion. The fragmentary pottery consisted mainly of sherds of four finely decorated Bipartite Bowls and numerous sherds of plain, coarse flat-bottomed pots. Sherds of coarse ware, all possibly from the one pot, came from the body of the cairn on its long axis along with some charcoal. Charcoal also from the body of the cairn provided a radiocarbon date of 1742-1526 BC and might indicate a second millennium BC date for the plain pottery. The remains of a cist, a small slab-built sub-rectangular structure measuring about 1m in internal length, was found near the northern end of the cairn. No capstone survived and the cist had been rifled in the past: no trace of any burial was found but it did contain a few sherds of a Goodland bowl, a flint flake and a flint javelin head.[52]

Exceptional information has been recovered from the portal tomb at Poulnabrone, in the Burren, Co. Clare. Excavation by Ann Lynch in 1986 and 1988 revealed that the side stones of the rectangular chamber simply rested on bedrock and were kept in place by the weight of the large capstone. A broken sill stone between the portals had been set in a gryke or crevice; its original height is unknown but it could have been large enough to have closed the entrance. Three slabs had been set on edge just outside this entrance and formed a small antechamber which had been filled with earth and stones and marked the limit of the edge of the cairn; its purpose is not clear. The surrounding cairn was approximately oval in plan and consisted mainly of large limestone slabs extending about 3m from the tomb and laid against the sides of the chamber. No trace of a kerb was found and it seems that the cairn may never have been more than about 55cm in height. It would have mainly served to support the chamber orthostats and the tomb with its soaring capstone would have always been visible. The soil in the chamber was about 25cm in depth and this deposit and the grykes beneath contained numerous unburnt human bones and some animal bones; the latter included bones of cattle, pig, sheep or goat, dog, hare, stoat, pinemarten, woodmouse and bird. The human remains represented at least 22 individuals, 16 adults and 6 children. The bones, many of which had been jammed into the grykes, were disarticulated and had obviously been deposited in a defleshed condition. Since no cut marks were noted, deliberate defleshing seems unlikely and, since even smaller bones were represented, exposure (allowing the bones to be dispersed by scavenging animals and birds) may not have been practised either. It is thought the remains were probably buried elsewhere and later exhumed, and then transferred with some care to the tomb.

Ten radiocarbon dates obtained from samples of human bone have provided interesting information about the extent and duration of burial practice. Excluding the complete skeleton of one newborn child buried in a gryke beneath the antechamber which proved to be a later, second millennium insertion, the dates indicate that burials were deposited at regular intervals over a period of 600 years between about 3800 and 3200 BC. The fragmentary state of the bones made it difficult to age and sex them accurately. Males and females were equally represented among the eight adults whose sex could be determined. Most of the adults were quite young, dying before the age of 30; only one was more than 40 years old. Apart from a couple of infants, most of the children were aged between 5 and 15. The numbers and the age and sex profile suggest that the remains are those of a select sample of a community chosen at various times over some six centuries for the special privilege of being reburied in this tomb. Some of the bones were scorched and the burning pattern shows that this was done when the bone was dry: they may have been purified by fire as part of the reburial process.

Why just some adults and children were selected is not obvious. Evidence of arthritic conditions indicates that the adults led physically active lives carrying heavy loads and though they merited special treatment after death, they were not spared the normal stresses and strains of everyday existence. One adult male had the tip of a flint or chert projectile embedded in a hip bone; there was no trace of infection or healing so the wound occurred at the time of death. Two healed fractures, one on a skull, the other on a rib, were the sort of injuries usually produced by aggressive blows rather then by accidents. Dental wear suggested a diet which included stone-ground cereals. Artefacts placed with the burials included a triangular bone pendant, part of a mushroom-headed bone pin, a polished stone axe, two stone beads, several flint and chert implements and over 60 sherds of plain coarse pottery.[53]

Traces of burials have been found in several other portal tombs – usually small quantities of cremated human bone. Burnt bone was recovered from the disturbed chamber at Drumanone, Co. Roscommon, but it was too fragmentary to permit any estimate of the number of individuals represented. The only other significant find in the chamber was a small polished stone axe of Antrim porcellanite which was found close to the inner face of the large closing slab. Cremated human bone was also found in excavations at Aghnaskeagh, Co. Louth, and Ballyrenan, Co. Tyrone, for example. Finds of pottery of Lyles Hill style and of Bipartite Bowl style from these tombs are similar in quite a few respects to those from court tombs.[54]

Stone implements have also been found of course, but again not in great numbers. The polished stone axes from Drumanone and Poulnabrone have been mentioned and flints include a small number of leaf-shaped arrowheads, convex scrapers and concave scrapers from several tombs. A chert concave-based arrowhead comes from a tomb at Kiltiernan, Co. Dublin. A few stone beads are known: simple disc shaped beads were found in Poulnabrone, in Clonlum, Co. Armagh, and Ballyrenan, Co. Tyrone; the latter tomb also produced two longitudinally perforated ovoid beads of polished schist similar to those from the court tombs at Bavan, Co. Donegal, and Tully, Co. Fermanagh.

Some relationship between court tomb and portal tomb has long been recognized and various writers have thought the latter evolved from the former. In 1960, De Valera suggested that the origins of the portal tomb lay in the subsidiary chambers found in the cairns of some court tombs. Both have a similar relatively simple plan: both are single chambered, of sub-rectangular form, and both are entered through a pair of portal stones with a sill stone or closing stone between. The fact that both subsidiary chambers and most portal tombs lack forecourts was considered significant as was the mutual usage of long cairns. While some portal tombs are of massive construction, others are quite small and in general the internal dimensions of the type are said to be closely comparable to those of the subsidiary chambers of court tombs. Other minor shared features can also be cited. On the basis of these morphological resemblances an origin for portal tombs has been sought in central Ulster (in south-west Donegal, and Derry and Tyrone) where these tombs and court tombs with subsidiary chambers are both well represented. This hypothesis would allow for the contemporary construction and use of both portal tombs and some court tombs. Poulnabrone is firmly dated to the fourth millennium BC and would confirm the notion of contemporaneity.

While a relationship to court tombs is not disputed, there are alternative views on the question of origins and development. The fact that they are essentially simple tombs was one reason for a belief that they could be of early date and it has been proposed that a simple structure like a portal tomb could be the primary stage in the development of the court tomb: the placing of a second chamber in front of the hypothetical primary structure would result in a two chambered burial gallery requiring only a long cairn and concave facade to give the basic court tomb form. Though there is evidence from some Irish court tombs for separate constructional phases, an evolutionary sequence such as this, from simple to complex, has yet to be clearly demonstrated. It is worth noting that finds of early pottery from a portal tomb at Dyffryn Ardudwy, Merioneth, Wales, and early dates for this sort of pottery elsewhere have prompted ApSimon to suggest that portal tombs are among the earliest megaliths dating from about 3800 to 3500 BC.[55]

WEDGE TOMBS

With over 500 examples recorded, the Wedge Tomb is the most numerous megalithic tomb in Ireland, representing about one third of the total. It is so-called because many though not all examples have a chamber of a relatively narrow wedge shape or trapezoidal plan which decreases both in height and in width from front to rear (Figs 42-43). This main chamber is constructed of orthostats and roofed with one or more capstones which, in the majority, rest directly on the side stones. Some tombs have a short orthostatic portico or antechamber at the front and some have a small closed chamber at the rear. The division between antechamber and chamber is usually by a slab inset at the sides and of roof height. Occasionally a pair of jambs, or more rarely a sill stone, occur instead of this closing slab. The chamber is frequently flanked by one or more lines of outer orthostatic walling which taper in plan to form a straight or U-shaped rear end. A straight orthostatic facade is found at the front of the tomb, which consistently faces west. Cairns may be approximately round, oval or D-shaped, sometimes with a kerb.

These tombs vary considerably in size: the chamber at Labbacallee, near Glanworth, Co. Cork (Fig. 42A), measures some 9m in overall length while some particularly small tombs in Co. Clare have chambers of 2m or less in length. The well-known Labbacallee tomb is a large well-preserved example which was excavated in 1934. Some ancient disturbance at the western, front end of the tomb has meant that the original form of this part of the monument is uncertain: two straight lines of orthostats may have formed a double facade in front of the chamber. The long narrow chamber decreases in both height and width towards the eastern rear end. It is 1.8m high at the western end and is constructed of double rows of orthostats with a further row of outer walling 0.5m to 1.2m from either side, the intervening space being filled with cairn stones. An orthostat 1.45m high separates a small end chamber from the rest of the gallery. This slab effectively sealed the small chamber except at one of its upper corners which may have been knocked away to provide some limited access; however, the single three-ton capstone which neatly covered this chamber, as the excavators discovered, was capable of being moved aside with relative ease and thus access to both chambers was possible. One very large and one smaller capstone roofed the rest of the tomb. The rear of the tomb was supported by three buttress stones.[56]

The contents of the main chamber had suffered some human and animal disturbance but they included a 60cm deep fill of earth and stones with numerous animal bones, fragments of the unburnt bones of a young male adult and a child, as well as the skull of a female; fragments of one well-made pottery vessel with incised decoration (of uncertain type) and of some coarser flat-bottomed pottery were also recovered. Fragments of coarse pottery

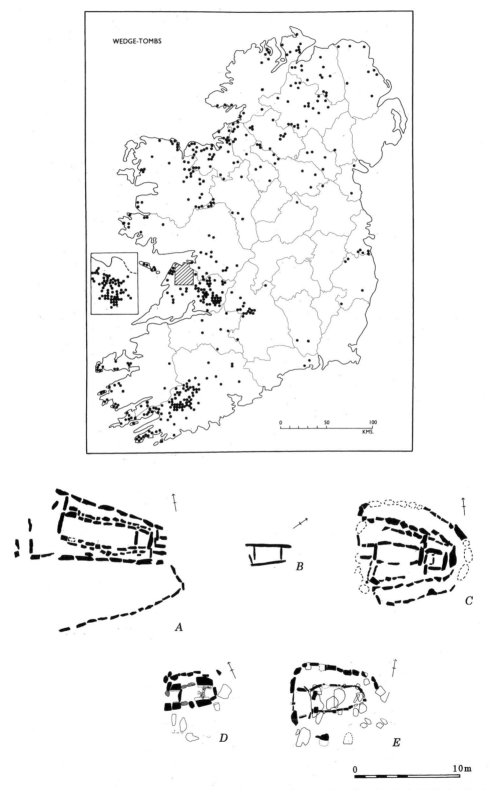

Fig. 42. Above. Distribution of wedge tombs. Below. Plans of wedge tombs. A. Labbacallee, Co. Cork. B. Parknabinnia, Co. Clare. C. Ballyedmonduff, Co. Dublin. D. Kilhoyle, Co. Derry. E. Loughash (Giant's Grave), Co. Tyrone.

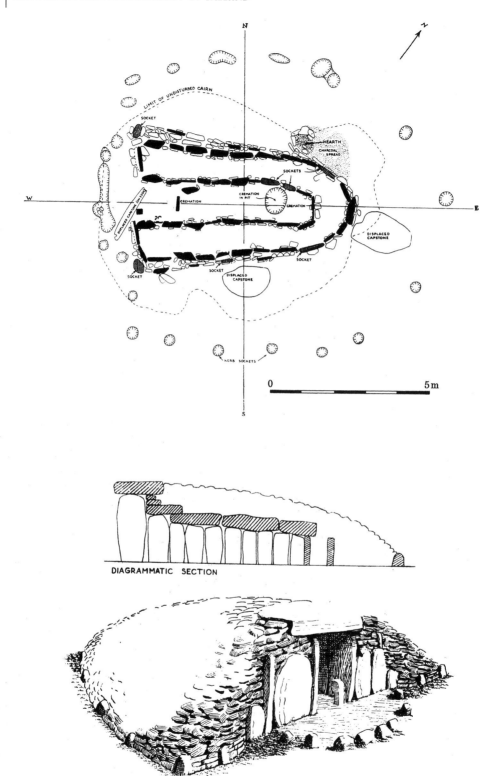

Fig. 43. Plan, section and reconstruction of a wedge tomb at Island, Co. Cork; the cairn as shown probably represents a later extension of the original monument and the reconstruction is not precisely to scale.

and a perforated piece of animal bone were found along with cremated human bone in the earth and stones which filled the small end chamber and below these, on the floor, lay the unburnt remains of a headless skeleton. These unburnt bones were those of an adult female and, since they were partially in articulation, it seemed that the body had been partly decomposed when buried. A skewer-like bone pin was found with the bones and it was suggested that the skull from the large chamber belonged to this skeleton.

Over 50 years after the excavation, radiocarbon dating of samples of unburnt bone has shed further light on the Labbacallee burials. A long bone from the headless skeleton in the end chamber provided a date of 2456-2138 BC while the two skeletons in the main chamber were dated to 2458-2038 BC and 2202-1776 BC respectively. A date in the second half of the third millennium BC for these primary burials is indicated, the three being placed in the tomb at intervals over several hundred years. The cremated bone was a secondary deposit and it has been suggested that the animal bone and the coarse pottery also represent secondary use of the chamber.

The wedge tomb at Kilhoyle, near Drumsurn, Co. Derry (Fig. 42D), examined in 1937, is a much smaller example about 4.6m in length. Excavation did not ascertain the original shape of the cairn which, like the burial chamber, had suffered considerable disturbance. The tomb consisted of a main chamber with outer walling surviving on one side and a small antechamber separated from the larger chamber by a large slab of almost roof height. It faced approximately west and decreased in height from about 1.6m (excluding missing capstones) at the front to 0.6m at the rear. Both chambers had been extensively disturbed. The antechamber produced fragments of cremated human bone, sherds of Beaker pottery and a bowl, a flint concave scraper and a barbed and tanged arrowhead. The main chamber also yielded cremated bone, fragments of Beaker and of flat bottomed, coarse, straight-walled ware. Possible cup marks occurred on one orthostat. The outer walling at Kilhoyle may once have formed a rounded, U-shaped rear end, a feature of a number of wedge tombs such as Loughash (Giant's Grave), Co. Tyrone, Ballyedmonduff, Co. Dublin (Fig. 42C) and Island, Co. Cork. At Loughash (Fig. 42E) entrance to the antechamber was impeded by a centrally placed orthostat (bearing a dozen cup marks) with a low sill stone on either side of it and a pair of jamb stones separated the antechamber from the main chamber. Jamb segmentation has been noted in a number of tombs in the northern half of the country and in a few in the south-west. Here an orthostat of almost roof height (sometimes called a septal stone – a term used of slabs which, unlike sill stones, are high enough to prevent normal passage from one area to another) is more usual. Cup-marked stones are known from a number of other sites including Ballyedmonduff and Baurnadomeeny, Co. Tipperary.

At Island, south of Mallow, Co. Cork, the antechamber was separated from the main chamber by a single small pillar stone and a 7cm high sill stone (Fig. 43). Excavation has shown that the denuded cairn of this tomb had been approximately D-shaped with a maximum length of about 11.5m. A series of small sockets of varying depths spaced around the cairn were interpreted as sockets for kerb stones. The entrance to the tomb, on the south-west, was marked by a pair of tall portal stones 1.65m in average height and its length (including antechamber) was 5.74m Its height decreased considerably from antechamber to main chamber. The small pillar stone 0.68m high stood just inside the entrance: its purpose is unknown though during the excavation it became known as the 'sentinal stone'. A socket for a similarly placed and, presumably, ritual stone was found in the antechamber at Ballyedmonduff. A stone standing in the centre of the tomb entrance is a feature of several sites in Ulster (including Loughash mentioned above) and elsewhere.

At Island the characteristic outer walling of the tomb formed a rounded rear end and at the front was joined to the portals of the antechamber by a straight orthostatic facade. The two metres of cairn on either side of this facade gave a slight concavity to the front of the monument. The upper fill of the tomb consisted of a 35cm thick deposit of loose soil and stones cleared and thrown in from the surrounding field since the original cairn cover was removed. Below was a firmly packed layer of soil and small boulders which had been laid on the old ground surface where the original turf line was readily recognisable. Beneath this layer a circular pit was found near the eastern end of the chamber; it contained charcoal, some finely fragmented cremated human bone, and part of a burnt flint implement, perhaps a knife.

A little burnt human bone and two flint scrapers were found on the tomb floor and a shallow pit just inside the sill stone contained the cremated bones of an adult female of 60 to 70 years of age. Some charcoal collected from a hearth site on the old ground surface outside the kerb stones provided a radiocarbon date of 1730-1000 BC which was generally thought to be both unreliable and too young for the construction of the monument. But a duplicate sample from the same location and another of charcoal from the socket of one of the kerb stones have been dated in recent years: the respective dates of 1412-1226 BC and 1430-1274 BC confirming the original late date. According to Anna Brindley and Jan Lanting these dates may be related to a later enlargement of the monument; it may be that the tomb proper dated to the early second millennium but that a secondary phase of activity in or about the 14th century BC, indicated by the radiocarbon dates, consisted of the addition of the D-shaped kerb.[57]

Single chambered wedge tombs, lacking an antechamber (or the rarer end chamber), are also recorded. In Co. Kerry, for example, one of several tombs at Coomatloukane may simply have had a narrow wedge-shaped chamber with outer walling and an orthostatic facade at the broader western end. However, it is possible that a slab found at the entrance may once have segmented the chamber. Excavations produced only a small quantity of cremated bone in the centre. The availability of easily quarried sandstone slabs in west Cork and Kerry allowed the construction of neat sub-rectangular monuments. Similarly built tombs are well known in Co. Clare (Fig. 42B) where their apparent simplicity is also accentuated by the local availability of large tabular pieces of limestone which facilitated the construction of rather box-like monuments with perhaps just one or two slabs for side-stones and capstones. In the absence of excavation certainty about details of tomb plan is often impossible but only a few of these megaliths have traces of likely antechambers or end chambers and the majority appear to have been single chambered. Many display a decrease in height and width from front to rear and the broader, front end consistently faces approximately west. Outer walling is visible in quite a number of cases and closure of the western end is sometimes by one large slab and sometimes by two overlapping slabs, one wider than the other. The use of such multiple

closing stones may indicate that repeated access was intended. In a few instances one upper corner of the closing stone at the eastern end has been knocked or chipped away. A few of these openings may be fortuitous but others may be an original feature and some tombs may have been entered from the eastern end.[58]

Whether there is any significant difference in purpose and function between such small simple chambers and longer more monumental galleries like Labbacallee is not clear. The orientation of wedge tombs in general is remarkably consistent: they almost invariably face somewhere between west-north-west and south, a majority being aligned to the south-west and west towards the general position of the setting sun. Their distribution too has a western bias (Fig. 42): over 75% of them occur in the west and south-west of the country with significant concentrations in Sligo, in Clare and Tipperary, and in Cork and Kerry. The latter south-western group includes clusters of over 30 tombs on the major peninsulas of the indented coast from Mizen Head to Dingle. In the north, these tombs are to be found in some numbers in Donegal, Derry, Antrim and Tyrone, as well as Cavan, Fermanagh, Leitrim and Monaghan. A few scattered examples occur in Leinster.

The relatively small number of wedge tombs excavated to date cannot be said to provide a clear picture of the funerary ritual and grave goods of the class as a whole. Just over twenty examples have been investigated and some have produced evidence of burials and a variety of artefacts notably fragments of pottery. Cremation seems to be the dominant burial rite, though unburnt bones have been found in several instances and a number of tombs have yielded no trace of burials at all. Whether the absence of burials at sites such as the possible wedge tomb at Kilnagarns Lower, Co. Leitrim, and several tombs at Coom and Coomatloukane, Co. Kerry, is due simply to disturbance or to the decay of unburnt bones is not known. Very small quantities of cremated bone have been found at sites such as Ballyedmonduff, Co. Dublin, Boviel, Co. Derry, Kilmashogue, Co. Dublin, and Moylisha, Co. Wicklow. Clogherny, Co. Tyrone, produced 'many fragments' of cremated human bone. They were mixed with charcoal through a layer of yellowish clay 30cm in average thickness and the excavator surmised that the cremation pyre had been shovelled into the chamber along with some of the soil beneath it. Fragments of burnt bone were recovered from both antechamber and chamber at Kilhoyle, Co. Derry, and at least three persons were represented. At Largantea, Co. Derry, the cremated bones of at least six adults (male and female being represented), a twelve year old child and an infant were found; the cremated bones of at least four persons came from the main chamber at Loughash (Cashelbane), Co. Tyrone, while some more burnt bone was recovered from two small chambers behind the main chamber; and at Loughash (Giant's Grave), Co. Tyrone, the antechamber contained some burnt bones of an adult male while the burnt bones of two persons were found in a pit at the rear of the main chamber. The nature of the burial deposits in these tombs raises many problems: for example, the range of pottery styles represented (see below) suggests the likelihood that they were re-used over a period of time. However, it is probable that the cremation in a pit at Loughash (Giant's Grave) was primary; this was true of the similar pit containing unidentifiable cremated human bone at Island, already mentioned. The small quantity of cremated bone from the centre of the gallery of one of the Coomatloukane tombs may be primary too.[59]

A complex sequence of deposition of cremated bones was observed in and around the wedge tomb at Baurnadomeeny, near Rear Cross, Co. Tipperary. This monument comprised a chamber and broad antechamber set in a round cairn with kerb. A septal slab separated the chambers and the main eastern chamber had been completely dug out in modern times; nothing survived of the original deposit except a few minute scraps of cremated bone. The antechamber did contain burials, two of which were apparently primary: a rectangular slab-built structure constructed against the southern side contained fragments of cremated bone (possibly of an adult female) and thirty-three potsherds, and another deposit of cremated bone was found at old ground level covered by two thin slabs. Three other deposits of cremated bone were found on a packing of boulders around the slab-built structure and are thus later, though perhaps not much later, than the primary deposits. Outside the tomb some fourteen other deposits of bone were found all on the southern side of the monument. All were cremated and five were in diminutive rectangular or polygonal slab-built cists set in pits in the old ground surface. A sixth small cist was empty, this

possible grave and three of the cremations were found under the cairn. Six other cremations were possibly primary and four were secondary; one of the latter had been inserted into the cairn and the rest were outside the kerb. Thus at least part of the funerary ritual at Baurnadomeeny seems to have involved, as far as can be judged, the deposition of the burnt bones of separate individuals within and without the tomb over a period of time and the deposits outside the tomb were seemingly token deposits some deliberately mixed with soil and charcoal. Because acid soil had damaged the bones, little information was gleaned from their study: adult males and females as well as adolescents were represented.

Unburnt burials have been recorded in a few cases. Labbacallee, Co. Cork, has already been mentioned, unburnt bones being found both in the main chamber and the end chamber. Here, the cremated bone from the fill of the end chamber may be secondary. A wedge tomb at Lough Gur, Co. Limerick, produced a considerable quantity of pottery, a few fragments of cremated bone from antechamber and main chamber and numerous unburnt human and animal bones. The contents of the tomb had been greatly disturbed and the unburnt remains were in a very fragmentary condition. The human bones from the main chamber represented at least eight adults (a figure based on the number of second cervical vertebrae found). Bones of children were also found both inside and outside the chamber, and some adult remains occurred outside the tomb too. The animal bones were mainly those of cattle and pig. A burial of the skeleton of a young ox was found to the south of the tomb and considered contemporary. A series of radiocarbon dates from unburnt bone suggest a series of burials over a period of several centuries from about 2500-2000 BC. Nineteenth century investigations in a wedge tomb at Moytirra, Co. Sligo, are said to have yielded the unburnt bones of at least six individuals including one child, a 'long thin piece of bronze' and fragments of Beaker pottery. Both cremated and unburnt human bones were found on the site of a destroyed wedge tomb at Breeoge, Co. Sligo.[60]

A remarkable sequence of ritual activity which sheds considerable light on the later use of wedge tombs has been identified by William O'Brien in two tombs near Toormore Bay, near Schull, in west Cork. One megalith in Altar townland was a simple trapezoidal orthostatic gallery 3.42m long, wider at the front western end. The monument seemed to have been aligned on Mizen Peak 13km to the south-west and it has been suggested that this was an orientation towards the setting sun at Samhain in early November. Excavation produced a little cremated bone (just 15g) of a human adult found near the entrance, a single unburnt tooth, some charcoal from two pits near the rear of the chamber and some deposits of shellfish such as periwinkles and limpets. No artefacts were recovered. At first glance these results might be considered unpromising but a programme of radiocarbon dating of a number of samples from a variety of carefully selected contexts revealed a remarkable pattern of depositional events:

– the unburnt tooth dated initial activity to 2316-1784 BC.
– charcoal from a small pit near the centre of the chamber was dated to 1250-832 BC and might indicate some sort of depositional activity which could have included offerings of food or some other perishables.
– charcoal found near the rear of the chamber provided slightly later dates of 998-560 BC and 766-404 BC.
– charcoal from a small pit on the south side of the chamber dates to the period 356 BC - 68 AD.
– a deposit of periwinkle and limpet shells inside the entrance is of later date: 2 BC - 230 AD.
– a pit in the centre of the chamber contained various deposits of shells (periwinkle and limpet) and fishbones (wrasse and eel); three dates for the upper fill place some of this activity in the 2nd century AD.

The ritual sequence at Altar initially seems to have involved just the deposition of token deposits of human remains but the placing of food offerings, including fish and shellfish, may have figured prominently particularly in later prehistoric times. It would appear that the depositional emphasis may have shifted from human remains to other votive offerings in the course of the second millennium BC. Obviously late prehistoric communities (who otherwise remain archaeologically invisible in the region) also regarded the monument as a sacred place.

The second tomb, in nearby Toormore townland, had suffered considerable damage in the past but also revealed early and late prehistoric activity. A small deposit comprising a decorated bronze axe and two pieces of copper had been placed as an offering at the tomb entrance, it and some radiocarbon-dated charcoal indicate ritual practice in the general period 1800-1600 BC. Further charcoal from the tomb was dated to 1368-1002 BC and 818-412 BC.[61]

Fragmentary pottery is the commonest artefact in wedge tombs generally and about half of the excavated examples have produced sherds of one sort or another. A puzzling variety of pottery types occurs and at some sites at least this indicates the use of the tomb for some length of time. Beaker pottery and coarse ware are the two pottery classes most frequently represented, each being recorded from some eight or nine tombs. The coarse ware includes flat bottomed, plain pots as from Kilhoyle, Co. Derry, from the two tombs at Loughash in Co. Tyrone and from Largantea, Co. Derry, as well as other coarse wares from Ballyedmonduff, Co. Dublin, Lough Gur, Co. Limerick, and Baurnadomeeny, Co. Tipperary. Apart from the last mentioned, these tombs have also yielded sherds of Beaker pottery of various types, as have Moytirra, Co. Sligo, Aughrim, Co. Cavan, and Kilnagarns, Co. Leitrim (probable Beaker sherd). It has been suggested that the Beaker pottery (and the occasional barbed and tanged flint arrowhead) firmly date the beginnings of the wedge tomb type to the later third millennium but a few tombs have contained sherds of pottery hinting at earlier use: sherds of a Goodland Bowl, a polished stone axe and a concave scraper from Boveil, Co. Derry, as well as some decorated pottery from Lough Gur and two sherds from Largantea which may be pre-Beaker in date.

Much of the artefactual material and the radiocarbon evidence now indicates a complex pattern of use throughout the later third and the second millennia, and even later. Bowl Tradition pottery, so-called 'food-vessels', were found in sherds in the tomb at Loughash (Cashelbane) and at Largantea; sherds of one were discovered in the chamber and in the cairn at Kilhoyle, and bowl fragments also come from the Lough Gur wedge tomb. These finds are presumably secondary – this is certainly the case with two bowls in two cists inserted into or added to the cairn of a wedge tomb at Kilmashogue, Co. Dublin. Sherds of urn from a few sites also indicate further secondary activity. Fragments of cordoned urn were found in the antechamber at Largantea, encrusted urn in

Loughash (Giant's Grave), possible vase urn in Kilhoyle, and a complete encrusted urn containing cremated bones in Craigarogan, Co. Antrim, all demonstrating activity in the tombs in question well into the earlier second millennium. The occasional metal find is confirmation of this.[62]

The earlier use of some wedge tombs, perhaps from about 3000 BC, seems possible but further excavation is necessary to clarify the very hazy picture of their earliest use and until this is achieved the vexed question of their origins and development will remain no nearer an answer. Over the years many writers have seen parallels between Irish wedge tombs and certain megalithic tombs in western France. Indeed, at one stage the builders of northern wedge tombs were thought to have arrived in the Mayo-Sligo area and those of the southern wedge tombs were believed to have landed in Counties Cork and Kerry, both groups coming from a common focus probably in western France. More recent historical events seemed to add plausibility to this suggestion: 'historic landings from France and Iberia in both these areas are well known'. Further research, however, appeared to show that wedge tombs in general formed a single class and a single point of entry in the south-west was then postulated.

Beaker, barbed and tanged arrowheads and coarse flat-bottomed pottery were seen as the characteristic finds and the narrow rectangular megalithic tombs of the *allée couverte* type in Brittany (with the occasional antechamber and outer walling) were thought to be excellent prototypes. It is also true that Beaker pottery in some parts of Europe seems to be contemporary with the acquisition of the knowledge of metalworking and some of the wedge tombs in west Cork and Kerry are situated not too far from copper deposits. This, coupled with the supposed Breton connection, led to the theory that these tomb builders were copper workers and a major element in the introduction of this new technology to Ireland. This hypothesis has its deficiencies not least the absence of supportive evidence from the excavated south-western wedge tombs. The Toormore deposit does establish a connection between tomb builders and metal users but at a stage when the tradition of wedge tomb building was well established.

The Beaker pottery comes only from a minority of tombs mainly in the northern half of the country. Furthermore, this pottery is of types which, if not peculiarly Irish, are best paralleled in Britain. The Breton tombs themselves differ in important respects from the Irish examples: many are not wedge shaped but rectangular and many face east not west. It is true that there are parallels, antechambers and outer walling occur sporadically in Brittany and some tombs may face west. It is, in the absence of other evidence for contact, a question of attempting to gauge the relative significance of the morphological differences and resemblances. The parallels, if not coincidental, may indeed be an indication of Irish contact with Brittany but it does not follow that the origins of the largest class of Irish megalithic tomb can be attributed to the same source. Features such as jamb stones in some wedge tombs raise the question of some relationship with court tombs and the possibility of indigenous development.[63]

The four major classes of Irish megalithic tombs are remarkable expressions of prehistoric social organization, engineering ability and ritual obligation. They were certainly the most permanent and they were probably the most conspicuous objects in the contemporary landscape. They were something more (or perhaps on occasion something other) than just burial places for there are obviously more economic and no less effective ways of disposing of the dead. Since in some cases at least these monuments were situated on or near the farming land of the people who built them, they may have had a social and ceremonial role as significant as any funerary one. They may have been special repositories for sacred ancestral bones. It has been suggested, for example, that they were territorial markers, an expression of the community's claim to their land and possibly serving as ceremonial centres. It is interesting to speculate that aside from the disposal of the dead some megalithic tombs may have been locations for such activities as ceremonial gift exchanges, fertility rituals, ancestor worship and the observation of celestial events. The anthropological study of modern and recent primitive societies has always proved to be a particularly fruitful source of inspiration for possible explanations of archaeological phenomena and in recent years it has provided a number of social and economic models with interesting archaeological applications, some in the realm of megalithic tomb studies.[64]

If the concept of territoriality was developed in early prehistoric Ireland, then some tombs may indeed have served as the symbolic and functional centre of a community; in any event they may have been expressions of communal solidarity. It has been argued that the tendency of court tombs generally to occur in isolated and scattered locations reflects the dispersed distribution of the social units of a segmentary society. Such societies are small acephalous communities lacking the centralized hierarchical structure of the chiefdom or state; the communities (or segments) are politically and economically autonomous and not subordinate parts of a larger political and economic entity. Anthropological studies indicate that populations usually range from about 50 to 500 persons living in a village or in a small number of dispersed houses. It is thought that the variety in plan of broadly contemporary court tombs could be a mark of a segmentary society where a broad hierarchical control of tomb design would of course be absent. The spread of innovations in details of tomb plan between communities could be aided and encouraged in a variety of ways, kinship ties, population movement, and especially local and long distance trade are all likely factors. In contrast, passage tombs, it has been suggested, may be the products of a different sort of society and part of a wider burial tradition in western Europe which may imply wider ritual organization. The use of cemeteries in particular is considered significant, possibly implying denser population concentrations and a form of social organization other than a segmentary one. A hierarchical society has been postulated – conceivably one in which a group rather than an individual exercises control. This centralized control could explain the relatively limited variation in passage tomb plans and may be expressed too in the substantially greater input of labour represented by the largest monuments such as those in the Boyne Valley and at Loughcrew.[65]

But there are other possible explanations. Alison Sheridan has argued that the construction of ever larger passage tombs reflects the ambitions of various communities to enhance their power and status (and she draws an analogy with the ostentatious funerary practices of Victorian Britain). Different groups attempted to outdo each other in their treatment of the dead by building bigger and better monuments and by devising more elaborate rituals which included the introduction of novel and exotic elements into the ceremonial repertoire. These elements could include architectural features or artefacts borrowed from abroad and here we may have an explanation for architectural parallels with, for instance, passage tombs in Wales and the Orkneys and for the presence of objects such as the stone maceheads at Knowth.[66]

The distributions of various types of tomb overlap and there is also evidence that different types were in contemporaneous use with no neat chronological succession of tomb types. Thus the development of complex forms of court tombs in the north-west, for instance, could be seen as a regional development similar to the passage tomb aggrandizement in the Boyne Valley but one for which another design option was chosen. Different tomb types may not represent different cultural groups but different responses, some regional, to various social and ritual imperatives. It is possible that communities may have had allegiances to more than one tomb type and in this respect the existence of small groups of tombs of different categories may be significant: for example, two court tombs, a portal tomb and a wedge tomb at Wardhouse, Co. Leitrim (between Bundoran and Cliffony) form a small cemetery; a group at Fenagh, also in Co. Leitrim, comprises two passage tombs, a court tomb and a portal tomb, and there is a concentration of wedge tombs as well as other monuments in Parknabinnia and adjacent townlands near Kilnaboy in the Burren in Co. Clare.[67]

Instead of just studying monuments such as court tombs and passage tombs as expressions of territoriality, for instance, it may also be useful to try and assess them from the standpoint of their users: the different tomb plans reflecting different ways of controlling access and using space. Portal tombs with their simple plans were relatively unsophisticated in this respect and may have mainly served to proclaim 'the presence of the ancestral remains in the landscape'. The linear segmentation of court tomb galleries demonstrates increasing emphasis on the division of space and it is possible that social divisions were imposed as well – some people, such as women or uninitiated males, being excluded. The longer passages, some with sill stones, and the various cells of the more elaborate passage tombs would also dictate patterns of movement and allow for distinctions to be made between different classes of material deposited.[68]

It is an interesting possibility that while the earliest farmers seem to have felt no compelling need to build such megalithic monuments, certain factors such as a rising population and pressure on land resources, as well as competition for other commodities, may have compelled some agricultural communities to do so particularly if these tombs also served as territorial markers, demonstrating and reinforcing their ownership of the land and acting as public expressions of the group identity as well as the wealth and status of the community. If this was so the form of monument adopted would probably depend on a range of factors and might well comprise architectural features borrowed from adjacent regions with idiosyncratic local modifications.

LINKARDSTOWN GRAVES AND OTHER BURIALS

In the 1940s a megalithic grave was discovered in the course of ploughing in the townland of Linkardstown, south-south-east of Carlow town, and this name is now applied to a small group of fourth millennium burials. At Linkardstown, a low circular mound some 75cm high and 25m in diameter had a kerb of low stones and covered a large centrally-placed grave. This megalithic cist was polygonal, formed of large inward sloping granite blocks, roofed with two capstones and built on the old ground surface which formed the floor of the grave. The disarticulated unburnt bones of an adult male were found and mixed with them were sherds of five incomplete bowls. The skull displayed several ancient fractures. A polished stone axe was also found. The most complete pot was a large round-bottomed bowl with grooved or channelled ornament and a heavy rim; the remaining sherds represented parts of one plain vessel and of three highly decorated pots, including two Bipartite Bowls. Some half a dozen other graves are assignable to the Linkardstown type: each consists of a round mound covering a large cist containing one or two burials and few grave goods apart from highly decorated round-bottomed pottery vessels. The cists, built on the old ground surface and covered by circular mounds, often have inclined walling and contain the remains of one or two unburnt bodies but cremation is also recorded. The burials seem to be usually those of males.

At Ballintruer More, near Baltinglass, Co. Wicklow (Fig. 44), the destruction by bulldozer of a circular mound with kerb revealed a polygonal cist with a floor of fine sand and which contained some disarticulated and apparently broken bones

representing part of the skeleton of an adult male. An empty pottery vessel had been placed in the centre of the grave immediately to the west of the bones. This pot, like a number of vessels from other burials of this type, is a fine Bipartite Bowl. A large polygonal cist in a round cairn at Ardcrony, near Nenagh, Co. Tipperary, contained the unburnt skeletons of two men, one aged about seventeen, the other aged about forty. The bones were disarticulated and the individuals were placed in separate deposits on a paved floor on either side of a similar pottery vessel found empty and mouth upwards in the centre of the grave. The cairn, which measured 33m in diameter, was not excavated and a report that it was once surrounded by a bank and ditch was not confirmed.

The remains of a mound at Jerpoint West, Co. Kilkenny, were excavated with some intriguing results. The circular mound, about 24m in diameter, covered a centrally placed polygonal cist and partial excavation uncovered two arcs of small stones resting on the old ground surface. The arcs were concentric with the edge of the tumulus which was delimited by a kerb of small limestone flags too slight to have been a retaining wall. Radially set stones occurred between the arcs. Various stone settings, including arcs of stones, have been found in and beneath the mounds of a number of satellite passage tombs at Newgrange and at Knowth and arcs with radially set stones were uncovered beneath the mound of the undifferentiated passage tomb at Townleyhall, Co. Louth. It is thought that some of these puzzling settings of relatively small stones may have demarcated different stages in the construction of the mound but they may also have had some ritual purpose prior to this. The central cist at Jerpoint West had a roughly paved floor and contained some cremated bone, the unburnt bones of a young adult male, some sherds of plain pottery and fragments of a highly decorated bowl, part of a leaf-shaped flint arrowhead and part of a bone object, possibly a pin. The contents of the cist had suffered some disturbance, possibly by rabbit activity, but it was clear that the adult male had lain in an extended position with head to the north. It was thought too that this burial and the cremation were contemporary.

A polygonal cist beneath a damaged circular mound at Baunogenasraid, Co. Carlow, contained some disarticulated unburnt bones of an adult male of large stature with a decorated bowl nearby; a

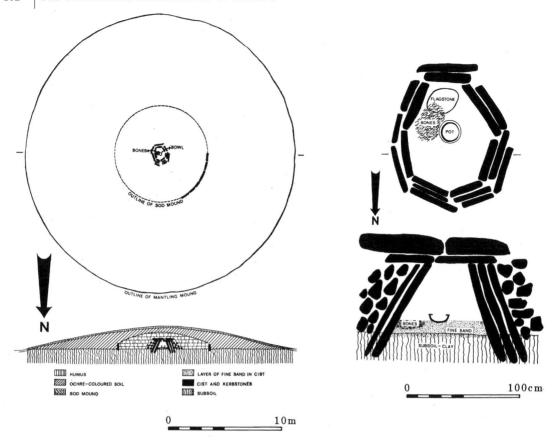

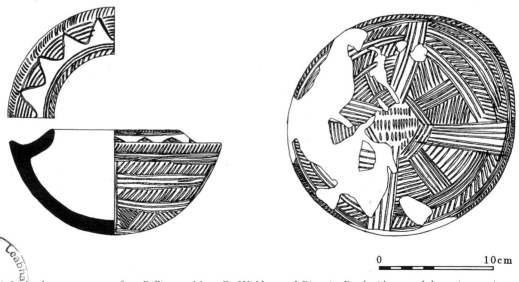

Fig. 44. Linkardstown type grave from Ballintruer More, Co. Wicklow, and Bipartite Bowl with grooved decoration on rim, body and base.

worked, pointed piece of animal bone and small perforated object (a toggle?) of lignite were the only other finds in the grave. The cist was built of five granite blocks which sloped inwards and a sixth stone, of limestone, which had no part in supporting the capstone. This stone, the smallest of the six, seems to have been selected for ease of movement to seal the 30cm gap between the two adjacent granite blocks. The cist was almost completely surrounded by a near-circular platform of stones 30cm high at its edge rising to 1.2m at the centre where it did not cover the tomb. This arrangement recalls the stone packing which Burenhult found at Carrowmore for example and which he thought to have been all the cairn there was at these sites. At Baunogenasraid the rudimentary cairn was covered by a mound of turves with a maximum height of some 2m above ground level. Several penannular stone settings seem to have had some role in retaining parts of the stone platform and sod mound. At some later date, in the early second millennium, the mound was enlarged to incorporate at least eleven simple burials. A mound at Drimnagh, Co. Dublin, had an even more complicated history but the large primary mound some 22m in diameter covered an arc of stones, a cup-marked stone and a polygonal cist containing the unburnt skeletal remains of a male adult (possibly flexed) and a highly ornamented Bipartite Bowl (Fig. 19, 10). Very little is known about a mound at Norrismount, Co. Wexford, which was almost completely destroyed. It covered a rectangular cist with inclined side stones which contained the unburnt skeletal remains of a male adult (possibly flexed) and another highly ornamented Bipartite Bowl.[69]

FUNERAL FEASTS

At Ashleypark, Co. Tipperary, just south-east of Ardcrony, a large mound was partly excavated and found to consist of a cairn with a mantle of clay surrounded by a pair of concentric banks each with an internal ditch with an overall diameter of about 90m. The cairn covered a rectangular open-ended stone structure with inclined side stones which incorporated part of a natural rock outcrop and contained a deposit of clay about 60cm deep through which were mixed unburnt human and animal bones and some sherds of pottery. The human bones were disarticulated and represented an elderly adult male and a child, the animal bones

were those of cattle, sheep and pig, and the pottery fragments were from a Carinated Bowl style vessel, a Decorated Bowl and a pot with grooved decoration, possibly a Bipartite Bowl. More animal bones were found in the cairn and the context of these bones is particularly interesting. Such bones from megalithic tombs are sometimes assumed to be the remains of offerings or of funeral feasts (as in the passage tomb at Fourknocks I, for instance) but direct association with the monument and food consumption is often difficult to prove. At Ashleypark the mantle of clay which covered the cairn was obtained from the surrounding ditches and sealed the animal bones found among the cairn stones. These bones represented three fully grown cattle, a small number of other cattle bones and a single pig femur, and in many cases were split or broken for marrow extraction and sometimes displayed butchering marks indicating that they were discarded food remains. Thus the consumption of food seems to have been part of the rituals enacted here and a radiocarbon date for a cattle bone indicates that this activity may well have been contemporary with the deposition of the human remains and pottery fragments in the grave shortly after 3500 BC. The bones with the burials, a single pig bone, a sheep or goat bone and a few cattle bones did not represent joints of meat and could have been token offerings perhaps representing the three most important domestic animals of the community.[70]

The occurrence of the remains of individual unburnt male burials accompanied by complete or fragmentary pottery vessels in these Linkardstown Graves, the use of a large round mound, polygonal cist and other details of monument construction all indicate a distinctive burial ritual in Leinster and Munster for a number of centuries in the fourth millennium. Radiocarbon dates from the human bones from sites such as Ardcrony, Ashleypark, Ballintruer More, Baunogenasraid and others suggest a timespan of about 3600 to 3300 BC and demonstrate their contemporaneity with megalithic tombs such as court tombs and passage tombs. These graves also demonstrate a preference for a form of individual expression by some persons or groups at a time when some others, for whatever reason, often practised a collective rite. The consistent inclusion of finely decorated pottery vessels suggests these pots had some particular significance and they may have denoted special status and, like some stone axes, may have been the insignia of male community leaders. It is worth noting that the inturned necks of these pots renders them unsuitable for the consumption of food and drink and they may have been suspended containers for some other purpose.

A variety of other burials are known, some clearly related to the Linkardstown type. The primary burial in a cairn at Poulawack, in the Burren, Co. Clare, was a polygonal cist containing the disarticulated bones of an adult male and female, a child and an infant; a concave scraper, a boar's tusk and two sherds of unclassifiable pottery were also found. Radiocarbon dating indicates contemporaneity with Linkardstown Graves. At Martinstown, Co. Meath, fragments of a highly decorated Bipartite Bowl were found along with the unburnt human bones of an adult male in a sand and gravel ridge. Unfortunately no details of the burial were recorded though it seems to have been in a simple pit. A pit at Clane, Co. Kildare, contained the unburnt bones of two adolescents, a Decorated Bowl and a piece of polished lignite. In contrast, a rectangular double cist grave at Rath, Co. Wicklow, contained a similar bowl in one compartment and the cremated bones of a young adult male in the other. Other burials with pottery are known from Annagh, Co. Limerick, Cahirguillamore, Co. Limerick, Lough Gur, Co. Limerick, and possibly Knockaulin, Co. Kildare.[71]

NOTES

1 Useful general surveys have been published in recent years by Harbison 1988, O'Kelly 1989, Twohig 1990, and Mallory and McNeill 1991. Detailed surveys: De Valera and Ó Nualláin 1961, 1964, 1972, 1982; Ó Nualláin 1989. The most recent general figures have been published by Twohig 1990 and Walsh 1995. Tombs in Connemara: Gibbons and Higgins 1988; Gosling 1993.

2 Megalithic tomb siting and passage tomb cemeteries: Cooney 1983, 1990; Ó Nualláin 1968; Herity 1974. Knocknarea, Co. Sligo: Bergh 1995, 236. Ballycarty, Co. Kerry: Connolly 1996.

3 'Druid Stone', near Ballintoy, Co. Antrim: Mogey 1941. Baltinglass Hill, Co. Wicklow: Walshe 1941. Carnanmore, Co. Antrim: Chart 1940, pl. 58. Townleyhall, Co. Louth: Eogan 1963. Carriglong, Co. Waterford: Powell 1941. and Harristown, Co. Waterford: J. Hawkes 1941; also Ó Nualláin and Walsh 1986.

4 Newgrange, Co. Meath: O'Kelly 1982.

5 Knockroe, Co. Kilkenny: O'Sullivan 1993a, 1996, where a cairn contained two passage tombs and was faced with quartz at the entrance to the eastern example; the passage of the western tomb was aligned on the setting sun of the midwinter solstice. Solstice phenomenon at Newgrange: Ray 1989. Preliminary computer simulations of the acoustic properties of chambers such as Newgrange indicate that male chanting (or even a contribution from 'deep-chanting women') may have been possible: Devereux and Jahn 1996.

6 Mitchell 1992.

7 Newgrange radiocarbon dates: 4425 ± 45 BP (3316-2922 BC, GrN-5462-C) and 4415 ± 40 BP (3304-2922 BC, GrN-5463); the basal turf layer in the mound produced one anomalous date (UB-360) of about 300 BC (possibly because the loose structure of the mound permitted penetration by younger material) and one date of 4535 ± 105 BP (3510-2920 BC, UB-361). A date from the pre-mound turf layer on the north, 4480 ± 60 BP (3350-2930 BC, GrN-9057) offers a terminal date for the large mound.

8 Sweetman 1985; Simpson 1988.

9 Newgrange satellite tombs: O'Kelly et al. 1978.

10 Knowth, Co. Meath: Eogan 1967, 1968, 1969a, 1974b, 1984, 1986, Eogan and Roche 1997a.

11 Knowth radiocarbon dates: charcoal from redeposited turves at the base of the mound: 4745 ± 165 BP (3940-3040 BC, UB-357), a terminal date for its construction. Charcoal believed to be contemporary with the commencement of construction: 4490 ± 60 BP (3358-2932 BC, GrN-12358) and 4405 ± 35 BP (3292-2922 BC, GrN-12357); Eogan 1991, 126.

12 Millin Bay, Co. Down: Collins and Waterman 1955. Knowth radiocarbon dates: charcoal in the mound of satellite Site 2: 4158 ± 126 BP (3090-2400 BC, BM-785); Site 16: 4399 ± 67 BP (3334-2910 BC, BM-1078); Site 9: 4415 ± 50 BP (3316-2920 BC, GrN); Eogan 1991, 126.

13 Dowth, Co. Meath: O'Kelly and O'Kelly 1983.

14 Fourknocks I, Co. Meath: Hartnett 1957; Twohig 1981, 221.

15 Cooney 1992.

16 Fourknocks II, Co. Meath: Hartnett 1971; charcoal from the trench has produced an unexpectedly late date: 3480 ± 140 BP (2200-1460 BC, D-45): ApSimon 1986. Burial rite: Cooney 1992. Fourknocks I and II: Cooney 1997.

17 Mound of the Hostages, Tara, passage tomb: Newman 1997, 71; Herity 1974, 252, fig. 33. Radiocarbon dates (ApSimon 1986, 10): pre-tomb palisade trench: 4260 ± 160 BP (3355-2465 BC, D-43); pre-tomb burnt vegetation: 4080 ± 160 BP (3035-2145 BC, D-42); hearth in front of the tomb: 3880 ± 150 BP (2875-2800/2780-1945 BC, D-44).

18 Loughcrew, Co. Meath: Twohig 1981, 205; McMann 1993 and 1994.

19 Carrowkeel, Co. Sligo: Macalister et al. 1912; Bergh 1995, 46. Mullaghfarna settlement: Herity 1974, 61; Grogan 1996a; Bergh 1995, 60, who notes positive results of a limited phosphate survey.

20 Carrowmore, Co. Sligo: Burenhult 1980; 1984. The numbering system is that of Bergh 1995, 181. The art

on Carrowmore 51 has been published by Curran-Mulligan 1994.

21 Radiocarbon dates (ApSimon 1986; Bergh 1995, 102): Carrowmore no. 7: 5240 ± 80 BP (4330-3820 BC, Lu-1441); Carrowmore no. 27: 5040 ± 60 BP (3980-3706 BC, Lu-1698), 5000 ± 65 BP (3970-3694 BC, Lu-1808), 4940 ± 85 BP (3962-3530 BC, Lu-1818) accepted by Bergh; Carrowmore no. 3: 5750 ± 85 BP (4838-4400 BC, Lu-1840), 4320 ± 75 BP (3306-2666 BC, Lu-1750).

22 Carrowmore no. 3 (Bergh 1995, 182) is Burenhult's no. 4.

23 Caulfield 1983; ApSimon 1986. Croghaun, Co. Sligo: 6680 ± 100 BP (5640-5490 BC, Ua-713), 5685 ± 85 BP (4675-4460 BC, St-10453) both from pine charcoal associated with cremated deposits: calibrated dates from Bergh 1995, 104, 225. The reliability of these early dates is defended by Burenhult 1995.

24 Slieve Gullion, Co. Armagh: Collins and Wilson 1963.

25 Eogan and Richardson 1982; it is an ovoid macehead belonging to Simpson's (1988, 1989a, 1996a) Early Series; the example from the western tomb is a pestle macehead also of the Early Series; technique of manufacture: Fenwick 1995.

26 McMann 1994, 540.

27 Art: Twohig 1981; Eogan 1986; O'Sullivan 1986 and 1993; Eogan and Aboud 1990; Twohig 1996.

28 Eogan 1986, 152, has tentatively suggested that there are some 16 principal motifs.

29 The suggestion is from Herity 1974, 106, 185, where interpretative hazards are also clearly exemplified by a composition of arcs and circles in a passage tomb at Sess Kilgreen, Co. Tyrone, which moved the same writer to ask 'Is it face or vulva that is represented?'

30 Entoptic imagery: Bradley 1989; Lewis-Williams 1993; Dronfield 1995, 1995a, 1996; Twohig 1996.

31 Breton origins: Herity 1974, 203. Iberian parallels: Eogan 1990.

32 Sheridan 1986. Craigs, Co. Antrim: Williams 1987. Slieve Gullion, Co. Armagh: Collins and Wilson 1963; ApSimon 1986.

33 Renfrew 1973.

34 O'Kelly 1982, 122.

35 Court tombs: De Valera 1960; 1965; Ó Nualláin 1976; 1977; 1989.

36 Creevykeel, Co. Sligo: Hencken 1939. Browndod, Co. Antrim: Evans and Davies 1935. Goward, Co. Down: Davies and Evans 1933. Kilnagarns Lower, Co. Leitrim: Corcoran 1964. Bavan, Co. Donegal: Flanagan and Flanagan 1966. Tully, Co. Fermanagh: Waterman 1978. Ballymacdermot, Co. Armagh: Collins and Wilson 1964; radiocarbon dates: a series of charcoal samples have been radiocarbon dated (UB-207, 693-5, 697-8, 700, 702-3, 705) and several late dates suggest the monument was disturbed in Viking times but two separate charcoal samples from the burial gallery produced dates of 4717 ± 190 BP (3940-2930 BC, UB-698) and 4830 ± 95 BP (3898-3372 BC, UB-694).

37 Ballyalton, Co. Down: Evans and Davies 1934. Cohaw, Co. Cavan: Kilbride-Jones 1951. Ballymacaldrack, Co. Antrim: Evans 1938; Collins 1976. Clady Halliday, Co. Tyrone: Davies and Radford 1936. Barnes Lower, Co. Tyrone: Collins 1966. Aghanaglack, Co. Fermanagh: Davies 1939. Creggandevesky, Co. Tyrone: Foley 1988.

38 Audleystown, Co. Down: Collins 1954 and 1959a; Cooney 1992.

39 Annaghmare, Co. Armagh: Waterman 1965; radiocarbon date: 4395 ± 55 BP (3308-2914 BC, UB-241).

40 Case 1973.

41 Ballymarlagh, Co. Antrim: Davies 1949. Browndod, Co. Antrim: Evans and Davies 1935. Shanballyedmond, Co. Tipperary: O'Kelly 1958a.

42 Ballymacaldrack, Co. Antrim: radiocarbon dates of 4940 ± 50 BP (3930-3640 BC, UB-2029) and 5130 ± 90 BP (4226-3708 BC, UB-2030) from the trench. A sample from the lower part of the forecourt blocking produced a date of 4630 ± 130 BP (3690-2930 BC, UB-2045).

43 Goward, Co. Down: Davies and Evans 1933. Malin More, Co. Donegal: Lacy 1983, 32; Twohig 1981, 235, fig. 281.

44 Bavan, Co. Donegal: Flanagan and Flanagan 1966. Ballyrenan, Co. Tyrone, portal tomb: Davies 1937.

45 Radiocarbon dates: ApSimon 1986; Ballybriest, Co. Derry: 5045 ± 95 BP (4038-3644 BC, UB-535), 4930 ± 80 BP (3952-3528 BC, UB-534); Tully, Co. Fermanagh: 4960 ± 85 BP (3970-3542 BC, UB-2115), 4890 ± 65 BP (3908-3520 BC, UB-2119); Shanballyedmond, Co. Tipperary: 4930 ± 60 BP (3938-3544 BC, GrN-11431).

46 De Valera 1960; 1965.

47 The French connection still figures, as a possibility, in a recent account of the Céide Fields in north Mayo: Caulfield 1992.

48 For example Davies and Evans 1962; Case 1969; Collins 1973; Waddell 1978.

49 Scott 1969; Henshall 1972; Corcoran 1972.

50 Ó Nualláin 1983.

51 Portal tombs: Ó Nualláin 1983; Ballykeel, Co. Armagh: Collins 1965; Ballyrenan, Co. Tyrone: Davies 1937; Malin More, Co. Donegal: Lacy 1983; Melkagh, Co. Longford: Cooney 1987; Ticloy, Co. Antrim: Evans and Watson 1942; Aghaglaslin, Co. Cork: De Valera and Ó Nualláin 1982.

52 Ballykeel, Co. Armagh, radiocarbon date: 3350 ± 45 BP (1742-1526 BC, UB-239).

53 Lynch 1988; Lynch and Ó Donnabháin 1994.

54 Drumanone, Co. Roscommon: Topp 1962; Aghnaskeagh, Co. Louth: Evans 1935; finds from portal tombs: Herity 1964; 1982.

55 Portal tomb origins: De Valera and Ó Nualláin 1972; Flanagan 1977; Corcoran 1972; ApSimon 1986.

56 Wedge tombs: De Valera and Ó Nualláin 1961. Labbacallee, Co. Cork: Leask and Price 1936; Brindley *et al.* 1988; radiocarbon dates: 3805 ± 45 BP (2456-2138 BC, GrN-11359); 3780 ± 70 BP (2458-2038 BC, OxA-2759) and 3630 ± 70 BP (2202-1776 BC, OxA-2760): Brindley and Lanting 1992.

57 Kilhoyle, Co. Derry: Herring and May 1937. Loughash, Co. Tyrone: Davies 1939a. Ballyedmonduff, Co. Dublin: Ó Ríordáin and De Valera 1952. Island, Co. Cork: O'Kelly 1958; radiocarbon dates: charcoal from hearth: 3110 ± 140 BP (1730-1000 BC, D-49); recent dates (Brindley and Lanting 1992): 3050 ± 35 BP (1412-1226 BC, GrN-10631) and 3090 ± 30 BP (1430-1274 BC, GrN-10632). Baurnadomeeny, Co. Tipperary: O'Kelly 1960; Cooney 1992a.

58 The question of access has been studied by Paul Walsh 1995.

59 Kilnagarns Lower, Co. Leitrim: Corcoran 1964. Coom and Coomatloukane, Co. Kerry: De Valera and Ó Nualláin 1982. Ballyedmonduff, Co. Dublin: Ó Ríordáin and De Valera 1952. Boviel, Co. Derry: Herring and May 1940. Kilmashogue, Co. Dublin: Kilbride-Jones 1954. Moylisha, Co. Wicklow: Ó h-Iceadha 1946. Clogherny, Co. Tyrone: Davies 1939b. Kilhoyle, Co. Derry: Herring and May 1937. Largantea, Co. Derry: Herring 1938. Loughash (Cashelbane), Co. Tyrone: Davies and Mullin 1940. Loughash (Giants' Grave), Co. Tyrone: Davies 1939a.

60 Lough Gur, Co. Limerick: Ó Ríordáin and Ó h-Iceadha 1955; radiocarbon dates: 3830 ± 80 BP (2560-2040 BC, OxA-3274, etc.; Brindley and Lanting 1992). Moytirra, Co. Sligo: Madden 1969. Breeoge, Co. Sligo: Rynne and Timoney 1975.

61 Altar and Toormore, Co. Cork: O'Brien 1993a, 1993. Altar radiocarbon dates: unburnt tooth: 3670 ± 80 BP (2316-1784 BC, OxA-3289); charcoal from pit: 2820 ± 70 BP (1250-832 BC, GrN-17504); charcoal from rear of chamber: 2660 ± 70 BP (998-560 BC, GrN-17499) and 2440 ± 50 BP (766-404 BC, GrN-17505); charcoal from pit on the south side of the chamber: 2070 ± 70 BP (356 BC - 68 AD, GrN-17503) deposits of shells and fishbones: GrN-17506-8. Toormore radiocarbon-dates: 3330 ± 70 BP (1870-1450 BC, GrN-18492); 3395 ± 35 BP(1870-1618 BC, GrN-18496); 3250 ± 70 BP (1730-1412 BC, GrN-18493); later dates: 2940 ± 55 BP (1368-1002 BC, GrN-18495) and 2540 ± 70 BP (818-412 BC, GrN-18494); hoard: O'Brien et al. 1990.

62 Aughrim, Co. Cavan: Channing 1993. Craigarogan, Co. Antrim: Lawlor 1915. Kilmashogue, Co. Dublin: Kilbride-Jones 1954. Metal finds: De Valera and Ó Nualláin 1982, 119.

63 Wedge tomb origins: the quotation is from De Valera 1951, 180; De Valera and Ó Nualláin 1961; Waddell 1978; O'Kelly 1983.

64 Renfrew 1976; Orme 1981.

65 Fleming 1972, 1973; Darvill 1979; Hodder 1984; Bradley 1984.

66 Sheridan 1986; Simpson 1988.

67 Cooney 1990; Parknabinnia area: Ó Nualláin 1989, 117ff.

68 Cooney and Grogan 1994; Thomas 1990.

69 Linkardstown Graves: Brindley et al. 1983; Brindley and Lanting 1990; Ryan 1973; B. Raftery 1974; Herity 1982. Linkardstown, Co. Carlow: J. Raftery 1944a. Ballintruer More, Co. Wicklow: J. Raftery 1973; radiocarbon date: 4800 ± 70 BP (3776-3376 BC, GrN-10469). Ardcrony, Co. Tipperary: Wallace 1977; radiocarbon date: 4675 ± 35 BP (3606-3368 BC, GrN-9708). Jerpoint West, Co. Kilkenny: Ryan 1973; radiocarbon date: 4770 ± 80 BP (3770-3372 BC, OxA-2680). Baunogenasraid, Co. Carlow: B. Raftery 1974; radiocarbon date: 4735 ± 35 BP (3632-3376 BC, GrN-11362). Drimnagh, Co. Dublin: Kilbride-Jones 1939. Norrismount, Co. Wexford: Lucas 1950.

70 Ashleypark, Co. Tipperary: Manning 1985; radiocarbon date obtained from the femur of the adult male: 4765 ± 40 BP (3684-3378 BC, GrN-11036), from a sample of cattle bone: 4385 ± 110 BP (3370-2700 BC, GU-1779); McCormick 1986.

71 Poulawack, Co. Clare: Hencken 1935; Brindley and Lanting 1990 and 1992a for radiocarbon dates: 4695 ± 35 BP (3614-3373 BC, GrN-12622) for central grave. Martinstown, Co. Meath: Hartnett 1951; radiocarbon date: 4720 ± 35 BP (3624-3376 BC, GrN-12271). Clane, Co. Kildare: Ryan 1980a; radiocarbon date: 4470 ± 35 BP (3338-2940 BC, GrN-12276). Rath, Co. Wicklow: Prendergast 1959. Annagh, Co. Limerick: Ó Floinn 1992 and 1993; Cahirguillamore, Co. Limerick: Hunt 1967. Lough Gur, Co. Limerick: Ó Ríordáin 1954, 371. Lough Gur, Co. Limerick: Cleary 1995; radiocarbon date: 4740 ± 60 BP (3644-3370 BC, GrN-16825). Knockaulin, Co. Kildare: Johnston 1990. Also Knockmaree, Phoenix Park, Dublin: Herity and Eogan 1977, 84; bone dated to 4650 ± 70 BP (3630-3110 BC, OxA-2678): Brindley and Lanting 1990. Several other 18th and 19th century discoveries are noted in Ryan 1981 and Manning 1984.

4

Sacred Circles and New Technology

Various megalithic tombs continued to be the focus of ritual activity in the third and in succeeding millennia. However, other forms of ritual expression emerge and, in time, a new metal technology had a profound effect not just on economy and society but in the ritual sphere as well.

Excavations in Goodland townland, just over 3km south-east of Fair Head in Co. Antrim, revealed a complex of pits, ditches, and other features in the subsoil beneath an area of blanket bog. A series of irregular stretches of shallow ditches of varying lengths with gaps of different sizes between them appear to have delimited an oval area about 14m by 12m (Fig. 45). The segments of ditch were formed by pulling out weathered blocks of rock which accounted for their very irregular shapes; depths varied from 20cm to 65cm and it seemed that they were quickly and deliberately filled with soil. Boulders with pottery sherds packed around them or deposits of pot sherds and flints were either incorporated in or inserted into the fill of these ditches. Numerous shallow pits were found both inside and outside the enclosed area, none deeper than 40cms, and post-holes and stake-holes were found for the most part within the ditch system. Many of the pits contained identical deposits to those found in the ditches: boulders packed round with sherds and flints. Some pits contained little except soil and these occurred mainly outside the enclosure to the east. There was clearly a sequence of activity: at least one pit was earlier than a segment of the ditch and pits sometimes intersected each other. The pottery included Decorated Bowls and Goodland bowls.

Flint implements included leaf-shaped arrowheads and convex and concave scrapers. The ditched area, the contents of the pits within it and the absence of hearths or other traces of habitation all suggested to the excavator, Humphrey Case, that 'it is hardly possible rationally to look beyond a ritual explanation for the enclosure and many of its associated pits'. There was evidence for flint knapping to the east and to the south-west of the site: large quantities of struck flint were found and it seems that nodules of flint were dug out of the boulder clay and the upper few centimetres of the underlying chalk. Judging from the waste material present, knapped pieces of flint were removed to be worked elsewhere. It seems that this activity had begun before the digging of the ditch and its enclosed pits, and it continued during the use of the enclosure.[1]

Judging from one radiocarbon date obtained from charcoal in a pit the ritual activity at Goodland may have begun in the later fourth millennium and, in Case's opinion, involved the deposition in pits of material such as pot sherds, flints, scraps of animal bone and phosphate-enriched dark soil which was derived from settlement debris. He suggested that the contribution such material might make to the fertility of the land would have been fully appreciated by prehistoric farmers and it thus might be deliberately buried as part of some fertility ritual. At Goodland, the purpose may have been to encourage the land to continue to produce nodules of flint for the nearby flint knapping.

The identification of a ritual site is often problematic and negative evidence such as the absence of unambiguous traces of domestic or

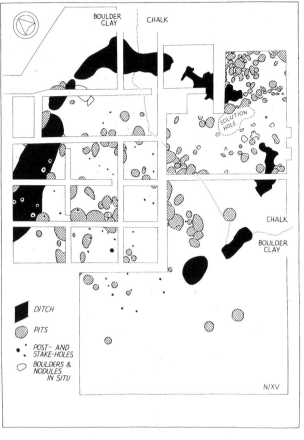

BOULDER CLAY

CHALK

SOLUTION HOLE

CHALK

BOULDER CLAY

DITCH

PITS

POST- AND STAKE-HOLES

BOULDERS & NODULES IN SITU

N/XV

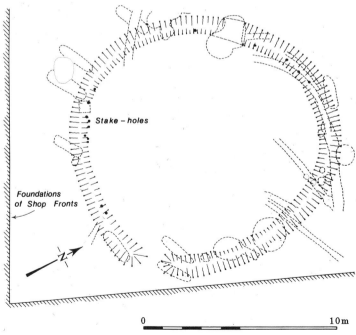

Stake-holes

Foundations of Shop Fronts

0   10m

Fig. 45. Above. Plan of ritual site at Goodland, Co. Antrim. Below. Plan of penannular ring ditch (disturbed by later features) at Scotch Street, Armagh.

economic activity or formal burial is sometimes a consideration. A partially excavated site at Langford Lodge, Co. Antrim, situated on a promontory jutting into Lough Neagh at Gartree Point, illustrates some of these interpretative problems. Five small pits and a larger shallow depression were found within an area of about 8m by 6m. A number of stake-holes each about 5cm in diameter occurred and some small boulders may have been purposely placed on the ground. The pits contained fragments of plain pottery, including Lyles Hill ware, some struck flint and quartz, a few flint implements and charcoal. Numerous small fragments and crumbs of pottery had been trodden into the natural surface around these features. This surface was covered with a deposit of sandy clay up to 30cm thick through which were mixed more charcoal, pottery and flint, as well as two fragments of a porcellanite axe. Traces of a ditch, producing similar material, were found about 10m east of the pits and stake-holes. Only a short segment was excavated and it was not established that this ditch enclosed the site.

A penannular ditch, about 1.1m wide and deep, did enclose a circular area with an internal diameter of some 12m at Scotch Street, Armagh (Fig. 45). Nothing survived within the circle but the ditch contained silt, redeposited soil, charcoal, flints, animal teeth and many hundreds of pottery sherds including fragments of Decorated Bowls (and a little Carrowkeel ware). Radiocarbon dating suggests the ditch was dug around 2800 BC and some later wooden stakes were inserted in its fill.

A very low circular mound at Rathjordan, east of Lough Gur, Co. Limerick, was surrounded by an annular ditch with outer bank. This site (Rathjordan I) had an overall diameter of about 13m and excavation demonstrated that the mound covered a small area of burning and a pit (measuring about 70cm by 50cm and 50cm deep) which contained charcoal, some small pieces of burnt bone, possibly of pig, and sherds of part of a plain round bottomed Limerick style bowl. Another similar ring barrow nearby (Rathjordan II) covered three pits and produced sherds of similar pottery, some burnt animal bone, and three fragments of polished stone axes. A third site (Rathjordan IV), which seemed to consist of a mound with encircling ditch but no external bank, also covered a number of small pits and yielded some pottery sherds, fragments of polished stone axes and a little burnt animal bone. Again a ritual explanation may be appropriate, as

with the segmented ditch system at Goodland, a penannular or annular ditch or an annular ditch with external bank could also serve to demarcate an area of special importance.[2]

Although the circular kerbs of some passage tombs and the banks and internal ditches at Ashleypark, Co. Tipperary, for instance, are indications of the importance of large stone and earthen circles in funerary ceremonial in the fourth millennium, circular enclosures seem to assume new significance in the following millennium. Some larger and more elaborate open circular areas offer greater space for more complex depositional and other practices.

EMBANKED ENCLOSURES

There are a number of earthworks in the Boyne Valley which were possibly built by the tomb builders or their successors but which, in the absence of excavation, are of unknown date and purpose but may well have had a ritual function. These include several more or less circular enclosures. A large and impressive oval enclosure near Dowth is well known: located about 1.5km north-east of the passage tomb (Fig. 27), it has a maximum overall diameter of about 180m and consists of an oval area some 165m in greatest diameter surrounded by an earthen bank 3m to 5m high in places and with an average width of 20m. Today, there are two gaps in the bank but only one, that on the south-west, seems likely to be original. Apart from a hollow outside the bank on the northern side, there is no trace of a surrounding ditch either outside or inside the bank and it would seem that the material for the bank had been scooped up from the interior. This was the case at an embanked enclosure, some 3km north of Newgrange, in Monknewtown townland. Only a segment of the earthen bank of this circular enclosure survived but originally the monument was about 107m in overall diameter. The bank, about 1.5m in height and about 11m wide at its base, was constructed by scarping between 1m and 1.5m of material from the interior. Excavation of part of the interior on the north revealed a dozen pits within some 15m of the bank. Some of these pits contained stones but no finds of any description, small deposits of burnt bone were found in or near eight of them; in one shallow pit a small amount of cremated bone (of a child) had been placed in a Carrowkeel bowl, in another pit a plain bucket-shaped pot contained some cremated bone. In the south-western quadrant of the enclosure, the remains of a flat-bottomed pot and some burnt bone were found in a pit at the centre of a small annular ring-ditch. Traces of a hut site associated with Beaker pottery were found 3m to the south-east. Charcoal from around a hearth in this hut produced a radiocarbon date of 2456-2138 BC. However, samples of charcoal said to be from the remains of hearths in the area of the pits and burials produced a series of dates which ranged over several thousand years and contamination of some of the samples is a possibility. It is also possible that the site had a long and complicated ritual history. The occurrence of Carrowkeel pottery would seem to indicate that passage tomb builders were associated with it and a small passage tomb is situated just 150m to the south-east. This may be true, too, of the Dowth earthwork and other circular enclosures such as one at Micknanstown located 0.6km from the passage tomb at Fourknocks, Co. Meath.[3]

Embanked enclosures such as Dowth, Monknewtown and Micknanstown belong to a well-defined group of earthworks characterized by their large size with maximum external diameters exceeding 100m. These and ten others in the Boyne region have been surveyed by Geraldine Stout who notes their oval or circular plan, a slightly raised centre or hollowed interior (due to the scarping of material to build the bank), and a flat-topped earthen bank generally with a single entrance. They are located on good agricultural land in river valleys and sometimes occur in groups of two or three. Small to medium sized examples with diameters of 106m to 160m tend to have circular plans while the four largest sites, with maximum diameters of 180m to 275m (like Dowth and Rath Maeve, at Belpere, near Tara) tend to an oval plan. Internal features have been noted in some examples: a burial mound is located in one near Newgrange, circular features have been recorded in several, including Rath Maeve, and limited geophysical analysis has revealed an arc of a possible trench or ditch 3m-4m wide inside the bank at Micknanstown and at another 160m wide enclosure at Balrath, Co. Meath. A number of similar embanked enclosures, usually with smaller overall diameters ranging from 35m to 96m, have been identified elsewhere and may be related monuments, as indeed may be a number of large earthworks with banks and internal ditches.[4]

The great earthwork known as the Giant's Ring at Ballynahatty, Co. Down, just south of Belfast, is an exceptionally large example of an embanked enclosure. With an approximately circular plan, it has an overall diameter of about 225m with an earthen bank about 4m high and of an average width of 19m which was built of material scarped from the interior (Fig. 46). A small polygonal passage tomb lies just east of the centre. Various prehistoric burials were found in the general area in the 19th century mainly to the north-west of the enclosure and aerial photography and excavation has shown that the Giant's Ring is just the largest of a complex of prehistoric ring ditches and other monuments in an area of at least 33 hectares. This may have been a ritual landscape where most activity was ceremonial and funerary rather than domestic. A large oval enclosure has been identified about 100m to the north-west of the Giant's Ring and partial excavation suggests it is just one of a number of timber circles in this part of the complex; this oval enclosure was formed of a double ring of timber posts with a maximum diameter of about 90m. The paired timbers were each about 30cm in diameter and set in pits with an average depth of 1.8m; each pit had a substantial ramp to allow the timbers to be slipped into the holes and raised to a vertical position and the excavator, Barrie Hartwell, has pointed out that there was no trace of any structure between them and they could have been as much as 6m high. A small rectangular setting of timbers, 2m by 3m, was found just inside the line of these double posts. Another smaller timber circle was found within the large enclosure and it too consisted of a double ring of timbers (Fig. 46). This structure had several constructional stages and the cremation of an adult female in a shallow pit was associated with its primary phase. When completed, it consisted of a central square timber feature, perhaps a platform, with four large timber posts set in 2m deep pits a short distance from either corner; the surrounding double ring of timbers, set in deep post-holes, had timber planking infill between the posts near the entrance. This timber circle, about 15m in diameter, may have been the focus for ceremonial activity over a period of time but was eventually burnt to the ground. Judging from the way in which the stumps of some timbers were dug out and the holes deliberately filled with charcoal-rich soil, flints and other material, the structure was destroyed on

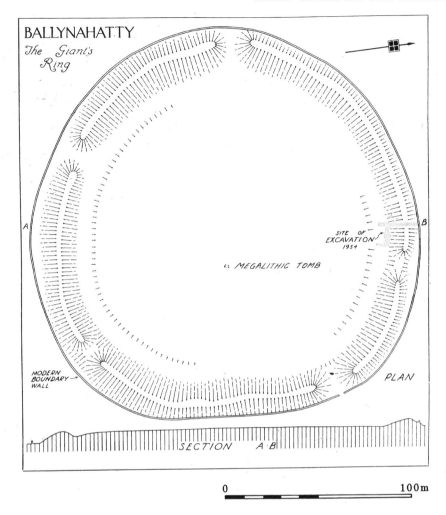

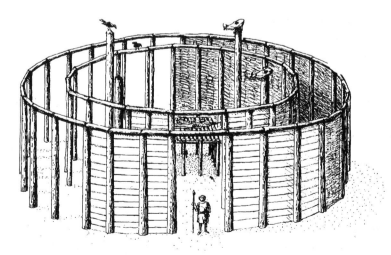

Fig. 46. Above. Large embanked enclosure known as the Giant's Ring, Ballynahatty, Co. Down. Below. A reconstruction of a double timber circle (found within a larger timber circle) excavated to the north-west of the embanked enclosure at Ballynahatty (not to scale).

purpose. What form the rituals took is uncertain, some Grooved Ware, animal bones (notably pig), flint scrapers and stone balls were found. It is possible, as Hartwell has suggested, that the central timber structure may have served as an exposure platform where corpses were defleshed by the elements or by carrion birds.

A smaller timber post structure, of slightly oval plan and about 8m across, has been found at Knowth about 10m from the entrance to the eastern tomb; sherds of Grooved Ware, broken fragments of flint flakes and an unusual number of convex scrapers were deliberately deposited in some of the post-holes. It has been firmly radiocarbon dated to the middle of the third millennium BC.[5]

Limited excavation to the south-south-east of the large passage tomb at Newgrange has uncovered a series of concentric arcs of pits and some post-holes which may have formed a large oval enclosure with an overall diameter of about 100m and which would have encompassed the destroyed satellite passage tomb Site Z. An outer arc of holes seems to have been dug to hold large spaced timber posts and this was traced for just over 9m of its circumference but only occasional post-holes identified elsewhere. However, concentric rows of pits have been traced for a circumferential distance of over 130m; some large pits were deliberately lined with clay and contained charcoal, burnt clay and redeposited boulder clay, other rows of pits contained token deposits of burnt animal bone sometimes on or under layers of small rounded stones. Charcoal spreads, paving, post- and stake-holes, Beaker pottery and Grooved Ware were found within the lines of pits and a series of radiocarbon dates suggests that this activity and the pits date to the later third millennium. David Sweetman has argued that the stone circle, which partly surrounds the large mound, is later than this pit circle. Further limited excavation 50m to the west of the large passage tomb has revealed a double arc of post-holes. Two main phases of activity were identified, the first consisting of a series of small and large pits some of which displayed traces of extensive burning and produced Beaker pottery. In a second phase some pits were used as post-holes and other post-holes were dug to form what seemed to be a double timber circle with an outer diameter of about 20m.[6]

A well-known monument at Grange, near Lough Gur, Co. Limerick, demonstrates the general relationship between stone circles and embanked enclosures. The Grange circle was excavated in 1939 and consists of a large circle of 113 contiguous stones set immediately within a penannular earthen bank with an internal diameter of about 46m. Most of the stones are level with the top of the bank but some are higher: two massive portal stones flank the entrance to the circle which is via a narrow stone-lined passage in the bank on the north-east. The portal stones average about 2m in height and a closely-set pair of equally tall stones occur on the opposite side of the stone circle. Several other exceptionally tall stones occur elsewhere on the perimeter, the largest being 2.6m high and weighing over 60 tons. These larger stones may mark various significant alignments across the circle and it has been claimed that the axis from portal stones to the opposing pair was aligned on the moon's minimum midsummer setting. Excavation revealed a small post-hole in the centre of the enclosure and the excavator, Seán P. Ó Ríordáin, claimed that this was the point from which the circumference of the inner bank was marked out. As there is no ditch the material for the bank was presumably scraped from the surface of the surrounding area. Abundant finds included flint arrowheads and convex scrapers, a number of petit tranchet derivative implements, a polished stone axe and fragments of two others, and thousands of sherds of pottery both from under the earthen bank and from the interior. No structures were found but two hearths, a few unburnt human bones and some animal bones, mainly cattle, were discovered. Much of the pottery came from the interior of the circle and mostly consisted of Beaker and later Bowl Tradition wares.[7]

These large circles of the third millennium, whether of timber, earth, stone or delimited by pits, are linked by a number of features of which the delineation of a circular space is only the most obvious. Limited excavation does suggest a ritual purpose but to what extent the rituals may have replaced the functions of megalithic tombs and represent, for instance, a shift from the worship of ancestral remains to some other form of religious expression is not clear; human bones are occasionally reported but the occurrence of pottery sherds and animal bones may indicate the consumption of food and drink in non-funerary ceremonies. Some new pottery types, such as Grooved Ware and Beaker pottery, may have had specific roles in such activities. There is also a pattern of deliberate deposition in pits of certain materials such as charcoal and soil, and burnt animal bones as at Ballynahatty and Newgrange. But it would be unwise to assume that all these different circles had similar functions and there may be important regional differences. What is evident in the case of the very large monuments in Co. Meath and Co. Down, is that large amounts of labour were mobilized for their construction and this may imply a greater degree of political centralization in these areas. Analogous circles and embanked enclosures are known in third millennium Britain.

Smaller stone circles were also built. At Millin Bay, on the Ards peninsula in Co. Down, an oval setting of large standing stones surrounded an oval mound which covered a long stone-built grave containing the disarticulated bones of fifteen individuals. Some Carrowkeel pottery and some art carved on a number of stones indicated a relationship with passage tombs. Partial excavation of a stone circle at Ballynoe, near Downpatrick, in the same county revealed a complex multi-period monument comprising a large circle of closely-set orthostats which enclosed a long low oval cairn containing two chambers, and an oval arrangement of stones partly surrounding the cairn. The cairn and its associated stones were eccentrically placed within the larger stone circle and the relationship of the two is uncertain. Ballynoe is similar in some respects to Millin Bay and like the latter site it also produced a little Carrowkeel ware.

A circle at Castlemahon, Co. Down, consisted of half-a-dozen widely spaced orthostats enclosing an area about 20m in diameter. A large circular pit near its centre had contained a hot fire of ash wood which had been quenched with a layer of clay. Nearby a burnt plano-convex flint knife and a few cremated bones of a child were found in a small cist; a pit on the perimeter contained oak charcoal, a few worked flints and some sherds of plain round bottomed pottery. Excavation of the remains of a possible stone circle at Kiltierney, Co. Fermanagh, revealed no less than seven cremated burials on its perimeter and within the interior. Near the centre a spread of cremated bone contained several pendants (two of baked clay and one of stone) and a few sherds of Carrowkeel ware. Below this deposit a pit contained another cremation along with two stone and four amber beads. Only two of the remaining burials had any associated artefacts: a few sherds of pottery were found with one and a small

quantity of burnt bone near the perimeter was covered by an inverted cordoned urn of the early second millennium BC. A number of regional groups of small stone circles of second millennium date will be considered in Chapter 5 and it seems that stone circles of different types were constructed over a long period of Irish prehistory.[8]

INNOVATION AND CHANGE

The chronological period conventionally named the 'Neolithic' lasted in calendar years from at least 4000 to about 2400 BC, a period of at least sixteen centuries. Within this long time-span tomb building fashions and pottery styles, for instance, clearly changed and no doubt some of these changes reflect social and demographic developments. Population may well have increased and some change may have occurred in social structures too. The fact remains that until much more is known about the chronological limits of the various megalithic tomb types and about the settlement and economy of their builders, evaluation of factors such as social and economic organization will remain little more than speculative exercises. Major technological change and significant changes in pottery and burial fashions occur towards the end of the third millennium BC and these and other developments mark the commencement of the period which has traditionally been called the 'Bronze Age'.

The period of the later third and much of the following millennium coincides with the latter half of the Sub-Boreal vegetation zone in which temperatures continued to be slightly higher on average than those of today. There may have been some increase in rainfall because there are indications in the pollen record, as at the Céide Fields for example, of a growth of blanket bog from the early third millennium BC. High rainfall may leach a soil of nutrients like iron and may produce an acid podsol with a basal layer of impervious iron pan causing waterlogging and peat formation. Farming activity such as over-grazing, can also cause nutrient loss and soil degradation with similar results. Thus peat formation may not be an indication of higher rainfall and the contribution of human activity to the formation of upland peat may have been significant.[9] Along with the development of blanket bog, the process of deforestation and regeneration initiated over two thousand years before continued of course, though much of Ireland remained heavily forested. Elm never achieved its former status and pine, in particular, shows a decline in the second millennium.

BEAKER POTTERY

The appearance of Beaker pottery in the latter part of the third millennium, about 2400 BC, is one ceramic innovation which is still imperfectly understood. Several types of Beaker pottery have a fairly widespread if irregular distribution in western and central Europe and more localized types are also recognized in various regions from Hungary to Ireland. On the Continent and in Britain, these pots are often found in graves usually accompanying the unburnt skeletal remains of one individual lying in a crouched position. Sometimes these graves also contain other distinctive items notably copper knives, barbed and tanged flint arrowheads, stone wrist-guards or bracers (to protect an archer's wrist from the recoil of the bowstring), and buttons with a distinctive V-shaped perforation.[10] For over a century the concept of a 'Beaker Folk' was generally accepted in European prehistoric studies and some believed that this pottery and other artefacts, and the rite of single burial, represented the movement of early metalworkers from a homeland in Iberia or central Europe to other parts of the Continent as well as to Britain and Ireland. In recent years, as we shall see, the theory of a distinct Beaker culture or folk has come under increasingly critical scrutiny and alternative explanations have been offered for the widespread if somewhat discontinuous European distribution of interrelated types of Beaker pottery.

Various Beaker pottery types have been recognized both in Britain and Ireland and several classifications have been proposed. Humphrey Case's division of different groups of insular Beaker pots into three styles and a number of regional groups is a useful simplification and a convenient way of summarizing a complex phenomenon.[11] The Beaker pottery tradition comprises a range of forms, fabrics and sizes, and vessels were evidently used in everyday life and for special occasions. There is a wide range of sizes in both fine and coarse wares and the fact that so many survive with capacities ranging from about 0.5 to 2 litres is probably because this was the preferred size for deposition with burials; many of these may well have served as drinking vessels while coarse Beakers may have been used as storage and cooking pots as well.

Fine Beaker pottery is well-made and profusely and sometimes attractively decorated. Pots usually have a sort of S-shaped profile and for this reason are sometimes described as 'bell-shaped'. A common and distinctive type of decoration is 'comb' ornament produced by impressing a toothed implement (probably of bone) into the wet clay before firing but other decorative techniques are used too and include grooved or incised lines and impressions of twisted cord; many Beakers bear characteristic geometric ornament in horizontal zones. A range of fine and coarse wares come from very different contexts including burials and settlements but a considerable amount of Beaker pottery from Ireland is not readily classifiable and to a great extent this is because of the fragmentary nature of much of the material coming as it does from settlement or other non-funerary contexts.

If the evidence from Britain and elsewhere applies to Ireland the earliest Beaker is likely to be the so-called all-over-cord (AOC) style which may have persisted throughout the Beaker period. These vessels (Case's Style 1) are usually decorated from rim to base with fairly closely-set horizontal lines of twisted cord impressions and they are related to another style of Beaker with all-over ornament (AOO) which may take various forms including horizontal grooving and comb-impressed lines (Fig. 47). Fragments of all-over-ornamented Beaker have been found in settlements of Beaker-using people at Newgrange, Knowth, Dalkey Island and Lough Gur. Sherds of all-over-cord Beaker come from Newgrange and Dalkey Island, and have also been reported from later settlement at Ballynagilly, Co. Tyrone, and from sandhills at Whitepark Bay, Co. Antrim. A few such sherds occurred in the Beaker material in the wedge tomb at Loughash (Cashelbane), Co. Tyrone. The relatively small quantity of all-over-cord Beaker from Ireland represents the westernmost distribution of a widespread bell-shaped Beaker type, one also found in Scotland, England, Brittany, the Netherlands and in Germany in the middle Rhineland. In Britain and the Rhineland these Beakers are fairly frequently found complete and accompanying crouched unburnt burials in flat graves or beneath burial mounds; in Brittany they have been found in megalithic tombs.[12]

Style 2 Beakers in Case's classification include well-made bell-shaped vessels, often red in fabric, decorated with comb-impressed or incised ornament, the European (E) Beaker as it has been called. Decoration is sometimes distinctive:

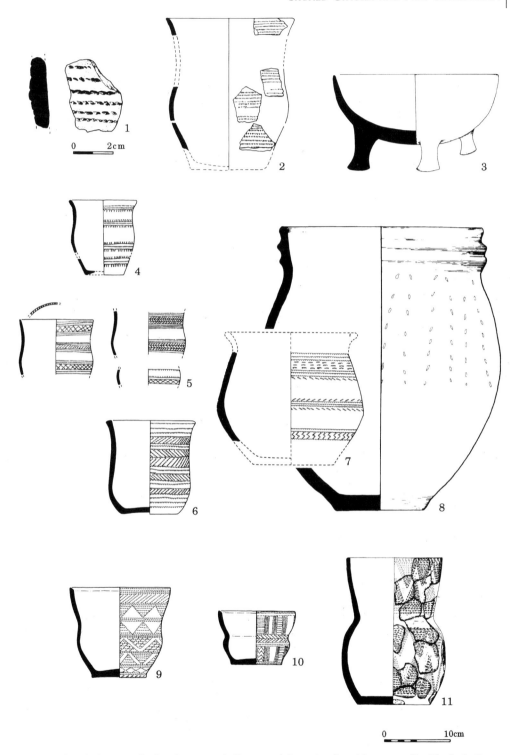

Fig. 47. 1-2. Style 1 beakers. 1. Sherd with impressed all-over-cord decoration from Newgrange, Co. Meath. 2. Reconstruction of a beaker with comb impressed all-over-ornament from Newgrange. 3. Wooden polypod bowl found in a bog at Tirkernaghan, Co. Tyrone. 4-8. Style 2 beakers: 4 and 6. Newgrange. 5. Three beakers from Moytirra wedge tomb, Co. Sligo. 7. Knowth, Co. Meath. 8. Cluntyganny, Co. Tyrone. 9-11. Style 3 beakers: 9-10. Largantea wedge tomb, Co. Derry. 11. Grange stone circle, Lough Gur, Co. Limerick.

multiple horizontal zones are usually alternately plain and decorated. The decorative motifs employed are invariably simple: horizontal, vertical, or oblique lines (the latter sometimes forming a herringbone design); lattice and zig-zag (chevron) motifs are also found. Horizontal lines of cord-impressions may occasionally occur. Sherds have been reported from settlements such as Newgrange and Dalkey Island, in the Loughash (Cashelbane) wedge tomb and in other similar tombs at Moytirra, Co. Sligo (Fig. 47), and Lough Gur. Again the quantity is small and fragmentary – and as with all-over-cord Beakers there are interesting contrasts with the British and Continental evidence. The consistent association of these Beakers with crouched unburnt burials in single graves in Britain, for instance, is a striking difference in funerary context. It is true that the unburnt bones of two adults and a child were found along with some of the decorated Moytirra sherds but the 19th century account of this discovery is brief and direct association less than certain. In any event, it was not a classic Beaker burial and the same can be said of the few other Beaker burials now known from Ireland (below). Other Beaker types assigned by Case to his Style 2 include various examples related to rather loosely defined regional groups in Britain which display in form and particularly in decoration some affinities with cross-channel Beakers in certain areas of the Rhineland.[13] Shapes vary somewhat but relatively tall slender curving profiles are frequent and everted necks sometimes occur. While simple decorative motifs such as herringbone and lattice are also used, new motifs and decorative styles are evident. Motifs in common use include the filled triangle, a zone of short vertical lines (ladder motif), oblique or vertical short lines delimiting zones (fringe motifs) and simple panelled designs. Broad zones of ornament (sometimes consisting of paired or trebled narrow zones) are favoured and in some cases decoration contracts into just three broad bands of ornament. Incision, grooving and comb impression occur and plain vessels are also known.

Coarse pottery of various sorts presumably served as domestic wares. Carbonaceous matter adhering to the surface of some pottery at Newgrange suggests they functioned as cooking pots. Decoration may consist of impressed lines or fingernail impressions and one or more cordons, or raised ribs, may occur just below the rim. A very large and complete pot of this sort (with a height of over 41cm) was found in Cluntyganny, near Cookstown, Co. Tyrone (Fig. 47), and sherds also come from sites such as Monknewtown, Co. Meath, a possible camp-site at Rockbarton, Co. Limerick, the Lough Gur and Dalkey Island settlements and the Kilhoyle, Co. Derry, wedge tomb. Bowls also occur and Newgrange produced fragments of polypod bowls, a rare type also known from Britain, the Rhineland and further east and which may be a pottery rendering of a wooden form with several legs. Several wooden examples have been discovered in Ireland: a circular five-legged wooden bowl found at a depth of 4.5m in a Monaghan bog at Lacklevera, north-east of Killeevan, is probably of prehistoric date and another found in a bog at Tirkernaghan, just south of Dunnamanagh, Co. Tyrone (with two small wooden round-bottomed cups), has been radiocarbon dated to the third millennium (Fig. 47).[14]

Beakers assigned to Case's Style 3 are mainly insular fashions. These Beakers vary in shape: from pots with a curving body and convex neck to those with a biconical body and straight everted neck. Broad zones of ornament are common and comb-impressed and incised decoration occurs. There is a wide range of motifs including filled triangles and chevrons. Reserved decoration is sometimes prominent (decorative motifs juxtaposed with plain or reserved designs notably triangles and chevrons). Fragments come from the Largantea, Co. Derry, Loughash (Giant's Grave) and the Ballyedmonduff, Co. Dublin, wedge tombs, sherds of possible examples bearing incised ornament were found in the lowest levels of a cairn in Moneen, Co. Cork, on the Dalkey Island settlement site and in the Grange stone circle at Lough Gur, Co. Limerick.[15]

Much of the Irish Beaker so far discovered comes from a variety of excavated settlement, burial and ritual sites in the northern half of the country. To some extent this northern bias in distribution is a reflection of the pattern of archaeological excavation. The excavated Beaker from the Lough Gur area, from Moneen in Co. Cork, Longstone, Co. Tipperary, and Ross Island, Co. Kerry (below), indicates a significant southern presence. Beaker pottery has also been found at Parknabinnia, near Kilnaboy, in Co. Clare, associated with a house site and field system.[16]

SETTLEMENT AND ECONOMY

Mention has been made of sherds of Beaker pottery from a number of settlements: aside from the several sandhill sites, these settlements include Dalkey Island, Co. Dublin, Lough Gur, Co. Limerick, Knowth, Co. Meath, Monknewtown, Co. Meath, Newgrange, Co. Meath, and Ballynagilly, Co. Tyrone. At Dalkey Island excavation revealed traces of intermittent settlement from about 4000 BC to the early Historic period. The scattered Beaker ware – with no trace of any houses – suggested temporary occupation; some coarse ware was associated with a small shell midden. The Beaker finds at Knowth consisted of five separate pottery concentrations; in one or two instances these were associated with hearths or pits but no evidence of structures was uncovered. However, scraps of flint indicated flint knapping on site and a layer of dark soil was probably the result of accumulated habitation refuse. Domestic activity of some description, perhaps of a seasonal or temporary nature, is likely though George Eogan did remark that the layers of darker earth and the amount of evidence for flint work and pottery usage indicate a great deal of activity for a seasonal occupation. A similar puzzling picture of hearths, pits and stake-holes but no clear trace of houses was excavated at Ballynagilly. This scarcity of 'Beaker structures' is a well-known phenomenon and not confined to Ireland; it is just as true of Britain and elsewhere and it seems likely that many of the huts and houses were lightly built. Structures of roughly oval or circular form have been recognized at a few sites.

At Monknewtown, Co. Meath, extensive traces of habitation were found in the south-western sector of that embanked enclosure which had also been used for burial and ritual purposes. A roughly oval area about 7m by 4.5m had been dug out to the underlying gravel leaving a broad shallow pit containing some 50cm of occupation debris: dark soil heavily impregnated throughout with charcoal and pot sherds. The pottery from the upper levels was similar to that from the lower levels. An approximately circular hearth about 1m in diameter and partly stone-lined lay on the underlying gravel near the centre of the pit which also contained an irregular series of possible post-holes. The excavator, David Sweetman, suggested that these had held timbers supporting a conical house of more or less oval plan. Pottery fragments included fine Beaker (mainly with incised decoration) and coarse pottery,

some decorated. Very little flint and stone work was found: a few flint blades and convex scrapers, and three concave scrapers. The absence of animal bone may have been due to acid soil conditions.

Excavation to the south of the major passage tomb at Newgrange revealed later activity beyond the limits and on top of the material that had slipped from that mound. There was evidence of considerable occupation: some seventeen hearths were found usually of rectangular plan and often bounded by carefully laid stone settings. Numerous pits, some post-holes, short stretches of foundation trenches, concentrations of Beaker sherds, flints and animal bones were also discovered. The post-holes and trenches, however, did not provide any clearly identifiable house plans though the existence of circular houses with central hearths has been postulated. An arc of post-holes found just west of a stone-lined rectangular hearth may have been some sort of screen or shelter. As in some other hearths, this one contained no ash but heat-cracked stones and soil oxidized to a bright red colour indicated considerable heat. O'Kelly surmised that this was an outdoor hearth and the ash had eventually blown away. Other nearby post-holes formed no coherent plan. Three oval pits contained charcoal and two contained Beaker ware. One produced fragments of all-over-ornamented Beaker and charred grains of barley and emmer, and charcoal which was radiocarbon dated to 2488-2284 BC. Another contained fragments of plain bowls and charcoal which yielded a comparable date. A few metres to the north-east of the hearth lay two boulders, one so picked and abraded that the excavator thought it must have served as a metalworker's anvil. The discovery of a bronze axe and a number of stone tools, a perforated granite hammer, a quartzite hammer, and a rubbing stone showing traces of use as a polisher, raised the possibility that at least some metal hammering and finishing had taken place on site, probably by the users of the Beaker pottery. However, the date for the Beaker activity is a century or two earlier than the generally accepted date for bronze production of this sort and the correlation of axe, putative metalworking activity and the other Beaker-period features must remain tentative.[17]

Elsewhere the occupation evidence included an L-shaped foundation trench thought to be part of a rectangular structure (though no other traces of this rectangle were detected). Here, in and near this trench, the pottery comprised some sherds of Grooved Ware, and Beaker ware including polypod bowl fragments. Besides pottery, pits in this area also contained much flint waste, flint artefacts and animal bones. The flint material found indicated that knapping had taken place on the site and the raw material was probably small nodules collected from the glacial drift in the locality. In relation to waste flakes and cores, the percentage of finished implements was 8.6%. Scrapers of various sorts were the commonest implement type, convex scrapers being particularly frequent but side scrapers, concave scrapers, and other forms were represented too. Also found were petit tranchet derivative implements (or knives), as well as a few barbed and tanged and other arrowheads.

The animal remains were preponderantly those of domesticated cattle and pig. Cattle bones comprised about 58% of the total and it seemed that most were killed when they were between three and four years old suggesting they were reared primarily for meat and secondarily for milk. The absence of older cows suggests that milk and dairy products were not a significant dietary component. Bull calves may have been castrated and, though direct evidence was lacking, a small proportion of the docile results of this procedure may have been used for traction. Pig bones (about 35%) came from a large breed and with a few exceptions they were killed at two to two and a half years; they too were clearly an important food source. Only about 3% of the identifiable bones were of sheep or goat and some dog bones were identified. Also found were some bones of horse (about 1% of the total). It is difficult to distinguish between the bones of wild and domestic horse. Wild horse is recorded from a considerable number of early sites in Britain but, in contrast, there is no certain evidence for native postglacial wild horse in Ireland. Thus the Newgrange horse bones are tentatively considered to represent a domesticated stock imported in the later third millennium, one of the several innovations which seem to coincide with the appearance of Beaker pottery. A small quantity of wild animal bones (1%) was also found and included wild cat, brown bear, wild boar and red deer. It should be noted that it is not certain that all of this Newgrange activity represents normal domestic occupation, it may be a part of the ritual practices demonstrated by the pit and timber circles there and the animal bones recovered may not be representative of the economy of the Boyne region in the later third millennium.[18]

As already mentioned Beaker pottery has been associated with a house site and field system at Parknabinnia, Co. Clare, and – as we shall see – at Ross Island, Co. Kerry, with a copper mining work camp. Evidence for Beaker period settlement was also discovered at Lough Gur. Stray finds of this pottery occurred on several sites in this complex but only at Site D was there Beaker in any quantity. The post-holes of two timber houses of irregular plan were associated with several thousand sherds of Limerick style and Beaker pottery. One house, with hearth, had a roughly oval ground plan measuring about 7.3m by 6m, the other, also with hearth, was somewhat D-shaped in plan and measured about 5.5m by 5.5m. The excavator believed that these two houses and the earlier Limerick style sherds were coeval but the houses may be contemporary with the Beaker ware. The evidence is inconclusive. A range of pottery and a sequence of occupation were identified at the enclosed Site L at Lough Gur and it has been suggested that the later settlement there was contemporary with Beaker pottery which represented over 60% of the sherds recovered. Other evidence for enclosure occurs at Donegore, Co. Antrim, where a stockade, dated to about 2000 BC, is reported.[19]

Beaker burials

Allusion has already been made to the intriguing differences in Beaker funerary practice between Britain and Ireland. In England, Scotland and Wales Beakers are consistently associated with crouched skeletons in graves. In Ireland the situation is very different. Fragments of Beaker pottery have been found in a minority of excavated wedge tombs which more often than not have also produced some cremated bone, though tombs such as Lough Gur and Moytirra, for instance, did yield unburnt human bones. Other Beaker burials are rare. The cremated bones of an adult and a child were placed in the passage of one of the satellite tombs at Knowth and sherds of a Beaker were found in and close to the burial; the pot is a well made bell-shaped vessel without decoration. To what extent the Beaker deposits in wedge tombs are similar secondary insertions is uncertain. Three small sherds with incised zonal ornament found with a cremation in a stone circle at Kiltierney Deerpark, Co. Fermanagh, have been compared to Beaker and fragments of a small necked pot associated with cremated bones in cist at Knockmullin, Co. Sligo, have been claimed to be Beaker but classification is debatable. The varied nature of these burials and the uncertainties about some of them only emphasize all the more that difference in funerary custom. In Ireland, it is some makers of pottery of the Bowl Tradition of the late third millennium who adopt the practice of crouched unburnt burial with accompanying pot in classic Beaker fashion.[20]

THE BEAKER ASSEMBLAGE

The widespread European distribution of some Beaker pottery, the occurrence in many areas of a consistent burial rite and the recurrence in these graves of a variety of artefacts such as copper knives, archer's wrist-guards, buttons and arrowheads, have all helped to give credence to the concept of a culturally distinct 'Beaker Folk'. True, this Beaker assemblage came mainly from graves but when, as in Britain for instance, the broad-skulled or brachycephalic skeletons from those graves appeared to differ from the narrow-skulled or dolicocephalic remains from earlier contexts, then arguments for a new intrusive population group seemed persuasive.[21] In addition to pottery, other elements of what has been called the Beaker assemblage are found in Ireland, though not, of course, in direct association in single graves.

Over 100 wrist-guards (or bracers) are known, most of them unfortunately stray finds without any documentation about their archaeological context and many without even their provenance recorded. The great majority of the Irish examples (95%) are of slender rectangular or sub-rectangular shape, of more or less flat or of plano-convex cross-section with two holes, one at either end (Fig. 48, 1). This type is a western European fashion, found in the Iberian peninsula and France and well represented in Britain. A very small number are of broader rectangular shape, of flat or concave-convex cross-section, have four perforations, two at either end. Wrist-guards of this sort are frequent in central Europe but examples have been found in Britain and the Netherlands too. Irish specimens are made from quite a variety of polished stone including jasper, siltstone, porcellanite, sandstone, porphyrite and slate; and there seems to have been some preference for stones of a reddish colour. Of the provenanced examples a remarkable number, no less than two-thirds, come from Co. Antrim with the

remainder scattered as far west as Co. Galway and as far south as Co. Limerick. This Antrim concentration is extraordinary but it may in part be due to the activities of a number of antiquarian collectors in that part of the country. As mentioned, the find circumstances of most of these objects were not recorded and only one certain example comes from a burial; at Longstone, Co. Kildare, a large stone-lined grave at the foot of a standing stone contained fragments of a two-holed bracer, a few coarse pot-sherds, a flint, a stone bead and cremated bones. A number have been found in bogs and two grey siltstone wrist-guards from a bog at Corran, about 10km south of Armagh, were found in 1833 'in a box bound with a gold band, together with some gold circular plates, and several jet beads of various shapes'. Unfortunately no more precise details are recorded and only the wrist-guards appear to have survived though it has been suggested that an unprovenanced gold disc may be one of the lost circular pieces (Fig. 52, 6).[22] A possible wrist-guard was found in a court tomb in Ballywholan, Co. Tyrone, and another possible and rather plump example was found in the excavation of Site C at Lough Gur in association with coarse pottery. It is generally accepted that most of these objects were either intended to protect the archer's wrist from the recoil of the bowstring or were decorative versions of such a protective device. The Corran find indicates that some were highly prized, certainly many were carefully made and polished and the finest examples may have been emblematic rather than functional items.[23]

Buttons of various types are known in Beaker contexts in Europe and in Britain where the commonest form is conical with a basal V-shaped perforation and where examples of jet and amber have been found singly or in pairs mainly in later Beaker graves. A small number of these V-perforated buttons from Ireland may be of Beaker period or later date. Of jet, shale, steatite and bone, most are stray finds. Three (one of shale and two of jet) are reported from the passage tomb in the Mound of the Hostages at Tara, Co. Meath (Fig. 48, 3) where they were apparently associated with secondary burials. One bone example was found with cremated bones and a bone pin in a grave at Kinkit, Co. Tyrone.[24]

Another innovation attributed to Beaker-using people is the barbed and tanged arrowhead. In Britain, flint arrowheads of this variety occur in

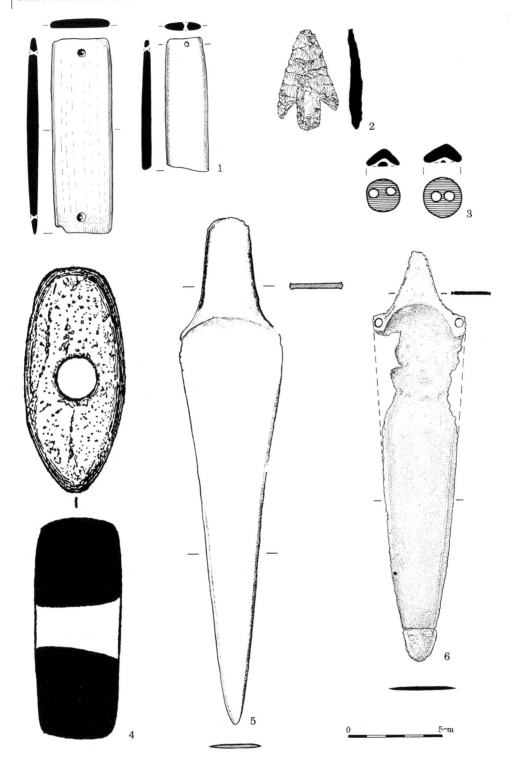

Fig. 48. 1. A pair of stone wrist-guards found at Corran, Co. Armagh. 2. Barbed and tanged flint arrowhead from a hoard of flints at Ballyclare, Co. Antrim. 3. Two V-perforated buttons of jet found in the Mound of the Hostages, Tara, Co. Meath. 4. Stone battle axe from Drumeague, Co. Cavan. 5. Tanged copper knife from Blacklands, Co. Tyrone. 6. Tanged copper knife with rivet holes in the shoulders from Derrynamanagh, Co. Galway.

Beaker contexts and, like buttons, continue in use in post-Beaker times. A number have been recovered from Irish wedge tombs and Beaker settlements such as Ballynagilly and Newgrange. Among the numerous stray finds several have been found with part of their wooden shafts still attached: one from a bog at Tankardsgarden, near Newbridge, Co. Kildare, had an incomplete hazel shaft 42cm in length split for the insertion of the point and bound with animal sinew or gut, a second, from Gortrea, near Killimor, Co. Galway, is said to have had an alder shaft and a third such find comes from Ballykilleen bog, near Edenderry, Co. Offaly. Different types of barbed and tanged arrowheads have been identified including large and small forms and one large type named after a find from Ballyclare, Co. Antrim (Fig. 48, 2), seems to be a favoured Irish type. The Ballyclare discovery consisted of a hoard of twenty-two finished arrowheads and seventeen roughly oval flint flakes which have been interpreted as blanks or rough-outs from which other arrowheads could be made, the finished examples have an average length of 6.5cm. The later use of the barbed and tanged arrowhead is demonstrated by its association with a cremation and a collared urn at Galgorm Parks, Co. Antrim. A perforated stone axe, a so-called 'battle axe', is another item occasionally associated with Beaker pottery in Britain and some Irish examples may be of this period too but none come from dateable contexts (Fig. 48, 4).[25]

An important and novel artefact occasionally found with Beaker pottery abroad is a tanged copper knife, one of a series of metal objects and trinkets recorded in such contexts from Britain to central Europe. It was associations such as these which inspired the belief that the 'Beaker Folk' were the first metalworkers in certain parts of western Europe including Ireland and Britain and it was once widely believed that wholesale migrations of these people were responsible for innovations like copper working, new funerary customs like single burial and even the introduction of domesticated horses. Tanged copper knives are amongst the earliest metal objects known in Ireland but like wrist-guards and V-perforated buttons they have not been found in direct association with Beaker pottery. Most of these knives, and they are few in number, are stray finds often from bogs. They are simple flat implements of copper with a rather rounded point and sometimes with bevelled cutting

edges; the sides of the tang are occasionally serrated to give better purchase to a hilt of some organic material (Fig. 48, 5-6). A few related knives have one or two holes for rivets to improve the stability of the hilt. Two tanged knives come from important hoards containing other metal types which of course provide a possible indication of some of the range of implements in contemporary use. At Knocknagur, near Tuam, Co. Galway, a 19th century bog find comprised one tanged copper knife, three flat copper axes and three copper awls (Fig. 49, 1). At Whitespots, just north of Newtownards, Co. Down, a very corroded tanged knife was discovered in a rock crevice along with an axe and a riveted copper blade variously considered to be a dagger or a halberd. The Corran find mentioned above is just one piece of evidence which suggests that some sheet gold work was manufactured at this time as well and it is contended that some gold discs, lunulae and ear rings could be 'Beaker work'.

It was not until the early 1930s that excavations in a number of wedge tombs in the north of Ireland revealed the existence of Beaker pottery in any quantity in Ireland. Thereafter it was generally assumed that 'the Beaker Folk' must have been a significant element of the population and some believed these people introduced the knowledge of metalworking and in effect initiated a copper or bronze age. The traditional concept of 'a Beaker Folk' has received considerable scrutiny in recent years and various attempts have been made to re-assess the significance of the widespread geographical distribution of 'the Beaker assemblage'. It has become increasingly clear that there are significant differences between regional Beaker-using groups and this is particularly evident in the settlement material. To a lesser extent these regional differences are also apparent in funerary contexts (the differences here between Britain and Ireland being a good example). One common link is the bell-shaped Beaker vessel itself but, as already noted, the material from single-graves also includes some other widely distributed objects, such as wrist-guards, tanged copper daggers and buttons, which are rare in settlement contexts. The wide-ranging objects, however, are not subsistence-producing tools; the Beaker pot may often be finely made and decorated, and items such as the polished stone wrist-guards were probably highly prized pieces more for display than protection. If this limited series of artefacts was an indication of the

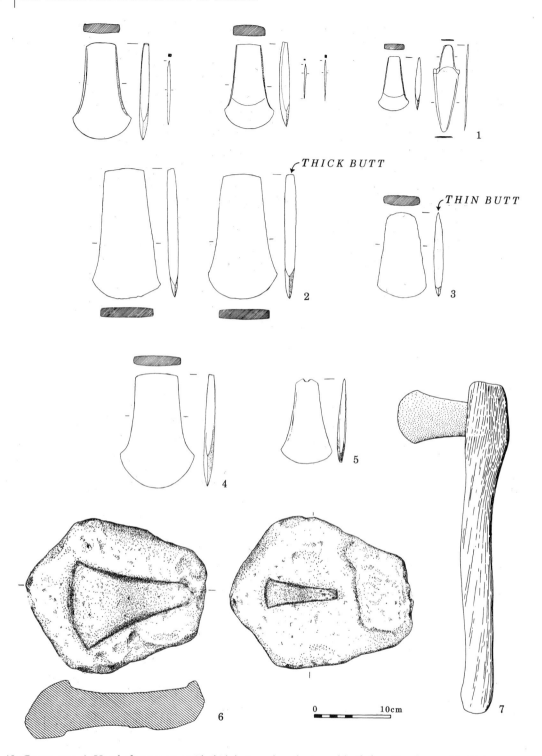

THICK BUTT

THIN BUTT

Fig. 49. Copper axes. 1. Hoard of copper axes with thick butts, awls and a tanged knife from Knocknagur, Co. Galway.
2. Two axes from the Castletownroche, Co. Cork (the example on the left is a straight-sided trapezoidal specimen and both
have thick butts). 3. Straight-sided axe with thin butt from Growtown, Co. Meath. 4. One of the thick-butted axes from the
Lough Ravel hoard, Co. Antrim. 5. The one surviving thin butted axe from the Ballybeg, Co. Cork, hoard. 6. Stone mould
for two flat axes from Lyre, Co. Cork. 7. Axe mounted in a club-shaped wooden haft.

social status of the deceased in life, then their function was primarily a social one. As emblems of status, items such as copper knives could have been exchanged, traded and copied over wide areas by late third millennium societies in which individual ranking and social differences were becoming more marked. If the attractive Beaker was also associated with the ceremonial drinking of some alcoholic brew such as beer or mead, its importance would only be enhanced. Indeed, the residue in one Beaker from a Scottish grave, at Ashgrove, Fife, has been identified as mead made from fermented honey flavoured with meadowsweet. Since pollen indicated that this honey derived from lime trees, which then as now only grow further to the south, it may have been an imported and presumably costly funerary offering. Some association with alcohol and possibly with ceremonial drinking or even with the consumption of plant-derived hallucinogens would offer a plausible explanation for the widespread distribution of Beaker pottery. That said, the regular occurrence of this pottery in settlement contexts suggests regular usage for more mundane drinks as well.[26]

The hypothesis of a distinct population group, 'the Beaker Folk' of older archaeological literature, has therefore been replaced by a functional model in which various artefacts including Beakers are considered as expressions of individual status. While this model does not preclude the possibility that some users of Beaker pottery travelled from place to place, it does obviate the need to presuppose complex population movements to account for the European spread of 'the Beaker assemblage'. As far as Ireland is concerned, the adoption of certain Beaker period fashions by some of the indigenous population seems to be a reasonable explanation. Like the Beaker pot and the stone wrist-guard, it is possible that the knowledge of metalworking was gained at this time as part of the same acquisitive process but the Irish evidence at present is rather equivocal. If the tanged copper knife was the principal copper artefact of the period then the argument that it and the knowledge of copper working and Style 2 Beakers were all interrelated would have much to recommend it. However, there may be important differences between the earliest Irish and British metal industries and, in Ireland, the scarcity of Beaker pottery associations means that the importance of this pottery type as a status symbol is very difficult to estimate. Other objects,

like the more numerous copper axes or some of the goldwork or some perforated stone battle axes, for instance, may have played a more important role in this sphere. What evidence there is suggests that most Beaker pottery was locally made and not widely distributed. At Newgrange, scientific analysis of clay and grit tempering of the Beaker pottery indicated local production. Some petrological analysis of the grit tempering of the Knowth and Monknewtown Beaker ware as well as small samples from Dalkey Island and Lough Gur all point to local manufacture.[27] An increased emphasis on status and display may be only part of the explanation, domestic coarse Beaker wares may not have been particularly significant in this respect and when fine and coarse Beaker pottery is considered together, it is possible that a whole range of pottery types became familiar over large areas primarily through a constant pattern of seasonal movements and exchanges between small communities, a pattern of interaction as old as the fourth millennium.

NEW TECHNOLOGIES: COPPER, BRONZE AND GOLD

With significant copper and gold resources, Ireland was one of the important metal producing areas in early prehistoric Europe. The large number of copper and bronze axes and gold objects which have been found are testimony of this. The morphological developments of various metal types have been studied and these changes in form when coupled with evidence for relative contemporaneity provided by hoard deposits and grave groups permit the construction of a theoretical sequence of overlapping metalworking traditions and several typo-chronological schemes have been proposed. The most primitive copper axe is a typologically simple, flat, almost straight-sided implement: the sides are straight for most of its length but curve very slightly outward near a slightly convex cutting edge; the butt is flat and thick. The shape is almost trapezoidal. Peter Harbison in a study of flat copper and bronze axes includes these trapezoidal examples along with axes with more curving sides (like those from Knocknagur: Fig. 49, 1) in the one category named after a find at Lough Ravel, Co. Antrim (below) but Colin Burgess has argued that the simple straight-sided trapezoidal axes in this Lough Ravel category represent a copper working tradition which predates the curving-sided flat axe and tanged knife tradition as found at Knocknagur. A study of over 200 flat, thick-butted axes noted a very small number (about 4%) of straight-sided specimens which compared closely in their proportions to early Continental trapezoidal copper axes, some from Beaker or possibly pre-Beaker contexts. Axes with more or less straight sides (showing only a slight curvature) and still displaying some resemblance to Continental trapeze-shaped axes comprised about 30% of the total sample. These axes have been found mainly in Ulster, Leinster and Munster, the latter province producing almost as many as the other two combined. Given their rarity in Britain, they may represent, according to Humphrey Case, an archaic Munster copper industry inspired by some unspecified Continental early Beaker tradition. Burgess has also argued for such an early Munster industry and has named his first phase of early metalworking the Castletownroche stage after a possible hoard of four axes found near Mallow in Co. Cork. Agreeing with Case that the source of this putative primary industry is uncertain, he would not rule out inspiration from Atlantic Europe, possibly even the Iberian peninsula. The principal problem as far as this Irish material is concerned is that it is undated. The one hoard containing trapeze-shaped axes is not particularly helpful: only two of the Castletownroche axes survive: one is trapezoidal but the other has slightly curving sides (Fig. 49, 2)

departing from the primitive Continental straight-sided form and foreshadowing the preferred shape of Irish and British axe makers. The significance of these trapeze-shaped copper axes remains a puzzle as indeed do the earliest beginnings of Irish copper working.[28]

The long debate on the origins of Irish metallurgy has been reviewed by Alison Sheridan who thinks it more plausible that this innovation is contemporary with the spread of Beaker pottery and related fashions from about 2400 BC. Two sources are possible, one from the Iberian peninsula perhaps via Atlantic France, the other from the Middle Rhineland to Britain and Ireland. Trapeze-shaped copper axes do occur in Iberia and France, of course, but the rarity of other artefacts of likely Iberian extraction in Ireland may be important negative evidence. But the very occasional parallel may indicate sporadic southern contact through the medium of an overlapping network of Atlantic coastal traffic. The bulk of the evidence, however, seems to point to Britain and ultimately the Rhineland and claims that the makers of Style 2 Beakers had some role to play in the transmission of the new technology may be the likeliest explanation. Again the evidence is fairly tenuous and in the main comprises a small number of copper objects, notably tanged knives, and sheet gold artefacts which have parallels in Beaker burials

Phases Ireland	Harbison	Burgess	Needham (Britain)	Approximate dates
Knochnagur Phase	Knocknagur Phase	Stage 1 Castletownroche	Metalwork Assemblage I and II	2400BC – 2200BC
	Frankford-Killaha-Ballyvally Phase	Stage 2 Lough Ravel		
		Stage 3 Frankford		
Killaha Phase		Stage 4 Killaha	Metalwork Assemblage III	2200BC – 2000BC
Ballyvally Phase		Stage 5 Ballyvally	Metalwork Assemblage IV	2000BC – 1600BC
		Stage 6 Scrabo Hill	Metalwork Assemblage V	
Derryniggin Phase	Derryniggin Phase	Stage 7 Derryniggin	Metalwork Assemblage VI	1600BC – 1500BC

Table 3. Metalworking phases of the traditional earlier Bronze Age.

in Britain. It is fair to say that the appearance of selected metal items in a funerary context there may not reflect either the true chronology or the full extent of the spread of this new technology. The large number of Irish copper axes and halberds (below) raises many questions, a number prompted by the fact that these artefacts are relatively scarce in Britain. This contrast between the Irish and British copper industries is one reason why some writers are reluctant to see both having a similar Continental source.[29]

Both Colin Burgess and Peter Harbison have attempted to divide the metalwork of the late third millennium and the earlier second millennium into a series of chronological and metalworking stages. In both schemes the typological development of axes and daggers in particular is the basis of a sequence which in very general terms is supported by associated finds in a very small number of significant hoards. A chronological framework of metalwork assemblages proposed by Stuart Needham and based on the metrical analysis of axe morphology is broadly similar (Table 3). All this evidence is fragile in the extreme and while the broader sequence of metalworking development is clear, the postulated phases of development are less easily verifiable. As already mentioned, Burgess has suggested an early copper industry producing trapeze-shaped axes, his Castletownroche phase but Harbison has placed both trapeze-shaped and curving-sided copper axes in the one typological category and in the one Knocknagur Phase. This name is retained here for the earliest stage of Irish metalworking including the production of the primitive Castletownroche axes.[30]

METALWORK OF THE KNOCKNAGUR PHASE

The copper axe is the principal metal artefact of the Knocknagur Phase. The typological evolution of Irish copper and bronze axes broadly conforms to the classic developmental sequence first recognized in the 19th century. This progressive sequence, from broad flat copper axe to narrower forms of flanged bronze axe is generally believed to reflect a desire for improved efficiency both technological and functional. In a general way this sequence has also some chronological significance, albeit a quite imprecise one as we shall see. Over 2000 early copper and bronze axes have been recorded by Harbison; unfortunately over 56% of them are

unprovenanced with no record of where and in what context they were discovered. Of those with some information about these circumstances, almost 95% are isolated finds. Four types of copper axe have been identified:[31]

Type Castletownroche: the straight-sided form of copper axe with a broad straight thick butt (Fig. 49, 2 left).

Type Growtown: another straight-sided axe named after a find of two copper axes (found with two rounded stones and a boar's tusk) near Dunshaughlin, Co. Meath; it differs from Castletown Roche type axes in having a thin butt and some examples are broader and shorter (Fig. 49, 3).

Type Lough Ravel: named after a group of five axes (considered a possible hoard because of their similar coloration or patina) from a bog midway between Toome and Randalstown, Co. Antrim. These are flat copper axes with broad thick butts and slightly curving sides (Fig. 49, 4). There are two important associated finds with tanged copper knives: the axe in the Whitespots hoard and two of the three axes in the Knocknagur hoard are of this type.

Type Ballybeg: a similar flat copper axe with slightly curving sides but having a thin butt is a type named after a Co. Cork hoard (Fig. 49, 5). A mixture of thick and thin butted axes was found in a hoard from Carrickshedge, Co. Wexford, and in the Knocknagur find one of the three axes has a butt which, as Harbison puts it, 'could almost be described as thin'; clearly the identification of a thin butt sometimes presents difficulties and may sometimes be a subjective assessment. However, the association of thick and thin butted forms indicates that some measure of contemporaneity is likely. Some are also contemporary with a typologically more developed form of dagger: several Ballybeg type axes and a Lough Ravel type were found with a small riveted dagger and a halberd in a hoard found together in 1892 at a depth of 10m in a bog at Frankford, near Birr, Co. Offaly.

The large number of Castletownroche, Growtown, Lough Ravel and Ballybeg copper axes (over 400 are known) is generally considered to demonstrate Ireland's importance as a centre of early copper working particularly when compared with Britain where some 40 examples are recorded in northern England and Scotland. Indeed the latter mostly have the distinctive Irish copper composition and may even be the product of some early metal exchanges across the Irish Sea.

All the Irish axes are usually quite small, 10cm to 15cm in length, and they were possibly mounted in club-shaped wooden hafts (Fig. 49, 7). They could have been cast in simple open stone moulds (Fig. 49, 6) and some axe-shaped objects called 'ingots' with a plano-convex cross section may be unfinished axes. Metallurgical analyses have indicated that while a few axes were made of unalloyed copper (a relatively soft metal) a greater number were made of copper with significant traces of arsenic and other trace elements such as antimony and silver. Copper with a moderate content of arsenic (about 4%) is better able to withstand a process of cold-hammering to produce, for instance, a hard strong cutting edge (not greatly inferior to bronze) and is also less likely to suffer porosity in the casting process. Considered by some to be a deliberate alloy it now seems likely that in most cases early copper smiths purposefully selected arsenical copper ores. Ores containing arsenic and trace elements of antimony and silver include the *fahlerz* or grey copper ores of Counties Cork and Kerry which were exploited at Ross Island, Killarney, Co. Kerry, at this time. These particular Munster ores may have been the main source of early Irish copper and the importance of this region is demonstrated by the fact that 34% of all provenanced copper axes (and a number of important hoards) come from this part of Ireland. The new and effective copper axe may have been rapidly and widely adopted; timbers used in bog trackways at Corlea and Annaghbeg, Co. Longford, dating to shortly before 2000 BC were cut with copper or bronze blades.[32]

Apart from the three copper awls in the Knocknagur hoard, the only other copper artefact assigned to this early metalworking phase is the tanged copper knife. A small number are known and apart from the Knocknagur and Whitespots examples, all are isolated finds. Like Knocknagur some have come from watery contexts and may have been votive depositions. One from Blacklands, near Fivemiletown, Co. Tyrone, was found at a depth of 1.2m in a bog (Fig. 48, 5). They were probably cast in simple open stone moulds; one such mould, possibly from Ireland, is preserved. Developed variants include examples with one or more rivet holes in the tang or with a rivet hole in each shoulder. A bog find from Derrynamanagh, near New Inn, Co. Galway, is a fine example of the latter (Fig. 48, 6), in addition to the two rivet holes,

it displays differential corrosion indicating the former presence of an organic haft and the tang bears characteristic hammered indentations to give it greater purchase in the hilt. A dagger with a single rivet hole and a total of five rivet notches in the sides of the tang was recovered from the Sillees River, near Enniskillen, Co. Fermanagh, and like most of these tanged daggers has the typical arsenic-antimony-silver impurity pattern of early Irish copper. The Killaha dagger (below) is one exception, with a pair of rivet holes in the shoulder as on the Derrynamanagh variant, it has grooves on its blade which recall the grooving found on some British tanged daggers and it is interesting to note that its composition, with high arsenic, some nickel and almost no other impurities, also finds parallels in Britain.[33]

METALWORK OF THE KILLAHA PHASE

The Killaha Phase marks the commencement of the widespread adoption of bronze. It is named after a hoard from Killaha East, near Kenmare, Co. Kerry, found in 1939 under a limestone slab below a sandstone outcrop, which comprised the tanged copper dagger just mentioned, a halberd, four axes, one or two unfinished axes and a fragment of another. Like the Frankford hoard, this find suggests that axes, daggers and halberds continued to be the principal metal products. The four bronze axes are examples of Type Killaha and it seems that most axes of this type may well be made from an alloy of tin and arsenical copper or copper. They are of broad and approximately triangular shape with a shallow crescent-shaped cutting edge which is occasionally clearly bevelled (Fig. 50, 1). Most are flat but slight hammered-up flanges are found on a few examples; butts are thin and rounded. These large, broad-bladed axes with evenly curved sides have a length to maximum width ratio of 1.5 or less to 1 and the largest example, found in the ruins of Kilcrea Castle, near Ovens, Co. Cork, measures 31cm in length, 22cm in width and is 9mm thick. As was the case with some polished stone axes, large bronze examples like this may have had a ritual purpose. A hoard of ten or eleven axes found at Carhan, Cahersiveen, Co. Kerry, was probably a votive deposit: the find was made when an attempt was made to remove a large stone in the middle of a small channel of a river; this stone (which served as a stepping stone between an area of marshy

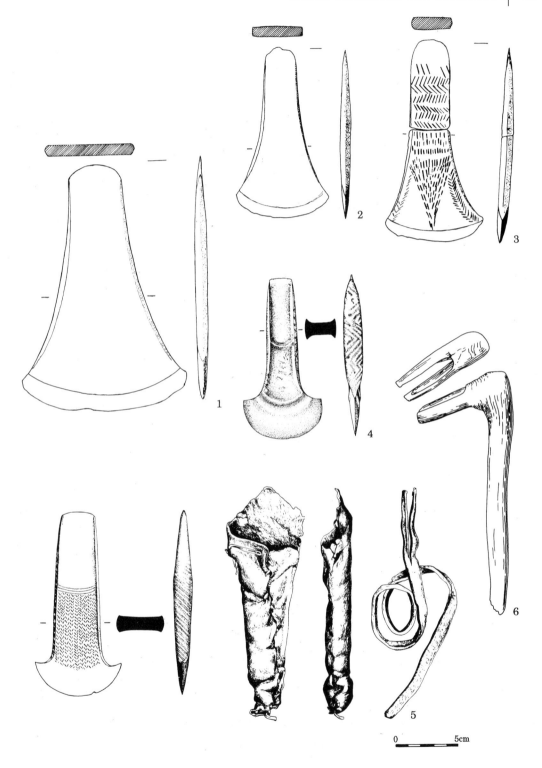

Fig. 50. Bronze axes. 1. One of the axes from a hoard at Killaha East, Co. Kerry. 2-3. Two of four axes from a possible hoard at Ballyvally, Co. Down. 4. A Derryniggin Type axe with flanges and stop-ridge from Clondalkin, Co. Dublin. 5. A decorated Derryniggin Type axe from Brockagh, Co. Kildare, found in a leather sheath. 6. A split knee-shaped wooden haft for flanged axes (not to scale).

ground and dry land) contained a slab-covered hollow in which the axes were arranged in a circle, cutting edge outwards, around a deposit of wood ashes and small fragments of deer bones. Only four of these axes are preserved: two are of Type Ballybeg and two of Type Killaha, suggesting a measure of contemporaneity between the two types. A ritual use for some bronze axes should not obscure the fact that experiment has shown that these bronze implements are about twice as efficient as stone axes and the appearance of such superior tools must have contributed to major developments in wood-working.[34]

A few Type Killaha axes bear decoration which usually consists of longitudinal grooving possibly produced by grinding and polishing. Their general distribution provides no clue as to the whereabouts of any manufacturing focus if such there was and unfortunately just over 70% have no recorded provenance. Analyses demonstrate that the tin content in these bronzes varies somewhat (from about 7% to 15%) but a majority contain in the region of 10%. The continued use of arsenical coppers is evident and since 24% of these axes with known provenance (and the majority of the half dozen hoards containing such axes) come from the south-west, this part of the country evidently continued to be an important source of copper and a significant metalworking region.

The origins of the new alloying technique are uncertain. Continental inspiration for bronze working has been assumed given the scarcity of tin in these islands and a Central European stimulus for this new process of alloying copper with tin is generally accepted. There may have been wide ranging trade and exchange in tin and copper and the rich tin resources in south-western England, in Devon and Cornwall, were probably utilized.[35] Alluvial tin mainly in the form of pebbles of cassiterite was presumably the first source to be exploited but tin ores near the surface were possibly mined as well. Early smiths could well have fortuitously discovered the benefits of including pebbles or grains of cassiterite when smelting copper or could even have perceived the improved casting properties of the rarer mineral stannite, an ore containing both copper and tin. Unfortunately, evidence for early tin mining is all but absent, much of it conceivably destroyed by later working. While south-western England may have been an important source of tin for the Irish bronze

industry, it is possible that local sources existed and were exploited. While it has been argued that alluvial cassiterite known from the Gold Mines River in Co. Wicklow (and other rivers in this area) would have been sufficient to meet the demands of early bronze smiths, evidence for the exploitation of tin in Ireland is lacking.[36]

AXES OF THE OF THE BALLYVALLY AND DERRYNIGGIN PHASES

Developed flat axes are the principal artefacts of the Ballyvally and Derryniggin metalworking phases and are the result of a developmental trend from broad simple and more or less triangular axes to narrower forms with straighter parallel sides. This trend is discernible in axes of Type Ballyvally named after a find of four axes on Ballyvally Mountain, east of Newry, Co. Down, in 1843. Nothing more is recorded about the discovery but it was possibly a hoard. Axes of this type (and various subdivisions of this category)[37] are flat or slightly flanged with thin rounded butts, sides are more or less parallel for about half the length and they then diverge gently towards the cutting-edge. They are usually 15cm to 20cm in length with a maximum width to length ratio of 1 to more than 1.5. About 50% are decorated, usually with fairly simple hammered or engraved geometric motifs: herringbone and stroke ornament being particularly common (Fig. 50, 2-3). The presence of slight hammered flanges or a median thickening or both on some examples is an indication of a change or improvement in hafting methods: it is believed that these axes were intended to fit into the split or forked end of a knee-shaped or angled wooden haft (Fig. 50, 6). The narrow flanged portion would fit firmly into the split end and a median thickening would help to prevent the axe being driven further into the haft. The differential colouring of the patina of the Newgrange axe retained traces of this sort of haft. The Ballyvally type of axe is the commonest Irish form: over 800 are recorded. Most occur in the east and north-east of the country. The small number of hoards is widely distributed: the only concentration is to be found in the north-east and there is a possibility that this region was a centre for their manufacture. Ritual deposition is attested at the Toormore wedge tomb, Co. Cork, where a developed flat axe with faint traces of decoration on faces and sides and two pieces of raw copper were placed as an offering near the tomb entrance.[38]

A range of developed axes was included by Harbison in his Type Derryniggin. This Co. Leitrim hoard was found in a bog near Newtown Gore in the course of turf cutting and comprised two fragmentary axes and two plano-convex flint knives. The deposition of parts of broken axes is unusual and – if not scrap bronze – may recall the ceremonial destruction of some axes noted in Scotland.[39] The Derryniggin type axe is fairly small, under 13cm in length with straight and more or less parallel sides which curve out abruptly to an expanded crescentic cutting edge. Butts are usually flat, low hammered flanges are present in many cases, though a few axes are flat; a median thickening or ridge often occurs. A number of axes have flanges several millimetres high (possibly cast) and a few have a true stop-ridge (Fig. 50, 4). Decoration occurs on a majority of examples. The presence of high flanges on both faces is a significant development for it may imply the use of a bivalve or two-piece mould. No stone moulds for these axes are known at present and baked clay moulds may have been used but it is also possible that high flanges could have been produced by laborious forging and grinding.[40]

Many of these bronze axes of the period 2200-1500 BC were presumably used for wood-working and tree felling, or even as weapons, but again not all of these axes may have been functional. A decorated Derryniggin type axe in mint condition from Brockagh, near Robertstown, Co. Kildare (Fig. 50, 5), was found in a leather sheath at a depth of 4m in a bog; the sheath was slit for attachment to a strap or belt and it seems the axe was not hafted but carried around in this fashion perhaps as a ceremonial object or a status symbol. The overall decoration on some other examples may imply that they too were meant to be seen in an unhafted state on certain occasions.[41]

HOARDS

Axes occur in about 90% of early metal hoards and over 40 hoards containing at least one axe have been recorded. Almost 60% of these are hoards of axes only, the largest being a find of 25 found in a bog at Clashbredane, near Ballineen, Co. Cork; all but two are lost and the survivors belong to Type Lough Ravel. Deposits containing other objects are not common, a few axes were accompanied by copper cakes, or pieces of copper as at Toormore. Other implements are rare and the small number of

hoards, such as Knocknagur, Killaha, Frankford and Derryniggin, containing a range of items such as knives, daggers, halberds and awls are the exception. The frequent occurrence of axes in hoards is also in marked contrast with their rarity in graves. Clearly axes had some particular significance at this time. As with some stone axes, copper and bronze examples may have been an important element in a system of competitive gift exchange in which social prestige was enhanced by the acquisition of highly prized objects in a display of wealth and munificence. If this was so the deliberate deposition of hoards containing axes may have been votive offerings for communal gain; of course they could also have served to increase individual status if publicly perceived as an act of conspicuous generosity, a pattern of activity prominent in later prehistory.

While a majority of hoards have been found in dry-land contexts, often on or protected by stones, almost half have been found in wet conditions usually in bogs. Indeed individual axes may have been deposited in this fashion as well; of those whose context has been recorded no less than half come wet contexts such as river, lake or bog, and as the Carhan find demonstrates such contexts were evidently deliberately chosen on some occasions. Various trends are detectable in the practice of hoard deposition: the smaller numbers of typologically later axes (and the fewer axes in these later hoards) may denote a decline in the custom. There is also a suggestion that a greater number of typologically later axes may come from wetland contexts, a preference which also becomes particularly marked in later prehistoric times.[42]

HALBERDS

The halberd, a pointed, dagger-like metal blade mounted at approximately right angles to a haft, is an intriguing object (Fig. 51). It was fashionable in various parts of Europe in the third and second millennia BC, in areas as widely different as Ireland, Iberia and central Europe. A relatively large number have been found in Ireland: over 170 have been recorded of which, unfortunately, over half are unprovenanced. In some cases it is difficult to distinguish halberds from daggers but most halberds are heavy, broad, slightly asymmetrical blades, usually of copper rather than bronze, with low rounded midribs to strengthen the blade and holes for stout rivets. Where differential patination reveals traces of a haft, this invariably forms a straight line

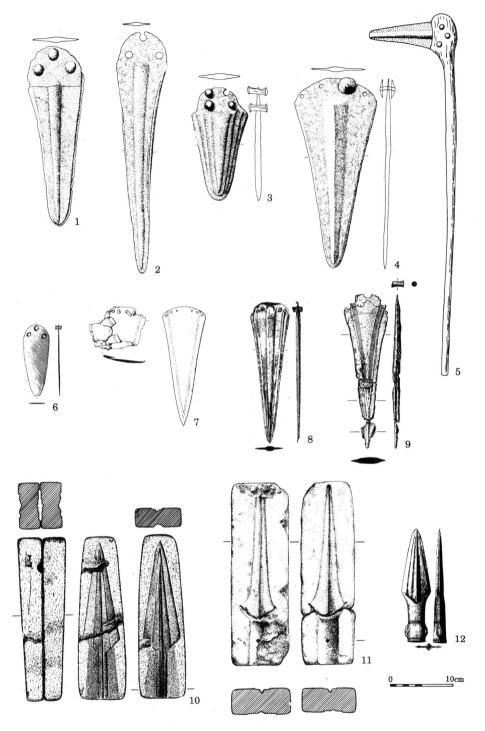

Fig. 51. Halberds, daggers and spearheads. Halberds: 1. Carn, Co. Mayo. 2. One from a hoard at Cotton, Co. Down. 3. Clonard, Co. Meath. 4. Breaghwy, Co. Mayo. 5. The Carn halberd mounted on a copy of its original wooden haft: not to scale. Daggers: 6. River Blackwater at Shanmullagh or Ballycullen, Co. Armagh. 7. Grange, Co. Roscommon (with reconstruction). 8. Gortaclare, Co. Clare. 9. Kiltale, Co. Meath. Spearheads: 10. Stone two-piece mould for casting a tanged spearhead from Omagh, Co. Tyrone. 11. Stone two-piece mould from Omagh, Co. Tyrone, for an early socketed spearhead. 12. End-looped spearhead found near Ballymena, Co. Antrim.

across the butt in contrast to the more or less concave hafting mark sometimes found on daggers.

A majority of halberds belong to two closely related types: Type Carn and Type Cotton. A bog in Carn townland near Ballina, Co. Mayo, yielded an example with at least part of its wooden haft still attached. As found the oak haft was about 1m in length and riveted at right angles to the blade by means of three large cylindrical, round-headed rivets. The blade, 24.6cm long and 8cm in maximum width, has a straight, rounded midrib on both faces and is slightly asymmetrical: one edge being very slightly concave (Fig. 51, 1 and 5). This sort of asymmetrical blade (possibly grooved) with straight midrib and a rounded butt with a triangular arrangement of three rivet holes are the distinguishing features of Type Carn halberds. Type Cotton, named after three examples found in a bog south-east of Bangor, Co. Down, is similar but has a curved midrib corresponding to the curvature of one side of the blade (Fig. 51, 2). About a dozen examples are assigned to a Type Clonard, named after a single Co. Meath find, which has a squared or shouldered butt with four large rivet holes arranged more or less in a rectangle (Fig. 51, 3). A halberd found in a bog near Castlebar, Co. Mayo, has given its name to a Type Breaghwy: a small group characterized by a fairly straight blade and a rounded butt with three or more narrow rivet holes arranged in a shallow arc (Fig. 51, 4). One of this type of halberd was also reportedly found with its wooden haft still attached but this was not preserved. In contrast to the other types most Type Beaghwy halberds are of bronze and the one rivet surviving on the eponymous example suggests that the narrow rivets may have been three-piece objects with conical caps on a slender stem – a rivet type common on the Continent. One Type Cotton halberd bears similar but stouter three-piece rivets.

It is not certain if the various halberd types form a chronological sequence. A few typological straws have been grasped by several writers: the use of bronze as well as multiple narrow rivets (as found on developed bronze daggers) have prompted the suggestion that Type Breaghwy is late in a developmental series. Harbison has claimed that some evidence of re-hafting indicates that narrow rivets were a later fashion than large rivets. Since the halberd with a straight midrib is the Continental norm, the earliest Irish type (assuming Continental inspiration) may have been Type Carn. The closely related Type Cotton was presumably partly contemporary. The inadequacy of this sort of evidence is widely recognized and needs no further comment here. Unfortunately the few associated finds are not very enlightening. Halberd hoards are not common: a hoard of seven (two of Type Carn, the rest of Type Cotton) was found in 1850 at Hillswood, near Kilconnell, Co. Galway; they were discovered stuck point downwards in a bunch in the ground beneath some bog and may well have been a ritual deposit. In two instances other objects have been associated with halberds: in the Frankford hoard one copper halberd (Type Cotton) was found with five axes (of Types Lough Ravel and Ballybeg) and a flat riveted dagger. The Killaha hoard included four bronze axes, a bronze halberd of Type Breaghwy and that tanged and riveted grooved dagger. Harbison has tentatively suggested a halberd sequence commencing with Type Carn, followed in turn by Types Cotton and Clonard and culminating with Type Breaghwy. While Ireland, Iberia, Italy and Central Europe have all been suggested as the original centre where these objects were invented, he finds a German origin most likely.

The substantial midribs of Irish halberds imply that they were cast in bivalve moulds of stone or clay (none of which survive). These large extravagant and unwieldy blades would have made clumsy weapons and it is generally believed that they had some ceremonial or emblematic function. Conceivably they represent a parade weapon tradition akin to that of the polished stone macehead or battle axe; the persistent use of copper might also be an indication of the special nature of these objects. The relative shortness of the surviving rivets may denote fairly slender wooden hafts: the rivets on the Carn halberd for instance indicate that its oak haft had a total thickness of only 2cm where it enclosed the butt. Yet it has been claimed that a number of Irish halberds have displayed signs of wear at the points and may have been re-sharpened at the cutting edges and this suggests that at least some of these puzzling objects may have been put to some practical use.[43]

DAGGERS

Although flat axes and halberds together represent the bulk of the material of the early Irish copper and bronze industry, the repertoire of early metalworkers also included a series of knives or daggers ranging from the early tanged copper knives to typologically advanced bronze examples with riveted hafts, midribs and grooved blades. Quite a variety of forms were manufactured and Peter Harbison has attempted a classification and identified nine separate types and several miscellaneous categories. Because of the paucity of associated finds these are, in the main, imprecisely dated but a very general typological sequence is apparent. To simplify matters, a four-fold classification is summarized here. The earliest form, the tanged copper knife (Harbison's Type Knocknagur) has been briefly described (Fig. 48, 5-6). Flat riveted daggers (Type Corkey) are a more developed type: most if not all of these simple flat daggers are of bronze; they vary in shape from short triangular specimens to longer, rather tongue-shaped blades and may have a U- or V-shaped hafting mark. Butts are rounded and contained two to six rivets to affix an antler or bone haft (Fig. 51, 6). The Corkey example was found in a cist grave near Loughguile, Co. Antrim, and, along with a bowl, accompanied an unburnt burial (Fig. 55, 4).

A series of grooved daggers are not easily classifiable but two major groups are identifiable with some intermediate forms and variants: grooved triangular daggers (such as Harbison's Type Topped Mountain) comprise a small number of daggers with a gently rounded butt and straight cutting edges giving a triangular form. Blades may be almost flat, have a central thickening (giving a biconvex cross section) or even have a distinct midrib. Two or more grooves run parallel to the edges and four or six slender rivets are placed in a very shallow arc in the butt. An unprovenanced dagger and an interesting find from a grave at Grange, near Tulsk, Co. Roscommon (Fig. 51, 7) each have fairly flat grooved blades and six rivets, disposed in pairs of three. Both are comparable to a well-known group of six-riveted daggers in southern England and Brittany. The Topped Mountain dagger is a smaller version with four rivets; it was probably associated with a secondary unburnt burial in a grave in Co. Fermanagh; a fragment of sheet gold was also found.[44] The piece of gold is generally believed to have once decorated the organic hilt or its pommel. A dagger from Gortaclare, Burren, Co. Clare (Fig. 51, 8) probably had six rivets as well as a prominent midrib.

Grooved ogival daggers (various types in Harbison) are slender blades usually with a curved outline, expanding in a gentle curve from point to butt. Sometimes the curve is pronounced but occasionally so slight as to give an almost triangular shape; usually three or more grooves run parallel to the cutting edges and reflect their curvature. Cross-sections of the blade are occasionally biconvex but frequently display a fairly distinct midrib. Butts are often trapezoidal usually with two rivet holes; a few have three or more rivet holes and an indentation in the heel of some, as on an example from Kiltale, Co. Meath, may have been for a notch for a third rivet (Fig. 51, 9). Some are decorated with engraved triangles or lozenges on the upper blade. Miscellaneous daggers include small nondescript blades, some flat, some with midribs, of various shapes and sizes, and include several with triple midribs.[45]

Except for the riveted flat daggers of Type Corkey, a simple type which may have been in use for much of the earlier second millennium, there is some evidence to suggest a typological sequence obviously commencing with the tanged copper dagger but followed in turn by grooved triangular daggers and then grooved ogival daggers. It is this sort of typological succession for axe, dagger or halberd, when combined with the slender evidence of associated finds – be they from Irish hoards or British graves – which provide the basis for the various overlapping typo-chronological phases from Knocknagur to Derryniggin. The gold work, pottery and burials as well as some of the later bronze types (such as the earliest bronze spearheads) can be loosely correlated with this sequence from 2400-1500 BC.

EARLY SPEARHEADS

The bronze spearhead was an important development in the Derryniggin Phase but the lack of associated finds makes it difficult to relate it to other bronze types and to accurately chart its development. The typologically earliest form of spearhead was a tanged blade, a development of grooved ogival daggers in southern England. A few examples have been found in Ireland and their manufacture is indicated by the survival of a bivalve or two-piece stone mould from near Omagh, Co. Tyrone (Fig. 51, 10) with matrices for a dagger as well as a tanged spearhead. This is one of a group of stone moulds found about 1880. A second mould demonstrates the contemporary manufacture of a typologically more advanced form of spearhead with a hollow socket (Fig. 51, 11). To prevent the shafts of tanged spearheads splitting it would have been necessary to bind them with leather at this vulnerable point or to provide them with a bone or metal collar and a third mould from Omagh is for the production of a detached metal collar (with side loops) which would have served as just this sort of a strengthening device on the top of the shaft. An obvious typological improvement was the casting of collar and spear-blade in one piece to produce a socketed weapon. The casting of a collar or socket would have entailed the use of a core, perhaps of charcoal, in a complex two-piece mould and represents the earliest attempts at hollow casting. The socketed bronze spearhead quickly became a relatively popular weapon and different forms were fashionable at different stages throughout much of later prehistory. The first socketed spearheads in this long typological sequence display features recalling the dagger blades and the separate collars which inspired their development. These include ogival blades and rare features such as oval sectioned sockets and small bosses or dummy rivet heads on the socket emulating the rivets which once attached the separate collars to the wooden haft. They invariably have a pair of cast loops near the mouth of the socket, a consistent feature of the standard type.

The standard type is a small weapon with a solid-cast, channelled or broadly grooved blade, a short circular socket (terminating at or near the base of the blade) and loops near the socket mouth (Fig. 51, 12), this has been named the end-looped spearhead and was popular not just in Ireland but also in Scotland and Wales in particular. A stone mould for one of these end-looped spearheads (and a small lugged chisel) was found at Inch Island, Co. Donegal, and another mould for several examples comes from Lough Gur, Co. Limerick. Derryniggin type axes and end-looped spearheads are the two principal products of the Irish metalworking industry at this time and the manufacture of both may well have continued into the succeeding metalworking phase which is distinguished by further developments in axe, dagger and spear, and loops of one sort or another remain a distinctive feature of insular spearheads for many centuries.[46]

GOLD

In early times, as today, gold was doubtless a highly prized and prestigious metal. Yet despite its ancient and modern value a remarkable number of Irish gold objects of early prehistoric date has survived. Unfortunately, most are isolated finds with no recorded archaeological contexts: the gold strip found with the Topped Mountain dagger and the gold discs found with the Corran wrist-guards are two exceptions. The invariable preference, as we shall see, was for the manufacture of objects of sheet gold, in the main ear rings, decorative discs and collars or lunulae.

Two Irish ear rings are of the basket ear ring type but now consist of a slender flattened plaque of sheet gold with a narrow tang for attachment to the ear. Both are plain and may have formed a pair but their findspot is unknown (Fig. 52, 1). Half a dozen pairs are known from Beaker graves in Britain. A third sheet gold ornament is a roughly oval disc of thin sheet gold with a tang found at Deehommed, Co. Down (Fig. 52, 2). It has been considered a basket ear ring and more oval, less elongated, forms are known from Britain but its simple repoussé dotted ornament around the edge finds a close parallel in a pair of tanged gold ornaments from late Beaker contexts in Portugal and it may be an Iberian import.[47]

Some twenty decorated discs of sheet gold are also thought to date to the Beaker period but are invariably poorly documented finds. In about half a dozen cases they form matching pairs and they vary in diameter from about 4cm to about 11cm. All are of thin sheet gold and bear repoussé decoration (Fig. 52): on several this consists of a few concentric circles, including on occasion circles of zigzags or dots or short lines, pressed up with a pointed implement from behind. A majority also bear a cruciform design, usually a simple double cross with a ladder pattern set within a circle. A well-known pair from Tedavnet, Co. Monaghan, found between the roots of an old oak tree, and the surviving specimen of a pair from Ballyshannon, Co. Donegal, have somewhat more complex cruciform decoration with triangles in the quarters of the circle. On some of the more elaborate discs decoration is raised on both faces: on the Tedavnet pieces, for instance, the repoussé linear decoration is carefully raised from the back and emphasized by dots punched from the front. Centrally placed pairs of perforations were presumably for attaching these discs to something and some minute holes or nicks near a part of the circumference of discs from Kilmuckridge, Co. Wexford (said to have been found near a great stone) and Castle Treasure, Co.

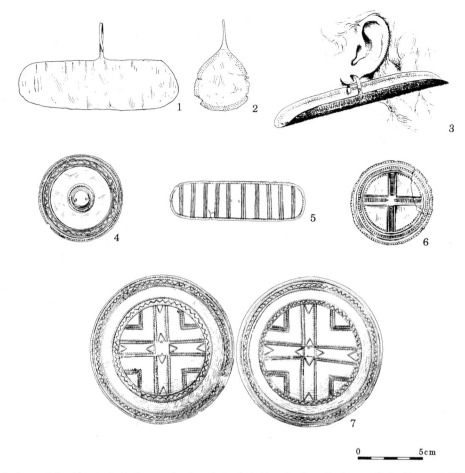

Fig. 52. Beaker period goldwork. 1. Basket ear ring from Ireland. 2. Ear ring from Deehommed, Co. Down. 3. Wearing a basket ear ring. 4. One of a pair of gold discs from Cloyne, Co. Cork. 5. Gold plaque from Bellville, Co. Cavan. 6. A gold disc with no recorded provenance but possibly one of the discs from Corran, Co. Armagh. 7. Pair of gold discs from Tedavnet, Co. Monaghan.

Cork, have been thought to imply some additional stitching to give extra security. Pairs of these discs may have been permanently attached to some perishable substance such as cloth or leather. It has also been suggested that the cross and circle motif was inspired by Continental decorative pin fashions: a series of bronze disc-headed pins in central Europe have a cruciform pattern very similar to that on the Kilmuckridge disc and on a pair from Ballina, Co. Mayo. The symbolism of this motif is unknown but the use of pairs of these discs from time to time may indicate they were for personal adornment. Four narrow gold plaques may have had a similar purpose. At least three of them were found in a stream at Bellville, near Crossdoney, Co. Cavan, and all have centrally placed pairs of perforations and simple linear repoussé ornament; they too may once have been attached to something.[48]

LUNULAE

The numerous gold lunulae represent the greatest volume of insular gold of this period. The name, a diminutive of the Latin *luna*, 'moon', was first given to these crescent-shaped objects in the middle of the 18th century. Just over 85 examples have been found in Ireland and of these just 50 have their provenance recorded. About a dozen have been found in Britain, notably in Cornwall and Scotland, and about 18 have been found on the Continent, mainly in north-western France. None of the Irish finds comes from an archaeological context. Some were found on dry land, a few in bogs and some were seemingly associated with prominent landmarks such as large stones. One, from Newtown, Crossdoney, Co. Cavan, was found at a depth of about 2m in a bog and was contained in a two-piece oak box. A number of lunula hoards are known: four from Dunfierth, north-east of Carbury, Co. Kildare, were said to have been found together 'with several bones' in hard gravel thought to be the remains of an ancient bog trackway, three were found in a bog at Banemore, south of Listowel in Co. Kerry, and two were found at a depth of 60cm in a field at Rathroeen, near Ballina, Co. Mayo. None have come from certain burials.

A typical lunulae is a decorated, crescent-shaped object of burnished, thin, sheet gold with impressed or incised geometric ornament on one face only where it is invariably confined to the horns of the crescent and the edges of the widest part (Fig. 53). The horns end in flat, expanded, oval or sub-rectangular terminals usually turned at right angles to the plane of the lunula. Internal diameters are generally about 14cm-16cm. Joan Taylor's detailed study of shape and decoration has revealed three lunula styles: Classical, Unaccomplished and Provincial. Analysis of the thickness and the width of the sheet gold at the widest part of the crescent has shown that Classical lunulae have the thinnest and widest collars, the Unaccomplished are of broadly similar thinness but noticeably narrower and the Provincial examples are of thicker sheet gold and overlap both the others in width.[49]

The thinner and wider Classical lunulae are superb examples of sheet gold craftsmanship. They were skilfully beaten from a single rod, then polished and decorated with precision. Most were worked to give a thicker inner edge to provide greater strength. On lunulae generally the decoration was applied with a fine pointed implement and impressed or incised with the sheet gold being firmly held in a bed of resin or pitch or some such, for in a few cases it has come through on the other face. On Classical examples the commonest motifs are triangles, lozenges, zig-zags and lattice patterns, all carefully executed. The latter two motifs often occur on the edges of the broadest part of the lunula which is otherwise plain. All four motifs and others are found in complex zonal patterns on the crescent tips, on some the whole tip is filled with zonal ornament, on others three major decorated panels are separated by undecorated zones. This juxtaposition of plain and decorated areas is also frequently found in the patterned zones where reserved triangles, lozenges and chevrons are prominent. The overall effect of balance and contrast thus produced is elegant and restrained. Taylor has demonstrated that symmetry was an important decorative consideration: the decorative scheme on one horn of the crescent is more or else the mirror image of that on the opposing horn. On some examples one half of a horn's decoration is a mirror image of the other half – divided on a central longitudinal line.

The Unaccomplished lunulae are inferior but close relatives of the Classical type, they are narrower and more crudely decorated. Symmetry was still sought but only roughly achieved as over-run lines, truncated designs and misapportioned spaces show. A broadly similar range of motifs is used and sometimes placed in the familiar zones or panels; sometimes the decoration is placed in a novel fashion longitudinally along the centre of the horn of the crescent. A small number bear no decoration.

While there is a scatter of these lunulae in the south-west, the majority of both types have been found in the northern half of the country. If this distribution pattern of provenanced examples (about 60% of the total) is any guide then the gold resources of the north, in Donegal, Derry, Tyrone and Antrim, may have been exploited rather than the better known Wicklow sources. No Unaccomplished lunula has been found outside Ireland but three Classical examples have been found in Cornwall, one possibly found with a Provincial example near Harlyn Bay.[50] Classical lunulae are generally believed to have been manufactured in Ireland and exported.

With the single exception of a lunula found in a bog at Cooltrain, near Enniskillen, Co. Fermanagh, all Provincial lunulae have been found outside Ireland – hence their name. They are characterized by their thickness and scanty decoration; they also often have distinctive deep crescentic terminals. Ornament may be linear: several incised lines parallel to the edge, perhaps with a simple zig-zag. When uncomplicated panelled ornament occurs it is usually executed in the dot-line technique (an incised line embellished with punched dots). Like some Classical lunulae, these Provincial pieces were also traded or exchanged: the Provincial specimen from Harlyn Bay is identical to one from a hoard of three lunulae from Kerivoa in northern Brittany and all of these may have been manufactured by the one craftsman whose patron or patrons were one link in a chain of contacts which extended from Ireland to southern England to north-western France.

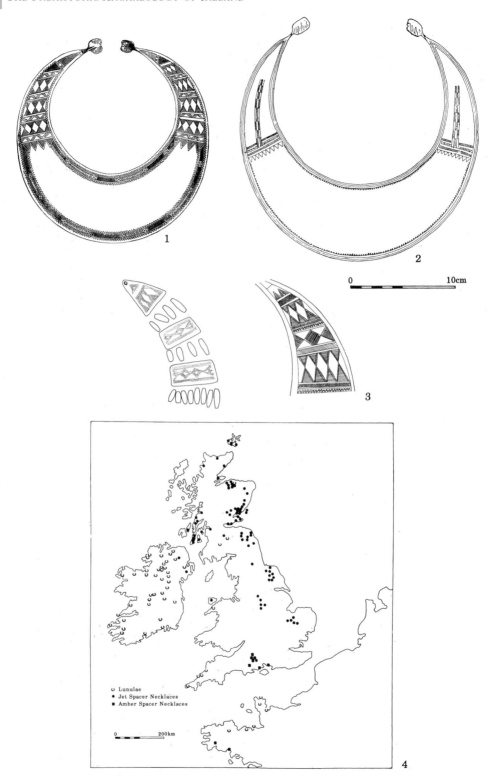

Fig. 53. Gold lunulae. 1. Classical lunula from Killarney, Co. Kerry. 2. One of four Unaccomplished lunulae found at Dunfierth, Co. Kildare. 3. Comparison of part of a jet necklace with spacer beads from Mount Stuart, Bute, Scotland (left), with a lunula from Blessington, Co. Wicklow (right). 4. General distribution of gold lunulae and necklaces of jet and amber.

Though some antiquarian commentators believed lunulae may have served as diadems, their shape and size have long convinced many writers that they must have been decorative collars. However, obvious signs of prehistoric use have been detected on only two and Taylor suggests they may not have been used as personal ornaments very often, if at all, and they may even have decorated inanimate objects like wooden idols. Since they do not occur in burials as personal grave goods, she suggests they may have been the property of the community serving as the insignia of a chieftain or a priest.

The absence of associated finds makes dating of lunulae particularly difficult but the fact that Beaker pottery decoration, in Britain in particular, offers a parallel for every motif found on Classical lunulae prompted Taylor to suggest a Beaker date for this goldwork. Motifs such as hatched triangles, lozenges, lattice patterns, and zig-zags or chevrons are shared, as is the preference for reserved designs and for symmetrical presentation. Stylistic parallels are uncertain dating evidence and lunulae also show a close resemblance to a somewhat later series of necklaces of jet and amber well-known in Britain in the early second millennium and more or less contemporary with Ballyvally and Derryniggin Phase metalwork. The decorated sub-rectangular spacer beads of the jet necklaces in particular recall the panelled decoration of the goldwork. Such necklaces are rare in Ireland but the general distribution pattern does suggest that lunulae may be an Irish version in gold of a widespread fashion for crescent-shaped neck ornaments which finds a commoner expression in either jet or amber in Britain (Fig. 53, 4). These were probably the personal possessions of a minority but all were probably prestigious and symbolic objects. The amber and jet necklaces from graves in Britain are seen as expressions of high status, a further indication of the increasing significance of certain materials in the definition of social relations. The greater use of gold in Ireland may be another expression of this phenomenon and the wide distribution of the lunula fashion, whatever its precise date, may denote, like the distant contacts suggested by other metalwork, a continuing interest by social elites in the acquisition of prestigious objects and a wider network of reciprocal contacts to further this objective.[51]

EXCHANGE AND PRODUCTION

Three Classical lunulae from Cornwall including the one from Harlyn Bay and the parallel, already mentioned, between the Provincial lunula from that site and the example from Kerivoa in Brittany are just some of the indications of far-reaching trade and exchange in the early second millennium. Cornish tin, Irish copper and gold, as well as some finished objects may have travelled considerable geographical distances. Like the polished stone axes of Antrim porcellanite of earlier centuries, metal axes and other items may have been exchanged in various social circumstances. A number of halberds of Irish type have been found on the Continent. An Irish axe found at Dieskau, Germany, may have passed through many hands before being finally deposited in an enormous hoard of bronzes there and several axes from Denmark and southern Sweden have been claimed to be of Irish origin. Reciprocal contacts no doubt allowed Continental fashions to reach these shores and here, perhaps, lies the source of the inspiration for Irish halberds. It is possible that finished products were not the only objects exchanged. The so-called ingots, if that is what they were, may have been a means of transporting raw metal and the presence of broken items or scrap metal in a small number of hoards may reflect some collection and recycling of metal at this early date.[52]

Few certain tools for metalworking have been recognized. The copper and bronze as well as the sheet gold work demonstrate that highly skilled hammering was a very common and important technique as indeed was the subsequent grinding and polishing. Stone or metal hammers were probably used. It has been claimed that some perforated stone implements of sub-rectangular or oval shape were metalworkers' hammers and it will be remembered that part of a perforated, oval, granite hammer was found at Newgrange along with a bronze axe, a quartzite hammer and a rubbing or polishing stone, and these were considered to be the equipment of a metalworker. Two rounded sub-rectangular polished pieces of stone from the north of Ireland have been compared to similar objects from Beaker contexts on the Continent where cushion stones, as they are called, seem to have served as hammers and anvils.

Evidence of early casting methods is provided by a number of stone moulds. Mostly of medium-grained sandstone or similar stone, many are for the production of flat axes. One such mould from Lyre, near Carricknavar, Co. Cork, has two matrices or cavities, for a large and a small axe (Fig. 49, 6). The irregularity of the surfaces around each matrix on this and other similar moulds shows that they are single-piece, open moulds for no cover or lid could have effectively converted them into closed moulds. The objects cast can only have been rough-outs requiring further working: according to M. J. O'Kelly 'a thick rough-out would be drawn out to a larger size than a thin one in the hammer finishing, as one may legitimately assume that the smith did not waste scarce and valuable metal by unnecessary grinding away. In fact, different sizes and shapes of axe can be produced from the same matrix by pouring in more or less metal and by drawing out to a greater or lesser extent in the hammer finishing'. The Newgrange axe, for instance, was shaped by extensive hammering. This is just one of the difficulties facing any attempt to identify the products of a particular matrix in the surviving axe population. Since crucibles of fired clay were presumably a necessary part of the casting process, clay moulds were possibly used at this early date too, but none have yet been found. It is also conceivable that moulds of some substance like sand mixed with animal dung were used and these, not surprisingly, would rarely if ever survive. The cast flanges on some Derryniggin axes, the high midribs on both faces of some halberds all imply the use of two-piece moulds at an early date; the development of the early spearheads with tubular metal collars or short sockets indicates more complex hollow casting.[53]

Important evidence of prehistoric mining activity comes from the south-west where the earliest copper mining in western Europe has been identified at Ross Island on the eastern shore of Lough Leane, Killarney, Co. Kerry, and where over thirty mine workings have been recognized on Mount Gabriel, near Schull, Co. Cork. Excavations by William O'Brien at Ross Island have demonstrated that some early mine workings have survived modern 18th and 19th century mining activity there. Mineralized exposures in the limestone were mined in the period 2400 to about 2000 BC and the workings consist of cave-like openings, the walls displaying evidence of fire-setting to weaken the rock face. Numerous stone hammers were found and these were used at the mine face to crush the extracted rock to allow the sorting of the copper fragments. Charcoal-rich spoil outside the mines contained large numbers of these stone hammers, some modified to take flexible withy handles, and shoulder blades of cattle which were used as shovels. A contemporary work camp was discovered nearby and produced evidence for ore smelting, crushed limestone from the mine workings, traces of several timber huts, animal bones, flints and Beaker pottery. Fragments of stone hammers, anvil stones and comminuted rock indicated that the copper ore was crushed and sorted on part of the site and copper slag testified to smelting in the locality, pit furnaces being used to reduce the concentrate to metal. The arsenic-rich ores at Ross Island were probably an important source of raw material for the copper and bronze artefacts of the Knocknagur and Killaha Phases. In contrast, the arsenic-free copper from the Mount Gabriel mines on the Mizen peninsula in west Cork was mainly exploited in the period 1700-1500 BC.[54]

The Mount Gabriel mining complex has provided a wealth of information about early mining and copper extraction. Some 32 mines have been identified, mostly on the eastern slopes of the hill just below the summit, where beds of copper ore are exposed in the near-vertical rock outcrops. These workings consist of short inclined openings or tunnels which followed the ore-bearing green sandstones in the hard siliceous rock (Fig. 54). The relatively low grade copper necessitated the extraction of large quantities of rock and sizeable spoil heaps outside the bigger mines are characteristic. Mines are up to 10m in length depending on the amount of copper present and on problems posed by water seepage. Workings are small, able to accommodate only a few workers at a time. The smooth concave profiles of the mine walls are one of the telling signs of the use of fire-setting – in which wood fires were lit against the rock face to cause heat fracturing which might be aided by sudden water quenching. Rock was then removed by pounding with stone hammers or mauls. These are mostly rounded sandstone cobbles, about 10cm by 15cm and generally weighing 1000 to 2000g, and very likely collected on the coast at Schull some 4km to the south. Tens of thousands were probably used; easily broken, large quantities of fragments of these hammers were recovered. They were hand-held or hafted and some show light pecking or abrading around part of the circumference to give purchase to a wooden haft; the remains of a flexible twisted withy, possibly of hazel, was found in one

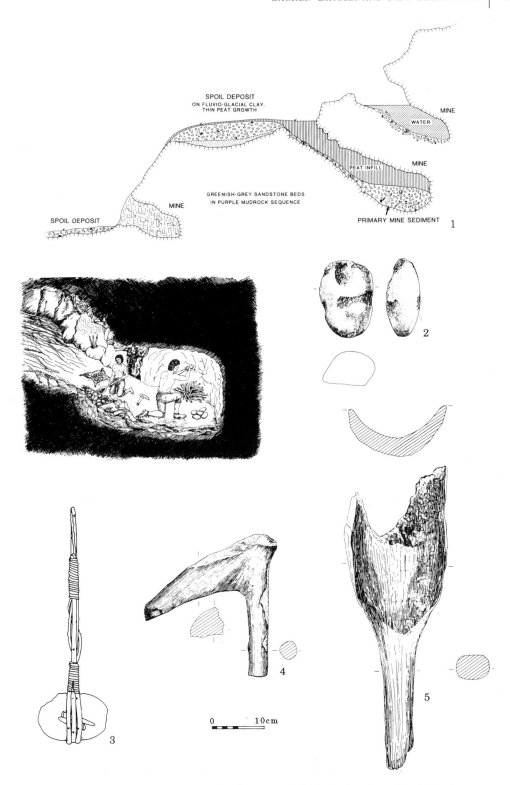

Fig. 54. Mount Gabriel copper mines. 1. Schematic profile of a Mount Gabriel mine based on mines 1-4 and a reconstruction of underground mining with hand-held stone hammers and pine lighting chips (no scale). 2. Stone hammer with modification for hafting. 3. Reconstruction of the hafting mechanism with a flexible withy. 4. Hazel pick. 5. Alder shovel.

mine. Pointed hazel sticks were used to help prize out the heat-shattered rock which was then removed with the aid of wooden shovels and containers of some kind. Pine splints were used as torches at Mount Gabriel and, though none were found, ropes and ladders were probably used as well.

The mineralized rock extracted from the mines was crushed nearby and the ore removed elsewhere for smelting. The location of smelting sites associated with the Mount Gabriel mines remains unknown; they may have been on the mountain or near the coast. Certainly the ten or so wedge tombs on the Mizen peninsula, including those at Altar and Toormore, indicate extensive second millennium settlement there.

The size of the mine workings and the mounds of spoil provide a general indication of the amount of rock extracted but it is difficult to estimate annual ore production. Over a 200 year period the mines as a whole may have yielded anything from 1.5 to 26.5 tonnes of copper but in any one year the production was more likely to have been in kilograms rather than in tonnes. O'Brien suggests that Mount Gabriel may have produced as little as 15–20kg per year, enough to make 40 to 50 bronze axes and requiring a kilogram or less of tin. Tin, a vital raw material in bronze production, must have been obtained through some exchange mechanism, possibly from Co. Wicklow, where cassiterite is associated with alluvial gold. Cornish sources are another possibility. Though the Cork-Kerry region may not have been the only source of copper at this time, the distribution of contemporary metal products such as the developed axes of Types Ballyvally and Derryniggin, which are mainly concentrated in the midlands and the north-east of the country, suggest that ore from Mount Gabriel could have had a wide circulation. The concentration of Type Ballyvally axes along with stone moulds for their manufacture in Antrim and Down suggests important metal workshops in this region and they may very well have been supplied by a long distance metal trade. It is possible that various local communities had access to the Mount Gabriel ores in much the same way that Antrim porcellanite may have been exploited at Tievebulliagh, but given the more complex technology and the fact that axes generally display considerable uniformity, it is more likely that both access and production were controlled and organized. Communities in the locality may have

mined the ore and smelted it into either ingot form or finished products or both which were then transported by land into the Cork hinterland or by boat along the coast. The social differentiation implied by finely crafted objects such as lunulae and reflected in the burial record (below) serves as a reminder elite individuals or groups may have had a controlling role in these metal exchanges.

INNOVATIONS IN THE FUNERARY RECORD

While the wedge tombs of the west and north demonstrate the continuing importance of megalithic tombs in ritual and funerary practice towards the end of the third millennium and early in the second millennium BC, this period also saw the development of novel burial customs and ceramic types. Some of the significant innovations in pottery and in funerary practice were inspired by Beaker fashion, others correspond to contemporary developments in Britain. The burial evidence is varied and complex, some of this diversity in grave form or content reflects changing fashions over a period of time, some variations are regional and others may denote differences in social status. Pottery vessels of different types are the commonest artefacts found with these burials and provide one way of summarizing this diverse body of evidence.

These different pottery types and burial customs overlap with one another and are broadly contemporary with metalworking phases Knocknagur to Derryniggin but because metal artefacts were rarely placed in graves it is still difficult to correlate the major categories of metal objects with the various pottery types from funerary contexts. Our understanding of burial ritual is hampered too by the unfortunate fact that many graves have been casual discoveries in the course of agricultural activities or gravel digging and have often been less than adequately recorded. The scarcity of settlement evidence is also a serious problem. Notwithstanding these difficulties, material from these graves reveals new ceramic fashions and social customs and bone and charcoal are susceptible to radiocarbon dating. Four major pottery and burial traditions are evident: almost a thousand pottery vessels may be assigned to either a Bowl Tradition, a Vase Tradition, a Collared Urn Tradition or a Cordoned Urn Tradition, a ceramic and funerary patterning which implies the existence of ordered social groups.

THE BOWL TRADITION

The pottery of the Bowl Tradition, the so-called 'bowl food-vessels' of some writers, consists mainly of several forms of highly decorated, hand-made bowls usually 8cm to 15cm in height. The exterior is almost always covered with impressed or incised designs and bases and rims are sometimes decorated too (Fig. 55). Impressed ornament is particularly characteristic and the use of comb-impressed lines (as on Beaker pottery) is noteworthy, as is the technique of false-relief in which a line of impressions executed with a triangular-pointed or spatulate implement gives a raised zigzag or chevron or other pattern. The principal forms comprise simple and bipartite bowls, necked bipartite bowls, tripartite bowls and ribbed bowls. The decoration

on simple and bipartite examples is sometimes quite distinctive being often dominated by two broad horizontal zones of the same motif, one on the upper and one on the lower half of the vessel. These zones may contain grooved or whipped cord or comb impressed vertical lines; other motifs such as chevrons in false relief occur occasionally. Necked bipartite bowls, so called because they have a slightly out-turned rim and neck, bear somewhat similar decoration. Multiple horizontal zones of decoration usually executed in false relief or comb-impressed are frequent on tripartite and ribbed bowls and a quite limited series of motifs is repeated in various ways. The principal designs are zones of parallel horizontal lines, chevrons in false relief, short vertical or oblique lines, often forming a

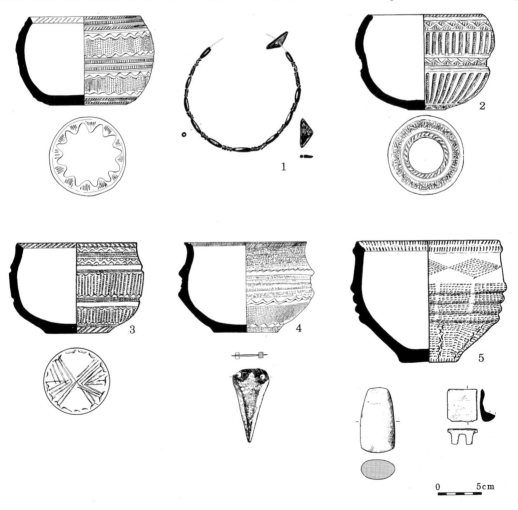

Fig. 55. Pottery of the Bowl Tradition. 1. Simple bowl found with a necklace of jet beads at Oldbridge, Co. Meath. 2. Bipartite bowl with no recorded findspot. 3. Necked bipartite bowl from Crumlin, Co. Dublin. 4. Tripartite bowl and bronze dagger from Corkey, Co. Antrim. 5. Ribbed bowl from Killycarney, Co. Cavan, found with a miniature stone axe and a bone belt hook.

herringbone pattern. Lugs occur on a significant number of tripartite bowls and are rare or absent on other forms. They are usually just low imperforate bosses placed between the horizontal ribs: some were applied, some may have been pinched-up. Four or perhaps six are commonest, equally spaced around the circumference, and a few are perforated. Most of these lugs and particularly those imperforate or minutely perforated examples are obviously decorative renditions of one-time functional features. It is possible that they and false-relief ornament are elements borrowed from the wood-workers' craft. The majority of lugged bowls come from the north of Ireland.

Bowls have been mainly found in the north and east of the country: notably in counties Antrim, Derry, Down and Tyrone, and in Meath, Westmeath, Dublin, Kildare and Wicklow (Fig. 56). Sherds have also been found on a few habitation and ritual sites but the majority are known from funerary contexts. A small number have been found in megalithic tombs: one in the Audleystown, Co. Down, court tomb and several in various passage tombs. These were secondary depositions either in the tomb or inserted into its mound or cairn. Two bowls were found in the Loughash (Cashelbane), Co. Tyrone, wedge tomb and were also considered to be secondary deposits by the excavators; in Kilhoyle, Co. Derry, sherds of the one bowl came from various levels both inside and outside the tomb. Two bowls from Kilmashogue, Co. Dublin, were found in cists which were secondary to the wedge tomb. Fragments of bowl, possibly associated with late Beaker pottery, came from the wedge tombs at Largantea, Co. Derry, and Lough Gur, Co. Limerick.

By far the greater number of bowls has been found in cists or pits, and graves such as these, when they contain a crouched unburnt skeleton

0   1m

Fig. 56. 1. Large rectangular cist grave in a cemetery at Keenoge, Co. Meath, containing the crouched skeleton of an adult female with a bowl placed in front of the face. 2. General distribution of pottery of the Bowl Tradition.

accompanied by a pot, are the classic Irish representatives of the single-burial tradition so popular, for instance, among Beaker communities in Britain. However, the Bowl Tradition burial rite is more varied: about 43% of these bowls have been found with unburnt burials and about 57% with cremations. The unburnt corpse was almost always placed on its side in the grave in a crouched position with the bowl usually in front of or behind the skull. Bowls have been found with the remains of adult males and females, as well as with children. Unburnt burial was popular in the midlands and the south-east; it was occasionally practised in the north but here cremation was commoner. Again these pottery vessels were usually placed beside the pile of burnt bone but on occasion they contained some of the bone as well. In a few rare instances bowls have been found placed mouth downwards with cremated burials. The relatively few cases in which the cremations have been scientifically examined and successfully aged and sexed demonstrate that both adults and children were cremated and now and then the remains of several individuals have been noted in the one grave. Details of burial ritual such as this will be considered further when the interesting and varied funerary ritual of the cemeteries of this period is examined. Since bowls of all types have been found with both unburnt and burnt human remains it would appear that both burial rites were in contemporaneous use and each must have had important and different symbolic significance.

Grave types differed too. Approximately 78% were stone built cists and 22% simple pit graves. Cists were usually short, rectangular slab-built boxes at most large enough to contain an adult corpse in a crouched position: usually with a capstone, they sometimes had paved floors as well (Fig. 56). Some cists were flat graves placed in the earth below ground level with no surviving superimposed monument, others were above ground level but covered by a mound of earth or stones. Why some individuals were accorded very different rites remains an intriguing puzzle: there is some evidence that unburnt burial of both adult males and females in well-made cist graves was a mark of special status. Such graves seem to be in a minority and, from time to time, occupy focal positions in cemeteries.[55]

Some graves may have been isolated single burials, others have been found in cemeteries. At Carrickinab, Co. Down, for instance, a cist was discovered when a plough struck its capstone, it was a small slab-built box, some 70cm in length and 35cm in width internally, and it had a paved floor. It contained a bowl, the cremated bones of an adult (possibly male), a copper or bronze awl, a small flat bronze knife in a fragmentary condition, and two flint scrapers. In contrast a cist at Keenoge, Co. Meath (Fig. 56) contained the crouched skeleton of an adult female and a bowl and was one of fourteen graves in a flat cemetery in which the majority of graves were pit graves (below). A mixture of burial rites and pottery types is a fairly common and puzzling feature of such cemeteries but now and then just the one pottery tradition is represented. A cemetery mound at Corrower, south-east of Ballina, Co. Mayo, consisted of a low circular mound some 13m in diameter without any encircling ditch. It was found to contain nine graves. Eight burials survived and all of these were cremated; five were accompanied by one or more bowls. A majority were unprotected, perhaps placed in small pits; four, however, were in cists. One cist, slightly off-centre, seems to have been the principal grave; this was a small polygonal structure with capstone and paved floor. Three bowls stood mouth upwards on this floor and, in an unusual ritual, they and the cist were filled with fine sand through which were mixed the cremated bones of at least five persons.

There were three burials with bowls in a flat cemetery of some nineteen burials at Edmondstown, Co. Dublin (Fig. 61) which displays much of the funerary variety so frequently found. Two short rectangular cists each contained crouched skeletons with a bowl placed in front of the face while a third contained a deposit of cremated bone also accompanied by a bowl. The other burials were all cremated and the majority lay south and south-west of the cists mentioned. Other pottery included encrusted urn and collared urn.

Artefacts of stone or bronze are now and then found with bowls: flint scrapers (as at Carrickinab) or flint knives (some of the plano-convex type) have been placed in the grave on a small number of occasions. Flint leaf-shaped arrowheads and small polished stone axes have been recorded too. Bronze is surprisingly rare: the small flat bronze riveted dagger from Corkey, Co. Antrim, was found in a cist with an unburnt skeleton and a tripartite bowl (Fig. 55, 4). The much corroded flat bronze blade from Carrickinab is believed, judging from the one rivet recovered, to have been a riveted specimen as well. A small bronze knife, two bowls and several flints, came from a pit grave in that cemetery at Keenoge, Co. Meath. A small hooked bone object, a bowl and a miniature stone axe came from a double-grave at Killycarney, Co. Cavan (Fig. 55, 5); the bone artefact is thought to be a belt-hook and finds a counterpart in gold in a rich contemporary grave, Bush Barrow in Wiltshire. Another exceptional find comes from a double-grave at Oldbridge, Co. Meath, which produced a bowl and a necklace of over sixty jet beads (Fig. 55, 1).[56]

It is possible that bowls contained a funerary offering of food or drink but evidence is lacking; the inturned rims of simple and bipartite bowls would seem to render them unsuitable as drinking vessels. However, the makers of bowls also manufactured a range of vessels: smaller miniature vessels and larger pots have been found. The miniature bowls occur only very occasionally in burials and like other small cups or 'pygmy' cups some specific ritual purpose seems quite likely. Larger vessels are also rare but this may be due to the scarcity of settlement evidence. Sandhills at Magheragallan, Co. Donegal, have produced sherds of some large vessels up to 25cm in height which, judging from the presence of false relief ornament may have affinities with bowls from funerary contexts.[57]

Sherds have been found on various sandhills sites in the north of Ireland including Ballintoy and Whitepark Bay, Co. Antrim, Castlerock and Portstewart, Co. Derry, Ballykinlar and Dundrum, Co. Down, and on a few other habitation sites such as on Dalkey Island, at Lough Gur and on Coney Island in south-western Lough Neagh. On Coney Island traces of prolonged prehistoric occupation were obscured by subsequent activity notably of Medieval and later periods. A few sherds of bowls were associated with what appeared to be rectangular structures, a number of pits and a hearth. In the very small area examined: 'two more or less rectangular cuts into the sand contained compact very dark sandy or clayey charcoal-bearing soil ... In the more easterly cut lines of silt-like white soil were found ... Associated with the white soil in places were very dark patches; and nearby were substantial blocks of apparently burnt timber'. It was suggested that the white soil was decomposed and leached sod representing a sod wall, the dark patches and timber remains being the burnt remnants of posts. Judging from the position of the hearth (believed to have been close to a wall) and of the one possible sod wall, the house – if such it was – may have measured at least 6m in length but only a little over 2m in internal width. To the west, 2m away, lines of dark soil and some stones were thought to indicate a second structure more than 3m long but again only a little over 2m in width. Whatever these features represent, both were associated with sherds of bowl.[58]

As already mentioned, the distribution of these bowls is essentially a northern and eastern one and their scarcity or absence in the west and south is possibly because the use of megalithic wedge tombs was the dominant funerary ritual in these areas. A significant number occur in south-west Scotland and attest to the importance of cross-channel contacts. The development of this Bowl Tradition was clearly stimulated by Beaker practices: the use of comb-impressed ornament and the custom of placing a pot near the head of a crouched unburnt corpse were probably inspired by fashions in northern Britain. But the preference for the use of bowl forms, the choice of a limited range of Beaker decorative motifs, as well as a predilection for cremation reflect a strong non-Beaker element. The Bowl Tradition was a parallel development in Ireland to the Beaker phenomenon (as found in Britain) presumably with a similar funerary purpose and social significance. A series of radiocarbon dates indicates that it was contemporary with some Irish Beakers from wedge tombs and with some vases and dates approximately to the period 2300 to 1950 BC.[59]

THE VASE TRADITION

There is no doubt that the makers of pottery of the Vase Tradition did manufacture a range of pottery sizes for they had occasion to place both small pottery vessels, so-called 'vase food vessels', and large vessels or 'cinerary urns' in graves. In contrast to the Bowl Tradition where the one pot type was placed with either an unburnt or a cremated burial, in this tradition a small vase or a larger vase urn or encrusted urn are all usually found with cremated burials. Unburnt burial is rare, though it does occur with a relatively small number of vases.[60]

Vases are small hand-made, well-decorated pottery vessels usually 11cm to 16cm in height. There are two main forms (Fig. 57, 1-2). One is a tripartite vase with an angular profile, having an everted or even a vertical neck above a sloping shoulder. The distinct neck, shoulder and body give the characteristic tripartite shape. The other is a bipartite vase with a slightly everted rim and a biconical profile often with a rounded shoulder. A small number bear imperforate or perforate lugs on the shoulder; these are found, for the most part, on bipartite vases. The great majority of all vases bears incised decoration on most of the exterior; impressed decoration occurs occasionally (including comb and cord impressions). The principal motifs employed are simple herring-bone patterns, zones of vertical or oblique short lines, and filled triangles.

Like bowls, vases have been frequently found in the east and north but a significant concentration of bipartite vases is found in the west, in Galway and Mayo, and tripartite vases have a curious two-fold distribution pattern, one major group scattered across the north of the country, the other in the east and south-east. Some fragments of vases come from likely habitation sites but most finds come from funerary contexts. A few have been associated with megalithic tombs: sherds of vases were found in court tombs at Ballymacaldrack, Co. Antrim, and Clontygora, Co. Armagh. Like bowls, of course, most have been found in cists or pits. While a small number accompanied unburnt burials (notably in Counties Galway and Mayo), the majority were placed in the grave with cremated remains and here there is some variety in funerary practice. A majority of vases were placed in a short rectangular cist, mouth upwards beside a deposit of burnt bone. This was the case, for instance, in cist discovered at Ballynahow, near Fermoy, Co. Cork (Fig. 57, 3): a slab-built cist (placed in a pit below ground level) was found in the course of ploughing; unfortunately the contents were disturbed but it seems that a miniature vase and a bipartite vase stood mouth upwards on either side of a small amount of cremated bone placed on a floor slab; the bones, unfortunately, were not preserved. In some graves, vases contained some cremated bone or were placed mouth downwards beside the bones (indicating that these pots probably held no offering of food or drink). Vases have been found with the bones of adults as well as children and analysis of the burnt remains has sometimes revealed the presence of bones of more than one individual in the one grave. Vases have sometimes been found as isolated burials but often in cemeteries. While most of these cemeteries have produced a range of pottery types, a small number such as Cloghskelt, Co. Down, and Clonshannon, Co. Wicklow, may possibly be attributed to the Vase Tradition alone.

While objects of stone and metal are also occasionally placed along with vases as grave offerings in burials, the commonest item is another pottery vessel, either a second vase, a larger vase urn or an encrusted urn. This triangular pattern of association contrasts with the relatively infrequent direct associations between other pottery types, and these funerary associations and the typological resemblances between vases, vase urns and encrusted urns are the two reasons for the identification of a distinct Vase Tradition. Just as the proponents of the Bowl Tradition had a varied burial ritual embracing both unburnt burial and cremation, so too those of the Vase Tradition who not only practised cremation and some unburnt burial but also favoured the use of urns. These larger bucket-sized vessels, of sufficient size to hold a deposit of burnt bone, were intended to be either containers for or perhaps when inverted protective coverings for cremated burials. In this the contrast with many vases is apparent – for vases more often than not were placed beside the human remains. This distinction between urns as containers for bones and both vases and bowls ('food-vessels') as supposed containers for food has been emphasized by Rhoda Kavanagh who sees the difference as having 'important cultural connotations'. This sort of explanation, with its traditional view of separate 'food-vessel' and 'urn' communities, presents the related vase urns and encrusted urns as the result, at least in part, of some sort of process of cultural fusion between 'food-vessel' and 'urn' groups.[61]

Other artefacts occasionally found with vases include plano-convex flint knives (like those from Currandrum, Co. Galway: Fig. 57, 2) and, more rarely, bone pins. A faience bead was found with a tripartite vase and a cremation (mixed through a 15cm fill of clay) in a rectangular cist at Ballyduff, Co. Wexford. A small triangular dagger and an awl were found with a bipartite vase and a cremation in a similar cist at Annaghkeen, near Headford, Co. Galway, and a well-known grooved dagger and a strip of gold, possibly decoration for the haft or pommel, were found with an unburnt burial in a cist in a cairn on Topped Mountain, near Enniskillen, Co. Fermanagh, the cist also contained a tripartite vase (Fig. 57, 1) and a cremation possibly representing an earlier burial in the same grave. A series of radiocarbon dates for vases suggest broad contemporaneity with bowls. Like bowls, these pottery vessels were seemingly used as domestic

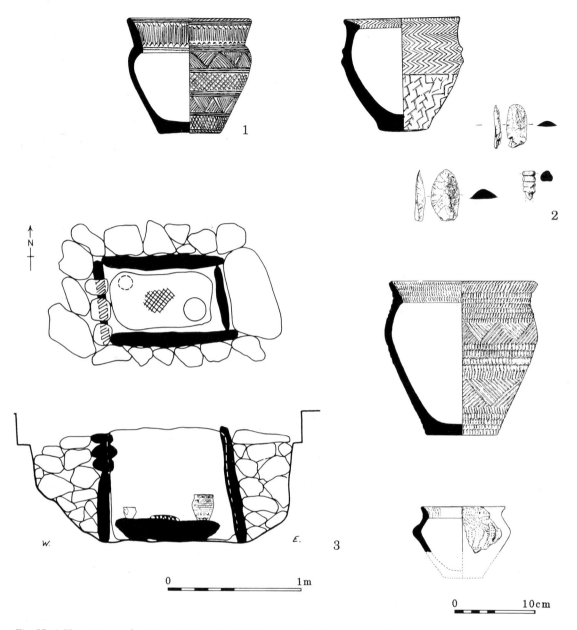

Fig. 57. 1. Tripartite vase from Topped Mountain, Co. Fermanagh. 2. Bipartite vase from Currandrum, Co. Galway, found with two plano-convex flint knives and the head of a bone pin. 3. Bipartite vase and miniature vase found accompanying cremated bone in a rectangular cist at Ballynahow, Co. Cork.

vessels as well, sherds of vase are reported from sandhills sites in the north and from a settlement context on Dalkey Island, Co. Dublin. Possible vase also comes from sandhills at False Bay, near Ballyconneely, Co. Galway.[62]

Vase urns, which have sometimes been called 'enlarged foodvessels' or 'food-vessel urns', are large vessels invariably over 20cm high and average just under 30cm in height (Fig. 58, 1). Though obviously larger than vases and of thicker and coarser fabric, there is a clear typological relationship in both form and ornament between the two. Both the angular form of tripartite vases and the slack, curving profile of bipartite vases are found in the vase urn category. Some of these urns have the sharp shoulder and everted or near-vertical neck of the former and are usually decorated with incised lattice, filled triangle or herringbone motifs. Others have a round

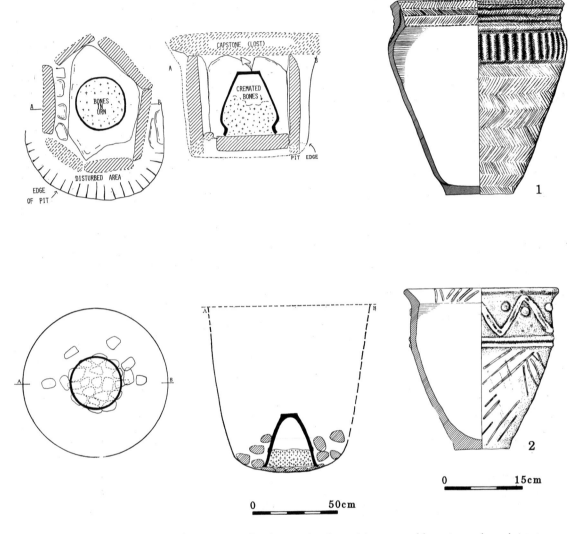

Fig. 58. Urns of the Vase Tradition. Above. Vase urn found inverted and containing cremated bones in a polygonal cist at Ballinvoher, Co. Cork. Below. Encrusted urn found inverted and containing cremated bones in a large pit at Coolnahane, near Kanturk, Co. Cork.

shouldered form with a slightly everted rim, again with a predilection for incised decoration, notably herringbone designs. The distribution of vase urns (and encrusted urns) broadly coincides with the distribution of vases. Minor differences do exist, however; for example, the absence or rarity of these urns in parts of the west from Galway to Donegal, where there is a significant cluster of bipartite vases, is puzzling.

Most vase urns come from funerary contexts: both from simple pit graves and from cists. A few cists were short and rectangular but the majority were polygonal and just big enough to contain the urn. In most cases the vessel was inverted, as at

Ballinvoher, near Castletownroche, Co. Cork (Fig. 58) where a polygonal cist was discovered in the course of bulldozing work on a farm. A vase urn containing the burnt bones of at least one adult and one child had been deposited mouth downwards on the floor-slab of the cist. Presumably a cloth covering or some such had been placed over the mouth of the urn to keep the bones within it. A partly stone-lined pit at Knockroe, near Sion Mills, Co. Tyrone, contained an inverted vase urn which in turn held the cremated remains of five individuals, an adult male, an adolescent female and three children; a fragment of a flint blade, part of a tubular bone object, some burnt animal bones and a plano-convex flint knife were also found in the vessel. Most of these plano-convex flint knives from burials have been found with pottery of the Vase Tradition. A secondary pit burial in a cemetery mound at Grange, near Tulsk, Co. Roscommon, contained an inverted vase urn which held the cremated bones of a young adult male; in the bone deposit lay the twisted remains of a bronze grooved dagger (Fig. 51, 7) and its bone pommel, the dagger had been deliberately twisted and ritually destroyed and burnt on the funeral pyre. Here, though the urn was a crudely-made vessel, the dagger – related to a well-known type found in rich burials in southern England – suggests an individual of exceptional importance. Sherds of vase urn were found in a court tomb at Clontygora, Co. Armagh, and in the Kilhoyle and Largantea wedge tombs in Co. Derry: all were secondary deposits. A secondary cist in the cairn of the Kilmashogue wedge tomb, Co. Dublin, contained an urn of this type also.[63]

Encrusted urns are so called because they bear distinctive encrusted, or applied, ornament (Fig. 58, 2). By and large they tend to be slightly taller and broader than vase urns: over two-thirds have heights and rim diameters in excess of 32.5cm (to a maximum of about 40cm). The larger examples also tend to be the most ornate as far as applied decoration is concerned. A typological relationship to vases and vase urns is evident: a small number of encrusted urns have the familiar angular tripartite form, but a majority have a rounded curving, profile which recalls bipartite vases, sometimes with the slightly everted rim, sometimes with a distinct neck. Encrusted ornament consists of applied strips or bosses of clay and ranges from simple zig-zag or wavy motifs to complex net-like designs on a number of urns which recall vessels suspended in rope netting; applied strips with short incised lines on them may be echoes of strips stitched to leather containers. Incised ornament is also common and simple impressed decoration occurs too. A few of these urns are of such coarse and friable fabric it is a reasonable assumption they were made specifically for burial purposes.

A small number of encrusted urns have been found as secondary burials in or near megalithic tombs of court, wedge and passage tomb type but the great majority have been found inverted (with cremated bones) in pit or cist graves. As with vase urns, simple pits and polygonal cists are the preferred grave types; a small number have been found in rectangular cists. A number of urns have been found with the bones of adults but cremations of children are also reported and occasionally more than one individual is represented. An example from Ballyveelish, near Clonmel, Co. Tipperary, was found inverted in a stone-lined pit along with two cups and the cremated bones of two adults and three children; the grave lay at the centre of a ring ditch and was protected by a timber structure which Martin Doody has interpreted as a mortuary house.[64]

The occurrence of vase and urns of the Vase Tradition in the one grave suggests contemporaneous usage but a number of radiocarbon dates, including a date range of 1890 to 1700 BC for the Grange dagger burial and vase urn, indicate that the urns of this tradition continued in use at least to the end of the 18th century BC. Urns have been recovered from possible habitation sites: sherds of vase urn were found on Dalkey Island, Co. Dublin, and fragments of vase urn and encrusted urn are recorded from various northern sandhills, from contexts which presumably can be described as non-funerary and possibly domestic. The abundant evidence for settlement by makers of vase urns and encrusted urns in Scotland, at Kilellan, Islay, and at nearby Ardnave, for example, shows how reasonable this supposition is.[65]

The Vase Tradition can justly be described as the major pottery tradition of the later third and earlier second millennia in Ireland and, like the Bowl Tradition, it is essentially an indigenous development. The presence of pottery vessels of both these traditions in western and south-western Scotland confirms, if such were necessary, the fact that the narrow stretch of water between north-eastern Ireland and the adjacent parts of Scotland linked the two areas inextricably together. Various commentators have suggested that features on Irish vases such as a shoulder groove with lugs (a characteristic feature of vases in northern England) indicate either contact with or even derivation from the vase series there. The sharing of certain traits may well reflect the exchange of information and material among and between communities through an extensive network of contacts. Two important British urn traditions, represented in Ireland, are probably good examples of this process and a further illustration of cross-channel links. One of these, the Collared Urn Tradition, is the major urn tradition in Britain and has been credited more than once as the general inspiration for the rite of urn burial generally. Arthur ApSimon, for instance, believed the Collared Urn 'culture' responsible for the adoption of urn burial by his 'Food Vessel Group' and the hypothesis that encrusted urns and vase urns are developments of the vase ('foodvessel') under the impact of another urn types is an attractive one, for it could offer an explanation, not only of the vase features of vase urns and encrusted urns, but also of the very rite of urn burial itself in Ireland. But it is quite clear that the urns in question, in their shape or ornament, show no hint of influence from a Collared Urn source. The recognition that this Collared Urn series, the largest urn group of all, had its origins in the third millennium Peterborough ceramic tradition in Britain, supports the notion that urn burial is probably an indigenous insular development, even if a precise inspiration for the custom of placing burnt bones in a pottery vessel is difficult to identify. As the deposition of a cremation in a Carrowkeel pot at Monknewtown, Co. Meath, shows, this was an occasional occurrence at an earlier date, but the practice of consistently inverting an urn remains difficult to explain.

The suggestion that the Irish urns of the Vase Tradition originated in northern Britain has little to recommend it. The dating evidence suggests broad contemporaneity making it rather difficult to convincingly derive one group of urns from another. The majority of Scottish and northern English urns, in fact, echo local vase forms and appear to represent a post-Beaker development parallel to the Irish one, the two traditions displaying clear evidence of reciprocal contacts. Future research may well reveal the significant role that pottery traditions such as Grooved Ware and Beaker coarse wares played in the development of some vases and related urns.[66]

THE CORDONED URN TRADITION

Cordoned Urns are so named because they usually have one or more horizontal cordons or raised ribs encircling their exteriors, with a simple (almost straight-sided or slightly barrel-shaped) or a slightly bipartite profile, and a single horizontal zone of ornament on the uppermost part of the exterior (Fig. 59). The cordons are usually applied or pinched up and, since these vessels are coil built, it has been suggested that cordons might have been made to mark coil junctions; while this may be true

in some cases the presence of narrow, closely-set multiple cordons on some urns and the occasional presence of false cordons, produced by grooving or by impressing pairs of lines, indicates that some were intended to be decorative. This is evident on the superbly-made urn found in a pit in the centre of a small penannular ring ditch at Urbalreagh, Co. Antrim, where the decoration is produced by fine whipped cord impressions. It and the urn from a cemetery mound at Knockast, Co. Westmeath, are examples with simple, slightly curving profiles with simple rims (Fig. 59, 1 and 4). The Knockast urn has an internal cordon just below the rim, an occasional feature of the type. An urn from Laheen, north-east of Ballyshannon, Co. Donegal (Fig. 59, 2), is an example with a bipartite profile. Most cordoned urns are about 30cm or more in height but a number of miniature examples 12cm to 15cm high are known.[67]

As already mentioned, decoration is usually confined to one broad zone below the rim and cord impressed designs are usual, occurring on about 75% of examples. Incised decoration is found on a minority of pots. Other techniques such as comb ornament are rare. Filled triangles, chevron and lattice patterns are favoured motifs and it is worth noting that reserved designs, sometimes in elegant panels as on the Urbalreagh vessel, are a feature of over a third of these urns. A few are undecorated.

The great majority came from burials and the simple pit grave is the commonest type, few have been found in cists. Cremation is the invariable rite and most urns were inverted; a minority stood mouth upwards. Bones of adults both male and female as well as those of children have been identified. Some urns have been found in cemeteries and several interesting instances are known where cordoned urns have been found to be the principal and, sometimes, the only burial in burial mounds. The Pollacorragune urn was found in the centre of a small circular mound; the urn was inverted, half full of cremated bone, and also contained a decorated, tanged bronze razor (Fig. 59, 3).

Sherds of cordoned urns have been recovered from settlement contexts. At Downpatrick, Co. Down, traces of two roughly circular timber houses were uncovered. The remains of an important and extensive habitation were revealed in the course of the construction of a housing estate. Sadly, despite the efforts of archaeologists, the construction work was not postponed and most of the archaeological

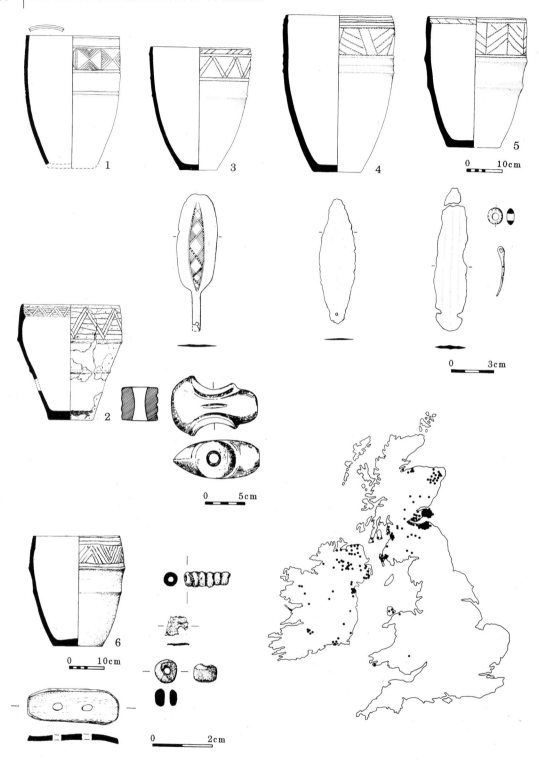

Fig. 59. The Cordoned Urn Tradition and distribution in Ireland and Britain. 1. Urbalreagh, Co. Antrim. 2. Laheen, Co. Donegal, and stone battle axe. 3. Pollacorragune, Co. Galway, and tanged bronze razor. 4. Knockast, Co. Westmeath, and bronze knife or razor. 5. Harristown, Co. Waterford, and bronze knife, quoit-shaped faience bead and bone pin. 6. Kilcroagh, Co. Antrim, and segmented faience bead, stone bead, perforated bone object and fragment of a bronze knife or razor.

remains were destroyed. Only a narrow cutting, for the most part 2m wide and some 42m long, could be excavated, and this only with difficulty. The excavation revealed the greater part of two approximately circular timber houses set about 18m apart, and a few pits, a hearth and some isolated post-holes. A complex stratigraphy survived in the north-eastern half of this cutting revealing at least two separate periods of occupation. The primary, lowest, level (layer 7) rested on the natural sandy boulder clay and consisted of a black layer of charcoal and burnt stone, perhaps evidence of extensive cooking or industrial activity. On either side of this confined spread, a thin stratum of brown clay (layer 6) also rested on the subsoil and contained much charcoal and numerous fragments of pottery. On top of this (layer 5) was a deposit of sandy clay with hardly any charcoal; this was interpreted as a natural deposit, possibly hill-wash onto this low-lying site, indicating a temporary abandonment of part, at least, of the habitation area. Layer 4 was similar to layer 7, containing dark soil and many burnt stones. Layer 2, like layer 4, was an occupation level but both layers produced only a few pottery fragments, a few scraps of burnt bone and a burnt flint. Layer 1, which sealed the site, was a thick deposit of sandy clay, representing more hill-wash.

The bulk of the stratified cordoned urn fragments came from layers 6 and 7 and the former layer covered the floor of the larger of the two structures found (House B). House B had an irregularly circular ground plan and a diameter of about 6.8m; on the north-east its wall was marked by a shallow trench and some stake-holes and post-holes with two posts of a possible porch beyond; more substantial post-holes occurred on the south-west and two pairs on the south suggest the replacement of structural timbers. Two post-holes in the centre presumably helped to support a roof, the purpose of a number of stake-holes is uncertain. This structure was considered contemporary with the adjacent layer 7, charcoal from which provided two radiocarbon dates ranging from about 2400 to 2000 BC. However, charcoal from layer 2 yielded dates of about 1750 to 1500 BC or somewhat later which seem more appropriate for the cordoned urn pottery and agree with broadly similar dates for cordoned urn burials at Altanagh, Co. Tyrone, and Kilcroagh, Co. Antrim.

Only about half of the smaller House A was uncovered: post-holes (one of which contained part of an axe of Tievebulliagh porcellanite) delimited a structure with a diameter of about 4m with a central hearth. Several pits, some with associated stake-holes, were also investigated. Unfortunately, acid soil conditions precluded the survival of any animal remains other than a few cattle teeth. Of particular interest was the fact that though a greater variety of decorative techniques were used, the pottery in general did not differ in any significant way from the funerary series. Perhaps in this instance it is possible to tentatively suggest that a particular pottery style may well be the material expression of a particular community. Sherds of cordoned urn have been found on destroyed habitation sites at Ballyrenan and Sheepland, Co. Down, as well as at Moynagh Lough, Co. Meath, and on a number of sandhill sites in Counties Antrim, Derry and Down.[68]

The Cordoned Urn is an Irish-Scottish type: in Ireland there is a distinct concentration in the north-east, in Counties Antrim, Derry, Down, Tyrone and Louth. Scattered examples extend from Donegal to Inis Oírr, Aran, in Co. Galway, to Counties Limerick and Waterford. The number recorded in Scotland is about double the Irish figure and their general distribution is another indication of Irish-Scottish contact: a scatter of finds links a south-western group of urns in Ayrshire and Wigtownshire (including Arran and Kintyre) with major concentrations in the east and north-east. A few examples are known in northern England, the Isle of Man and Wales. Again the origins and development of this urn group are imperfectly understood. Once thought to be a devolved or degenerate form of the collared urn, it is now considered a distinct tradition different in form but, as far as the evidence goes, broadly contemporary.

Associated finds with cordoned urns are intriguing. The rarity of bronze artefacts in burials generally has been readily apparent but the Cordoned Urn Tradition offers an unusual exception. Some fifteen small bronze knives or razors have been found with as many of these urns and they and a limited range of other artefacts are probably tokens of particular importance.

PRESTIGIOUS TOKENS

The small knives or razors found with cordoned urns may have been male equipment; in the few cases where the cremated bones have been analysed it seems they did accompany male burials. They do occur, albeit rarely, with other pottery types but seem to be a favoured artefact in this burial tradition, both in Ireland and in Scotland. A fine tanged and decorated razor (Fig. 59, 3) was found with the Pollacorragune urn and a somewhat similar but plainer tanged example was associated with a vase and vase urn burial in a cemetery mound at Knockast, Co. Westmeath. The commonest type of blade is a simple, more or less oval, flat knife less than 9cm long usually with one or two rivet holes in a rounded or broadly tanged butt for the attachment of a hilt (Fig. 59, 4). While the name razor may be justly applied to tanged implements like that from Pollacorragune, the purpose of the miniature knives is less apparent. Some were burnt on the cremation pyre and some were not. Their use is uncertain, they may have been shaving implements or have been used for cosmetic mutilation; they do seem to have had some symbolic significance. It is interesting to note that one cordoned urn in a small cemetery at Kilcroagh, Co. Antrim, contained the cremated bones of a male teenager and an adult female, a bronze knife or razor in the urn may have been a male offering, a small faience bead may have accompanied the female. A second similar burial in the same cemetery also contained a fragment of a razor and a faience bead (Fig. 59, 6). In addition to knives or razors and those beads of a glassy substance called faience, a number of bone pins, a few plano-convex flint knives and other flints, and two stone battle axes have also been found with these urns.

While the significance of small bronze blades or single beads may be difficult to determine, the finely made and often highly polished perforated battle axes are evidence of a considerable investment in time and craftsmanship and presumably were items with considerable prestige value. The cordoned urn found at Laheen, Co. Donegal, had been inverted in a pit and contained cremated bones; the stone axe had been placed beside the urn and showed some traces of use: its cutting edge was slightly blunted and its flat butt was slightly abraded (Fig. 59, 2). Another cordoned urn from Ballintubbrid, near Kilmuckridge, Co. Wexford, contained a burnt perforated axe of simpler form and another battle axe, also burnt in the pyre, was found in a collared urn burial in a cemetery in the Mound of the Hostages at Tara. Several types of perforated battle axes are known in

Ireland though – compared to Britain – they are not particularly common. The Laheen and Tara battle axes belong to a distinctive Irish form, the Bann type, characterized by a widely-splayed, crescentic blade, a deeply cut waist, and a truncated-conical butt; decoration, usually in the form of a carved moulding on the sides, also occurs. A number of battle axes from Scotland have affinities with this Bann type and experiments have shown that it takes several days of intensive pecking, drilling and polishing to produce one example. These axes, like the various flint knives, scrapers and other implements occasionally found with other burials, are a reminder that stone work still had significant uses in an age of metal. Indeed for many stone may still have had a predominant role.

The faience beads found in the cordoned urn burials at Kilcroagh, Co. Antrim, are two of a small number of such finds; similar associations with cordoned urns are recorded at Carrig, Co. Wicklow, Longstone, Co. Tipperary, and Harristown, Co. Waterford. At the latter site one of three cordoned urns in a small cemetery contained a faience bead, a bronze knife and a bone pin. Other faience bead finds include Ballyduff, Co. Wexford, where one was found with a cremation and a vase and at the Mound of the Hostages at Tara where an unburnt burial was accompanied by a bronze knife and a necklace of faience, jet and amber beads and of beads of bronze tubing. A biconical cup, a faience bead, a cremation and a (lost) urn was found at Knockboy, near Ballymena, Co. Antrim (Fig. 60, 1). Most Irish beads are of a segmented tubular variety as at Kilcroagh, those from Harristown and Knockboy are circular and flat, a form sometimes called quoit-shaped, and a few are star-shaped. In prehistoric archaeology the term faience is given to a synthetic substance widely distributed in Europe and the Near East in the second millennium in particular. Beads made of powdered quartz or sand with a surface glaze coloured with copper salts to produce a blue-green glassy finish were evidently highly prized and, like amber, some may have been exchanged over considerable distances. Various analyses demonstrate regional groups and production and X-ray fluorescence spectroscopy indicates that Irish beads, for the most part, have a similar tin content to British finds.

The Carrig, Co. Wicklow, association is particularly interesting because the deposition of faience beads was part of a complex ritual sequence.

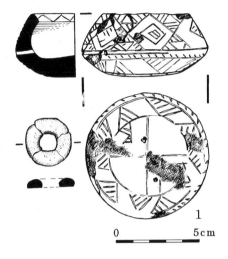

Fig. 60. 1. Biconical cup found with a quoit-shaped faience bead and an urn at Knockboy, Co. Antrim. 2. Collared urn found inverted in a pit at Killeenaghmountain, Co. Waterford, and general distribution.

A rectangular cist grave in a damaged cemetery mound south-east of Blessington was seemingly used on no less than six separate occasions and contained two vases accompanying cremated bones which were covered by a clay filling through which small pockets of burnt bone were mixed; these deposits were followed by three further cremations in inverted cordoned urns inserted into the fill and a final token deposit of a few cremated bones and some coarse pot sherds (Fig. 61, 3). Two of the cordoned urns produced bronze knives or razors, and one also contained a star-shaped and segmented faience beads.[69]

Miniature pottery cups are a rare find with urns of all types; like the limited range of metal and stone artefacts, no cup form is clearly restricted to any one of the major pottery traditions but several have been discovered with cordoned urns. While some of these puzzling cups are evidently miniature bowls or vases, the commonest form is a small biconical vessel no more than 6cm high. Incised geometric decoration is common but a number are plain. About half of these have a pair of small perforations in the shoulder as in the Knockboy cup found with the faience bead. A few related cups have larger triangular perforations in their sides giving them an openwork appearance and these and the perforated cups inspired the suggestion that these small pots were meant to hold a pleasant-smelling substance (such as incense) and they have been variously called 'incense cups' and 'pygmy cups'. Their purpose is unknown but it has also been suggested that they may have served as burners for narcotic substances. Though the evidence is limited, they frequently have been found with the remains of adults, both male and female.[70]

THE COLLARED URN TRADITION

Over 2000 collared urns have been recorded in Britain by Ian Longworth who lists just under sixty from Ireland. A distinguishing feature of these urns is a collared rim above a concave neck (Fig. 60, 2) which gives the vessel a distinctive, angular, tripartite profile. Rims are often broad and flat, or bevelled, and are sometimes expanded internally and externally. Simple rims, as on cordoned urns, are rare. Collars are often concave, sometimes straight and the curvature of the neck may vary from pronounced to slight. The collars and necks are frequently decorated with cord impressed or incised designs; both techniques are more or less equally popular in

Ireland. Lattice, filled triangle and herringbone are the commonest motifs. In a few cases the body below the shoulder is decorated usually with a lattice design. A number of urns are plain.

The majority of these urns (no less than 72%) have been found in the north and north-east, in Counties Antrim, Derry, Down and Tyrone; the remainder have a scattered distribution in the east and south of the country. The general distribution pattern clearly shows how a British fashion impinged on the eastern half of the country. While sherds have been recovered in domestic as well as funerary contexts in Britain, in Ireland they have so far only been discovered in burials, sometimes singly, occasionally in cemeteries. By far the greater number occurred inverted in pit graves and containing cremated bones. Very few were in cists and few were placed mouth upwards. The urn from Killeenaghmountain, near Kilwatermoy, Co. Waterford, is fairly typical: found in the course of gravel working, it had been placed on a flat stone in a pit and protected by another stone on the base. It contained a small quantity of burnt bone, possibly the remains of a child. Bones of adult males and females have been found in these urns too. At Ballymacaldrack, Co. Antrim, where an urn contained the cremated bones of a female and a burnt barbed and tanged arrowhead, it was suggested by the excavator (since an arrowhead seemed an inappropriate funerary offering for a woman) that the flint may have been the cause of her death. At Creggan, Co. Antrim, a plain urn reportedly held the burnt bones of three persons: an adult female, a child, and an infant.

Associated finds with collared urns are relatively few but some are of interest. Several contained small bronze daggers: a small dagger of Type Corkey was found with another Creggan, Co. Antrim, urn, and two collared urns in the cemetery in the Mound of the Hostages, Tara, contained daggers, burnt and broken or twisted out of shape. The burnt stone battle-axe mentioned above was found in one of these urns which was accompanied by an inverted vase. Another bronze dagger was found in an inverted urn at Bay Farm, Carnlough, Co. Antrim, along with a shell button and carved piece of chalk.[71]

In Britain the radiocarbon evidence suggests that the Collared Urn Tradition was prominent from about 2000 to 1500 or 1400 BC, their chronological position in Ireland is less certain but may have been similar.

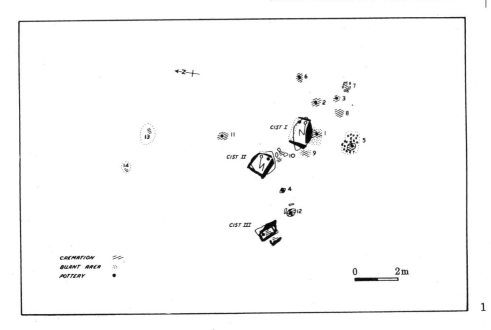

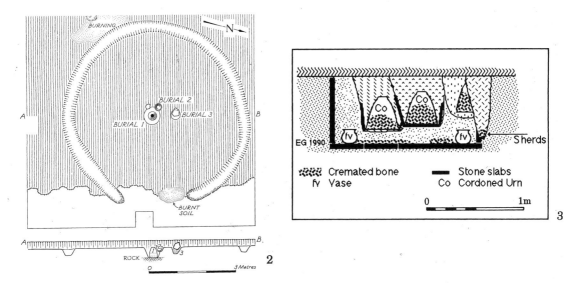

Fig. 61. 1. Simplified plan of a flat cemetery at Edmondstown, Co. Dublin. 2. Ring ditch containing three urn burials at Urbalreagh, Co. Antrim. 3. Cist grave containing successive burials in a cemetery mound at Carrig, Co. Wicklow.

These burials with their occasional grave goods were the interments of representatives of small agricultural communities whose settlements remain elusive but were presumably nearby. Most of the burials and pottery mentioned in the preceding pages were casual discoveries in the course of ploughing, gravel digging and other such activities, and many, unfortunately, were disturbed and further damaged by the finders. This was particularly the case with flat graves – cists or pits *in* the ground

with no surviving superimposed monument or marker – but mounds containing burials were frequently damaged too. Thus an enormous amount of information about details of burial ritual has been irretrievably lost. Some burials appear to have been isolated, solitary interments, a number occur in small groups of two or three, and others were grouped in small cemeteries. Whether those solitary burials were actually just one of a group destroyed in the past or one of a group just not detected is often an unanswerable question. The last-mentioned certainly has happened: at Cloghskelt, Co. Down, two urn burials were accidentally found many decades before an excavation in the area in 1973 undertaken after a further accidental discovery revealed that the old finds were but two graves in a flat cemetery of over twenty burials. Charles Mount has shown how the circumstances of discovery have significantly influenced the present picture: it is clear that pit graves are under-represented because ploughing in particular has led to the discovery of more cists than pits. Thus small groups of cists are probably the remnants of larger cemeteries where pits were not recognized. Solitary burials do occur however, some burial mounds which have been carefully excavated have produced just one grave: Pollacorragune, Co. Galway, with its cordoned urn burial mentioned above, and a vase urn burial found at the centre of a very low mound with encircling ditch at Lissard, Co. Limerick, are just two examples; it is clear that some flat graves may indeed have been isolated ones. Such may have been the case at Ballyveelish, Co. Tipperary, where an encrusted urn was found with the cremated bones of five individuals and where the one grave was, in effect, a small collective burial.

Judging from the poorly documented evidence, sites with just two or three graves are surprisingly numerous (comprising about 58% of all multiple grave sites). Small cemeteries of four to ten graves represent about 32%, larger cemeteries of eleven to nineteen graves about 8%, and more extensive sites of more than twenty are rare: only about 2%. Mount has shown that in the south-east of the country the average number of graves is four and three is the most common number but many of these are sites with only cists recorded. In the mixed cemeteries (those with cists and pits) the average number is higher, about six. Thus the relatively large number of very small sites is due in part to inadequate or incomplete excavation and to the failure to discover or recognize pits. However, it is still apparent that in most instances only small numbers were given formal burial and not everyone was entitled to this privilege.

There are two contrasting forms of cemetery: flat cemeteries where the graves have no surviving superimposed monument, and cemetery mounds where a round mound or cairn may contain a number of graves. Since many burials were not accompanied by a pottery vessel, be it bowl, vase or urn, a summary of the pottery traditions is not a summary of burial fashions. The cemeteries of the time offer a clearer picture and a number of well-excavated examples are excellent illustrations of the remarkable diversity of burial practice and provide important information about the social significance of some of the complex variations in the funerary record.[72]

FLAT CEMETERIES

Most flat cemeteries have been incompletely or inadequately recorded but Cloghskelt, Co. Down, is one of the few to have been excavated in recent years. In addition to an encrusted urn burial, and a vase urn 'in a small stone cist', found years before, the flat cemetery contained a further twenty-three graves within an area measuring about 13m by 5m. One grave was a small and approximately polygonal cist holding a vase urn and a vase, another, possibly the remains of a long cist, contained two vases. The other graves were pit graves, some protected by one or more stones. Nine contained no pottery and, apart from a few stray sherds of bowl found, all the pottery was of the Vase Tradition, mostly vases but a vase urn and several encrusted urns as well. Other grave offerings were few: a plano-convex flint knife and a flint convex scraper, for instance. An interesting feature of the site was the apparent division of the cemetery into two areas: a southern concentration of burials consisted of urns and vases, while only vases were found in a northern group. Whether this reflects some social distinction or is of chronological significance is not clear. Excavation also revealed the possible cremation site; a thick black deposit containing minute fragments of burnt bone covered an area about 9m by 6m. Evidently at least some of the dead were buried near the remains of their funeral pyre.

While a very small number of cemeteries seem to contain just one pottery tradition, in most cases a mix of traditions is present. This was the case at the Edmondstown, Co. Dublin, flat cemetery. Here it seems four rectangular cists may have formed the nucleus of a cemetery of some nineteen burials (Fig. 61). Cist I contained the crouched skeleton of a young adult male lying on his right side with a bowl mouth upwards in front of the face. An irregular hole had been cut in the left side of the skull and may be an early instance of trephination – an operation sometimes performed to relieve pressure on the brain after injury.[73] Cist II contained the crouched skeleton of a teenager with a bowl standing in front of his or her face; the cist was almost filled with soil containing both burnt and unburnt bone. A mixture of clay fill and cremated bone (of a young adult male) was found in Cist III along with another bowl. Cist IV was a small addition to III and just contained the cremation of an adult male. Most of the other burials were situated south and south-east of the cists and were all cremations. Some of these were just scatters of bone but others were pit burials; the accompanying pottery included complete or partially complete vase urns, encrusted urns and collared urns. One of the pit burials with an inverted encrusted urn contained the bones of four individuals and another burial was a collared urn containing the cremated bones of three persons. Several cremations had no accompanying pottery.

Apart from the two unburnt individuals in Cists I and II, the cremated remains represented 27 individuals including four adult males, one adult female and six adults of uncertain sex, four children, three to four infants and eight deposits of bone which were unidentifiable. All the burials in the cists were adults and all but the youth in Cist II were positively identified as male. These were the only burials associated with bowls. This contrasts with the treatment of women and children who were all cremated, though some adult males were cremated as well. A similar pattern occurs in the cemetery mound at Knockast (below). Another interesting feature at Edmondstown was the number of multiple burials in the one grave: three of the nineteen (16%) contained the remains of more than one person and these were mostly children and infants with the occasional adult. This pattern of adult males predominating in single interments and women and children figuring more in multiple burials has also been noted by Charles Mount in southern Leinster generally and by Martin Doody in Munster.[74]

At Keenoge, near Duleek, Co. Meath, a flat cemetery of 14 graves was gradually uncovered in a low esker from 1929 to 1936 in an area measuring about 14m by 10m. A mix of cist and pit burials was found and only a minority was cremated. Two small cists simply contained cremations, a third contained the unburnt remains of an infant, several pit graves held crouched skeletons – none of these accompanied by any pottery. A polygonal cist contained a cremation and

an encrusted urn and a vase urn. Bowls and crouched skeletons occurred in three pit graves and in two rectangular cists. One of these pit graves was distinguished by a paved floor and contained the crouched skeleton of an adult female, two bowls, a small bronze knife and several flints; a small deposit of cremated bone was found beneath and behind the head of the skeleton. One cist was built of massive stones (Fig. 56, 1); it contained the crouched skeleton of an adult female and, in addition, to a bowl in front of the skull, had two more placed outside it, on either side. These two burials would seem to have been the most important in the cemetery but a simple pit contained the crouched skeleton of a young adult female with a necklace of 40 jet beads around her neck, an unusual grave offering. Like at least two of the cremations and six other unburnt burials this grave contained no pottery and while it might be assumed that the crouched skeletons should be assigned to the Bowl Tradition, certainty is not possible and they could be of earlier or later date. A minimum of 26 individuals were represented in the cemetery with adult males predominating (64%) and children and infants clearly under-represented. However, it is also evident that when some women were accorded formal burial they sometimes received exceptional treatment. The high proportion of multiple burials is also noteworthy, with five single and nine multiple interments (69%). Some of the graves may have been used for successive burials, as was so clearly demonstrated at Carrig, Co. Wicklow (Fig. 61, 3). Judging from a number of radiocarbon dates for human bone samples, the Keenoge cemetery was used for at least 500 years, and possibly for as much as 760 years perhaps with just one or two burials taking place in each generation.

Given the limited extent of excavation at sites such as Keenoge it is unclear if cemeteries were normally enclosed or not. At Urbalreagh, south-east of Portrush, Co. Antrim, a penannular ring ditch with a diameter of about 6m surrounded three burials (Fig. 61, 2). The central pit burial (no. 1) was a fine inverted cordoned urn (Fig. 59, 1) containing the burnt bones of a male and the remains of a possible razor or knife. A secondary urn (no. 2) and the burnt bones of a child were placed in the upper levels of this pit and a third cremation (no. 3) representing part of the remains of a juvenile were placed in a pit just to the north. The positions of these burials may once have been marked by very low mounds. On the south-west, the ring ditch had cut through an area of intense burning which produced some small pieces of cremated bone and may have been the site of a funeral pyre.[75]

CEMETERY MOUNDS

A number of cemetery mounds have been scientifically excavated but many have been less than adequately recorded in the past. The term embraces earlier mounds re-used for multiple burials in the later third and second millennia, as well as circular mounds specifically constructed to cover several burials, or perhaps built to cover just one or two graves with secondary burials inserted at a later date. On present limited evidence there seems to be no great difference in the variation in numbers in cemetery mounds or flat cemeteries, though two cemetery mounds are exceptional in having over forty burials: Knockast, Co. Westmeath, and the Mound of the Hostages, Tara, Co. Meath. Presumably the unusually large number at the latter site, at least, is in some measure an indication of Tara's exceptional importance in early as well as later prehistory. At Tara, as occasionally elsewhere, an earlier monument was re-used as a burial place. The primary monument here was a small undifferen-tiated passage tomb covered by a circular cairn with 1m thick covering of clay. Some of the original contents of the tomb had been cleared out to make room for several unburnt crouched burials with bowls and a large number of other secondary burials were inserted into the mantle of clay. Some forty burials were found, all but one cremated. The one unburnt burial is of unusual interest: it was the unprotected skeleton of a youth, lying on its back with the legs flexed. There was no pottery but a necklace of beads of jet, amber, faience and bronze tubing lay in the neck area and a small bronze knife and a pin or awl had been placed beside the corpse. Among the urn burials were encrusted and collared urns, and two cups were also found. Important grave goods included the necklace just mentioned, a stone battle axe and bronze daggers.

The re-use or augmentation of older mounds is recorded elsewhere too: at Baunogenasraid, Co. Carlow, a mound covering a Linkardstown type grave was enlarged to contain at least ten burials, all in shallow pits protected, in a few cases, by some small stones. Both cremated and unburnt crouched burials occurred in the secondary mantling and two

of the latter (one with a bowl) were disturbed by subsequent cremations. The remains represented both adults and children. The well known passage tomb at Fourknocks I, Co. Meath, was also used as a later cemetery. A secondary mantling of clay was spread only over part of the northern half of the original mound. This covered four of five cists which had been constructed in pits dug into the primary mound. No bones were found in one cist but four held the unburnt remains of children, one with a bowl. Three pit burials were also found: fragments of a bowl and some human teeth were all that survived of one, the other two were cremations in inverted vase urns. Bowl and urn also accompanied secondary burials placed at the periphery of the mound of the undifferentiated passage tomb at Harristown, Co. Waterford. Here a bowl contained cremated bones and the three urns found were of the Cordoned Urn tradition; one of these (Fig. 59, 5), in addition to the burnt bones of a young male adult, contained a small bronze blade, a bone pin and a quoit-shaped faience bead.[76]

The radiocarbon dating of some material from a 1934 excavation of a cemetery mound at Poulawack, in the Burren, Co. Clare, suggests the possibility of remarkable ritual persistence in some cases (Fig. 62). The primary burial on the site was a polygonal cist related to the Linkardstown type of grave and dated to 3614-3373 BC (Graves 8 and 8A) which was probably covered by a low cairn and encircled by a stone wall or kerb with a diameter of about 10m. A thousand years later, towards the end of the third millennium, a rectangular cist (Grave 4) containing the unburnt remains of an adult and a child was inserted into the cairn at a point where some of the kerb may have been removed. Two other cists (Graves 5 and 6) were inserted about this time as well and these various acts could have taken place over several generations. Towards the middle of the second millennium BC, the cairn was enlarged, it was heightened by about 1m and extended by about 2m around its circumference. Judging from the radiocarbon evidence Graves 1 and 3 were added or incorporated at this time and Graves 2 and 7 were then evidently inserted into the enlarged cairn. Far from being a simple and relatively short-lived cemetery containing the remains of some 16 people, mostly unburnt, with no significant grave goods, this complex monument had a protracted ritual significance for at least 1800 years. The evidence suggests three periods of funerary activity

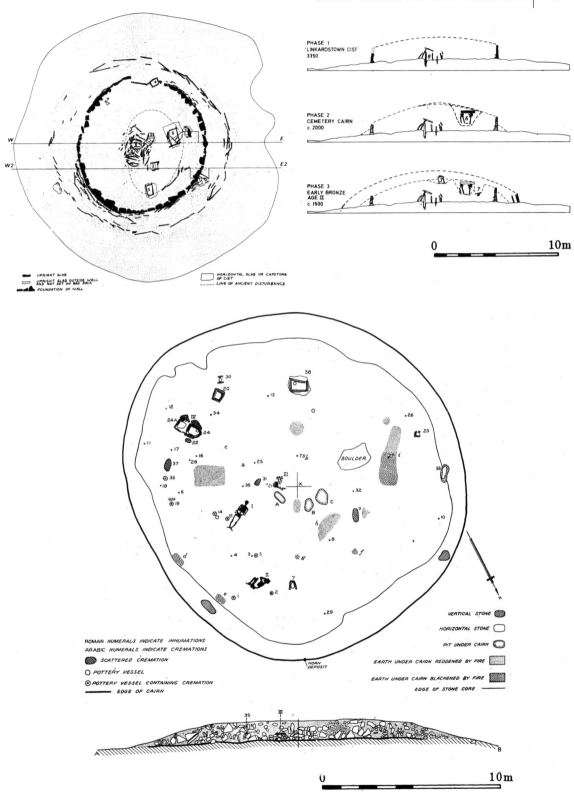

Fig. 62. Above. Cemetery mound at Poulawack, Co. Clare, with simplified section showing sequence of burials.
Below. Cemetery mound at Knockast, Co. Westmeath.

in this long timespan but during this millennium and a half Poulawack, a prominent monument on a broad limestone plateau, may well have been a focus for other sorts of ritual observance which have left no archaeological trace.[77]

A shorter span of activity of several centuries probably obtained at Moneen, just south of Glanworth, Co. Cork, where a circular cairn enclosed by a shallow annular ditch covered four cists. A primary, central cist was of massive megalithic construction and it contained the unburnt bones of a male and a possible female, placed on a paved floor. At some later date, these were displaced and the cremation of a youth spread on the floor. This cist was surrounded by a kerb of large stones, one inturned slab on the north-east conceivably being the remains of an entrance. Three subsidiary cists lay to the west of the central grave; two on the pre-cairn surface, one partly on this surface and partly on the lowest layer of cairn material. The latter contained the disturbed unburnt bones of an adult male, a diminutive cist was empty, and a third (only about 90cm by 55cm internally) held the disarticulated unburnt bones of a male, a female and a child, whose remains must have been stored for a period elsewhere, and defleshed, to allow them all to fit in this grave. Two further burials were found near the cairn on the south-west, one an encrusted urn burial had been placed within an arc added to the annular ring ditch which encircled the cairn; the other a cremation and bowl sherds had been disturbed when this added arc was dug. Several pits, some spreads of charcoal, Beaker pottery, a few fragments of a human skull (some burnt), a few flints and a scatter of stake- or post-holes were found beneath the cairn and within the area of the ring ditch. This activity could have been either temporary occupation or of some ritual significance and radiocarbon dating now places it to the period 2854-2294 BC. The central grave is radiocarbon dated to 2284-2046 BC (from human bone). The other cists are probably broadly contemporary and the two other burials associated with the extension to the ring ditch are somewhat later.[78]

The cemetery mound at Knockast, near Moate, Co. Westmeath (Fig. 62) was a broad, low, flat-topped, kerb-less, circular mound just over 18m in diameter and with a maximum height of 1.2m. It was situated on the summit of a low but conspicuous hill. Excavation in 1932 revealed a core of clay and stones covered by dark soil. Burials were found both on the old ground surface and at different depths within the cairn. One unburnt, extended, adult male skeleton found about 50cm beneath the surface in the eastern half of mound disturbed two cremated burials and because it differed somewhat in physical type from the other unburnt burials, it was thought to be of different date. In fact its date is unknown and while extended burial is unusual in early prehistory, it does occur. Burial 2 was the unburnt skeleton of a man in the more usual crouched position which lay at the base of the cairn. This unfortunate individual suffered from chronic arthritis and as a youth had an abscess of the inner ear which had left his face badly distorted. The only find in the grave was a pig's tusk. Unburnt burials 3 and 4 were disturbed by subsequent cremations. In addition to these four unburnt burials, thirty-nine cremations were found, the majority of all burials being in the eastern half of the mound. The cremations were placed in cists in a few instances, in spaces between the stones of the cairn, on the earth at the base of the cairn, or in small pits made in the old ground surface. Ten cremations were accompanied by pottery, in some cases so decayed as to be unrecognizable, but which included bowl (cremation no. 28), encrusted urn (no. 2), vase and possible vase urn (no. 14), vase urn (no. 15) and cordoned urn (Fig. 59, 4) found with cremation no. 36. The latter was the cremated burial of an adult male accompanied by a small bronze knife or razor. Other grave goods included a small decorated bronze knife and a plano-convex flint knife with cremation 18 and small bone cylinders (no. 6). The excavator noted that the burials accompanied by non-pottery artefacts such as these were confined to a restricted area near the south-eastern edge of the cairn. Some two dozen cremations had no accompanying grave goods of any description.

A study of the cremated bones revealed the remains of 20 males, 8 females and 12 individuals among whom sex characteristics were not clearly defined, probably because these bones were more fragile and had disintegrated more in the intense heat of the pyre. If these were the remains of females, the unusual preponderance of males over females would be reduced. Only two female burials (nos 2 and 30) were accompanied by pottery and all the bronze items were found with male burials. Of the forty individuals identified in thirty-nine burials (one was a double burial) only eleven could be identified as having reached middle or old age (that is over 36 years of age). A high mortality rate up to and in early adulthood would be normal in early prehistoric societies. In studying the Knockast bones, Movius detected an interesting difference between the people who were buried unburnt who were of larger and more rugged appearance, and those who were cremated who were of a smaller and more light-limbed physical type. He thought this pointed to a racial difference between the two, but socio-economic circumstances, or better diet or different work patterns, could be a causal factor too. Beneath the Knockast mound there were three clearly defined pits containing earth, charcoal and bones of cattle, horse, and sheep or goat; there were also patches of well burnt earth and charcoal, and some fragments of plain pottery of possible fourth millennium date.

There was no obvious primary or focal burial in the Knockast cemetery but since a few graves disturbed others, there clearly was a sequence of burials there. Other cemetery mounds such as Cornaclery, Co. Derry, with five graves and Corrower, Co. Mayo, with nine graves had more or less centrally placed primary graves with the majority of the other burials being placed on the eastern and southern sides of the mound respectively.[79]

The variation in numbers of burials, in types of grave, in the rituals practised, and in the range of grave goods found is a remarkable feature of cemeteries, both flat cemeteries and cemetery mounds. They offer a conspectus of the variety of burial rite and funerary pottery of the period. Some, such as Knockast, could have been the communal burial place of a small community, the different pottery types perhaps reflecting changes in ceramic fashion through time, or different social caste or ancestry, or even family affiliation. A relatively small number of cemeteries have contained pottery of just one tradition but more commonly two or more pottery traditions are represented. There is evidence that only a fraction of the members of a family or community were formally buried, others presumably disposed of in other ways. There is also growing evidence that some individuals had special status though clear evidence of a social hierarchy is still lacking. The occasional mixture of pottery types, particularly in small burial groups such as Harristown, Co. Waterford, with a bowl and three cordoned urns,

suggests that some mixed deposits may have had some magico-religious, social or political significance, rather than just a funerary one.

It is perhaps not surprising that pottery fashions and burial customs such as these should eventually cease. What is intriguing is that they are apparently not followed or replaced to any extent by new pottery or equally visible funerary customs. Once again the nature of the archaeological record, at least as we perceive it today, undergoes a significant change. The decline in formal burial practice was possibly a gradual one and may have varied from place to place. The date of the demise of the different types of urn is not yet clear and the significance of this change is uncertain. Cremations placed in plain coarse bucket-shaped urns, as at Tankardstown, Co. Limerick, for instance, are often considered to denote the end of the urn burial tradition. There is no suggestion of social decay or economic disintegration. Other less visible or less easily detectable forms of disposal of the dead were presumably adopted. Simple cremations in pits, or token burials of very small amounts of burnt bone, may have become the norm and several burial sites or possible burial monuments may be assigned to this period. A U-shaped ring ditch at Shanaclogh, near Croom, Co. Limerick, enclosed several pits some of which contained minute quantities of burnt human bone. Some 20 low barrows or ring ditches were investigated by S. P. Ó Ríordáin in 1935 in the vicinity of Lissard, near Galbally, Co. Limerick, and only one produced a few fragments of cremated bone. Excavation of a ring cairn at Carnkenny, near Ardstraw, Co. Tyrone, which consisted of a low annular bank of stones encircling a small central cairn, revealed that the cairn covered a series of small pits containing earth, charcoal and scraps of burnt bone. A small annular ring ditch just under 3m in diameter at Ballybeen, Dundonald, Co. Down, enclosed a very small scatter of cremated bone and no burial was found in a ring barrow at Cahercorney, north-east of Lough Gur, Co. Limerick. A series of barrows at Mitchelstowndown West, Knocklong, Co. Limerick, also produced no evidence of burial and Eoin Grogan has suggested that a tradition of token burial had there progressed to the stage where barrows became cenotaphs without formal burials.[80]

From at least 1500 BC, contemporary in part with this period of funerary change, new developments in bronze types are characteristic of the metalwork of the Killymaddy Phase. The relative scarcity of settlement evidence means greater emphasis is still placed on the study of the surviving metalwork in this phase and indeed in the later prehistoric period generally. More so than ever

before the archaeological evidence consists of a wide range of metal types whose study offers interesting insights into society and technology and new interpretative challenges as well.

NOTES

1 Goodland, Co. Antrim: Case 1973; radiocarbon date from pit: 4575 ± 135 BP (3630-2920 BC, UB-320E), a general terminal date is provided by a sample of basal blanket peat dated to 4150 ± 200 BP (3340-2150 BC, D-46). Herity 1982, 265, 359, considers Goodland a problematical habitation site; however, the ritual interpretation is a plausible one. Ritual deposition is a widespread phenomenon: Thomas 1991, 56.

2 Langford Lodge, Co. Antrim: Waterman 1963. Scotch Street, Armagh: Lynn 1988. Rathjordan, Co. Limerick: Ó Ríordáin 1947a and 1948. The annular ring ditch at Moneen, Co. Cork, is now believed to post-date the cairn: Brindley et al. 1988. Case 1961 has suggested that various sites including Langford Lodge and deposits found beneath a variety of prehistoric burial mounds and megalithic tombs were ritual Goodland-type monuments and, of course, 'places recognized as sacred can be made permanent by monument building' (Cooney 1994, 35). Most but not all pre-court tomb activity is judged habitational by Herity 1987.

3 Monknewtown, Co. Meath: Sweetman 1976; radiocarbon dates (*Radiocarbon* 16, 269): 3810 ± 45 BP (2456-2138 BC, UB-728) from hut; from hearths: 4750 ± 65 BP (3688-3372 BC, UB-732), 2445 ± 40 BP (764-406 BC, UB-729), 2495 ± 70 BP (798-410 BC, UB-730), 1130 ± 70 BP (716-1022 AD, UB-731), 2440 ± 65 BP (768-404 BC, UB-733), 3465 ± 80 BP (2028-1536 BC, UB-734).

4 Stout 1991; also Banagher, Co. Cavan: O'Donovan 1995, 13; Carn and Creevagh South, Co. Mayo: Lavelle 1994, 11, 60; Knockadoobrusna and Ballinphuill, near Boyle, Co. Roscommon: Condit 1993a; and possibly Dun Ruadh, Crouck, Co. Tyrone, where the ditch has a terminal radiocarbon date of 2137-1940 BC (UB-3047): Simpson 1992, 1993a; Coogaun, Co. Clare: Condit et al. 1994; Clashwilliam, Co. Kilkenny: Gibbons 1990, 6; and Longstone, Cullen, Co. Tipperary: Raleigh 1985.

5 Ballynahatty, Co. Down: Giant's Ring: Collins 1957a; timbers circles: Hartwell 1991, 1994. Knowth, Co. Meath, timber structure: Eogan and Roche 1997a, 101; radiocarbon dates obtained from charred material attached to the interior of sherds of Grooved Ware from post-holes: 3985 ± 35 BP (2588-2458 BC, GrA-448) and 4130 ± 35 BP (2876-2594 BC, GrA-445).

6 Newgrange pit circle: Sweetman 1985; a series of 13 radiocarbon dates range from 4070 ± 40 BP (2866-2502 BC, GrN-11800) to 3885 ± 70 BP (c. 2500-2200 BC, GU-1619). Newgrange 20m timber circle: Sweetman 1987; radiocarbon dates from pits: 4000 ± 30 BP (2590-2464 BC, GrN-12828) and 3930 ± 35 BP (2568-2340 BC, GrN-12829).

7 Grange, Co. Limerick: Ó Ríordáin 1951; Burl 1976, 227; Ó Nualláin 1995, 19.

8 Millin Bay, Co. Down: Collins and Waterman 1955. Ballynoe, Co. Down: Groenman-van Waateringe and Butler 1976. Castlemahon, Co. Down: Collins 1956. Kiltierney, Co. Fermanagh: Daniells and Williams 1977.

9 O'Connell 1990.

10 Harrison 1980.

11 Influential studies of insular Beakers include Clarke 1970, Lanting and Van der Waals 1972, Gibson 1982, and Case 1993, 1995, 1995a.

12 Style 1 Beakers (AOO or AOC): Newgrange: O'Kelly et al. 1983, fig. 23; Knowth: Eogan 1984, 263 ff; Dalkey Island: Liversage 1968; Lough Gur: Ó Ríordáin 1954; Whitepark Bay, Co. Antrim: ApSimon 1969, 58; Loughash (Cashelbane), Co. Tyrone: Davies and Mullin 1940, pot C; see also Clarke 1970.

13 Style 2 Beakers: Clarke's 1970 European (E) Beaker incorporating the Continental Maritime Beaker type, and Wessex-Middle Rhine, North-Middle Rhine, North-North Rhine and Primary North British-Dutch Beakers. Moytirra, Co. Sligo: Madden 1969. Lough Gur: Ó Ríordáin and Ó h-Iceadha 1955.

14 Cluntyganny, Co. Tyrone: Brennan et al. 1978. Monknewtown, Co. Meath: Sweetman 1976. Rockbarton, Co. Limerick: Mitchell and Ó Ríordáin 1942. Tirkernaghan, Co. Tyrone: Earwood 1992; 3960 ± 100 BP (2870-2150 BC, OxA-3013); the small cups are illustrated in Bigger 1917, fig. 3.

15 Case's Style 3 includes Clarke's 1970 later Northern and Southern Beakers. Moneen, Co. Cork: O'Kelly 1952; Brindley et al. 1988. Ballyedmonduff, Co. Dublin: Ó Ríordáin and De Valera 1952.

16 Longstone, Cullen, Co. Tipperary (unpublished): Raleigh 1985, 17. Parknabinnia, Co. Clare: Jones 1996.

17 Beaker settlements: Knowth, Co. Meath: Eogan 1984; Eogan and Roche 1997a; Monknewtown, Co. Meath: Sweetman 1976; Newgrange, Co. Meath: O'Kelly et al. 1983, radiocarbon dates: sample no. 3 with AOO sherds: 3885 ± 35 BP (2488-2284 BC, GrN-6342); sample no. 4 with plain bowls: 3990 ± 40 BP (2850-2458 BC, GrN-6343); metalworking activity: O'Kelly and Shell 1979; animal bones: Van Wijngaarden-Bakker 1974, 1986a. Cooney and Grogan 1994, 79, fig. 5.2, suggest a cluster of about 14 circular or oval houses 5-6m in diameter.

18 Mount 1994.

19 Site D, Lough Gur, Simpson 1971. Site L, Lough Gur: Grogan and Eogan 1987, 385. Donegore, Co. Antrim: Mallory and McNeill 1991, 95.

20 Kiltierney Deerpark, Co. Fermanagh: Daniells and Williams 1977. Knockmullin, Co. Sligo: Madden 1968.

A partly disarticulated brachycephalic burial found in a shell midden on Dalkey Island produced a radiocarbon date of 4250 ± 150 BP (3340-3220/3200-2490 BC, BM-78): Liversage 1968, 103, 176.

21 Such differences in cranial morphology remain unexplained: Brodie 1994. For Taylor 1994 the physical and the archaeological evidence denote a mobile and intrusive Beaker population.

22 Corran gold disc: Case 1977.

23 Harbison 1976. Longstone, Co. Kildare: Macalister *et al.* 1913. Corran, Co. Armagh: Wilde 1857, 89; the association is plausible, two small gold discs were found with a Beaker, a bracer and a tanged copper knife in a grave at Mere, Wiltshire: Clarke 1970, fig. 130. Ballywholan, Co. Tyrone: Kelly 1985. Site C, Lough Gur: Ó Ríordáin 1954, 347, fig. 23, 20.

24 Harbison 1976. Kinkit, Co. Tyrone: Glover 1975. Jet is a black stone related to lignite or brown coal; possibly often confused with shale, it and jet-like materials were more widely used in Britain: D. V. Clarke *et al.* 1985, 204; Davis 1993.

25 Barbed and tanged arrowheads: Green 1980, 45, 410, 412, 411. Gortrea, Co. Galway, is also illustrated in Brindley 1994, pl. 15. Ballykilleen, Co. Offaly: Wilde 1861, fig. 164, was reportedly found at a depth of over 2m on a wooden trackway with a perforated antler axe: O'Leary 1902, 331, pl. 3, 10; for a perforated antler hammer or macehead: Liversage 1957. Ballyclare, Co. Antrim: Flanagan 1970b. Galgorm Parks, Co. Antrim: Kavanagh 1976, fig. 5. An uncertain association is reported from Carrivemurphy Mountain, Co. Antrim, where a barbed and tanged arrowhead may have been found in a bog with a bronze riveted dagger: Harbison 1969, 9. Battle axes: Simpson 1990 (his Early and Intermediate series of battle axes).

26 Harrison 1980. Drink and drugs: Scott 1977a. Sherratt 1991 has made the interesting suggestion that cord impressed ornament might reflect the use of hemp fibres and the use of cannabis. Pollen and seeds of black henbane, a narcotic which can induce intoxication or hallucinations, have been identified in residues on a sherd of Grooved Ware at Balfarg, Fife: Barclay and Russell-White 1993, 108.

27 Eogan 1984, 331.

28 Copper axes: Case 1966; Burgess 1980, 72; 1979; Schmidt and Burgess 1981.

29 Sheridan 1983; O'Brien 1995a; Iberian contacts: Harrison 1974; Taylor 1980; Schmidt and Burgess 1981, 27.

30 Burgess 1974, 1979; Harbison 1969, 1973. Schmidt and Burgess 1981. Needham *et al.* 1985. Associated finds are described by Harbison 1968. The find-spot of the Knocknagur hoard is given as 'Knocknague' in these studies; it was found at Knocknagur probably in Kilcreevanty townland: Waddell 1986.

31 Harbison 1969, modified by Schmidt and Burgess 1981; comments by Northover in O'Brien *et al.* 1990.

32 Munster ores: Craddock 1979; O'Brien 1994, 188. Woodworking techniques at Corlea 6 and Annaghbeg 1, Co. Longford: O'Sullivan 1996a, 314; Corlea 6 has been dendrochronologically dated to 2259 ± 9 BC.

33 Tanged copper daggers: Harbison 1969a. Blacklands, Co. Tyrone: Harbison 1978. Derrynamanagh, Co. Galway: Rynne 1972a. Sillees River, Co. Fermanagh (and metallographic analyses): Sheridan and Northover 1993. British tanged daggers: Gerloff 1975. Stone mould from 'Ireland' for a tanged dagger and three flat axes: Schmidt 1979, Abb. 3; Megaw and Hardy 1938, pl. LIII, C (one face); see Schmidt and Burgess 1981, 27, who compare the axes on the mould to an Iberian type.

34 Coles 1979, 168.

35 The 19th century discovery of a Killaha Type axe at Harlyn Bay in Cornwall suggests contact; the discovery of an Irish-type gold lunula and a second lunula on the site may indicate the manufacture of these sheet gold objects at this time as well but the association of axe and lunulae is uncertain: Pearce 1983, 417; D. V. Clarke *et al.* 1985, 260; for other evidence of contact: Needham 1979, 271, and O'Brien 1994, 247.

36 Irish ore sources: Jackson 1979; Briggs *et al.* 1973.

37 Harbison's 1969 Type Ballyvally is modified by Schmidt and Burgess 1981, 61, who also identify Types Glenalla, Falkland and Scrabo Hill in Ireland.

38 Toormore, Co. Cork, deposit: O'Brien *et al.* 1990. Other axes associated with burial mounds include Tully, Co. Fermanagh, court tomb: Waterman 1978; Newgrange, Co. Meath, passage tomb: O'Kelly and Shell 1979 and Carrowlisdooaun, Co. Mayo, ditch of second millennium mound: Waddell 1990, 70. Only two or three have been found with burials: Waddell 1990, 22; an axe and an unburnt burial is reported from Jordanstown, Co. Meath: Cooney and Grogan 1994, 118.

39 Broken axes occur in hoards such as Killaha East, Co. Kerry and Monastery, Co. Wicklow: Harbison 1968; Scotland: Coles 1969.

40 Schmidt and Burgess 1981, 65, attempt a more precise definition of Type Derryniggin axes which they re-name Type Bandon; they would also prefer to distinguish between axes with hammered flanges and those with higher and cast flanges (some of which are categorized as Type Balbirnie) but recognize the difficulties involved.

41 Brockagh, Co. Kildare: Rynne 1963. Deposition and non-utilitarian role of axes: Needham 1988; Dickins 1996. Axe contexts: Cooney and Grogan 1994, 102, 116.

42 The contents and contexts of early metal hoards have been analysed by O'Flaherty 1995; not all the hoards included in his study would be accepted as such.

43 Halberds: Harbison 1969a, 1973, 105. Burgess 1980, 75, has noted 175 from Ireland, 10 from England, 8 from Wales and 40 from Scotland. Halberd and haft from Altnamackin, Co. Armagh: Flanagan 1966a.

44 The Topped Mountain grave also contained a cremation and a vase; a radiocarbon date of 3220 ± 70 BP (1680-1326 BC, OxA-2663) for the unburnt bone suggests that the dagger and the unburnt burial were a secondary interment in the grave already containing the cremation and vase: Brindley and Lanting in Hedges *et al.* 1993.

45 Daggers: Harbison 1969a; a number of his ogival daggers are classed as dirks by Burgess and Gerloff 1981. Unprovenanced dagger: Harbison 1970. Gortaclare, Co. Clare: Lucas 1970. Miscellaneous daggers: Harbison l969a, 15; Lucas 1971, 216; Kavanagh 1976, 307; Ramsey 1992. Dagger pommels: Hardaker 1974.

46 Tanged spearheads: Flanagan 1961; Gerloff 1975, 253; Harbison 1967a, 97; Needham 1979b; Omagh moulds: Coghlan and Raftery 1961, nos 26-29, 40. End-looped spearheads: Burgess and Cowen 1972. Moulds: Inch Island, Co. Donegal: Coghlan and Raftery 1961, no. 22; Lough Gur, Co. Limerick: Evans 1881, 436.

47 Basket ear rings: Eogan 1994, 18; Armstrong 1933, nos 348-349, pl. XVIII, 423-424; Taylor 1980, pl. 3g; for a discussion of the claim that these objects were not ear rings but hair ornaments worn around plaits, see Russel 1990. Deehommed, near Katesbridge, Co. Down: Taylor 1979, pl. 6, and 1980, 22, compare her pl. 3h and i with pl. 3j from Ermegeira, Torres Vedras, Portugal.

48 Gold discs: Case 1977; Taylor 1980, 23, and 1994; Eogan 1994, 19. Kilmuckridge, Co. Wexford: Cahill 1994b. A tiny disc of very thin sheet gold found on Site D at Lough Gur (which also produced Beaker pottery) may be related; though it does have a pair of perforations, it is only 11mm in diameter and is undecorated: Ó Ríordáin 1954, 410, pl. XLVIb, 31. Gold plaques from Bellville, Co. Cavan: Armstrong 1933, nos 391-393, pl. X, 53, 55-56.

49 Lunulae: Eogan 1994, 30; Taylor 1970, 1980. Dunfierth, Co. Kildare: Armstrong 1933, 51, nos 4-7. Banemore, Co. Kerry: Cahill in Ryan 1983, 78. Rathroeen, Co. Mayo: Lucas 1968, 118.

50 Two Classical examples in Scotland may be imports from Ireland in recent times: Eogan 1994, 124. One of the Cornish finds, the Classical lunula from Harlyn Bay, may have been found with a Provincial lunula, a Migdale Type flat bronze axe was also recovered; the 19th century account of this discovery is unsatisfactory and the association of axe and lunulae is uncertain: Macalister 1949, 139; Pearce 1983, 417; D. V. Clarke et al. 1985, 189, 191, 260.

51 Harding 1993. Jet spacer-bead necklaces are recorded from Rasharkin, Co. Antrim, and Cumber, Co. Down: Jope 1951a; Brindley 1994, pl. 23; various unprovenanced spacer-beads are also known: Harbison 1973, 112.

52 Continental finds: Butler 1963; Cordier 1969; Harbison 1968a; Harrison 1974. Hoards containing broken objects include Killaha East, Co. Kerry, Derryniggin, Co. Leitrim, and Monastery, Co. Wicklow; both the latter find and Carrickshedoge, Co. Wexford, contained copper cakes: Harbison 1968.

53 Stone hammers: the function of pebble hammers and axe hammers is difficult to determine: Simpson 1988, 1990a, 1996a. Cushion stones: Butler and van der Waals 1966, 73, fig. 17; D. V. Clarke et al. 1985, 306. Stone moulds: Coghlan and Raftery 1961; Collins 1970; Williams 1980; Eogan 1993a. Lyre, Co. Cork, mould: O'Kelly 1970. Study of the products of moulds: Flanagan 1979; see Tylecote 1973 who noted

that even the one bivalve rapier mould was unlikely to produce identical weapons. Other types of mould: Goldmann 1981. Casting of halberds in bivalve moulds: Allen et al. 1970, 247.

54 Ross Island, Co. Kerry: preliminary accounts in O'Brien 1994a, 1995, 1995a, 1996, 1996a; radiocarbon dates extend from 3910 ± 40 BP (2562-2298 BC, GrN-20224) to 3580 ± 50 BP (2128-1776 BC, GrN-19623). Mount Gabriel, Co. Cork: O'Brien 1990 and 1994; for radiocarbon dates see Brindley and Lanting in O'Brien 1994, 281, those for wood associated with the working of Mine 3 extend from 3430 ± 30 BP (1876-1682 BC, GrN-13667) to 3260 ± 30 BP (1626-1506 BC, GrN-13980).

55 Pottery and burials of the Bowl Tradition: Ó Ríordáin and Waddell 1993; Waddell 1990; Mount 1995 has also demonstrated how pit graves generally are under-represented in the archaeological record because ploughing, for instance, has tended to uncover cists closer to the surface and not reveal deeper graves especially pits.

56 Carrickinab, Co. Down: Collins and Evans 1968; Ó Ríordáin and Waddell 1993, no. 145. Corrower, Co. Mayo: Raftery 1960; Waddell 1990, 118.

57 Evidence from a small number of graves in Scotland suggests the possibility of a cereal-based food offering: a vase from Strathallan, Perthshire, contained a little cereal pollen and traces of pollen of meadowsweet, perhaps a porridge or a fermented ale flavoured with meadowsweet flowers or extract; in other graves amounts of meadowsweet pollen have been interpreted as floral tributes or coverings or wrappings of plant fibres: Tipping 1994. Inturned rims may have been intended to retain the solids when sucking the boozy juice of a sort of alcoholic porridge: Hawkes 1981. Bowl Tradition cups: Kavanagh 1977, nos. 9, 57 and 62; Ó Donnabháin and Brindley 1990. Magheragallan, Co. Donegal: Evans 1941, 71, fig. 2.

58 Coney Island, Lough Neagh (preliminary report only): Addyman 1965.

59 Radiocarbon dates for bowls include: Halverstown, Co. Kildare: 3820 ± 40 BP (2456-2142 BC, GrN-12950), Keenoge, Co. Meath: 3685 ± 45 BP (2264-1946 BC, GrN-12272), Annaghkeen, Co. Galway: 3660 ± 25 BP (2136-1972 BC, GrN-11357), Betaghstown, Co. Meath: 3745 ± 30 BP (2282-2042 BC, GrN-11357), Haylands, Co. Wicklow: 4095 ± 30 BP (2868-2518 BC, GrN-11901), Ploopluck, Co. Kildare: 3735 ± 35 BP (2282-2038 BC, GrN-11353), Bolinready, Co. Wexford: 3620 ± 60 BP (2190-1784 BC, GrN-9321), Milltown, Co. Westmeath: 3755 ± 35 BP (2292-2042 BC, GrN-11903), Oldtown, Co. Kildare: 3655 ± 35 BP (2138-1944 BC, GrN-11902), Riverstown, Co. Westmeath: 3645 ± 30 BP (2134-1944 BC, GrN-9322), Sliguff, Co. Carlow: 3475 ± 35 BP (1888-1698 BC, GrN-11352), Stonepark, Co. Sligo: 3665 ± 35 BP (2184-1958 BC, GrN-11356), see Ó Ríordáin and Waddell 1993, 37; Grange, Co. Roscommon: 3620 ± 80 BP (2268-1756 BC, OxA-2761) and 3770 ± 70 BP (2458-2032 BC, OxA-2664), see Hedges et al. 1993; Straid, Co. Derry: 3810 ± 40 BP (2454-2140 BC, GrN-15491), 3840 ± 35 BP (2458-2202 BC, GrN-15492), 3845 ± 40 BP

(2460-2202 BC, GrN-15493), Brannon *et al.* 1990; Keenoge, Co. Meath: Mount 1997.

60 Pottery and burials of the Vase Tradition: Ó Ríordáin and Waddell 1993; Waddell 1990; Kavanagh 1973.

61 Kavanagh 1973, 1976.

62 Radiocarbon dates for vases include: Carrowlisdooaun, Co. Mayo: 3695 ± 35 BP (2198-1978 BC, GrN-11900), Carrowntober East, Co. Galway: 3755 ± 30 BP (2284-2046 BC, GrN-11354), Moyveela, Co. Galway: 3755 ± 35 BP (2292-2042 BC, GrN-12273), Stonepark, Co. Mayo: 3625 ± 30 BP (2128-1918 BC, GrN-12275), Tremoge, Co. Tyrone: 3570 ± 45 BP (2108-1774 BC, GrN-11446), Foley 1985, Drumnakeel, Co. Antrim: 3255 ± 80 BP (1740-1404 BC, UB-2639), Williams 1985, see Ó Ríordáin and Waddell 1993, 37; Topped Mountain, Co. Fermanagh: 3220 ± 70 BP (1680-1326 BC, OxA-2663) for the unburnt bone and dagger which may post-date the vase and cremation: Brindley and Lanting in Hedges *et al.* 1993. False Bay, Co. Galway: McCormick 1995; McCormick *et al.* 1996.

63 Vase urns: Waddell 1976; 1990, 11. Ballinvoher, Co. Cork: O'Kelly and Shee 1974. Clontygora, Co. Armagh: Davies and Paterson 1937. Knockroe, Co. Tyrone: Williams and Wilkinson 1988. Grange, Co. Roscommon: Waddell 1990, Ó Ríordáin and Waddell 1993; radiocarbon date from charcoal: 3480 ± 35 BP (1890-1700 BC, GrN-9709).

64 Encrusted urns: Kavanagh 1973; Waddell 1975a; radiocarbon dates from charcoal include: Strawhall, Co. Carlow: 3420 ± 80 BP (1920-1526 BC, OxA-2657) and 3440 ± 70 BP (1940-1534 BC, OxA-2658), Shanahoe, Co. Laois: 3540 ± 70 BP (2124-1696 BC, OxA-2679), Hedges *et al.* 1993. Ballyveelish, Co. Tipperary: 3580 ± 50 BP (2128-1776 BC, GrN-11657), Doody 1987; the fill of the pit also contained some burnt bones of a large dog or wolf.

65 Vase Tradition pottery from northern sandhills: ApSimon 1969. Kilellan, Islay: Burgess 1976; Ardnave, Islay: Ritchie and Welfare 1983.

66 Urn burial origins: ApSimon 1969; Kavanagh 1973. Lynn 1993a suggests that inverted urns were representations of the circular houses of the living.

67 The Cordoned Urn Tradition: Kavanagh 1976; Waddell 1995a.

68 Downpatrick, Co. Down: Pollock and Waterman 1964; radiocarbon dates from charcoal from layer 7 or equivalent: 3575 ± 70 BP (2134-1746 BC, UB-471) and 3795 ± 75 BP (2464-2038 BC, UB-472) and charcoal from a stone-packed trench and from layer 2 provided dates of 3265 ± 80 BP (1742-1412 BC, UB-473) and 3325 ± 75 (1870-1442 BC, UB-474), and the gap between the two sets of dates was thought to reflect the presence of the sterile layer 5 on the site (*Radiocarbon* 15, 213) but only the last two dates are considered to date the cordoned urn pottery. Altanagh, Co. Tyrone: 3465 ± 30 BP (1882-1700 BC, GrN-11448), 3330 ± 60 BP (1864-1460 BC, GrN-10556) and 3360 ± 30 BP (1740-1534 BC, GrN-11449), Williams 1986. Kilcroagh, Co. Antrim: 3420 ± 70 BP (1900-1528 BC, OxA-2673), Williams *et al.* 1992. Ballyrenan, Co. Down: ApSimon 1969. Sheepland, Co.

Down: Waterman 1975. Moynagh Lough, Co. Meath: Bradley 1991, radiocarbon date: 3460 ± 35 BP (1882-1692 BC, GrN-11442). Sandhill sites: ApSimon 1969.

69 Knives and razors: Kavanagh 1991; Williams *et al.* 1992. Battle axes: Simpson 1990, 1996a. Laheen, Co. Donegal: Ó Ríordáin 1967. Faience beads: Magee 1993; Harding 1984. Carrig, Co. Wicklow: Grogan 1990. Harristown, Co. Waterford: Hawkes 1941. Ballyduff, Co. Wexford: Hartnett and Prendergast 1953. Mound of the Hostages, Tara, Co. Meath: Ó Ríordáin 1955. Knockboy, Co. Antrim: Rynne 1964a.

70 Cups: Kavanagh 1977; Ó Donnabháin and Brindley 1990. Use as narcotic burners: Sherratt 1995, 27.

71 Collared urns: Longworth 1984; Kavanagh 1976. Bay Farm, Co. Antrim: Mallory and McNeill 1991, 97, fig. 3-16. Killeenaghmountain, Co. Waterford: Ryan 1975.

72 Lissard, Co. Limerick: Ó Ríordáin 1934. Cemeteries: Waddell 1990; Mount 1995. Environmental siting of burials in Co. Kildare: Mount 1995a.

73 Other Irish instances of trephination or trepanning are Medieval in date: Buckley and Ó Donnabháin 1992.

74 Cloghskelt, Co. Down: Waddell 1990, 78, fig. 41. Edmondstown, Co. Dublin: Mount and Hartnett 1993. Burials in southern Leinster: Mount 1991, 1995; Munster: Doody 1987.

75 Keenoge, Co. Meath: Mount 1997. Urbalreagh, Co. Antrim: Waterman 1968.

76 Mound of the Hostages, Tara, Co. Meath: Ó Ríordáin 1955; Kavanagh 1973, 1976, 1979. Baunogenasraid, Co. Carlow: B. Raftery 1974. Harristown, Co. Waterford: J. Hawkes 1941.

77 Poulawack, Co. Clare: Hencken 1935; Brindley and Lanting 1992a for radiocarbon dates. The possible use of a deliberate sealant of marl and sand for the boulder core of a burial mound at Clogher Lower, Co. Roscommon, may represent a different sort of constructional and ritual complexity: Shimwell *et al.* 1996.

78 Moneen, Co. Cork: O'Kelly 1952; Brindley and Lanting 1988 for radiocarbon dates and a revision of O'Kelly's interpretation: early activity, 3960 ± 60 BP (2854-2294 BC, GrN-10629 from charcoal), central grave, 3755 ± 30 BP (2284-2046 BC, GrN-11904 from human bone).

79 Knockast, Co. Westmeath: Hencken and Movius 1934; early prehistoric extended burial: Waddell 1990, 16. Cornaclery, Co. Derry: May 1942. Corrower, Co. Mayo: J. Raftery 1960.

80 Tankardstown, Co. Limerick: Gowen and Tarbett 1988. Shanaclogh, Co. Limerick: Gowen 1988, 68 (and Manning 1988). Lissard, Co. Limerick: Ó Ríordáin 1936, 177 (no details published). Carnkenny, Co. Tyrone: Lynn 1974; radiocarbon date from charcoal from a possible cremation area beneath the bank: 2815 ± 50 BP (1126-842 BC, UB-599). Ballybeen, Co. Down: Mallory 1984a; charcoal from the ring ditch provided radiocarbon dates of 2660 ± 70 BP (998-560 BC, UB-2640) and 2530 ± 70 BP (810-410 BC, UB-2641). Cahercorney, Co. Limerick: MacDermott 1949. Mitchelstowndown West, Co. Limerick: Daly and Grogan 1993. Burials with later metalwork are rare: Burgess 1976a.

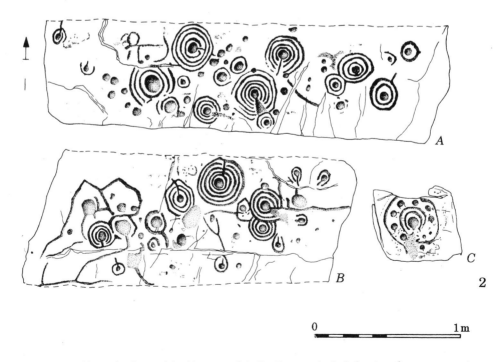

Fig. 63. Rock art. 1. A rubbing of a decorated boulder at Reyfad, Co. Fermanagh. 2. A drawing of art on two sections (a and b) of a boulder at Derrynablaha, Co. Kerry, and on a small detached boulder (c) nearby.

5

Enigmatic Monuments

Embanked enclosures, timber circles, burials, burial mounds and artefact hoards are not the only evidence of ritual activity in the third and second millennia BC. A series of monuments including rock carvings, stone circles, standing stones, and stone alignments testify to other ceremonial preoccupations and a puzzling group of boulder-monuments seem to combine some elements of the megalithic tradition with the custom of token burial.

ROCK ART

The carving of symbols on some exposed rock surfaces may have been a means of imbuing natural rock outcrops or certain parts of the landscape with special significance. Rock art, sometimes called rock carvings or petroglyphs, is found in several locations in Ireland and seems to be part of a wider western European or Atlantic fashion. Five stones at Reyfad, north-west of Boho, Co. Fermanagh, are fairly typical. They are low rock outcrops on high rising ground and there are wide and impressive views to the east. The largest rock measures over 3m in length and its surface is covered with a profusion of cup-and-ring motifs (Fig. 63). This combination of a hill slope siting and a viewpoint is a feature of some rock art sites. A major complex of over 20 stones occurs at Derrynablaha, Co. Kerry, about 12km north-east of Sneem; it lies at the head of the Kealduff river valley and some of the stones, located at heights above sea level of over 200m, also command extensive views. Cup marks and cup-and-ring marks, some with radial lines, are common. This is one of over 40 finds of rock art on the Iveragh peninsula where most examples have

been found in elevated positions around the 180m contour and towards the upper reaches of river valleys. Elsewhere a majority of sites are found below 133m. Other concentrations have been identified, for example in the Dingle peninsula, in Inishowen in north Donegal, in Co. Louth and in south Leinster, mainly in Co. Carlow, and, in all, rock art has been recorded at over 100 sites in Ireland.

This art is executed by picking with a stone or metal implement often on flat or gently sloping rock surfaces. Compositions may be widely or closely spaced, motifs may be linked or unconnected to one another. A quite limited range of basic abstract motifs occurs: particularly common are cup marks, cup marks with a tail or radial groove, cup-and-ring marks, sometimes with a radial groove and sometimes with multiple rings, and cup and penannular rings – again sometimes with a radial groove and with multiple rings. On sloping surfaces the radial grooves often run downwards and circular motifs are often conjoined. Less common are rectilinear motifs such as parallel lines sometimes in sub-rectangular fields, circles of cup marks and cruciform designs. True spirals are rare if not absent. This detail is not unimportant because the question of the relationship of rock art to the art on passage tombs is crucial in any consideration of the date of this phenomenon. There are some parallels between the two, cup marks, dot and circles and concentric circles with a radial line do occur in the passage tomb repertoire but the sum of the differences is considerable. There are certainly significant differences in both context and distribution and the variety of passage tomb motifs is not found in rock art. The relationship between the two styles remains uncertain and the mutual occurrence of cup marks may be of little significance in this respect. Stones bearing cup marks have a long history in western Europe, appearing as early as 4000 BC and continuing in fashion until about 2500 BC, and various writers would distinguish between stones with rock art (including cup marks) and stones with just cup marks by themselves.

The concentration of rock art in the south-west has prompted suggestions of some connection with copper mining but the distributions of art and copper are for the most part mutually exclusive and there seems to be no connection between them. Some carved motifs on the capstones of several cists, including a rectangular cist at Moylough, Co. Sligo, which contained a cremation and a halberd, have suggested a second millennium date for rock art but the arcs, rough lozenges and concentric circles found on these cist stones have, if anything, closer parallels with passage tomb art and in some cases may even be re-used stones. The precise date of rock art remains quite uncertain though a third millennium date is usually assumed.

There has been much theorising on the possible meaning of individual motifs, the cup-and-ring marks on the Reyfad stone were thought to be 'votive sun symbols', for instance, and fertility interpretations have been freely offered too but no satisfactory explanation has emerged. The motifs undoubtedly had some special meaning and it may be that the circle and the cup mark, if derived from passage tomb art, were selected because they were especially potent symbols in their own right and lost none of their significance when deployed in a very different context. The size, spacing and intricacy of the design elements may have conveyed complex information too. Recent studies have emphasized the role this art may have played in the ordering of the landscape. A majority are within 50m of fresh water, usually a river or lake, and, while many are situated in rocky areas, they are, in some cases, on the margins of land that would probably have been suitable for agriculture and may have overlooked or have been adjacent to settlement sites. Some of the more complex sites at higher altitudes, like Reyfad and Derrynablaha, may mark routeways or boundaries.[1]

Irish rock art finds parallels in Scotland and northern England and some of its motifs such as cup-and-ring marks are also found in the rock art of Portugal and north-western Spain, in Galicia in particular, where strikingly similar compositions of concentric circles also occur. Galician art, however, also contains figures of daggers, halberds and animals such as deer. To what extent the abstract motifs form an international Atlantic art style or to what extent they reflect a common ancestry in the symbolic art of megalithic passage tombs is not clear.

STONE CIRCLES, STONE ALIGNMENTS AND STANDING STONES

The term stone circle is applied to ritual monuments consisting of a circular or almost circular area delimited by a number of stones which are usually spaced but are occasionally contiguous. The area within the circle is usually open as in the Grange stone circle briefly described in Chapter 4 but, as we have also seen, some circles may have surrounded cairns like Newgrange and in some cases circles of contiguous stones may be the kerbs of denuded cairns.

Various types of stone circle are widely distributed in Ireland and different forms include circles with widely spaced stones, examples with almost contiguous stones, and circles combined with an earthen bank. Scattered examples occur in Connacht and Leinster and major concentrations are found in Ulster and Munster. Apart from a small group in Co. Limerick, the majority of Munster examples are situated in Cork and Kerry where over 90 are recorded. Here recumbent-stone circles are the typical form: these are circles of free-standing orthostats arranged symmetrically and varying in number from five (five-stone circles) to a greater number (multiple-stone circles). The entrance to the circle is through a pair of matched portal stones, usually the tallest in the circle. Opposite the entrance is a stone called the 'recumbent' or 'axial' stone normally the lowest in the monument. The recumbent stone is so called because in many cases it appears to be a long stone placed on its side rather than on end and often having a horizontal upper edge. The other stones decrease in height from portal to recumbent stone. The main axis of these circles is considered to extend from the middle of the gap between the entrance stones to the centre of the recumbent stone and divides the monument into more or less symmetrical parts. This axis consistently lies approximately south-west to north-east with the recumbent stone on the south-western side and the portals on the north-east. The orientation in fact shows a general splay of 107°, the axes of the recumbent stones for example varying from 6° west of south to 230° north of west suggesting an alignment in the direction of the rising or setting sun. About half of the Cork-Kerry recumbent stone circles are multiple-stone circles with seven or more stones. These have uneven numbers of stones, 9, 11 or 13 stones for the most part, and internal diameters vary from almost 3m to 17m. The other half of the series comprises five-stone circles which often have a rather irregularly circular or D-shaped plan (in which the recumbent stone forms the straight line of the D); their maximum dimensions on their main axis varies from 2.3m to about 4m. Half a dozen of the southern circles have been excavated: one five-stone circle at Kealkil, Co. Cork, and one multiple stone circle at Reanascreena South, Co. Cork, produced no artefacts at all.

Drombeg stone circle, near Glandore, Co. Cork, is situated on a natural terrace overlooking a shallow valley with the Atlantic visible to the south. Excavation showed that it had originally consisted of seventeen stones set in an almost perfect circle 9.3m in diameter (Fig. 64). A pair of portal stones on the north-east averaged 2m in height and the recumbent stone on the south-west was an almost flat-topped slab 2.1m long and 90cm high. The upper surface of this stone bears a cup mark and a second cup mark nearby is set within a carved oval shape which has been compared to a stone axe. The axis of the monument, from portal to centre of recumbent stone, seems to have been aligned on the mid-winter sunset. Two of the orthostats (nos 14 and 15) in the northern half of the circle differed noticeably from the others: one was a carefully-erected, large, lozenge-shaped boulder flat on its inner face, the other, beside it, was a small pillar stone standing just over 1m in height and the smallest stone in the monument. The excavator believed that these stones may have had some fertility significance representing respectively the female and male sexes. A similar sort of juxtaposition has been noted in an avenue of paired stones at Avebury in Wiltshire.[2] The interior of the Drombeg circle was found to have been covered with a compact layer of pebbles and gravel. Five pits were discovered beneath this layer: three (C-E) contained mainly stones, one (B) contained a

deposit of dark soil and a few flecks of charcoal and, in the centre, a 82cm wide and 28cm deep circular pit (A) contained a cremated burial. The bones of an adolescent were very fragmentary and may have been broken up after burning; these bones had been placed along with some sweepings from the funeral pyre in a broken pottery vessel which, the excavator suggested, had been wrapped in some organic material before being placed in the pit. The pot which lacked its base and most of its rim was of plain, coarse ware. Charcoal scraped from the pot yielded a radiocarbon date range of 1124-794 BC.

A stone circle at Bohonagh, near Ross Carbery, Co. Cork, not far from a boulder-monument described below, was a multiple stone circle of thirteen stones. In the centre a small very low mound covered a cup-marked slab and a shallow pit containing soil, pebbles and flecks of burnt bone; the pit had been disturbed. The Reanascreena circle, about 6km to the north-west, also of thirteen stones, had a soil-filled pit at its centre and a few metres to the north a second pit near the edge of the circle contained some minute fragments of cremated bone. The stone circle was surrounded by a ditch with external bank and the monument had an overall diameter of 24m. Charcoal from the cremation pit suggested a date range of 1004-844 BC. At Cashelkeelty, near Lauragh, Co. Kerry, a circle of eleven or thirteen stones had been greatly disturbed; the only find was a flint convex scraper. A second circle at Cashelkeelty was a five-stone monument situated about 80m east of the multiple-stone example; a slab-covered pit in the centre contained the cremated bones of an adult of 25 to 30 years. A short alignment of four stones stood just south of this circle. Stone implements found in or near the circle and alignment included a leaf-shaped flint arrowhead, a barbed and tanged flint arrowhead, two scrapers and part of a sandstone point but direct association with the monuments was impossible to prove. Two radiocarbon dates indicate the possibility of a date around 1000 BC for the circle and a slightly earlier date may be indicated for the stone alignment on stratigraphical evidence.

Standing stones and stone alignments are associated with a small number of circles. At Kealkil, Co. Cork, a pair of standing stones had been erected just north-east of the circle, one was originally over 6m in height. Nearby a small cairn covered a ring of stones and sockets, some set radially. Most stone alignments are isolated monuments.

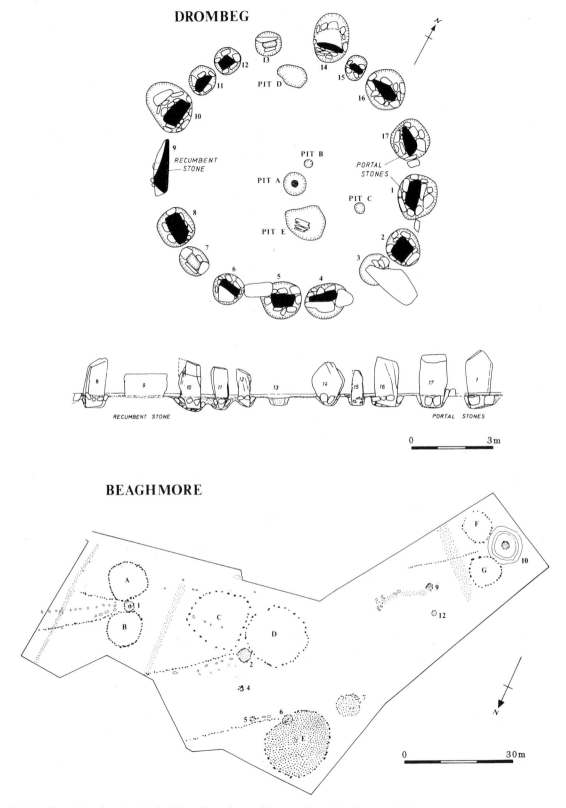

Fig. 64. Above. Drombeg, Co. Cork. Below. Plan of part of the complex at Beaghmore, Co. Tyrone.

'... A SPECTACULAR CONJUNCTION OF ENERGY AND MATTER'

A stone alignment is a row of three or more standing stones, intervisible and in a straight line. Three to six stones is the norm in stone alignments in west Cork and in Kerry and many have the stones graded in height with the tallest stone at either the eastern or western end; in the Iveragh peninsula the tallest stone is often found at the western end. Their purpose is obscure and excavation at both Cashelkeelty and at Maughanasilly, Co. Cork, revealed nothing about this aspect of these puzzling monuments. At the last mentioned site a row of five standing stones was excavated and two charcoal samples believed to represent the burning and clearance of the area produced identical radiocarbon dates of 1678-1438 BC. At Dromatouk, Co. Kerry, charcoal which provided a date range of 1740-1520 BC has been tentatively related to the construction of a three stone alignment. Ann Lynch has suggested that a circle and alignment at Cashelkeelty, Co. Kerry, and an alignment at Maughanasilly, Co. Cork, were erected on marginal farmland whose soils were degenerating (as evidenced by developing podzolization) and the settlements of their builders, which were not located in the immediate vicinity, may have been several kilometres away.

Two standing stones, of course, may form an alignment too and over 100 stone pairs have been identified in Counties Cork and Kerry. A pair of standing stones at Ballycommane, Co. Cork, set 3m apart and situated a few metres from a boulder-monument, was aligned in a north-north-east to south-south-west direction; one stone had a very small stone-lined pit nearby which contained two thin deposits of fine clay containing flecks of charcoal separated by a thin lens of boulder clay and a small flat stone. An unusual double stone alignment with a similar orientation has been found at Askillaun, west of Louisburgh, Co. Mayo. An alignment of a row of six quartz boulders at Gleninagh, Connemara, Co. Galway, points to a high pass between two mountain peaks to the south-south-west and the setting of the midwinter sun, sliding down into the gap between the mountains, has been described as 'a spectacular conjunction of energy and matter'. This alignment is located on the crest of a low morain both to be visible and to offer a view of the surrounding valley and therefore 'marks the intersection of an astronomical constant with a constant of human spatial awareness'.[3]

Alignments and circles appear to be related (particularly in the north of Ireland) and in the Cork-Kerry area evidence suggests a chronological range of about 1700 to about 800 BC. Both monument types may have had some related ceremonial and ritual purpose. The circles are an expression in stone of the idea of a sacred ceremonial circle which had a long life in various forms in different parts of prehistoric Britain and Ireland – and it is an intriguing fact that recumbent stone circles find their closest affinities in north-east Scotland. The belief that the occasional deposits of cremated bone in the stone circles are dedicatory seems reasonable and a fairly consistent pattern of south-west to north-east orientation suggests some preoccupation with the position of the rising or setting sun. Claims that circles were accurately aligned on certain significant lunar and stellar events are disputed, however. As already mentioned the axis of Drombeg when projected to the horizon coincides with the point of sunset at the winter solstice, the Bohonagh circle may have been orientated on sunset at the equinoxes. Reanscreena South has a general south-west to north-east axis but seems to have had no more precise astronomical focus. Study of the stone alignments in the south-west has also indicated a general south-west to north-east orientation and some were focused on certain prominent hilltops which were also locations on the horizon where the moon rose or set.[4]

A group of some fifty or so monuments in the south-west, in Counties Cork and Kerry, have been named 'boulder-burials' by Seán Ó Nualláin and evidently have some connection with the stone circles of the region. Here called boulder-monuments, they consist of a large boulder or a thick slab usually 1m to 2m long set above three or more very low flat-topped stones which rarely form a recognizable chamber. A few of these low monuments have small stones inserted between the supporting stones and the capstone. Covering cairns or mounds are not recorded. In eight instances boulder-monuments are placed within stone circles, two are present in one, while four are set within a large stone circle at Breeny More, near Kealkil, Co. Cork. At Bohonagh, the boulder-monument is situated 18m to the east of the stone circle. The boulder, which rested on three low stones, measured 2.9m by 2.4m and 1.1m in thickness.

Two of the supporting stones were of quartz, the other stones (including capstone) of sandstone. Beneath the boulder a shallow pit contained a few fragments of cremated bone. The underside of this stone bore at least seven cup marks. Two boulder-monuments at Cooradarrigan, near Schull, Co. Cork, each covered a pit, while a third, in Ballycommane, near Durrus, Co. Cork, covered a thin layer of what may have been burnt clay. Some charcoal from the pit beneath one of the Cooradarrigan monuments provided a radiocarbon date of 1426-1266 BC and though no human bones were found, a funerary association is possible because it is conceivable that the burnt material was a token deposit from a funeral pyre.[5]

The second major concentration of stone circles (and alignments) in Ireland is to be found in mid-Ulster, in Counties Tyrone, Derry and east Fermanagh. These circles are very different from the south-western examples being often of irregular plan and built of a greater number of quite small stones rarely over 50cm in height. The alignments are different too being constructed of closely-set small stones as well. The circles often occur in groups as at Beaghmore, Co. Tyrone.

A small number have been excavated. At Drumskinny, near Kesh, Co. Fermanagh, a circle with adjacent alignment and cairn which had been partly obscured by upland bog has been examined; the stone circle originally comprised 31 stones set in a fairly accurate circle with a diameter of just over 13m. The stones varied considerably in shape and size, usually between 60cm to 1.2m in height, and were normally placed 30cm to 60cm apart. There was no clearly defined formal entrance to the circle though there were slightly larger than usual gaps between stones at three points in the perimeter; any one of these could have served the purpose. The only finds within the circle were a flint convex scraper, a flake and a burnt blade. These came from the natural clay surface as did a minute fragment of pottery found near one of the stones. Immediately north-west of the circle a small circular cairn with kerb had a diameter of just 4m. Nothing was found but a burnt flint flake and a crude concave scraper beneath a small spread of stones adjoining the cairn. The alignment of small stones ran north-south and at its nearest point this row of 24 uprights was only 1.2m from the circle; heights ranged mainly from about 30cm to 60cm. Some of the stones had been set in

shallow sockets but others stood more or less on the natural surface. The few finds from Drumskinny give little or no indication of the date or purpose of the monuments.

A similar group of monuments has been partially examined at Castledamph, near Plumbridge, Co. Tyrone, on the southern slopes of the Sperrin Mountains; like some other northern circles these were apparently first revealed when some two metres of peat were cut away in the late 19th century. A circle of low stones measured about 19m in diameter; the stones were set almost contiguously and enclosed a semi-circle of similar stones within which was a low cairn. A small cist in this cairn had been disturbed: some cremated bone was recovered and represented one eighteen year old individual. A cup-marked slab was found near the grave. An alignment of relatively large stones, about 1m high, ran southwards from the circle. A nearby small cairn was trenched but produced no finds and a second subsidiary alignment was observed to the west of the main stone row.

A complex of nine circles has been recorded at Copney Hill, Co. Tyrone, and is associated with a standing stone, a cairn and an alignment; at least three of the circles enclosed a low cairn containing a robbed cist. Some 11km away is the well known group of circles, alignments and cairns at Beaghmore, north-west of Cookstown (Fig. 64), first uncovered in the course of turf cutting. It is located on the eastern slopes of the Sperrin Mountains about 195m above sea level and the monuments so far exposed include seven stone circles, eight stone alignments (and the sockets of a ninth), and a dozen small cairns. Some have been excavated. At least two other circles and cairns have been recorded in the vicinity and one cairn just to the south-west has produced some cremated bone. Three pairs of stone circles (A-D, F, G) occur along with one unusual isolated circle (E). Associated with each pair, and with circle E, are at least one stone alignment and one small cairn. Most of the stones of circles and alignments are of quite small boulders or slabs. Several of the alignments run over lines of stony rubble – possibly the remains of collapsed field walls or the results of field clearance. The small cairn (no. 1) between circles A and B measured 3m in diameter and contained a small cist in which was found a porcellanite axe. Circles C and D with average diameters of some 16m are quite irregular and to some extent this irregularity seems to have been intentional. Circle C, for example, seems to extend eastwards to enclose a flat stone and three stones which form part of a bulge on the south-west were, for some reason, set on a bank of small stones. Two pits within this circle contained charcoal, stones, sherds of Lyles Hill pottery and a few flints. The nearby small cairn (no. 2) was also excavated and found to contain a small cist but apart from what may have been the very last vestiges of a pot sherd, the contents – if any – had been destroyed by peat water.

No bones were found in cairns 4 and 9 but a few decayed particles were found beneath no. 5 while nos 6 and 12 produced some cremated bone. An intriguing feature of cairn 4 was a small stone lined pit containing a short section of an oak tree trunk. No. 10 proved to be the most elaborate cairn on the site: a small cairn with kerb was covered with a clay capping and this was surrounded by a ditch and external bank with an average overall diameter of about 10m. The cairn contained a small cist empty but for a few decayed fragments of bone. A second small and empty cist was found outside the kerb. The soil under the cairn contained enough charcoal to give a radiocarbon date of 1950-1684 BC and organic material from a sample of the lowest layer of peat which had formed in the encircling ditch provided a date of 990-808 BC. The monument's construction lies between the two dates. A small hoard of pieces of flint, including several cores, was found near the stone alignment which ran north-eastwards from cairn 10 and charcoal from the soil in which they were embedded gave an early second millennium radiocarbon date. This is a possible date for the flints and the nearby stone row but, of course, the dated sample was not directly associated with either. Charcoal from a hearth found near the alignment running from cairn 6, when radiocarbon dated, suggested activity in the period 2900-2500 BC. The small hoard of flints recalls a larger cache of over 60 flints, including convex scrapers, knives and points, which was found at the base of one of the stones of another circle at Cuilbane, near Garvagh, Co. Derry.

The cremation in cairn 6 was unusual: bones were deposited in two lots, one on the floor of a small cist, the other on a flat stone outside it near the centre of the cairn; it is possible that the latter deposit represented just the skull of the individual in the cist. This cairn was incorporated in the puzzling monument called circle E which is in fact an oval arrangement of over 880 closely-set stones with a maximum diameter of 18m. Its purpose is unknown – and even the ritual epithet so often applied on the basis of negative evidence to ostensibly non-utilitarian sites seems not very illuminating here. Whatever rituals took place in and around the various sites at Beaghmore, it has been argued that astronomical practices do not seem to have been a part of them. The irregular shapes of the circles, and the small size of the stones used would appear to support the suggestion that no significant celestial observations could have been made.

The date for the Beaghmore complex as a whole is uncertain, some monuments such as cairn 10 were built between 1800-800 BC (a date-range similar to those so far obtained for the circles in the south-west). The discovery of Lyles Hill pottery in circle C and the possible date of 2908-2504 BC for the hearth should not be forgotten and indicates earlier activity there though not necessarily connected with the stone circle. Palynological work at Beaghmore has shown clearance of pine and elm and cereal cultivation there from about 3800 BC, a phase which lasted for several centuries (until approximately 3400 BC) and during which cereal cultivation was superseded by grazing.[6]

Smaller clusters of stone circles are found elsewhere in Ireland. In Co. Cavan, in Banagher townland, south-east of Stradone, two circles (one surrounding a possible passage tomb) are part of a small complex of monuments including megalithic tombs, ring barrows and an embanked enclosure. At Killycluggin, south-west of Ballyconnell, a decorated late prehistoric pillar stone once stood in or near a stone circle but the relationship of the two monuments and the construction date of the circle are not known. A small group of four stone circles occurs just north-east of Cong, Co. Mayo, and is part of a scattered complex of monuments including a large circular enclosure and several cairns. A number of standing stones, numerous cairns and small circles of stones are among a series of ritual monuments identified on the western side of the Monavullagh mountains, north of Dungarvan, in Co. Waterford. In the absence of excavation, it is difficult to assess the significance of complexes of prehistoric monuments like these but here, as at Beaghmore, and at Ballynahatty, Co. Down, and Tara, Co. Meath, whole landscapes may have had a prolonged ritual significance. Rituals in these locations may have been enacted at particular times of the year and monuments such as mounds, cairns, stone circles, alignments and standing stones provide a link between the megalithic tombs of earlier times and other special centres of ceremonial activity in later prehistory such as hilltop enclosures. But man-made monuments are not the only evidence of the persistent importance of ritual, the second millennium also sees natural features such as rivers, lakes and bogs becoming increasingly significant as special places for the ceremonial deposition of metalwork (Chapter 6).[7]

Numerous isolated standing stones were also markers of special places but on a smaller scale. Though the particular significance of an individual stone is more difficult to assess, many are considered to date to the second millennium. It is probable, however, that this monument type spans a long period of time from at least the third millennium to the later centuries BC and had a variety of functions. Standing stones are widely distributed with over 200 recorded on the Iveragh and Dingle peninsulas alone, where they range from 1m to 3m in height. Some 300 have been noted in Co. Donegal and an equally large number in west Cork. More modest numbers are recorded elsewhere and a few bear cup marks. Relatively few have been excavated. A 3m tall monolith at Carrownacaw, Co. Down, stood adjacent to a ring ditch; a number of petit tranchet derivative flints were found. A squat 1.37m high stone in Drumnahare, near Loughbrickland, Co. Down, had a few fragments of cremated bone in the very shallow pit in which it stood. Burials have been associated with some: for example, a small deposit of cremated bone was found in a pit at the base of a stone at Killountain, near Bandon, Co. Cork; disarticulated unburnt human bones were found at the base of another at Ballynamona, Co. Offaly; and small standing stones occurred beside vase urn and cordoned urn burials at Culmore, Co. Antrim, and Aghascrebagh, Co. Tyrone, respectively. But some stones, such as one near Newgrange and another at Ballybeen, Dundonald, Co. Down, had no direct funerary purpose. The latter, known as the Long Stone, did stand about 50m to the west of a small annular ring ditch and, if there is any connection between the two, it is possible that the stone served as a boundary marker or marked the route to the ring ditch. Some standing stones may be recent monuments; it is often claimed that some were erected as scratching stones for cattle and some, situated near large houses in Co. Galway, may have been erected or re-erected as 18th or 19th century ornamental features.[8]

THE ENIGMA OF THE BURNT MOUNDS

If excavated settlements of the second millennium are still a rarity, the same cannot be said of one enigmatic monument type of the period which has been recorded in extraordinary numbers in various parts of the country. The *fulacht fiadh* or burnt mound has been identified in almost every part of the island with over 2000 recorded in Co. Cork alone. About 110 have been recorded in Co. Kerry and in the north of the county at least 16% of those noted were levelled by ploughing and survived as black spreads of earth in the fields. Some 300 have been reported in Co. Clare, mainly in the Burren, and 200 in Mayo but elsewhere numbers are smaller and they seem to be fairly rare in northern Ireland. Over 4500 are known altogether but this number will undoubtedly increase considerably with further field survey. Indeed fieldwork on Clare Island, Co. Mayo, has revealed that a majority there had no surface trace being fortuitously exposed as layers of burnt stones in drainage ditches, stream banks or in turf cutting. These inconspicuous sites are the commonest prehistoric monument in Ireland. The term *fulacht* or *fulacht fian* is found in early Irish literature from at least the 9th century AD and refers to open-air cooking places often associated with the young warrior-hunters of the *fianna* and the legendary Fionn MacCumhail. The name *fulacht fiadh* was sometimes used in the 19th century and thereafter applied to mounds of burnt stones believed to be the remains of these ancient cooking-places which were then, of course, dated to late prehistoric and early Historic times.

The classic burnt mound is a relatively low grassy mound of crescent or U-shaped plan. Survey in Co. Cork has demonstrated there that about 44% have this shape, 34% being circular or oval, 2% D-shaped and the remaining 20% irregular in form. Often small and inconspicuous, most are 1m to 2m high and may range in greatest dimensions from a few metres to over 20m in a few instances. They are usually close to water, often near a stream, or by a lake or river, or in marshy ground. They sometimes occur in groups, clusters of two to six occasionally located within quite a small area.[9]

Two burnt mounds at Ballyvourney, Co. Cork, were the first to be scientifically excavated. They were investigated by M. J. O'Kelly in 1952 who in a classic piece of practical experimentation also demonstrated how they could have served as cooking places. One of these mounds, Ballyvourney I (Fig. 65) proved to be a roughly oval accumulation of burnt stone measuring just over 12m in maximum width and about 60cm in maximum height; this dump of burnt material partly surrounded a rectangular wooden trough, two hearths, a stone-lined pit and a series of post-holes. The mound consisted of some 27 cubic metres of burnt and broken sandstone with abundant charcoal and some ash. The sub-rectangular trough was 1.8m long and 40cm deep and constructed of branches of birch and oak, an oak plank and stones; it had been set into the peat which lay beneath the mound and it naturally filled with about 450 litres of water from the surrounding bog. A hearth was found beyond the south-eastern end of the trough and this area of burnt material was partly delimited by a line of slabs. A second, later hearth was found at the opposite end of the trough and it too was delimited in part by an arc of slabs. Each hearth showed several phases of use. A nearby stone-lined pit displayed traces of burning and seemed to have been an oven. A series of inclining post-holes to the south of the trough formed an approximate oval and were interpreted as the foundations of a timber hut which had a central post as well. A pit, dug into the peat, four stake-holes forming a rectangle and a pair of post-holes were found inside the hut. Apart from five small stone discs and a stone pounder, there were no finds and no bones were discovered.

O'Kelly reconstructed the hut, the wooden trough and a hearth and determined, by experiment, that stones heated in the fire, removed with a long-handled wooden shovel and placed in the trough could bring the water to the boil in 30 to 35 minutes. Adding the occasional well-heated stone kept the water at boiling point and a 4.5kg leg of mutton wrapped in straw was cooked to perfection in three hours and forty minutes. After this process, it was found that the trough was about two-thirds full of cracked and broken stones, amounting to about 0.5 cubic metres in volume. This material and ash and charcoal from the hearth were thrown to one side to eventually form the stone dump. Assuming the stones were not used more than once, the size of the mound suggested some 54 cooking episodes. A further experiment demonstrated that the stone-lined pit could well have been an oven for another similar piece of mutton was equally well cooked by placing hot stones around and over it for a similar length of time. The boiling experiment has now been repeated many times.

A burnt mound at Drombeg, Co. Cork, situated just over 40m from the stone circle, had a stone-lined trough and a stone-built hearth enclosed by a penannular bank which was built piece-meal during the period of use of the site; at one time associated features included a substantial circular hut. While the question of permanent or temporary occupation could not be resolved, the lack of occupation debris suggested a prolonged though periodic use of the site and the excavator calculated that the volume of burnt stones indicated a minimum of 300 episodes of use. Excavation at a number of other sites has revealed wooden troughs and hearths: one of group of three at Killeens, Co. Cork (Site I) contained a plank-built trough but no formal hearth though there was evidence for fires in various places around the trough; the only find, from beneath the plank floor, was a fragment of thin gold foil which had once covered a tin ring A second mound at Killeens (Site II) had a trough formed from an oak tree trunk and a similar dug-out trough occurred at Ballyvourney II. A trough at Curraghtarsna, Co. Tipperary, was actually made from a re-used logboat. A third site at Killeens (Site III) was a very slight monument; its mound measured only 5m in maximum width, the burnt stone reached a height of only 51cm and its volume was calculated at just five cubic metres. Its trough was simply a shallow unlined pit dug through a thin layer of peat into the impervious gravel below. This site may have been used only half a dozen times and troughs like this could have been lined with leather.

Four burnt mounds were excavated at Ballycroghan, near Bangor, Co. Down. Three contained wooden troughs but one, a low mound of burnt stone and ash, just covered two shallow circular depressions in the underlying clay; these measured 53cm and 68.5cm in diameter respectively and were only 23cm deep. Because these depressions seemed too shallow to have been cooking pits, the excavator suggested that they could have taken the bases of cauldrons, and vessels of either wood or bronze are a possibility, their contents being heated with hot stones in the usual

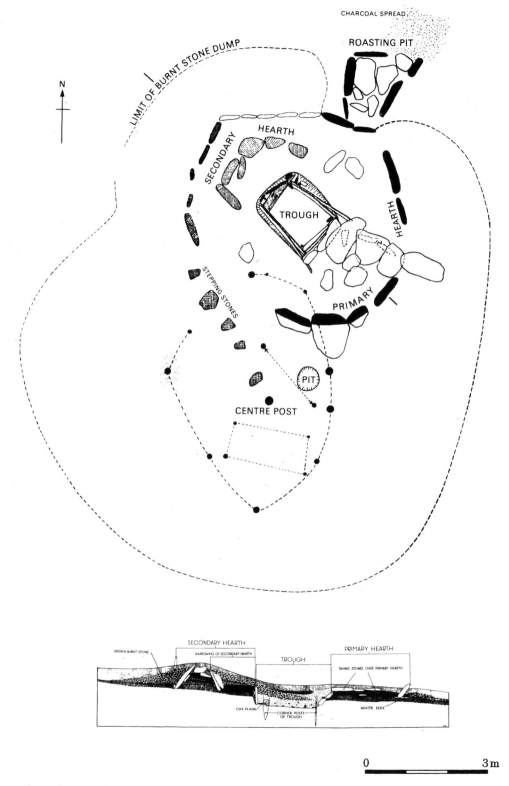

Fig. 65. Plan and section of a burnt mound with hearths, wooden trough, roasting pit or oven, and post-holes of structures at Ballyvourney, Co. Cork.

fashion. Burnt stones or 'pot boilers' from various settlement sites may reflect this practice.

While only a relatively small sample of burnt mounds has been excavated, a mound of heat-fractured stones, a trough, and traces of fires – sometimes a formal hearth – are consistent features. A distinct scarcity of artefacts and food waste such as animal bones seems equally characteristic as far as scientifically excavated sites are concerned. The widespread absence of bone cannot always be attributed to acid soil conditions, at the very least some pieces of burnt bone might be expected to survive. Of course, it could be that the cooking of joints of meat was subject to various sorts of ritual controls and food remains carefully disposed of. Some faunal remains have been recovered from one mound at Fahee South, near Carron, in the Burren, Co. Clare, where a mound with a wooden trough produced five cattle teeth, one deer tooth, two deer antlers, one horse jaw bone and other fragments. The horse bone had been chopped and two other bones showed breaks which might have been due to butchering. The survival of bone here may have been due to reduced soil acidity caused by the effects of carboniferous limestone on the soil and in the ground water.[10]

There is no agreement that burnt mounds were cooking places and the fact that experiment has shown that meat can be boiled in them does not prove that this was their main purpose. They do seem to have been used to prepare large quantities of boiling water and some were repeatedly used over a period of time with the resultant accumulation of quite large mounds of stones. It has been argued that they could have been covered by light structures and used as saunas or sweat-houses, or used for bathing, or for some semi-industrial purpose such as washing or dyeing large quantities of cloth or for dipping hides in hot water as part of the preparation of the leather. Far from suggesting that these sites are the result of the gastronomic activities or the rites of passage of roving bands of hunters, the large numbers so far identified and the clustering and large size of some examples suggests that they were an integrated part of a wider settlement pattern, one in which they served some particular but periodic function. Palynological evidence suggests that a number of burnt mounds on Valencia Island, Co. Kerry, may be broadly contemporary with a phase of closely-grazed grassland not far away and two burnt mounds may be part of a complex of field systems, cairns and wedge tombs near Carron, Co. Clare. There seems to be a puzzling distributional correlation between these mounds and standing stones in the Mooghaun region in Co. Clare.[11]

A relatively extensive series of radiocarbon dates places the majority of burnt mounds firmly in the second millennium BC. Some date to the earlier first millennium BC. Drombeg, for example, has produced a date of 766-410 BC from charcoal from the trough and 994-814 BC from charcoal from the mound, and probably dates to about 800 BC. The range of dates for burnt mounds generally extends from about 1800 to 800 BC and demonstrates that these sites have no connection with the cooking places of those hunter-warriors referred to in early Irish literature and also indicates that the Irish monuments are probably broadly contemporary with similar sites in England, Wales and Scotland.

NOTES

1 Rock art: Johnston 1991 and 1993; Bradley 1991, 1995 and 1997. Reyfad, Co. Fermanagh: Coffey 1911. Derrynablaha and the Iveragh peninsula, Co. Kerry: O'Sullivan and Sheehan 1993 and 1996, 91. Dingle peninsula: Cuppage 1986, 56. Cork: Power 1992, 96 and 1994, 51. Donegal: Lacy 1983, 98; van Hoek and van Hoek 1985; van Hoek 1987, 1988, 1993a and 1993b. Co. Louth: Buckley and Sweetman 1991, 82. South Leinster (Carlow, Wicklow, Kilkenny): Brindley and Kilfeather 1993, 15; Stout 1994, 16; Gibbons 1990, 27. Circles of cup marks: van Hoek 1990. 'Keyhole' motifs: van Hoek 1995. Spiral-like motifs: O'Sullivan and Sheehan 1993, 81; van Hoek 1993b. Cup marks: Burgess 1990. Rock art and copper deposits: O'Brien 1994, 225. Motifs on cist stones: Shee 1972. Astronomical significance of a decorated stone at Boheh, Co. Mayo: Bracken and Wayman 1992; van Hoek 1993. Some rock art at Clehagh, Co. Donegal, has had Christian symbols added: van Hoek 1993a.

2 Stone circles: Burl 1976, Ó Nualláin 1995, 1975, and 1984; variant circles perhaps related to ring cairns: Lynch 1979; other variant monuments: Ó Nualláin 1984a. Kealkil, Co. Cork: Ó Ríordáin 1939. Drombeg, Co. Cork: Fahy 1959; radiocarbon date from charcoal 2740 ± 80 BP (1124-794 BC, OxA-2683), a date of 1350 ± 120 BP (430-953 AD, D-62) is too young (Hedges *et al.* 1993); for the carving on the recumbent stone, see Ó Nualláin 1995, pl. 8. Reanascreena South, Co. Cork: Fahy 1962; charcoal from cremation pit 2780 ± 35 BP (1004-844 BC, GrN-17509), charcoal from beneath bank: 2895 ± 35 BP (1254-998 BC, GrN-17510), peat from near bottom of ditch: 1695 ± 30 BP (252-412 AD, GrN-17511), W. O'Brien 1992.

3 Bohonagh, Co. Cork: Fahy 1961. Cashelkeelty, Co. Kerry: Lynch 1981; stone circle radiocarbon dates: 2920 ± 60 BP (1362-936 BC, GrN-9173) came from charcoal embedded in the old ground surface which was sealed by a layer of stony soil used to level the ground before building the circle; the other, 1665 ± 50 BP (246-528 AD, GrN-9172) was provided by charcoal found in the layer of stony soil; the date of the circle lies between these two determinations. Stone alignments: Burl 1993, Ó Nualláin 1994, Lynch 1981; radiocarbon dates: Maughanasilly, Co. Cork: 3265 ± 55 BP (1678-1438 BC, GrN-9280 and GrN-9281), Dromatouk, Co. Kerry: 3330 ± 50 BP (1740-1520 BC, GrN-9346), Ballycommane, Co. Cork: W. O'Brien 1992. Askillaun, Co. Mayo: Corlett 1997; some other Mayo alignments: O'Hara 1991. Gleninagh, Co. Galway: Gosling 1993, 17, pl. 3; the quotations are from Tim Robinson's evocative account of site and sunset (1996, 200).

4 There is a large body of literature on the question of stone circles and alignments and on their possible astronomical significance: Burl 1976 and 1993; Barber 1973 for stone circles, disputed by Heggie 1991; Ruggles 1994, Lynch 1981a and 1982 for stone alignments.

5 Boulder-monuments: Ó Nualláin 1978; W. O'Brien 1992; radiocarbon date from Cooradarrigan, Co. Cork: 3080 ± 35 BP (1426-1266 BC, GrN-15716).

6 Stone circles in northern Ireland: Davies 1939c. Drumskinny, Co. Fermanagh: Waterman 1964. Castledamph, Co. Tyrone: Davies 1938. Copney Hill, Co. Tyrone: Foley 1983; MacDonagh 1995. Beaghmore, Co. Tyrone: May 1953, Pilcher 1969 and 1975; Brannon 1979; radiocarbon dates from cairn 10: charcoal under cairn, 3485 ± 55 BP (1950-1684 BC, UB-11), organic material from ditch, 2725 ± 55 BP (990-808 BC, UB-163), charcoal from soil near alignment, 3555 ± 45 BP (2034-1764 BC, UB-23), charcoal from hearth, 4135 ± 80 BP (2908-2504 BC, UB-603); Burl 1976, 249; Thom 1980 has claimed that some of the circles and alignments are geometrically and astronomically significant. Cuilbane, Co. Derry: Yates 1985.

7 Stone circles etc.: Banagher, Co. Cavan: O'Donovan 1995, 13. Killycluggin, Co. Cavan: Raftery 1978. Cong, Co. Mayo: Lavelle 1994, nos 4-7, 440, 20, 21, 33-35, etc.; Lohan 1993. Monavullagh Mountains, Co. Waterford: Moore 1995. 'Special places': Cooney and Grogan 1994, 209; as later evidence demonstrates even trees may mark special places: Manning 1988.

8 Standing stones: Iveragh peninsula: O'Sullivan and Sheehan 1996, 58. Dingle peninsula: Cuppage 1986, 43. Donegal: Lacy 1983, 333. Drumnahare and Carrownacaw, Co. Down: Collins 1957b. Killountain, Co. Cork: Twohig and Doody 1989. Ballynamona, Co. Offaly, Culmore, Co. Antrim, and Aghascrebagh, Co. Tyrone: Waddell 1990. Newgrange, Co. Meath: Shee and Evans 1965. Ballybeen, Co. Down: Mallory 1984a. Galway: Gosling 1993, 16. A modern scratching stone has been excavated in Ballygrennan, Co. Limerick: Gowen 1988, 141. A small pillar stone with rock art has been published by Connolly 1991.

9 Burnt mounds: Buckley 1990; Ó Drisceoil 1988, 1990 and 1991; the word *fulacht* means a cooking pit or place, *fian* may mean a roving band of hunters or warriors like the *fianna,* and *fiadh* may mean 'of the deer' or 'of the wild'. Co. Cork: Power 1990, 1992 and 1994. Co. Kerry: Cuppage 1986, 73; Toal 1995, 51; O'Sullivan and Sheehan 1996, 117. Co. Clare: Coffey 1985. Co. Mayo: Buckley and Lawless 1988; Lawless 1990; Higgins 1991. Clare Island, Co. Mayo: Gosling 1994. Slater *et al.* 1996 for successful geophysical analysis. Radiocarbon dates: Brindley *et al.* 1990.

10 Ballyvourney and Killeens, Co. Cork: O'Kelly 1954. Drombeg, Co. Cork: Fahy 1960; radiocarbon dates: 2460 ± 50 BP (766-410 BC, GrN-14718) and 2740 ± 50 BP (994-814 BC, GrN-14719). Other experiments include Fahy 1960, Ó Drisceoil 1988, Buckley 1990, 170, Lawless 1990 and Allen 1994. Curraghtarsna, Co. Tipperary: Buckley 1985; another re-used log boat was found at Teeronea, Co. Clare: Brindley *et al.* 1990. Ballycroghan, Co. Down: Hodges 1955. Other excavated examples are noted in Cleary *et al.* 1987, 45; Gowen 1988, 129; Buckley 1990, 27; Brindley *et al.* 1990. Stray and other finds from burnt mounds have been listed by Cherry in Buckley 1990, 49. Fahee South, Co. Clare: Ó Drisceoil 1988. Alternative uses: Barfield and Hodder 1987; Lucas 1965; alternative approaches: Ray 1990.

11 Valencia Island: Mitchell 1989; Hayden 1994. Carron, Co. Clare: Grant 1995. Mooghaun, Co. Clare: Grogan 1996.

6

Bronze and Gold and Power: 1500–900 BC

The changing pattern of bronze types produced in later prehistory allows part of the broad timespan from about 1500-900 BC to be sub-divided into a series of industrial and chronological phases. The absolute chronology of these phases is often somewhat uncertain and they are best considered no more than loosely delineated stages in the general picture of metalworking development. Their use, no doubt, masks considerable variation in the duration of some types from region to region, as well as considerable chronological overlap and uneven development. Nonetheless, they do offer a convenient means of assessing the changing character and context of artefact types and their relationships (particularly in hoards), and of correlating these developments with those in various parts of Britain and even further afield.

A group of stone moulds found during ploughing near Killymaddy, south of Ballymoney, Co. Antrim, includes moulds for socketed kite-shaped spearheads, dirks, sickles and tanged blades (Fig. 66) and has given its name to a metalworking phase dated to approximately 1500-1350 BC. Dirks and various flanged axes, palstaves and certain types of spearheads are characteristic products of this Killymaddy Phase.[1] Associated finds are very rare but it is possible to correlate, to some extent, developments in Ireland with those in Britain in particular (Table 4). It should be remembered that Derryniggin material continued in use and end-looped spearheads, for instance, were probably partly contemporary with the new kite-shaped and side-looped types.

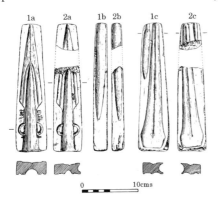

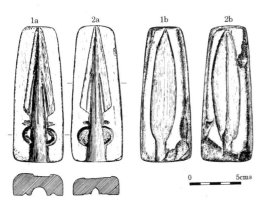

Fig. 66. Two of the stone moulds from Killymaddy, Co. Antrim, showing various faces with matrices for casting kite-shaped spearheads, tanged blades and a dirk.

METALWORK OF THE KILLYMADDY, BISHOPSLAND AND ROSCOMMON PHASES

SPEARHEADS

Kite-shaped spearheads are characterized by a kite-shaped (approximately lozenge-shaped) blade

Traditional Phases	Phases Ireland	England	Approximate Irish dates
Middle Bronze Age 1	**Killymaddy Phase**	Acton Park Phase	1500–1350 BC
Middle Bronze Age 2	**Bishopsland Phase**	Taunton Phase	1350–1200 BC
Middle Bronze Age 3		Penard Phase	1200–1000 BC
Late Bronze Age 1	**Roscommon Phase**	Wilburton Phase	1000–900 BC
Late Bronze Age 2	**Dowris Phase**	Ewart Park Phase	900–600 BC
Iron Age	**Dowris C/Athlone**	Llyn Fawr/Hallstatt	600 BC–400 AD
Iron Age	**La Tène**		

Table 4. Later prehistoric metalworking phases of the traditional later Bronze and Iron Ages.

usually with distinctive ribs or grooves parallel to the edges and sometimes with a median rib on the socket as well. A small hoard of three examples of this type was found in a bog at Tattenamona, south-west of Enniskillen, Co. Fermanagh (Fig. 67) and demonstrates the range of sizes commonly found. Anther common feature is a pair of rather lozenge-shaped side loops placed more or less mid-way along the socket. No longer does the socket terminate at or near the base of the blade as with end-looped spearheads: in a significant development the hollow socket extends into the blade, a technological improvement giving a stouter weapon with a longer socket. Several hundred examples of this type have been found in Ireland where it is widely distributed. It is only occasionally recorded in Britain and thus seems to be a product of the Irish bronze industry. It is very difficult to estimate its date with any accuracy because the type is rarely associated with other material. The Killymaddy moulds imply contemporary manufacture with early dirks and rapiers (below) yet two hoards hint at survival into the Dowris Phase, perhaps into the 9th century BC. At Ballinliss, Co. Armagh, an example was reportedly found with a socketed bronze axe and in Scotland with a bronze sword. Another kite-shaped spear was possibly found near Ballysadare, Co. Sligo, in a cist grave: 'in an artificial cave with partly charred human bones and a vessel of baked clay which fell to pieces on being handled'.[2]

Side-looped spearheads have a leaf-shaped blade which may be short and broad, or long and slender, and side loops usually placed midway on the socket may be leaf or lozenge shaped or semi-circular 'string loops'. Rare examples have been found in Ireland (Fig. 68, 1–2). One half of a stone mould for a leaf-shaped example (with the ribs on blade and socket reminiscent of those features on kite-shaped spearheads) comes from Ballyshannon, Co. Donegal. This leaf-shaped side-looped spearhead was the most popular form in Scotland, and in Britain generally. The preponderance of kite-shaped spears in Ireland and the preponderance of leaf-shaped examples in Britain suggests two broadly complementary and contemporary weapon traditions. The nature of the relationship between them is a matter of debate. The leaf-shaped blade has been variously thought to be of Continental inspiration or even derived from the Irish kite-bladed series. The limited hoard evidence from Scotland and southern Britain suggests a date more or less contemporary with the Bishopsland Phase.

A reminder of the lethal purpose of these weapons comes from a remarkable discovery at

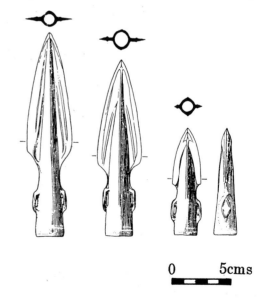

0 5cms

Fig. 67. A hoard of three kite-shaped spearheads with lozenge-shaped side loops from Tattenamona, Co. Fermanagh.

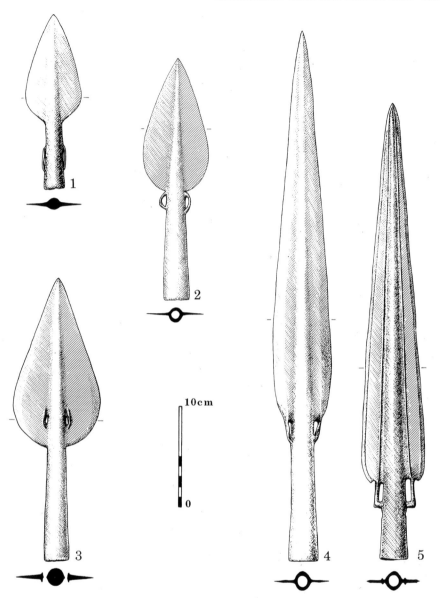

Fig. 68. 1. Side-looped spearhead with leaf-shaped blade from Edenvale, Co. Antrim. 2. Side-looped spearhead from Larkfield, Co. Leitrim. 3. Protected-looped spearhead from the River Bann, Co. Antrim. 4. Basal-looped spearhead from Toome, Co. Antrim. 5. Basal-looped spearhead with triangular blade: no provenance.

Tormarton, Gloucestershire, where the skeletons of two young men aged about nineteen were found. One had a hole in its pelvis apparently made by a lozenge-sectioned spearhead while the other also had the pelvis pierced in this fashion with part of a bronze spearhead still embedded in it but in addition had part of a second spearhead embedded in the lumbar vertebrae.[3] Evidently not all bronze spears were mere status symbols or used in the hunt.

The basal-looped spearhead, with loops at the base of the blade, is an interesting development (Fig. 68, 4-5). These loops may be incorporated in the lower part of the blade or be separate but joined to it. Blades with a slender leaf shape are common and usually have flattened loops which more or less complete the curve of the blade. On a few the loops are narrow rectangular appendages to the base of the blade which is long, slender and approximately triangular in shape. Blades often have a groove on either side of the midrib. Occasionally, a rib occurs on the midrib itself. A small number have blades which seem to have been modelled on the shape of the rapier (below). It is possible that placing the loops close to the base of the blade gave them greater protection. The basal-looped spearhead is an Irish-British form with some significant Continental concentrations notably in western France. The triangular form with a straight base has been called the Enfield Type after a Middlesex find and is also represented on the Continent.

A majority of examples (60%) come from rivers. Associated finds are very few and thus the chronology of these weapons is unclear. Three hoards, from Tempo, Co. Fermanagh, a possible one from Knockanbaun, Co. Sligo, and another from Kish, Co. Wicklow, show their continued use into the Dowris Phase. But evidence from Britain and the Continent indicates that the type had appeared at least by the Bishopsland Phase. The origin of these basal-looped type spearheads is uncertain. It has been suggested, for example, that they represent a hybridisation between British side-looped spears and the Continental leaf-shaped type or that they are an Irish development from the kite-shaped (side-looped) spearhead. In the earlier phases of its development the basal-looped type seems not to have exceeded 25cm to 30cm in length but the late hoards such as Tempo or Knockanbaun (with its spearhead 46cm in length) demonstrate that some late examples are very long. The tendency to lengthen the blade may have commenced as early as the Bishopsland Phase and presumably indicates some development in fighting practice. While the very longest examples may have been prestigious items primarily for parade and display, there is evidence that some were put to murderous use: the tip of a spearhead (with a groove on either side of the midrib) was found impaling the pelvis of a human skeleton at Dorchester, Oxfordshire, and is presumably part of a basal-looped weapon. A combination of long and short spear may have been used in combat: the short one used as a throwing spear, the long spear as a thrusting weapon as was the case in 1st millennium BC Greece.[4]

A series of bronze spearheads called protected-loop spearheads with loops set well within the blade as perforations (Fig. 68, 3) may be an Irish form as they are infrequently encountered in Britain. A raised outer edge to the perforations has prompted the term 'protected-loop' and it is believed they are a development of the side-looped and basal-looped types. The basal and protected loops can hardly have had a functional role and the size of some of these spears (over 60cm in maximum length) and the narrowness of the sockets suggests that they were mainly for display.

DIRKS AND RAPIERS

The second popular weapon type of the Killymaddy Phase (and the following Bishopsland Phase) was a narrow stabbing elongated version of the grooved dagger, the so-called dirk or rapier. The British and Irish examples have been studied by Colin Burgess and Sabine Gerloff and the name dirk is conventionally and arbitrarily applied to blades less than 30cm in length which could have served as cutting knives or daggers as well as a stabbing implement. The longer rapiers were probably specifically intended as thrusting weapons. Almost 1000 dirks and rapiers are recorded from Britain and Ireland and detailed study has shown that there is considerable variety. Indeed Burgess and Gerloff's typology comprises four major groups within which are some 60 types or variants plus quite a number of miscellaneous categories. It is debatable whether or not this sort of complicated typological scheme is really workable, particularly when some of the criteria such as butt shape and blade cross-section are occasionally subjective. Furthermore because butts were often made of thin metal and rivets were often positioned very close to the butt edge, the hafting mechanism (usually a handle of animal horn) often failed and numerous torn rivet holes testify to this. Many so-called rivet notches are in fact torn rivet holes. Six Irish examples retain their horn hafts (as Fig. 69, 3) and two Irish finds, from Kanturk, Co. Cork, and Belleek, Co. Fermanagh, have hollow cast metal hilts; the latter was separately cast and attached to the butt with rivets. One is known from southern England. Only two solid hafts (cast in one piece with the butt) are known, one supposedly from Co. Cork and one from a late hoard from Ambleside, Cumbria.

The four major groups (Groups I-IV) are distinguished by blade cross-section and, in broad general terms, they represent a chronological evolution. However, it is also likely that all of these groups overlap in time for evidence from several British hoards reveals that at least one example of each group has been found associated with an example of every other group, yet on typological grounds or on the evidence of associations with other metal types, most Group I blades are early and

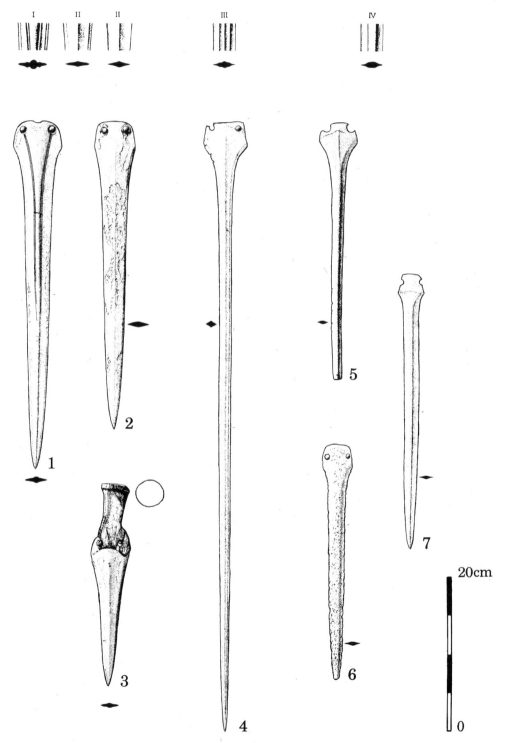

Fig. 69. Above. Blade cross-sections of rapier groups I-IV: I: rounded midrib usually with grooves and/or beading; II: flattened lozenge section with or without bevelled edges; III: triple ribbed; IV: flattened mid-section. Below. 1. Group I rapier from the River Barrow, Riverstown, Co. Kildare. 2. Group II rapier from Keelogue, Co. Galway. 3. Group II dirk with horn handle from a bog in Beenateevaun townland, Co. Kerry. 4. Group III rapier from Lissan, Co. Derry. 5. Group IV rapier from Cloonta, Co. Mayo. 6. Group IV rapier from Carndonagh, Co. Donegal. 7. Group IV rapier from Killukin, Co. Roscommon.

most Group IV blades are late. The four blade forms are fairly readily recognisable (Fig. 69, top): I is characterized by a rounded midrib which may be flanked by grooves, ribs and channels; II has a central ridge giving a slender lozenge-shaped cross-section and blade edges are sometimes distinctly bevelled; III has a triple-ribbed blade; and IV has a flattened or slightly rounded centre section.

In form and blade section, Group I rapiers (and particularly dirks) are close to earlier daggers. So close is the resemblance between some of the dirks and grooved daggers, it is sometimes impossible to distinguish between them. It is this resemblance which suggests that many, if not all, Group I weapons are early. Their lengths vary from 13cm to 58cm but are for the most part 20cm to 30cm; butts are rounded to trapezoidal in shape, mostly with two rivet holes though occasionally a central rivet notch or former river hole also occurs (Fig. 69, 1). A number bear engraved decoration. These weapons are known from Britain, notably from south of the Wash, and from Ireland where they were even more popular. Grooved daggers were evidently a significant element in their development but inspiration for the production of longer, slender, stabbing weaponry was probably of ultimately Continental origin where trapezoidal-hilted rapiers are common. The presence, notably in eastern and southern England, of some rapiers with Breton features presumably reflects this influence.

All the Irish examples are stray finds and unfortunately some 50% are unprovenanced. Of the provenanced pieces, a large number may have come from watery locations such as lakes, rivers or bogs. The absence of associated finds makes dating difficult but some British evidence suggests continued use into the equivalent of the Bishopsland Phase there. The possibility that the Group I examples in later hoards were heirlooms has been advanced by Burgess but the bulk of Irish finds may conceivably date to the Derryniggin and Killymaddy Phases. Two valves of a fine stone mould for casting one dirk and three rapiers of this Group come from Inchnagree, Co. Cork. This mould also contains a matrix for a small leaf-shaped tanged blade of the sort found on one of the Killymaddy moulds (Fig. 66). The important Killymaddy mould assemblage also contained matrices for casting Group II rapiers.

Group II rapiers, with their distinctive lozenge-shaped cross-section, usually have more or less trapezoidal butts with two rivet holes. Occasionally there are four rivet holes as on Continental rapiers. Blade edges are sometimes distinctly bevelled. Most are 20cm to 40cm in length, a few are over 50cm. The longer blade on one of the Killymaddy moulds is almost 38cm long. Those blades over 30cm long are thought with some justification to have been specifically made as thrusting weapons. Burgess and Gerloff attempt to identify several types of Group II rapiers, among them Type Keelogue named after two examples found in the River Shannon at Keelogue, near Portumna, Co. Galway. These are broad, heavy weapons with wide trapezoidal butts (about 6cm across), usually 30cm to 40cm long, and with two or perhaps three rivets (Fig. 69, 2). Almost two-thirds of them have been found in Ireland and, whenever find circumstances have been recorded, all have been found in watery contexts, in river, lake or bog. Group II rapiers are slightly more frequent in Ireland than in Britain (where there are two remarkable concentrations in the Thames area in and near London, and in the Fens of East Anglia). Apart from the Killymaddy mould there is a dearth of Irish dating evidence but typological similarities to Group I rapiers, as well as British and Continental associations, may imply development late in the Derryniggin period (alongside Group I) and use in the Killymaddy and Bishopsland Phases.

Weapons of Group III are almost all 30cm or more in length with a distinctive triple-ribbed blade (which very occasionally is difficult to distinguish from the Group II form with distinct blade edge bevelling). Butts are generally trapezoidal with two rivet holes near the corners. This group includes the longest and most elegant blades of the Irish-British rapier series, some being over 60cm in length. A well known example from a bog at Lissan, near Churchtown, Co. Derry (Fig. 69, 4) is 79.7cm long; its length and extraordinary slenderness must imply that it was made more for display than for stabbing. It shows hardly any signs of use and like many dirks and rapiers may well have been purposefully deposited, perhaps as a votive offering. Almost three-quarters of Group III rapiers have been found in England where a few hoards provide the main dating evidence and indicate a date equivalent to the Bishopsland Phase. A unique find from the vicinity of the Cutts, on the River Bann just south of Coleraine, Co. Derry, has a rod-like tang projecting from the butt. This feature, if inspired by a similar rod-tang on some early swords on the

Continent suggests continued Group III rapier manufacture in Ireland after *c.* 1200 BC.

More than half of all Irish-British rapiers belong to Group IV with a flattened or slightly rounded centre section. On the basis of butt form they are divided into two general categories: (a) weapons with archaic trapezoidal butts with corner rivet holes as in Groups II and III, and (b) what Burgess and Gerloff call weapons in the Appleby tradition which mark a distinct change in the insular rapier tradition. One identifiable type in the first category is Type Cloonta named after a bog find in Co. Mayo; in addition to the characteristic rivet holes near the corners of a trapezoidal butt, it has a vertical rib on the butt which broadens out as it extends onto the blade (Fig. 69, 5). Lengths vary from 25cm to over 50cm.

Several rapiers in a hoard from Appleby, Lincolnshire, display the characteristic features of the second category: smaller, less shapely trapezoidal butts now have rivet holes or notches (some of which are now genuine cast notches) in their sides, not their corners, and blade lengths are generally shorter, between 30cm and 40cm. They continue, of course, to have the more or less flattened centre section (Fig. 69, 6). Of a number of types identified, one, mainly Irish, is Type Killukin (named after a Roscommon find) characterized by small butts with side notches for rivets (Fig. 69, 7), a feature found on several other types. This butt form finds its ultimate development in a series of rapiers with deeply indented or constricted butts in which the traditional trapezoidal outline is lost completely. Many of these rapiers come from Ireland where a Type Cutts (named after another find from the River Bann) has a constricted butt and a slightly leaf-shaped blade showing the influence of early leaf-shaped swords.

Group IV rapiers in the archaic tradition are found both in Britain and in Ireland; those in the Appleby tradition are relatively scarce in Ireland where notched butt forms predominate and continued to be more popular. Indeed it is suggested that rapier manufacture ceased in the south and east of England with the development of the insular leaf-shaped sword *c.* 1200 BC there but elsewhere, in northern Britain and, possibly, in Ireland, the rapier continued perhaps for a number of centuries.[5] The absence of Irish associated finds means that dating again depends on the evidence of a number of British hoards containing rapiers.

Indeed the scarcity of hoards of bronzes in (and just after) the Bishopsland Phase generally means that chronological developments are uncertain. In any event the dirk and rapier fashion was a long-lived one, conceivably spanning at least six centuries throughout which designs – notably in butt and blade shape – continually changed. Ireland shared in a vigorous way in an widespread weapon fashion for slender stabbing implements. The fact that both short dirks and longer rapiers were in contemporary use raises the possibility, as Burgess and Gerloff note, that two-handed combat was practised with dirk in one hand and rapier in the other. The wetland context of so many finds is noteworthy as is the likelihood that some of the more splendid pieces (like Lissan) were made for display rather than practical use.

DEPOSITION OR LOSS?

It has been estimated that 45.7% of Irish rapiers with details of discovery recorded have been found on wet sites and the percentages from wetlands for Burgess and Gerloff's four main Groups are 26%, 38%, 45% and 51% respectively. If these Groups do represent a broad typological and chronological sequence then these figures possibly indicate an increase in the practice of wetland deposition through time. Rivers seem to have been the most desirable location (68%) followed by bogs (22%) and lakes (10%). It may be that the formal disposal of prestige bronzes was now more or less confined to wetland contexts, particularly in the open water of rivers, and certain rivers like the Shannon (notably at Keelogue), the Bann and the Barrow seem to have been particularly favoured. These bronzes were valuable commodities not lightly discarded and this, therefore, may well have been an elite ritual activity.

It is a great pity that the find circumstances of most dirks and rapiers are poorly recorded but given that so many of them have been recovered from such wetland contexts it does seem strange that only one scabbard has ever been recorded: traces of a wooden scabbard (made of flat laths of hazel bound with narrow bronze bands) were found with a Suffolk rapier from West Row, near Mildenhall. This scarcity of scabbards might support the belief that all or almost all of these finds are the results of ritual activity in which just the weapon figured. The high proportion of prehistoric weaponry from riverine contexts at certain times in prehistory is one of the principal arguments in favour of this thesis, and in the case of rapiers the numerical evidence is certainly compelling. That said, some finds may reflect the proximity of settlements and others may be the result of loss – for river systems were undoubtedly important route-ways and they may have also provided suitable locations for barter and exchange. Rapiers are the commonest bronze object found in the River Shannon at this time, and are replaced by spearheads in the following Dowris Phase; it does seem likely that at least a proportion of this material was ritually deposited. In contrast, a concentration of bronzes of various dates from the River Blackwater comes from just downstream of a ford and they may have been casual losses.[6] But it is also possible that some rivers served as boundaries between warring communities and became the focal points for confrontations.

AXES AND PALSTAVES

A series of axes and palstaves is the third major bronze product of this period. The Irish material has yet to be studied in detail. Derryniggin type axes and related forms continued in use in the Killymaddy Phase but were in time superseded by their typological successors, the short-flanged axes. Included in this category are what some writers have called haft-flanged axes with long low flanges rounded in side-view and wing-flanged axes with high flanges angular in side-view and sometimes bent inwards to grip the haft more firmly (Fig. 70).

Short-flanged axes are so-called because prominent flanges were shortened (presumably to economise on metal) and confined more or less to the upper hafted part of the axe with little or no continuation down the sides of the blade. Viewed from the side they often have a convex appearance. In typologically early specimens, the axe splays in plan from butt to broad crescent-shaped cutting edge. Later short-flanged axes have slender parallel-sided hafts and splay is confined to the lower blade. Some short-flanged axes have a stop-ridge, but on some typologically later ones the thinning between the flanges is accentuated and ends in a ledge-like stop. Early and late short-flanged axes display considerable variety of form. This variety contrasts with the more standardized Continental products of the time and perhaps implies smaller and more individualistic workshops in Ireland as in Britain. A significant number of Irish finds are unprovenanced and the virtual absence of helpful hoard associations means that dating is difficult. An early short flanged axe (of the haft-flanged variety) and a typologically later example (with wing-flanges) were seemingly found together in a bog at Doagh Glebe, near Derrygonnelly, Co. Fermanagh (Fig. 70, 1-2), in the last century and two wing-flanged specimens were found in similar circumstances at Kilnamanagh, near Collooney, Co. Sligo (Fig. 70, 3-4).[7]

The palstave is an implement which represents a development of the flanged axe principle but one burdened with an antiquated and ill-suited name.

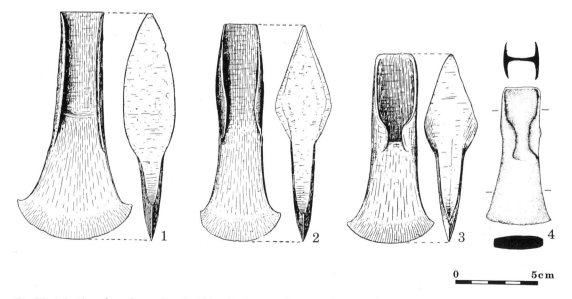

0   5cm

Fig. 70. 1-2. Short-flanged axes. Doagh Glebe, Co. Fermanagh. 3-4. Kilnamanagh, Co. Sligo.

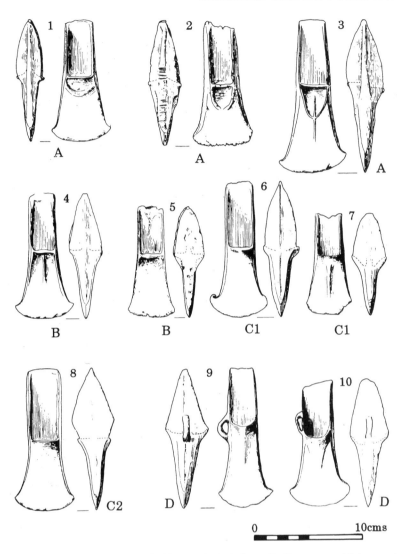

Fig. 71. *The Irish palstave series. 1-3. Group A (shield-pattern). 4-5. Group B (flanges extend below stop). 6-8. Group C (continuous flange-stop line). 6-7. C1, low-flanged; 8, C2, high-flanged. 9-10. Group D (looped, narrow blade). All 'Ireland': unprovenanced.*

This unfortunate term was borrowed from Danish archaeology in the 19th century and came originally from Icelandic *Paalstab*, a digging tool. Various definitions of a palstave have been offered. An important characteristic is a ledge stop or a bar-ledge stop with the blade below the stop being significantly thicker than the septum between the flanges; also important is the height of the stop which should be more or less the height of the adjoining flanges and all should usually form a continuous U-shaped feature (Fig. 71). This fusing of stop and flanges is a distinguishing feature of the palstave. Some examples of the so-called 'West European' palstave series occur in Ireland. This is a widespread form characterized by a broad blade and correspondingly narrow body with a cast U-shaped (shield-shaped) or Y-shaped motif below the stop. This form was particularly popular (instead of the flanged axe) in southern Britain including north Wales. Similar palstaves in north-western France, the Netherlands and northern Germany are testimony to a vigorous pattern of contact. However, the cross-channel impact of the Irish bronze industry declined in the Killymaddy Phase and, in the corresponding Acton Park Phase, north Welsh metal sources seem to have supplied much of England where the novelty of lead alloying makes its appearance for a relatively short period. The

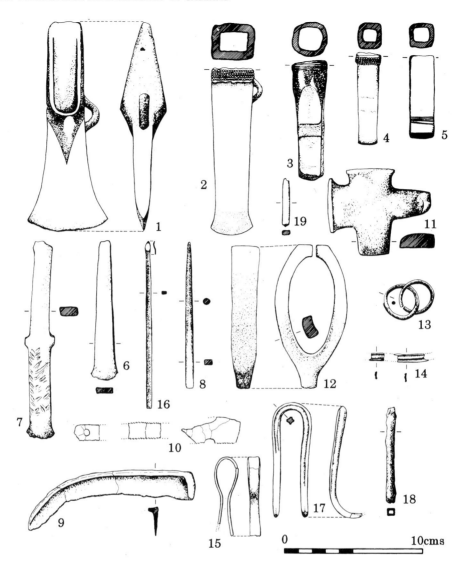

Fig. 72. The Bishopsland hoard, Co. Kildare.

addition of small amounts of lead (2% to 7%) to bronze improves its casting capabilities and lowers its melting point.

A number of these Anglo-Welsh shield pattern (also called Group I) and midribbed (Group II) palstaves occur in Ireland and a bronze mould for one of the former from 'Ireland' but with no precise provenance has been identified. A looped, low-flanged (Group III) palstave with a trident pattern below the stop comes from the Annesborough hoard (Fig. 73) and another with a midrib from a lost find in Co. Westmeath.

Most Irish palstaves have a distinctively local character tending to be short, squat pieces with deep stops and high flanges. An undercut stop

which acts as a type of socket for the haft is a distinctively Irish feature. A number of stone moulds are preserved. The typological development of these Irish palstaves broadly follows that of the British series and they are provisionally divided into four basic groups. Group A comprises shorter and broader versions of British shield pattern palstaves with the characteristic U-shaped motif below the stop; occasionally a vertical rib forms a trident pattern. Ledge and bar-ledge stops occur and flanges may extend below them, curving inwards to form the shield. Many have the peculiarly Irish feature of prominent casting seams on the sides, and flanges may vary from low rounded to high angular forms when viewed from the side. Group B are

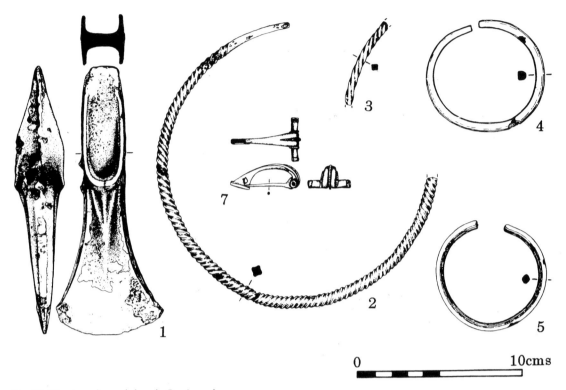

Fig. 73. The Annesborough hoard, Co. Armagh.

broadly similar but instead of a shield pattern have a vertical midrib (like British Group II palstaves) or are plain. Flanges extend below the stop and are usually rounded in side-view.

In Group C, flanges are not extended but may, in side-view, form convex curves from stop to butt (low-flanged: C1) or have their highest point above the butt and be often angular in outline (high-flanged: C2). This differentiation on the basis of the treatment of the flanges recalls British Group III palstaves but otherwise there are few similarities. Plain and midribbed specimens are known and blades may be splayed or narrow. Under-cut stops occur and are presumably the culmination of attempts to strengthen and improve the split haft method.

In Britain, the name Transitional palstave has been given to examples chronologically and typologically placed between broad-bladed palstaves of the Taunton Phase and later examples with narrower blades. Blades are only slightly expanded and often have a midrib; flanges, in side-view, form a straight line from butt to stop. A loop (presumably to help secure the object to its haft) is a characteristic feature. Group D seems to be the Irish

version of this Transitional type. They may have slightly expanded blades, usually with a midrib. A loop is a regular feature and flanges tend to have the straight line from butt to stop. A Group D palstave occurs in the Bishopsland hoard (Fig. 72) described below and a Transitional palstave was apparently found with a flange-twisted gold torc with recurved terminals at Croxton, Norfolk, which dates to the 12th century and the Penard Phase.[8] Again, associated finds are rare in Ireland and, as with short-flanged axes, the pattern of development and the date of these objects are difficult to assess. There is no Irish version of the British late, narrow-bladed and looped variety.

The range and diversity of short-flanged axes and palstaves is remarkable and, at least in part, may be due to a continuing concern to improve hafting methods. However, they also show considerable variation in size (52mm to 192mm) and weight (44gm to 903gm) and it is likely that they served a range of wood-working functions, though use as weapons is possible too. If they did have this multiplicity of purposes then a wider range of designs was likely and, moreover, they may not have been subject to the control of specialist weapons smiths (if such existed). They may have been valuable objects nonetheless: the average weight of a flanged axe (370g) and palstave (313g) is significantly higher than that for spears or dirks and rapiers, in other words they were not insignificant in terms of metal quantity.

THE BISHOPSLAND AND ANNESBOROUGH HOARDS

Two significant finds of bronzes are attributed to the Bishopsland Phase and indicate some correlation with the metalwork of the Taunton Phase in southern England, a phase, which is generally dated to *c.* 1350-1200 BC on the basis of a range of Continental parallels for the British material.

The hoard from Bishopsland, Co. Kildare (Fig. 72), was found in 1942, near Ballymore Eustace, during work on the Poulaphuca hydro-electric scheme. Unfortunately it was dispersed after discovery and may originally have contained items other than those recorded. As it stands it appears to be a remarkable hoard of the tools and other possessions of a smith. It includes such metalworking implements as bronze socketed hammers (nos 3-5), a possible vice (no. 12) and a miniature anvil with three work surfaces and a stem presumably for insertion into a block of wood. A small anvil like this would obviously have been used for delicate work. Other implements include two chisels (nos 6 and 7), and a double-edged saw (no. 10). Three items of particular interest are a sickle blade (no. 9), a simple form of flesh-hook (no. 17: so-called because such objects are thought to have been used for hooking meat from a boiling cauldron or cooking pit) and a square-mouthed socketed axe (no. 2). Several of these types find parallels in southern British hoards of the Taunton Phase. One such is the looped socketed axe, a small, narrow tool presumably used chisel-like for light wood or other work. This is the earliest socketed axe form and the multiple mouldings on the Bishopsland piece imply casting in a clay mould. Hollow cast sockets, of course, were familiar to the makers of bronze spearheads. This axe, like the three socketed hammers from the same hoard, should possibly be considered part of a general tradition of specialized craftsmens' tools. It has been suggested more than once that these tools were the equipment of a travelling smith, perhaps hidden for safekeeping, but little is known about the nature of

the socio-economic role of the metal worker at this time (below).

The Annesborough hoard, found near Lurgan, Co. Armagh, in 1913, raises other questions (Fig. 73). It was found at a depth of about 23cm when a tree-root was being removed and consisted of a low-flanged palstave, a bronze spiral-twisted neck-ring or torc, a fragment of another, two penannular bracelets (one of D-shaped, the other of lozenge-shaped cross-section), and a fibula or brooch of provincial Roman type. Apart from the fibula which dates to about the 1st century AD, all the objects find parallels in southern British hoards of the Taunton Phase where palstaves and bronze personal ornaments such as twisted torcs and bracelets, and plain bracelets often of lozenge-shaped cross-section, are among the characteristic finds.[9] For this reason it is generally assumed that the fibula is simply a later intrusion but it is also possible that a genuine ancient hoard, first discovered in the 1st century AD, was reburied with the addition of a fibula perhaps to personalize a later votive offering. It is worth remembering after all that a recurved terminal of a Bishopsland Phase gold torc bearing a Roman inscription was found at Newgrange.

A third small hoard found in 1959 at a depth of about 2m in a bog at Clooneenbaun, north-west of Roscommon town, Co. Roscommon, contained just two bronze objects: a bracelet of circular cross-section with tapered terminals and a small cast ribbed bracelet; they have Continental parallels and may even have been imports.[10]

GOLD WORK

A series of novel gold types form an important and remarkable addition to the range of Bishopsland Phase metalwork. Found singly and in a significant number of hoards, this gold work is evidence of exceptional gold-working skill and further testimony to wide-ranging contacts with Britain and with north-western Continental Europe. Various forms of what seem to be personal ornaments, torcs, bracelets, ear rings and tress rings are commonest, and gold bar work now represents a noteworthy innovation.

TORCS

Torcs or neck rings, usually made of twisted gold, include bar torcs, flange-twisted torcs, and ribbon torcs. Various writers have suggested typological classifications based on the nature of the spiral

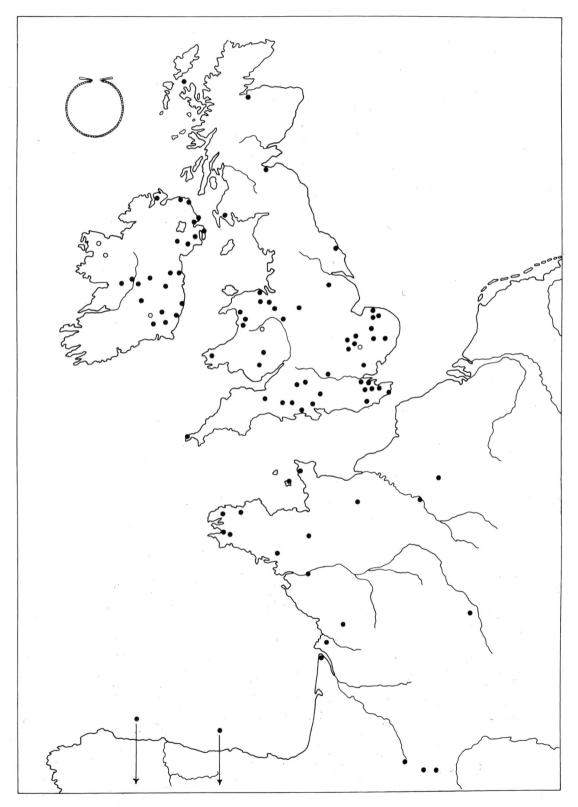

Fig. 74. Distribution of gold bar torcs.

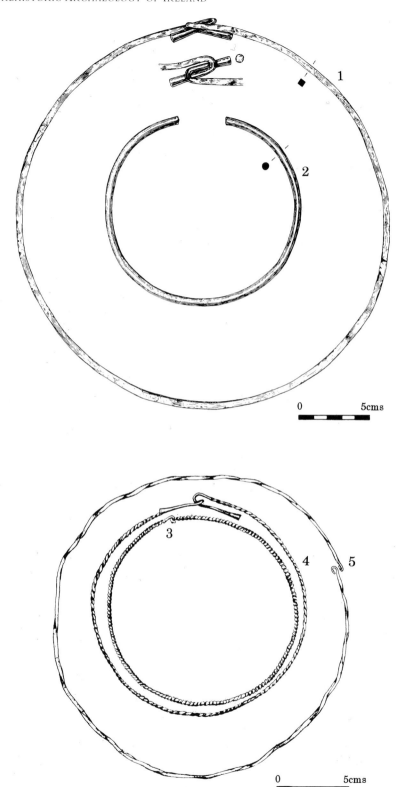

Fig. 75. Gold bar torcs. 1-2. Pair from Enniscorthy, Co. Wexford. 3-5. Bar-twisted torcs: 3. Unprovenanced. 4-5. Two bar-twisted torcs from Athlone, Co. Westmeath, one loosely twisted.

twisting and on terminal form and some would distinguish between torcs made from a stout wire and those made from a more substantial bar or rod but here the general term bar torc is used of both and also embraces both the bar-twisted and the flange-twisted varieties.

As their name implies bar torcs are made from a thick wire (up to about 3mm in thickness) or a more substantial bar of gold (usually 4mm–9mm in thickness) which may be of square, triangular, circular or oval cross-section. Square cross-sectioned bars are commonest. The great majority are elegantly spiral-twisted usually in a right-handed or clockwise manner and, as already mentioned, the torsion or twisting may be described as either bar-twisted or flange-twisted. All are penannular with terminals which are often hooked or re-curved and tapering, some have described them as club-shaped.

Some 38 bar torcs are recorded from Ireland, mostly from the east and north-east, almost 50 from Britain and a scatter of about 20 examples from the Continent, mainly in north-western France but extending as far south as Spain (Fig. 74). In Ireland many are fragmentary and almost 40% are unprovenanced or with county only recorded. Precise details of circumstances of discovery have been very rarely recorded.

Bar-twisting consisted of spiral twisting a bar of gold possibly holding one end in a vice and the other in a pliers of some sort. The results presumably gave the object greater aesthetic appeal allowing light to play in different ways on the surface and both fine tight twisting and looser twisting occur. A large untwisted example of square section with a diameter of about 27cm found (with a smaller gold torc) near Enniscorthy, Co. Wexford, is believed to be an unfinished piece (Fig. 75, 1).

About a dozen bar-twisted examples are recorded from Ireland and a slightly greater number in Britain; Irish finds include a bog find from Carrowdore, Co. Down, one unprovenanced example and two 19th century discoveries from near Athlone, Co. Roscommon, with diameters ranging from about 14cm to 20cm (Fig. 75, 3–5). All but one of these have simple hook-shaped terminals; one of the Athlone finds (like the large Enniscorthy example) has elongated recurved tapering terminals. It is generally believed that the bar-twisted gold torcs with simple hooked terminals in Ireland and in Britain are versions of the similarly twisted bronze form seen in the Annesborough and Bishopsland hoards and more widely distributed in southern England.[11]

FLANGE-TWISTED TORCS

Flange-twisted torcs are more intricate pieces of work: again an ingot of gold was forged to the appropriate length and diameter but then three or four deep longitudinal cuts were made in the bar which was hammered to a threefold or cruciform section with three or four protruding flanges, and finally spiral twisted (Fig. 76). This provided a deeper spiral and presumably accentuated the effect achieved by simple bar-twisting. Experimentation has shown that this sort of flange cutting can be done with a small chisel, a punch and an anvil and an even width may have been achieved by drawing the twisted torc through a die or by rolling it between two flat surfaces. It has also been suggested over the years by a number of writers that these torcs could have made by soldering or fusing or hammer-welding strips of gold together but this, if done at all, was rare; soldering on examples from Shropshire and Essex has been shown to be due to ancient repairs. A few Irish torcs of this type have hooked terminals, three flanges and are loosely twisted; these appear to be a specifically Irish form. Coolmanagh, Co. Carlow (Fig. 77, 1), though untwisted is a good illustration of the three-flanged form. Most flanged torcs, however, have tighter spiral-twisting with four flanges and invariably have tapering terminals. These terminals are usually round-sectioned and some were clearly made before the rest of the body was flange-twisted (as on the Enniscorthy example). Joan Taylor differentiates between these integral terminals, which are an integral part of the torc and usually associated with broad flanges and wider twisting, and separate terminals which were evidently soldered or fused to the twisted body. The latter torcs have an abrupt termination of the fluting caused by the flanges and usually have narrow, more tightly twisted flanges which have been hammered directly on the edge to produce a slight thickening or expansion of the edges themselves; she suggests that this form is a later development. A few terminals are faceted and one fine torc from Co. Mayo, with a diameter of about 27cm has its faceted terminals decorated with engraved herringbone ornament. Two exceptionally large torcs were found at the Rath of the Synods at Tara in the early 19th century, one has broad flanges, the other narrow flanges – but both have

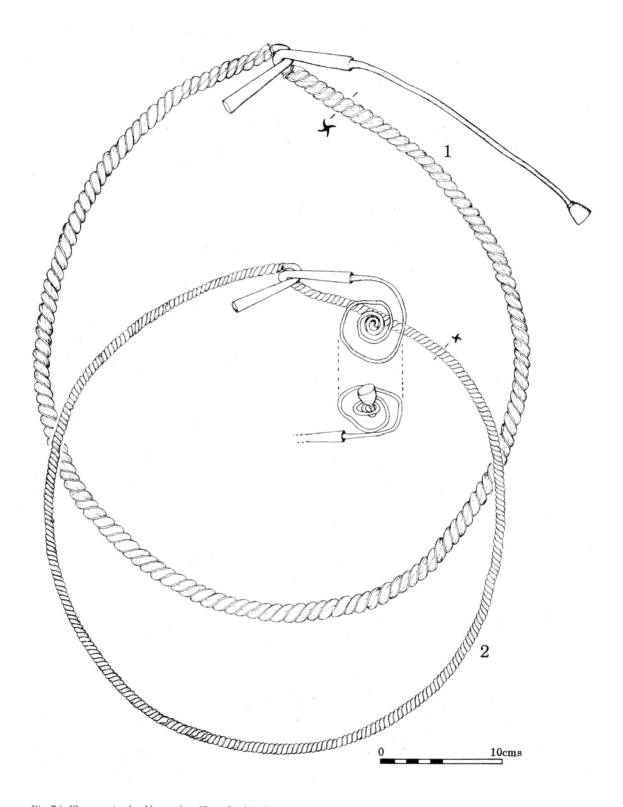

Fig. 76. Flange-twisted gold torcs from Tara, Co. Meath.

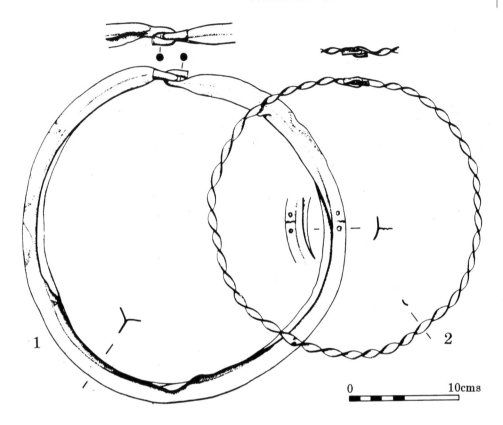

Fig. 77. Possible hoard from Coolmanagh, Co. Carlow. 1. Untwisted triple-flanged torc. 2. Ribbon torc.

separate terminals. One terminal on each example has curious sprouting extensions (Fig. 76). The largest of the Tara torcs has a diameter of some 42cm (and – if extended – a total length of about 167cm including the extension).

As their name suggests, it is generally assumed that these torcs were worn as neck ornaments but the Tara pieces and some others are large enough to be worn around the waist if indeed they were ever worn at all, and some English and French examples (found wound into several coils) may well have served as armlets.[12]

Flange-twisted torcs have, in the past, been labelled the 'Tara type' giving the impression of an Irish product but this is misleading because greater numbers have been found in Britain, with significant concentrations in Wales and East Anglia in particular where there may have been other important centres of production (Fig. 74). There is also a possible correlation between weight and distribution: large torcs have weights in the region of 750g and examples come from Tara, Wales and Jersey, but torcs in the weight range 567g to 316g are mainly found in Ireland and north-western France while examples in the range 200g to 275g are largely found in Wales and the Marches. The weight range 160g to 186g also seems to have a regional distribution but in southern and eastern England. The significance of these possible 'regional weight standards' is not clear, they may be a further indication of regional production centres or reflect regional fashions. The presence of the very large torcs in several of these regions may indicate a hierarchy of torcs and possibly a hierarchy of owners as well.

The resemblance between bar-twisted gold torcs and their bronze counterparts confirms a Bishopsland-Taunton Phase date and flange-twisted examples with similar simple hooked terminals (like Coolmanagh) may be broadly contemporary. English associations suggest that at least the majority of flange-twisted torcs with tapering terminals are somewhat later, belonging to the Penard Phase of the 12th-11th centuries BC. Peter Northover notes that there are differences in the silver content of these torcs: the earlier ones have a silver content of 10-12%, the Penard examples 17-19% which may indicate a change in gold sources and a move away from the Irish and Welsh ores perhaps towards a Continental origin. Richard Warner, on the basis of a review of copper and tin content, has argued that even a somewhat later date is likely for flanged-twisted torcs.[13]

RIBBON TORCS

Ribbon torcs are relatively simple ornaments made from a band of gold loosely or moderately spiral twisted. Terminals are hooked and most expand slightly sometimes forming small knobs but other shapes are known as well. There are some 64 examples from Ireland, from some 40 find-spots, all but two of them usually placed in the Bishopsland Phase. Some fifty examples are recorded from Scotland with one find each from Wales and from England (where two bronze specimens have also been found in Taunton Phase hoards). The type is clearly an Irish-Scottish one (Fig. 140) with a quite different distribution to the bar torc and presenting many problems both typological and chronological which have yet to be resolved. Scottish examples tend to be more rigid, thicker and narrower in the ribbon and have simple hooked terminals while the Irish pieces are more flexible with knobbed terminals and also tend to have a more acute angle to the spiral twist than the Scottish. Dimensions vary too, from as little 8cm (presumably armlets) to over 21cm. Most could have served as neck ornaments but examples have been sometimes found in cut fragments and may have had a role as a form of currency at some stage.

The unique Coolmanagh association of a flange-twisted torc and a ribbon torc (Fig. 77) would seem to confirm that some gold ribbon torcs belong to the Bishopsland Phase but even here there are problems. These two objects were found together in 1978 in the course of disc-harrowing a field but the finder reported finding 'similar pieces' six years before this and throwing them away. It is uncertain, therefore, if the two torcs are a closed find, they could be re-discoveries and one or both of them might be part of another find. This uncertainty is important because while ribbon torcs have been found in other hoards they have usually been found with other ribbon torcs. There are two significant exceptions and these are two definite associations, a gold ribbon torc from Somerset, south of Ballinasloe, Co. Galway, was found with several decorated bronze mounts and other objects dated to the 1st century BC or the 1st century AD (Fig.

139), and the other from Knock, Co. Roscommon, was found in a wooden box with a superb gold torc and generally dated to about 300 BC (Fig. 138). The Knock ribbon torc has unusual hollow pear-shaped terminals and it has been claimed that those of the Somerset torc (straight and square-sectioned) may be later additions. It is possible that these are re-used or re-modelled pieces and that the bulk of ribbon torcs do belong to the Bishopsland Phase or perhaps a fashion for ribbon torcs was revived in the later centuries BC. Significantly, gold analyses have shown that ribbon torcs contain a platinum trace of not more than 0.012% in common with other later gold objects like the Broighter torc. When the evidence of the platinum trace is combined with the values for copper and tin, this goldwork appears to be completely distinct from the gold of the Bishopsland Phase and, when the flimsiness of the archaeological evidence is also considered, a date in the last few centuries BC is more likely.[14] Ribbon torcs are therefore considered again in Chapter 8.

EAR RINGS

Various sorts of penannular gold ear rings are another innovation of the Bishopsland Phase and amongst these are bar-twisted and flange-twisted examples. There are some 16 recorded from Ireland, a few in Britain and about 20 from France. Two bar-twisted examples, each slightly different, were acquired by the National Museum in 1927 and are said to have been found at Tara, Co. Meath 'with some bronze objects, since lost' (Fig. 78, 1). Another bar-twisted example was found with a spiral finger ring at Ardmayle, Co. Tipperary. These and the half a dozen other Irish bar-twisted examples have parallels in France where acceptable associations are known.

A flange-twisted pair is said to have been found near Castlerea, Co. Roscommon (Fig. 78, 2) probably in the 18th century but their find circumstances are not recorded. They and the one other Irish find of this sort all come from the same 19th century collection and are remarkably similar to gold ear rings from Senegal, west Africa, some of which date to the last few centuries and where bar-twisted forms also occur. Whether these Irish flange-twisted ear rings (and indeed some or all of the French finds) and the African examples represent the convergent development of the same type of ornament in different places at different times or whether they and the French specimens

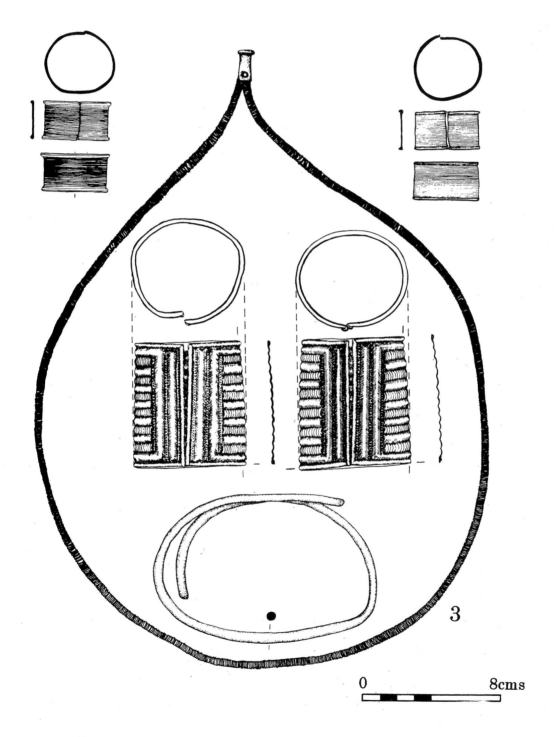

Fig. 78. 1. Pair of bar-twisted gold ear rings from Tara, Co. Meath. 2. Pair of flange-twisted gold ear rings said to have been found near Castlerea, Co. Roscommon. 3. The Derrinboy hoard, Co. Offaly.

are recent imports (from a former French colony) remains to be seen. Another type of ear ring is a beaded form: one of the two recorded is unprovenanced, the other was found in a bog near Macroom, Co. Cork.[15]

It has been argued that the technique of flange-twisting, be it on torc or ear ring, was inspired by a supposedly Mediterranean technique termed 'strip twisting' (in which two V-shaped strips of gold were soldered apex to apex and then twisted) but this particular suggestion has been discounted.[16] It is possible that flange-twisting may be just an ingenious way of achieving a deeper spiral twist with a greater contrast of light and shade and, while bar-twisting in gold may indeed have been inspired by Continental fashions for spiral-twisted bronze work, the practice of decorating a leather piece with spiralled gold wire, as on the composite necklet in the Derrinboy hoard, may have been a contributing factor.

THE DERRINBOY HOARD

A unique discovery was made in a Co. Offaly bog in 1959. Turf cutting in Derrinboy, near Ballyboy, uncovered a hoard of objects at a depth of about 4m. It comprised two gold cuff-shaped bracelets, two tress (or hair) rings also of gold and a composite necklet (Fig. 78, 3). All the items were found within a circle about 13cm across formed by a piece of stout copper wire. The necklet consists of a leather core just over 90cm in length, a strip folded over and sewn with gut, covered with closely coiled gold wire. The core measures 4mm across and the gold wire, of D-shaped cross-section is 1mm wide and 0.5mm thick. Unwound, the wire, apparently hammered in several pieces, has a total length of 15.25m. The other objects are made of sheet gold: two small items, formed of a rectangular sheet of gold are bent into a circular shape just 37mm in diameter, are assumed to be tress rings; they are 27mm wide and the outer surfaces are decorated with fine horizontal grooves. Two larger pieces, also of sheet gold, are similarly formed cuff-shaped bracelets with average diameters of about 65mm; they bear ribbed repoussé decoration. Two similar bracelets are known: one found at the base of a stone along with a piece of pottery and a copper object at Dysart, Co. Westmeath, the other found at Skrene, Co. Sligo.[17]

The Derrinboy hoard would appear to be a set of personal ornaments deliberately deposited in boggy ground presumably as a votive offering of some sort. This ritual explanation may also apply to the other hoards of gold objects of the period and perhaps to many of the single finds as well.

BRACELETS

Bracelets, be they of sheet gold as at Derrinboy or made from a bar of gold, are the commonest ornament. Those made from a penannular bar belong to a common form of bracelet in later prehistoric Ireland and Britain but one with many different types of terminal and forms of cross-section. Dating is often difficult, depending – particularly in the case of the simpler types – on typological details and a few associations. The earliest examples of this penannular form are found in the Bishopsland Phase. They usually have simple unexpanded terminals and the body may vary in cross-section: simple circular cross-sections, lozenge-shaped cross-sections and square cross-sections with spiral twisted body are all recorded. Some 20 examples of the type with circular cross-section with simple terminals (that is plain or at most very slightly but evenly expanded) are known from half a dozen hoards, the majority coming from two found on Cathedral Hill, Downpatrick, Co. Down (Fig. 79).

The Downpatrick hoards are rare instances of well documented discoveries. Hoard no. 1, found in the course of grave-digging in 1954, had been carefully deposited in a very small pit, 20cm in greatest diameter, covered by some stones; it consisted of eleven bracelets and part of a neck ring which had been carefully stacked one upon the other, the smaller ones at the bottom, the three largest at the top and separated from the rest by an inch of clay filling. Five of the bracelets had lozenge shaped cross-sections, six had circular cross-sections. One of these (no. 11: several times heavier than the others) was represented by just one half and a chisel mark clearly showed that it had been partly cut by such an implement. Another (no. 9), also more massive than the rest, had some decoration on the terminals: engraved concentric rings on the flat end and engraved triangles on the body. Only about half the neck ring (no. 12) had been deposited and it too had been partly cut with a chisel and one terminal hammered back against the body. Whether this represented ritual destruction is not clear but two of the three heaviest pieces in the hoard were singled out in this way. The neck ring was decorated with panels of engraved herringbone ornament and it

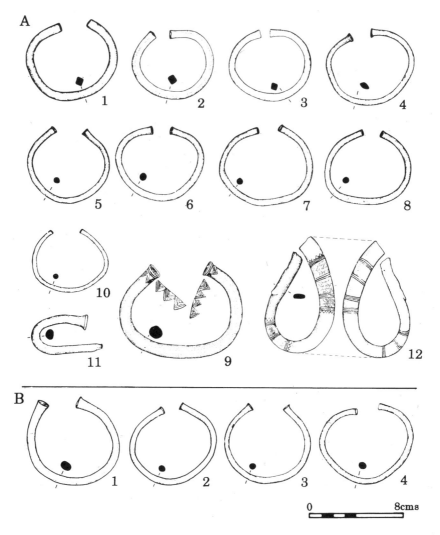

Fig. 79. Two gold hoards from Downpatrick, Co. Down. A. Hoard no. 1. B. Hoard no. 2.

may be that it is related to Iberian decorated neck rings of Berzocana type.

Hoard no. 2 was discovered in similar circumstances two years later some 20m from the site of the first. This time four bracelets had been stacked in a very small pit and three small stones had been placed in the pit on top of them. All four are of more or less circular cross section with slightly expanded terminals.

Both hoards were found within some 20m of the site of limited excavations undertaken on the south-western side of the hill in the 1950s. These excavations had revealed extensive traces of late prehistoric occupation mainly in the form of coarse pottery but whether hoards and settlement are contemporary is uncertain and the site was not a hillfort as was once thought.[18]

The association of the rare form of lozenge sectioned bracelet with those of circular cross-section at Downpatrick implies the contemporaneity of the two types and the chronology of the Bishopsland Phase goldwork rests in great measure on the evidence of a limited number of hoards as well as on typological parallels with material elsewhere. A poorly documented hoard found in 1858 at Saintjohns, near Castledermot, Co. Kildare, contained five gold ornaments: a circular sectioned bracelet, two spirally twisted armlets and two tress rings of grooved sheet gold. In this instance the so-called tress rings were both large and heavy enough to be bracelets (Fig. 80). Like Downpatrick hoard no. 1, it provides a crucial, if tenuous, link between several different types of gold work. Unfortunately, most of the dozen or so gold hoards attributable

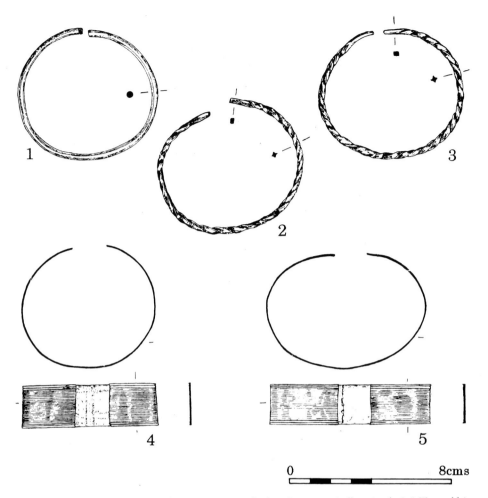

Fig. 80. Gold hoard from Saintjohns, Co. Kildare. 1-3. Penannular bracelets: two spirally twisted. 4-5. Two gold 'tress rings' or bracelets.

with some degree of plausibility to the Bishopsland Phase are inadequately documented or questionable in some other way. Trustworthy associations between different types are surprisingly few and dating rests on this sort of slender evidence (Table 5).

GIFTS TO THE GODS?

The practice of depositing hoards of metal objects in the ground is not a new departure. Axes and halberds were the favoured objects at an earlier date but hoard deposition was not common in the ensuing Killymaddy Phase though single finds of rapiers, for example, may in some cases represent another sort of depositional pattern in wet locations. What is new in the Bishopsland Phase is the range of personal ornaments and the predilection for the use of gold. The belief that these are valuable possessions buried for safekeeping in a time of danger is an old one but it should not be

Hoard	Braclet lozenge section	Braclet circular section	Braclet spiral twisted	Groooved 'tress ring'	Bracelet ribbed
Downpatrick 1 Co. Down	●	●			
Saintjohns Co. Kildare		●	●	●	
Derrinboy Co. Offaly				●	●

Table 5. Associated gold finds of the Bishopsland Phase.

dismissed entirely because it may yet be testable if, for instance, settlement excavation ever demonstrates a contemporary concern with fortification in turn suggesting political instability. But at present it seems to be a less than adequate explanation. Why conceal just a selection of gold objects and not some prized bronzes as well? The restricted range of artefacts, and the rarity of combined finds of gold and bronze artefacts indicate that other factors may apply.

It has been suggested that the decline in urn burial may have ushered in an alternative cult of the dead which demanded the burial of some of an individual's prized possessions instead of the corpse – which was presumably disposed of in some way which left no archaeological trace. This is a possibility though it should be recalled that flamboyant grave offerings were not a feature of earlier times and now the range of objects is so restricted it is not even possible to know if we are dealing with sets of male or female ornaments. A ritual explanation, though not necessarily one associated with death, seems plausible and ritual activity might well increase in times of social or economic stress. Such a ritual purpose could explain the selectivity but there are other possibilities too. It is by no means certain that all the objects are simply personal ornaments, they like earlier lunulae could have had other social roles, perhaps as emblems of caste or rank. The votive offering of special objects may have been one way for an individual or a group to distinguish themselves from others. Offering 'gifts to the gods' in this fashion could have had the coincidental effects of combining the symbolical and the practical by placating the otherworld and conferring status on the donor.[19]

The contemporary bronze work should not be forgotten. There is an intriguing contrast between the deposition of weapons such as rapiers in wet locations and the tendency to deposit many (though not all) gold ornaments on dry land. If casual loss is an inadequate explanation for river finds, then these contrasting contexts offer very different instances of processes of selective deposition which have yet to be analysed. Detailed study may yield surprising results: there is, for instance, too little information to gauge the significance of the total weights of gold hoards but it has been suggested that there may have been precisely calculated units of weight. The weight of the combined pieces in the Downpatrick hoard no. 1 (1037.98g) finds some comparisons in a number of other European hoards which are multiples or fractions of 1037.25g.[20]

The wide distribution of the finer types such as flange-twisted torcs does suggest an elite fashion in prestigious metalwork and demonstrates that the eastern half of Ireland had contacts with areas such as north Wales, southern England and East Anglia. Indeed finds of Irish bronze metalwork in Hampshire and Dorset as well as in East Anglia may be significant as well though the nature of the patterns of exchange and circulation, like the patterns of deposition, is far from clear.[21]

The Penard Phase in Britain is probably contemporary with the later Bishopsland Phase and overlaps with its successor, the Roscommon Phase as George Eogan has named it. As already indicated, this Penard Phase (*c.* 1200 to 1000 BC) not only contains indigenous developments like the later flange-twisted torcs with tapering terminals and Group IV rapiers but it also witnessed important new developments. These included such significant types as the leaf-shaped sword (which had probably inspired the earliest Irish swords of Ballintober type by about 1100 BC), the bronze shield and large vessels of sheet bronze all of which are just part of a large body of evidence for frequent and diverse contacts with the Continent. The novel type of sword implies new forms of personal combat and the earliest expressions of this important development and the innovations of the Roscommon Phase may be summarized together. However, most of the developments at this time had profound consequences in succeeding centuries and will be examined when the metalwork of the following Dowris Phase is considered.

THE ROSCOMMON HOARD: A 'FIND OF BROKEN THINGS'

In 1880, a Cork antiquarian and collector, Robert Day, reported that in January 1870 he had inspected a collection of bronze objects acquired by a dealer in Mullingar. This consisted of 'a hoard of bronze fragments, about two hundred in number, and weighing over sixteen pounds, which had all been found together, somewhere in the county of Roscommon, by a labouring man'. Unfortunately, the exact location of this discovery was not recorded and, because the dealer demanded too high a price for the whole hoard, Day only purchased a selection. Fragments of eleven broken socketed axes, a part of a sword blade, fragments of three long slender chapes (mounts for the tips of scabbards), three mould 'gates' (waste bronze pieces cast in the channel through which molten metal flows into a mould) and 21 pieces of bronze, some evidently waste, are preserved. Day also referred to 'numerous small portions of spear-heads and bronze vessels' or 'bowls' and he identified the hoard as the stock-in-trade of a 'bronze founder'.

This large hoard of scrap bronze, if genuine, is an exceptional find in an Irish context (Fig. 81) and, while Day undoubtedly acquired it in Mullingar, how and where the dealer got it is unknown. It may even have come from a settlement site. This sort of collection has numerous parallels abroad notably in southern England and on the Continent. Like the Guilsfield hoard, found in Montgomeryshire in south Wales, which also contained over a hundred items including spearheads, chapes, socketed axes as well as palstaves, other objects and scrap bronze, this is a bronze smith or founder's hoard.[22] These hoards, containing a significant quantity of broken objects and bronze fragments, as well as casting residues, are a noteworthy feature of the Wilburton Phase or industry in southern England. Such deposits of scrap metal have prompted discussion about the role of the bronze smith and the nature of the metal industry at this time. But one hoard of scrap metal and one collection of craftsman's tools (Bishopsland) do not shed much light on bronze production in Ireland.

THE ELUSIVE SMITH

While a votive explanation is possible for the Roscommon hoard, it and other founder's hoards may have been buried with the intention of recovery and may have been part of an efficient system of collection and recycling, a suggestion perhaps supported by the scarcity or absence of bronze on settlement sites like Lough Gur, Co. Limerick, Rathgall, Co. Wicklow, Dún Aonghasa, Co. Galway, or Lough Eskragh, Co. Tyrone, which have produced evidence for metalworking usually in the form of fragments of clay moulds. It has often been assumed that prehistoric bronze workers were itinerant high status specialists but this is by no means certain: metalworking may not have been a full-time occupation and could have been a local seasonal event, or even one regularly practised by particular kin groups. In England, it has been suggested that smiths – whether travelling or settled – produced material such as tools, small spears and ornaments on a local basis for communities within a radius of 15km to 20km but in addition there were wider regional weapon industries producing rapiers, large spears and eventually swords.

There could even have been both itinerant full-time and settled part-time bronze smiths in prehistoric Ireland and the situation may well have been a complex one. The belief that smiths were persons of high status in society is commonly held but their position may have been ambiguous and surrounded by taboos. It is possible that the supply of raw materials to the smith was controlled and the general scarcity of metalworkers' tools such as hammers, tongs and anvils and the puzzling absence of metalworking debris on sites where moulds have been found may point to some procedures of selection and exclusion.[23]

ROSCOMMON PHASE METALWORK

The Roscommon Phase was considered as 'an extension of the Wilburton industry to Ireland' by George Eogan but the amount of southern English material is limited and a larger body of bronze types has closer comparisons with material in northern England which Colin Burgess has called the Wallington Tradition where Transitional palstaves and square-mouthed socketed axes with flat collars are also found. As already mentioned, Group IV notched-butt rapiers probably continued in use if not in production and the same may be the case with various types of spearheads such as basal and protected-looped. Though their beginnings are unclear, spears with lunate (half-moon shaped) openings in the blade, thought to be derived from the protected-looped type, probably appeared at this time and were a long-lived weapon type which continued into the Dowris Phase. If significant Wilburton influences did reach Ireland then the flange-hilted sword, a common weapon of the Dowris Phase, may have appeared too replacing the primitive Ballintober sword.

The appearance of the first chapes is presumably another reflection of this growing interest in weaponry and related fitments: of thin cast bronze they would have served as both protective and decorative extensions and guards for the tips of sword scabbards of wood or leather. The so-called tongue-shaped chapes of the Roscommon hoard (Fig. 81, 2-4) are long slender objects (up to 28cm

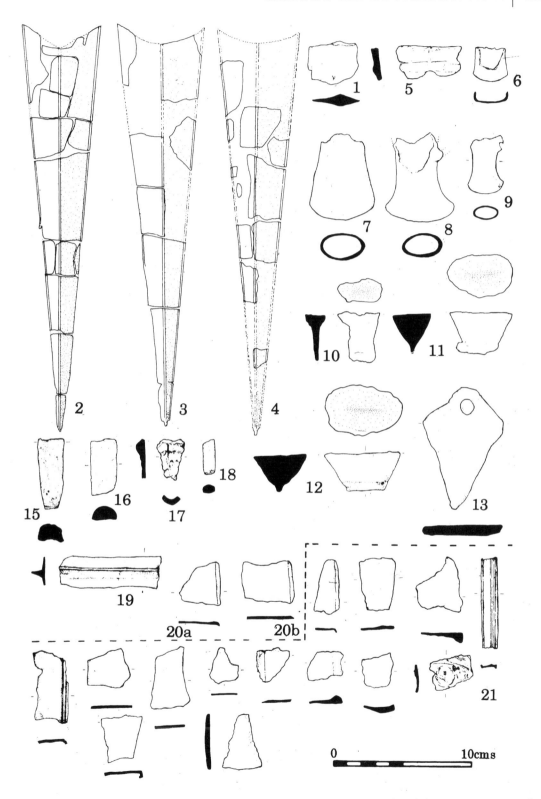

Fig. 81. The Roscommon hoard. 1. Fragment of a sword blade. 2-4. Fragments of tongue-shaped chapes. 5-9. Fragments of socketed axeheads. 10-12. Mould gates. 13 and 15-20. Bronze fragments. 21. Pieces of waste bronze.

in length and 6cm in greatest width), of flat lozenge-shaped cross section with curving mouths, midribs and a short projecting tip. Two or three related chapes of a shorter form have also been found in Ireland. What are thought to be spear butts of bronze of long almost cylindrical or tubular shape may also appear at this time, again occurring in hoards like Guilsfield. They would have served as ferrules or metal guards and extensions for the butts of wooden spear shafts and may have been inspired by similar objects of conical shape of the Penard Phase in Britain.[24]

THE BALLINTOBER SWORD

The first sword in Irish prehistory designed as a slashing weapon is named after a find from a bog in Ballintober, Co. Mayo (Fig. 82). The type has a flat rectangular hilt or tang usually with four rivet holes in two pairs; this tang broadens to pointed shoulders. Below these, on about half the examples, the blade edge is blunted to form a ricasso (a blunted indentation replacing the sharp edge). Blades are slightly leaf-shaped, sometimes with bevelled edges, and usually have a ridged, narrow lozenge-shaped, cross-section. Lengths vary from about 43cm to 61cm. Compared to the rapier, the hilt or tang obviously provided an improved hafting mechanism. The leaf shape is also significant because with the greater weight of the weapon in the lower part of the blade it is clear that these weapons were designed more for slashing blows rather than stabbing and thrusting in rapier fashion. It is

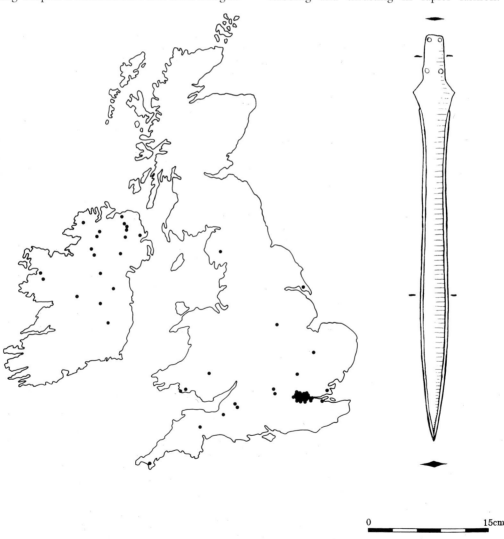

0   15cm

Fig. 82. Sword from Ballintober, Co. Mayo, and general distribution of the type.

assumed that this indicates an important change in fighting methods.

Some two dozen are recorded but only half have even brief details of find circumstances documented: almost all of these come from rivers or bogs. Distribution is mostly confined to the northern half of Ireland but examples in Britain show a remarkable concentration in the Thames valley which from about 1200 BC emerges has a major centre of bronze production and of Continental imports and influences. Sporadic finds occur elsewhere including in the Penard hoard in Glamorgan with its early Rosnoën sword, narrow socketed axe and leaf-shaped spearhead. Contacts between Ireland and the Thames valley may have been via south Wales. British examples of the Ballintober type tend to have less prominent and less widely splayed shoulders (with a variant having a flat or rounded cross-section with bevelled edges) and using these criteria it is possible to identify Irish pieces in Britain and *vice versa*.

Ballintober swords have long been considered the result of a process of hybridization between rapiers and early leaf-shaped swords, and their cross-sections do recall the lozenge and flattened lozenge cross-sections of Group IV rapiers. However, the earliest swords in Britain are the north-west French Rosnoën swords with sub-rectangular riveted hilts and more or less parallel-sided slender blades, and the slightly broader and ever so slightly leaf-shaped Ambleside swords, both responses to early central European sword fashions. One or both of these could have prompted the development of Ballintober swords or at least their distinctive hilts. It may be that their leaf-shaped and lozenge-sectioned blade was inspired by early rod-tanged swords of the type recovered from the site of a possible shipwreck at Moor Sand, Salcombe, but the chronology of Ballintober swords is so uncertain it is possible that the leaf shape may have been inspired by the earliest leaf-shaped (and flange-hilted) swords which appear in the Thames valley in the Penard Phase in the 12th century BC and are derived from imported Continental leaf-shaped swords.[25]

This preoccupation with swords is but one facet of a wider interest in weaponry and may well be an indication of an increase in martial activity. It is also necessary to remember that while some weapons were undoubtedly functional (and lethal), others were for show. This may imply the emergence of a warrior aristocracy with an interest in diverse 'heroic' activities such as raiding and ostentatious display. This evidence and the appearance of defended enclosures as well as a possible hierarchy of settlement types may point to significant social change towards the end of the 2nd millennium BC.

SETTLEMENT, ECONOMY AND SOCIETY 1500–900 BC

Evidence for settlement and economy in the period 1500-900 BC is not abundant but excavation in the last two decades in particular has greatly advanced our knowledge in this field and has begun to reveal a remarkable diversity of settlement forms and activities. This progress has been mainly due to factors such as the archaeological monitoring of major construction projects like the natural gas pipeline work in the 1980s, archaeological survey and research projects such as the work of the Navan Research Group and the Discovery Programme.

Hilltop enclosures, lowland and wetland settlements and temporary occupation sites have all been identified and they are beginning to illuminate a complex area crucial to a better understanding of a society which did not live by bronze and gold alone. However, the evidence is still very fragmentary and the study of economy and of settlement patterns barely begun. Thus the correlation of settlement with metalwork production and distribution remains an unresolved but important problem. Too little is still known about the agricultural base, the contemporary landscape and territorial organization though, as already mentioned, some evidence of a range of settlement types hints at increasing social complexity.

BALLYVEELISH, CO. TIPPERARY

Excavations on the Cork to Dublin gas pipeline in 1981-82 at Ballyveelish, just north of Clonmel, Co. Tipperary, revealed part of a subrectangular enclosure which may have measured about 47m north-south by 25m east-west (Fig. 83). No trace of the site was visible before excavation and less than half of its southern area lay within the pipeline corridor; only this section was examined. The site had suffered considerable damage in more recent times (some of it associated with a nearby Medieval moated site) and the surviving features were clearly truncated: if, for instance, an occupation horizon containing domestic refuse had existed within the enclosure, it had been stripped away. The enclosure

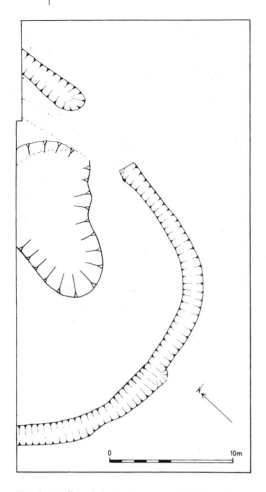

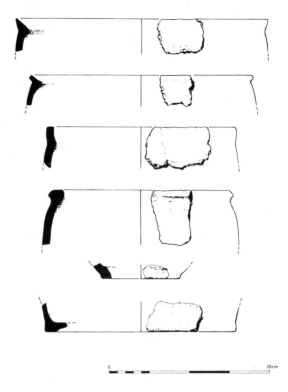

Fig. 83. Ballyveelish, Co. Tipperary. Left. Plan of excavated part of sub-rectangular ditched enclosure. The central hollow was the site of a natural spring later filled with stones. Right. Coarse flat-bottomed pottery.

consisted of a shallow V-sectioned ditch about 1.8m wide at the top and 50cm wide at the base with a maximum depth of 1.2m: its upper layers had been removed too so it may once have been somewhat more substantial. No evidence of an internal bank was found and a gap in the ditch on the east may have been an entrance. The recovery of a quantity of animal bones and sherds of coarse pottery from the fill of the ditch provided the main evidence for occupation. Indeed the excavator had the impression that the ditch had been deliberately allowed to fill with silt and domestic refuse and it was this refuse that offered the most useful information about the site's inhabitants. Two samples of wood charcoal from the ditch provided radiocarbon dates which suggest occupation around 1130–810 BC.

The animal bones demonstrated that cattle were the most important livestock (about 42.9%). Next in significance came pig (about 35.7%) and caprovines (sheep or goat: about 16.7%). Since cattle provide more meat than pig it is possible that beef may have been by far the major component of the meat diet. Large numbers of broken bones were evidence of marrow extraction. Many of the cattle bones represented mature animals but the presence of numbers of immature specimens may be important: it has been argued that the presence of calf bones in quantity indicates that dairying was not important, an argument partly based on the premise that primitive cows needed their calves to maintain lactation. The Ballyveelish economy may well have been cattle-based and focused on beef production but whether it can be inferred from the limited evidence from this and a few other prehistoric sites that dairying (as the basis of the economy) had yet to develop remains to be proven.[26]

Horse and dog bones were found in small numbers and, since they too were broken, these animals may have occasionally formed part of the diet. Hunting seems to have been of minimal importance but red deer was occasionally hunted and eaten on site. Cereals were also cultivated, processing of a soil sample from the ditch by water flotation and sieving produced a number of grains of barley and one possible grain of wheat.

Over 200 sherds of coarse plain pottery were recovered including some fragments of rims, shoulders and bases. These suggested flat-bottomed bowls and squat jars (Fig. 83). Only one sherd was decorated with a few incised lines. The pots were coil-built and some had sooty accretions suggesting some were cooking vessels. A detailed study of fabric demonstrated a range of possible uses: a majority of the sherds (95%) were 10mm-18mm thick and were tempered with varying amounts of calcite grits. The amounts of temper may relate to function: the greater the degree of tempering (to produce a coarser textured pot) the better the capability of the vessel to withstand the thermal shock of an open fire. Petrological analysis indicated local manufacture. A minority of sherds (5%) were about 22mm in thickness and were tempered with crushed pottery (variously termed grog or chamotte) to produce a vessel with a dense texture suitable as a dry-goods container. Some of the sparsely tempered calcite gritted pots could have had a similar function. The thicker pottery was calcite-free and the clay used probably originated outside the Ballyveelish area, thus a little pottery – or perhaps just the clay – was imported.

Other artefacts were few. Two small stone chisels or adzes, two stone spindle whorls, a fragment of a lignite bracelet and three bone points were found. The evidence indicates a relatively simple and self-contained agricultural community, living in a small enclosed settlement, who were engaged in cattle raising and cereal cultivation with some other activities such as spinning and pottery making.

A larger oval ditched enclosure at Chancellorsland, near Emly, Co. Tipperary (Site A), measuring about 60m by 50m, has also produced extensive and possibly long-term occupation evidence along with coarse pottery and faunal remains. The enclosure was surrounded by a double ditch but only one of these may have been open at a time. Traces of a timber palisade were found inside the inner ditch. Remains of several circular and rectangular huts representing a number of phases of activity were revealed; two contained hearths and one had a hearth outside the building. The only metal objects found were two copper or bronze awls but tool marks on some timbers from the ditch indicated the use of metal axes.[27]

CURRAGHATOOR, CO. TIPPERARY

Gas pipeline work revealed another settlement at Curraghatoor, Co. Tipperary, south-west of Cahir, and again there were no surface traces of the archaeological remains. Excavation in 1982 and from 1987 to 1991 uncovered at least half a dozen circular structures and part of a timber palisade.[28] The full extent of the settlement was not determined but even these features represented more than one phase of settlement activity: the timber palisade may have surrounded some of the structures and went out of use with further expansion of the settlement. The largest structure named Hut 1 was 6.5m in diameter and consisted of a circle of ten post-holes set about 2m apart and each measuring about 20cm-30cm in diameter and depth; these stout posts had stakes between them. A dense layer of charcoal and an area of fire-reddened earth seem to represent a central hearth (with associated stake-holes) but this hearth covered a post-hole which may or may not have been part of the circular timber structure (Fig. 84). Huts 2 and 3 were smaller and of different construction, each having a shallow circular foundation trench containing four to five post-holes, and 4m and 3m in diameter respectively. Topsoil removal by the pipeline construction workers had destroyed any occupation layer in Hut 2 and only the very bases of the post-holes (the last 10cm) survived; there were no finds from either but it was suggested that the trenches could have supported a light timber structure, one with a central timber support, in the case of Hut 2, one perhaps like an upturned basket in the case of Hut 3. Two fragments of coarse pottery were found in one of the pits in Hut 1 and a hammer stone was found near the hearth.

Acidic soil conditions meant that little animal bone survived but charred seeds were recovered and these were identified as wheat (emmer and possibly spelt) and barley. The presence of cereal straw and seeds of weeds of cultivation indicated crop processing on site. A series of radiocarbon dates suggests that this settlement dates to the late second and early first millennia BC but also indicates some earlier occupation.

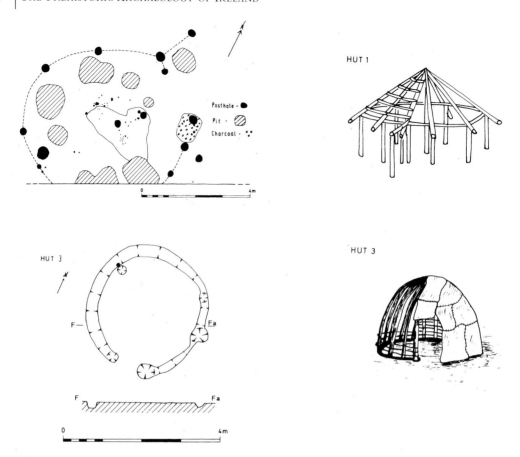

Fig. 84. Curraghatoor, Co. Tipperary. Plans and suggested reconstruction of structures.

LOUGH GUR, CO. LIMERICK

Broadly similar settlement has been identified on the northern slope of Knockadoon at Lough Gur, Co. Limerick, where several timber structures represent a sequence of occupation over a period of time from about 1200 to 800 BC judging from a series of radiocarbon dates. This settlement was situated in the shelter of a cliff and overlooked the lake to the north-west. It was not enclosed but Knockadoon may have been almost an island in prehistoric times so the location may have offered some natural security.

The earliest structure identified on the site was formed of a circle of six post-holes, set about 1.8m apart, with a diameter of 4.9m. Some missing post-holes on the south may have been destroyed by later activity. Charcoal implied that the timbers used were mature ash and elm, and hazel twigs were also present; it was suggested therefore that the walls may have been made of wickerwork covered with daub.

Eight other post-holes were interpreted as the remains of a later rectangular structure measuring about 2.9m in width and at least 3.8m in length (it may have extended further beyond the limits of the excavation). There was an internal hearth and again it seemed that the walls could have been of wicker and daub. Various stake-holes belonged to other flimsier structures possibly circular in plan. These features were sealed by a compact layer of chert fragments conceivably laid down as a trackway or floor, which in turn was partly covered by a layer of burnt limestone and sandstone fragments which were not burnt in place but came from elsewhere. The presence of charred ash from mature timbers suggests that this material may be the remains of a demolished burnt structure but it could also be the result of some domestic or industrial process somewhere to the east of the area excavated. This layer produced most of the animal bones and pottery found.

A deliberately laid platform of layers of soil was then constructed at the southern end of the excavated area and seven post-holes on this level area were considered to represent an oval timber house measuring 4.8m by 5.3m (Fig. 85). Numbers of internal stake-holes may have been for divisions or screens and one pit contained a fragment of an infant's skull, perhaps a dedicatory offering. Some pits found on the site may have been storage pits. Based on evidence from various British excavations including Black Patch, Sussex, Cleary has suggested that the timber posts of this oval house and those of the earlier round and rectangular structures may have been internal roof supports but not external walls: she argues the external walls may have been quite low and built of material which would leave little or no archaeological trace like turves or plastered wickerwork. If the surviving post-holes were those of internal structural supports, this would certainly be an explanation for the rather wide spacing of these timbers and their relatively modest diameters.

Analysis of the faunal remains produced unexpected results. In contrast to earlier periods at

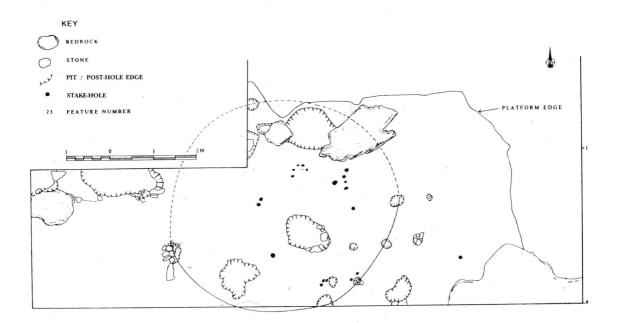

KEY

⬭ BEDROCK

⬭ STONE

PIT / POST-HOLE EDGE

• STAKE-HOLE

23 FEATURE NUMBER

PLATFORM EDGE

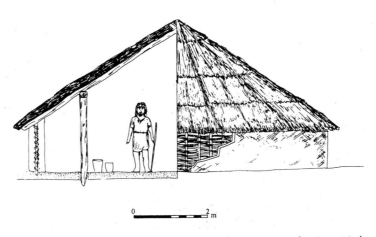

Fig. 85. Lough Gur, Co. Limerick. Plan of an oval house with a suggested reconstruction showing vertical posts acting as internal supports rather than an external wall.

Lough Gur pig bones now formed 50.5% of the assemblage followed by cattle (38%) and sheep or goat (10%). The remains of dog, horse and red deer also occurred but in negligible quantities. There were deliberate slaughtering strategies: all pigs were killed before they reached 3.5 years of age (mature height) and only 27% and 33% of cattle and sheep or goat respectively were allowed to reach maturity. The killing of such a high proportion of immature cattle is again taken to imply meat production rather than dairying. The sheep or goat population was mainly slaughtered between 3 and 3.5 years and since prehistoric sheep probably started breeding at the age of two years, it is possible that they were kept for wool or milk or both. Clearly pig and cattle were the major components of the economy. Even with the large quantities of charcoal recovered, there were no charred plant remains and cereals may have had a minimal role, if any.

Very few stone implements were found including a small number of simple flint scrapers and blade fragments. Sherds of pottery were the commonest artefact; plain coarse flat-bottomed bowls and squat jars were the principal forms, one small cup was also found in a post-hole of the rectangular structure where it may have been a votive offering. Limestone tempering was the norm (74%) though other crushed stones such as basalt (20%) and chert were used as well; all were locally available. One sherd with greywacke (coarse sandstone) temper may have been a cooking pot imported from outside the region. The general coarseness of the tempering suggested that the pots were intended for this sort of domestic use. Five other sites on Knockadoon have produced similar coarse pottery and may have been occupied around this time too.[29]

CARRIGILLIHY, CO. CORK

Excavation at Carrigillihy, near Union Hall, Co. Cork, was undertaken to try and find the permanent settlement of the builders of a nearby coastal promontory fort which seemed to have been unoccupied. In the event, Carrigillihy produced evidence of much earlier and presumably unrelated activity. A small oval enclosure measured 24m by 21m internally and consisted of a stony bank some 2.7m wide with an entrance, with post-holes for a gate, on the east facing the sea (Fig. 86). The excavator estimated that the bank may have

originally been about 1.4m in height. Within was an oval house 10m by 6.7m internally. It too was stone-built with a 1.5m thick wall faced with boulders and with a core of small boulders and earth. It survived to a maximum height of about 54cm and an asymmetrical arrangement of post-holes in the interior provided roof support. Before this house was completed a level surface was made on the east by filling a natural hollow there with soil scooped from the immediate vicinity. No hearth was found but the floor was covered with a layer 10cm to 15cm thick of black habitation refuse including charcoal and pottery.

It is often difficult to determine if occupation inside an enclosure is contemporary with the surrounding bank or wall. In this instance, since the dark habitation layer inside the house extended in an unbroken stratum through the door and abutted the bottom courses of stones of the enclosure wall and since the house and enclosure had parallel axes and their entrances faced in the same direction, the excavator, M. J. O'Kelly, concluded that both were contemporary.

The occupation layer contained numerous fragments of pottery: 166 sherds represented at least nine coarse flat-bottomed vessels. Many sherds were carbonized and were evidently cooking pots; their tempering was similar to the pottery from Lough Gur. A small number had rudimentary decoration (a line of impressed twisted cord or grass) below the rim. Because of acid soil conditions, no animal bones survived but a small quantity of periwinkle shells showed that the resources of the nearby coast were exploited. O'Kelly compared the Carrigillihy pottery to the Class II ware from Ó Ríordáin's excavations at Lough Gur and suggested that the settlement should be dated to the early second millennium BC but subsequent radiocarbon dating of charred twigs from a pit in the house and from the habitation layer indicated a later date: two samples provided dates with calibrated ranges of 1510-1220 and 1130-850 BC.[30] Thus a fragment of a bronze socketed axe, a stray find in modern rubble covering the site, may have come originally from the later prehistoric settlement. A later rectangular house (with opposed doors) was built on the site, probably in early Medieval times, and used stone robbed from the earlier house and the enclosing bank; it was separated from the earlier occupation by a thick layer of archaeologically sterile soil leached to a grey-white colour.

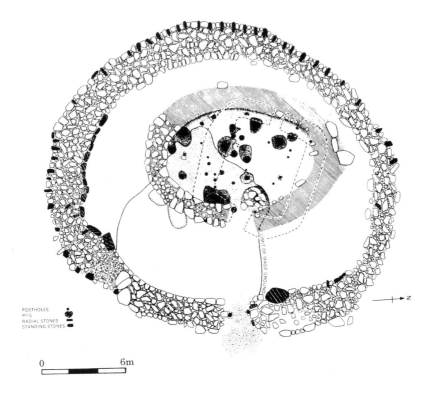

POSTHOLES
PITS
RADIAL STONES
STANDING STONES

0   6m

Fig. 86. Carrigillihy, Co. Cork. Oval house in oval stone-built enclosure. A later rectangular house built on the site is dotted on the plan.

CLONFINLOUGH, CO. OFFALY

Another oval enclosure of a very different sort has been excavated at Clonfinlough, Co. Offaly. Here, investigations by the Irish Archaeological Wetland Unit in a midland raised bog have added an important dimension to the varied and fragmentary settlement picture of the period. On the southern shore of Finlough, just over 2km south-east of the River Shannon and Clonmacnoise, a palisaded enclosure had been built on shallow peat on the lake shore. It had been revealed at a depth of 2m to 3m in the bog in the course of mechanical peat extraction which had unfortunately caused considerable damage and destroyed most of any occupation levels.

A stoutly-built but irregularly oval palisade enclosed an area some 50m by 40m (Fig. 87). The ashwood posts were closely set and were 16cm to 20cm or more in diameter; in places they were set in a trench but sometimes driven up to 2.5m into the shallow peat and lake marl below. The pointed ends of the timbers showed cut marks of bronze axes with blades 4cm to 6cm across. It was thought that these posts could have formed a stockade 1m to

1.5m in height and probably open on the east at the lake edge. Within the enclosure four timber platforms, three of which probably supported circular houses, and the remains of several timber trackways were found. The platforms, up to 60cm or 70cm deep, were built to provide a dry surface above the damp ground.

Platform 1, to the south-east, was the best preserved. It measured 9.35m in diameter and was a carefully constructed complex structure of layers of wood including ash posts and split oak timbers, brushwood, stones and gravel. There was a roughly circular central hearth built of large stone slabs and several layers of sand and clay along with ash and charcoal suggested a number of re-lining episodes. Pockets of occupation debris did survive and consisted of charcoal with burnt and unburnt animal bone. An amber bead and sherds of coarse pottery were also found.

The floor of this platform underwent one major reconstruction and layers of split oak planks was laid down, the uppermost around a square slab-built hearth. The platform was surrounded by a double post and wattle wall, the tightly woven wattle walls

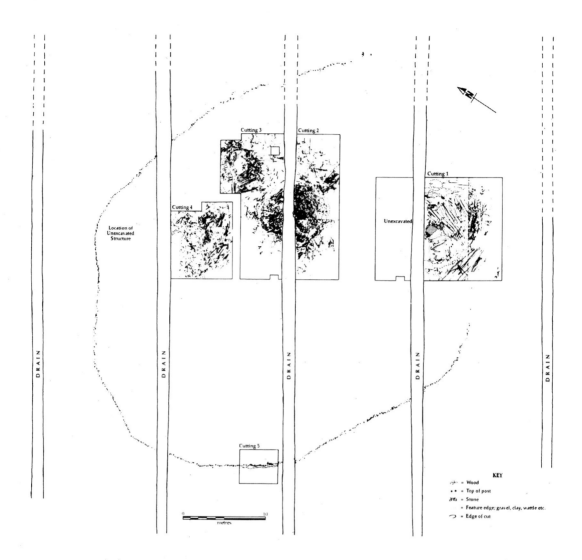

Fig. 87. Above. Plan of palisaded enclosure at Clonfinlough, Co. Offaly, showing from right to left Platform 1 in Cutting 1, Platform 2 in cuttings 2 and 3, Structure 4 in the northern corner of Cutting 3 and Hut 3 in Cutting 4. Below. Reconstruction of Clonfinlough.

being about 30cm apart on average. Whether this outer wall supported a roof is unclear but there could also have been internal roof supports simply resting on some of the stone slabs. There was a stepped entrance-way on the north-east. Dendrochronological analysis of some oak timbers demonstrated that this platform had been constructed in the period 917-899 BC.

Platform 2, 10m to the south-west, was badly damaged but of broadly similar construction. It too was surrounded by a double post and wattle wall with an outer diameter of 7.2m. Part of a central slab-built hearth survived as did some occupation debris including pottery and charcoal. There was also a stepped entrance on the east with a brushwood path or trackway leading to it. Two broken wooden paddles (Fig. 88, 6-7) were found beneath this path and a saddle quern was discovered near the entrance (Fig. 88, 8). Timber from the upper level of the entrance produced a felling date of 886 BC. A smaller structure (called Hut 3) was uncovered 6m to the west. With a diameter of 5.2m it consisted of a platform of several layers of timbers with a central slab-built hearth (rebuilt on a number of occasions) and surrounded by many posts. A small, perforated wooden disc (Fig. 88, 5) was found in the upper timbers here and it bears some resemblance to the perforated lids of modern milk churns of the dash churn variety.

A fourth platform (structure 4), 4.4m in diameter, may have been a work area; there was no sign of a hearth but organic material, charcoal, burnt and unburnt bones were found here. A second amber bead was found nearby.

A site like Clonfinlough would probably have been a part of a network of settlements and its inhabitants evidently had wider contacts and were able to acquire relatively exotic items. The two amber beads (Fig. 88, 1-2) are small but significant discoveries. Amber probably originates in the Baltic region or on the eastern coasts of Scotland or England and there is a discernible increase in the exchange of this prized material from the Penard Phase onwards. It is highly likely that proximity to the Shannon was an important factor in whatever social communication there was and the two paddles were probably used to row or scull some sort of wooden or hide-built craft on the waters of this major routeway. Logboats were probably a common feature on rivers and lakes. In addition there may have been an important fording place near Clonmacnoise. It is also possible that Clonfinlough was a part of a widespread network of timber trackways. The period of use of a trackway at Annaghcorrib, Co. Galway, 10km to the east across the Shannon, is partly contemporary, with a dendrochronological determination of 892 ± 9 BC.[31]

Besides the paddles and the perforated wooden disc, parts of possible wicker baskets were recovered and there was, of course, abundant evidence for wood-working. There was also evidence for woodland management. Ash was the dominant species exploited (75%) and was deliberately selected in two sizes: brushwood 3cm-6cm in diameter and roundwood 12cm-24cm across. The brushwood used showed particular uniformity and indicated the coppicing of ash rods of similar ages. It appeared that a stand of 1 to 2 hectares of ash was carefully grown and periodically cut to provide the necessary sort of wood over a period of time.

Other finds were mundane: stone objects were few and included a whetstone, an axe-like object of siltstone and the saddle quern mentioned above. The pottery was the familiar coarse flat bottomed ware, some with sooty accretions and used for cooking. At least two vessels were quite large and one broad basin-like pot (Fig. 88, 3) with a complete profile was found to have a capacity of 11.5 litres.

Much of the animal bone was burnt and fragmented and identification was necessarily tentative. As at Ballyveelish and other sites cattle was clearly dominant (62.5%) with pig, sheep or goat and dog each having similar but much smaller percentages (12.5%). It is worth noting that these percentage figures conceal the fact that the bone sample recovered here was very small: the minimum number of individual animals identified was eight, five (62.5%) of which were cattle. These showed butchery marks and long bones were broken for marrow extraction but age and slaughter patterns could not be determined. Some sheep bones also showed cut marks.

The dendrochronological evidence suggested that the construction and occupation of the Clonfinlough settlement could have extended from 917 to 886 BC, perhaps representing one or two generations of an extended family. The substantial platforms and hearths do seem to imply permanent occupancy but intensive seasonal occupation, and some specialized economic purpose, is also a

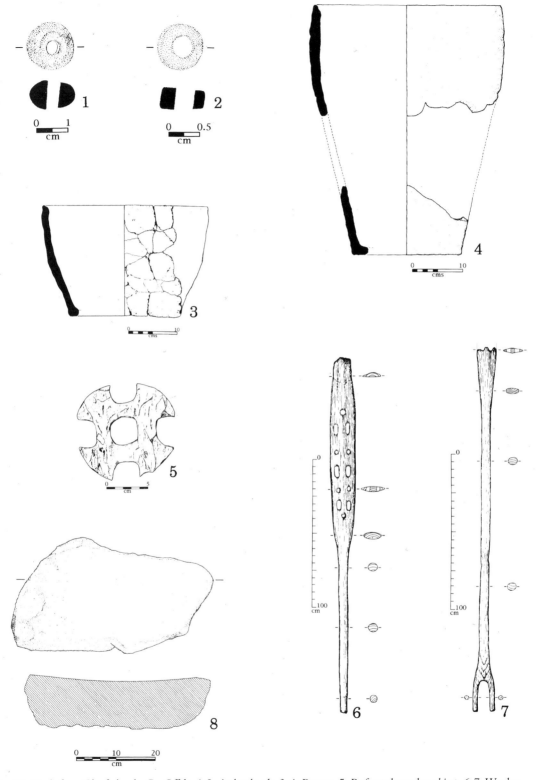

Fig. 88. Finds from Clonfinlough, Co. Offaly. 1-2. Amber beads. 3-4. Pottery. 5. Perforated wooden object. 6-7. Wooden paddles. 8. Saddle quern.

possibility. However, such a wetland location may have had a particular attraction as a permanent settlement because of the security it offered. While the stockade could have served to keep animals in or out, like the stone wall at Carrigillihy, it was not a defensive measure. The Clonfinlough settlement was naturally protected being situated in an area of bogland with a lake to the north and a large raised bog to the south. A strip of dry land to the east could have been reached by a path or trackway which would have allowed restricted access. If it can be established that there was a significant increase in the occupation of naturally defended wetland sites at this time, then the latter part of the second millennium BC may well have been a time of unrest and increasing social pressures. But for the inhabitants of Clonfinlough there may be simpler explanations: the proximity of the Shannon offered several advantages, the possibility of trading contacts being but one. There was no surviving evidence that the rich wildlife of the area was exploited but this may have been another factor, there certainly was vegetation suitable for cattle.

One similar though smaller site was excavated at Cullyhanna, Co. Armagh, in 1956. A lake-shore enclosure of irregular oval plan, about 20m in maximum dimensions, was formed by a line of oak stakes. Within was a circular hut about 6m across with a central hearth on a timber platform. Just south of this hut an outdoor hearth protected by a screen or windbreak was found. The only artefacts recovered were a few flint scrapers and the excavator thought the site was a hunting camp of the early Historic period. However, timber samples taken from the site in 1969 provided both radiocarbon and dendrochronological dates; the latter demonstrated that hut and palisade were contemporary and with the completion of the Belfast master tree-ring chronology Cullyhanna was eventually dated to 1526 BC. Though now securely dated, its purpose remains a puzzle and it may well have been a temporary and specialized site.[32]

Sites like Ballyveelish, Lough Gur, Carrigillihy and Clonfinlough offer a revealing picture of the very diverse locations chosen for settlement. Varied though they are, some enclosed, some not, these lowland, lake-side, wetland and coastal sites share a number of significant features. Though the rarity of faunal remains is a problem and often makes assessment difficult, they would seem to have been modest agricultural settlements. The little evidence

there is at present suggests a mainly pastoral lifestyle with some cereal cultivation. Coarse pottery is frequently found and at first glance bronze might be considered a scarce commodity. It was clearly used at Clonfinlough but its absence might just be an indication of its value. What is evident on these sites is the absence of metal working.

Evidence for metalworking on or near settlement sites is rare but a number of significant discoveries have been made. At Site D, Lough Gur, Co. Limerick, S. P. Ó Ríordáin excavated a hut site, partly stone-built against a cliff face, on the southern side of Knockadoon. This hut (House 1) was quite small measuring about 5m by 3m and of partly oval plan. There was no trace of a hearth inside or immediately outside. The discovery of part of a stone mould for a looped palstave inside and another fragment of the same mould outside on the north-east, and the further discovery of ten fragments of clay moulds for casting spearheads (one possibly basal-looped) led Ó Ríordáin to conclude that the occupants were engaged in bronze working. If this was indeed the case then bronze casting here may have been an activity undertaken somewhere in the vicinity and some distance from any settlement, as was the case at Lough Eskragh, Co. Tyrone (Chapter 7). At Site F at Lough Gur a rectangular structure was found to contain a hearth and finds included fragments of clay moulds for casting spears and rapiers and waste pieces from bronze casting. A part of a stone mould for a palstave was found with a quantity of coarse pottery in a curving segment of ditch at Raheen, Co. Limerick.[33] Nearby sections of other ditches there may be contemporary and form part of an enclosure but it is not certain if they are the remains of a settlement or a ritual site. Some minute fragments of gold suggesting fine metalworking were recovered at Haughey's Fort, Co. Armagh, and clay moulds for casting various bronze objects have been found at the ritual site known as the King's Stables nearby and at Dún Aonghasa, Aran, Co. Galway.

HAUGHEY'S FORT

Haughey's Fort, named after a local land-owner, it is situated on a low but prominent hill just over 1000m west of the celebrated Navan enclosure, commonly called Navan Fort, in Co. Armagh. Several seasons of excavation have revealed evidence for occupation in the general period 1300–900 BC.

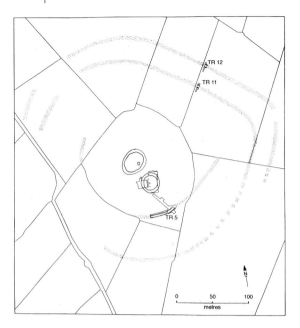

*Fig. 89. Schematic plan of Haughey's Fort, Co. Armagh,
showing position of Trench 5 which sectioned the inner
ditch, Trench 11 at the middle ditch and Trench 12 at the
outer ditch. The approximate positions of the two circular
structures in the inner enclosure are indicated.*

The fort was trivallate with an approximately oval outer ditch measuring some 340m by 310m in diameter (Fig. 89). The inner enclosure was first recorded in the 19th century when it may still have been visible on the ground but today no superficial trace survives and the two outer ditches were only identified through aerial photography in 1989. The middle ditch is 25m from the outer one with the inner ditch a further 55m upslope and enclosing an area measuring *c.* 150 by 140m in diameter.

No traces of an earthen bank survived near any of the ditches but the excavated ditch sections revealed the slip of material from the interior indicating the former existence of internal banks and it seems that the site was a defensive one, a hillfort. The ditches were substantial, more or less V-shaped in section, 2.3m to 3.2m in depth. A small palisade trench was found near the lip of the inner ditch. This innermost ditch was waterlogged and yielded a considerable quantity of faunal and floral remains. Samples of short lived organic remains (small branches, twigs, etc.) from the base of the ditch provided a number of high-precision radiocarbon dates. These demonstrated that the filling of this ditch began in the period 1160-1042 BC. A sample extracted from 1m above the base of

the ditch produced a date of 1047-941 BC and another 30cm above this yielded a date of 841-806 BC which suggests that the defences may have been established about 1100 BC and that abandonment of the site may have occurred within a century or two, perhaps around 900 BC.

Limited excavation of the interior of the fort has revealed numerous small stake-holes presenting no clear structural pattern as well as three lines of stake-holes and small post-holes running in an arc from north to south-east, perhaps part of a stockade. Radiocarbon dates from two of the posts indicated a date range of *c.* 1250 to 900 BC (but others produced a series of seemingly anomalous dates from 2450-1550 BC and whether all are contemporary or not remains uncertain). Two possible lines of pits were also found: these measured about 1m or more in depth and at least 1m in diameter. There were no traces of posts in the pits which produced quantities of coarse pottery, carbonized grain and fragments of gold and bronze suggesting that they had been filled with occupation debris. The enhancement of a series of vertical aerial photographs indicates that the excavated pits actually form part of a double ring structure about 25m in diameter. The excavator suggests that the large pits may be the remains of a dismantled double-ringed timber structure, the timbers having been removed from their post-pits with the subsequent accumulation of settlement debris therein. A radiocarbon date from one of the pits has a calibrated range of 1260-910 BC. Aerial photography also revealed a second and slightly larger double-ringed structure with a diameter of some 30m just to the north-west of the first.

A number of pits containing pottery, carbonized grain and hazel nut shells, burnt bone, fragments of quern stones and metal artefacts with radiocarbon dates ranging from 1250 to 900 BC indicate occupation broadly contemporary with that of the ditches and post-pits. Some later occupation on the site (possibly transitory) is also indicated by fragments of iron and later glass beads in a few of the pits. One pit, which contained a small iron object, possibly a strap handle, produced two charcoal samples which provided radiocarbon dates ranging from *c.* 400-200 BC and demonstrate that the latest evidence for occupation at Haughey's Fort is more or less contemporary with the complex timber structures at the Navan enclosure (Phase 3ii) to be described in Chapter 9.

Artefacts recovered included a considerable quantity of pottery, generally classic coarse ware. A number of pots could be reconstructed and were about 30cm to 40cm in height with rim diameters of about 23cm to 32cm. Analysis of organic deposits on the interior of some of the vessels suggested that carbonized residues were produced both by a cellulose material derived from plants and from the meat or skins of cattle. The fact that some large vessels, with capacities of as much as 16 litres, showed traces of plant remains suggested they may have been part of some manufacturing process, perhaps tanning leather.

Metal finds included some minute fragments of gold leaf or wire recovered after flotation of material from the large post-pits. One complete object was a gold stud about 4.5mm in diameter from the post-pit radiocarbon dated to 1260–910 BC. These might indicate fine metalworking on site. Bronze items included a sunflower pin, a fragment of a possible bracelet and three rings. A number of glass beads were found. The largest stone object recovered was a cup-and-ring marked block of sandstone found in a shallow pit containing charcoal radiocarbon dated to *c.* 1250–900 BC. Carved with a double ring with a groove running from the centre to the outer edge of the stone, this sort of rock art is normally dated to the third millennium BC but being portable this stone could obviously have been brought to the site from elsewhere and need not be evidence of early prehistoric activity there. A few saddle quern stones and rubbing stones were also discovered.

Evidence of woodworking included poles made of alder and hazel, split-wood oak used for structural purposes, two perforated handles of ash (possibly for socketed bronze axes which would have had wooden dowels in their sockets set into mortises in the hafts) and fragments of a round-bottomed bowl.

Faunal remains were mainly those of cattle (54.33%) with some pig (33.8%) and only few traces of sheep or goat (3.1%), horse and dog. A single red deer, a fox and a wild pig were the only evidence for hunted animals. The cattle are identified as short horned some with a shoulder height of 100cm–112cm (comparable to cattle from the early Historic period). A few larger animals, one with an estimated shoulder height of 129.5cm, may denote selective breeding. The pigs were large with some up to 77.2cm at the shoulders. The horns of two goats measured 344mm and 348mm respectively, considerably larger than other recorded examples. The presence of unusually large animals is also evident in the dog remains where several skulls represent the largest canine skulls known from prehistoric Ireland. Measurements suggest heights of *c.* 63cm and 65cm for some of these animals. It has been suggested that animals of large stature may be one of the criteria for the identification of a high status site since such elites might well be engaged in the selective breeding of larger animals or be the recipients of very large animals as prestigious gifts.

The interior ditch also yielded the remains of an insect assemblage: a preliminary report identified diverse species of beetle some of which are generally associated with water or at least wetland areas while a variety of dung beetle is associated with decaying animal and plant remains. This suggests that a certain amount of dung may have been deposited in the ditch from time to time, while much of this may have been from herbivores it is also possible that the ditch could have been used as a latrine and was certainly used as a dump for rotting vegetable matter.

The environment of the Navan complex has been studied by David Weir mainly through pollen samples from nearby Loughnashade. This work has revealed a series of prehistoric clearance episodes culminating in the period *c.* 1400 to 1000 BC when there was a significant reduction in elm, hazel, ash and oak. The increasingly open landscape appeared to be primarily for grassland. Arable agriculture was also important as evidence for cereals, present since *c.* 1760 BC, rose to reach levels of *c.* 6% which are among the highest known from Irish prehistoric contexts. The recovery of large quantities of carbonized barley from the pits at Haughey's Fort is further evidence of the importance of this cereal. Preliminary analysis indicates that these samples are free of contaminants and may indicate that the grain was processed elsewhere before being brought to the fort. The wood and seed remains, and an apple, from the lower levels of the interior ditch provide additional botanical evidence for the period *c.* 1100-900 BC. Pollen from both rye and flax was identified in the contemporary levels of the lake cores. The end of the major clearance phase occurs about 1000 BC and more or less coincides with the fort's abandonment. Hazel scrub was the first to recover but by *c.* 850 BC, ash and elm began to expand again and grass values fall.

It was first thought that Haughey's Fort may have been the secular component of the Navan complex with Navan Fort itself being the ritual centre of the area. This division between the sacred and the profane has not been supported by the radiocarbon dating which shows that the main floruit of Haughey's Fort preceded most of the activity so far uncovered at Navan Fort. The possibility that the two large double-ringed enclosures in Haughey's Fort could be ritual structures is a reminder that the fort may have been more than just a settlement. Indeed the food remains could be interpreted as the debris from occasional ceremonial feasting and the relatively pure barley might be the offerings of farmers who lived in the area but not in the enclosure. But settlement and ceremony are not incompatible activities on the one site. The faunal evidence, the size and hilltop location, the bronze artefacts and the limited evidence for fine metalworking, and even the possible indications of some ritual practice might all be considered as indicators of a high-status settlement. Ritual practices are certainly attested at the so-called King's Stables nearby.[34]

THE KING'S STABLES

The monument traditionally known as the King's Stables was once described as a sort of a 'ringfort with a sunken floor' and was popularly thought to be the site where the ancient kings of Ulster stabled and watered their horses. It lies just below and to the north-west of Haughey's Fort and is a flat-surfaced and approximately circular sunken hollow about 2m below the surrounding ground surface and surrounded by a low, broad penannular earthen bank about 1m high and up to 10m wide with a broad gap on its western side. The interior filled with water in wet weather but normally the surface appeared as a soft moss. A very small part of the site (about 5%) was excavated with intriguing results. It proved to be an artificially constructed flat-bottomed basin with steeply sloping sides and a diameter of about 25m and depth of 3.5m to 4m. The surrounding bank was formed by the upcast from the interior. Stratification in the basin basically consisted of a layer of fibrous peat on top of about a metre of mud on bedrock and some 50cm of clear water above the peat had a layer of floating vegetation on top of it. The depth of the basin and the high level of the modern watertable suggest that it must have originally contained a considerable depth of standing water.

The limited excavation produced eighteen fragments of clay moulds all for the manufacture of leaf-shaped bronze swords, two sherds of coarse pottery, a small plank of alder, two items of worked bone, some animal bones (mostly cattle, dog and pig) and a cut portion of the skull of a young adult human, probably male. Twigs from the basal silt and charcoal from beneath the earthen bank produced three radiocarbon dates which suggest contemporaneity with Haughey's Fort. Indeed there is a possible entrance through the outer ditch of the fort aligned on the King's Stables.[35]

The King's Stables seems to have been an artificial pond deliberately constructed for cult purposes which included offerings of animal and human remains as well as material associated with bronze working. What prompted this ritual development and the construction of the nearby hillfort is not clear. It has been tentatively suggested that both fort and pond were in some way a response to various economic and social pressures precipitated by climatic deterioration caused by the eruption the Icelandic volcano Mount Hekla. This event (known as Hekla 3) and the ensuing dust-veil has been dated to about 1150 BC but, as already mentioned, the pollen record suggests a steady increase in land-use at this time and Weir thought the hillfort a response to the social stresses caused by over-population. J. P. Mallory speculated that the hillfort might have been constructed by aristocratic intruders and Richard Warner pointed out that these various explanations are not mutually incompatible since local over-population could well be caused by population displacement from northern and western regions of Britain, including Scotland, where the consequences of climatic deterioration might be more severe. Fluctuations in prehistoric climatic conditions are notoriously difficult to determine and their social and economic consequences even more difficult to assess. Short-term climatic problems might not be recognizable in coarse pollen records, yet a quick succession of poor harvests might be disastrous for a community dependant on arable agriculture. If there was significant and widespread climatic deterioration, societies with a predominantly pastoral economy may have been able to accomodate its consequences to a greater degree.[36]

DÚN AONGHASA

One of the surprises of the excavations initiated by the Discovery Programme at the great stone fort of

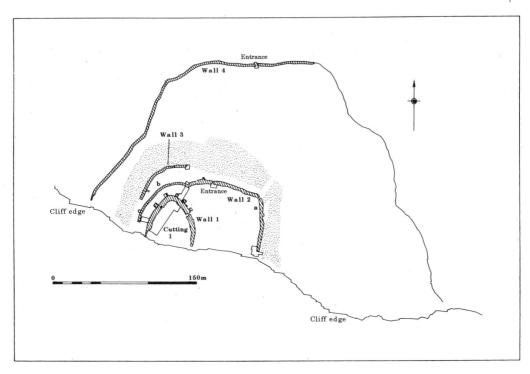

Fig. 90. General plan of Dún Aonghasa, Aran, Co. Galway. Excavation cuttings indicated.

Dún Aonghasa on the Aran Islands, in Co. Galway, was the discovery of prehistoric settlement there long before the celebrated fort visible today was built. This well known monument stands dramatically on the edge of a sheer sea cliff 87m high and dominates the lower lands of Kilmurvey to the north-east. It consists of an inner stone-built fort surrounded by two outer walls, a fragment of a third and a stone *chevaux-de-frise*.[37] Its outer defences enclose a total area of 5.7 hectares (Fig. 90). The rampart of the inner fort survives to a height of 4.9m and has a slight external batter, that is it slopes inwards from base to top to give greater stability, and has a maximum thickness of over 5m. The low, narrow, lintelled entrance is on the north-east. This inner fort is of irregular U-shaped plan, with an average internal diameter of about 47m and open to the Atlantic at the southern cliff edge. Presumably the enclosure was once an oval or at least D-shaped with a wall or rampart on the seaward side.

Excavations conducted from 1992-1995 have revealed occupation broadly dating to the period 1300-800 BC within the inner enclosure of the fort and in the middle enclosure between the inner rampart (Wall 1) and the next rampart (Wall 2). The remains of a number of circular huts and other structures have been identified in the inner

enclosure (Fig. 91). These include the remains of certain or possible hut foundations (nos 1, 2, 5 and 8), paved areas possibly the remains of dwellings (nos 4 and 6), paved areas possibly representing work areas (the 'North area' with a large hearth) and traces of walling (no. 3).

Hut 1 was about 4.8m in diameter and survived as several lines of low edging stones (all that remained of the foundation course), part of a paved floor and a stone-lined hearth; a horizontal slab marked the entrance on the east. An occupation layer of compact charcoal-flecked clay on the paving contained limpet shells, animal bones, sherds of coarse pottery, fragments of clay moulds (Fig. 91) and two crucibles. A sample of animal bone, when radiocarbon dated, suggests occupation in the period 1063-924 BC but traces of earlier occupation were found beneath the floor of Hut 1 and extended beyond its limits.

Finds included more coarse pottery and clay mould fragments, bone pins, four small hollow bronze rings and a small bronze chisel. Again, animal bone indicated date ranges of 1379-1127 and 1266-1092 BC. This earlier occupation, *c.* 1300-1000 BC, was traced elsewhere under walls and paving but further radiocarbon dates suggest that the other structures, like Hut 1 itself, date to

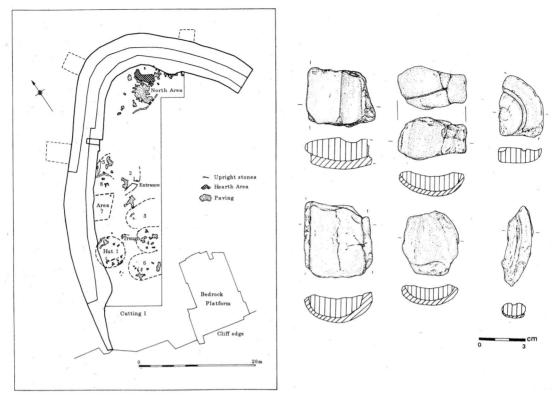

Fig. 91. Left. Area excavated in inner enclosure at Dún Aonghasa. Right. Fragments of clay moulds for casting a bronze sword, spearhead and bronze rings or bracelets.

the period 1000-800 BC. Not all were in use at the same time, the foundations of Hut 5 partly overlay Hut 8, and there clearly was a sequence of occupation on the site. A stone built trough was found to the east of Hut 1; it had been constructed in pre-existing occupation debris. The large hearth uncovered in the 'North area' measured 3.6m by 1.8m and was up to 17cm deep and produced coarse pottery and a number of bone points as well as animal and fish bones.

Traces of similar occupation were also found outside the rampart in the middle enclosure to the north. The foundations of a stone wall were uncovered here running for a distance of 9m in a north-east to south-west direction. It was 2m in average width and survived to a maximum height of 50cm. Occupation material containing animal bone, limpet shells, pottery, part of a bronze ring, bone pins and some stone artefacts abutted the eastern face of this wall and continued southwards under the foundations of Wall 1. Two radiocarbon dates from the upper level of this material provided a date range of 900-540 BC for this occupation and also provided a terminal date for the wall

foundations and a terminal date after which Wall 1 was built.

Determining the relationship of the occupation to the enclosing walls was not an easy task. In the middle enclosure, no trace of any habitation material was found to the west of the wall foundations uncovered north of Wall 1 or outside Wall 1 on the west between it and Wall 2b. Occupation material (animal bone and coarse pottery) was found in a small cutting abutting Wall 1 in the middle enclosure near the entrance to the inner fort, near the entrance through Wall 2a and, to the east, in a cutting excavated near where Wall 2a runs to the cliff edge. Here the material extended in under the inner face of the wall for a distance of 30cm-40cm. In effect the late prehistoric occupation seems to have been confined to what is now the inner enclosure and to that part of the irregularly-shaped middle enclosure east of the wall foundation found running from Wall 1 to the junction of Walls 2b and 2a.

The excavation in the inner enclosure demonstrated that the occupation material ran under the inner side of the rampart (Wall 1). It seems as if this massive rampart had been built of a series of vertical walls of masonry and its construction may have begun with a double-faced core wall (now contained within the thickness of the rampart) with additional skins of masonry added later to each face, the innermost skin resting on the interior occupation. The core wall would have been part of the original enclosing wall of the late 2nd millennium BC settlement. It is possible that this original enclosure consisted of a stone wall which ran, on the west, along the line of Wall 1 to join with the foundation wall uncovered in the middle enclosure and then joining an earlier element of Wall 2a. The enclosing wall must also have extended along the Atlantic side of the settlement to provide essential protection from the elements.

It has been suggested that the outer wall (Wall 4) may have been contemporary with this enclosure but whether this was a multivallate monument remains uncertain. What does seem clear is that the great stone fort as it stands today represents a large-scale remodelling of the original enclosure but when this took place is also uncertain. Quite limited material indicates activity on site in the last century or two BC and in the early Historic period but there is no evidence of extensive occupation at these times.

The finds from the inner and middle enclosure excavations are particularly intriguing. Preliminary analysis of the animal bones has indicated a considerable emphasis on sheep-rearing (52.3%) with cattle (33.5%) and pig (12.4%) of lesser importance. About 34% of the sheep were killed at less than one year of age and only 20% were more than three and a half years at death, suggesting that this animal was reared primarily for its meat rather than for secondary products such as wool.

While the pottery conforms to the usual coarse flat-bottomed fashion, the fragments of clay moulds demonstrate the casting of bronze swords, spearheads, rings or bracelets and pins on or near the site. At first glance a cliff-top location on the edge of the Atlantic might seem to be an unlikely location for this sort of work. If the spectacular cliff setting is ignored, Dún Aonghasa is actually located in a commanding position almost but not quite at the highest point of the southern end of a north-south ridge which dominates lower land to the north-east and east. This prominent location is only 15m or so higher above sea level than Haughey's Fort and was probably occupied for much the same reasons. Status, prominence and possibly defence were in all likelihood intertwining factors in the choice of location for both these monuments.[38]

A HIERARCHY OF SETTLEMENT

The exceptional bronze and gold objects in the Bishopsland Phase have prompted the suggestion that they were the prized possessions of an elite element of society and it is possible that social ranking is reflected in the broadly contemporary settlement evidence as well. If it is correct to consider Haughey's Fort and Dún Aonghasa as higher status sites, possibly at the top of a hierarchy of settlement, then Clonfinlough, Ballyveelish and Carrigillihy may represent lesser orders of habitation site. The evidence is very limited but a range of distinguishing characteristics may be tentatively identified. For important sites, these include a prominent hilltop location possibly chosen for defensive reasons but also chosen for visibility – as a proclamation of status and even as a focus for the organization of the surrounding landscape. Scale may be important too: both the size of the enclosure and the presence of one or more ditches, banks, walls or palisades will indicate a greater measure of labour investment.

Given the importance of bronze and gold at this time, the possession of metal objects may be revealing. Since the evidence for metalworking seems particularly scarce, the presence of items like clay moulds is probably significant and since weapons such as rapiers, swords and spears were sometimes of symbolic significance, evidence for weapon manufacture may denote special importance. More difficult to quantify is access to exotic materials. Prized materials, like the amber beads from Clonfinlough, may find their way into the archaeological record only in exceptional circumstances. The same is true of faunal assemblages which are only preserved in special conditions. Cattle, in both size and quantity, may have been a major indicator of wealth and status.

Since cooking and storage were universal activities it is probably not surprising that so many settlements should share the same coarse cooking pottery, what is curious is that the supposedly more important sites should lack finer wares especially since the clay moulds show that the capability to manufacture finer pottery did exist. Most of the coarse pottery was locally made but a small amount at Ballyveelish and Lough Gur, for instance, was made of different clays and may have come from further afield.

Finally, the evidence from Haughey's Fort and from the nearby King's Stables is a reminder that ritual activity in or near a settlement may be a mark of special status as well. Too few sites have been excavated and too little is known about economic and territorial organization to clarify the picture. It is possible that we are seeing the emergence of powerful community leaders, even theocratic chiefdoms in which tribal leaders had both a political and religious role. The control of long-distance exchange networks, which become even more marked in the succeeding Dowris Phase, may have been an important factor in the development and maintenance of these social hierarchies. Elite power and control was possibly enhanced by complex depositional rituals which themselves may have been monopolized by a chiefly element. The appearance of the bronze sword, in particular, suggests that warfare, or at least aggressive and combative activities such as persistent raiding, may also have become a prominent part of a male-dominated system.

NOTES

1 Burgess and Cowen 1972 proposed the name Killymaddy Phase for the metalworking industry of what some archaeologists have considered to be the first phase of the traditional Middle Bronze Age. Killymaddy moulds: Coghlan and Raftery 1961, nos 17-19, 33, 37 and 39.

2 Kite-shaped spearheads: Mitchell et al. 1941; Ramsey 1995. Tattenamona, Co. Fermanagh: Eogan 1983, no. 2, fig. 4B. Ballinliss, Co. Armagh: Eogan 1983, no. 43, fig. 21A. Scotland: Corsbie Moor, Berwickshire: Colquhoun and Burgess 1988, 51, no. 230. Ballysadare, Co. Sligo: Waddell 1990, 131.

3 Side-looped spearhead mould from Ballyshannon, Co. Donegal: Coghlan and Raftery 1961, no. 21. Britain: Coles 1964, 106; Ehrenberg 1977, 8; Rowlands 1976, 51. Tormarton, Gloucestershire: Knight et al. 1972 with radiocarbon date of 2927 ± 90 BP (1394-918 BC, BM-542); Rowlands 1976, 192, 273.

4 Basal-looped spearheads: Ramsey 1995; O'Connor 1980, 64; Evans 1933; Rowlands 1976, 57; for the Enfield, Middlesex, spearhead, see Burgess 1968, fig. 5:1; Continental distribution: Schauer 1973. River finds: Cooney and Grogan 1994, 167. Hoards from Tempo, Co. Fermanagh, Knockanbaun, Co. Sligo, and Kish, Co. Wicklow: Eogan 1983, nos 80, 130 and 155. Dorchester, Oxfordshire: Ehrenberg 1977, 37, pl. 1.

5 Dirks and rapiers: Burgess and Gerloff 1981; Ramsey 1993; 1995. Late usage of rapiers: Burgess 1995. See Coles 1984 for a review of Burgess and Gerloff's typology.

6 Wetland deposition: Cooney and Grogan 1994, 139; 62.4% of unprovenanced rapiers show water patination. West Row, Suffolk: Trump 1968, 213, pl. 3; Coles and Trump 1967. River finds: Bradley 1979; 1990, 23. River Shannon: Bourke 1996. River Blackwater: Ramsey et al. 1992.

7 Short-flanged axes: the term is employed by Schmidt and Burgess 1981. See Armstrong 1915 and 1917; Collins 1964. Eogan 1983, nos 1 and 4, fig. 4 A and D. Stone mould from Sultan, Co. Tyrone: Williams 1980.

8 Palstaves: Schmidt and Burgess 1981, 115, 164. Ramsey 1995. Burgess 1974, 201, 310, 312. Metallurgy: Northover 1980, 233; 1982. Stone moulds: Coghlan and Raftery 1961; Collins 1970; Eogan 1993a. Croxton, Norfolk: Needham 1990.

9 Burgess 1974, 203. Eogan 1994, x, favours a timespan of about 1300 to about 1150 BC for the Irish products of what he named the Bishopsland Phase in 1964. Taunton Phase material: Smith 1959. Anvils: Needham 1993. Narrow socketed axes are named the Taunton Type by Schmidt and Burgess 1981, 172, and though generally believed to have been inspired by northern German axes, they may be an insular development; Rowlands 1976, 42; see Jockenhövel 1982 for related socketed hammers.

10 According to Eogan 1983, no. 26, fig. 15C. E. P. Kelly 1985 suggests a decorated penannular bronze bracelet from Grangeford, Co. Carlow, is a Continental import.

11 Goldwork: Eogan 1994. Torcs: Hawkes 1932; Northover 1989 who would distinguish between torcs made from a stout wire and a more substantial bar or rod but here, following Eogan 1967a, 1994 and Taylor 1980, the general term bar torc is used. Carrowdore, Co. Down: Taylor 1980, pl. 37b.

12 Torc manufacture: Taylor 1980, 12, 61, pls 38, 40 and 41; Lang et al. 1980; Northover 1989; Meeks and Varndell 1994. See also Eluère 1982, fig. 95.

13 Torc weights and metallurgy: Northover 1989; Warner 1993. Date: Needham 1990.

14 Ribbon torcs: Eogan 1994, 53; 1983a; Taylor 1980, 63, for the Scottish examples; for differences in the form of spiral twist compare her pls 44b and 44e. Coolmanagh, Co. Carlow: Manning and Eogan 1979. J. Raftery 1971a; Warner 1993 favours the later date.

15 Ear rings: Eogan 1994, 59. For Ardmayle, Co. Tipperary, see Cahill 1983, 22; for the few other Irish bar-twisted examples, all poorly documented, see Hawkes 1961; Armstrong 1933, nos 315-5; Taylor 1980, pl. 31i. Senegalese examples: Eluère 1981. Macroom, Co. Cork: Taylor 1980, pl. 40e, left and right respectively.

16 Mediterranean origins argued by Hawkes 1961 and discounted by Taylor 1980, 62. The gold wire on the Derrinboy necklet is well illustrated in Brindley 1994, 42.

17 Dysart, Co. Westmeath: Eogan 1983, fig. 15F; Skrene, Co. Sligo: Armstrong 1933, no. 410.

18 Bracelets: Eogan 1994, 50. Downpatrick hoards: Proudfoot 1955 and 1957. For the hilltop occupation: Proudfoot 1955 and 1956; Hamlin and Lynn 1988, 61.

19 Hoards: Eogan 1983, 7, suggests a cult of the dead. See also Bradley 1982; 1990, 135.

20 Spratling 1980.

21 Rowlands 1976, 144.

22 Roscommon hoard: Day 1880; Eogan 1983, no. 32, fig. p. 325. Guilsfield hoard, Montgomeryshire: Savory 1980, no. 268, figs 32-38; Davies 1967.

23 Lough Gur, Co. Limerick: Ó Ríordáin 1954, 420; Rathgall, Co. Wicklow: Raftery 1976; Dún Aonghasa, Co. Galway: Cotter 1993, 1995, 1996; Lough Eskragh, Co. Tyrone: Collins and Seaby 1960, Williams 1978. Metalworking organization: Rowlands 1971; 1976; Barrett and Needham 1988. Eogan 1993a provides a list of clay and stone moulds.

24 Roscommon Phase metalwork: Eogan 1964; Burgess 1968; 1968a; Burgess et al. 1972. Chapes: Eogan 1965, 168, fig. 91; Burgess et al. 1972. Spear butts: Eogan 1964, 290, fig. 1:8; O'Connor 1980, 141; Needham 1982, 38.

25 Ballintober swords: Eogan 1965, 5: Class 1; Pryor 1980, 18. Colquhoun and Burgess 1988, 19. Early swords: Needham 1982. Moor Sand, Salcombe, Devon: Muckelroy 1981. Rowlands 1976, 79, sees some comparisons between some Ballintober sword hilts and those of the flange-hilted sword.

26 Ballyveelish, Co. Tipperary: Doody 1987; radiocarbon dates: 2550 ± 130 BP (980-960/940-390 BC, GrN-11445) and 2770 ± 60 BP (1088-810 BC, GrN-11658) from charcoal from ditch. Faunal remains: McCormick 1992; 1994. The study of the cattle bones from Knockaulin, Co. Kildare, by Crabtree 1990 revealed a large number of immature animals and some older females which seemed consistent with milk production, young calves being killed to allow more milk for consumption and elderly females being killed when no longer milk producing. However, McCormick would argue that the presence of so many calf bones implies the rearing of cattle primarily for their meat.

27 Chancellorsland, Co. Tipperary: Doody 1993a; 1995; 1996; 1997.

28 Curraghatoor, Co. Tipperary: Doody 1987a for 1982 excavation; preliminary reports of later work: Doody 1988-1992; 1993; 1997; published radiocarbon dates include: 2759 ± 35 BP (992-838 BC, GrN-11660) from charcoal in pit in Hut 1; 2940 ± 50 BP (1310-1006 BC, GrN) and 2730 ± 50 BP (990-810 BC, GrN-19562).

29 Lough Gur, Co. Limerick: Cleary 1995; Grogan and Eogan 1987, 487; pottery: Cleary 1993, 119. Black Patch, Sussex: Drewett 1982.

30 Carrigillihy, Co. Cork: O'Kelly 1951; pottery: Cleary 1995; coarse ware in general: Cleary 1995a; radiocarbon dates (O'Kelly 1989, 222): 3100 ± 50 BP (1510-1220, GrN-12916) and 2810 ± 50 BP (1130-850 BC, GrN-12917). Exploitation of coastal resources in the period 1400-1260 BC is also indicated at a midden at Culleenamore, Co. Sligo: Burenhult 1984, 131, 326.

31 Clonfinlough, Co. Offaly: Moloney 1993. Some would distinguish between settlements built on natural knolls or promontories in or near lakes and surrounded by light piling and the crannogs of early Historic times which are substantial defended structures encircled by a stockade of deep-set piles: Crone 1993; Kelly 1991. Amber: Beck and Shennan 1991, 101. Logboats: Lanting and Brindley 1996; Robinson et al. 1996. Annaghcorrib, Co. Galway: B. Raftery et al. 1995.

32 Cullyhanna, Co. Armagh: Hodges 1958; Hillam 1976; Baillie 1982, 236; Mallory and McNeill 1991, 108. A worked timber from a probable lake-side settlement at Imeroo, Co. Fermanagh, has been radiocarbon dated to 3310 ± 50 BP (1900-1300 BC, UB-2330) and dendro-chronologically dated to 1478 ± 9 BC: Baillie 1985.

33 Sites D and F, Lough Gur, Co. Limerick: Ó Ríordáin 1954, 384, 400. Raheen, Co. Limerick: Gowen 1988, 84.

34 Haughey's Fort excavations: Mallory 1991, 1994, 1995; Hartwell 1991; Mallory et al. 1996. Faunal remains: Murphy and McCormick 1996; McCormick 1994. Insect remains: Anderson 1989. Pottery: Boreland 1996. Wood remains and palaeobotanical evidence: Neill 1996; Hawthorne 1991; Weir and Conway 1988; radiocarbon dates (Mallory 1995) include: 2877 ± 60 BP (1260-910 BC, UB-3386), 2865 ± 25 BP (1124-943 BC, GrN-15481), and 2920 ± 25 BP (1256-1032 BC, GrN-15482) all from charcoal from internal pits or hearths; 2253 ± 26 BP (384-209 BC, UB-3384) and 2221 ± 26 BP (386-198 BC, UB-3385) both from charcoal from the pit containing the iron object; and 2872 ± 47 BP (1255-918 BC, UB-3380) from charcoal from the pit containing the cup-marked stone. Selective breeding: Warner 1988. Pollen analysis: Weir 1987, 1993, 1994; in Lynn 1997, 111.

35 The King's Stables, Co. Armagh: Lynn 1977; radiocarbon dates: 2765 ± 75 BP (from charcoal, 1122-800 BC, UB-2123:); 2585 ± 80 BP (from twigs, 900-429 BC, UB-2124); and 2955 ± 45 BP (from twigs, 1374-1024 BC, UB-2157).

36 Climatic factors and consequences: Mallory and Warner 1988; Baillie 1995, 77. Burgess 1985 has argued for a late second millennium population contraction. Weir 1993; Mallory 1991a; Warner 1994.

37 The name chevaux-de-frise is used to describe wooden stakes or upright pointed stones placed in the ground to hinder attackers and it is said to derive from spikes used by Frisians to impede enemy cavalry in the late 17th century. For chevaux-de-frise see Harbison 1971; Mytum and Webster 1989. The scatter of small stones at the promontory fort at Doonamo, Aughernacalliagh townland, Co. Mayo, interpreted as a chevaux-de-frise may in fact be the protruding stones of a children's burial ground (information from Markus Casey).

38 Dún Aonghasa: Cotter 1993, 1995, 1996, 1996a for preliminary reports; radiocarbon dates include: 2084 ± 25 BP (1063-924 BC, GrN-20226); 3165 ± 30 BP (1379-1127 BC, GrN-20228) and 2955 ± 25 BP (1266-1092 BC, GrN-20229) all from animal bone from Hut 1 and area; date from animal bone from occupation layer abutting wall: 2625 ± 60 BP (900-669 BC, AA-10276) and from animal bone from under face of Wall 1: 2585 ± 60 BP (842-540 BC, AA-10270).

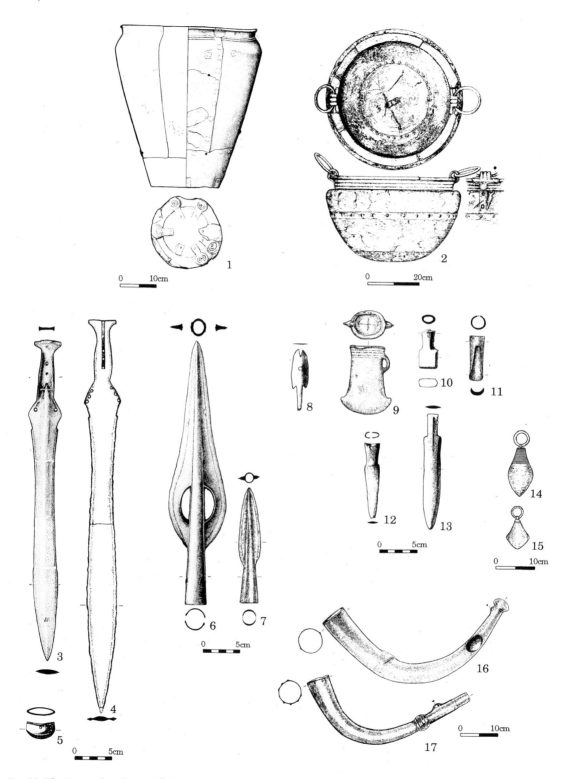

Fig. 92. The Dowris hoard, Co. Offaly, selected bronze objects. 1. Bucket. 2. Cauldron. 3-4. Swords. 5. Scabbard chape. 6-7. Spearheads. 8. Razor. 9. Socketed axehead. 10. Socketed hammer. 11. Socketed gouge. 12-13. Knives. 14-15. Pendants. 16-17. Horns.

7

The Consolidation of Wealth and Status: 900–500 BC

METALWORK OF THE DOWRIS PHASE

The first half of the last millennium BC saw the culmination of many of the developments in ornament and weaponry initiated in the preceding centuries. There seems to be a significant increase in the amount of metal in circulation and a considerably greater variety of objects manufactured. Some writers have seen this as a time of conspicuous wealth expressed in a remarkable range of weaponry and gold ornaments. Certainly some of the most outstanding pieces of prehistoric gold and bronzework belong to this period. Technological skills develop as well with the production of exceptional examples of hollow cast and sheet metalwork. This is also a time which saw the consolidation of a warrior and aristocratic society with an even greater emphasis on ostentatious display and on depositional cult practices. Indeed almost 80% of the metal hoards of Irish prehistory, including some of the most remarkable, belong to the metalworking phase which George Eogan named the Dowris Phase after a major find of bronze artefacts in the midlands.

THE DOWRIS HOARD: 'A HORSE-LOAD OF … BRONZE ANTIQUITIES'

What has become known as the Dowris hoard is the largest collection of bronze objects ever found in Ireland and originally it may have comprised over 200 objects; it was described in one early report as 'a horse-load of gold-coloured bronze antiquities'. The discovery was made in the 1820s in the townland of Whigsborough, approximately 8km north-east of Birr, Co. Offaly, and the name Dowris

derives from that of an adjacent townland called Doorosheath. The find was poorly recorded but may have been made in the course of potato digging in reclaimed bogland. No precise details of the original contents exist and some of the collection was dispersed. Today 110 bronze objects are preserved in the National Museum and a further 67 in the British Museum (of which most though not all probably came from the find); the latter collection also contains two pieces of waste bronze and six sandstone rubbing or polishing stones. Of the surviving items (Fig. 92) the most numerous are hollow-cast bronze pendants (48), spearheads (36), socketed axes (35), cast bronze trumpets or horns (26), knives (7), swords (5), socketed gouges (5), buckets (3) and cauldrons (3) of sheet bronze, and razors (3). A socketed hammer and a scabbard chape are also preserved.

Many of the surviving objects are complete or in reasonably good condition. All of the swords are damaged or broken, but most of the axes, apart from half a dozen broken and incomplete examples, are, like the spearheads, well preserved. A majority of the horns are complete or nearly so, though six are represented only by parts or fragments. Two of the surviving buckets and two of the cauldrons are represented by parts or fragments as well. It is said that the complete cauldron had contained 'an assortment' of bronzes. The pendants are in good condition except for two which seem to be broken and flawed castings.

Though generally described as a hoard, given its unusual size this assemblage of bronzes may not have been a single deposition but could have accumulated over a period of time as a result of a prolonged sequence of ritual activity perhaps in a lake or pool. The deposition of musical instruments, such as horns, is a new departure which may echo northern European customs. The bronze bucket is a remarkable object which had been repaired several times and was probably a number of centuries old when deposited. This bucket and a number of other types in the collection, such as the cauldron, horns and pendants, are good illustrations of some of the significant metalworking developments of the Dowris Phase.[1]

THE DOWRIS BUCKET

The intact bucket from Dowris is one of two which stand at the head of an accomplished sheet bronze industry in late prehistoric Britain and Ireland. It and a bucket from Arthog, Merioneth, south Wales, are generally considered early imports from Central Europe, perhaps in the Penard Phase, which inspired insular craftsmen to produce local forms of flat bottomed buckets and round bottomed cauldrons of similar riveted multi-sheet construction.

Made from very thin sheet bronze (0.8mm thick), it is over 40cm high and in good condition, apart from missing handles and a number of riveted repairs and patching (Fig. 92, 1). It is constructed of three pieces of sheet bronze, the lower part is a single sheet beaten into a tub shape with a slightly dished base surrounded by a foot ring. The upper body consists of two overlapping sheets of bronze of equal size riveted together along two vertical seams and riveted to the basal portion. The edge of the everted rim was bent around a bronze wire to strengthen it and there are two low corrugations on the neck. Two opposed handles (which would have held solid-cast bronze rings) were originally riveted to the vessel at the top of the vertical seams and the basal foot ring was originally protected externally by six equally spaced base plates consisting of a small decorated disc with a tab or strap-like extension.

Parallels between the Dowris and Arthog buckets and buckets of Hosszúpályi type in Hungary and Romania are intriguing: the latter are of similar size, manufactured of three riveted sheets of bronze, with deep tub-shaped lower portions, riveted strap handles and, on rare occasions, what may be similar protective base plates. These Hosszúpályi vessels (Fig. 93, 1-2) are a variant of the smaller Kurd buckets (named after another Hungarian find) which occur further west. They were probably important status symbols, one Kurd bucket was found in a chieftain's cremation grave of about 1100 BC at Hart, in Bavaria, associated with a bronze cup and a strainer, and bronze fitments from a four-wheeled wagon. It has been suggested that such buckets, cups and strainers may have been special drinking sets, even connected with wine drinking and it is possible that the insular buckets may also have served as containers for some alcoholic drink perhaps of a ceremonial nature.

Two other Irish buckets are of Continental form but have had their original riveted strap handles replaced by cast-on handles, a distinguishing feature of the locally produced examples. One has no precise provenance, the other comes from Derrymacash, north-west of Lurgan, Co. Armagh.

It is possible that buckets like Dowris and Arthog are not imports and it indeed may be difficult to determine whether buckets such as these are actual imports or close copies of a Continental fashion, the difficulties in distinguishing between the two are often considerable. However, they do seem at least to demonstrate the long distance transmission of material fashion and are just one element in a much larger body of evidence, which includes bronze swords and shields, for interaction between elite societies in Ireland, Britain and Continental Europe at this time. Not everyone is convinced that insular buckets were necessarily inspired by Central European types; Stephen Briggs suggests that both may have had a common ancestry in wood or more probably leather forms. Certainly wooden cauldrons were being manufactured at this time: an unprovenanced round-bottomed wooden cauldron, probably from the north of Ireland, has been radiocarbon dated to 1055-795 BC.[2]

A fine bronze bucket from a bog at Cape Castle, Co. Antrim, now in the Hunt Museum, Limerick, is a local product judging from its shape, wheel-shaped base plate and cast-on handles. The wheel-shaped base plate replaced a series of separate angular base plates and seems therefore to be a later development. There is repoussé geometric decoration on the shoulder of this bucket (Fig. 93, 3) which recalls central European fashions and prompted the suggestion that its Irish maker must have been acquainted at first hand with the modes and methods of Continental schools of workmanship. Similar repoussé decoration occurs on a bucket, with riveted staples and a corrugated base, acquired by a 19th century collector and said

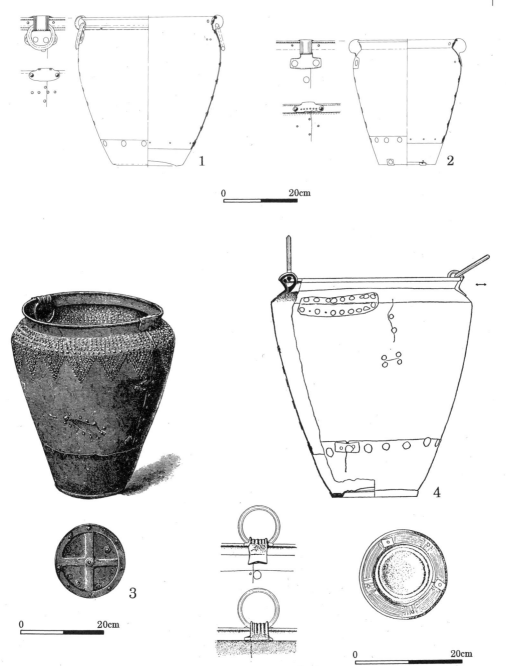

Fig. 93. Bronze buckets. 1-2. Hosszúpályi, Hungary. 3. Cape Castle, Co. Antrim. 4. Magilligan, Downhill, Co. Derry.

to have been found near Ballymoney, Co. Antrim, but this could be a Continental find given an incorrect Irish provenance.

Other Irish-British buckets are for the most part of evident local manufacture and include some seven other buckets or fragments thereof from Ireland and ten from Britain (Fig. 94). The Irish fragments include the tub-shaped lower part of one

and two angular base plates of another in the Dowris hoard.

The principal distinguishing features of locally manufactured buckets are the presence of cast-on rather than riveted handles and developed base plates. A complete example found at Magilligan, Downhill, Co. Derry, is made of the usual three sheets of bronze each about 1mm thick (Fig. 93, 4).

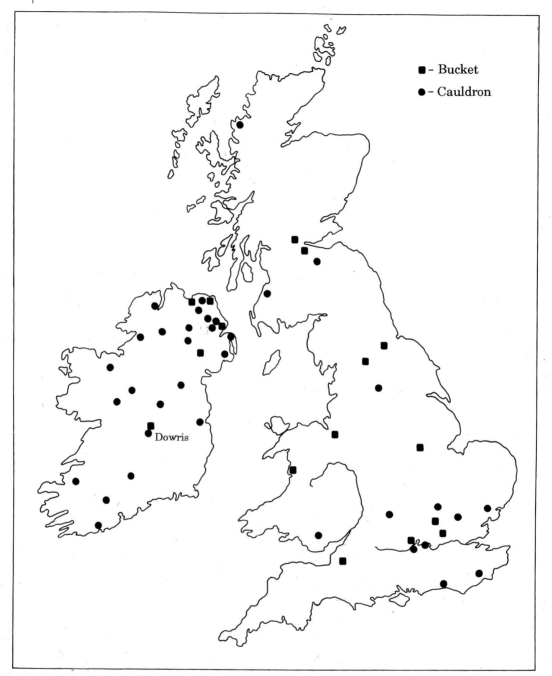

Fig. 94. General distribution of buckets and cauldrons in Britain and Ireland.

The skill required to hammer each of these from a heavy piece of cast metal was considerable; the basal part of the bucket is estimated to weigh a little under 1.2kg and was beaten into shape on a matrix using a metal hammer at least in the final stages. The rivets used have flat heads beaten tightly against the body. Several riveted patches are later repairs. The two handles (or staples as they are sometimes called) are cast onto the rim and neck and each projects inwards, forming a semicircular loop, to hold a free-riding bronze ring. These cast staples and rings are typical of insular bronze cauldrons and it is far from clear why this sort of complicated attachment was preferred on both buckets and cauldrons to a simpler riveted one. The casting-on must have been a difficult process perhaps undertaken in more than one stage; great care was needed to see that the molten metal did not burn through the thin sheet bronze and the bronze ring (cast separately) had to be carefully held in place. This sort of complex metalworking probably denotes the existence of specialized craftsmen who may have worked for aristocratic patrons. The Magilligan bucket has its base reinforced by a circular, ribbed, cast bronze fitment which fits over and is riveted to the foot ring. This type of protective base ring or plate may be a development of the wheel-shaped base plate found on the Cape Castle and other insular buckets.[3]

CAULDRONS

The complete cauldron from Dowris (Fig. 92, 2) belongs to a well-known series of round bottomed sheet bronze vessels found in Ireland, Britain and in western Continental Europe in Denmark, France and the Iberian peninsula which have been called 'Atlantic cauldrons' to differentiate them from various bronze vessels found elsewhere in Europe. They have been divided into two classes, an earlier Class A and a later Class B, with various subdivisions, and the earlier examples have been studied by Sabine Gerloff. The Dowris cauldron is a Class A example characterized by a spheroid or slightly conoid body usually with a corrugated neck and a rim which is turned sharply inwards to give a flat top. Two staples consisting of semicircular ribbed tubes are cast onto the rim and hold ring handles which are usually (but not always) of circular cross-section. The body is always made of three bronze sheets riveted together: two upper sheets with vertical seams set inside and riveted to a bowl-shaped bottom part (Fig. 95, 1). Other sheets invariably represent later additions and repairs. The Dowris cauldron has suffered some damage but was originally made in this way and the lowest basal part is a later and rougher addition. It is just over 50cm in external diameter with a characteristic corrugated neck and inturned flat rim rolled around a bronze wire. Both corrugations and wire served to strengthen the sheet bronze. The staples are cast triple-ribbed tubes and hold cast rings.

Gerloff has assigned Class A cauldrons in Ireland and Britain to four types, the earliest of which are represented by finds from England, one example coming from Colchester, Essex, and another from Shipton-on-Cherwell, Oxfordshire. The Dowris cauldron belongs to her Tulnacross Type, named after a bog find in Co. Tyrone about 5km south-east

of the Beaghmore stone circles. The Tulnacross example itself (Fig. 95, 2) is a much repaired piece with a conoid body and a maximum height of about 47cm. The lip of the inturned flat rim is rolled around a bronze wire in the usual fashion and the several later repairs to the body may reflect distinct phases of work. What was thought to be a strengthening iron band inside the rim has proven, on analysis, to be an organic deposit.

Found mainly in Ireland, this Tulnacross Type usually has a rather conoid body with heights of 33cm to 40cm and a capacity of 35 to 45 litres, there are three corrugations on the neck and characteristic cast-on staples in the shape of a half tube with three ribs, a staple form which 'in its entirety represents a triple-ribbed arch on two T-shaped supports'. Staples of this sort have been found in a huge founder's hoard from Isleham, Cambridgeshire, of the Wilburton Phase, and this association and several other strands of evidence have convinced Gerloff that the manufacture of Tulnacross cauldrons began about 1000 BC. The distinctive triple-ribbed staples may be a development of the staples found on the earlier English cauldrons of Colchester and Shipton Types which are not ribbed tubes but formed of two or three closely-set but separate three-quarter rings. One Irish cauldron from a bog at Derreen, near Bellanagare, Co. Roscommon (with ring-handles of lozenge-shaped section) seems to have staples which consist of three separate rings simply fused together and thus, typologically at least, may represent an intermediate stage between the primitive Shipton and later Tulnacross forms. The Tulnacross Type and later cauldrons are remarkable products of the bronzesmith's craft displaying familiarity with sophisticated casting techniques, seemingly using lead-alloyed bronze for handle fitments and unleaded bronze for the carefully beaten sheet work and rivets.

The Portglenone Type is named after two finds from a bog at Portglenone, Co. Derry (Fig. 95, 3). The triple-ribbed staples now have a flange at either end and a basal element usually formed by two transverse bars across the rim with a small space between them (this bracing presumably strengthened the attachment and protected the flat rim from contact with the free-riding ring handle). One of the cauldron fragments from the Dowris hoard is a staple of this type. The neck of these cauldrons has two rather than three corrugations

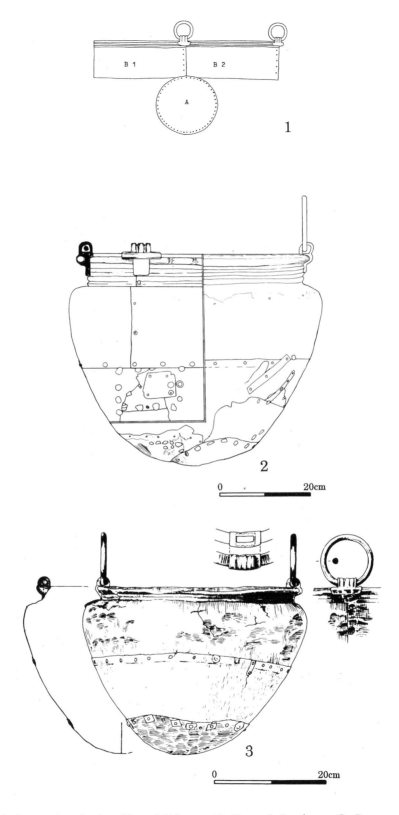

Fig. 95. 1. Method of construction of early cauldrons. 2. Tulnacross, Co. Tyrone. 3. Portglenone, Co. Derry.

and, judging from the complete examples, it seems as if the type is generally smaller: 29cm to 35cm in height with a capacity of 20 to 38 litres.

A significant number of complete cauldrons have been found in bogs but details of their discovery are all too rarely recorded. One, revealed at a depth of about 1m in the course of turf cutting, in Barnacurragh townland, near Tuam, Co. Galway, had the lip of its rim rolled around a wooden rod rather than a bronze wire. This cauldron had been deposited in an inverted position but nothing else was found and nothing was noted in the vicinity when more of the bog was cut away.

According to Gerloff, a number of associated finds indicate that cauldrons of the Portglenone Type are firmly dated to the Dowris Phase and the corresponding Ewart Park Phase in Britain. Since all the complete cauldrons have been found in Ireland (and the one complete Scottish example – of Tulnacross Type – from Hattenknowe, Peebleshire, may be an Irish export) and since the British finds and one from a large western French hoard at Vénat, near Angoulème in the Charente, are represented by fragments, Gerloff also suggests that cauldron production may have been confined to Ireland at this time, the fragments reflecting a trade in scrap metal.

The most detailed assessment of Class B cauldrons remains a brief study by Leeds in 1930. These are bronze round-bottomed vessels of multi-sheet construction but without a corrugated neck. Now the rim is everted with rolled lip (sometimes rolled around a bronze rod or tube) and the staples are cast onto the inner part of the slanting rim. The staples are the familiar ribbed tubes with pronounced flanges at either end, but the T-shaped element is now usually confined to the exterior and various sorts of external or internal riveted struts or stays may be added (Leeds B1). The rim may be decorated with corrugations and repoussé dots. The fragment of the third cauldron from the Dowris hoard is a part of a rim with repoussé ornament. Conical-headed rivets sometimes occur and are occasionally purely decorative; these are believed to be inspired by north German and south Scandinavian fashion and are also found on some of the bronze horns of the period. There is some greater elaboration of handle rings which may be fluted or ribbed. A small number of vessels have staples (of half-tube form with a base and with quite pronounced flanges) which were cast

separately and then affixed to the neck by various means including riveting (Leeds B2).

A cauldron found at a depth of some 3m in a bog at Lisdrumturk, Co. Monaghan, has a body basically made from three large sheets of bronze, a lower saucer-shaped piece with two broad sheets above, but the upper body and rim is formed of two further pieces and also bears several triangular attachments (Fig. 96, 1). All are riveted together with flat-headed and conical-headed rivets. Most of the vertical seams of rivets are decorative. The ribbed and flanged staples (B1) with faceted ring-handles are cast on and a number of patches on the interior are ancient repairs. An intriguing feature of this cauldron is the presence of what seem to be iron rivets. A dozen or so have been noted on different parts of the vessel. There is no good evidence for the date of the first use of iron in Ireland but its use in Britain and on the Continent is well attested after 700-600 BC. Some of the iron rivets may be repairs or replacements but some may be original and may imply that the cauldron was made around or about 600 BC.

A second good example of a Class B cauldron was found in a bog at Castlederg, Co. Tyrone, and is also made of multiple bronze sheets and bears conical rivets, a large number of which form purely decorative seams, some with a reinforcing bronze strip on the interior. The handle-rings are of octagonal cross-section (Fig. 96, 2). Another cauldron of this class was found in a bog in Raffrey townland, near Killinchy, Co. Down.[4]

CAULDRONS OF PLENTY?

A number of writers have speculated on the purpose of these large bronze vessels and have been particularly struck by references to the special significance of cauldrons and their role in feasting in Medieval Irish and Welsh literature. It has been claimed there is some evidence that they may have been used as media for commercial barter in ancient times and legend has it that some cauldrons were magical vessels providing the right amount of food for an assembled company and sometimes miraculously large enough to hold the carcasses of several sheep or hogs. Medieval legend is probably an unreliable guide to late prehistoric practice but David Coombs has noted the magical properties and aristocratic associations of cauldrons in other contexts: 'It is possible to see the cauldron as epitomising the chief and his power. "The main

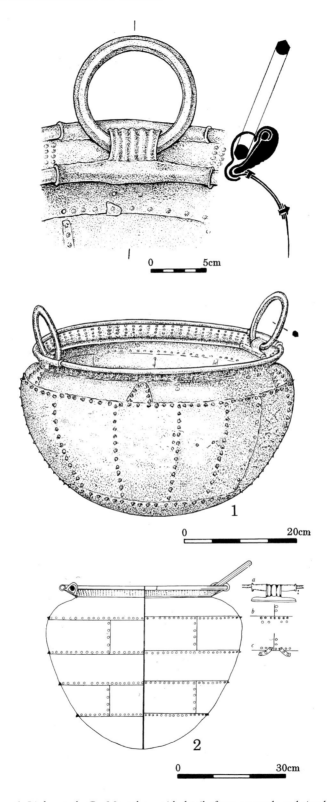

Fig. 96. Class B cauldrons. 1. Lisdrumturk, Co. Monaghan, with detail of cast-on staple and ring handle. 2. Castlederg, Co. Tyrone.

symbol of being powerful is to be wealthy and of wealth is to be generous" sums up the redistributional chiefdoms known from anthropological studies. The giving away of selected portions of food out of the cauldron during certain ceremonies could have symbolized the whole process of the power of the chief to redistribute wealth'.[5]

Bronze cauldrons were valuable objects as demonstrated by the technical skills required in their manufacture which demanded a knowledge of complex casting processes as well as beating and riveting. The care with which they were repaired from time to time is a further indication of just how prized they were. It is reasonable to see them as aristocratic possessions which were put to periodic use and the fact that so may of them seem to have been single deposits in bogs may denote a special ritual significance. Their considerable capacity suggests the boiling of meat and, if primarily cooking vessels, this may have been for ceremonial purposes only. An early cauldron (of Colchester Type) found while ploughing a field at Feltwell Fen, Norfolk, contained a bronze flesh-hook. This is a socketed single hook, a more developed version of the simple double-pronged hook found in the Bishopsland hoard (Fig. 72) and at the settlement at Ballinderry, Co. Offaly (below). These different types of bronze hooks, as the name 'flesh-hook' implies, are believed to have been used to pick pieces of boiled meat out of a vessel or a cooking pit though use as goads is also a possibility.[6] Whether these cauldrons were set in the ground and their contents heated with hot stones like the contents of a trough at a burnt mound, as has been suggested, remains uncertain. The attention given to neck and handles may imply that suspension was the norm and of course they could have been used to hold liquids too.

If bronze cauldrons were used to prepare special ceremonial food or drink, they may have been the centre-pieces at ritual meals or at elaborate feasts which were occasions for conspicuous hospitality and social competition conducted by a wealthy elite. The eventual votive deposition of a cauldron in a bog or some other place could have been the ultimate way of breaking an economically exhausting cycle of competitive feasting. What rituals may have accompanied such an event are unknown but more than metalwork may have been involved on some ceremonial occasions at some bog sites. Ritual locations may have been demarcated in

some way but nothing like the small rectangular wooden cult building found in a bog at Bargeroosterveld in the Netherlands has been found in Ireland. However, a crudely carved wooden idol found in a bog at Ralaghan, near Shercock, Co. Cavan, has been radiocarbon dated to 1096–906 BC. This primitive and sexually ambiguous figure (Fig. 97) stands just over 1m in height and when discovered it had a basal tenon which was inserted into a square block of wood which was not preserved. It is conceivable that it had once formed part of some larger structure. The bog of Cullen, Co. Tipperary (below) which produced an enormous quantity of gold and bronze objects over a number of years in the 18th century also yielded – at the same time as a bronze sword was found – a 'fragment which was said to be part of an image ... of black wood entirely covered and plated with thin gold'. Also found was 'another fragment of the same kind of wood' which contained some golden studs or rivets (which could have been bronze) and which was described as 'of an human form ... of sufficient size to make a gate-post, to which use it was applied'. Unfortunately, it did not survive this treatment.[7]

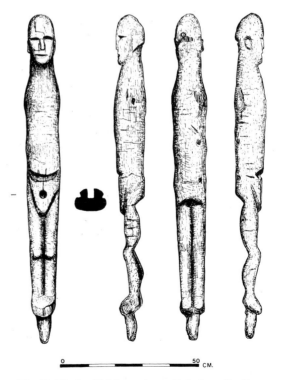

Fig. 97. Wooden idol from a bog at Ralaghan, Co. Cavan.

Horns

It is probably not surprising that fine metalwork, like sheet bronze vessels, should be associated with status and ceremony and the same appears to be true of a remarkable series of cast bronze horns or trumpets which were a particularly Irish development. The Dowris hoard contained at least 26 examples, the largest assemblage of these objects found and it contained examples of the two principal forms, those blown through an aperture on one side and those blown through a mouth-piece at one end (Fig. 92, 16–17). Over 120 horns have been recorded and over 90 of these are extant.

These objects were recognized as wind instruments in the 19th century, a development which may have produced Ireland's first (and only) martyr to archaeology: an antiquarian, Dr Robert Ball of Dublin, demonstrated that these could be blown as musical instruments and he produced 'a deep bass note, resembling the bellowing of a bull'. Sadly 'it is a melancholy fact, that the loss of this gentleman's life was occasioned by a subsequent experiment of the same kind. In the act of attempting to produce a distinct sound on a large trumpet ... he burst a blood-vessel, and died ...'. The most detailed study of these horns is that of John Coles who happily survived to produce a comprehensive report.

The horns were cast in two-piece moulds formed of two outer clay halves and a clay core: the technology was complex and inventive. Presumably wooden models or actual cow horns were used to form the moulds because some pairs of horns exist and suggest the production of identical castings. No clay mould fragments have yet been found.

A summary of Coles' classification is a convenient way of describing the basic features of these instruments; he divided the horns into two classes, each class containing end-blow and side-blow examples (Fig. 98). Class I end-blow horns are slender curving horns with both the bell (or wider) end and body either plain or simply decorated with ribs, grooves, bosses, or small spikes like conical rivets. The characteristic feature is a tubular piece at the narrow end designed to fit inside a short tube which usually formed the mouth-piece. Most of these short tubes are removable but a few are cast on. The latter horns, those with the cast-on mouth-tube, are the longest examples known, measuring almost 1m in length. Side-blow horns in this class may also be plain or decorated in a similar simple fashion. Their closed end is either flat or knobbed and most have one or two loops. All Class I horns have at least one loop and are generally smaller than Class II.

Class II end-blow horns are characteristically decorated with large cast conical spikes at the bell end and often have perforations as well; they have a narrow tubular end, often with four holes, enclosing (rather than fitting inside) the tubular straight piece which has a narrow inserting collar at either end each with four holes. These perforations may have served to lock the horn and tube, and sometimes a mouth-piece (none of which survive) together. The tube is decorated with ribs and conical spikes and has a loop and ring. The perforations at the bell end may have been used to fasten an extension. The same is true of the side-blow horns, they too have plain bodies and the mouth usually has conical spikes and, sometimes, four perforations. The closed end is shaped like a stepped cone with a loop and ring. Another ring occurs on the body between the end and the mouth-hole.

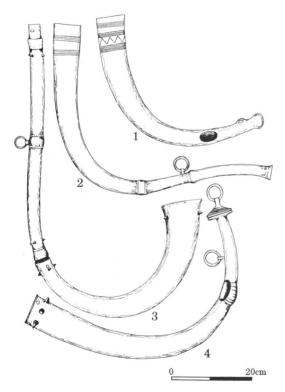

Fig. 98. Bronze horns. 1. Class I, side-blow: no provenance. 2. Class I, end-blow: Drumbest, Co. Antrim. 3. Class II, end-blow: Clogherclemin, Co. Kerry. 4. Class II, side-blow: Derrynane, Co. Kerry.

This classification confirmed an interesting two-fold fashion in horn design and an equally divergent distribution (Fig. 99) which later proved to be part of two major regional schools of both bronze and gold working in the Dowris Phase. Class I end- and side-blow horns have a northern distribution while Class II examples are a distinctly south-western phenomenon. The Dowris hoard is one instance where the two classes overlap. Indeed over half the number of known Class I horns are from Dowris. The only other northern horn found in the midlands was found at Griffinrath, near Maynooth, Co. Kildare, in 1725.

These horns are a distinctively Irish type: only two finds are recorded in Britain, a Class I end-blow from Battle in Sussex in south-eastern England and a fragment of a side-blow horn from Innermessan, Wigtownshire.

They are rarely associated with other types of bronze objects. Apart from the Dowris hoard, the only other associated find of this kind is a small hoard of bronzes from a bog at Boolybrien, south-west of Ennis, Co. Clare, which contained a Class I end-blow horn, a hilt fragment of a sword, two socketed axeheads, a sunflower pin, a chain and several rings. But in about eleven instances horns have been simply deposited with other horns. This is a curious exclusivity, even more so when it is remembered that there is a noteworthy number of finds of large numbers of horns. Unfortunately details are scanty but these finds include, for example, four horns found in a bog at Drumbest, Co. Antrim, in 1840; six found near Chute Hall, near Tralee, Co. Kerry, thought, when discovered in the course of turf-cutting, to be parts of 'an ancient distilling apparatus'; eight ('four of one make, four of another') from near Dungannon, Co. Tyrone; and 13 or 14 found in a bog between Cork and Mallow around 1750. There are several pairs of more or less identical horns: the two side-blow and two end-blow horns from Drumbest may be the best examples. Coles has also suggested that the two side-blow horns from this hoard and two other finds may be, in either case, products of the same moulds. Finds of two horns, from a bog at Drunkendult, north of Ballymoney, Co. Antrim, and from Macroom, Co. Cork, where each find contained one end- and one side-blow, might indicate that on some occasions these two forms may have been played together.

Nineteenth century writers sometimes referred to these horns as war trumpets and believed they

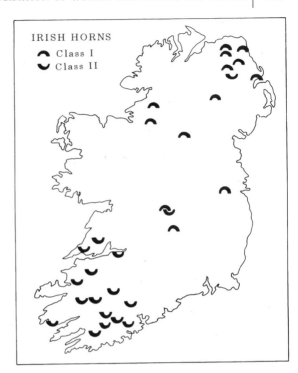

Fig. 99. Distribution of bronze horns in Ireland.

could have been cast away in the haste of retreat by war parties. Today the contexts in which they have been found and the nature of the horns themselves, including their musical capabilities and the occasional pairing, suggest to most writers that they were ceremonial pieces.

In 1963 Coles thought that side-blow horns were effectively one-note instruments and that the end-blow examples – judging from the two examples with cast-on mouth tubes which can be considered proper mouth-pieces – were capable of producing four or five notes at most and possibly yielded only two notes with any clarity. However, experimentation has since shown that trying to blow these like modern instruments, and attempting the impossible in trying to achieve melodic higher notes, may not be the best way to proceed. Different blowing techniques may have been used. If played like the Australian *didjeridu*, with lips given greater freedom of movement, considerable variation is possible in both pitch and tone-colour and much greater harmonic and rhythmic variety is possible. Modern replicas of both a Drumbest end-blow and side-blow horn together, and original horns from Drunkendult, Chute Hall and elsewhere, have produced impressive rhythmic effects.[8]

The horns were an indigenous development and were essentially translations into bronze of the simple curving cattle horn. Some very different bronze horns in northern Europe are unconnected: the production of metal versions of animal horns presumably occurred in those areas where casting techniques were sufficiently advanced.

BULLS AND RATTLES?

The Dowris hoard included a collection of bronze pendants (Fig. 92, 14-15) and it has been argued that these objects and the horns were part of a wider European bull cult in the last millennium BC. This suggestion was prompted in part by the fact that horned helmets or other horned head-dresses are recorded from Iberia to northern Europe (though not in Ireland) in bronze or in rock art and by the belief, at the time, that Irish horns produced a very limited range of bull-like sounds and could, of course, be representations in bronze of a bull's horn.

A further element in this argument was the pendant. These hollow cast bronze objects are unusual and puzzling artefacts. They have been called crotals, an antiquarian term adapted from the Latin *crotalum* (rattle), are somewhat pear-shaped and often contain a loose piece of bronze or perhaps stone. The largest number (48) come from the Dowris hoard itself and, surprisingly, only two seem to have been found elsewhere. One was reportedly found in the ditch of a fort at Calheme, east of Ballymoney, Co. Antrim, and the other has no recorded provenance. They vary slightly in shape and size and are usually about 12cm long with 12 or 14 grooves on the upper part with a suspension loop and ring above. Since they were meant to be suspended, one commentator thought they may have formed a sort of musical *Glockenspiel* struck in scalar sequence with a hammer. According to Coles they are heavy objects, weighing about 270g, and are thus unlikely to have been attached to clothing. He was struck by a resemblance between these supposed rattles and the scrotum of a bull, and it was this that inspired his suggestion of a cult with bull-horn and rattle, the latter being the 'outward sign of the virility of the beast'. He does note that the rattling sound produced is very faint and indeed it has been claimed that this is accidental being caused by nothing more than bits of loose metal.

It does seem likely that the horns were used for musical rituals and indeed a combination of end-blow and side-blow may have been employed but any association with 'rattles' rests solely on the Dowris evidence and remains uncertain. The purpose of the so-called rattles is equally unclear and for that reason the term pendant is employed here. The suggestion that they bedecked the necks of prize cattle in parade has as much, if not more, to recommend it at present. A series of hollow balls of heavy sheet gold, perforated for suspension, found at Tumna, Co. Roscommon, near Carrick-on-Shannon, in 1834, may have served a similar purpose.[9] Judgement both on a bull cult and on rattles is best suspended.

WEAPONRY

The Bishopsland Phase saw the development of the earliest Irish swords of Ballintober type by about 1100 BC and ensuing developments in sword production and in other forms of weaponry give a distinctly war-like cast to a large section of the corpus of metalwork of later prehistory, particularly in the Dowris Phase.

SWORDS AND CHAPES

The flange-hilted leaf-shaped sword has generally been considered an important improvement in sword making: the manufacturing of a broad hilt with flanges (to take a riveted haft of bone or some other organic material) cast in one piece with the blade was a major step. This combination of improved hafting mechanism and blade form produced a much more effective slashing and cutting bronze weapon which remained in use, with relatively minor changes, for over half a millennium.

The earliest flange-hilted leaf-shaped swords in Britain are concentrated in south-eastern England, notably in the Thames valley, where, after the introduction of different types from the Continent, native forms emerged. These early swords include imported or local copies of swords of Hemigkofen Type with short, wide leaf-shaped blades and high-flanged terminals with short projecting wings and poorly formed rivet holes. Erbenheim Type swords are similar but the flanged hilt has curving sides (and a distinctive small projection to support a pommel) and blades are of long, slender leaf shape. A well formed ricasso is absent in both types. Local versions with minor variations exist. Swords with convex (or U-shaped) shoulders − instead of the usual Erbenheim straight shoulder − represent a later British development as do short heavy swords with straight (V-shaped) shoulders considered to develop from Hemigkofen swords. Some other early British flange-hilted swords have a curved ricasso and hilt slots, a feature of the later Wilburton swords which have a slightly wider currency.

The only detailed account of Irish bronze swords is Eogan's 1965 classification (Fig. 100) which requires revision. His Class 1 is the Ballintober sword type already described (Chapter 6). His Class 2 contains versions of the British Erbenheim-derived swords and his Class 3 swords are versions of Hemigkofen-derived forms. Some of them bear comparison with Wilburton swords in Britain. It is not until the Ewart Park and Dowris Phases that indigenous flange-hilted swords of various sorts are widely distributed. Eogan's Class 4 contains over 400 flange-hilted leaf-shaped swords which evidently demand further study. These are the Irish counterparts of the equally numerous British Ewart Park Type (named after a Northumberland find) and, though a significant number of Irish examples

are fairly short weapons, they share a series of basic features which include hilts which are generally slightly convex-sided (sometimes lacking flanges) with expanded straight or flat terminals, steep straight shoulders usually with a straight (or sometimes slightly concave) ricasso, slots are rare – a variable rivet pattern being preferred, blades usually have a gently rounded mid-section flanked by a slight concavity and then slightly bevelled cutting edges. One example, just over 50cm long, found at Mullyleggan, near Loughgall, Co. Armagh, has part of its deer antler hilt-plate still attached (Fig. 100). No scabbards have been found but bronze chapes of slender elongated form and lozenge-shaped section, and small purse-shaped chapes are known. One of the latter type was found in the Dowris hoard (Fig. 92, 5). Swords of Eogan's Classes 5 and 6 are described in Chapter 8.

The relatively short size of some Irish swords is surprising, given the technological skills of the

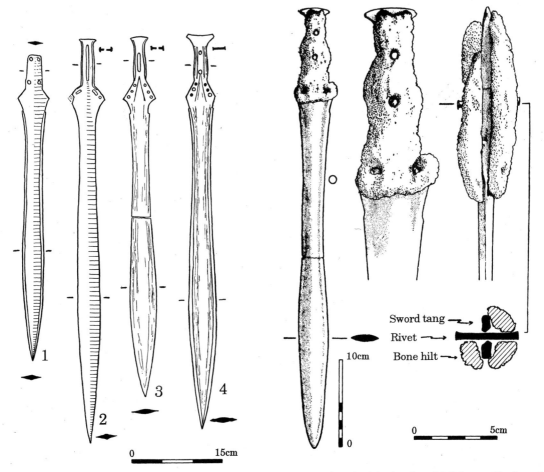

Fig. 100. Bronze swords of Classes 1-4 and (on right) a Class 4 sword with antler hilt-plate from Mullyleggan, Co. Armagh.

bronze smiths longer weapons could surely have been made if required. Judging by the measurements given in Eogan's corpus, they range in overall length from just over 40cm to a little over 60cm, the average being 52.7cm. Only some 22% are 60cm or more in length. The smallest comes from Knocknalappa, Co. Clare, with a length of 40.5cm, while the longest, at 66.5cm, is said to have been found with four other swords in Co. Tyrone.

While the leaf-shaped sword may denote a change in fighting methods, from stabbing and thrusting in rapier-like fashion to cutting and slashing, the depositional pattern of the swords remains the same, the greater number coming from river, lake and bog. A significant number of hoards of the Dowris Phase also come from bogs and, in contrast to the Bishopsland Phase, 26% of them contain weapons.

A small number of weapons hoards are known, mostly containing just two or three objects. Eogan has noted fourteen finds, seven of swords alone, four of swords and spears, one of a sword, spear and axehead, and two containing sword fragments and other items including spears, axeheads, and several tools. The association of sword and spear reflects the popularity of these weapon types at the time (Fig. 101) and is a common enough association in Britain. One might speculate that a small hoard of such weapons could be the grateful votive offering of a happy warrior but this was not always, if ever, the case. One hoard, from Ballycroghan, near Bangor, Co. Down, may have been deposited near the site of a former wetland settlement by a bronze smith: it consisted of three swords cast in moulds from the same model and in various stages of completion, one a raw casting straight from the mould with unperforated dimples instead of rivet holes.[10]

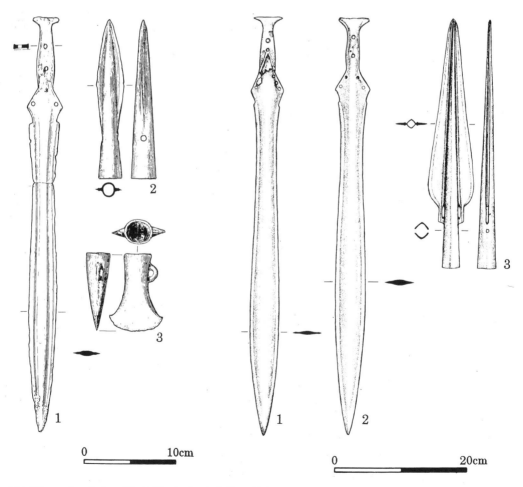

Fig. 101. Weapon hoards from Blackhills, Co. Laois (left) and Tempo, Co. Fermanagh (right).

The association of a weapon such as a sword or spear and a socketed axehead, as at Blackhills, Co. Laois, is rare but does raise the question were some socketed axes used as weapons too?

SPEARS

Different types of spear were fashionable and the Tempo discovery as well the find from Kish, near Arklow, Co. Wicklow, and the possible association at Knockanbaun, south of Easky, Co. Sligo, demonstrate that the basal-looped type continued in use in the Dowris Phase. The Knockanbaun find, with a length of 46cm, was probably a parade weapon. Also current were spears with lunate openings in the blade – undoubtedly related to the protected-loop form (Fig. 68, 3); a good example occurs in the Dowris hoard (Fig. 92, 6). Found in both Ireland and Britain (where it occurs in Wilburton hoards) this type also continued in later use in Scotland. A number are known in France and Spain. Some are elegantly ribbed and some are exceptionally long, that from Dowris is almost 40cm in length and there are others that exceed this figure such as an unprovenanced example from Ireland with gold band decoration on its socket (Fig. 102, 4).

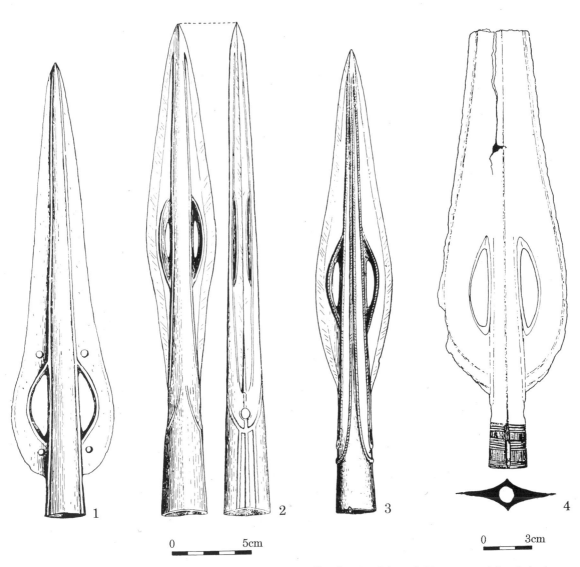

Fig. 102. Spearheads with lunate openings in the blade. 1. Near Ballinasloe, Co. Galway. 2. Unprovenanced from Ireland. 3. River Shannon. 4. Unprovenanced from Ireland with gold band decoration on the socket.

Many spearheads of the simple leaf-shaped type, whether long or short, were probably more functional weapons. This type, also with peg or rivet holes in the socket to attach it to a wooden haft, is a very widespread form and may have been introduced into Britain from the Continent in the Penard Phase. It is well represented in the Dowris hoard which contained 35 examples (Fig. 92, 7) and there is one in the Blackhills hoard as well (Fig. 101). Some very small examples are known: one 4cm in length was found at Navan, Co. Armagh, but many are 15cm-25cm in length and longer ones, though rare, are recorded. One splendid example found near Belturbet, Co. Cavan, is 53.6cm long. This, like a leaf-shaped spearhead with gold band ornament on its socket from Lough Gur, Co. Limerick, which is 41.7cm long, was probably primarily intended for display.[11]

SHIELDS

A small number of circular shields of various materials have been found. The development of a defensive device like a shield is probably one telling indication that many of the swords and spears we have been considering were sometimes put to effective use and the basic equipment of a warrior may have consisted of sword, spear and shield. Ireland has provided some remarkable evidence for the use of leather shields and these are reminders that leather helmets and body armour may have been worn as well and that, across Continental Europe, the bronze helmets, shields and breastplates found there had more functional leather counterparts too.

A unique leather shield was found during turf cutting in 1908 at Cloonbrin, near Abbeyshrule, Co. Longford. It is made of a piece of leather about 50cm in original diameter and 5mm-6mm thick. It has a hollow, oval central boss capped externally with another sewn-on leather piece and inside the boss is a leather handle. Decoration consists of a raised penannular rib around the boss and two other concentric ribs each with a V-shaped indentation or notch (on the same axis as the handle); between the ribs are four sets of three bosses (Fig. 103, 1). When found it was assumed to be a quite ineffective object but John Coles has shown, by experiment, that soaking a suitable piece of leather in cold water, repeatedly hammering it with wooden punches, pressing it with weights on a mould over a period of several days, and finally impregnating it with wax,

produces a very hard and inflexible shield which is both capable of withstanding heavy blows with a sword and is impervious to water.

Two wooden moulds for the production of leather shields are known, both apparently made from circular slabs of wood cut from the trunk of a tree but now badly shrunk. One comes from Churchfield, Co. Mayo (Fig. 103, 2), the other from Kilmahamogue, near Ballycastle, Co. Antrim. Both have central depressions (to produce a central boss) surrounded by deeply grooved circles with V-shaped notches. The Kilmahamogue mould has produced the surprisingly early – but not impossible – radiocarbon date of 1950-1540 BC.

It is an intriguing fact that shields with V-shaped notches have only been recorded in Ireland (in organic form) and in western Iberia (in stone) where a series engravings on stone slabs depict, in a schematic fashion, a range of objects including shields, swords, spears, and the occasional human figure, representing a warrior and his equipment. The decorated slab from Brozas, Cáceres, in western Spain (Fig. 103, 4) bears a shield (with handle on the same axis as the notches) which is very similar to Cloonbrin.

The distribution of V-notched shields has naturally encouraged speculation about direct contacts between Iberia and Ireland but other explanations have been offered for the striking parallels. It has been suggested that notches may have been cut in early leather prototypes to achieve a slight convexity as the material shrank during processing and shields may have been constructed of several layers of leather of diminishing size placed one on top of the other, a structure eventually reflected in multiple notches and concentric ribs. If this became traditional shield decoration, it could be copied in leather (as on Cloonbrin) and in other materials. The divergent distribution of V-notched shields, surviving in unusual circumstances in both regions, might then be unrelated images of a more widespread prototype.

Two curious wooden shields carved from slabs cut from tree trunks are also preserved. One find from Annadale, south-east of Drumshanbo, Co. Leitrim, was found 3m deep in a bog; it shrunk as it dried and now measures 66cm by 52cm but originally may have been nearly circular and about 10cm thick. A handle has been cut out of the alder wood behind a raised central boss. Decoration on the front consists of seven very narrow concentric

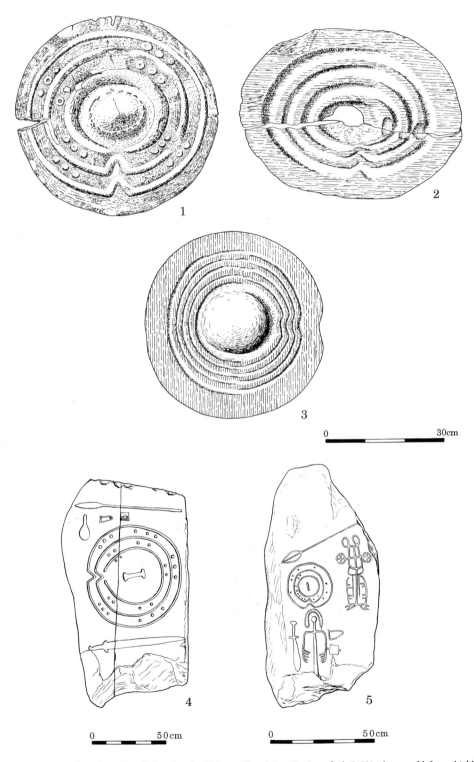

Fig. 103. Shields with V-shaped notches. 1. Leather shield from Cloonbrin, Co. Longford. 2. Wooden mould for a shield from Churchfield, Co. Mayo. 3. Wooden shield from Cloonlara, Co. Mayo. 4. Engraved slab of 8th-7th century BC date from Brozas, Cáceres, Spain, depicting a shield with V-notched ribs and bosses, a sword, spear, fibula, comb and mirror; the vertical line is a break in the stone. 5. Engraved slab with two-wheeled chariot and helmeted warrior with equipment from Cabeza de Buey.

ribs which are purely ornamental, six have shallow U-shaped notches. A second, also of alder, from Cloonlara, near Swinford, Co. Mayo, is slightly smaller but has quite a high central boss with cut-out handle behind (Fig. 103, 3). Four narrow ribs each have shallow U-shaped notches and on both shields the handle axis is at a right angle to the notches. The Cloonlara object has been radiocarbon dated to about 1200 BC. These wooden shields could have been functional, they could even have been leather-covered, but equally they may even have been votive models made for ritual deposition. Bronze ribbed shields with U-shaped notches are known in central and northern Europe and again, it is possible that this notch is a decorative echo of a leather feature.

The surviving bronze shields from Ireland find their closest analogies in Britain. One type of bronze shield, the Yetholm type named after a Scottish find, is well represented in Britain. Generally of large size (averaging 60cm in diameter) they are characteristically decorated with concentric ribs and rows of small bosses as on a well known example from Lough Gur, Co. Limerick. This superb sheet bronze object was found in a bog near Lough Gur and may have been wrapped in a textile when deposited (Fig. 105, 1). It has a diameter of 71.3cm and bears multiple repoussé ribs

and bosses; on the back there is a riveted handle and a pair of perforated bronze tabs for a suspension strap presumably to allow the shield to be slung from the shoulder. A second bronze shield, said to have been found in Co. Antrim, is similar with a diameter of 66cm. A third, also decorated with ribs and bosses, was found in the River Shannon, near Athlone, in 1987.

Three other circular bronze shields (Fig. 105, 2-4) are of very different form. They are quite small, from 27cm to 35.5cm in diameter, and have only one or two raised ribs and one or two sets of large bosses around a prominent central boss. One, with two rings of bosses, was found near Athenry, Co. Galway, with a large spearhead (now lost) and another similar shield was found on the shores of Lough Gara, Co. Sligo. The third, recovered from the River Shannon at Athlone in 1981, has a stepped central boss, encircled by four bosses and one rib; the bosses are, in fact, large domed rivet heads. The four rivets secure a handle and two suspension tabs on the back. Features such as size, stepped boss and domed rivets indicate some relationship to Continental Nipperwiese shields which also inspired a small number of British bronze shields. These, it has been argued, may be as early as the Penard Phase.

Bronze shields, whether small or large, are generally considered to be prestigious items for ceremonial purposes. Experimentation has confirmed their non-utilitarian nature, using a modern copper replica of comparable thickness and hardness revealed that the point of a leaf-shaped bronze sword could easily penetrate the metal and a slashing blow could cut completely through the shield.[12] The bronze shields, along with some other exceptional bronze weapons, may indicate the existence not just of a hierarchical society whose elite had sufficient wealth and patronage to commission the finest craftsmanship and follow the latest fashion but one dominated by a warrior aristocracy preoccupied as much with flamboyant display as with warlike activity.

GOLD

The finest goldwork of the Dowris Phase is a good illustration of a propensity for spectacular exhibitionism and three objects in particular are excellent examples of this: a group of sheet gold neck ornaments called gorgets, the so-called lock-rings, and dress-fasteners. The greatest number of

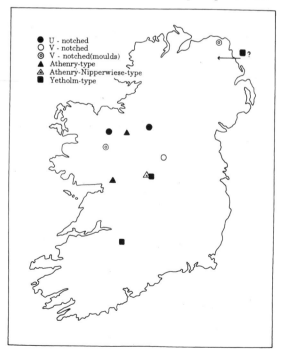

Fig. 104. Distribution of Irish shields.

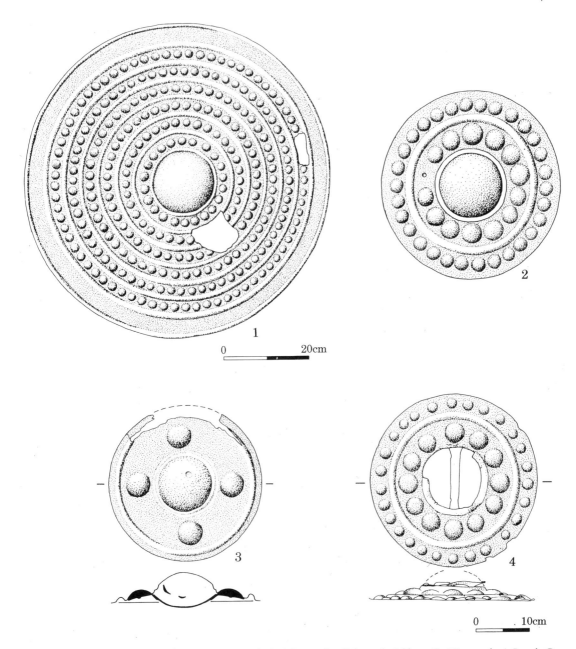

Fig. 105. Bronze shields. 1. Lough Gur, Co. Limerick. 2. Athenry, Co. Galway. 3. Athlone, Co. Westmeath. 4. Lough Gara, Co. Sligo.

prehistoric gold objects date to this period and a number of types, particular made of sheet gold, are uniquely Irish.

The gorgets are impressive ornaments and six more or less complete examples and one fragmentary find are preserved and provenanced; five others are recorded and have uncertain provenances and as many as four may have been found in the large assemblage of objects found at Cullen, Co. Tipperary.

They basically consist of a broad crescentic collar of beaten sheet gold with elaborate decoration (Fig. 106). A series of concentric semicircular ribs in high relief usually have narrow rows of rope moulding between them, produced by a combination of repoussé and chasing techniques. The edges of some collars are reinforced by wrapping them around gold wire. The circular terminals are double discs attached to one another by lapping the edges of the larger

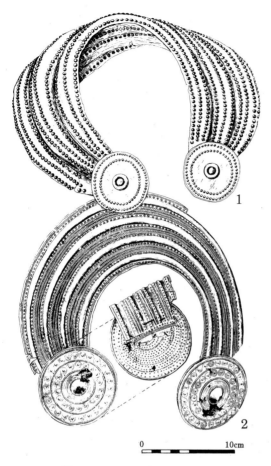

Fig. 106. Gold gorgets. 1. Co. Clare. 2. Borrisnoe, Co. Tipperary.

back disc around the edge of the front disc; these terminals are usually stitched to the collar with gold wire and the uppermost discs are decorated with finely stamped concentric circles, round or conical bosses and raised herring-bone or rope patterns. There is some evidence that gorgets may have been worn: a small perforation on either side of the inside upper edge probably held a cord or light chain to go around the back of the neck of a wearer. One from a bog at Borrisnoe, Co. Tipperary, has one link of a gold chain in one of these holes. Details of discovery are usually scanty, examples from Ardcrony, near Nenagh, Co. Tipperary, and from Shannongrove, near Pallaskenry, Co. Limerick, were each found in a bog.

A well preserved example was found in 1932 in a rock fissure at Gleninsheen, in the Burren, Co. Clare, it measures 31.4cm across and is decorated with characteristic ribbing which includes seven plain ribs with intervening rows of triple rope mouldings produced by working the gold from the

front. The terminals bear a large central conical boss within concentric circles surrounded by a pattern of similar boss and circle ornament. It has been described as one of the finest achievements of the goldsmiths of the period.

The only associations occur in a hoard of gold ornaments found at Gorteenreagh, Co. Clare. This hoard was found beneath a large slab just below the surface in a field south-west of Feakle and comprised six gold objects, a gorget, two lock rings, two bracelets and a plain dress fastener. The gorget is an unusual piece (Fig. 107) in so far as the collar is composed of three broad ribs with lines of punched dots between them. Though of stout sheet gold, its edges are also strengthened by wrapping them around a gold wire. The terminals bear the familiar conical boss and concentric circle decoration and were apparently deliberately torn from the collar before deposition. The bracelets are penannular with expanded cup-shaped terminals, one is of circular, the other of lozenge-shaped cross section. The dress fastener and the two lock rings are gold types which will be considered below. With the possible exception of the bracelets, the way in which all the objects were actually worn is uncertain, nonetheless the hoard seems to be a set of personal ornaments. The gorget may have been ritually mutilated before being placed in the ground but it has also been suggested that this damage might hint at violence and plunder.

The distribution of gorgets is quite confined: they have been found mainly in Counties Clare, Limerick and Tipperary and form one element in a remarkable regional industry which includes other gold objects such as lock rings, bowls, boxes, and other collars and some of the largest gold hoards ever found (Fig. 110). Sheet gold seems to have been particularly popular here.

Gorget origins are disputed. General shape and the concentric circle decoration in particular have suggested north European inspiration and George Eogan sees other objects such as certain types of pin including sunflower pins, U-notched shields and amber as further evidence of Nordic influence. For Joan Taylor, however, this influence is a myth. Others have noted the possibility of leather prototypes and remarked how the broad ribs of a gorget found somewhere in Co. Clare (Fig. 106) resemble the stiff folds of a leather collar (like a horse collar) and how the embossed ornament on this gorget recalls studded leather.[13]

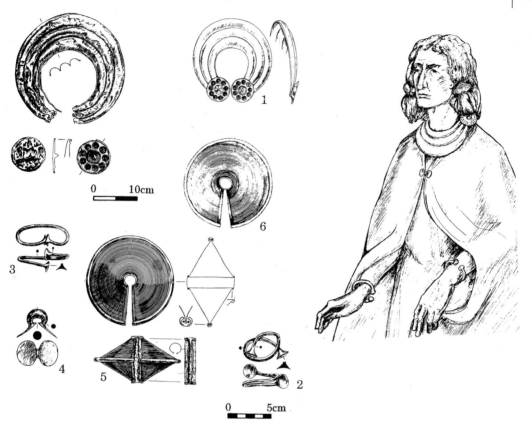

Fig. 107. Left. Hoard of gold ornaments from Gorteenreagh, Co. Clare: 1. Gorget with reconstruction on right. 2-3. Bracelets. 4. Sleeve fastener. 5-6. Lock rings. Right. Suggested manner of use of the Gorteenreagh gold ornaments – the gender of the wearer is suitably ambiguous.

DRESS FASTENERS AND LOCK RINGS

The term dress fastener has been used to describe a series of puzzling penannular gold objects with large terminals of various sorts which are assumed, on no certain evidence, to have served as garment fasteners. Small examples, like that from the Gorteenreagh hoard (depicted as a cloak fastener: Fig. 107) have been called sleeve fasteners or cuff fasteners and have been studied by Eogan who does allude to the fact that the discovery of just one in such a hoard does not help in determining function. These are small hoop-shaped objects some of which may be hollow, others cast. They invariably have elegantly grooved bows and a narrow zone of engraved lattice ornament between the bow and the terminals which are expanded and often disc-shaped. The terminals may be cast in one piece with the bow, and then expanded by hammering, or they may be soldered on; decoration on the terminals is rare occurring on only a few examples. A number of examples without terminals exist and these have been called 'striated rings'.

Various writers have accepted that sleeve fasteners could indeed have served as a garment fastener, in cuff-link style, the discs being slipped through eyelets in the clothing (Fig. 109, 4) but the space between the terminals of some is so narrow that only the thinnest clothing could pass through it. Over 80 of them are known and the type seems to be an Irish fashion (Fig. 111), being a smaller version of the large dress fastener which has a wider distribution.

The larger penannular dress fasteners, or cup-ended ornaments as they have also been called, are no less puzzling. A broad hoop of gold, which may be either solid or hollow, ends in prominent concave or cup-shaped terminals (which lie almost horizontally more or less on the same plane – as in Fig. 109, 2-3). Decoration occurs on a small number. A general relationship between the simpler examples and penannular bracelets with expanded terminals has long been recognized and both are represented in a small hoard of objects found at a depth of over 3m in a bog at Lattoon, north-east of

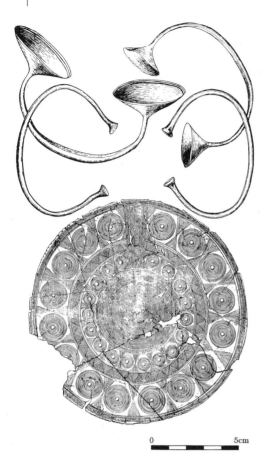

Fig. 108. Armstrong's (1933) illustration of a gold hoard of two dress fasteners, two bracelets and a disc from Lattoon, Co. Cavan.

Ballyjamesduff, Co. Cavan (Fig. 108). The dress fasteners vary in size and Mary Cahill has studied 20 extraordinary examples which are distinguished by their large size and weight (from 311g to 1353g). Weights obviously depend on whether bows are hollow or solid and three specimens of solid gold, all weighing over 1000g, could never have been worn. Presumably of symbolic significance, at the very least they must have represented considerable wealth: the heaviest known is an example found near Dunboyne, Co. Meath, which weighed about 1353g (over 43 ounces) and contained enough gold to make between 20 and 40 lunulae. A well known example from Clones, Co. Monaghan, which is unusual in that it also has very fine decoration which includes dot and concentric circle motifs, weighs 1031.5g.

Some 80 gold examples of dress fasteners of all sizes (and two bronze specimens) have been recorded from Ireland and 18 gold and one bronze from Britain (Fig. 111). It is generally claimed that dress fasteners are an adaptation of a Nordic fashion, being inspired by north European bronze fibulae (formed of separate pin and bow) which have convex disc-shaped terminals (Fig. 109, 1) but it has also been argued that the large gold dress fasteners and the bronze fibulae are each the exaggerated culmination of two independently evolving and unrelated ornament fashions.

As the name and the Gorteenreagh reconstruction suggest (Fig. 107) gold lock rings are believed to have been hair ornaments. They have been studied by Eogan who does note that it has not been established that they were used in this fashion. The only merit of the name lock ring is that it is a little more convenient than the descriptive 'penannular hollow ornaments of triangular section' used by other writers who also thought they could be ear rings.[14] Whatever their purpose, they are complicated objects. Two penannular conical plates are held together by a narrow C-shaped binding strip to form a large biconical bead-like piece, a penannular tube, usually of sheet gold, fits in the centre, but triangular side

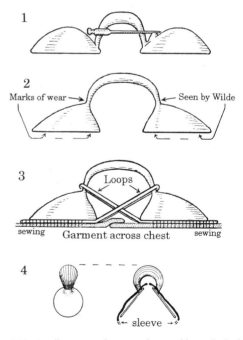

Fig. 109. An illustration depicting the possible method of attachment of a gold dress fastener (2 and 3) and the prototypical Nordic bronze fibula (1). The method of attachment of a sleeve fastener (4) is also shown.

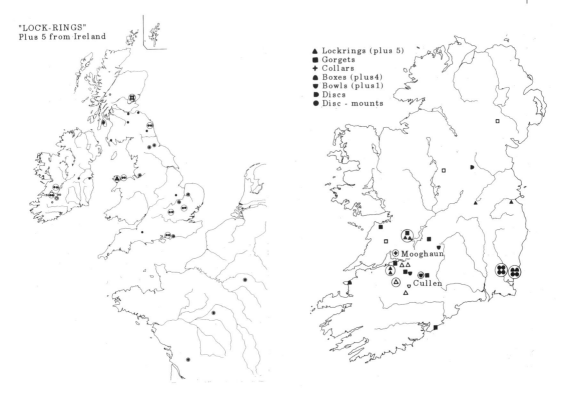

Fig. 110. Left. Distribution of lock rings in Ireland, Britain and France. Right. Distribution of gorgets and other gold work.

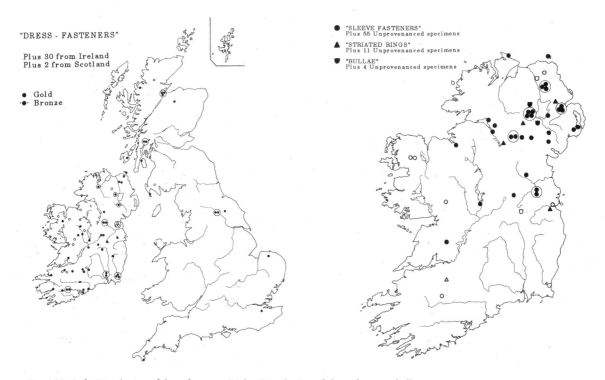

Fig. 111. Left. Distribution of dress fasteners. Right. Distribution of sleeve fasteners, bullae, etc.

plates (in the gap or slot) rarely survive and may not always have been used. In a small number of cases, including the Gorteenreagh specimens, repoussé bosses occur in the central tube and it is suggested that these might have helped to hold locks of hair in place. The method of manufacture of the conical plates is their most remarkable feature: in one Irish case these are of sheet gold decorated with light repoussé ribbing but in most instances each plate has been constructed of concentric rings of gold wires joined together with an average of about three to the millimetre. This work of extraordinary delicacy is unparalleled and it is a good illustration of specialized craftsmanship in which patronage and wealth are expressed in the creation of exclusive and exceptional objects.

These lock rings were clearly an Irish-British fashion and the region of the lower Shannon may have been the main centre of production in Ireland (Fig. 110) but they are also well represented in north Wales, northern England, Scotland and south-eastern England with a few known in northern France. Outside of Ireland conical plates of sheet gold, plain or with engraved ornament, are commoner in Britain and sheet gold covered bronze is found in France. The type does seem to be an insular innovation, prototypes elsewhere are unknown. Eogan would see them as an Irish development but he suggests the possibility of some Mediterranean inspiration – from a part of the world where hair ornaments such as small penannular round-sectioned hair rings are found.

HAIR RINGS, RING MONEY AND BULLAE

Dress fasteners and lock rings are not the only puzzling artefacts in the repertoire of the Dowris Phase goldsmiths. Even more enigmatic are the unfortunately named ring money and bullae. For many years the name ring money has been given to series of small thick penannular gold or gilded rings because it was thought that a series of standard weights could be identified among them. However, standard weights have yet to be satisfactorily demonstrated. These rings have also been compared to Egyptian hair rings, and there is a striking resemblance, but connections are difficult if not impossible to prove. For want of a better name, the term hair ring is now employed. These little hair rings are of circular cross section, about 2.5cm in diameter, and may be of solid gold or may be composite pieces with cores of copper, tin or lead covered with gold (Fig. 112). It has been claimed that some striped examples have been inlaid with silver or electrum. Over 170 have been recorded, the great majority, over 125, from Ireland but some also from Britain, France, Belgium and the Netherlands. This remarkably widespread distribution may indicate, notwithstanding their small size, that these were highly prized and sought-after objects. One was found in a pit near the centre of a circular house at Rathgall, Co. Wicklow: it and a small token deposit of burnt human bone had been placed in a layer of carbonized organic material and may have been a foundation deposit.

A small group of larger decorated penannular rings of oval section are clearly related and consist of a lead core (or in one or two cases cores of tin or clay) encased in thin sheet gold decorated with geometric motifs including filled triangles and lattice patterns (Fig. 112). Examples of these gold or gilded penannular rings have been found in hoards at Tooradoo, near Athea, Co. Limerick, which also contained bronze rings and amber beads and at Rathtinaun, Lough Gara, Co. Sligo, with bronze rings, amber beads, boars' tusks and other items.[15] These large penannular rings have also been called crescent-shaped bullae and their decoration and lead cores may indeed suggest some relationship with bullae of pendant form.

Named after a type of Roman pendant or amulet, bullae are heart-shaped objects consisting of a lead core covered with decorated thin sheet gold with a transverse perforation for suspension. Decoration may include filled triangles and concentric circles. A U-shaped motif on one face of a find from the Bog of Allen, Co. Kildare (Fig. 113) has been variously described as phallic and anthropomorphic. Five examples are recorded, all from Ireland. One found on the edge of the River Bann was said, after a 19th century chemical analysis, to have contained traces of blood.[16] Another may have been associated with a number of sleeve fasteners and gold discs near Arboe, Co. Tyrone (below). Needless to say the purpose of these mysterious objects is unknown but they are further testimony of the capabilities of those innovative goldsmiths and the suggestion that they and some of the other puzzling artefacts, like hair rings, might be magical charms has as much to recommend it as any other. Though obviously difficult to quantify, much of the goldwork under consideration probably had a symbolic role.

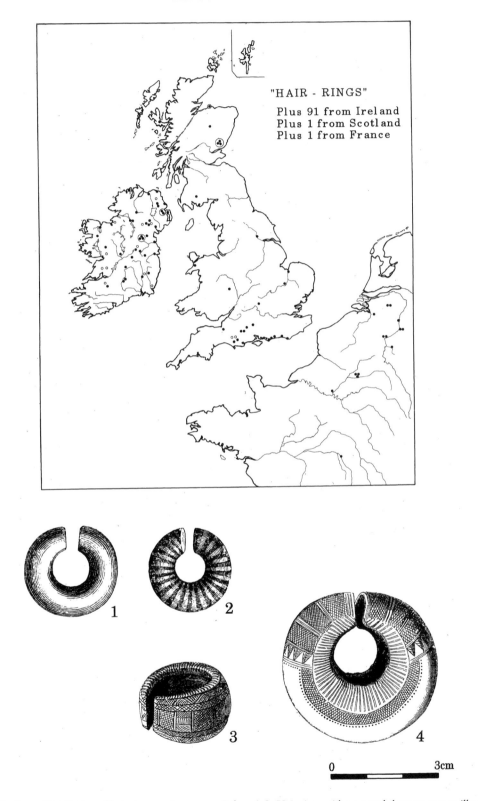

Fig. 112. Above. Distribution of hair rings or ring money. Below. 1-2. Hair rings with no recorded provenance as illustrated by Wilde in 1862. 3-4. Larger penannular rings or crescent-shaped bullae with no provenance.

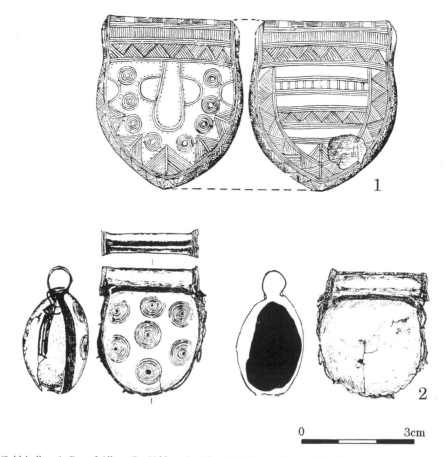

Fig. 113. Gold bullae. 1. Bog of Allen, Co. Kildare. 2. Arboe, Co. Tyrone, front and back.

BRACELETS

The great diversity of personal ornaments is one of the noteworthy features of the Dowris Phase. Most numerous of all is a series of gold penannular bracelets. Three principal types have been identified and over 300 examples recorded. The first comprises examples formed of a thin rounded or oval bar of gold with evenly expanded solid terminals like those found in the Lattoon hoard (Fig. 108); over 150 may have formed part of 'the great Clare find' at Mooghaun (below). A second type is similar but has hollowed terminals as in the Gorteenreagh hoard (Fig. 107, 3) and in another small hoard of personal ornaments found at Drissoge, near Athboy, Co. Meath (Fig. 114). The third type, also represented in the Drissoge hoard, is a larger bracelet with a thick body of rounded or oval cross-section, which may be solid or hollow, with hollow terminals set at a marked inclination to one another. Rare bronze examples of all three types have been found and a bronze version of the last-mentioned was found in a hoard at Mount

Rivers, near Fermoy, Co. Cork, which, along with other items, also contained two gold dress fasteners neatly illustrating the difference between these and the bracelets (Fig. 114). Hoards like this containing a mix of bronze and gold are fairly rare.

A number of each type has been found in Britain (Fig. 115), mainly in Scotland, and one large gold bracelet has been found in a pottery vessel at Gahlstorf, near Bremen, in northern Germany, and has been often cited as a further indication of Nordic contacts. Ribbon-like bracelets of British type are rare in Ireland where round or oval-sectioned solid or hollow forms are the norm. Of the various sorts of gold and bronze penannular bracelet found in Britain, only three have been recorded in Ireland, two with a flat ribbon-like body with expanded terminals, a third, is of similar form but has coiled ends. A small hoard of ribbon-shaped gold bracelets with simple terminals found in a bog at Vesnoy, in Strokestown demesne, Co. Roscommon, in 1849, may be related.[17]

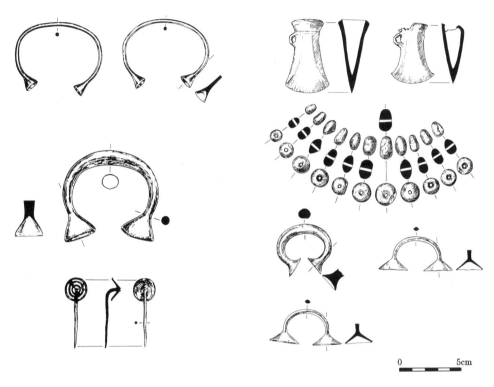

Fig. 114. Left. Hoard from Drissoge, Co. Meath, containing two gold penannular bracelets, a larger gold bracelet with a hollow body and inclined terminals and a small gold sunflower pin. Right. Hoard from Mount Rivers, Co. Cork, containing two bronze socketed axes, amber beads, a large bronze penannular bracelet and two gold dress fasteners.

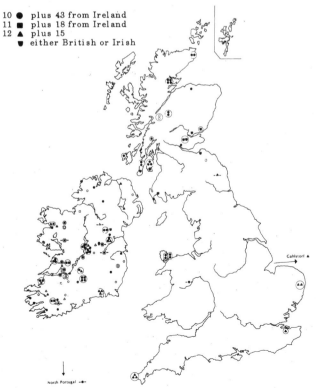

10 ● plus 43 from Ireland
11 ■ plus 18 from Ireland
12 ▲ plus 15
▼ either British or Irish

Fig. 115. Distribution of penannular bracelets of Irish type.

REGIONAL TRADITIONS

Another noteworthy feature of the Dowris Phase is the identification of what appear to be regional metalworking traditions. Local fashions probably existed at an earlier date and may yet be revealed by detailed analysis. But the study of distributional densities of widespread artefact types is a crude analytical method and naturally hampered by a range of circumstances not least patterns of retrieval and collection. For example, the concentrations of rapiers, swords and spearheads in the Irish midlands and in central Ulster have been compared to weapon concentrations in the Thames Valley and contrasted with areas of northern Britain and Wales where weapons are less common[18] but they cannot be said to form a well defined Irish weapon zone. Nonetheless, typological differences may offer useful evidence of broad regional patterning particularly if chronological questions can be resolved. Two broad regional concentrations of bronze horns have already been noted (Fig. 99) and in 1974 Eogan demonstrated that not only Class I horns but also buckets, cauldrons of Class A and sleeve fasteners had a primarily northern distribution while Class II horns, lock rings, gorgets and a series of gold bowl-shaped objects had a mainly south-western focus (Fig. 116). More tentative, perhaps, is his identification of a Midland province mainly reflected in the distribution of penannular bracelets (Fig. 115).[19]

Such localized patterns may well hint at distinct production centres or even reflect regional identities but, in the absence of contemporary settlements and workshops, it must be remembered that these distribution maps, since they are often a record of gold finds in bogs, may be essentially maps of varied depositional practices.

There is no doubt about the significant concentration of fine goldwork in the north Munster region and it may be argued that the lock rings and gorgets alone would suggest that the lands about the Shannon estuary were an important and wealthy gold working centre in the Dowris Phase. The presence of a number of exceptional hoards would seem to support this.

'The great Clare find', as it has been called, was made in 1854 by labourers working on the Limerick to Ennis railway in the townland of Mooghaun North, near Newmarket-on-Fergus, Co. Clare. Sadly, details about the discovery and the original contents are scanty. It may have been buried in a burnt mound near Mooghaun Lough. The hoard was dispersed, a considerable portion was melted down and its full extent will never be known. It is known that at least 146 gold objects were displayed at a meeting of the Royal Irish Academy a few months after the discovery but today the whereabouts of only 29 gold objects are known though casts of the rest of the items displayed survive. The original pieces include two

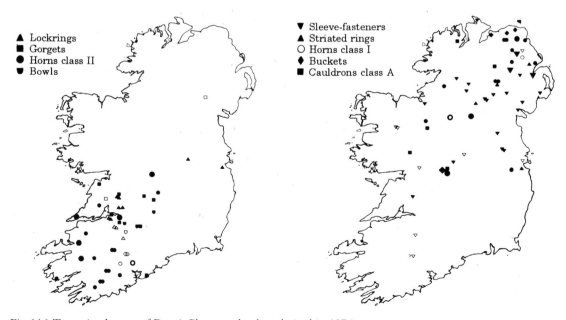

Fig. 116. Two regional groups of Dowris Phase metalwork as depicted in 1974.

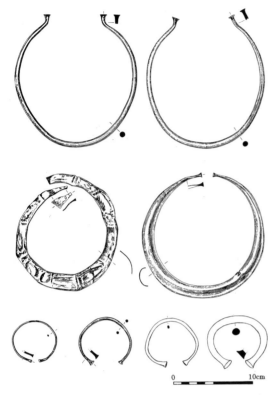

Fig. 117. A selection of gold neck rings, collars and penannular bracelets from 'the great Clare find' near Mooghaun.

penannular neck rings and six collars (Fig. 117), the neck rings of circular section with expanded terminals and the collars of C-shaped cross-section are of types otherwise unknown though a somewhat similar neck ring of bronze was found in a hoard from Ballykeaghra, south of Tuam, Co. Galway. Twenty-one penannular gold bracelets, casts of 137 more and casts of two gold ingots are also preserved. This is all that survives of what has been described as 'by far the largest associated find of gold objects found in Ireland and also in Bronze Age Europe outside the Aegean'. Yet another large collection of both gold and bronze objects came from 'the golden bog of Cullen', north-west of Tipperary town, in the 18th and 19th centuries and possibly included gorgets, a gold bowl, a gold disc, as well as a bronze cauldron, swords and spearheads. A gold bracelet and two lock rings may have been found near Askeaton, Co. Limerick.[20]

MISNAMED AND MYSTERIOUS: BOXES, REELS AND BOWLS

A number of other puzzling objects also demonstrate the exceptional nature of the gold working tradition of north Munster but also show that innovative gold work is found further afield in the south of the country (Fig. 118). Seven gold boxes and two gold bowl-shaped objects are known from Ireland. Except for two recent discoveries, they are all old finds and poorly documented. Of the seven small boxes of sheet gold, the circumstances of discovery of only three are recorded. One was found in boggy land at Ballinclemesig, near Ballyheige, Kerry. It is a small circular object, only 6.5cm in diameter and 1.8cm in maximum height; both top and base are separate pieces but attached by overlapping the edges of the sides and are decorated with repoussé boss and concentric circle ornament. Four other boxes, all fairly similar, are unprovenanced and appear to be two pairs; they may be small gold versions of larger organic boxes, the rope moulding on the lid of one of them has been compared to the stitching on larger bark containers from Denmark. A pair was found in a dump of topsoil at Ballinesker, near Curracloe, Co. Wexford, along with two gold 'reels', two dress fasteners and a bracelet. It seems these boxes were meant to be sealed and removal of any one of the closing discs would damage them. The Ballinesker pair each contained two small beads of solid gold. Their purpose is a mystery and the term 'box' seems a less than adequate term.[21]

The gold reels also defy explanation at present. These objects have the appearance of two discs joined together by a very short cylinder but each face consists of two discs (joined in the same way as gorget terminals) and the faces are joined to each other by short cylindrical collars of a lesser diameter. The Ballinesker discovery led to the recognition of other examples: an unprovenanced piece of sheet gold which had been simply called a 'hat-shaped gold plate' (Fig. 118, 1), may be one of four discs found near Enniscorthy, Co. Wexford, in the 18th century (two of which do survive), and an example found near Cashel, Co. Tipperary, which also contained a solid gold bead. Both the decoration and method of manufacture of these curious reel-shaped pieces indicate some relationship to gorgets.[22]

A series of bowl-shaped objects may be gold vessels but only one of these supposed bowls survives and it is a shallow, circular, dish-shaped fragment of sheet gold now 11.3cm in diameter and obviously once somewhat larger. Repoussé decoration consists of a small central boss surrounded by concentric circles (Fig. 118, 3). It bears some similarity to a gold object found in the 17th century in a bog near Devilsbit Mountain, north-west of Templemore, Co.

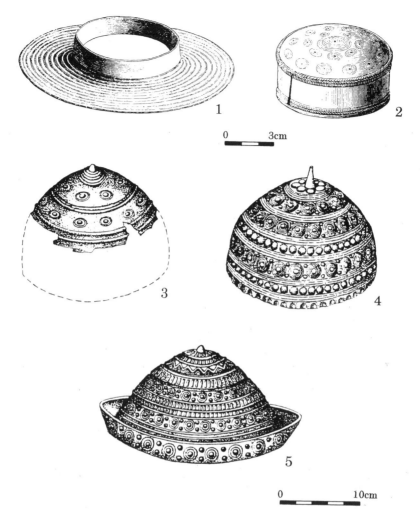

Fig. 118. Gold objects. 1. A 'hat-shaped gold plate' now recognized as one half of an enigmatic gold reel possibly found near Enniscorthy, Co. Wexford. 2. Unprovenanced gold box (as illustrated by Wilde). 3. Unprovenanced sheet gold bowl-shaped object from Ireland. 4. Sheet gold hat or crown from Rianxo, Corunna, Spain. 5. Gold hat or crown from near Devilsbit Mountain, Co. Tipperary.

Tipperary, and depicted in an 18th century engraving (Fig. 118, 5). The four others are known only from vague references to 'crowns' in the literature and include 'a golden crown weighing 6 ounces' found in that golden bog at Cullen. It has been suggested that the two Irish bowls could have been head gear – sheet gold objects which may have been crowns or hats of both skull-cap and conical shape are known elsewhere in Europe.[23]

PINS

A wide range of other ornaments and implements were produced by the bronze smiths of the time. Chief among the bronze personal ornaments are different pin types and for the first time the bronze pin becomes a relatively common feature of the Irish archaeological record. Whether this is just another ornamental expression of a widespread predilection for display or some indication of a change in dress fashion is not known. In short, since none have been found with unburnt burials for example, questions such as how these pins may have been worn and whether a long established practice of using buttons or toggles, if such existed, became unfashionable cannot be answered.

The majority of pins are divided into two major classes: disc-headed and cup-headed pins. The disc-headed variety includes both pins with straight stems and a horizontal circular head and those pins with a bent stem and circular heads placed at right

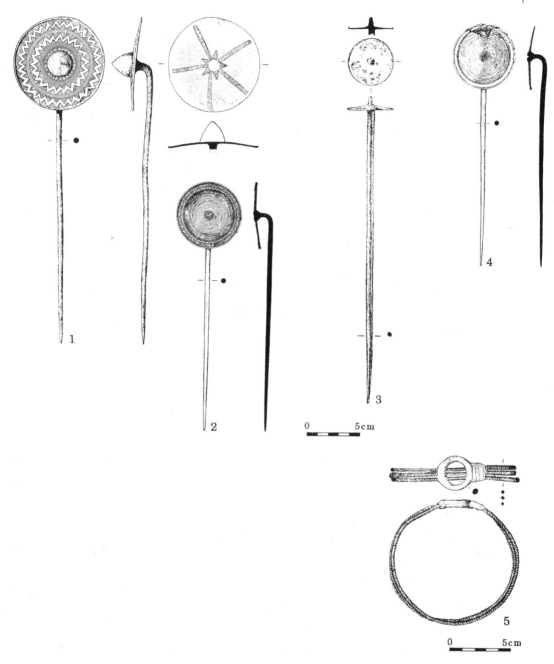

Fig. 119. Bronze pins and a bracelet from a hoard found in a sandpit at Ballytegan, Co. Laois, which also contained two bronze socketed axeheads and numerous bronze rings of various sorts. 1. Sunflower pin. 2 and 4. Sunflower pins with gold foil decoration. 3. Disc-headed pin with horizontal head. 5. Triple bracelet.

angles to the length of the stem – the so-called sunflower pins. Both are represented in a hoard from Ballytegan, near Portlaoise, Co. Laois (Fig. 119). Disc-headed pins with straight stems have discs with a central conical boss which are otherwise plain or simply decorated with concentric circles, other motifs being rare. Pins of

this general type are scarce in Britain but well known in northern Europe particularly in Denmark and northern Germany and Irish examples with small heads, small hemispherical central bosses and concentric circle ornament are, in Eogan's opinion, closest to the Nordic forms and some may even be imports.

Sunflower pins are generally more elaborate objects: the head, at right angles to the stem, provides a field for more complex ornament which in addition to a central boss and concentric circles may include filled triangles, lattice and chevron patterns. Simply decorated examples occur and one small plain pin, lacking even a boss on its disc, from Knocknalappa, Co. Clare, is a very down-market piece. However, a unique gold sunflower pin with an abnormal conical head from Drissoge, Co. Meath (Fig. 114) is even smaller. In contrast, two of the three Ballytegan examples are particularly ornate, the patterns on the large heads (one with a prominent conical boss) may have been engraved in the bronze rather than cast and this was then reproduced on a thin covering of gold foil fitted to the head and pressed into the underlying decoration. Other gold foil decoration of this sort has been noted in a hoard from Arboe, Co. Tyrone.

Again pins with small hemispherical bosses and concentric circle ornament are held to be earlier than those with large conical bosses and these have been called primary and secondary series pins respectively. Sunflower pins are found in Scotland where they differ in having a recurved neck. They also occur in Denmark and northern Germany and those of the primary series are deemed to be closest to the supposed Nordic prototype.[24]

The second major class of pin is the cup-headed variety which is not particularly common and mainly recorded from the northern half of the country. These are invariably undecorated though one from Arboe, Co. Tyrone, has a small conical boss in the centre of the cup (Fig. 120). This is an interesting minor detail, a few pins with somewhat cup-shaped heads are known from Britain and one from a hoard at the Point of Sleat on the Isle of Skye has a similar pointed cup, a detail which has

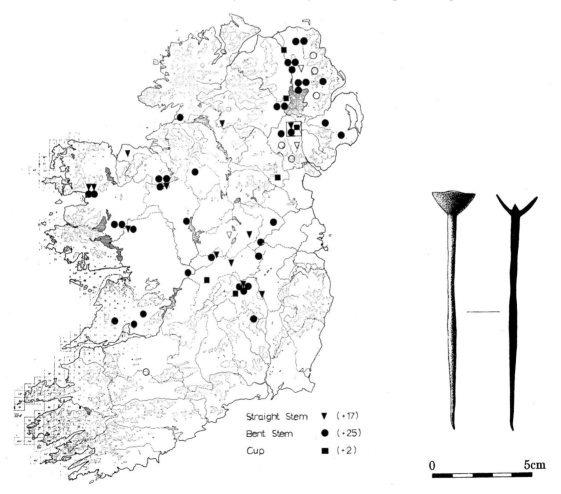

Straight Stem ▼ (+17)
Bent Stem ● (+25)
Cup ■ (+2)

0   5cm

Fig. 120. Distribution of disc- and cup-headed pins and (right) a cup-headed pin from Arboe, Co. Tyrone.

been noted on the Sintra gold collar from Portugal and on other Iberian ornaments. Cup-shaped decoration, derived from Iberian floral-cup ornament and has been claimed to be just one indication of venturers, perhaps even goldsmiths and their gold, along the Atlantic sea-ways.[25]

THE ATLANTIC SEA-WAYS

The words of R. A. S. Macalister, who once declared that Britain was essentially an island of the North Sea and Ireland an island of the Atlantic Ocean, are sometimes quoted when the thorny question of the role of the Atlantic sea-ways in Irish prehistory is discussed. There has been a long-held belief that this island on the Atlantic border of Europe had important contacts by coastal sea-routes with France, Spain and the western Mediterranean on the one hand, and with Scotland and Scandinavia on the other. This belief has found some support in the archaeological evidence which is sporadically intriguing, if not exotic. It has also found occasional support in quainter and less reliable sources such as early origin legends: Goidelic Celts, for instance, were said to have come from Scythia via Spain, being preceded by various other invaders including the Fir Bolg from Greece. A belief in direct and influential contacts with France and Iberia must have had attractions too for some nationalist minds in the 19th and 20th centuries. For them a non-British source for the main cultural influences to impinge on these shores had obvious attractions.

Egyptians, Phoenicians, megalithic tomb builders and missionaries, prospectors, early metal workers, and stone fort builders (with or without *chevaux-de-frise*) have all been credited with use of the Atlantic sea-ways at one time or another. History, of course, from time to time seemed to lend credence to some of these claims. In a 1951 discussion of the origins of some megalithic tombs, for example, a sea-borne movement of peoples from western France to the Mayo-Sligo coast on the one hand and to the Cork-Kerry region on the other was postulated with the comment 'historic landings from France and Iberia in both these areas are well known'. The archaeological evidence continues to inspire debate. Parallels have been drawn between Irish passage tombs and their Iberian counterparts, Iberian elements have been claimed in some early pottery types, careful consideration has been given to the possibility that early copper metallurgy may have been inspired by Atlantic contacts, some early metal objects and Irish and Galician rock art have been studied and some of the claims for contact with the Mediterranean world in the last two millennia BC have been reviewed.

Even though the argument that Class A Atlantic cauldrons had Mediterranean prototypes is no longer tenable other evidence continues to raise the question of Atlantic contacts. The decorated gold neck ring from Downpatrick, Co. Down, may be related to Iberian decorated neck rings of Berzocana type and may indicate connections with western France before 1000 BC. Later contacts may be demonstrated by a range of interesting parallels many of which demand careful assessment and include such disparate stylistic details as V-shaped notches on shields and Hawkes' floral-cup ornament. A bronze penannular bracelet with evenly expanded hollow terminals from an unrecorded location in northern Portugal is considered an Irish type by Eogan who also notes the resemblances between golden bowl-shaped objects in Ireland and northern Iberia. He suggests connections with north Munster, the gold working traditions in this region possibly containing elements of both north European and southern fashion. Terence Powell provided a measured assessment of the conflicting stylistic parallels offered by the gold gorgets of the Shannon area where the decorated circular terminals with their northern inspired ornament find no parallels on bronze neck ornaments in northern Europe. He tentatively suggested that in shape and position they could be more splendid versions of the smaller floral-cups of Iberia.[26]

The importance of the Atlantic sea-ways as a means of long-distance communication in Irish prehistory may have been exaggerated in the past but there is no denying the probability of contacts along shorter stretches of the Atlantic coasts in prehistoric times. Short coastal journeys between communities must have been common and could well have formed an interconnecting chain of contacts extending considerable distances along the Atlantic coasts of Europe. This is neatly illustrated by an Irish-British spearhead with lunate openings in the blade found in the great Huelva hoard in south-western Spain along with swords, spears, ferrules and other material. This example is remarkably similar to one found near Ballinasloe, Co. Galway (Fig. 102, 1)[27] and is a reminder that Ireland, southern Britain, western France and south-western Spain could have been linked together by a network of coastal connexions. Such a process of exchange from coastal community to community was possibly the means by which objects and ideas were transmitted along the Atlantic facade and this may also have been the way a bewildered North African ape found its way to Navan, Co. Armagh, some centuries later.

AMBER AND THE NORDIC QUESTION

The wealth of gold in the Bishopsland and Dowris Phases has tended to eclipse the less spectacular amber bead but amber seems to have been particularly popular in Ireland in the latter phase especially. Over 30 finds have been recorded and beads of spherical, oval and disc shapes are common. A series of hoards which contained numbers of amber beads have already been mentioned: Mount Rivers, Co. Cork (Fig. 114: 11 beads), Tooradoo, Co. Limerick (105 beads) and Rathtinaun, Co. Sligo (31 beads). In addition to these, 109 beads were found with a cup-headed pin and a number of bronze rings near Portlaoise, Co. Laois, and several finds totalling over 200 amber beads (one at least with a bronze spearhead) were made in Ballycurrin Demesne, on the shores of Lough Corrib, north-west of Headford, Co. Galway. A gold dress fastener, a bronze penannular bracelet and two bronze rings were found with a necklace of 125 beads near a large rock at Meenwaun, near Banagher, Co. Offaly. Even larger collections of beads have been found: at Derrybrien, east of Gort, Co. Galway, over 500 beads and a small fragment of sheet gold were found scattered over an area about a metre square at the bottom of an upland bog; the beads vary from 3cm to 6mm in diameter and the presence of a number of doubly-perforated spacer beads suggest a complex multi-strand graduated necklace. Another large necklace of over 400 beads was found in a bog at Kurin, just south of Garvagh, Co. Derry. Smaller finds occur, of course, such as the ten beads from Ballylin, near Ferbane, Co. Offaly.

The relatively large quantity of Dowris Phase amber recovered in Ireland is interesting because this material seems to have been less common in Britain at this time. The amber found in British and Irish contexts is 'Baltic amber', that is amber derived from natural deposits extending from eastern Scotland and England to Holland, Scandinavia, northern Germany and the eastern Baltic. This general north European source has been confirmed by infra-red

spectroscopy but more precise origins cannot be identified. It is impossible to distinguish between a British and a Scandinavian origin for example but since it is probable that fairly small amounts of amber were available in eastern Britain, importation form the Continent was more likely than not. To date the evidence would appear to discount claims that Irish sources may have been used.

The exchange of Baltic amber extended over wide areas of Europe in the second millennium BC in particular and it was clearly a highly prized material occurring in rich graves in the south of England, in central Germany and Poland and in Mycenean Greece. Aside from any possible magical properties, its value in these locations may have been amplified by its far distant source, a cosmic charge enhanced by geographical distance. For these reasons it may have been an item strictly controlled by elite societies. Its association with gold finery in several Irish hoards and its occasional votive deposition as a single item indicate it had a special significance in the Dowris Phase but why it should seem to be less important in Britain is not easy to explain.[28] Because it was readily available, and control was therefore difficult, amber was less of a status symbol in the Baltic region than elsewhere, it was valuable, however, because it could be exchanged for coveted metal. A similar situation may have obtained in eastern Britain at this time and those penannular bracelets may have been one sought-after Irish item exchanged for exotic amber.

A whole series of objects and decorative motifs, and of course amber itself, have long prompted the widespread belief that there were pronounced and sometimes direct contacts with northern Europe. A few writers have alluded to the possibility of contact in early prehistoric times and some comparisons between megalithic tombs in Ireland and Scandinavia and some later ceramic parallels have been claimed and questioned. It is not until the last millennium BC that significant contacts are thought to have developed: as Eogan put it: 'during the initial stages of the Dowris Phase, Ireland came into direct contact with the Nordic world, particularly Denmark and the north German plain'.

Some of the evidence has already been mentioned and amber, of course, may have been one of the links in a chain of Nordic contacts. A range of decorative features such as U-shaped notches on shields, concentric circle ornament and conical bosses or rivets have been traced to

Scandinavia. The well-known gold disc from Lattoon, Co. Cavan (Fig. 108) with its central boss surrounded by concentric circle decoration has been compared by to the famous Trundholm gold disc from Denmark mounted on a vertical bronze disc on a six-wheeled model bronze wagon and generally accepted as a solar symbol. An unprovenanced small bronze disc from Ireland, with ornament similar to Lattoon, has prompted a similar comparison. Concentric circle ornament also occurs on gorget terminals whose collar shape has also been ascribed to Nordic prototypes. Dress fasteners too are seen to have been inspired by northern fibulae and the gold-plated sunflower pins in the Ballytegan hoard have been considered imports from northern Europe – though this has been disputed. Two small bronze bar toggles, one from Rathgall, Co. Wicklow, the other from Navan, Co. Armagh, are thought to be imports also.

Others have considered northern influence to be superficial, if not quite exaggerated and very debatable. It is claimed that the parallels so often cited are generalized and unconvincing, and it is worth noting that there are chronological discrepancies as well. The absence in Ireland of the spiral ornament which is such a striking feature of some Scandinavian metalwork (including the Trundholm disc) is one noteworthy difference. It has been argued that northern Europe had no great impact on British-Irish material culture, particularly goldwork, and what contacts there may have been were casual and over a long period of time. It may be that we are witnessing parallel analogous developments.[29]

It is not easy to resolve the conflicting opinions on the Nordic question but two important factors are worth considering. On present evidence much of the amber in Ireland may be of Baltic origin. It could conceivably have arrived in this island via a network of coastal traders and communities around the coast of Scotland and the presence of a Scandinavian type socketed axehead in both south-western Scotland and in Co. Antrim is a reminder that this is a possibility.[30] Even though the abundant evidence in bronze and gold for Irish-British contacts across the Irish Sea and across the North Channel makes a route across northern Britain seem more plausible, it should not be presumed that prehistoric trade or exchange would take the shortest route and the discovery of a number of amber beads at a strategically located settlement at Runnymede on the Thames, Berkshire, and at a number of other locations in southern England and north Wales is a reminder that amber might have come via southern England too. Clearly those involved in Britain seem to have had little use for amber themselves, but if amber travelled so could other objects and stylistic inspiration. The transmission of stylistic elements is an elusive phenomenon but it was probably a constant fact of prehistoric communication. From time to time it may have become an especially important fact, particularly when stylistic features, with a symbolic significance we may never recapture, could serve the eclectic needs of craftsmen and their patrons. It is surely significant that the evidence for supposed long-distance contacts, whether with Iberia or northern Europe, survives in what must be the material culture of a wealthy elite ever anxious to express their exclusive status in novel ways.

BRONZE TOOLS AND IMPLEMENTS

A series of bronze tools and implements had more mundane roles in society though their occasional presence in hoards suggests they may sometimes have been symbols of social position and have had a ceremonial use. Double-edged knives including socketed and tanged examples, socketed sickles, gouges, punches or hammers, chisels (both socketed and tanged), razors and tweezers, have been recorded. The commonest implement is the socketed axe.

A small number of hoards containing two or three bronze items such as socketed axes, gouges, and knives, in varying combinations, and sometimes a few other bronzes, suggest that some groups of objects had some special significance, perhaps as a mark of caste or trade. Examples include a hoard from Enagh East, near Mooghaun, Co. Clare, comprising three axes, a gouge, a knife and several rings; a small hoard found in a bog at Crossna, near Boyle, Co. Roscommon, containing three axeheads, a knife and a gouge; and another bog-find at Ballinderry, Co. Westmeath, containing an axehead, a tanged and a socketed chisel, two gouges, a knife and three rings (Fig. 121). A hoard containing a socketed axe, a socketed gouge, a razor and a pin found in a bog at Cromaghs, near Armoy, Co. Antrim, had apparently been wrapped in a textile and the razor was contained in a leather pouch. The textile remains are unique in the Dowris Phase and comprise a large piece of plain woven woollen

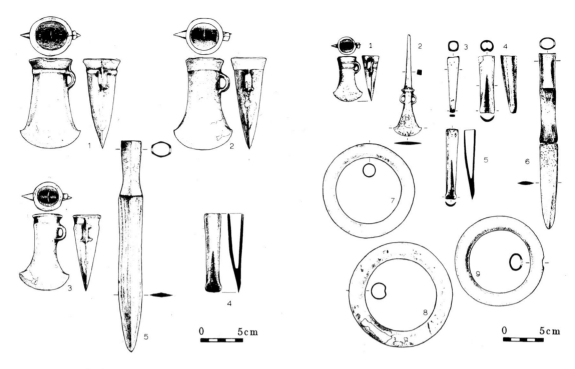

Fig. 121. Hoards of tools (including socketed gouges and a tanged and looped chisel or leather knife) and other bronzes from Crossna, near Boyle, Co. Roscommon, and Ballinderry, Co. Westmeath.

fabric, possibly a bag, and several pieces of a woven horsehair belt. Two socketed axeheads, a gold bracelet and a gold dress-fastener were found under the corner of a large stone at Kilbride, near Newport, Co. Mayo, and both bronze and gold may have been equally prized.[31]

While some axes and knives may have been put to offensive use on occasion, and a socketed knife was reportedly found driven into a human skull discovered near Drumman More Lake, north-east of Armagh, it is probably safe to assume that most of them, like gouges and chisels, were used for more conventional tasks. Gouges were wood-working implements and are widely distributed. Socketed chisels were undoubtedly wood-working tools as well. Some tanged examples with curved blades (as from Ballinderry) may have been for leather-working, they too are found in Britain and France. A number of different types of knives, both socketed and tanged, have been identified (Fig. 122): a Thorndon type has a straight base to the socket as on the example from the Ballinderry hoard; a Kells type has a socket narrowing to pronounced shoulders and a Dungiven type has an indentation at the base of the socket, a simple classification which does not take varied blade

cross-sections into account. A few curious knives with curved blades may have had some specialized purpose. These socketed knives are widely distributed in Ireland and Britain with a number in western France. They, like the tanged type, appear to be an Irish-British form. The great majority of small tanged razors in Ireland belong to a Type Dowris, named after an example in the well known hoard (Fig. 92, 8). Bronze anvils are rare but include the example in the Bishopsland hoard (Fig. 72, 11). Their small size suggests they were used for delicate work and one British find had traces of gold embedded in its surface and was evidently used by a goldsmith.[32]

Irish bronze sickles are a varied lot and have a relatively long history. Over 30 examples of what presumably was an important agricultural implement are recorded. Some early stone mould fragments for casting sickles are known from Killymaddy, Co. Antrim, and the Bishopsland hoard contained a bronze sickle with a knobbed haft. This primitive form may have been replaced by a ring- or cylinder-socketed type around 1200 BC in which the blade is more or less at right angles to the socket (Fig. 122, 1). A tanged form (with a perforation in the tang) found with a leaf-shaped

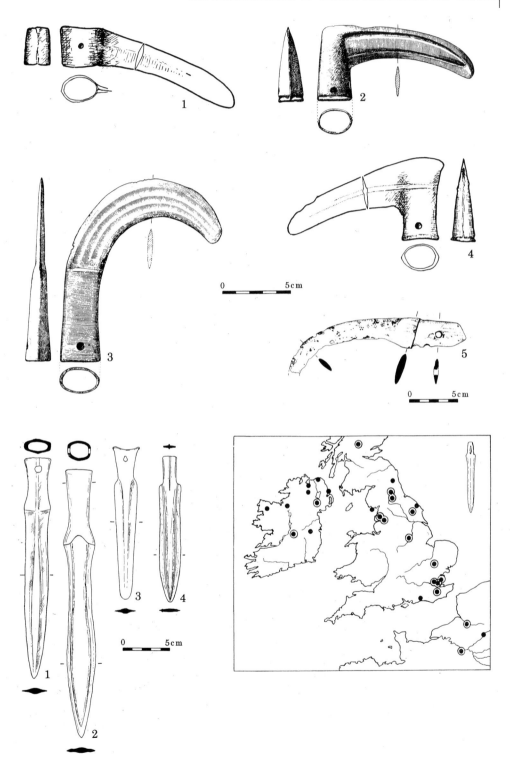

Fig. 122. Above. Bronze sickles. 1. Ring-socketed sickle from Lawrencetown, Co. Meath. 2. Socketed example with blade at right angles from Ballygawley, Co. Tyrone. 3. Sickle with blade rising vertically from the socket from Athlone, Co. Westmeath. 4. Heeled example: unprovenanced. 5. Sickle with perforated tang from Ballygowan, Co. Kilkenny. Below. Socketed bronze knives: 1. Ireland. 2. Kilmore, Co. Galway. 3. Co. Antrim. 4. Tanged knife from the Dowris hoard with the distribution of this type.

spearhead and some bronze rings in a hoard from Ballygowan, Co. Kilkenny (Fig. 122, 5) may be related to British and Continental examples.

Socketed sickles are an insular fashion and two basic forms have been recognized in Britain and Ireland, in one the blade springs almost vertically from the socket, in the other the blade is set at right angles as already mentioned. A small number of the latter in which the outer edge of the implement continues across the top of the socket to produce a projecting heel is particularly interesting because this type was copied in iron in a hoard from Llyn Fawr, Glamorgan, and may represent the final form of the bronze sickle. While ceremonial usage for some small slender examples cannot be excluded, experimentation has shown that these implements could cut cereals with reasonable success but were noticeably less effective than iron examples.[33]

SOCKETED AXES

Many hundreds of socketed axeheads have been found and there is considerable variety in form and great variety in size. Classification is often difficult and only a summary of the principal types is presented here.

Early examples include the narrow rectangular Taunton Type in the Bishopsland hoard and the sturdier Rossconor Type, named after a Co. Down find (Fig. 123, 1) which is typologically similar. The latter has a slender rectangular body with parallel sides and a slightly expanded cutting edge; a flat collar is a distinguishing feature with a stout loop below. Dating is problematic because they do not occur in hoards in Ireland but examples from the Wallington hoard in Northumberland suggest a 10th century BC date.

The Irish socketed axe series is dominated by small and large 'bag-shaped' socketed axeheads with an oval, sub-rectangular or circular mouth, a body of oval cross-section and a widely splayed cutting edge. Loops are positioned at varying distances below the mouth which may be plain (Fig. 123, 2) or surrounded by one or more mouldings or a collar. Examples occur in the Roscommon hoard (Fig. 81) and are well represented in the Dowris hoard (Fig. 92). Similar axeheads occur in northern England and Scotland. The axehead in the Blackhills hoard (Fig. 101) is a good example of a slender variant.

A socketed axehead with multiple mouldings of unequal width sometimes running through the loop (Fig. 123, 3) has been called the 'Dungiven type' and several examples identified in Scotland and in the north of Ireland; the axe in the Ballinderry hoard (Fig. 121) is of this general form. This pattern of mouldings is found on axes in northern Germany and Holland and an imported example occurs in a hoard from Minnis Bay, Kent.[34]

A series of faceted socketed axeheads includes examples of octagonal and hexagonal cross-section (Fig. 123, 4-5) with an oval to circular mouth and collar or moulding below. This is a widespread type, found in Britain, notably in the south and east, and in western Continental Europe. A small number of socketed axeheads of rectangular section and decorated with vertical ribs (Fig. 123, 6) have been compared to a well-known axe, the Yorkshire Type, found as its name implies in Yorkshire, and in Lincolnshire, East Anglia and Scotland as well. Ribbed socketed axes of this sort are also found in the south of England. A few Irish ribbed axes with the loop springing from a prominent collar (Fig. 123, 7) may be versions of the South Welsh axe which is looped in this manner like Continental axes.

These axeheads have generally been considered to have been used for carpentry and tree felling and in many instances this seems a reasonable supposition. However, the great diversity in size and shape suggests a variety of functions and it is even conceivable that some were mounted not in the assumed symmetrical way in a bent knee-shaped wooden haft (Fig. 123) but in adze-like fashion for some specific purposes. It is also possible that socketed axeheads were mounted on a wooden piece which was in turn inserted into a mortised handle. A number of miniature examples, only a few centimetres in length, can hardly have been functional pieces. The most notorious non-functional socketed axeheads are the Breton *haches armoricaines* known in their thousands in that part of France. Of slender trapezoidal shape and rectangular cross-section, with a prominent biconical collar, these small axes are made of such thin metal with a high lead content it is doubtful they ever had any functional use, but they were manufactured in such quantity it is assumed they were made specifically for trade or barter. Their association with iron in Brittany indicates survival into the 7th century BC. Just over a dozen have been found in Ireland and the British distribution, not surprisingly, is concentrated in southern England.[35]

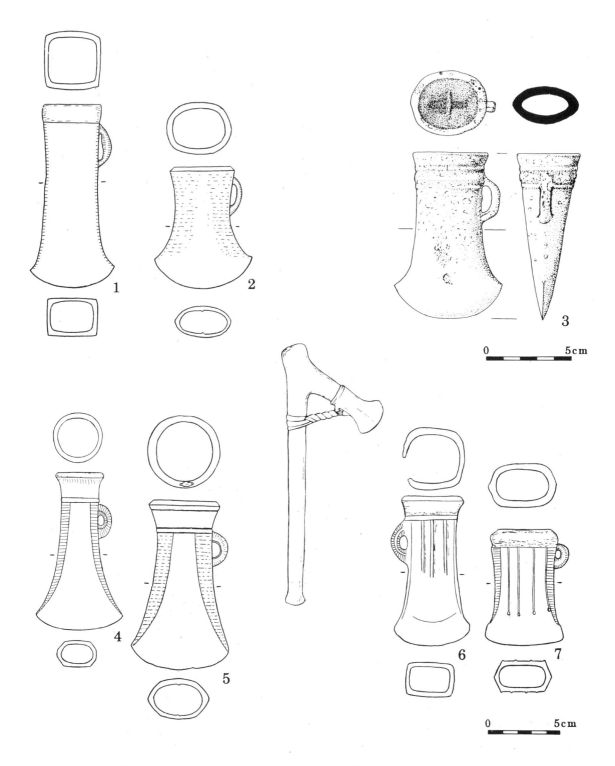

Fig. 123. Bronze socketed axeheads. 1. Rossconor Type: from Rossconor, Co. Down. 2. Bag-shaped type: Glenstal, Co. Limerick. 3. 'Dungiven' axehead: found near Armagh. 4-5. Faceted axeheads: Kish, Co. Wicklow and Mount Rivers, Co. Cork. 6-7. Ribbed axeheads: Crevilly, Co. Antrim and Keeloge, Co. Galway.

SETTLEMENT AND SOCIETY 900–500 BC

A small number of settlements are assigned to the Dowris Phase but shed only a little light on social and economic matters. The same variety of settlement sites found in the later 2nd millennium BC continues to be represented and ranges from large hilltop enclosures to small wetland sites. Some are imprecisely dated on the basis of artefactual evidence alone.

LOUGH ESKRAGH, CO. TYRONE

A wetland site at Lough Eskragh, near Dungannon, Co. Tyrone, was investigated in 1953 and in 1973. Three areas of timber posts were found projecting from the lake mud on its eastern shore (Site A) and two smaller areas of timber piles (B and C) were discovered further to the north. A linear concentration of timber posts (D) was noted near the western shore.

Site A consisted of two separate concentrations of timber piles, mostly birchwood with some ash and about 12cm in diameter (Fig. 124). One of these concentrations, to the north-west, was approximately circular with a diameter of 10.5m and constructed of brushwood, horizontal timbers and vertical piles to consolidate the brushwood. The discovery of two complete coarse pottery vessels, a cylindrical two-piece wooden vessel, a number of sandstone saddle querns, a polished stone axehead and part of a jet bracelet indicated occupation. This would seem to have been a small settlement accessed by boat and two flat-bottomed dug-out logboats of oak (one containing fragments of another tub-shaped wooden vessel) were found closeby.

The two tub-shaped wooden vessels, both of alder, from Lough Eskragh are further reminders that two-piece containers of wood were in common use. Another two-piece cylindrical vessel with at least three perforated lugs for suspension, also of alder, was found in a bog at Altanagh, near Carrickmore, Co. Tyrone. These are early examples of wooden vessels with the circular base held in a groove cut near the lower edge of the inner wall. The Altanagh vessel has been radiocarbon dated to between 838–408 BC.

An elongated 35m long concentration of almost 600 birch and ash piles, situated some 15m to the south-east of the settlement and between it and the lake-shore, produced the surprisingly large number of 16 sandstone saddle querns and one large granite example but no other domestic artefacts. This puzzling pile structure may have been used for some specialized activity but the suggestion that the querns could have been used to grind ore for metal production has yet to be proven.

Site B was located just over 108m to the north-east of Site A. This was an approximately circular structure, 9m in diameter, built of brushwood with horizontal timbers on top and vertical piles defining its perimeter. It seems to have been a lake-side platform with a clay floor surrounded by a wattle fence which seems to have eventually been destroyed by fire. This too was a site for specialized activity: fragments of clay moulds for casting bronze swords, a single-edged tool (perhaps a sickle) and a socketed axe were found as well as some baked clay fragments, possibly part of a pouring gate for a mould, and pieces of crucibles. Fragments of several saddle querns were also discovered and their presence here might support the ore grinding hypothesis. A flat-topped boulder showed traces of hammering and may have served as an anvil. No furnace was found but only a limited area was excavated. A small bronze finger ring was the only metal object recovered though a socketed axe found on the lake shore may have been made on the site.

Sites C and D were not investigated in any detail. An oak plank from the settlement at Site A was radiocarbon dated to 960–800 BC and confirmed by a tree ring date of about the 10th century BC. The elongated pile structure to the south was radiocarbon dated to 790–400 BC and a timber from Site B provided a radiocarbon date of 1520–1150 BC which may be anomalous being somewhat too early for the swords and axes manufactured there.[36]

BALLINDERRY, CO. OFFALY

Excavations in 1933 by Hugh Hencken of the Harvard Archaeological Expedition in Ireland revealed that a crannog of the early Historic period had been preceded many centuries before by a lake-side settlement of the Dowris Phase which survived as a thin black layer about 10cm in thickness. This was in turn sealed by a layer of mud deposited by rising lake waters which extended over an irregular area about 45m by 25m. The main late prehistoric features comprised two rectangular timber structures (Fig. 125). One on the north-west was a very large and approximately rectangular timber platform situated on slightly

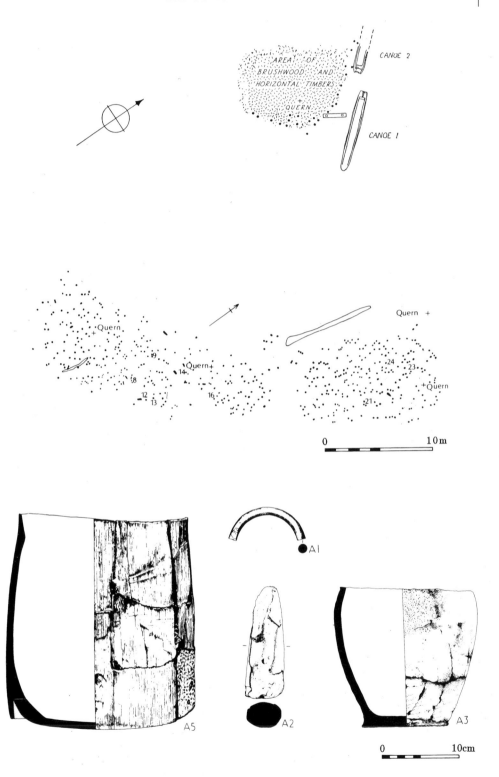

Fig. 124. Lough Eskragh, Co. Tyrone. Above. Plan of Site A showing on north-west a small settlement with dug-out canoes and to south-east a pile structure with tree trunk. Below. Cylindrical wooden vessel, part of a lignite bracelet, polished stone axehead and pottery vessel.

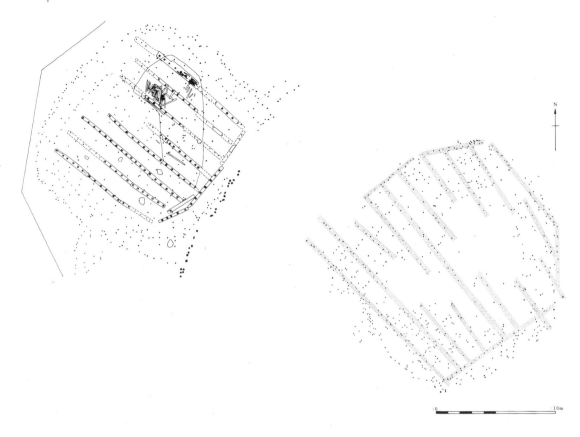

Fig. 125. Plan of Ballinderry, Co. Offaly: the rectilinear plank and post stucture is on the north-west and a series of posts (their lines accentuated with stippling) may represent the remains of a similar structure on the south-east.

higher ground. It measured 11.5m in length and consisted of eight rows flat oak planks of varying lengths and measuring 5cm-10cm in thickness and 20cm-60cm in width. These were embedded in the black layer and lay about 1.5m apart. Each plank had a row of squarish holes set at intervals of about 40cm and containing the remains of narrow posts 6cm-7cm across. There was no trace of any wickerwork but a thin layer of brushwood and a thin layer of gravel covered different parts of this structure which was partly surrounded by a number of lines of light wooden posts. Its purpose is far from clear but it was possibly meant to be a foundation platform for a house. According to Conor Newman, who has re-evaluated the excavation evidence, a series of timber posts to the east may represent a second rectilinear wooden structure of broadly similar dimensions.

Artefacts recovered included sherds of coarse pottery, a bronze socketed knife, two flesh-hooks, the stem of a sunflower pin, two awls and two rings. Two amber beads, fragments of lignite bracelets,

bone and stone spindle whorls, a bone toggle, a saddle quern, rubbing stones, part of a wooden bowl, other unidentifiable wooden pieces and some fragments of leather were also found. Animal bones from this level were predominantly those of cattle (around 80%) with a little pig, less sheep or goat and some horse. A few bones of wild animals such as red deer and some wild fowl were also recovered. While the finds suggest that this may have been a domestic settlement of some significance, ritual activity was attested by the presence of two human skulls and a portion of a third found at the base of the occupation layer. These were considered to be foundation deposits. All were of adults, two probably male and one probably female. One of the male skulls had part of the frontal bone deliberately removed after death and the other was just represented by a cut rectangular fragment. These and other finds of fragmentary skulls, including the cut portion from the King's Stables, suggest there may have been some special significance attached to the human skull in later prehistory.[37]

KNOCKNALAPPA, CO. CLARE

A lake-side settlement at Knocknalappa, on Rosroe Lake near Newmarket-on-Fergus, Co. Clare, was excavated in 1937. The site was a mound some 40m long and 15m-20m wide constructed of redeposited peat, brushwood and stone on top of lake marl. Timber piling occurred mainly on the lake foreshore side on the west where a double row of stout piles and some timber planks appeared to form a jetty (Fig. 126). Excavation produced a range of artefacts including a very small bronze sword, a gouge, a small sunflower pin, a bronze ring, a polishing or rubbing stone, a polished stone axehead, several amber beads, a lignite bracelet, a bone spindle whorl, bone toggles, two saddle querns and some coarse pottery. Animal remains recovered included bones of cattle, pig and a large dog, scanty remains of sheep and some red deer antler. No structures or hearths were found.

Polishing and rubbing stones and hammer stones were obviously in common use and the presence of stone implements like polished stone axeheads here and at Lough Eskragh, for example, suggests that the use of these stone tools alongside bronze implements was an occasional fact of later prehistory. The amber beads, the metal finds including the sunflower pin and the bronze sword, small though it is, suggest a settlement of some importance. The sword is not a unique settlement find: Island MacHugh, near Baronscourt, Co. Tyrone, has produced a larger example and radiocarbon dating of timber piles indicate some construction there just before, or early in, the Dowris Phase.[38]

Evidence for lake-side settlement of some importance at Moynagh Lough, Co. Meath, which probably dates to about the 9th century BC, included post-holes, hearths, and stone spreads (many showing signs of heat fracturing). Bronze pins, two leaf-shaped bronze spearheads, parts of lignite and shale bracelets, lignite and amber beads, sherds of coarse pottery and an antler toggle were found. A settlement on the shores of Lough Gara, west of Boyle, at Rathtinaun, Co. Sligo, was excavated between 1952 and 1955, and produced evidence of occupation at various times from the Dowris Phase to the early Historic period. Little survived of the earlier settlement but parts of wooden vessels, sherds of coarse pottery and bronze objects including tweezers, several rings, a razor and disc-headed pins were found. Some clay mould

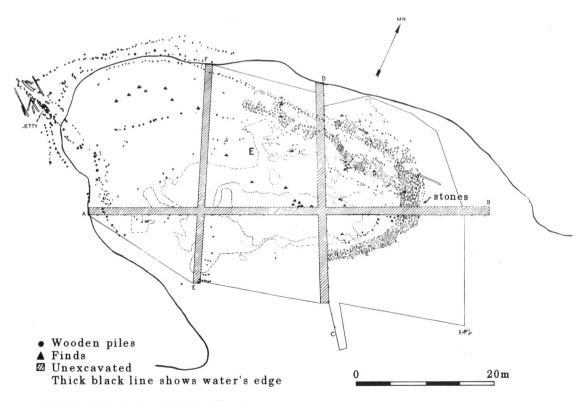

- ● **Wooden piles**
- ▲ **Finds**
- ▨ **Unexcavated**
  Thick black line shows water's edge

0　　　　　　　20m

Fig. 126. Plan of Knocknalappa lakeside settlement.

fragments, a penannular gold hair ring and a hoard of bronze objects in a wooden box (comprising rings, tweezers, a pin as well as several hair rings, amber beads and boar's tusks) were also recovered. The discovery of wooden models for the manufacture of clay moulds for casting spears, a socketed hammer and socketed axeheads in a bog near the village of Tobermore, Co. Derry, if not a votive offering might imply a nearby wetland settlement.[39]

AUGHINISH, CO. LIMERICK

Small enclosures, similar to Carrigillihy, Co. Cork, were also occupied. Two on Aughinish Island, near Foynes, in the Shannon estuary, were excavated in 1974. Both enclosures were about 35m in overall diameter with a bank faced internally and externally with limestone slabs and with a rubble core. Site 1 was built on bed rock and no post-holes were found but the ground had been levelled presumably for a house. Traces of occupation included shell-filled pits, coarse pottery, two saddle querns, a bronze tanged chisel and a bronze knob-headed pin, and the remains of an iron object, possibly a bridle bit. The iron object was a significant find but was heavily corroded; it had one surviving circular ring and one link with the openings at either end set at right angles to each other but it is not clear whether it was originally a two- or three-link bit. Site 2, about 200m to the south-east, also contained pits filled with shells and produced coarse pottery; the plan of a circular house 8m in diameter was recovered.

Limited excavation at Carrownaglogh, west of Ballina, Co. Mayo, revealed part of a farmstead dated to around the 9th century BC. Now covered by blanket bog, a combination of probing and excavation suggested the existence of an irregular stone-walled enclosure about 2.2 hectares in maximum extent. Traces of a robbed stone wall in the south-western part indicated that it had been enlarged at some time and a small hut some 7m across with a central hearth was reportedly found in the northern half. Much of the enclosure was occupied by well-marked spade cultivation ridges averaging 1.5m in width. Further cultivation ridges were found outside the enclosure on both north and south. Pollen analysis supported by radiocarbon dates demonstrated an intensive phase of both arable (wheat and barley) and pastoral agriculture which probably lasted for about 250 years. Pre-bog

field systems at Derryinver, Renvyle, Connemara, are somewhat later, radiocarbon dated pollen analyses indicate a 6th century BC date.[40]

MOOGHAUN, CO. CLARE

The hillfort at Mooghaun, near Newmarket on Fergus, Co. Clare, is the most prominent monument in that part of south-east Clare and, though situated on a low hill about 80m above sea level, it commands wide views of the Shannon estuary. It is a large enclosure with three stone ramparts encompassing a total area of almost 12 hectares (Fig. 127). All three ramparts were of broadly similar construction. Excavation in the inner enclosure demonstrated that the rampart here was of more or less dump construction with no significant stone facings or revetments. In size it measured 4m to 6.5m in width and 1m to 1.5m in height above the interior but it was built to take advantage of the natural slope and on the north-eastern half of the site in particular there was a steep drop outside the rampart. The outer rampart was of similar rudimentary construction and some burning on the old ground surface before it was built provided a

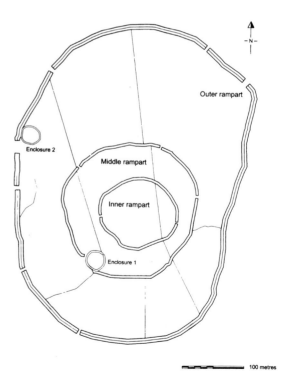

Fig. 127. Plan of Mooghaun hillfort, Co. Clare: the small circular enclosures are later features.

radiocarbon date of 1260-930 BC. This date is a terminal date after which this outer rampart was built but the excavator, Eoin Grogan, believed that no great span of time separated the two events and it was likely that all three ramparts were contemporary.

Only meagre evidence for settlement has been found but a little coarse pottery and animal bone, sealed beneath the inner and middle ramparts, indicates some domestic occupation prior to the construction of the hillfort. The purpose of the monument is difficult to determine. Its construction clearly demanded a considerable expenditure of human resources but it cannot be described as a high status settlement site and the term hillfort may be inappropriate as well. Nonetheless it was deliberately built as a prominent and focal monument in the landscape and presumably had some role in the social and economic organization of the surrounding territory. It appears to dominate a lakeland zone to the north and east of Newmarket-on-Fergus and a natural route-way extending from the Fergus and Shannon estuaries to Broadford, north of Limerick, where the Broadford river valley runs westward to Formoyle Hill, crowned by another trivallate hillfort, 10km south-west of Killaloe.[41]

There is an important concentration of late prehistoric material in the Mooghaun lakeland zone, the great Clare find being the most noteworthy. The deposition of this great collection of gold in a burnt mound near Mooghaun Lough some 750m to the north-east has prompted comparisons with both Haughey's Fort and Navan, Co. Armagh, both of which also have lakes or ponds with associated ritual depositions on the north-east. It may be that large and important sites like Haughey's Fort and Navan had associated pools for 'the insertion of special items into the natural order' but whether the deposition near Mooghaun is comparable is uncertain.[42]

Though not of the same scale as Mooghaun itself, a number of defended hilltop enclosures and some smaller enclosures which may be contemporary occur in this area and hint at a hierarchy of settlement. The lake-shore site at Knocknalappa is located about 4km south-east of Mooghaun.

The wetlands of the Shannon and Fergus estuaries were probably significant elements in flexible farming economies which also utilized the diverse resources offered by river bank and estuarine marsh at various dates including the Dowris Phase. An intertidal wooden structure on the eastern side of the upper Fergus estuary, adjacent to the townland of Islandmagrath, Co. Clare, was built of two parallel rows of closely spaced stout roundwood posts. It was over 35m in length and at least 2m in width with interwoven wattle between the posts. Horizontal panels of hurdlework were laid down between the two lines of posts and pinned to the underlying clays with sharpened pegs. A sample of hazel rod provided a radiocarbon date of 793-553 BC. This structure may have been a hard for beaching boats or a jetty or causeway giving access to the lower part of the shore.[43]

Coastal environments were also exploited as the radiocarbon dating of a hearth in a shell midden to 770-600 BC at Culleenamore, near Sligo, has demonstrated. The discovery of fragments of clay moulds for casting bronze swords in the sandhills at White Park Bay, Co. Antrim, is further evidence. Nothing is known about the precise context of these finds but sandhills evidently continued to be the scene of occasional or seasonal visits and these fragments raise the question was this particular metalworking exercise a seasonal one. Clay mould fragments have also been found on Dalkey Island, Co. Dublin. The moulds were for the casting of bronze swords, spears and socketed implements. Again the occupation here may have been seasonal though the evidence indicates that the island was occupied for a long prehistoric timespan and it is uncertain whether this was continuous or intermittent. There is a possibility that some promontory sites may have been occupied too: the early Historic defences at the promontory fort of Dunbeg, Co. Kerry, were preceded by a ditch which cut off part of the promontory and charcoal from this feature produced a radiocarbon date in the earlier half of the last millennium BC.[44]

The absence of significant evidence for settlement at Mooghaun is intriguing and it is possible that it too was seasonally or intermittently occupied. While hilltop sites such as Haughey's Fort, Co. Armagh, and Rathgall, Co. Wicklow, have produced extensive evidence for late 2nd and early 1st millennium BC occupation, others may have had functions other than defended settlements.

A small hillfort at Freestone Hill, Co. Kilkenny, with a single stony bank and external ditch enclosing an area of about 2 hectares, was excavated in the late 1940s. It produced some provincial

Roman bronzes and a coin of Constantine II of the middle of the 4th century AD and the latter was believed to offer a central date for the occupation. Some glass beads and coarse pottery were also found and parallels between the pottery from here and from Rathgall, Co. Wicklow, have prompted the suggestion that there may have been Dowris Phase occupation on Freestone Hill as well. The recognition that some of the glass beads could be early and the dating of an old sample of charcoal from the site to 810-550 BC confirms this.[45]

Downpatrick, Co. Down, is another hilltop which may have been occupied at this time. Limited excavation yielded coarse pottery of the same general sort found at Rathgall but in the absence of other evidence more precise dating is difficult and the picture is complicated by later activity. A hilltop settlement at Clogher, Co. Tyrone, was reportedly defended by a crude timber and stone rampart at this time too and has produced traces of structures and coarse pottery; a number of radiocarbon dates confirm Dowris Phase occupation.[46]

RATHGALL, CO. WICKLOW

The multivallate hillfort of Rathgall is situated on the western end of a low but prominent ridge some 137m above sea level in south-west Co. Wicklow (near Tullow, Co. Carlow). Four more or less concentric ramparts enclose an area of some 7.3 hectares (Fig. 128, upper). The inner enclosure is surrounded by a polygonal stone rampart 45m in average diameter; 27m to 53m outside this are two further ramparts set 10m to 12m apart. The irregular outer rampart is much denuded but had a diameter of about 310m. Excavations in the central enclosure, and on the southern slope of the hill beyond the outer rampart, have shown that the story of Rathgall was quite a complex one. The various ramparts have not been securely dated and the inner stone enclosure may be of Medieval or more recent date but it is possible that the three other ramparts are contemporary with late prehistoric occupation on the hilltop which lay in part beneath the late stone enclosure.

Excavation within the late stone monument revealed an annular ditched enclosure surrounding a large circular house which produced evidence for occupation and bronze working. The ditch was circular with an internal diameter of 35m but somewhat irregularly dug with depths varying from 50cm to 1.5m. There was no entrance causeway so

it may have been crossed by a timber bridge possibly facing the eastern entrance to the house. The house was particularly large, 15m in diameter, and built of timber posts set in a bedding trench 15cm-25cm deep. Two large posts flanked an entrance on the east and the walls turned inwards to form a small porch with a second inner doorway. Many post-holes were found in the interior and presumably served as roof supports but no coherent plan was discernible, though there did appear to be a parallel row of posts leading from the doorway towards the centre of the house.

A large oval pit, which measured 1.75m by 1.25m and 40cm in depth, was located just north of the centre of the house; its base and sides had been lined with some organic material and it contained a large boulder which had been carefully sealed in the pit with sandy soil. A very small scatter of burnt human bone and a gold hair ring were found beneath the boulder in the basal carbonized matter. This was interpreted as a foundation deposit contemporary with the construction of the house which was thus dated to the Dowris Phase. Several other irregularly dug pits were discovered and, except for a small fire-reddened area in the north-eastern part, no clear traces of a hearth were found.

Numerous pits and post-holes were found outside the house and within the enclosure. One pit just to the south-east of the house entrance contained traces of a wicker basket which had been renewed once if not twice and was evidently a storage pit. A series of hearths were found mainly on the north-east and several of these had associated post-holes suggesting shelters of some description. The bedding trench of the house cut into one of these so some of them at least may belong to an earlier phase of activity. For some, however, a Dowris Phase date is confirmed by a series of radiocarbon dates; potsherds and bones found in several hearths suggested domestic use but clay mould fragments were found in one.

Large quantities of coarse pottery were discovered, a little of it decorated in simple fashion. Other artefacts included saddle querns and stone rubbers, a bronze bar toggle of north European type (Fig. 129, 1), bracelet fragments, and a bronze conical rivet of the type found on some cauldrons. A large number of glass beads were an exceptional discovery. Most are simple annular beads of blue or greenish-blue colour but some are decorated with circle or concentric circle designs. Chemical

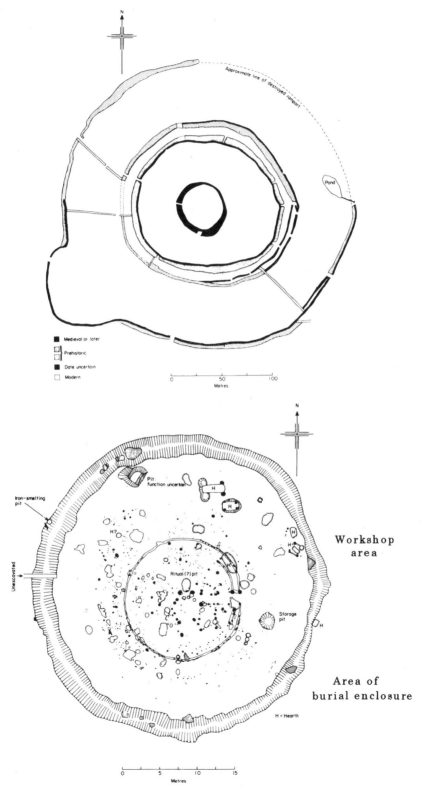

Fig. 128. Rathgall, Co. Wicklow. Above. General plan of multivallate hillfort. Below. Enclosure with circular house, pits and hearths. The workshop and burial areas are indicated.

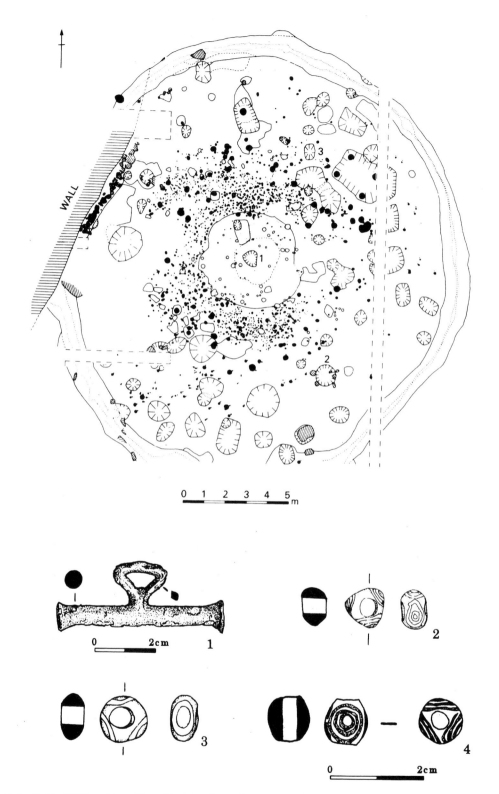

Fig. 129. Rathgall, Co. Wicklow. Above. Plan of burial enclosure showing central cremation pit (1) with U-shaped setting of stake holes. Below. Exotic material from Rathgall. 1. Bronze bar toggle. 2-4. Glass beads with inlaid concentric circle or circle ornament.

analysis has shown that most of these beads are of a low magnesium high potassium type found in Continental Europe but whether these are exotic imports or of local manufacture is still uncertain.

Some of this material came from the enclosure ditch on the east and was derived from a workshop area found just outside it where there were deposits of organic material up to 35cm deep. Numerous post-holes may be the remains of a number of timber structures reflecting a series of phases of activity. There were hundreds of fragments of clay moulds for weapons, including swords and spearheads, and for probable socketed axes and gouges or chisels. There was also a mould fragment for a flanged implement. Some lumps of waste bronze were found here and artefacts such as a small socketed gouge, a tanged punch and other bronze objects. Bracelets of jet or lignite, numerous glass beads, some small pieces of amber, saddle querns and whetstones were also recovered. Gold objects included a biconical gold bead, another hair ring – a penannular bronze ring covered with gold foil – and a finely made cylindrical bead or pendant consisting of a dark green glass bead with a gold inset.[47] This was evidently a major workshop which produced weapons on a significant scale and probably manufactured finer prestigious items as well.

Because burials of this period are very rare, the presence of several cremated burials proved to be another exceptional feature. To the south of the workshop area, a circular ditch 19m in diameter enclosed a series of features including a central pit containing the cremated bones of a young adult (Fig. 129). This pit had been dug into an area of reddened burnt soil enclosed by a dense U-shaped arrangement of some 1500 closely-set stake-holes. Fragments of human bone in this burnt earth suggest that the cremation had taken place on site. Elsewhere in the enclosure, the cremated bones of a child were found in a small pit at the end of one of the arms of the U-shaped setting, a coarse bucket-shaped pot placed mouth upwards in a second pit contained the cremated bones of an adult and child, and a third contained a hoard of bronzes comprising a small chisel, parts of a spearhead and a sword blade. Later activity is attested by a small bowl-shaped furnace for iron working dated to the period 180 to 540 AD.[48]

Further evidence of settlement was found on the southern slope of the hill outside the outer rampart. This included the foundations of a small D-shaped

hut and another larger circular structure with associated coarse pottery. Nearby pits contained more pottery, parts of saddle querns and fragments of clay moulds, and the remains of hearths were also discovered. A small annular ditch enclosed a few post-holes, one associated with some fragments of burnt human bone, and a pit, and may be a ritual site.

The sheer quantity of metalworking evidence, the weapon manufacturing, the gold, the glass beads, the amber fragments, the cremated burials and associated ritual, and the hoard of bronzes all combine to set Rathgall apart from other settlements of the time. These factors, the unusual ritual evidence and its prominent hilltop location clearly imply a site of considerable status.

WARRIOR ARISTOCRATS?

It is generally believed that significant social changes occurred in prehistoric Europe in the third millennium BC. The importance of ancestry, kinship and lineage may have diminished and it is suggested that social relationships were increasingly defined in terms of alliances and competition in which material goods played an important role. Prestigious artefacts were key factors in defining social relationships and since in some areas such artefacts could only be obtained through contacts with other societies with similar preoccupations a pattern of reciprocal demand developed.[49] In Ireland this process may have been a long and uneven one. The appearance of symbolic objects like stone battle axes, halberds, gold lunulae, and of individual burials in pits and cists with distinctive pottery and the occasional flint knife, bronze razor or faience bead suggests it could have commenced by about 2300 BC.

Metalwork and metalworking may have given greater impetus to the development of social hierarchies and the scarcity of evidence for metalworking on the admittedly few settlement sites may be an indication of its exclusive character. From about 1400 BC objects such as exceptionally long bronze rapiers and spearheads and finely executed goldwork represent both greater technical specialism and an increasing concern with ostentatious display by an elite minority. The appearance of prestige weaponry is revealing and when the martial repertoire consists of sword, spear and bronze shield, some evidently symbolic, then it may well be that the elite was a warrior aristocracy (who could possibly have sported some of the

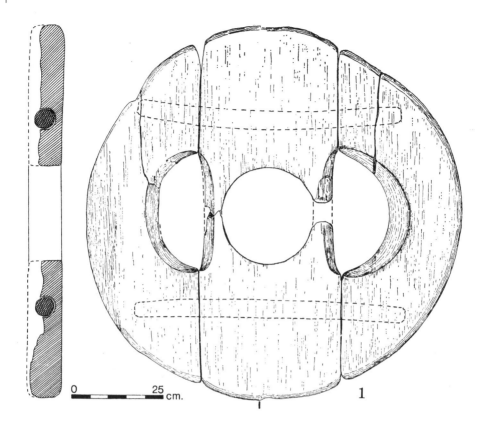

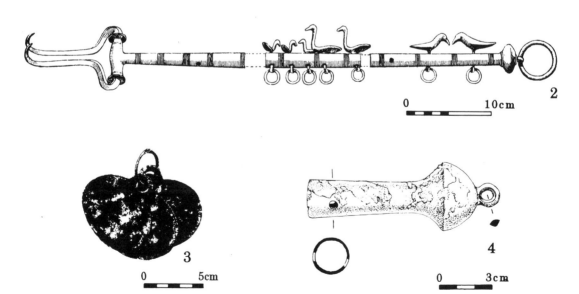

Fig. 130. 1. One of a pair of block wheels found in a bog at Doogarymore, Co. Roscommon. Three large pieces of alder are held together by two large dowels of yew, originally circular with a diameter of about 1m. 2. Bronze flesh-hook or goad from Dunaverney, near Ballymoney, Co. Antrim. 3. Rattle-pendant from Lissanode, Co. Westmeath. 4. Bronze ferrule possibly for a goad from Moynalty Lough, Co. Monaghan.

contemporary gold ornaments as well). This material may have been the insignia of chieftains and ritual leaders who rarely indulged in actual combat. Some of the swords and spears, and leather shields, were eminently functional of course, and these may have been the property of a fighting elite of lesser status, a differentiated warrior aristocracy may have existed.

Since the control of rituals such as hoard deposition and ceremonial feasting is also an important mechanism for the maintenance of power, these activities may have been the preserve of the elite as well. The presence of tools such as gouges and chisels in a small number of hoards indicates that certain craftsmen had high status and were also entitled to representation in the ceremonial sphere.

It is tempting to speculate that the two-wheeled cart or chariot may have been another status item, but Irish evidence is lacking. It is a possibility since there is abundant evidence elsewhere including carved representations of two-wheeled vehicles in such diverse locations as Iberia (Fig. 103) and Scandinavia. The use of wooden ceremonial carts with block wheels and drawn by either a pair of horses or oxen is conceivable. The remains of a pair of massive wooden block wheels found in a bog at Doogarymore, near Kilteevan, Co. Roscommon (Fig. 130, 1) are radiocarbon dated to 760–260 BC; a metre long piece of perforated timber found 3m away may have formed part of the vehicle. An unprovenanced wooden ox yoke has been dated to 920-780 BC. Some tubular knobbed ferrules may have been handles for goads and it is possible that the so-called flesh-hooks may have been used in this fashion too.[50]

There is very little evidence for metal horse trappings: a bronze phalera, a small circular bronze mount thought to be for horse harness, possibly of 7th century BC date, was found on Inis Cealtra, near Mountshannon, Co. Clare. A second is reported from Rathtinaun, Co. Sligo. A series of bronze discs considered to be rattle-pendants may be horse-gear too: several unprovenanced examples are recorded and a set of three suspended from a bronze ring were found at Lissanode, south-west of Ballymore, Co. Westmeath, along with bronze objects which may have been cheekpieces (Fig. 130, 3). Some bone or antler toggles may have served as cheekpieces. Both phalera and pendants have parallels in Britain and on the Continent. Bronze rings of various types are sometimes considered to be harness strap holders but obviously, like mounts and rattles, all were not necessarily placed on horses. Some, like a collar of bronze rings forming two broad chain-links, found in a former bog near the town of Roscommon, may have been personal ornaments.[51]

Whatever about the uncertainties of horse harness and the limited nature of the evidence for a hierarchical society, it may be tentatively suggested that prehistoric Ireland from the later 2nd millennium BC was populated by numerous small chiefdoms linked with one another (and with similar communities in western Britain) by an extensive system of alliances. It is not an unreasonable speculation that an elite stratum preoccupied with status, display and ritual was ensconced at the summit of a social hierarchy which also included warriors and craftsmen.

NOTES

1 Dowris Phase: Eogan 1964. Hoard: Eogan 1983, 117, no. 119, figs 64-79; Rosse 1984; Coles 1971b.

2 Buckets: Arthog, Merioneth, bucket: Savory 1980, 114.; unprovenanced Irish bucket of Continental form: Wright 1900, 285, fig.; Derrymacash, Co. Armagh: Armstrong 1924, 111, fig. 7, with secondary patches secured by iron rivets; Hawkes and Smith 1957; Briggs 1987; wine drinking: Piggott 1959. Hart, Bavaria: Müller-Karpe 1956. Wooden cauldron: Earwood 1989, 42, lower left, 2745 ± 70 BP (OxA-2427); Earwood 1993, 45.

3 Cape Castle, Co. Antrim: Doran 1978, 6; 1993, pl. 44; Briggs 1987, 184.; Ballymoney, Co. Antrim: Briggs 1987, 170, fig. 6; Magilligan, Co. Derry: Corcoran 1965; Rynne 1967.

4 Cauldrons: Hawkes and Smith 1957; Gerloff 1986. The Class A and B subdivision was proposed by Leeds

1930. Tulnacross, Co. Tyrone: Briggs 1987; Scott 1990, 60. Barnacurragh, Co. Galway: Costello 1921. Lisdrumturk, Co. Monaghan: Lucas 1968, 117; for the iron rivets see Briggs 1987, 174, fig. 10. Castlederg, Co. Tyrone: Ryan 1983, 24. Raffrey, Co. Down: Brannon 1984.

5 Hawkes and Smith 1957, 176, note 3; Green 1992a, 57. Macalister 1949, 217. Coombs 1975, 74, quoting Malinowski.

6 Feltwell Fen, Norfolk: Gerloff 1986, fig. 6iib. Flesh-hooks: Jockenhövel 1974. Goads: Piggott 1983, 134.

7 Bargeroosterveld, Netherlands: Waterbolk and van Zeist 1961. Ralaghan, Co. Cavan: B. Coles 1990, 326, 2830 ± 70 BP (OxA-1719); Mahr 1930. Cullen, Co. Tipperary: Pownall 1775, 357.

8 Horns: Coles 1963; 1967; Holmes 1979; Holmes and Coles 1981; Ó Duibhir 1988, 1994. Griffinrath, Co.

Kildare: Briggs and Haworth 1978. Boolybrien, Co. Clare: Eogan 1983, no. 55, fig. 26.

9 Pendants: Coles 1965; Megaw 1966; Eogan 1983, 136. Calheme, Co. Antrim: Weatherup 1975, 14, fig. 3, 4. Unprovenanced in Exeter Museum: Eogan 1964, 307. See also Macalister 1928, 141; Longworth 1985, 50. Tumna, Co. Roscommon, gold balls: Armstrong 1933, 37, 86, frontispiece; Wakeman 1888, 111.

10 Swords: Colquhoun and Burgess 1988, 24-39; Burgess 1969. Class 2: Eogan 1965, nos 24-33, 73; Class 3: nos 43-63, 276, 325, 326, 553. Knocknalappa, Co. Clare: Raftery 1942, 62, fig. 3.2; Eogan 1965, no. 114. Co. Tyrone: Eogan 1965, no. 478. Contexts: Cooney and Grogan 1994, fig. 7, 9 and fig. 8, 14. Hoards: Eogan 1983; Coombs 1975; Ballycroghan, Co. Down: Jope 1953.

11 Spears: Kish, Co. Wicklow: Eogan 1983, no. 155, fig. 96; Knockanbaun, Co. Sligo: Eogan 1983, no. 130, fig. 82. Scotland: Evans 1933, 197; Coles 1960, 25. See also Ehrenberg 1977, 13; O'Connor 1980, 100, 138, 181. Scott 1990, 42, considers small spears and axes as quite functional objects and no indication of an impoverished metal supply. Navan, Co. Armagh: Raftery in Lynn 1997, 91. Belturbet, Co. Cavan: Eogan 1983, no. 49, fig. 24; Ryan 1983, 95. Lough Gur, Co. Limerick: Coles *et al.* 1964, 191, also Coles 1971a.

12 Shields: Coles 1962; Raftery 1982; Graslund 1967; Bouzek 1968. Kilmahamogue, Co. Antrim: Jope 1951, pl. 4, 16; 3445 ± 70 BP (OxA-2429): Hedges *et al.* 1991. Cloonlara, Co. Mayo: radiocarbon date 3150 ± 90 BP (1672-1252/1246-1212/1180-1168 BC, OxA-3228), Hedges *et al.* 1993. Antrim shield: Doran 1978, pl. II; 1993, pl. 38. Shield usage: Coles 1962, 185. Needham 1979a, 113, 129, has noted that a distinctive perforation in the bronze Long Wittenham, Oxfordshire, shield could have been produced by a spearhead.

13 Gorgets: Eogan 1981, 364; Taylor 1980, 131. Borrisnoe, Co. Tipperary: Cahill 1995, pl. 13. Ardcrony, Co. Tipperary: Cahill 1995, pls 9-11. Shannongrove, Co. Limerick: Powell 1974, pl. 1; Eogan 1994, pls XIV and 25. Gleninsheen, Co. Clare: Cahill in Ryan 1983, 92 and pl. Gorteenreagh, Co. Clare: Raftery 1967. Origins: Powell 1974; Eogan 1994, 96; 1995, 133; Taylor 1980, 53. Leather prototypes: Gogan 1931, 88; J. Raftery 1967, 70.

14 Sleeve fasteners: Eogan 1972; 1994, 136. Dress fasteners: Cahill 1995, 67. Clones, Co. Monaghan: Cahill *op. cit.,* pl. 16; Ryan 1983, 83, pl. Taylor 1980, 67. Lock rings have been studied by Eogan 1969. Taylor 1980, 68, considers the size of the central tube and the penannular gap too great to keep hair in place but if the hair was braided this difficulty might be overcome. For 'penannular hollow ornaments of triangular section' see Proudfoot 1955.

15 Hair rings (ring money): Eogan 1997; listed in Eogan 1994, 137; Taylor 1980, 64. Silver or electrum inlay: Taylor 1980, pl. 33f and g, 189. Rathgall, Co. Wicklow: Raftery 1976, 342. Tooradoo, Co. Limerick: Eogan 1983, no. 103, fig. 58; Taylor 1980, pl. 36d and f. Rathtinaun, Co. Sligo: Eogan 1983, no. 132, fig 84; Taylor 1980, pl. 36a-c, e. For the term crescent-shaped bullae see Taylor 1980, 65, following Wilde 1862, 85.

Eogan 1994, 89, calls them decorated thick penannular rings.

16 Bullae: Bog of Allen, Co. Kildare: Macalister 1949, 194, and Cahill in Ryan 1983, 88. River Bann: Armstrong 1933, 43.

17 Bracelets: Eogan 1994, 85, 148; Hawkes and Clarke 1963. The type with a flat ribbon-like body with expanded terminals (Armstrong 1933, pl. XVIII, 384) is Taylor's (1984) Potterne Type or Needham's Class B1 (Hook and Needham 1990). The type with coiled ends is of the latter's Class B2. Vesnoy, Co. Roscommon: Eogan 1983, 206, no. 4, fig. 108.

18 Ehrenberg 1989, 82.

19 Eogan 1974; 1993, 125; 1994, 97.

20 Mooghaun North, Co. Clare: Armstrong 1917a; Condit 1996; Eogan 1983, no. 58, figs 23-37. For Ballykeaghra, Co. Galway, see Eogan 1983, no. 83, fig. 44. Cullen, Co. Tipperary: Eogan 1983, no. 135; Taylor 1980, 112. The suggestion that a large hoard, possibly containing a gold ingot, two lock rings, bracelets and a gorget, may have been found near Askeaton, Co. Limerick (Eogan 1983, no. 99, fig. 57) may be without foundation: Cahill 1994a would only ascribe a bracelet and two lock rings to this find.

21 Eogan 1981; his pl. III has been compared to Danish bark containers by Earwood 1993, 226. Ballinesker, Co. Wexford: Cahill 1994; also 1995, 66.

22 Enniscorthy, Co. Wexford: Eogan 1981a, 148. Cashel, Co. Tipperary: Wilde 1862, 89, figs 625-626.

23 Possible vessels according to Eogan 1981; head gear according to Gerloff 1995.

24 Sunflower pins: Eogan 1974a; Knocknalappa, Co. Clare: Eogan 1974a, fig. 5, 28. Ballytegan, Co. Laois: Ryan 1983, 91, pl. Arboe, Co. Tyrone: Eogan 1983, no. 138, fig. 88. Hodges 1956, 43, argued that pins with small hemispherical bosses and concentric circle ornament were earlier than those with large conical bosses and Eogan calls these primary and secondary series pins. Scotland: Coles 1959; two pins in Eogan's 1974a corpus have this so-called swan's neck feature: his fig. 4, no. 9 and fig. 5, no. 25).

25 Hawkes 1971, 41.

26 Atlantic sea-ways: the quotations are from Macalister 1928, 52 and De Valera 1951, 18. Passage tombs: Eogan 1990; pottery: Savory 1978; early metallurgy: Sheridan 1983; early metal objects: Harbison 1967; Irish and Galician rock art: Bradley 1995 and 1997; contact in later prehistory: Eogan 1990a. Powell 1972 saw only meagre traces of Iberian influence in the Irish Sea region in early prehistory, in contrast to more extensive relationships evident at a later date. Some aspects of the significance of later long distance exchanges along the Atlantic seaboard have been considered by Ruiz-Gálvez 1991, the claims for Irish contacts by Raftery 1992; see also Bowen 1972. Gold and Iberia: Eogan 1994, 53, 104; Almagro-Gorbea 1995; Powell 1974.

27 Hitherto unprovenanced but 'found in a gravel pit near Ballinasloe, Co. Galway', according to the caption to an illustration of the weapon by William Betham in National Library of Ireland Ms 4458. Huelva hoard: Almagro 1958; Savory 1968, fig. 74, l.

28 Amber: Eogan 1994, 85. Portlaoise, Co. Laois: Eogan 1983, no. 97, figs 54-55. Ballycurrin Demesne, Co. Galway: Eogan 1983, no. 107; Briggs 1997. Meenwaun, Banagher, Co. Offaly: Eogan 1983, no. 117, fig. 63; 1994, pl. XVI; Whitfield 1993. Derrybrien, Co. Galway: Prendergast 1960; Eogan 1994, pl. 20. Kurin, Co. Derry: Flanagan 1964. Ballylin, Co. Offaly: Kelly 1984. Continental source: Beck and Shennan 1991, 37; Irish source: Briggs 1976, 10; 1984 [appendix to Kelly 1984]; 1997. Britain: Pearce 1977.

29 Ireland and northern Europe: Eogan 1964, 316. For supposed megalithic tomb and ceramic parallels see Herity 1974; Herity and Eogan 1977; Herity 1981; questioned in Waddell 1978. North European contacts are claimed by Hencken 1951, 57. For comparisons with the Trundholm disc: Armstrong 1933, 49, and Smith 1920, 110. Dress fasteners: Hawkes and Clarke 1963; Eogan 1994, 96. Ballytegan hoard: Raftery 1971a, questioned by O'Connor 1980, 204. Rathgall, Co. Wicklow, and Navan, Co. Armagh, bar toggles: Raftery 1975. Parallels and contacts questioned by Butler 1963, 229; Savory 1971, 258; Taylor 1980, 55; Thrane 1995.

30 Scandinavian axes: Schmidt and Burgess 1981, 179: axes of Type Højby from Carse Loch, Kirkcudbrightshire, and from Co. Antrim.

31 Bronze tools and implements have been briefly noted by Eogan 1964, 293; 1983, and their wider context studied by O'Connor 1980. Enagh East, Co. Clare: O'Carroll and Ryan 1992. Cromaghs, Co. Antrim: Eogan 1983, no. 38; Jørgensen 1992, 19, 215; this hoard is a reminder that perishable materials may have formed a part of many deposits: O'Flaherty 1996. Kilbride, Co. Mayo: Cahill 1988.

32 Drumman More Lake, Co. Armagh: Waddell 1984. Gouges: Eogan 1966. Tanged chisels: Burgess et al. 1972; Roth 1974. Knives: Hodges 1956; Burgess 1982. Tanged razors: Jockenhövel 1980. Bronze anvils: Ehrenberg 1981; Needham 1993.

33 Sickles: Killymaddy, Co. Antrim, moulds: Coghlan and Raftery 1961, nos 36-37. Tanged sickles: O'Connor 1980, 177. Socketed sickles: Fox 1939; Steensberg 1943; Harding 1976; Raftery in Lynn 1997, 91. Llyn Fawr, Glamorgan: Savory 1980, 123, no. 291, fig. 46, 8.

34 The principal types of socketed axe have been outlined by Eogan 1964, 293, and studied in Scotland and northern England by Schmidt and Burgess 1981. Bag-shaped axes in northern England and Scotland are Types Portree and Dowris etc. of Schmidt and Burgess. The 'Dungiven type' of socketed axe, not to be confused with a similarly named type of socketed knife, was identified by Coles 1960, 44. The Minnis Bay, Kent, axe: Schmidt and Burgess 1981, 201.

35 Faceted and ribbed socketed axeheads: Needham in Martin O'Connell 1986, 44; Needham 1993a. Axe usage: Harding 1976. Hafting mechanisms: a bent haft of yew and a socketed axe from Kinnegad, Co. Westmeath, is illustrated in Coles et al. 1978, fig. 2, 2; for a mortised wooden haft from Haughey's Fort, Co. Armagh: Neill 1996. Miniature non-functional axes ranging from about 2.5cm to 5cm in length: for

example Wilde 1861, 386, no. 524, and Lucas 1961, 80; but see Scott 1990, 42, for a contrary view. Breton socketed axeheads: Flanagan 1959, 52; Dunning 1959; Eogan 1964, fig. 11, no. 9.

36 Lough Eskragh, Co. Tyrone: Collins and Seaby 1960; Willliams 1978, 2475 ± 45 BP(700-400 BC, UB-965), 2690 ± 45 BP (960-800 BC, UB-2047), 3105 ± 80 BP (1520-1150 BC, UB-948), 2360 ± 45 BP (750-290 BC, UB-950); Hodges 1954 for moulds. Altanagh, Co. Tyrone: Williams 1983, 2550 ± 85 BP (UB-2434); Earwood 1993, 57, 265. Saddle querns: Connolly 1994.

37 Hencken 1942; this site is also known as Ballinderry 2 and is situated just east of Moate; it is not to be confused with the nearby crannog of early Historic date of Ballinderry 1 in Co. Westmeath. Hencken believed that nine circular wicker basket-like structures, of uncertain purpose, were also of late prehistoric date but Newman would assign these to the early Historic period (information from Conor Newman). Skull burial: Cooney and Grogan 1994, 147.

38 Knocknalappa, Co. Clare: J. Raftery 1942. Island MacHugh, Co. Tyrone: Ivens et al. 1986; Simpson 1986, 2770 ± 80 BP (1150-800 BC, HAR-6821).

39 Moynagh Lough, Co. Meath: J. Bradley 1991, 1997; a radiocarbon date of 2650 ± 80 BP (1004-536 BC, GrN-12359) was obtained from charcoal. Rathtinaun, Co. Sligo: Raftery 1994, 32-35; Eogan 1983, no. 132, fig. 84, for the bronze hoard. Tobermore, Co. Derry: Hodges 1954.

40 Aughinish, Co. Limerick: unpublished: Kelly 1974; Raftery 1976a, 192. Carrownaglogh, Co. Mayo: unpublished, preliminary report: Herity 1981a; Fowler 1981, fig. 1; O'Connell 1986. Derryinver, Co. Galway: Molloy and O'Connell 1993.

41 Mooghaun, Co. Clare: Grogan 1993; 1995, 2895 ± 50 BP (1260-930 BC, GrN-20490); 1996; a period of intensive farming detected in the pollen record may be contemporary with activity at Mooghaun: Molloy 1997. Formoyle Hill: Condit 1995.

42 Cooney and Grogan 1994, 156.

43 O'Sullivan 1996, 2540 ± 20 BP (793-553 BC, GrN-20974).

44 Culleenamore, Co. Sligo: 2475 ± 100 BP (770-600 BC, Fra-63); other dates: 3060 ± 100 BP (c. 1400 BC, Fra-60), 3045 ± 100 BP (1390-1310 BC, Fra-65) and 2980 ± 60 BP (1370-1260 BC, Lu-2225): Burenhult 1984, 131, 326. White Park Bay, Co. Antrim: Collins 1970. Dalkey Island, Co. Dublin: Liversage 1968. Dunbeg, Co. Kerry: 2530 ± 35 BP (802-536 BC, UB-2216): Barry 1981.

45 Raftery 1969; 1976a; 1995, 2565 ± 35 BP (810-550 BC, GrN-21255); Henderson 1988.

46 Downpatrick, Co. Down: once thought to have been the site of a hillfort but the earthwork visible there is now known to be of Medieval date: Proudfoot 1956; Hamlin and Lynn 1988, 61. Clogher, Co. Tyrone: Warner 1988a; 2630 ± 45 BP (900-774 BC, UB-839), 2420 ± 100 BP (800-260 BC, UB-840), 2640 ± 45 BP (902-788 BC, UB-2176), Radiocarbon 21.

47 Rathgall, Co. Wicklow: Raftery 1973, 1974b, 1976, radiocarbon dates include 2470 ± 80 BP (788-408

BC, SI-1476), 2475 ± 80 BP (790-408 BC, SI-1477), 2560 ± 105 BP (900-410 BC, SI-1478), etc.; 1994, 58. Glass beads: Raftery 1987; Henderson 1988. Flanged implement: Raftery 1971, pl. 47c. Bead with inset: Raftery 1976, 346, pl. II on p. 533.

48 Iron working: Scott 1990, 160. Burials with metalwork: Burgess 1976a.

49 Various writers including Shennan 1982, 1982a; Kristiansen 1984, 1987.

50 Wheeled vehicles and goads: Piggott 1983. For ceremonial block wheeled vehicles as depicted in Scandinavia: Kristiansen 1987, 44. Doogarymore, Co. Roscommon: Lucas 1972 who suggested that the sophisticated construction and careful finish of the wheels may denote a vehicle of status or ceremonial use; 2315 ± 35 BP (400-260 BC, GrN-5990) and 2400 ± 35 BP (760-390 BC, GrN-5991). Unprovenanced wooden ox yoke in the Ulster Museum: 2660 ± 60 BP (OxA-2428), Hedges *et al.* 1991, 129.

51 Phalarae: O'Connor 1975; Raftery 1994, 34. Rattle-pendants and cheekpieces: Rynne 1962; Britnell 1976. Possible cheekpieces: : Knocknalappa, Co. Clare: J. Raftery 1942, fig. 3, 1; Ballinderry, Co. Offaly: Hencken 1942, fig. 5, 667; Moynagh Lough, Co. Meath: J. Bradley 1991, fig. 4, 252. Roscommon collar: Wilde 1861, 576, fig. 487.

8

From Bronze
to Iron

The date of 500 BC proposed for the end of the Dowris Phase and the commencement of the following iron-using period is only an approximation. The later first millennium BC and the early centuries AD are amongst the most obscure periods in Irish prehistoric archaeology. The decline of the bronze weapon industry and its replacement by iron sometime in the last millennium BC, and the disappearance of characteristic artefacts such as bronze swords and socketed axeheads, events which should theoretically mark the end of the Dowris Phase, are imperfectly understood developments to say the least. There is general agreement that the development of an iron technology was a significant factor in the eventual demise of bronze working on a large scale, but how, why and when this came about in Ireland is far from clear.

The use of iron on a modest scale is sporadically recorded in various parts of Europe from the second millennium BC onwards and iron implements were used with increasing frequency in central Europe from about 1000 BC.[1] Iron was in widespread use on the Continent by the 7th century BC. In Britain the earliest evidence for the new technology dates to about the middle of the 7th century: that iron copy of a bronze sickle in the Llyn Fawr, Glamorgan, hoard, being just one of a number of early instances. How long it took for the new technology to supplant bronze to any significant degree is uncertain and it is possible that the process may have taken several centuries. It is also possible, of course, that the appearance of iron had a more immediate effect on the value of bronze which in turn resulted in a

rapid reduction and eventually a cessation in wide-scale hoard deposition.

While some the bronze objects already considered probably denote contacts with Britain, and ultimately with the Continent, in the 7th century BC, a series of other bronze artefacts demonstrate further contacts in the 7th century continuing into the 6th; the spread of the knowledge of iron working was in all probability a consequence of these links.

THE GÜNDLINGEN SWORD

A series of bronze swords display some features which sharply distinguish them from the common Class 4 sword of the Dowris Phase. These are Class 5 swords in George Eogan's classification, the insular Gündlingen swords of J. G. Cowen. The Gündlingen sword, named after a possible grave-find in south-western Germany, is one of the classic Continental bronze sword types of the 7th century BC and was in contemporaneous use with iron swords. This sword has a number of quite distinctive features including a convex-sided hilt, usually flange-less, with a prominent perforated rectangular pommel-piece (an extension to take a large decorative pommel of bone or antler), narrow pin-like rivets (occasionally with a punched head with a central nipple), wide-angled shoulders and a long slender leaf-shaped blade of thick oval central cross-section with a beaded edge. The type was copied by Irish and British sword smiths.

While a few have sub-rectangular perforated pommel-pieces, versions of the bronze Gündlingen sword in Ireland and Britain are characterized by a distinctive pommel-piece with a notch in its upper

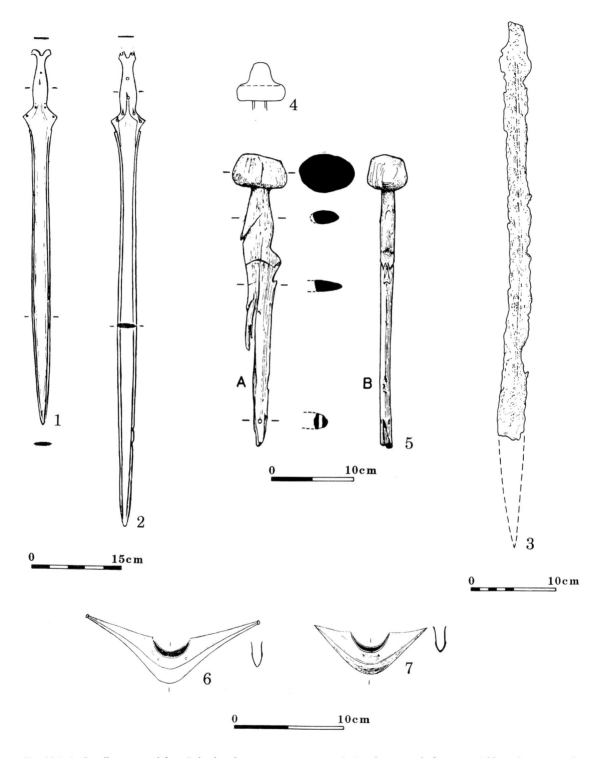

Fig. 131. 1. Gündlingen sword from Ireland with no precise provenance. 2. Another example from near Athlone. 3. Iron sword from the River Shannon, near Athlone (the slight bend is not ancient). 4. Possible pommel shape based on contemporary Continental forms: no scale. 5. Wooden model of a sword from Cappagh, Co. Kerry. 6. Winged chape from Ireland with no precise provenance. 7. Boat-shaped chape from Keelogue, Co. Galway.

edge or an even more exaggerated winged form in which the notch is widened and the ears extended outwards and downwards to form hooks (Fig. 131, 1). The hilt is usually flange-less and convex-sided with wide-angled shoulders below. The long slender blade may have the characteristic rounded central cross-section with a ridged or beaded bevelled edge but more often than not Irish examples have a simpler blade cross-section with a rounded or flattened centre with very wide, hollowed bevelled edges. Rivets are characteristically pin-like, some with the distinctive ring-punched head with central cone or nipple; the rivet pattern is apparently variable.

These swords are, on average, longer than Class 4: they vary from about 58cm to about 84cm in length, the average length being 67.3cm with 89% measuring 60cm or more. The longest known, with an original length of about 84cm, was dredged from the River Moy in Coolcronaun townland, north of Foxford, Co. Mayo. Surprisingly, associations of complete swords in hoards seem to be unknown: four swords are said to have been found with a few others 'upon an ancient battlefield near Athlone' and a number were recovered from the celebrated bog of Cullen, Co. Tipperary, but neither can be described as an associated find.[2]

A number of hybrid swords are known in Ireland, as in Britain, and they are possibly an indication of the willingness of sword smiths to experiment with various permutations of old and new features. A few have T-shaped terminals to the hilt, or combine features of Classes 4 and 5.[3] The distribution of the Gündlingen sword (Fig. 132) clearly depicts a widespread weapon type with an Irish, British and a Continental dimension, but the picture is more complex, typological differences

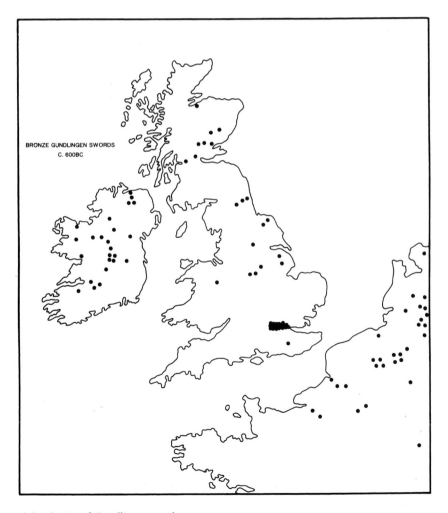

Fig. 132. General distribution of Gündlingen swords.

indicate regional forms and the type as a whole is part of a tradition of bronze sword-making over five centuries old. Over this timespan there was a continuous process of change in the forms of the weapons actually used and here we have the final regional expression of a long-lasting fashion for bronze sword usage. The distribution is a reflection of a shared fashion and the contact this implies.[4]

Though no scabbards have been found, a number of bronze chapes are known (Fig. 131, 6-7). Boat-shaped and winged types have been recognized and are of Irish-British forms inspired by Continental fashions. All are stray isolated finds but a boat-shaped example was found in the bog of Cullen (which also yielded a number of swords).[5]

It has been suggested that swords of the Gündlingen family were dual-purpose weapons, intended for use on foot or on horse-back, and the contemporary appearance on the Continent of horse equipment such as iron bridle bits might add some weight to this hypothesis. However, the belief that winged chapes were functional and capable of being hooked beneath the foot of a horse-riding warrior to facilitate the drawing of the sword seems implausible. The small size of the rivet holes for attachment to the scabbard tip suggests these objects could not have withstood robust treatment and were probably primarily decorative. Though no pommels have been found, some contemporary Continental swords had large decorated 'hat-shaped' pommels and this may have been the fashion in Ireland too: a small wooden sword found in boggy ground at Cappagh, Co. Kerry, has been claimed to be a model of a Class 5 example and it certainly has a quite prominent pommel (Fig. 131, 5). One of the bog of Cullen swords, found in 1748, is said to have had rivets about 2cm long still in place with 'a thin piece of gold' attached to one. Cowen accepts the description as that of a Gündlingen sword and it is possible therefore that some of these pommels were richly ornamented.

A number of other bronze artefacts are thought to reflect further contact with Britain or the Continent: these include a heavy knobbed bronze ring of Italian type said to have come 'from Co. Derry' which like a number of other stray discoveries of exotic objects could well be antiquarian acquisitions of recent centuries rather than ancient imports. A small bronze figurine of an Etruscan warrior 'found in a bog in Ireland' and another Italic bronze statuette 'from Sligo' could

conceivably be early imports but obviously, given the lack of information about the circumstances of their discovery, certainty is impossible.[6]

A small number of Italic safety-pin brooches or fibulae have been found, again as stray finds (Fig. 133). One is said to have been found in Co. Dublin, the others are unprovenanced but since a considerable number are known from Britain, the Irish finds could be genuine. When it is recalled that the exceptional flesh-hook or goad from a bog at Dunaverney, Co. Antrim (Fig. 130, 2), with its unusual iconography of a pair of swans and their cygnets and a pair of crows or ravens, has also been claimed to be an import (or to at least reflect Continental influence in the birds), it may be that there is a pattern of exotic imports awaiting identification in Ireland in or about the 7th century BC.[7]

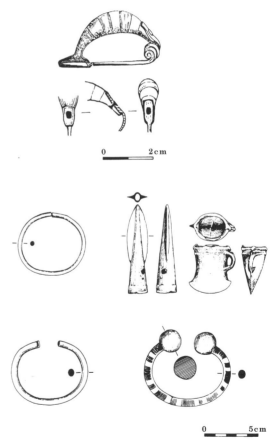

Fig. 133. Above. Italic leech-shaped safety-pin brooch or fibula from Ireland repaired with the addition of a riveted spring or pin. Below. Hoard with bronze spearhead, socketed axehead, two simple bracelets and an imported knobbed bracelet, from Kilmurry, Co. Kerry.

One find is relatively well documented. This is a small hoard of bronze artefacts from Kilmurry, near Castleisland, Co. Kerry, found in 1944 during quarrying operations (Fig. 133). It consisted of a small leaf-shaped spearhead, a bag-shaped socketed axehead, two simple penannular bracelets and a small knobbed bracelet with its outer body decorated with transverse grooves. Bracelets of this sort are known in the 7th and 6th centuries BC in various parts of France.[8] The association suggests that Dowris Phase bronzes may still have been in use around 600 BC or even 500 BC. However, the evidence for any later survival of Dowris Phase metalwork is very slight; the claim that a Class 4 sword bears traces of a scabbard form of the 3rd or 2nd century BC and is thus an indication of the very late survival of Dowris metalworking traditions should be treated with due caution; the same may be said of the miniature bronze socketed axe from Kilsmullan, Co. Fermanagh, associated with a stone

structure radiocarbon dated to 360-30 BC.[9] While the very late survival of Dowris Phase bronze working in some parts of Ireland cannot be ruled out, the limited evidence suggests that the late 7th century and the 6th century BC probably saw the displacement of bronze by iron.[10] This was a technological development which may well have initiated some significant social and economic changes.

THE EARLIEST IRON WORKING

A small number of iron objects have been considered to be early examples of the new technology and some are believed to be versions of well-known bronze types. Two looped and socketed axeheads are probably iron copies of the familiar bronze form but are from undated contexts. One, said to come from 'one of the Lough Mourne crannogs' in Co. Antrim (Fig. 134) has been made from a single piece of iron, forged flat, folded into a

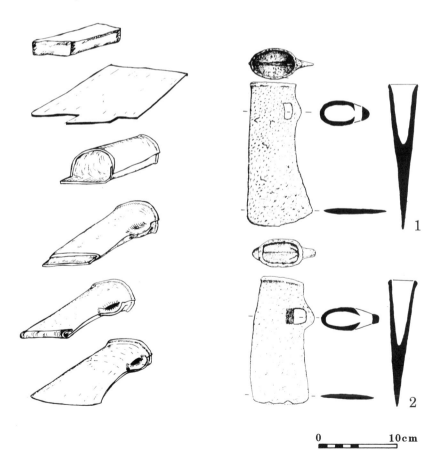

Fig. 134. Left. Method of manufacture of an iron socketed axe from Lough Mourne. Right. 1. Axe from Lough Mourne, Co. Antrim. 2. Axe from Toome, Co. Antrim.

cylinder, one end of which was then beaten flat. The loop was formed by pinching out a lobe of metal on one side of the completed socket and then punching a hole through it with a rectangular punch. It seems as if the smith went to considerable trouble to copy a bronze model even though a loop-less, rectangular-mouthed socketed form would have been simpler to make and equally effective, as an iron axe from Feerwore, Co. Galway, demonstrates.

The second example is from Toome, Co. Antrim (Fig. 134, 2) and was made in much the same way though the blade was formed not by folding over a tongue of metal but by welding the two faces together. Interestingly, even though older models were being copied, these two axes display a fairly sophisticated knowledge of the potential of iron to achieve a high degree of hardness when alloyed with carbon. The cutting edges of both have had carbon deliberately added, this carburization producing a superior metal approaching the quality of steel. Care was taken to position the carburized surfaces so that the steeled cutting edges were protected by more flexible metal with a lower carbon content.

Chemical analysis has shown that the Lough Mourne specimen was possibly made from Antrim ores and is unlikely to have been an import. Similar looped and socketed iron axeheads have been found in Britain where the same process of copying bronze prototypes occurred and where the earliest iron working is just as hard to find and equally difficult to date. The iron rivets identified on the Lisdrumturk, Co. Monaghan, bronze cauldron (Fig. 96) are obviously an instance of early iron working, though difficult to date precisely and possibly later repairs. The bronze patches secured with iron rivets on the Derrymacash, Co. Armagh, bucket are certainly secondary repairs. It has been claimed that a riveted sheet iron cauldron from Drumlane, Co. Cavan, may be early too though the use of multi-sheet construction and round-headed rivets is rather slender dating evidence.

An axehead from Feerwore, near Loughrea, Co. Galway, is of a simple socketed type (Fig. 135). Made from a single piece of iron, one end was forged into a blade while the rest was hammered out and folded over to form a rectangular socket, and here the smith had evidently mastered the

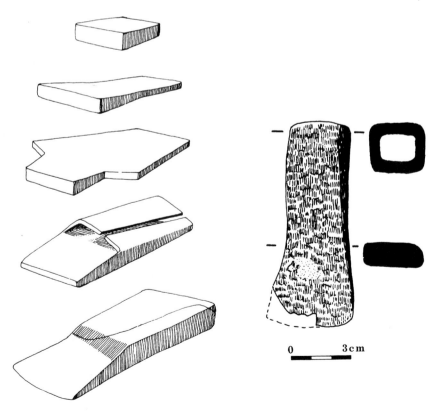

Fig. 135. Left. Method of manufacture of an iron socketed axe from Feerwore, Co. Galway. Right. The Feerwore axe.

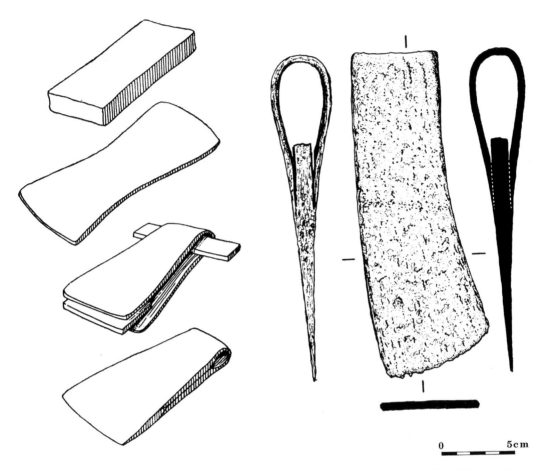

Fig. 136. Left. Method of manufacture of an iron shaft-hole axe. Right. One of three shaft-hole axes from Kilbeg, Co. Westmeath.

technique of expertly forging a right angle. It was found beneath the bank of a small ringfort and is not securely dated. Axes of this sort had a wide currency on the Continent from about the 3rd century BC and Barry Raftery suggests the Feerwore example might date to the late 2nd or early 1st century BC.

The date of a number of iron artefacts from the settlement at Rathtinaun, Co. Sligo, is uncertain but a shaft-hole axehead from there could possibly be of much the same date. It was rather crudely made but is nonetheless of complicated manufacture: a piece of iron was folded over and welded on to itself to make a socket, the welded area was covered by a flat plate hammered over both sides of the blade, the blade was then drawn down and folded back on itself and welded to the plate. As on the looped socketed axes, the blade edge was carburized.

Three other shaft-hole axes from Kilbeg, Co. Westmeath (Fig. 136) were of simpler manufacture being made of two pieces of iron, one folded over to form the socket with its two ends welded to the faces of a second which formed the blade. These were found with a pair of horse-pendants (one of bronze, one of iron), a type not easily dateable, but which may belong to the 1st century AD or thereabouts. These shaft-hole axes are a reminder that simple axe designs of a basic sort had a long lifespan and illustrate one of the consequences of the new technology. Percussive shaping reflecting the skills of individual smiths may now produce significant differences in shape in the one artefact type. Furthermore, the medium also imposed new and simpler lines on many artefacts producing basic forms of axe, chisel, knife and other implements which were to remain essentially unchanged for many centuries. A further complication, of course, is the susceptibility of iron to corrosion and decay which must explain to a great extent the scarcity of surviving material.

The problems of poor preservation are clearly demonstrated by the relatively small number of iron swords and spears which survive in comparison to the many hundreds of bronze examples. Indeed experimentation has shown that in certain bog conditions, the complete dissolution of an iron object could take place within a century.

An iron sword found in 1847 in the course of drainage in the River Shannon at Athlone, Co. Westmeath, has been claimed to be a 7th century BC Continental type (Fig. 131, 3) because, in particular, its haft was flat and its blade expanded towards the point and may have been leaf-shaped. But its triangular cross-section with slight midrib does not resemble the normal ribbed section of these iron swords as seen for instance on the only example known from Britain from the Llyn Fawr, Glamorgan, hoard. It is possible that the Athlone sword is an iron copy of an indigenous bronze Gündlingen sword and if its original length was about 60cm to 65cm then this would place it within the appropriate size range. Analysis also suggests that it could be an early piece, though low in carbon and therefore never a particularly effective weapon, its edges were cold-hammered to increase hardness, a technique which would have been familiar to a bronze smith.

The production of iron was a skilled process but required relatively simple equipment. Iron was extracted by heating the ore by burning charcoal in a small bowl-shaped furnace. This was a pit in the ground, covered in some way, possibly by clay or sods, with the required temperatures of 1100-1250° being achieved comparatively easily with a bellows. This smelting process would produce a deposit of slag which would accumulate at the bottom of the pit below a bloom. The bloom, a spongy mass of metallic iron, had to be reheated and carefully hammered to weld the iron particles together and to remove extraneous matter such as slag. Once this was done the smith had a piece of iron from which artefacts could be made. Small bowl furnaces have been found at Rathgall, Co. Wicklow, and Clogher, Co. Tyrone.[11]

If the Athlone sword dates to around 600 BC, and allowing for the poor survival rate of iron, it is still surprising that the next recognized group of iron swords should number only about 30 and should seem to date to a period spanning the last two or three centuries BC and the 1st century AD. An even smaller number of iron spearheads is preserved and, while many are virtually impossible to date with any degree of accuracy, a number

probably belong to this general period as well. The nature of the bronze industry changes too: in the main bronze is no longer used for weapons but is used instead for a range of personal ornaments, horse harness, ferrules and other decorative attachments.

The remarkable scarcity of archaeological material dateable to the period 600 to 300 BC is not solely an Irish problem, there is some decrease in the number of metalwork finds in Britain and in parts of the Continent as well. In Ireland, this scarcity seems more acute but this may be due to several factors including not just the virtual cessation of metalwork deposition but also the absence of a burial tradition which included the practice of placing grave goods with the remains of the dead and the failure to identify and excavate settlement sites in any number. The latter deficiency will, no doubt, be remedied in time.

DISCONTINUITY AND CHANGE OR CONTINUITY AND INNOVATION?

The apparent demise of the bronze industry at this time would seem to be a dramatic transformation reflecting at least some equally significant social and economic developments. This may well be what is implied by the disappearance of a whole range of gold and bronze types from the archaeological record. If, as seems likely, these metals had an important role in the maintenance of status relationships, then the adoption of iron working may indeed have disrupted this structure, reduced the value of gold and bronze in this sphere and precipitated a decline in associated customs like hoard deposition.

Why a new and potentially disruptive technology should be adopted is a difficult question. There are several possibilities and many years ago the answer seemed a deceptively simple one as, for example, when R. A. S. Macalister asserted that this change was brought about by the immigration of Celtic peoples about 400 BC: the invading Celts subduing the aboriginal inhabitants with superior iron weapons. But there is no good archaeological evidence to support the theory of an influx of new peoples on any scale. Another possibility is that a shortage of bronze might have prompted the search for some other metal – but it seems that local copper resources may have been sufficient for Irish requirements. Of course, if early iron objects had a prestigious value, then their acquisition along with the new technology would be just another step in a familiar acquisitive process by elite elements of society. But such prestigious early iron items are conspicuous by their absence and numerous bronze objects, notably the local versions of the Gündlingen sword, demonstrate both the continuing value of bronze and likely contacts with iron-using communities elsewhere. As already mentioned, these contacts, part of a long established network of communications between Ireland and Britain, are the probable mechanism by which knowledge of the new technology was eventually transmitted. There is the intriguing possibility that the impetus for the widespread substitution of one locally available metal for another came not from the elites but from other lower levels in the social hierarchy. Small though the sample is, it may be significant that socketed and shaft-hole axes should figure so prominently and it is possible that hewers of wood rather wielders of swords were the principal beneficiaries of the new iron technology and possibly its main proponents too. The potential of iron to supply a range of basic tools must have been quickly realized. If there were any disadvantageous differences in the relative hardness of bronze and iron edged tools, and this may not have been as significant as has been claimed, then these were offset by the ready availability of iron ore.

Iron ores are widespread in Ireland (Fig. 137) and sources include lateritic ores in Antrim basalts, pyrites in Co. Wicklow and siderite around Lough Allen in Co. Leitrim and at the aptly named Slieve Anierin or 'Iron Mountain' near Drumshanbo. Bog ores may also have been a plentiful source and theoretically ore can form in any peat deposit where conditions are suitable. Substantial quantities have been identified in recent times in Counties Donegal, Tyrone and Roscommon. To what extent these different sources were exploited in ancient times is not known but the general availability of iron must have offered many small communities the possibility of manufacturing their own tools and weapons free of the constraints imposed by the limited and controlled supplies of copper and tin.

This development would no doubt have caused some considerable discomfiture to those individuals or communities who controlled the raw materials of the bronze industry. If rank and power depended on this control then there could have been a collapse in the various exchange systems and

political alliances which linked communities, even leading to a more fragmented social landscape by the end of the 6th century BC as has been surmised elsewhere in Atlantic Europe.[12]

At present the Irish evidence provides few clues but it is possible that rank and power did not depend solely on access to supplies of a particular metal and dramatic though the disappearance of so many bronze artefact types appears to be, it does not necessarily follow that there was a wider socio-economic collapse since bronze was probably just one element, though admittedly a prestigious one, in a wider spectrum of activity. There may have been some dislocation but if, for instance, wealth and status also depended to a significant degree on cattle or sheep then another order may quickly have asserted itself.

There was some dislocation in the votive sphere as the halt in the deposition of fine metalwork indicates. It is possible that other materials may have replaced the gold and bronze or different rituals entirely may have developed. In any event offerings of fine metalwork reappear in the archaeological record after 300 BC but on a much reduced scale. The hiatus between the two episodes of metalwork deposition is one of the puzzles of Irish archaeology.

Fig. 137. Distribution of iron ores in Ireland with hatched areas depicting the major sources in Antrim and Wicklow.

THE PROBLEM OF THE CELTS

As already noted, the arrival of Celtic-speaking peoples was once a popular explanation for the beginnings of iron working and for the social and economic changes which followed. It was also a convenient explanation for the historical fact that by Roman times Ireland, like Britain and much of western Europe, spoke a Celtic language or languages. Since terms like 'Celtic Ireland' and the 'Celtic Iron Age' are popularly used to describe the Ireland of the last few centuries BC and the early pre-Christian centuries AD, and since the study of Celtic literature and our knowledge of the Celtic peoples of other parts of Europe have deeply coloured our interpretation of the archaeology of later prehistoric Ireland, the problem of the Celts must be briefly addressed.

It has long been believed that the Celtic languages, represented today by modern Irish, Welsh, Scots Gaelic and Breton, are descended from an ancestral language-family which developed in a Continental homeland from whence its speakers spread to various parts of the Celtic world including Britain and Ireland. This is an enduring belief and it is still claimed in some quarters that the first speakers of a Celtic tongue arrived in Ireland as late as about 200 BC. The problem with such assertions is that Irish prehistoric archaeology reveals no trace whatever of any significant incursion of new peoples. Rather it demonstrates a considerable degree of cultural continuity and invariably offers other more plausible explanations for the discontinuities that do exist in the archaeological record. There is simply no archaeological trace of the large-scale immigration necessary not just to implant a new language but also to eradicate virtually all traces of the pre-existing language as well.

The genetic, family tree, model of linguistic reconstruction, which implies fission and divergence from a common ancestor as the significant factor in language change has supported and has been supported by migratory archaeological theories. The inevitable equation of ancient Celtic languages such as Goidelic or Brittonic with a people such as 'Q-Celts' and 'P-Celts' or with aspects of material culture has had a long history. In Ireland, various writers have, in the past, equated 'the coming of the Celts' with the introduction of such diverse archaeological phenomena as the 'Beaker Folk', the appearance of bronze swords, the knowledge of iron or a Celtic La Tène art style. The debate has been a prolonged and convoluted one.

There seems to be general agreement among linguistic scholars that the Celtic family of languages emerged sometime in the last millennium BC, though ironically it is archaeological evidence that is often presented in support of this general date. With rare exceptions, however, there has been a great reluctance among Celtic linguists to consider alternative models of language diffusion and migrating Celts remain the favoured explanation.

Prehistoric archaeology, by its very definition, cannot reveal what languages were spoken at any time before written records appear, bronze swords are just as mute as stones. Archaeology can offer models of linguistic change which are at least in keeping with archaeological evidence and interpretation. A non-genetic model of the prehistory of European languages, in which the rate of the creation and demise of languages will change through time due to a variety of social processes, would envisage the existence of large language areas in early prehistoric times but with increasing sedentism and population growth and the formation of small, self-sufficient territorial groups, there would have been a considerable increase in the number of languages spoken in Europe from about 5000 BC. Language proliferation would have halted and then declined in the 3rd and 2nd millennia BC with the gradual formation of fewer, larger language groups.

The emergence of the Celtic languages in later prehistory would be due to an intensification of a complex series of processes operating across parts of Europe since the 3rd millennium BC: these would have included economic intensification, increasing polity size, developing gender and social stratification, and increasingly active trade along coasts and rivers. As Colin Renfrew has suggested, the European 'homeland' of the Celts would be constituted by the full extent of the area where Celtic languages came to be spoken. He proposed a process of parallel linguistic development precipitated by the interaction of the elite elements of ranked societies.

While Ireland had its own regional idiosyncrasies, there is good evidence that it participated at an elite level in wider European fashions in later prehistory and that the Irish Sea, far from being a barrier to communication, may have been a focal area for interaction and exchange, displaying evidence for recurring cycles of contact over long periods of time. The prehistoric reality may have been a constant pattern of communication which must have had interminable consequences in many spheres not least in terms of linguistic developments. The emergence of a Celtic language in Ireland was arguably not the result of mass immigration but the culmination of a long process of social and economic interaction between Ireland and Britain, and between these islands and adjacent parts of Continental Europe. This process does not exclude the possibility of movements of people, these may be difficult or impossible to detect in the archaeological record but if such movements did occur in later prehistoric times, then they only gave added impetus to diachronic linguistic developments long underway. Other possibilities have been suggested, of course, and it has been argued that changes were more abrupt and that influential immigrants did initiate significant language change in, for example, those enigmatic centuries between 600 and 300 BC.[13]

Whatever the outcome of this debate many archaeologists would consider it quite appropriate to speak of 'Celtic Ireland' after 300 BC and, if by these words is meant a 'Celtic-speaking Ireland', there would then be no further disagreement. But the distinction between these two phrases encapsulates yet another debate about another stimulating Celtic problem.

Celtic-speaking peoples occupied large areas of Europe in the last few centuries BC and there is no dispute that Ireland was a Celtic-speaking land at this time as well. To the Greeks, these *keltoi* were one of four great barbarian peoples of the ancient world and all of the known northern world was occupied by just Celts and Scythians. Even though they were linguistically related, it is disputable if the peoples whom the Greeks called Celts ever considered themselves to belong to an ethnically identifiable group. The modern definition of the ancient Celts is a scholarly and retrospective one and in great measure a relatively recent construct. The 19th century saw the development of both the genetic family tree model of linguistic development and the idea of distinct biologically-defined racial groups. The Celts were given an archaeological identity with the discovery of characteristic artefacts in a great cemetery at Hallstatt, near Salzburg, in Austria and at La Tène, on Lake Neuchâtel, in Switzerland.

These artefacts were part of the body of evidence which enabled the construction of the first detailed chronology of the 'Iron Age' which was divided into the two major phases named after these two sites. The discovery of La Tène swords, or brooches, or art, was then considered to be the material remains of the Celtic peoples known to Greek and Roman writers. Whether in Central Europe or in Ireland, La Tène material was simple confirmation of the presence of Celts and an illustration of how these people shared not just a material cultural assemblage but religious beliefs and social structures as well. This cultural-historical approach appeared to demonstrate the spread of Celtic peoples across a wide area of Europe and a Celtic 'homeland' was usually placed in the region of the upper Rhine and Danube where La Tène art styles developed. The concept of a 'Celtic World' extending from Ireland to central Europe and beyond is therefore of recent vintage and the extent to which, in this world, there were common factors in material culture, in rural economy and in social institutions is now the subject of some healthy scrutiny. Despite their common linguistic stock, there are great variations in subsistence and economy and in social structures discernible across the 'Celtic World'. The supposed homogeneity often implied by the adjective 'Celtic' is now being questioned by archaeologists conscious of these contrasts and concerned that its too ready acceptance has diverted attention from the difficult questions posed by difference and diversity.

Some elements of the fragmentary ethnographic accounts of Greek and Roman writers appear to be corroborated in evidence from early Irish and Welsh literature almost a thousand years later and these parallels may have given the 'Celtic World' a misleadingly cohesive and timeless image. The Classical references need to be assessed with caution; it is possible, for instance, that some references in Greek sources such as Poseidonius and some similar features in early Irish literature may have been quite separately inspired by heroic episodes in Homeric tradition. Other elements of the later Irish tales are probably imaginative fiction, they may be depictions of an ideal world for it seems as if the learned classes of Medieval Ireland thought it quite a proper thing to offer their perceptions of what the prehistoric past should have been like or even to rewrite the past to make a moral point or to support a political cause. Their accounts, like Homeric allusions, are obviously an unreliable guide to late prehistoric Ireland.

Nonetheless, in the last few centuries BC a Celtic-speaking Ireland was demonstrably in contact with a Celtic-speaking Britain, and possibly with the Continent as well, and the patterns of contact were probably broadly similar to the patterns that obtained since the later second millennium BC at least. The significance of these later prehistoric contacts needs to be critically assessed and doubtless, as in earlier times, there were similar or shared social and religious customs in later prehistory. Some would now argue that these are best identified or confirmed without the imposition of preconceptions about such things as a specifically Celtic society or a Celtic religion with a pan-European dimension.[14]

The period from about 300 BC to an ill-defined point in the early centuries AD has been variously called the Irish La Tène horizon and the Celtic Iron Age. It is a time when novel metal types, some – but by no means all – with British or Continental affinities, are once again prominent in the archaeological record. Equally remarkable, however, is the reappearance of a limited range of quite exceptional metalwork and, albeit on a reduced scale, the reappearance of depositional customs of the sort last encountered in the Dowris Phase. A small number of hoards, probably spanning a number of centuries, may faintly echo the extravagant practices half a millennium or more before.

THE KNOCK HOARD

Two gold objects were found in 1861 in the course of turf cutting in a bog in Knock townland, Co. Roscommon, about 8km north-east of Ballinasloe. They were found in a wooden box which was not preserved and for many years were believed to have been found near Clonmacnoise. The objects are torcs of quite different type, one is a buffer torc, the other a ribbon torc. The buffer torc is a celebrated and much discussed piece (Fig. 138) belonging a well-known British and Continental type of penannular neck ring with broad, flat, expanded, circular terminals or 'buffers'. The Knock example is a version where the terminals have been joined together to form a single element. It basically consists of two semicircular hollow tubes of sheet gold which fit into hollow decorative expansions at front and back. At the front (and worn beneath the chin), a biconical element, the conjoined buffers, is flanked by bosses one of which is perforated to take a pin which secured one detachable tubular section

of the torc. At the back, a rectangular element is decorated with pronounced convex mouldings which form in part a pair of interlocking oval loops ornamented with a sinuous pattern of applied gold wire. The decoration on the flanking bosses of the biconical element at the front consists of pairs of repoussé S-scrolls, that on the central part of the biconical piece consists of two narrow panels of irregular, asymmetrical, sinuous tendrils with spiral bosses. The background is finely stippled.

This type of torc and the repoussé ornament, in particular the asymmetrical tendril motif, find general parallels on the Continent in the early La Tène period and, if not an import as sometimes suggested, it was made by someone familiar with torcs and other fine metalwork in the Rhineland around or shortly after 300 BC.[15] It thus represents the earliest evidence for contact with or emulation of exponents of La Tène or 'Celtic' art. This remarkable art style developed in eastern France and western Germany, in the region of the Marne and the Rhine, in the 5th century BC and is found mainly on fine metalwork in rich aristocratic burials. Many of the motifs, like the tendril, are derived from Classical plant motifs, sometimes transformed almost beyond recognition. Some motifs are deliberately ambiguous and difficult to classify, and some may have had magical significance.

The gold ribbon torc is loosely twisted and has unusual hollow pear-shaped terminals.

THE SOMERSET HOARD

A second gold torc of the ribbon variety comes from a hoard of bronze and iron objects found in a field in the townland of Somerset, south of Ballinasloe, Co. Galway (Fig. 139). Unfortunately the hoard was dispersed after discovery and the iron objects were not preserved but several bronzes dating to the last century BC or the 1st century AD were recovered. These include five circular mounts, a fibula, part of a horse pendant and the handle of a bronze cup or bowl. The torc had been coiled and placed inside a sort of box formed by two of the mounts. It is fairly tightly spiral twisted and has unusual straight terminals of rectangular cross-section.[16]

The unique Coolmanagh association of a flange-twisted torc and a ribbon torc (Fig. 77) and the chronological difficulties posed by ribbon torcs themselves were briefly considered in Chapter 6. As

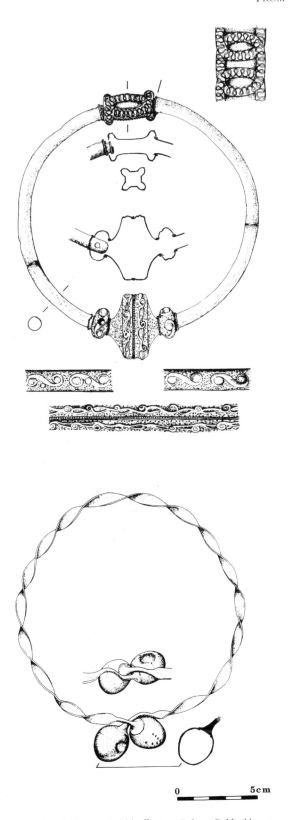

Fig. 138. The Knock, Co. Roscommon, hoard. Above. Gold buffer torc. Below. Gold ribbon torc.

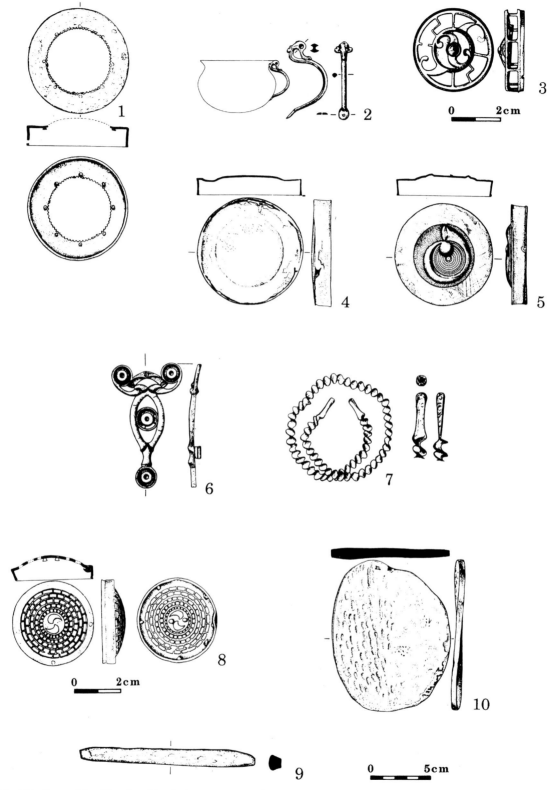

Fig. 139. Some of the objects found in the Somerset, Co. Galway, hoard. 1, 3-5, 8. Bronze mounts. 2. Cup handle. 6. Fibula of Navan type. 7. Gold ribbon torc. 9-10. Bronze ingot and cake.

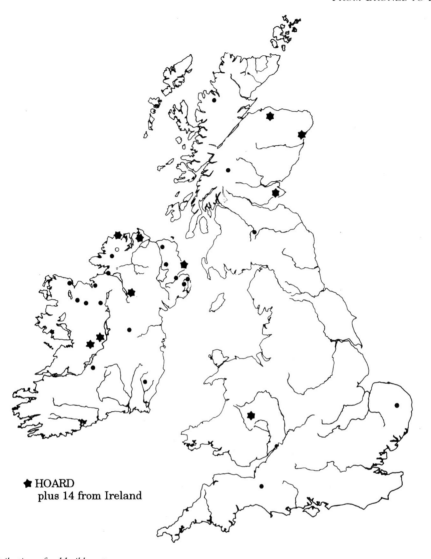

Fig. 140. Distribution of gold ribbon torcs.

we saw there are some 62 examples from Ireland which George Eogan would place in his Bishopsland Phase. There are also about fifty examples recorded from Scotland with a few from Wales and England (Fig. 140). Of all these Peter Northover notes only five examples, three from one Welsh find and three from Ireland, including the Coolmanagh find, which he feels can be fairly confidently dated to the Bishopsland Phase. Gold analyses have shown that ribbon torcs generally contain traces of platinum which when combined with the values for copper and tin demonstrate that the gold used is quite different from the rest of the gold of the Bishopsland Phase and Richard Warner is convinced that this confirms a date in the later centuries BC. There are other minor typological

clues to support this late date: a hooked terminal, as found on ribbon torcs, occur on two spiral twisted gold bracelets found with Roman material at Newgrange and a Scottish ribbon torc from Law Farm, Morayshire, has three decorative gold globules on one terminal akin to the granulated ornament on two imported necklaces in the Broighter hoard.

At present the claim for a late chronological position for a large number of ribbon torcs rests mainly on the evidence of gold analyses. If this evidence is accepted then the bulk of these objects could form a major component in the depositional rituals of a period in which gold objects and gold hoards are otherwise relatively uncommon. Poorly documented hoards, each containing a number of ribbon torcs, are recorded from Largatreany, Co. Donegal, Derryvony, Co. Cavan, and Ballylumford, Co. Antrim, two of them at least being dry-land finds.[17] Of the many single finds of ribbon torcs, several have been found in bogs but the majority have no details of discovery recorded. It would be unwise to simply assume a votive purpose but this does remain a possibility. Gabriel Cooney and Eoin Grogan have demonstrated how the contexts of other objects such as horse bits and pendants, and iron swords, follow Dowris Phase patterns with rivers, lakes and bogs continuing to serve as a focus for ritual offerings of metalwork.[18]

THE BROIGHTER HOARD

The most exceptional hoard of the period is undoubtedly that found at Broighter, near Limavady, Co. Derry, in 1896. Seven gold objects were discovered during ploughing near the shore of Lough Foyle and it is possible that they had been intentionally deposited at a spot on a raised beach which was originally just below the old shore line of the lough. The hoard comprised a fine buffer torc, a simpler twisted torc and a fragment of another, two gold wire necklaces, a small bowl of sheet gold and a model boat also of sheet gold (Fig. 141).

The miniature gold boat, just under 20cm in length, originally had nine benches for rowers and 18 oars with rowlocks, most of which survive along with one steering oar at the stern, three forked barge poles, a grappling iron or anchor and a mast with yard arm. It gives us a very general idea of what one type of sailing vessel of the 1st century BC may have been like, propelled by sail or oarsmen, or punted in shallow waters. It is usually assumed to be a model of a hide-built boat but, if it is to scale, the length of the original may have been about 15m and could therefore have been plank-built.

The small bowl-shaped vessel is more or less hemispherical and has four rings for suspension; it may be a model of a cauldron. The wire necklaces are imports from the Roman world, ultimately from the Mediterranean region, and may date to the period from the 1st century BC to the 3rd century AD. One is a triple strand necklace formed of single-looped gold chain work, the other is a single strand piece made of a chain of multiple loops.

The twisted torc and the fragmentary example are each made of a twisted gold rod of circular cross-section which was spiral twisted with a narrow gold wire. The terminals are of a hook and

eye type. This form of torc may be an Irish version of a type of neck ornament, made by spiral twisting two rods of gold together, found in Britain in the 1st century BC.

The buffer torc from the Broighter hoard is a magnificent object and one of the masterpieces of artwork in the La Tène style. It is a hollow tubular neck-ring of hammered sheet gold, now in two halves, with separate buffer terminals held in place by gold pins. The ends of the terminals could be locked together by rotating them and locking a T-shaped tenon on one into a corresponding slot on the other. A small number of tubular torcs of this general sort are known from Britain, Belgium, France and Switzerland, and are well dated to the 1st century BC.

The tubular portion of the torc is richly decorated with engraved and relief ornament. The motifs were defined by incised lines and were brought into relief by depressing the background, this was mainly done by hammering and the surface was subsequently polished to remove hammer marks. It is worth noting that this technique of working of gold from the front was part of the goldsmith's repertoire since the Dowris Phase. The superb relief design consists of a series of slender trumpet motifs, lentoid (pointed oval) bosses and spiral roundels. The overall pattern, mainly formed by the attenuated trumpets which distantly echo earlier vegetal tendrils, basically consists of two overlapping S-scrolls on each half of the torc. Though essentially a symmetrical composition, the effect of sinuous movement is accentuated by a static background of engraved compass-drawn cross-hatching.

The curvilinear decoration on the torc is undoubtedly insular and implies a skilled workshop somewhere in the north of Ireland shortly before or after the turn of the millennium with craftsmen who must have been in contact with others in Britain and even further afield. It has been suggested that the terminals were imported and added to a later piece of native work but this seems an implausible scenario, the granular decoration, for instance, could conceivably have been copied from that on the imported triple strand necklace.

Elusive or ambiguous imagery is a frequent component of La Tène art and Richard Warner has argued that some of the trumpet curves and spirals combine to represent stylized sea-horses (Fig. 141). He has also speculated that the hoard was a votive

Fig. 141. The Broighter, Co. Derry, hoard. 1. Gold buffer torc with (on right) suggested interpretation of some of the curvilinear motifs. 2-3. Gold twisted torcs. 4-5. Gold wire necklaces. 6. Gold model boat with oars and (on right) three barge poles and a grappling iron or anchor. 7. Gold vessel or model cauldron.

offering to an undersea god: the possible hippomorphic element having some connection with the sea god Manannán mac Lir who in various legends is associated with a horse capable of journeying over land and sea, with Lough Foyle, sea travel, and a large cauldron. It is quite possible that the various elements of the Broighter hoard had some individual and collective symbolism. The exceptional decorated torc may have been more than just a finely crafted status piece, it could have been a magical talisman, even a symbol of divinity. It has been suggested more than once that some special torcs may have been placed on idol rather than on human necks.[19]

HORSE HARNESS

It would be unwise to assume that most archaeological deposits of metal objects necessarily have a ritual explanation but when it comes to deciphering consistent patterns of deposition it is difficult to ignore this possibility. We tend to forget that in the prehistoric past, as in more recent Medieval times, the world and everything in it was richly invested with magical and superstitious meaning. After 300 BC a different spectrum of fine metalwork has a role in the votive sphere and items of horse harness, apparently highly prized objects, now seem to play a significant part in the resumption of depositional practices. A proportion of this metalwork was seemingly deliberately placed in river, lake and bog and harness hoards are now the commonest type of collective deposit: of 22 hoards, no less than 13 are hoards containing either bridle bits or pendants or both. Unfortunately approximately 68% of this material is unprovenanced and without details of discovery. Of the 27 horse bits with recorded provenance, three came from rivers, four from lakes and seven from bogs, in all about 52% from watery contexts. Of pendants with recorded contexts, the figure is about 75%.

BRIDLE BITS

The great majority of horse bits are of bronze and, surprisingly, they are the commonest surviving metal artefact from the period. Two bronze examples have iron rings and two iron bits are known, an unprovenanced fragmentary find and that possible example from Aughinish.

The typical bronze bit has a mouth-piece made of three links with two side rings for the attachment of the reins; the three-link section is formed of a small centre link of approximately figure-of-eight shape with two longer side links. Three-link bits of bronze or iron are also found in Britain but are rare on the Continent apart from a number in north-eastern France. In contrast to most British bits, the holes in the side links of Irish examples are in the same plane (Fig. 142, 1).

While there are differences in the shape of both centre links and rein rings, variations in the shape of the side links have formed the basis for the most recent classification but the degree to which these typological differences are of chronological significance is uncertain. The simplest and presumed early side links are few in number, they are hollow cast, sometimes retaining their clay casting cores, lacking any decoration and are horizontally symmetrical (Type A). An example found in a well-known votive deposit of metalwork in a bog at Llyn Cerrig Bach, Anglesea, Wales, may date to the 2nd or 1st century BC but the material from this find spans a number of centuries and obviously it provides no precise indication of date.

A common form of side link is slightly bowed and has a cast decorative V-shaped feature or moulding above the inner perforation which attaches to the centre link (Type B). This is the most numerous type (about 42% of the total) and there is considerable variety in detail, some side links are hollow cast but others are of solid bronze. Decoration on the outer ends is rare and while some V-mouldings are quite simple, others are more elaborate and occasionally seem to resemble duck's heads. That this ambiguous ornithomorphism was sometimes deliberate is demonstrated by an unprovenanced fragment (Fig. 143) which has what seems to be a bird's head at the inner end of the side links and an extraordinary stylized human mask at the other end of the one complete side link. Both motifs are ambiguous, however, and also resemble stylized plant forms found in earlier La Tène art. The bit shows evident signs of use and wear and the bird's head motifs would be invisible when the object was in use – and indeed any decoration on the outer ends would be obscured too. Why a bird's head design should be placed in a horse's mouth is mystifying but may imply that some of these designs were more than just ornamental and had some magical charge. Strange human or animal masks occur on the link ends of another unprovenanced bit.

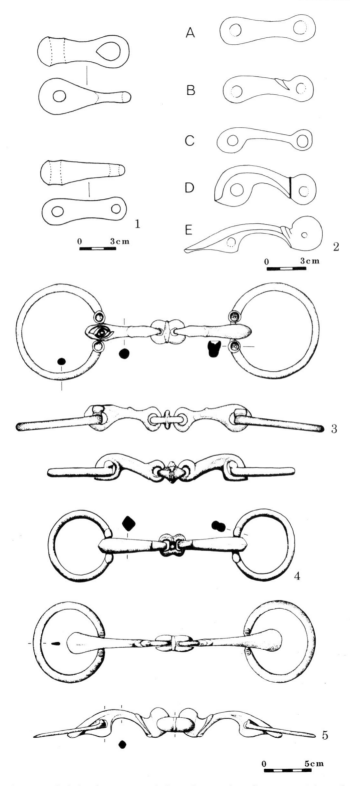

Fig. 142. Bronze horse bits. 1. Side links showing British form above with perforations at right angles and Irish form below with perforations in the same plane. 2. Typology (A-E) of side links. 3. Type B bit with asymmetrical ornament from Lough Beg, Co. Antrim. 4. Type D bit from Loughran's Island, River Bann, Co. Derry. 5. Type E bit from Tulsk, Co. Roscommon.

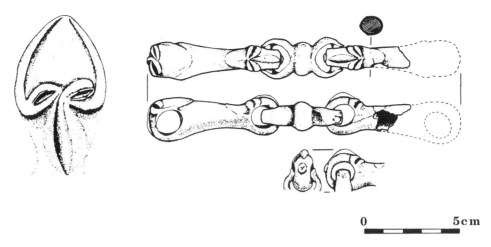

Fig. 143. Fragmentary bronze bit with stylized bird's heads at inner ends of side links and stylized human mask at the one surviving outer end.

A few simple, solid cast, very slender side links (Type C) are without decoration and if they have V-mouldings these are elementary. Links of Type D (representing about 21% of the total) are sharply bowed and are frequently decorated on their outer ends. This decoration may be either cast or incised but one unprovenanced link has its decoration created by cutting away a number of fields for champlevé, inlaid, enamel. The most developed side links (also about 21%) are markedly curved (Type E) with a pronounced central spine and they expand in width towards their outer ends. V-mouldings are prominent but only a few have cast decoration on their outer ends. Examples such as those from Attymon, Co. Galway (Fig. 145) probably date to the early centuries AD.

Most of these horse bits show signs of extensive wear and much skill and ingenuity were sometimes displayed in undertaking repairs. A pair of bits from Streamstown, Co. Westmeath, between them were repaired no less than twelve separate times. Their manufacture was a skilled process involving the casting and linking together of five separate elements. They were evidently highly valued and this may be one reason why they were eventually selected as votive offerings even in a fragmentary condition. Presumably their iron counterparts were commoner but were not favoured in this way. Of course, leather and wooden harness and items like antler cheek pieces could well have been widely used as well and may have had a long history. Thus the appearance of bronze bits in such numbers does not necessarily mean that horse riding suddenly became a popular pastime though they may indicate

a greater concern with expert horse management. Compared with two-link bits, the three-link type is considered to have a milder action, less severe on the horse's mouth, and may imply the use of a finer breed, more sensitive to skilled control. The centre link and the curved side links of Types D and E may have been designed to give greater adjustability, depending on how they were worn they offer a variable mouth-piece width of between 13cm and 16cm. While such general mouth-piece dimensions may indicate a relatively small horse of pony size, it is possible that mouth width may have no correlation with withers height and 'broad-faced' and 'narrow-faced' breeds may have co-existed.[20]

PENDANTS

A series of Y-shaped pendants are a peculiarly Irish type of harness piece, unknown elsewhere, and with one exception are all of bronze (Fig. 144). Various sorts of pendant pieces of horse harness are known on the Continent but nothing exactly like the Irish objects. These Y-shaped objects are puzzling artefacts basically consisting of a finely cast stem and a pair of prongs; the overall length is usually 28cm to 32cm and the distance between the prongs between 12cm and 16cm – but it may be as narrow as 7.8cm. Two basic types have been recognized: Type 1 are rarely decorated and have separate terminals cast onto the prongs; these terminals are usually hollow but of the same general design as the stem terminal and have inward projecting loops. Type 2 pendants have perforated prong terminals and decoration may occur on these and on the stem terminal which is often knobbed.

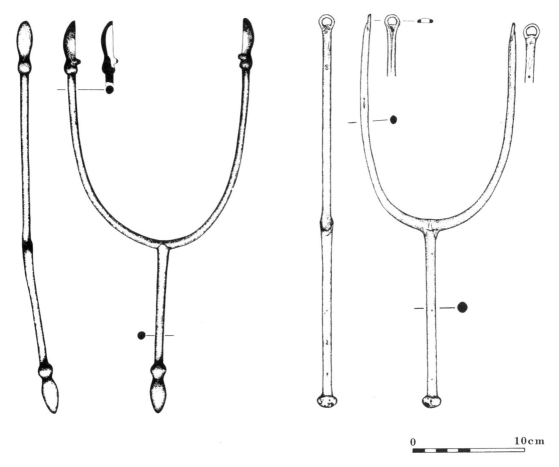

Fig. 144. Bronze pendants. Left. Type 1 from the River Boyne, Moyfin, Co. Meath. Right. Type 2 found in a ploughed field with a horse bit at Clongill, Co. Meath.

These objects were clearly meant to be attached to something, some apparently show signs of wear. Since they have been found with bridle bits, there is little doubt that they were some part of horse harness but their precise function remains uncertain. They have been thought to be head-pieces, curbs, leading pieces and even spurs but, as Barry Raftery has pointed out, the least unlikely explanation is that they were pendants, suspended beneath the horse's mouth and used as leading pieces on ceremonial occasions.

Not all bits and pendants were used in horse riding. Three matching pairs of bits and two pairs of pendants show that some at least may have been used for paired draught, worn by a yoked pair of horses presumably pulling a cart or chariot. Asymmetric decoration on a few bits (as on Lough Beg, Co. Antrim: Fig. 142, 3) and on a pendant may indicate that these pieces were parts of sets of two as well. A good illustration of this pairing is a hoard of two bits and two pendants found at a depth of over 7m near the bottom of a bog near Attymon, Co. Galway (Fig. 145). Both bits have identical cast curvilinear decoration and show signs of wear. Curvilinear decoration also occurs on the flattened perforated terminals and the knobbed stem terminal of the pendants. It is most unlikely that this discrete assemblage of just horse bits and pendants could be anything other than a deliberate votive offering placed at a considerable depth in a bog.

The general date of these bits and pendants is not easily determined. Bits may have been used from the 2nd century BC to the early centuries AD and the pendants were probably fashionable in the early centuries AD and possibly earlier. Decorative details, like the curvilinear designs on the Attymon bronzes, are obviously meagre dating evidence though the pattern on the side links finds parallels on Romano-British metalwork of the 2nd or 3rd centuries AD. The discovery of a copy of an Irish three link

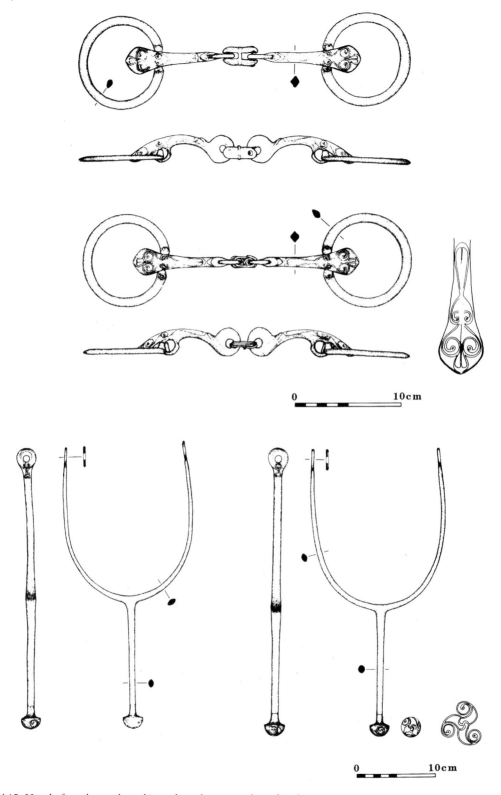

Fig. 145. Hoard of two bronze horse bits and two bronze pendants found near Attymon, Co. Galway. The illustrated details of the decoration on the ends of the side links and the stem terminals of the pendants are not to scale.

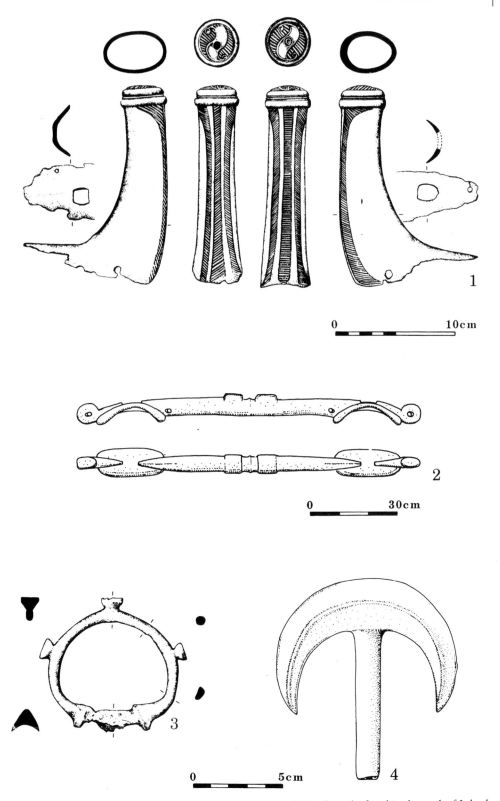

Fig. 146. 1. Two bronze yoke mounts from Lough Gur, Co. Limerick. 2. Wooden yoke found in the north of Ireland.
3. Bronze terret from Co. Antrim. 4. Bronze linchpin found near Dunmore, Co. Galway.

Type E bit in far-away Romania may reflect the movement of a Roman legion from Britain to that part of the Continent around 88 AD.[21]

CART OR CHARIOT FITMENTS

The pairs of bits and pendants just mentioned imply the use of pairs of horses for traction but fitments for the vehicles in question are remarkably scarce. Two-wheeled chariots are known from Britain and the Continent and were probably used in Ireland too but evidence is still lacking. Of course a scarcity of metal fitments does not mean a scarcity of wheeled vehicles and metal wagon fitments are not all that common in Britain or on the Continent either. Two bronze objects said to have been found on an island in Lough Gur, Co. Limerick (Fig. 146) are probably yoke mounts. Of cast bronze they are similar but not identical pieces each with cast S-shaped scrolls decorating their tips. Once thought to be horn caps or hand-grips at the rear of chariots, it is now believed objects like these decorated the upturned ends of some yokes and were similar to the wooden knobs found on some examples. An unprovenanced wooden yoke, found somewhere in the north of Ireland, is one of a number believed to date to this period.

One bronze terret, a guide for reins mounted on some types of yoke, was found somewhere in Co. Antrim and has close analogies in southern Scotland. The large rectangular perforations on the Lough Gur objects might have held attachments for terrets like this. A bronze linchpin for securing a wheel hub to an axle comes from Dunmore, Co. Galway.[22]

WEAPONRY

A limited number of swords and spears are known, a striking contrast with the large quantities recorded in the Dowris Phase. Some 30 iron swords form a varied and rather imprecisely dated assemblage. The inevitable problems posed by corroded iron mean that blade shapes are often difficult to determine and the identification of swords of late prehistoric date often rests on rudimentary distinguishing features such as short size and parallel-sided blades. However the presence of distinctive arched mounts or hilt-guards, a feature of Continental and British La Tène period swords, is an important characteristic detail (Fig. 147). Blades are parallel-sided, tapering gently to a point, with cross-sections of varied form which may be lozenge-shaped, a flat pointed oval or, in a few cases, with midrib and flanking grooves as on a fine example found in Ballinderry bog, Co. Westmeath (Fig. 147, 3).

The hilt-guards are usually curving pieces of hammered or cast bronze often with a campanulate or bell-shaped profile (which may be steeply arched or a shallow curve); a few are decorated and the Ballinderry example bears raised trumpet motifs on both faces. The hilt-guard on a sword from Knockaulin, Co. Kildare, is heavily corroded and may be of iron. A small group of swords have organic hilt-guards of materials such as antler and may represent a distinct type (Fig. 147, 1). One of these thicker organic hilt-guards is depicted on a small wooden model of a sword found in a bog at Ballykilmurry, Co. Wicklow, which also has a prominent sub-triangular pommel. Made of yew (with an unexplained projection on its blade), this may be a toy sword but is important because it appears to have a skeumorphic representation of an arched metal hilt-guard of La Tène type below the organic hilt-guard implying that those swords with the latter feature may be of this date too (Fig. 147, 4). A few other strands of evidence point to a possible late La Tène date for large oval antler pommels like that on a fragmentary sword found somewhere in the area of Edenderry, Co. Offaly, which has an organic hilt-guard as well as a tubular grip of bone (Fig. 147, 5). A couple of pommels of this sort have been found in Scotland and it seems probable that both these prominent pommels and organic hilt-guards are features of a late Irish-Scottish sword series perhaps dating to the early centuries AD.

A unique Irish find is a bronze sword hilt dredged up in a fishing net from the seabed in Ballyshannon Bay, Co. Donegal, about 1916. When found it still had its blade attached and this was completely encrusted with a marine deposit of sand and shells. The hollow cast bronze hilt is of stylized human form (Fig. 147, 6). Such swords with anthropoid hilts are known in Britain and on the Continent and the Ballyshannon find has been considered an import representing direct contact between the west of Ireland and France. This is by no means certain and it could even have been acquired in Britain or be a local copy. It certainly implies coastal traffic of some description in or around the 1st century BC.

The Irish swords are remarkable in one particular respect: where blade lengths can be established they vary from about 46cm, as on the Ballinderry

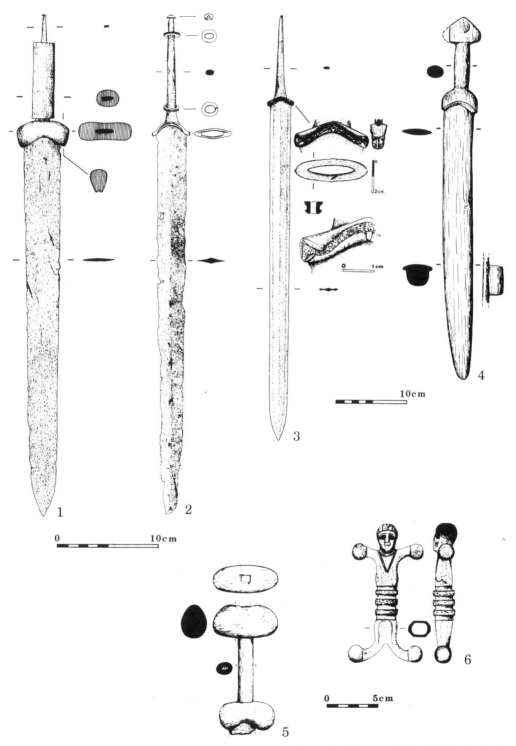

Fig. 147. 1. Unprovenanced iron sword with flat blade, bone grip and hilt-guard. 2. Iron sword found in the thatch of a derelict cottage at Cashel, Co. Sligo, with lozenge-sectioned blade and bronze hilt-guard of shallow bell shape. 3. Iron sword from Ballinderry, Co. Westmeath, with grooved and ribbed blade and decorated bronze hilt-guard. 4. Wooden model of a sword from Ballykilmurry, Co. Wicklow. 5. Hilt portion of an iron sword found near Edenderry, Co. Offaly, with bone grip and prominent deer horn pommel and hilt-guard. 6. Bronze anthropoid hilt from Ballyshannon Bay, Co. Donegal.

specimen, to as little as 29cm as on a sword from near Edenderry, Co. Offaly. In overall length, which varies from about 57.9cm to 41.8cm, they are notably shorter than the earlier bronze Gündlingen swords but all of them do fall comfortably within the lower range of the Dowris Phase (Class 4) sword series. However, their small size is in marked contrast to contemporary iron swords in Britain and, in particular, to those on the Continent which are effective weapons with an average overall length of 72cm and with later examples exceeding 1m in length. The Irish swords may have been intended for stabbing and hacking in close hand-to-hand combat but most of them are more appropriately described as elongated daggers rather than slashing swords. Their size has also prompted the comment that warfare in Ireland at this time may have been something of a ritual farce. Since it was technologically feasible to produce longer iron swords, sword size was probably dictated by fashion. If display was a paramount consideration, it is possible that decorated scabbards and hilts were more important than blade lengths. Indeed serious fighting may have been done with the spear.

It was a comparison of these short swords with those described in the epic *Táin Bó Cúailnge* that first demonstrated that heroic tales like this were not an accurate depiction of the material culture of a late prehistoric society, and were probably not 'a window on the Iron Age' to use K. H. Jackson's expressive phrase. The swords described in the *Táin* are akin to longer early Medieval swords and would be the weapons familiar to story tellers of the 7th century AD onwards when such tales were written down.[23]

THE IRISH SCABBARD STYLE

A series of finely decorated bronze scabbards provide clear evidence that some of these iron swords were the possessions of a warrior aristocracy who were preoccupied with decorative display and who were also the patrons of skilled iron workers, bronze smiths and artists. Presumably scabbards of organic materials were used as well but none have survived. Altogether eight bronze scabbards or parts of scabbards survive, two are plain and six have engraved decoration. One of the plain examples is of interest because it is the only substantially complete find, the others are represented by one scabbard plate only. The complete scabbard is one of four found at Lisnacrogher, Co. Antrim (below). This piece consists of two sheets of hammered

bronze held together by folding the edges of the front plate, which has a hammered midrib, over the edges of the back plate. There is a corroded iron blade within the scabbard and the scabbard tongue is protected by a cast bronze openwork chape. Two small perforations near the centre on both plates were probably for a suspension loop attached at different times to one or other of the scabbard faces (Fig. 148, 1). The second plain scabbard is represented by a single bronze plate from Toome, on the River Bann.[24]

Of the six decorated specimens, two are of less refined workmanship than the rest. One from the River Bann, near Coleraine (Fig. 148, 2), is decorated with an engraved curvilinear pattern which has been described as a design based on a running wave; this motif is a continuous and sinuous wave-like line with spiral off-shoots and is ultimately of Classical origin. Here the off-shoots form pelta shapes with tightly coiled spiral ends. Minor motifs include hatched triangles, leaf shapes, a crude step pattern along one edge and, in the spaces between the major curvilinear motifs, triangular arrangements of three dots.[25] The second, from the River Bann at Toome (Fig. 148, 3), bears a basic design of alternately disposed C-shaped motifs which are probably ineptly executed loose spirals. Minor motifs include leaf shapes, curves and circles which fail to form true spirals and parallel hatching. This decoration was not to someone's liking because the scabbard plate was cut down, reused with the decorated face turned inwards and some punched ornament added to the edges.[26]

The remaining four are finely crafted pieces. Three come from Lisnacrogher and one from Toome on the River Bann. Lisnacrogher 1 (Fig. 149, 1) has no midrib and the overall pattern is basically a sequence of four S-scrolls with spiral-filled comma leaf motifs filling the intervening spaces and touching the returned ends of the scrolls. The junctions between the scrolls are filled with spirals and triangles and parts of the stems of the scrolls bear pairs of minute almost lentoid motifs like eyes and are also emphasized with punched triangles. The scabbard edges are decorated with an engraved zig-zag line. A broadly similar basic pattern occurs on the scabbard plate from the River Bann (Toome 1) which has three large S-scrolls touching one another, the junctions filled mostly with spirals (Fig. 149, 2). The stems of the major S-scrolls expand and contain tiny loose spirals and the

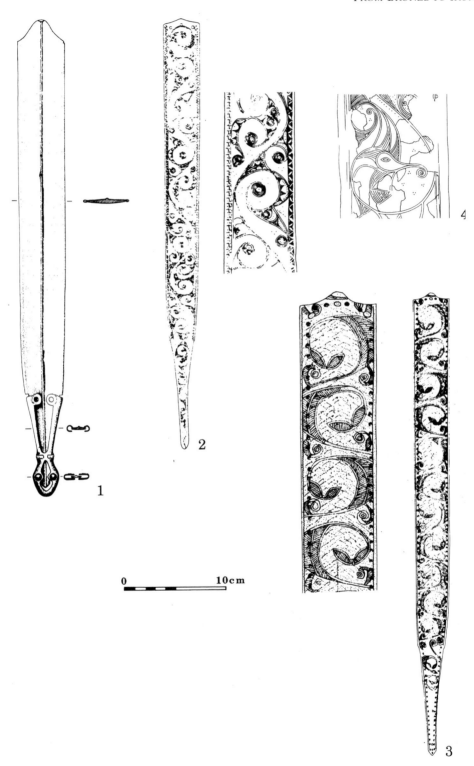

Fig. 148. 1. Plain bronze scabbard with chape from Lisnacrogher, Co. Antrim (Lisnacrogher 4). 2. Decorated scabbard plate from the River Bann, Co. Derry, with detail of decoration (Bann 1). 3. Decorated scabbard plate from the River Bann at Toome, Co. Antrim, with detail of decoration (Toome 3). 4. Detail of decoration on a scabbard from Cernon-sur-Coole, France, showing triple dot motif. Details of decoration not to scale.

Fig. 149. Decorated bronze scabbard plates with details of decoration. 1. Lisnacrogher 1. 2. Toome 1. 3. Lisnacrogher 2. 4. Lisnacrogher 3. Details of decoration not to scale.

ends of these S-scrolls finish in smaller scrolls with spiral ends. According to Jope the whole design was drawn free-hand without the aid of a compass and conceived with a great vigour and rhythm best appreciated when viewed horizontally with the tip to the right.

Lisnacrogher 2 is a scabbard plate which has retained its chape and which has an elegant and cleverly composed symmetrical pattern, arranged about a midrib and consisting of opposed S-scrolls forming a series of lyres in tiers – or, if viewed horizontally, a pair of opposed attenuated running waves with double pelta-shaped off-shoots filled with parallel hatching or other designs (Fig. 149, 3). As on Lisnacrogher 1 parts of the stems of the S-scrolls are accentuated by punched triangles. The overall decorative scheme has a further ambiguity: this is one of those compositions which can be viewed in either its positive (engraved motifs) or negative (background) design.

Lisnacrogher 3 is a scabbard plate with chape and a hammered midrib (Fig. 149, 4). The principal design is a series of large loose spirals touching one another, their junctions filled with small spiral motifs. This design is interrupted by the midrib and the motifs do not always precisely join each other. Near the top, the midrib has been used effectively to symmetrically divide the curvilinear ornament which includes a pair of pelta shapes with spiral ends. The larger motifs on the scabbard are filled with a few spirals, some parallel hatching and some so-called basketry work – in which small rectangular fields of parallel hatching are placed at right angles to each other. This is the only Irish scabbard with this sort of basketry motif.[27]

The art of these scabbards has inspired considerable comment and discussion, much of it concerned with stylistic affinities, origins and chronology. Though each one is different, they have a number of features in common including the accomplished use of the rocked-graver technique. Lines were engraved using a hand-held, pointed metal implement which when moved backwards or forwards with a rocking motion could produce deep fine lines cut with varied and slightly zigzag effects depending on whether the point was round or chisel-shaped, for example.[28]

Overall ornament is another shared characteristic and the principal designs are based on sequences of S-scrolls and spirals. There is a noteworthy preference for quite a range of minor motifs used to

fill the main figures and the spaces between them. Barry Raftery suggests that this Irish scabbard style contains two groups each the product of different craft centres. A Bann group consists of scabbards, usually of slender proportions, without midribs and with tongues which are slightly concave. Each of the decorated scabbards in this group also has pairs of small leaf shapes sometimes forming zigzag ornament. A Lisnacrogher group has midribs on three of the four examples and a sharp distinction between plate and tongue. The tops are usually of prominent bell-shape and the mouths of the decorated examples are outlined by punched zigzag decoration.[29]

Debate about the origins of these Irish swords and scabbards has mainly focused on the question of either direct British or Continental inspiration and, inevitably, has often involved consideration of minute decorative details. The discovery, in recent years, of a number of decorated scabbards in graves in Yorkshire has necessitated a complete reassessment of the problem. Four British scabbards have overall curvilinear ornament extending the full length of the scabbard plate in the Irish fashion, a trait rarely found on the Continent. The presence of centrally placed suspension loops on the Yorkshire scabbards and on the plain scabbard from Lisnacrogher is another insular feature. A few decorative motifs are shared too: the basketry motif on Lisnacrogher 3 is found on the Bugthorpe, Yorkshire, scabbard, for instance, and the zigzag motif along the edges of Lisnacrogher 1 is found on two scabbards from Wetwang, Yorkshire. These similarities suggest that the Irish swords and scabbards are broadly contemporary with those in Yorkshire, but there are significant contrasts. The slender Irish chapes are different from their heavier and often decorated Scottish and northern English counterparts and the profusion of ornament on the Irish scabbards and their propensity for employing a variety of minor filler motifs may be contrasted with the sparse, more open-textured style of the majority of the Yorkshire pieces. According to Barry Raftery certain minor motifs hint at the possibility of direct Continental links. These include the small motif like a pair of eyes on the stems of the S-scrolls of Lisnacrogher 1 and, in particular, the triangular arrangement of three punched dots found on Bann 1 and the way in which this motif is inserted into the voids between the tendrils. This unusual motif is found on three scabbards in Hungary and one in eastern France (Fig. 148, 4). Whether Continental inspiration came directly from Europe or through Britain and the nature of the relationship of the remarkable Irish and British scabbard styles will, no doubt, continue to be debated.[30]

SPEAR AND SHIELD

It is possible that spear and shield were the common attributes of the warrior at this time but once again the archaeological record is disconcertingly deficient. Part of the problem is a familiar one, the simple socketed iron spear is a weapon which remained essentially unchanged over many centuries and cannot be easily dated unless clearly associated with other material or decorated in some distinctive way. An iron spearhead found in a river near Inchiquin Lake, Corrofin, Co. Clare (Fig. 150, 1), has a pair of openwork bronze settings in the blade and traces of a rectilinear step-pattern on the socket. The perforations in the blade recall similar features in Dowris Phase bronze spearheads. Two large iron spearheads from Lisnacrogher, Co. Antrim (Fig. 150, 2) are presumably broadly contemporary with the swords and scabbards from that site. These are impressive objects, about 41cm and 47cm in length respectively, and if they were ever mounted on the sort of wooden shafts also found at Lisnacrogher which were about 2.4m in length, they would have been formidable weapons.

In contrast, two quite small bronze spearheads, about 14cm to 15cm in length, are known, one comes from a bog at Boho, Co. Fermanagh, the other from the River Blackwater, at Moy, Co. Tyrone (Fig. 150, 3-4). Both have decoration which recalls that on one of several cylindrical mounts from Lisnacrogher. These small weapons may have been for parade and display but could also have been throwing rather than thrusting spears.

Some 70 bronze spearbutts are recorded, no less than 25% of them coming from Lisnacrogher, Co. Antrim. These are bronze mounts of various shapes which are presumed to have been fitted as terminals to wooden spearshafts, most are hollow cast. Barry Raftery has divided them into four main groups. Type 1, the Lisnacrogher type, is a small waisted spearbutt with a convex base and a moulding below the mouth. One example from the eponymous site has La Tène ornament in relief on moulding and base (Fig. 150, 6). Type 2, the doorknob type, has a prominent rounded end and a slender cylindrical or funnel-shaped socket (Fig. 150, 7). Type 3, the

tubular type, is a long slender tapering mount (Fig. 150, 8). A small number have mouldings at top and bottom; five stand apart from the rest being made of hammered sheet bronze and include the longest known examples, up to 43cm in length. Some bear La Tène decoration. Type 4, the conical type, is a short cast form with a prominent and usually grooved moulding around the mouth (Fig. 150, 9). A number of Types 1 and 2 have been found in rivers and a significant number of Types 3 and 4 have been recovered from the Rivers Shannon and Bann.

Not one of these mounts has yet been found with a spearhead though some have been found with wooden shafts or retaining parts of these shafts. Some examples, notably of the Type 2 doorknob form have sockets of surprisingly narrow diameters, sometimes only a little more than 1cm. Wooden shafts of such slender dimensions must have been easily broken and it is questionable if the bronze mounts were functional pieces; they could have been mounts for ceremonial staffs and if they were spearbutts at all, they could conceivably have been primarily for display like the small bronze spearheads. Whether all of these mounts were butts for spears must remain uncertain but a couple of depictions of spears with bulbous ends to their shafts might be represen-tations of spearbutts of this sort. A stone carving from Maryport, Cumberland, one of a collection of carvings of Romano-British date, shows a horned figure with a shield and spear with a rounded butt. A silver plaque from Bewcastle, also in Cumberland, figures a Roman deity holding a spear with a rounded extension to the end of the shaft.

The distribution of spearbutts is interesting and at least as far as two types are concerned may suggest distinct Connacht and Ulster centres of production or fashion (Fig. 151). Type 1 seems to be a north-eastern type with a number of examples (or moulds for casting them) recorded in western Scotland while Type 2 has a scattered distribution including finds in Wiltshire and Scotland. The tubular and conical forms (Types 3 and 4) seem to be distinctively Irish types with the former strongly represented in the west.[31]

THE CLONOURA SHIELD

Only one complete shield is known but is an exceptionally interesting discovery. It was found in a near upright position in Littleton Bog, in Clonoura townland, south-east of Thurles, Co. Tipperary. The shield is rectangular with rounded

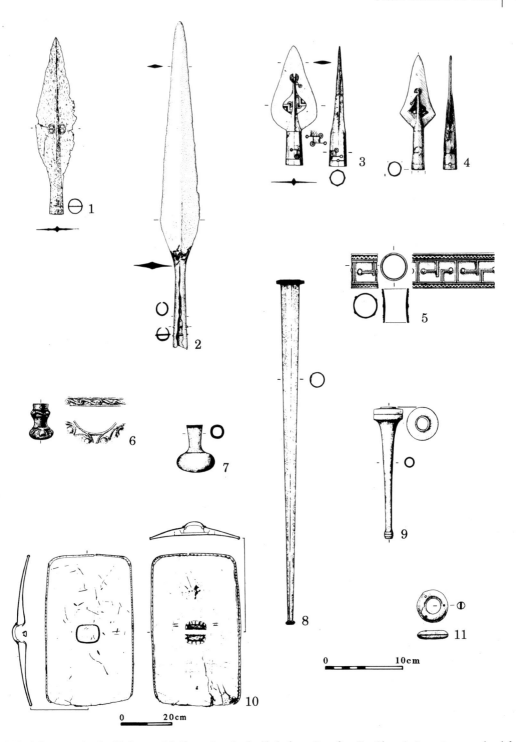

Fig. 150. 1. Iron spearhead with bronze inlaid openings in the blade from Corrofin, Co. Clare. 2. Large iron spearhead from Lisnacrogher, Co. Antrim. 3. Bronze spearhead from Boho, Co. Fermanagh. 4. Bronze spearhead from the River Blackwater, Moy, Co. Tyrone. 5. Decorated bronze ferrule from Lisnacrogher, Co. Antrim. 6. Type 1 spearbutt from Lisnacrogher, Co. Antrim. 7. Type 2 spearbutt from Derrymore Island, Lough Gara, Co. Sligo. 8. Type 3 spearbutt from the River Shannon at Carrick-on-Shannon, Co. Leitrim. 9. Type 4 spearbutt from the River Shannon at Banagher, Co. Offaly. 10. Shield of leather and wood from Clonoura, Co. Tipperary. 11. Hollow two-piece bronze ring from Lisnacrogher, Co. Antrim.

Type 1 △
Type 2 ▲
Type 3 +
Type 4 O

Fig. 151. General distribution of bronze spearbutts. Each symbol denotes one or more finds.

corners, 57cm by 35cm, and made of a slightly convex board of alderwood covered with a single piece of calf hide on both faces (Fig. 150, 10). These are fastened together with strips of leather stitched around the edges. There is a domed, alderwood boss or umbo on the front, covered with stitched leather, with a bar of oak behind to provide a grip. On the back a pair of incisions cut in the leather on either side of this grip were probably for the attachment of carrying thongs. It is interesting to note that the front of the shield displays haphazardly distributed ancient cut marks made by either sword blades or spear thrusts, dramatic evidence of combat usage and an indication that warfare may have been a serious activity for some elements of society. Composite shields of leather and wood may have been common and of different shapes, with metal attachments of various sorts, as a series of miniature hide-shaped shields from Britain demonstrates. The closest parallels for the Clonoura shield are to be found in depictions of shields in stone and metal of the early centuries AD in northern Britain.[32]

LISNACROGHER, CO. ANTRIM

The swords, scabbards and spearbutts from Lisnacrogher have been mentioned. These form a major part of a remarkable collection of objects recovered in the 19th century from a bog in or near the townland of that name, in the valley of the Clogh river, some 7km north of Ballymena, Co. Antrim. Nothing remains of the site and even its precise location is disputed. Numerous finds were made in the years 1882 to 1888 and the site was visited in 1883 by W. F. Wakeman whose published reports are not very informative. He noted timbers and encircling stakes and 'rough basket-like work' which may have been wattle work and listed many of the artefacts acquired by northern collectors such as Canon J. Grainger of nearby Broughshane. Robert Munro, whose short description of his visit in 1886 is the best contemporary account, wrote 'the bog in which these objects were found occupies the site of a former lake, which till recently, retained so much water as to prevent the working of the peat for fuel. To remedy this the outlet was deepened, and so new or undisturbed portions of the bog were brought within reach of the peat-cutters. The antiquities were found from time to time in a circumscribed area, within a small plot belonging to one of the neighbouring farmers. When attention was first directed to the locality, and the workers questioned as to the circumstances in which the relics came to light, it appears that some kind of wooden structure was encountered, which, however, had been entirely removed before being seen by anyone competent to form an opinion as to its nature'.

Munro questioned the farmer, who clearly recalled the existence of stakes and irregularly disposed oak beams and brushwood, and concluded having seen the remnants of some oak timbers containing mortises that there was 'little doubt that it was a crannog, but of no great dimensions'. He makes the important observation that 'as to the relics, there is no record of their association with the crannog beyond the fact of their being found in its vicinity'.

These relics, as we have seen, included one complete bronze scabbard and three extraordinary decorated scabbard plates, as well as at least three bronze chapes, two iron spearheads, four bronze ferrules for spearshafts, and some eighteen bronze spearbutts, several still attached to long wooden shafts. Other finds included three enigmatic hollow bronze rings, two bronze ring-headed pins, a simple bronze torc, several bronze bracelets and rings, a number of decorative bronze mounts, and an iron axe, adze and sickle. Two cauldrons made of sheets of iron are said to have been found but are not preserved. A gold ribbon torc is also said to have come from Lisnacrogher but this may not be a genuine provenance.

The three hollow two-piece bronze rings from the site (Fig. 150, 11) are the only known Irish examples of a puzzling artefact widely distributed on the Continent. One example is known from a cemetery at Kirkburn, Yorkshire, where it was found near the skull of a young woman who had been buried with a new-born infant. On the Continent they have often been found in male graves but some have been found in female burials too. The Lisnacrogher rings belong to an early riveted variety and might date to the 3rd century BC. They have been thought to be part of some mechanism for suspending a scabbard from a belt but seem too flimsy for this purpose; they may have been ornaments or amulets.

With so little information about the wooden structure or structures 'of no great dimensions', it is impossible to know if Lisnacrogher actually was a settlement or crannog, and even if there was a settlement there whether it had any connection with all the material recovered. This material has been considered the stock of a metalworker and the site has been thought to have been a chieftain's family armoury and workshop containing equipment accumulated over several generations.[33] The apparent absence of settlement debris may not be significant because mundane finds like saddle querns and metal fragments might well have held little or no interest for 19th century scavengers and collectors. All that can reasonably be said is that such an assemblage of metalwork has never been found on a prehistoric settlement of any date in Ireland and, on present evidence, the balance of probability is that the original lake here was an important focus for votive offerings like Loughnashade, Co. Armagh.

PERSONAL ORNAMENTS

Torcs, fibulae and pins are the commonest personal ornaments. Most are stray finds. The fine gold torcs from Broighter, Co. Derry, and Knock, Co. Roscommon, and the gold ribbon torcs, if worn as personal ornaments, were probably the possessions of an aristocracy, but many of the simpler bronze

fibulae and pins are also works of considerable craftsmanship and may have been status symbols too, albeit of a lesser nature. The fibula or brooch is a common type of dress fastener on the Continent where it is capable of subtle and chronologically-significant typological sub-division with variations assignable to different phases of the La Tène period there. To a lesser extent the same is true in Britain. In Ireland, however, the majority are local forms and are less easily dateable. Three principal Irish types have been recognized: rod-bow and leaf-bow safety-pin fibulae and Navan type brooches.[34]

Rod-bow fibulae have slender flat or arched bows formed of a rod of bronze; their foot curves back and touches or is attached to the bow and they usually have a double-coiled safety-pin type spring with an external chord or loop. (Fig. 152, 1-3). A decorated example found 3m to 4m deep in a bog at Lecarrow, Co. Sligo, has a typical spring with two coils and an external chord, the tip of the catchplate curves upwards to form an unusual ring from which the foot extends to the bow. At this point the foot forms a tiny bird's head. Another similar fibula, an old find from Clogher, Co. Tyrone, is decorated with cast trumpet curves and has three small settings which may once have held enamel. An iron example, much corroded, was found in the excavation of the ringfort at Feerwore, Co. Galway. The profile of most of these rod-bow fibulae, with an almost straight bow, is similar to that of the flattened-bow fibulae of southern England, and it is possible that their genesis may lie in contacts with the Wessex region as early as the 3rd century BC.

Leaf-bow fibulae usually have slightly curved profiles and characteristic bows which are cast or hammered to a broad flat slender leaf shape (Fig. 152, 4-5). Double coils and external chords are common but five-coiled springs are known as are internal chords. Decoration on the bow may be no more than a simple central line, but occasionally is a little more elaborate with elegant elongated arcs. The most ornate example has an openwork bow, the oval opening flanked by cast trumpet curves in relief, and was found with a cremated burial and some glass beads at Kiltierney, Co. Fermanagh.

A small number of fibulae, the Navan type brooches, named after two old finds at Navan Fort, Co. Armagh, form a distinctively Irish group (Fig. 152, 6). They have elaborate openwork bows with finely cast decoration with trumpet curves and lentoid bosses. One of the Navan finds and examples

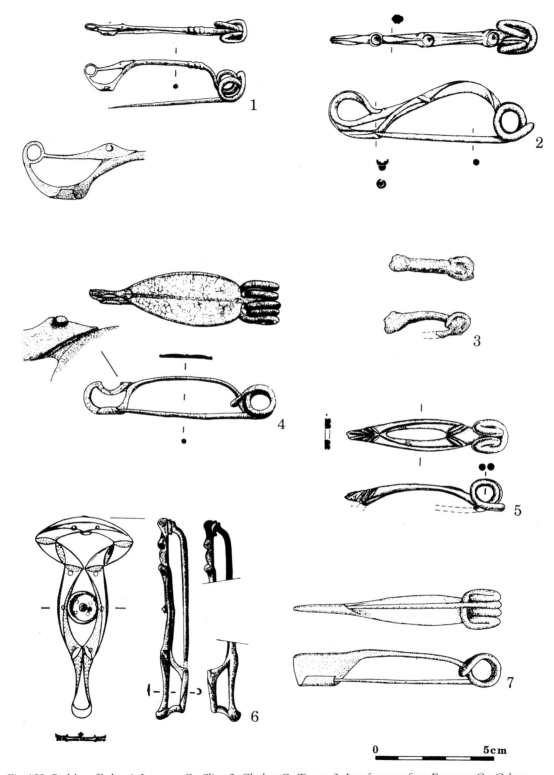

Fig. 152. Rod-bow fibulae. 1. Lecarrow, Co. Sligo. 2. Clogher, Co. Tyrone. 3. Iron fragment from Feerwore, Co. Galway. Leaf-bow fibulae. 4. Unprovenanced. 5. Kiltierney, Co. Fermanagh. 6. Navan type brooch from Navan Fort, Co. Armagh. 7. Nauheim-derivative fibula from Derrybeg, Co. Sligo.

from Lough Ree and from the Somerset hoard in Co. Galway (Fig. 139, 6) have circular settings for red enamel. The term brooch is often preferred because the fibula's characteristic safety-pin spring is replaced by a pin with an unusual and innovative ball-and-socket mechanism, or in one instance by a skeumorphic spring containing a spindle on which the pin swivels. It has been variously suggested that these brooches may have been influenced by late British fibulae, by openwork Roman brooches or clasps, or by larger openwork mirror handles known in southern England. Whatever their inspiration, a date in the late 1st century BC or the 1st century AD seems plausible.[35]

Among the few miscellaneous fibulae recorded, one from near Donaghadee, Co. Down, was found at a place called Loughey in about 1850 along with two glass bracelets, 150 glass beads, bronze rings, a bronze tweezers and a small bronze toggle. They were all found in a small pit and it is thought, on very slender evidence, that they had accompanied a female cremation. The fibula, with its solid catchplate, is a type well known in southern England and derived from a Continental Nauheim type.[36] It and the other items are imports and probably date to the 1st century AD. A similar fibula was found on the shores of Lough Gara at Derrybeg, Co. Sligo (Fig. 152, 7) and one was reportedly found with a cremation in a ring ditch at Ballydavis, Co. Laois.

Though there are a few finds of textiles nothing is known about late prehistoric clothing. Christopher Hawkes, prompted by the idea that novel dress fasteners might be connected with novel dress, did speculate that the appearance of the La Tène fibula in Ireland could have coincided with the introduction, also from southern Britain, of a male fashion for wearing ankle-length trousers of chequered pattern but so far, at least, evidence is lacking.[37] The few contemporary bog-bodies are unhelpful: a male found in 1821 at Gallagh, near Castleblakeney, Co. Galway, was buried wearing a short leather cloak but was otherwise naked. A pointed wooden stake had been placed on each side of the body and it is reported that there was a 'band of sally rods' around his neck which may have been either the means by which he was strangled or a symbolic torc.

It is interesting to note that dress pins were still popular and were evidently not displaced by the fibula. Indeed, if surviving numbers are any indication, they seem to have been marginally commoner but whether they represent a continuation in pin fashion from earlier times is uncertain. Most of the Irish examples are stray finds and there is considerable variety. The basic form is a pin with a ring-shaped head immediately above an angular bent neck (Fig. 153). They are normally of cast bronze and some heads are annular, others penannular. A number have bosses on the ring and

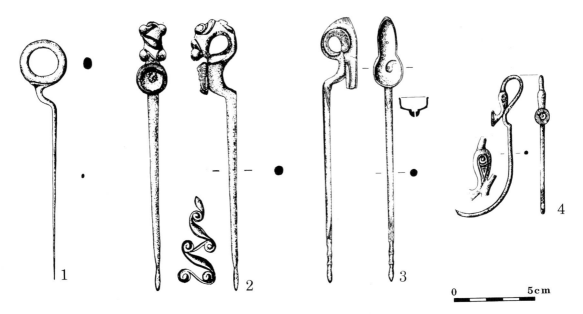

Fig. 153. Ring-headed pins. 1. No provenance. 2. Grange, Co. Sligo. 3. Roscavey, Co. Tyrone. 4. River Shannon.

some have curvilinear ornament in relief. One distinctive type has a large decorative setting for imposing studs of red enamel, another has a prominently forward curving head. Some of these pins have parallels in Britain but the precise chronology of the different types is unclear. There is an occasional hint of regional preferences: ring-headed pins are well represented in Co. Antrim, for instance, where rod- and leaf-bow fibulae are virtually absent.

DISCS AND HORNS AND SOLAR SYMBOLS

A series of bronze discs and horns are further testimony of the proficiency of the bronze smith and artist and some are, in their own right, remarkable expressions of artistic excellence. They are usually dated on stylistic grounds to the early centuries AD. The Bann disc, as it is generally called, is a small bronze disc only 10.5cm in diameter, which was dredged from the River Bann at Loughan Island, near Coleraine, in 1939. It is very slightly convex with three perforations, one containing a small bronze ring (Fig. 154, 1). It was probably a decorative mount of some description, though it has been suggested that it might be a pan from a weighing scales, and its convex face has an elegant composition of fine lines forming what is essentially a swirling three-limbed figure, a triskele, within a circle. The design is initiated by three raised lines radiating from a central circle and swirling in a clockwise direction, these lines, which are slender trumpet curves, join with other trumpet curves which swirl in the reverse, anti-clockwise, direction and terminate in stylized bird's heads. Based on compass-drawn curving lines, the overall design displays exceptional restraint and has a rhythmic quality suggesting 'an interplay of rotational forces caught in a moment of time'.

The bronze object known as the Petrie crown is so-called because it was once in the collection of the 19th century antiquary George Petrie, who did not record – or never knew – its provenance. It is a fragmentary piece now consisting of a band of openwork sheet bronze with a pair of slightly dished discs attached to the front (Fig. 154, 2). Each disc apparently supported a bronze horn, one of which survives. This horn is made of a sheet of hammered bronze folded to a conical shape. Each element of the fragment, the band, the discs and the horn, is very skilfully decorated with a symmetrical design of thin and elongated trumpet curves, some terminating in different sorts of bird's heads. The design on the disc below the surviving horn is particularly interesting because the bird's head terminals flank a circle set in a crescent form. This, like the design on a series of other bronze discs, is probably a solar symbol. With a maximum height and length of only 15cm, this metal object seems too small to be worn itself, but a row of small holes at the top and bottom of the band indicate that it was meant to be attached to something, perhaps a leather backing, and this could have been worn as a headpiece, though whether for display on a human head or in a ritual context on an idol is obviously unknown. An equally fragile bronze helmet with short conical horns, and also not a functional item, was found in the River Thames near Waterloo Bridge.

The object now called the Cork horns is another horned headpiece (Fig. 154, 3) though possessing three longer horns about 26cm to 29cm in length. It was found near Cork, in river mud, at a location which was originally probably in a tidal salt marsh, below the high water mark, and which recalls the findspot of the Broighter hoard in the north. This horned object is also incomplete: the three conical horns of sheet bronze were attached together by overlapping flanges and were once attached to a lost portion, probably of leather. Each horn bears a symmetrical design in low relief mainly composed of a pair of triskeles formed by attenuated trumpet curves. A more complex version occurs on the central horn where one limb of each triskele ends in a boss and spiral motif reminiscent of a bird's head. Triple horns are unusual and provide another useful reminder that some ornaments may not have been worn by human figures, animate or inanimate. Triple horns occur on images of bulls in England in Romano-British contexts and in Gallo-Roman France.[38]

Several features demonstrate that these three objects are closely related. They share a symmetry of composition, motifs such as slender trumpet curves and triskeles, and an elaborate technique of decoration in which at least part of the background was cut away to produce the relief ornament.[39] A variety of forms of stylized bird's heads link all three together as well: those on the Bann disc are quite abstract and mainly formed of tiny trumpet curves and lentoid bosses, three separate types are to be found on the Petrie crown while the pair on the Cork horns are perhaps the least bird-like. The

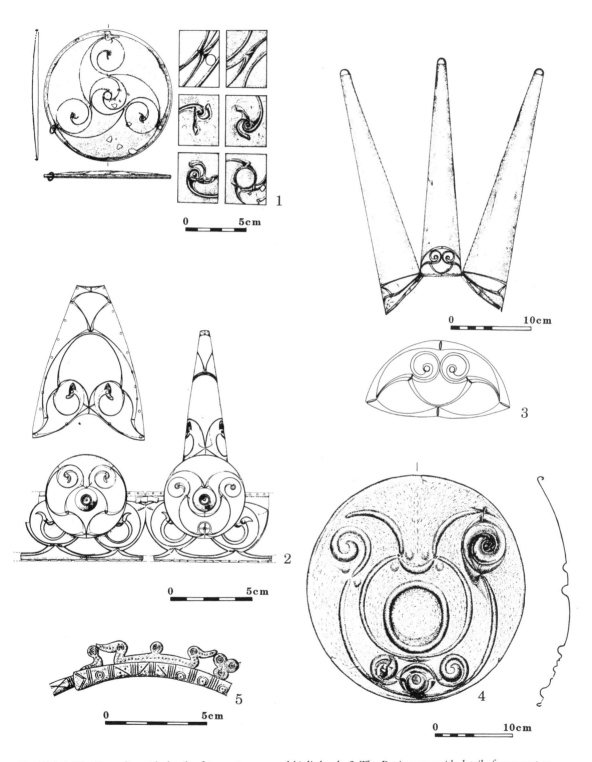

Fig. 154. 1. The Bann disc with details of trumpet curves and bird's heads. 2. The Petrie crown with detail of ornament on horn. 3. The Cork horns with detail of ornament on the central horn consisting of a pair of triskeles formed by trumpet curves. 4. Unprovenanced bronze disc of Monasterevin type. 5. Detail of an early bronze torc from Attancourt (Haute-Marne) showing solar boat with bird's heads.

decoration on the discs of the Petrie crown is also similar to the designs on a puzzling series of larger bronze discs.

A pair of large bronze discs found together at Monasterevin, Co. Kildare, has given the name Monasterevin type to a group of four complete and three fragmentary discs (Fig. 154, 4). All but the Monasterevin pair are unprovenanced and even they have no details of their discovery recorded. Made of sheet bronze, these discs are usually slightly concave and range in diameter from about 25cm to just over 30cm; their purpose is unknown. Decoration is similar but not identical and consists of bold repoussé work up to 10mm high. The overall pattern is a fairly consistent one: a large central circle or roundel, which varies from a slight concavity to a deep bowl-shaped hollow, is placed within a symmetrical field of trumpet curves forming an approximately U-shaped or semi-circular arrangement with spiral terminals which

contains a prominent circle. Given the positioning of a pair of spirals above a circle, it is probably not surprising that this design has been described as 'a geometrical fantasy' and compared to 'a grotesque face with large staring eyes'.

The bronze discs on the Petrie crown provide a clue to another more plausible explanation. The disc below the surviving horn shows a cross set in a crescentic shape which has spiral terminals with bird's heads and a circular device between them. This is a solar symbol, a stylized depiction of the boat of the sun drawn across the heavens by birds (Fig. 154, 5), the circular device representing the sun which is also symbolized by the wheel below. The larger motif is repeated in a more stylized manner on the second disc of the crown and on the Monasterevin type discs as well and illustrates just how a series of stylized forms may have been imbued with a magical significance which we can only dimly perceive today.[40]

NOTES

1 Early iron working: Champion 1980.
2 Gündlingen swords: Eogan 1965; Cowen 1967. Schauer 1971 and 1972 has proposed an insular origin and O'Connor 1980, 240, was inclined to agree. However, this claim has been rejected by Colquhoun and Burgess 1988. A ring-punched rivet head is clearly illustrated on a sword found near Athlone in J. Raftery 1951, pl. on p. 184. Athlone hoard: Eogan 1983, no. 124; 1965, nos 519-520; Cullen, Co. Tipperary: Herity 1969, pl. IX. An example has also been found in the River Corrib at Menlo, Co. Galway: Rynne 1984.
3 Hybrid swords: Eogan 1965, Class 6 and Class 4c; see Burgess 1969.
4 Champion 1982.
5 Chapes: Eogan 1965, 170; Meyer 1985.
6 Jope 1958. Some British finds are antiquarian acquisitions of recent centuries: Harbison and Laing 1974.
7 Fibulae: Jope 1962; Co. Dublin: J. Raftery 1951, fig. 213. Dunaverney, Co. Antrim: Powell 1966, 171; Scott and Powell 1969, 125, fn. Meyer 1985 has noted that the majority of Hallstatt imports in Britain are types found in male contexts on the Continent and are concentrated around the Humber, Ouse and Thames valleys.
8 Kilmurry, Co. Kerry: Eogan 1983, no. 90; bracelets: O'Connor 1980, 259.
9 Bronze sword with doubtful traces of late scabbard: Harbison 1970. Kilsmullan, Co. Fermanagh: Williams 1984, 2120 ± 45 BP (360-30 BC, UB-2173).
10 Champion 1971, 1989; but Warner's 1974 comments still have some validity.
11 Early iron working: Scott 1990. Britain: Manning and Saunders 1972. Drumlane, Co Cavan: Raftery 1984, 9, fig. 4, 228; Scott 1990, 48, fig. Feerwore, Co. Galway:

J. Raftery 1944, 33; Raftery 1984, 240. Rathtinaun axe: Scott 1990, 54, fig. Iron in bogs: S. Kelly 1995. Hallstatt C sword from Athlone: Coffey 1906; Rynne 1982; Scott 1990, 58. Rathgall, Co. Wicklow, radiocarbon dated to 1685 ± 70 BP (180-540 AD, SI-1480) and Clogher, Co. Tyrone, dated to 390-620 AD (UB-844, *Radiocarbon* 21): Scott 1990, 160; Raftery 1976, 347.
12 Macalister 1928, 16. Bronze resources: Northover 1982. Adoption of iron: Champion 1976; possible socio-economic consequences: Rowlands 1980, 45; Bradley 1990, 150. Iron ores: Scott 1990, 153.
13 The linguistic and archaeological debate has been summarized in Waddell 1991 and 1991a. Non-genetic linguistic model: Robb 1993; Renfrew 1987; Waddell 1992 and 1995. See also Mallory and McNeill 1991,171; Mallory 1984, 1989, 1991a, 1992; Warner 1991; Koch 1986, 1991.
14 Literature on Celtic problems includes: Aitchison 1987; Champion 1987, 1995, 1996; Chapman 1992; Collis 1997; Fitzpatrick 1991; Koch 1994; Megaw and Megaw 1995 and 1996; McDonald 1986; Mallory 1992a; Taylor 1991.
15 Knock hoard: some good detective work by Aideen Ireland 1992 has identified the correct provenance; Raftery 1983, nos 451 and 454; 1984, 177.
16 Somerset hoard: Raftery 1983, p. 286; the horse pendant is possibly part of the original discovery: Kelly 1993, 15.
17 Ribbon torcs: Eogan 1994, 53; 1983; 1983a; Northover 1989; Warner 1993; typological clues: Warner 1982; Carson and O'Kelly 1977 and Coles 1975. Raftery 1984, 180, notes two late ribbon torcs from Italy, one of gold and one of iron.
18 Cooney and Grogan 1994, 196.

19 Broighter hoard and torc: Warner 1982; Neill 1993; Raftery 1984, 181; Jope 1958a; 1975; Warner 1982; Kelly in Ryan 1983, 105; Kelly 1993, 10. Boat: most currachs are about 7.5m long and Tim Severin's Brendan replica was 11m long – close to the likely size limit imposed by this form of hide construction: Farrell and Penny 1975; but see McGrail 1987, 184, and 1995, 264, who considers that the Broighter prototype could have been a 20m long hide-built boat. Other torcs: R. R. Clarke 1954; Stead 1991; Eluère 1987.

20 Bridle bits are comprehensively studied by Raftery 1984, also Haworth 1971; contexts: Cooney and Grogan 1994, 196; Palk 1984 for Britain; Llyn Cerrig Bach: F. Lynch 1991, 285ff. Scott 1990, 63, suggests that the V-moulding may be a vestigial echo of the weld-seam produced when a piece of iron is folded over to create a perforation. The unprovenanced decorated bit is examined in detail in Raftery 1974a; Megaw and Megaw 1989, 224, stress the ambiguity of the designs: the ducks' heads if viewed upside-down 'can also be seen as a Pinocchio-nosed, mouthless human face' and the mournful twisted mask 'is one of the most shifting of the shape-changing figures found in Celtic art'. Masks: Raftery 1983, no. 49, fig. 5; 1984, fig. 11, 2. Streamstown, Co. Westmeath: Raftery 1977. Mouth width: Palk 1984, 100, pls VIII and IX; Piggott 1983, 219.

21 Pendants: Haworth 1971 with subdivisions proposed by Raftery 1984, 45; paired draught: Jope 1955. Type E bit and Romania: Warner 1976, 281.

22 Yoke mounts: Piggott 1969. Yoke from north of Ireland: Piggott 1949, though whether it was suitable for horses or oxen is uncertain: Fenton 1972; Raftery 1983, 80. Dunmore, Co. Galway: Pryor 1980, no. 167.

23 Swords: Rynne 1982 and 1983; Raftery 1984, 62, who distinguishes two types of sword: Type 1 with metal hilt-guards, Type 2 with organic hilt-guards. Rynne divides the swords on the basis of blade cross-section: Type A with lozenge-sectioned blade, Type B with a ribbed and grooved blade and Type C with an almost flat blade; Scott 1990. Ballyshannon, Co. Donegal: Clarke and Hawkes 1955, 215: 'it could quite conceivably have been made in Ireland.' It is also stated that the [overall] length was 49cm and that the iron blade was triangular. Jope 1971, 118, thought the well modelled ears to be very un-insular features (see Megaw 1970, pl. 229). Continental swords: Pleiner 1993, 63. Ritual warfare: Duignan, *Etudes Celtiques* 13, 1972, 628; also 'the popular image of the Irish Celt as always at war gains little support from archaeology': Megaw and Megaw 1989, 235, on the sparse evidence for chariotry. The sword in the *Táin*: Mallory 1982; 1992a.

24 Scabbards: Raftery 1984, 75; 1994a. The enumeration is that of Jope 1954 and Raftery. Plain scabbard Lisnacrogher 4: Raftery 1983, no. 265; 1984, fig. 48, 1; scabbards with centrally placed suspension loops are known in northern England and judging from a number of schematic chalk carvings of warriors from Yorkshire they could have been worn suspended from

a belt on the back or on the side: Stead 1988. Plain scabbard Toome 2: Raftery 1983, no. 267; 1984, fig. 48, 2. A pair of hammered lentoid facets at the tip hardly constitute decoration.

25 Bann 1: Raftery 1983, no. 270; 1984, fig. 51, 2. In the occasionally weird and often appallingly imprecise world of La Tène art terminology the term pelta or pelta-shape is sometimes used to describe a crescent shape with a point or stem emanating from the centre of its concave underside (see Fig. 181, 1E).

26 Toome 3: Raftery 1983, no. 269; 1984, fig. 51, 1. The incompetent craftmanship is clearly seen by comparing Megaw 1970, pls 249 and 248.

27 Lisnacrogher 1: Raftery 1983, no. 260; 1984, fig. 49, 1. The term comma leaf is sometimes used of a leaf-shaped motif (often plastic, that is three dimensional) with a circular or boss-like terminal. Toome 1: Raftery 1983, no. 268; 1984, fig. 50, 2; Jope 1954, 83. Lisnacrogher 2: Raftery 1983, no. 261; 1984, fig. 49, 2. Frey and Megaw 1976, 56, fig. 10, 2 and pl. 4, 2, suggest that the punched triangles, if read negatively, could be acanthus leaf borders. See Megaw 1970, pl. 248, for a good illustration of the foreground/ background or positive/negative ambiguity. Lisnacrogher 3: Raftery 1983, no. 263; 1984, fig. 50, 1. The pelta shapes with spiral ends are Raftery and Jope's 'trumpet finials'.

28 Lowery *et al.* 1971; see pl. XIV for Lisnacrogher 2.

29 Raftery 1994a.

30 See Piggott 1950, Jope 1954, Raftery 1984. Bugthorpe: Piggott 1950, fig. 2, 5, Fox 1958, fig. 26, and Raftery 1984, fig. 54, 5. The principal motifs on the Bugthorpe scabbard find parallels on the Turoe stone. For Wetwang, see Raftery 1994a, fig. 3, 1-2. According to Stead 1991a, 183, Irish chapes can be matched elsewhere in England as closely as on the Continent. Judging from the fine colour illustration in Kruta and Lessing 1978, pl. 94, the dots on the Cernon-sur-Coole scabbard more often than not form an irregular arrangement of multiple dots.

31 Spearheads and spearbutts: Raftery 1983, 1984. The problem posed by a lack of archaeological context is illustrated by an iron spearhead from Castleconnell, Co. Limerick, found 'doing duty as a poker in a country cottage' which may be either of Hallstatt date or a modern import from Africa: Rynne 1979; Raftery 1984, 108. Inchiquin, Co. Clare: Rynne 1982a, fig. 12. For further spearbutt subdivisions see Raftery 1984, 111; also 1982a. Three finds from the River Blackwater, two retaining parts of their wooden shafts, have been published by Bourke 1993.

32 Clonoura shield: Raftery 1983, 107; 1984, 128. British hide-shaped shields: Stead 1991b.

33 Lisnacrogher, Co. Antrim: Evans 1966, 48; Raftery 1983, 287 and references; Wakeman 1884, also 1889 and 1891; Munro 1890, 379. Hollow bronze rings: Raftery 1984, 105; also 1986 and 1988; Kirkburn, Yorkshire: Stead 1991, fig. 69. Jope 1971 suggested that Lisnacrogher was a chieftain's workshop and Warner 1983 noted that the assemblage contained several uncleaned castings for objects of types also present in

a finished state, mostly weapons and attachments, and suggested that the find was a metalworker's stock. O'Kelly 1989, 267, emphasized Wakeman's observational skills and knowledge of other crannog sites and accepted his identification of the site as a crannog.

34 Fibulae: Jope 1962; Hawkes 1982; Raftery 1984, 145.

35 Lough Ree: Raftery 1994, fig. 79c. Needless to say decorative ambiguity is also to be found on some fibulae: Jope 1962, fig. 6, compared the slender arcs on one leaf-bow specimen to folded-in bird-wings and Kelly 1993, 16, sees a 'bull-like outline' in the shape of one of the Navan brooches, for which see Raftery 1983, no. 390, 1984, fig. 82, 5. Raftery 1983, 141, suggests that the ring on the foot of the Lecarrow fibula might be read as a bird's head with the returned foot forming an elongated beak.

36 Loughey, Co. Down: Jope and Wilson 1957. Some of the glass beads may be of either Continental or local manufacture and the bracelets had a Continental source: Henderson 1987.

37 Textiles: Jørgensen 1992, 20, 215. A crouched unburnt burial in a cemetery at Betaghstown, Co. Meath, accompanied by iron penannular brooches of the 1st century BC and later, also yielded a bronze disc with traces of a fine woven horsehair gauze-like fabric on one side totally replaced by bronze oxides; see also O'Brien 1992, 135. Traces of a woven textile, probably linen, are preserved on a bronze amulet of Roman or earlier date found in a burial at Carrowbeg North, Co. Galway: Raftery 1984, 205; another textile impression

is preserved on a decorated circular bronze mount of Somerset type found near Navan Fort: Raftery 1983, no. 805. Dress: Hawkes 1982.

38 Discs and horns: Raftery 1983, 244, 259; 1984, 268. Bann disc: Jope and Wilson 1957a, 97. Thames horned helmet: Brailsford 1975, 32. Cork horns: O'Kelly 1961; it is recorded that a piece of material resembling decayed leather was attached to one of the horns when found. Triple horned images: Read et al. 1986; Green 1989, 180; 1992, 220; Megaw et al. 1992 who note the occasional triple-horned human head as well, as in Megaw and Megaw 1989, fig. 317.

39 Jope and Wilson 1957a originally suggested that the Bann disc and its design were both cast but later agreed with O'Kelly 1961 who argued that the relief design on this disc and on the Petrie Crown and the Cork Horns was laboriously created by cutting away or tooling down the background. Raftery 1994, 155, would not discount the possibility that some designs were cast and then finished by fine tooling.

40 Symbolism of Monasterevin discs: Megaw 1970, no. 269. Piggott and Daniel 1951, 20, also saw a grotesque face behind what was essentially 'a geometrical fantasy' but Duval 1977, 230, thought it could be deliberately ambiguous, a face or an open-mouthed fish. A face with an upturned curling moustache has been detected on the Petrie crown: De Wilde 1982, 104. The solar symbolism was recognized by Sprockhoff 1955 who pointed out the antiquity of the motif and how it extends beyond the 'Celtic world'; see also Kaul 1995.

9

Elusive Settlements and Ritual Sites

Although fine metalwork is eloquent testimony of a wealthy aristocracy and a proficient artisan class, and various ceremonial centres offer abundant evidence of constructional skills and organizational complexity, domestic occupation sites remain virtually unknown and our understanding of settlement, economy and social structure in the period from 600 BC to the early centuries AD is meagre in the extreme.

While ringforts are generally dated to the second half of the first millennium AD, to the early Historic period, excavation of a small number has revealed slight traces of earlier, pre-ringfort occupation of late prehistoric date. The simple iron socketed axehead, the fragmentary iron fibula, some occupation debris and other artefacts from Feerwore, Co. Galway, indicate settlement of some description on a gently sloping, low hill probably in the late 2nd or early 1st century BC. No associated structures were found and a ringfort was built on the site several centuries later. Traces of occupation, including gullies and hearths, radiocarbon dated to 90-320 AD, have been discovered beneath a ringfort at Dunsilly, Co. Antrim, and some stake-holes with associated charcoal, well stratified beneath a ringfort bank at Lisdoo, Co. Fermanagh, provided a date of 250-530 AD. At Millockstown, Co. Louth, limited excavation of a sequence of enclosures of early Historic date revealed that the earliest phase, an approximately oval ditched enclosure some 60m across, may date to 250-610 AD. Traces of late prehistoric activity of uncertain date but possibly of the late 1st millennium BC, along with coarse pottery and the trench of a large circular structure all pre-dated a ringfort at Ballyhenry, Co. Antrim. A

number of circular features, 3.6m to 4.6m in internal diameter, in a ringfort at Lislackagh, near Swinford, Co. Mayo, have been radiocarbon dated to 200 BC to 140 AD.[1]

A destroyed fort near Dungiven, Co. Derry, may have been a small vitrified fort in which a stone rampart containing strengthening timber beams had been set on fire fusing the stony material; judging from comparable sites in Scotland it may conceivably have dated to this general late prehistoric period. Charcoal from the wall trench of a hut circle on Scrabo Hill, Co. Down, which also yielded sherds of coarse pottery, has been dated to 180 BC to 340 AD. A series of small circular enclosures on the slopes of Knocknarea, Co. Sligo, are evidence of upland settlement in the first half of the first millennium AD. These sites, barely visible on the ground, were found for the most part through aerial photographic survey. They are small enclosures about 20m in diameter formed by a low stony bank and situated at about 275m above sea level. Two were partially excavated and produced extensive evidence of occupation including hearths, large quantities of sea shells, cereal grains, and some stone and iron artefacts. The few radiocarbon dates span many centuries, from before 100 BC to at least the 7th century AD, and suggest periodic settlement over a long period of time.[2]

Wetland locations were undoubtedly settled as well but evidence for the use of substantial lake settlements or crannogs has yet to be revealed. If there was settlement at Lisnacrogher the nature of the site remains uncertain. But while some occupation at Rathtinaun, Lough Gara, Co. Sligo, dated to both the Dowris Phase and to the early

Historic period, there was also activity there in the later centuries BC. The latter is attested by a series of radiocarbon dates for a deposit of charred cereals and number of wattle-built and clay-lined hearths which have a date-range of 490 BC to 230 AD. The construction of substantial bog trackways may be another indication of settlement in these locations or nearby. Knowledge of timber trackways has been immeasurably increased by the work of the Irish Archaeological Wetland Unit established in 1990 and by Barry Raftery's excavations at Corlea, in Co. Longford.[3] These excavations established that a massive timber trackway, justifiably termed a road, in Corlea townland was in fact part of a system which extended for some 2km into the neighbouring townland of Derraghan. Dendrochronological analysis determined that the oak timbers were felled about 148 BC. This Corlea-Derraghan roadway was constructed of large oak planks laid transversely on parallel lines of timbers of birch or ash placed on the bog surface. Up to 25 hectares of woodland were cleared in this huge undertaking and the whole process of felling, transport and construction was evidently a major coordinated effort by a local community or communities. To what extent, if any, a slave population may have been involved is unknown.[4] Alternatively the discovery of parts of two-piece tub-shaped wooden containers raises the possibility that feasting or drinking may have been a way in which work parties were mobilized. In any event these vessels and other pieces of finely crafted, slotted, mortised and tenoned timbers provide rare testimony of the carpenter's skill. The joiners and builders presumably lived in dispersed settlements in the general locality but where is not known. There are few finds from the area and the only significant contemporary artefact is a matching pair of bronze bridle bits found near Abbeyshrule, 12km to the east.

Coastal locations were occupied at this time too: radiocarbon dated charcoal from a shell midden at Glengarriff, Co. Cork, suggests the site was frequented in the period 370-20 BC. Some animal bone from a shell midden at Ballymulholland, Co. Derry, indicated a date range of 385-176 BC and some iron slag demonstrated nearby iron working.[5]

As we shall see, excavation at the royal sites of Navan and Knockaulin has produced abundant evidence for ritual activity but evidence for domestic settlement has yet to be clearly identified. None of the sites mentioned shed much light on the broader questions of settlement and economy but, excluding the latter two, a majority of them illustrate one striking fact. Admittedly the sample is very small and very varied but apart from a few iron artefacts and, even more rarely, some sherds of coarse pottery, these sites have not produced a consistent range of diagnostic artefacts. It is perhaps not surprising that prestigious bronze objects, like bridle bits, scabbards or spearbutts, should be absent but the scarcity of smaller metal objects and of pottery in any quantity is noteworthy. Most coarse pottery seems to date to the Dowris Phase and earlier and it is possible that pottery may simply have become an unfashionable and rare commodity, its domestic roles taken by containers of iron, wood and leather.[6] Wooden vessels were used and if there was now a greater reliance on perishable materials and if, as may be the case, few settlement sites were enclosed by substantial earthworks, then the elusive quality of later prehistoric settlement may be disconcerting but not surprising.

QUERN STONES

It would seem to be a reasonable assumption that the distribution of domestic artefacts might provide a significant clue as to the whereabouts of the elusive settlement sites. Since quern stones are likely to be discarded close to their place of use, these objects might be particularly informative. It is generally believed that the rotary quern was introduced to Britain in the 5th or 4th century BC. The earliest form is the beehive quern and the conventional assumption is that this type of quern appeared in Ireland in or about the 1st century BC, though the evidence for such a late arrival is slim. The appearance of this novel method of grinding cereals may have been an event of some significance because the new rotary method represented a considerable improvement on the saddle quern particularly because it crushed as well as ground the cereal and was therefore less onerous for the operator. Its appearance has sometimes been assumed to coincide with an intensification of arable agriculture.[7] Although it may have displaced the saddle quern for corn grinding purposes, the complete replacement of the saddle quern may have been a gradual one because these could have still been used for minor grinding tasks and for crushing nuts and suchlike.

The rotary quern consists of two circular stones, the upper stone, rotated with a handle, has a central hole which serves as a chute for the corn which is ground between the stones, working its way to the edge as it is ground (Fig. 155). The narrowness of the chute or feedpipe often implies the use of a metal spindle, this pivotal piece sitting in a socket in the centre of the lower stone. There are two basic forms of ancient rotary quern, those with thick grinding stones of relatively small diameter, the heavy upper one being slightly domed – hence the name beehive quern, and the flat disc quern, which, in Ireland, seems to have replaced the beehive form in the 1st millennium AD.

Irish beehive querns have been studied by Séamas Caulfield who recorded over 200 examples in 1977 and more have been found since then. The majority are 28cm to 36cm in diameter and invariably have flat grinding surfaces and a funnel-shaped perforation in the upper stone. The position of the handle socket varies, some are horizontally placed, others are vertical with a large proportion of them set in a projecting lug. There are some indications of regional trends, querns with horizontal sockets are concentrated in mid-Ulster,

in the upper Shannon region and northern Connacht, while those with vertical sockets are found mainly in the north-east, in north Leinster and in Tyrone, Antrim and Down.[8]

The general distribution of beehive querns is mainly confined to the northern half of the island with only a few examples found south of a Galway to Dublin line (Fig. 156, 1). The distribution is noteworthy in several respects. A number of concentrations of quern stones, around Belfast and Dublin, Draperstown, Co. Derry, and Bailieborough, Co. Cavan, for instance, reflect the activities of local collectors and antiquarians and do not represent clusters of possible settlements. The general northern bias of the beehive type is genuine however, and may be contrasted with the island-wide distribution of saddle querns and the later disc querns. Caulfield was intrigued by the similarity between this pattern and the northern distribution of material such as bridle bits, spearbutts and La Tène art (Fig. 156, 2). There is a broad similarity but even more intriguing is the fact that in this northern half of the country there is also evidence

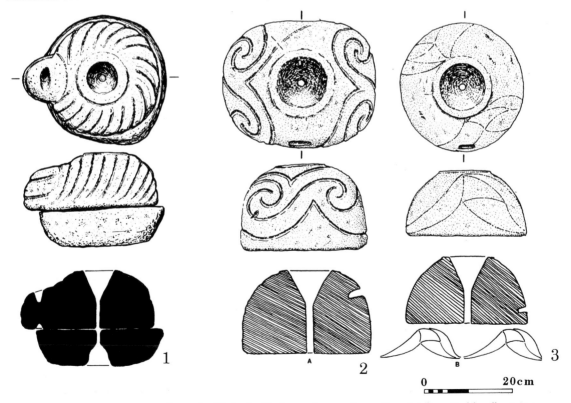

Fig. 155. Beehive querns. 1. From the north of Ireland with decorated upper stone with socket for vertical handle set in a projecting lug. 2. Decorated upper stone with 'horizontal' handle socket from Ticooly-O'Kelly, Co. Galway. 3. Decorated upper stone with 'horizontal' handle socket from Clonmacnoise, Co. Offaly.

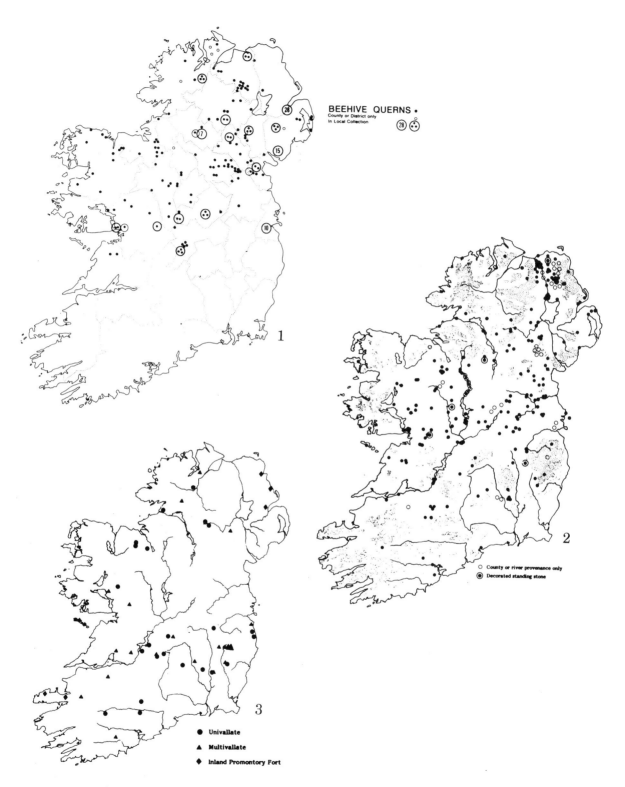

Fig. 156. Distribution maps. 1. Beehive querns. 2. Artefacts excluding querns. 3. Preliminary distribution map of hillforts.

of considerable mutual exclusivity. This is apparent in the north-east where most querns lie well to the west of the River Bann and the metalwork is concentrated in the Bann valley and to the east. It is also to be seen in north Connacht, where querns occur but metalwork is all but absent, and in the Monaghan-Cavan-Louth region. The significance of all this is far from clear.[9]

No beehive quern has been found in a datable context and the type is in effect undated. A small number were clearly special objects and are decorated with curvilinear La Tène ornament. For these at least the assumed date of 2nd century BC to 4th century AD may be appropriate if not very precise. If there is a correlation between rotary querns and an intensification in arable farming, then it is possible that their introduction could have occurred in the earlier centuries AD. Some pollen analyses have suggested a significant increase in tree growth in the period 200 BC to 200 AD with a consequent diminution in farming land. However, from about 200 AD the pollen record appears to demonstrate major land clearance and farming expansion but just how widespread this pattern of land-use contraction and expansion was is still uncertain and needless to say the role of the beehive quern in the story remains a puzzle.[10]

There is little doubt that this quern type originated in northern England and southern Scotland where querns of similar shape, size and handle socket configuration are well represented. Caulfield believed that their appearance was one significant piece of evidence for an immigration of people, but given the superiority and specialized nature of the rotary quern, its rapid adoption by farming communities would not be surprising and this is apparently what happened in Scotland.[11]

Since the introduction of the rotary quern is generally considered to be an important change in farming practice, one of the most puzzling features of the beehive quern in Ireland is its complete absence from settlement sites. Not one has been found in a ringfort, for example, which does suggest that the quern type had disappeared by the middle of the 1st millennium AD when ringforts became common but none have been found on earlier settlements either. They do show signs of use apparently, but where circumstances of discovery have been recorded, the great majority of these querns have been found in bogs. Inevitably this raises the question of ritual deposition and it is

possible that querns, like various metal types, were considered sufficiently valuable for this purpose. It is also possible, of course, that these querns were themselves special objects used only in specific circumstances, and not necessarily in a domestic context. If their primary role was an exceptional one, preparing grain for a special cereal-based alcoholic drink, for instance, the sort of drink that might have filled a fine wooden tankard found near Carrickfergus, Co. Antrim, then this might explain their distributional peculiarities and their eventual deposition in a particular way.

WOODEN AND BRONZE VESSELS

A small number of wooden and bronze vessels merely give a hint of the range of containers that were probably in regular use. Wooden vessels must have been very common and platters, a trough and fragments of several tub-shaped vessels (hollowed from tree trunks with inserted circular bases) were found beneath the Corlea roadway. The tankard found in a bog at Carrickfergus, Co. Antrim (Fig. 157, 1) was stave-built. Its base is a lathe-turned wooden disc and its body is formed of nine staves joined by the tongue-and-groove technique and held in place by a broad band of bronze around the upper exterior. It has one sheet bronze loop handle with a decorated D-shaped escutcheon above bearing engraved curvilinear ornament. It is very similar to a bronze-bound wooden tankard from a bog at Trawsfynydd, Merioneth, which has a bronze-decorated wooden base which was probably meant to be seen and to impress the happy user's drinking companions.

Two elegantly carved round-bottomed wooden bowls, each with one handle, are wooden versions of a type also known in bronze. One from Co. Armagh (Fig. 157, 2) has been radiocarbon dated to 213 BC to 61 AD and the other, from a bog near Cloughmills, Co. Antrim, has provided a broadly similar date of 174 BC to 134 AD. The finest bronze specimen is one found in the river just north Keshcarrigan, Co. Leitrim, which flows into Lough Scur (Fig. 157, 3)). Only 14cm in diameter, this small bowl, perhaps a ceremonial drinking cup, was either cast or beaten into shape and then finished and polished by being spun on a lathe. A graceful bird's head handle is soldered on. A similar handle was found in the Somerset hoard (Fig. 139, 2).

Cauldrons of iron, wood and bronze are known, though not all are securely dated. The Drumlane,

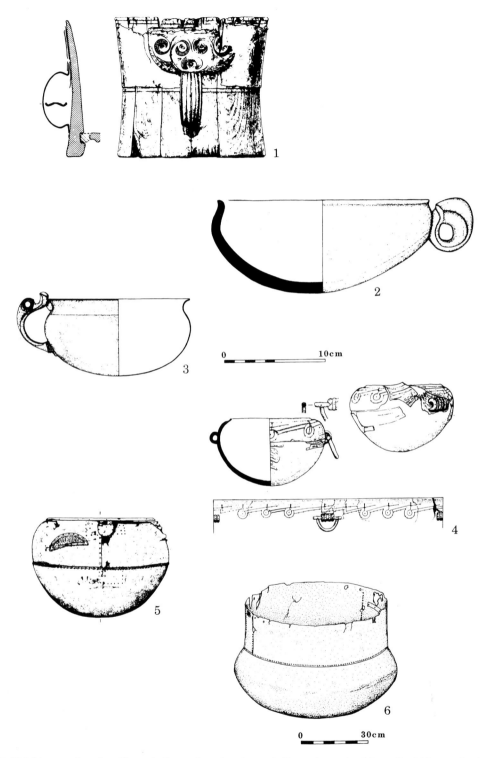

Fig. 157. Drinking vessels and cauldrons. 1. Bronze-bound and stave-built wooden tankard from Carrickfergus, Co. Antrim. 2. Wooden bowl from Co. Armagh. 3. Bronze bowl with ornithomorphic handle from Keshcarrigan, Co. Leitrim. 4. Wooden cauldron from Altartate, Co. Monaghan. 5. Bronze cauldron from a bog at Ballyedmond, Co. Galway. 6. Bronze cauldron of 'projecting-bellied' form from Ballymoney, Co. Antrim.

Co. Cavan, iron cauldron has already been mentioned, its multi-sheet construction recalling earlier bronze cauldrons has prompted suggestions of an early date. Cauldrons made of sheets of iron are said to have been found at Lisnacrogher but have not survived.

A wooden cauldron found in a bog at Altartate Glebe, near Clones, Co. Monaghan (Fig. 157, 4) is carved from a single piece of poplar and has two ribbed lugs one still containing a D-shaped handle of yew wood. It is difficult to date on stylistic grounds but the hemispherical shape of the body and the ribbed lugs have been compared to bronze Dowris Phase cauldrons and a frieze of incised parallel lines and dot and circle ornament below the rim has been compared to a motif on a British pottery vessel possibly of 4th century BC date. A broadly similar but undecorated round-bottomed wooden cauldron from Clogh, Co. Fermanagh, has been radiocarbon dated to 663-363 BC.

A small group of bronze cauldrons with parallels in England and Scotland may date to the early centuries AD. These include a globular specimen found in a bog at Ballyedmond, near Tuam, Co. Galway, and several examples with bulbous bodies and vertical necks, sometimes called 'projecting-bellied cauldrons' (Fig. 157, 6). Like earlier bronze cauldrons these could have served as containers for the preparation of either food or drink for special occasions. The uses to which the wooden cauldrons may have been put are unknown but it is worth considering the possibility that they in particular had a part to play in alcohol-related rituals. Evidence for convivial drinking has been claimed in various places at various times since the 3rd millennium BC and special drinking vessels, such as drinking horns, sometimes suggest a ceremonial aspect. The Carrickfergus tankard and the Keshcarrigan cup might well have fulfilled such a role and the recognition of drinking rituals remains 'a real challenge to archaeology'.[12]

ROYAL SITES AND HILLFORTS IN LATER PREHISTORY

Large monuments such as Haughey's Fort, Co. Armagh, demonstrate that hilltop enclosures and earthworks on a significant scale were constructed at least as early as 1100 BC. As we have seen, monuments such as this and sites like Rathgall, Co. Wicklow, may have been occupied by an aristocratic element and they seemingly had a ritual

component or a ceremonial role as well. The social developments, first detected in the Bishopsland Phase, are still in evidence and, indeed, there is some suggestion that exotic artefacts, display and ritual may have become even more important. Presumably some elite elements of society continued to have both a political and religious role, continuing to control long-distance exchange networks and to participate in ritual activities. It is still difficult to draw a line between the sacred and the secular and nowhere is this more in evidence than on certain 'royal sites' where archaeology of ritual and of settlement, and mythology and early history are all intertwined.

ROYAL SITES

A number of celebrated 'royal sites' figure prominently in early Irish literature and four, Tara (*Temair*), Navan (*Emain Macha*), Rathcroghan (*Cruachain*) and Knockaulin (*Dún Ailinne*) are identified as pre-Christian centres in the calendar of saints known as *Félire Óengusso* ('The Martyrology of Oengus') which dates to about 830 AD. A much quoted hyperbolic verse proclaims the triumph of Christianity and the abandonment of these pagan sites with the advent of the new religion in or about the 5th century. In a variety of early Medieval sources these sites are variously remembered as royal settlements or forts, cemeteries and assembly places. The presence of large, approximately circular earthen enclosures with bank or rampart and internal ditch at three locations has long provided archaeological support for the idea that they are in some way related. Survey and excavation now shows that these sites are related at least in so far as each of them has had a complex history of ceremonial and ritual activity in later prehistoric times. The convention of using their anglicized names (Tara, Navan, Rathcroghan, Knockaulin) is adopted here to distinguish between the physical or archaeological and the literary manifestations of these sites.

TARA, CO. MEATH

The Hill of Tara is situated about mid-way between the towns of Dunshaughlin and Navan in south central Meath. The monuments lie on a low ridge some 2km long and about 155m above sea level. The ridge drops steeply to the west with dramatic views over the central plain of the Irish midlands. The first recorded survey of the monuments at Tara

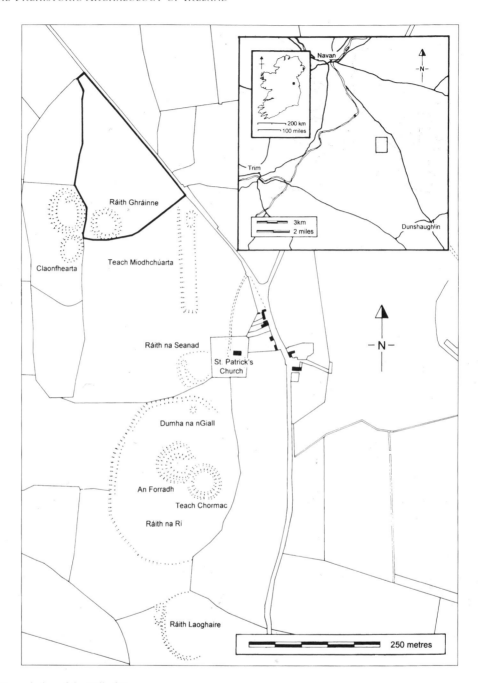

Fig. 158. General plan of the Hill of Tara.

is found in a collection of topographic texts known as *Dindshenchas* (the lore of placenames), the earliest version of which occurs in the *Book of Leinster* dating to about 1160 AD. Various monuments and natural features are named and tales about them recorded. The fanciful Medieval names were re-assigned to the monuments in the 19th century notably by John O'Donovan and George Petrie as part of their work for the Ordnance Survey. Some of these names, ultimately the result of what was a Medieval archaeological survey, are now in common usage and are applied to a variety of enclosures, burial mounds and linear earthworks. Over thirty monuments are visible on the hill and as many again have been identified through aerial photography or geophysical survey. The principal monuments extend over an area some 900m in length from south to north and include several enclosures and a large number of burial mounds (Fig. 158).[13]

To the south is a partly destroyed enclosure named Ráith Laoghaire ('the fort of Laoghaire', an early Historic king of Tara) with overall diameter of about 130m. It seems to consist of a rampart with internal ditch but there may be slight traces of another bank within the ditch.

The largest enclosure on the hill has been named Ráith na Rí (the fort of the kings). It is an earthwork of approximately oval plan measuring about 310m north-south and 210m east-west (Fig. 159). It encloses some 70,000m^2 of the summit and is one of those fairly rare hilltop enclosures characterized by an internal fosse and external bank, a type found at Navan and Knockaulin. At least five monuments are known to occur within Ráith na Rí: they include Dumha na nGiall (the Mound of the Hostages), Dumha na mBó (a mound noted on the first edition of the Ordnance Survey maps but destroyed by agriculture since then), the Forradh and Teach Chormac.

Part of the rampart of the enclosure has been incorporated into modern field boundaries and modified by the addition of a stone wall along the top. Examination of its ground plan reveals that at various points the rampart deviates from its elliptical curve. These aberrations cannot all be explained by local topographic anomalies, and it seems that some were created intentionally. Two of these bulges correspond with known monuments, namely Dumha na mBó and the Mound of the Hostages, and a third with a very low circular feature (*c.* 40m in diameter) due west of the Forradh revealed by aerial photography. It seems likely that the bulges result from a deliberate attempt on the part of the builders to accommodate earlier monuments. That the rampart had to deviate to enclose earlier sites might suggest poor forward planning but it may be that the deviations were intended to visibly proclaim the inclusion of these monuments by exaggerating the effect of their presence on the later enclosure. A section through the internal ditch was excavated by S. P. Ó Ríordáin in the 1950s and showed it to be a deep, V-shaped fosse dug to a depth of 3m into the bedrock; it had a deep vertical-sided palisade trench immediately inside it.

There are three possible entrances, one on the north-west, another on the east and geophysical survey has revealed a third on the south. The eastern entrance is just a gap in the very degraded rampart at this point but it seems to be aligned with the entrance to a ringfort known as Teach Chormac. Geomagnetic survey here has revealed a puzzling funnel-shaped feature, possibly palisade trenches, widening from about 8m near the entrance gap to about 20m towards the ringfort. Geophysical prospection has also confirmed the existence of the entrance on the south and has shown that a linear positive magnetic feature just inside the internal ditch there is also interrupted by a gap approximately 3m wide. This feature may be a continuation of the palisade trench identified by Ó Ríordáin but there is no corresponding gap in the internal ditch. The same is true of the ditch at the north-western entrance where geophysical survey has also failed to record a gap in the fosse even though there are positive magnetic traces of the possible palisade trench. Conor Newman suggests that the ditch at both the north-western and southern entrances was back-filled in order to create causeways, events possibly contemporary with the erection of the palisade and conceivably an indication of a more defensive role for the large enclosure in a later phase.

Two conjoined earthworks are the most visible monuments in Ráith na Rí. The circular earthwork now called Teach Chormac (Cormac's House: the supposed dwelling of the heroic king Cormac mac Airt) is a bivallate ringfort; the enclosed area is flat with a low sub-rectangular mound (traces of a house?) just off centre and is surrounded by two earthen banks with an intervening ditch. The overall diameter is 73m and the entrance, with causeway through the ditch, is on the north-east (Fig. 160). The Forradh (or 'royal seat') is a prominent flat-topped mound surrounded by a ditch and – for most of its circumference – by two banks with an intervening ditch. The internal arrangement of the ditches suggest that this is a large bivallate ring barrow, an impression strengthened by the fact that three small circular burial mounds have been deliberately incorporated into the larger inner bank (on the north-east, south-east and west). The outer bank is noticeably narrower and may be a later addition; since its size is similar to the outer bank of the adjacent Teach Chormac, it is possible that it represents an attempt to physically link the later habitation site to the burial complex. A similar conjoined earthwork

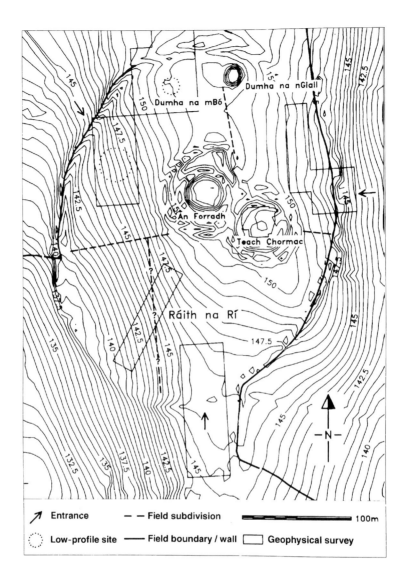

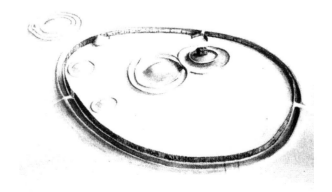

Fig. 159. Plan of Ráith na Rí and reconstruction.

Fig. 160. Above. The Forradh (centre) and Teach Chormac (right) with the Mound of the Hostages (top left). Below. Possible sequence of development of the Forradh and Teach Chormac.

occurs at Carnfree near Rathcroghan. A pillar stone of Newry granite on the summit of the Forradh stands 1.55m high and is said to have been originally located near the 'Mound of the Hostages' to the north. For this reason it is today believed to be the Lia Fáil, the 'stone of destiny': a stone which uttered a cry at the inauguration of a legitimate king of Tara.

The Medieval name Dumha na nGiall, 'the Mound of the Hostages', is applied to a large circular mound, 21m in diameter and 3.5m high, at the northern end of Ráith na Rí. Excavations in 1955-6 and 1959 have shown that it is an early prehistoric monument: a small undifferentiated passage tomb possibly built around 3000 BC (Chapter 3) was covered by a cairn which was later enveloped in a mantle of earth containing numerous later burials of the late third and early second millennia BC. Part of what may have been a trench for a timber palisade was found beneath this monument and is the earliest identified feature on the hill. Conceivably part of a late fourth millennium BC enclosure, this ditch has produced a radiocarbon date of 3355-2465 BC.[14]

The non-defensive internal ditch of the great enclosure, the presence of this complex prehistoric burial mound and of the ring barrow known as the Forradh (and the smaller mounds it incorporates) all suggest that Ráith na Rí was a monument with a major ritual purpose. If Teach Chormac is indeed a ringfort type settlement of the first millennium AD, then a ritual role was superseded or augmented by settlement activity, a sequence of events which also seems to have occurred at the Rath of the Synods.

The name of the 'Rath of the Synods' commemorates the ecclesiastical synods supposed to have been held at Tara by the early 8th century Adomnán. The monument suffered considerable damage between 1899 and 1902 when some lunatic diggings were undertaken by the British Israelites in an attempt to find the Ark of the Covenant. Though the monument has the appearance of a much disturbed multi-vallate ringfort, excavation by S. P. Ó Ríordáin in 1952-53 demonstrated that it had a complicated history (Fig. 161).

The first phase was funerary and consisted of an oval ring ditch measuring 27.5 by 32m with a low ring barrow (about 17m in diameter) to the north-west (now just visible between the middle and outer ramparts of the later ringfort). This ring barrow contained five primary cremations. Some time later, the top of the mound was levelled and four cremations and one crouched unburnt burial were placed at its centre. No dating evidence was found for either stage of burial activity. The second phase consisted of a series circular wall or palisade slots for timber-built structures varying in diameter from about 16m to 30m; at least four separate building phases as well as part of a circle of free-standing timber posts have been identified and such a multiplicity of circular wooden structures recalls Navan and Knockaulin. This phase was sealed by a layer of sterile yellow clay. A cluster of five unburnt burials and two cremations represented the third phase of activity.

The multi-vallate ringfort is the fourth and final phase and is dated to the period 300-500 AD. It consists of four ramparts each with external ditch and the inner enclosure was placed on the site of the phase one ring ditch, the ring barrow being incorporated between the outer two ramparts. The overall diameter is 83m. Traces of two rectangular timber houses were found in the interior and some finds (a lead seal, a glass inset for a ring or brooch and an iron barrel padlock) demonstrate contact with Roman Britain.

A long pair of parallel earthen banks just over 70m north of the multi-vallate ringfort is called the Teach Miodhchuarta or Banqueting Hall and was the subject of much Medieval speculation even to the nature of the seating arrangements. The parallel banks are slightly curved and run downslope from south to north for some 203m with a width of about 30m. Both banks were seemingly raised from material dug from the interior which is now below ground level; there are at least five gaps in the western bank and five or six in the eastern. There are slight traces of a closing bank at the southern end and the northern end is said to have terminated in an area of wet ground known in the *Dindshenchas* as 'the marsh of Tara'. Probably a ceremonial earthwork like the Mucklaghs at Rathcroghan (which also curve and terminate near a pond), it is also possible that this is a cursus, a ceremonial avenue (a monument type known in early prehistoric Britain) aligned on the Mound of the Hostages (though not on the passage tomb itself). It has been suggested too that it might be an Irish version of rectangular ritual enclosures known on the Continent and of various later prehistoric dates.[15]

Ráith Ghráinne, the supposed fort of Gráinne, the legendary lover of Diarmaid, is a large ring

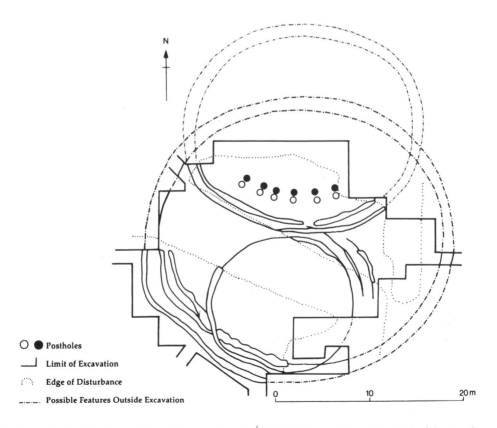

○ ● Postholes

⌐ Limit of Excavation

⋯ Edge of Disturbance

–·–·– Possible Features Outside Excavation

0   10   20 m

Fig. 161. Above. Rath of the Synods. Below. Schematic plan of Ó Ríordáin's excavations at the Rath of the Synods.

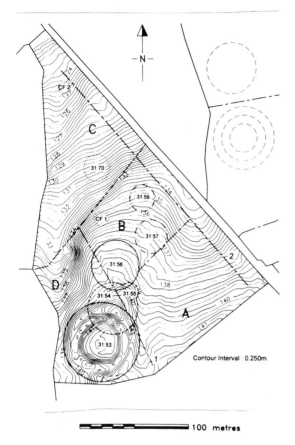

100 metres

Fig. 162. Ráith Ghráinne (31:53) and associated monuments.

barrow with central circular mound surrounded by a ditch with external bank (Fig. 162, 31:53). The mound measures about 32m in diameter and has a circular depression 13.5m in diameter with an encircling ditch and a low external bank (a small ring barrow) at its centre. The diameter of Ráith Ghráinne's external bank is about 70m diameter and it widens considerably in the north-east quadrant to incorporate a small mound. Geophysical and aerial survey has demonstrated an extraordinary sequence of ring barrow construction here: the latter small mound being, in fact, the central mound of a larger ring barrow (Fig. 162, 31:54) deliberately incorporated into Ráith Ghráinne. This larger ring barrow is about 60m in diameter and it too has a small circular mound *c.* 20m diameter with possible ditch (31:55) incorporated in its north-eastern quadrant. Geophysical survey suggests that the north-west quadrant of 31:54 has been erased by a larger ring barrow 31:56 which has a central circular area

(diameter about 26m) enclosed by ditch with low external bank (44m diameter approximately). Thus a possible sequence consists of the small mound 31:55 being incorporated into the large ring barrow 31:54 which is then partly erased by the later ring barrow 31:56 with 31:54 in turn being subsumed in part by Ráith Ghráinne (31:53). Five other low profile circular sites are located north and north-east of Ráith Ghráinne.

The Claonfhearta or so-called 'Sloping Trenches' lie north-west of the 'Banqueting Hall' on the steep western slope of the hill. One explanation prompted by their location considered them the remains of a royal residence which slipped down the hill when a king of Tara gave a false judgement. Both the northern and the southern 'Sloping Trenches' are large ring barrows 80m and 57m in diameter respectively. The northern monument has a small ring barrow incorporated in its bank on the north and a hole in the central mound indicates ancient disturbance. The southern has a small round mound on top of its central mound and there are three other small mounds placed between the two large ring barrows. Eight more small mounds lie in a line to the south along the ridge.

The practice of deliberately incorporating earlier monuments within the circuit of later ones has been noted at Ráith na Ríg, at the Rath of the Synods, the Forradh and Ráith Ghráinne (and in a different way at the Mound of the Hostages) and presumably means that earlier monuments were often considered important enough to warrant their inclusion in the new. The timespan between such different phases of activity may only be determined by excavation but, even if the chronology is not clear, these various monuments provide remarkable evidence of significant periods of carefully planned ritual continuity. At both the Forradh and Ráith Ghráinne the earlier mound is incorporated in such a way that it protrudes not on the inside but on the outside of the bank and therefore does not interrupt the curve of the internal ditch. In contrast, at the northern Claonfhearta, and possibly at the Rath of the Synods, the entire monument, bank, internal ditch and mound, seems to have been incorporated but here too the central mound is on the line of the bank and protrudes on its outside.

From the possible enclosure which pre-dates the passage tomb in the Mound of the Hostages to the late Roman contacts evinced in the Rath of the Synods, from before 3000 BC to 400 AD, the Hill of Tara has been the focus of activity, much of it funerary and ritual, for over three millennia. While various monuments clearly succeeded one another over time, it has yet to be demonstrated that this impressive prehistoric continuum is an unbroken one. Continuous or not, the long sequence of activity is a good illustration of how monuments and landscapes are enhanced or re-modelled by successive generations.

NAVAN, CO. ARMAGH

The name 'the Navan complex' has been given to a concentration of archaeological monuments in an area of intense late prehistoric activity stretching for just over a kilometre around Navan Fort in Co. Armagh. This complex is considered to be the archaeological manifestation of *Emain Macha*, the capital of the Ulaid in early Irish literary and pseudo-historical sources. Agricultural and other activities have damaged many of the sites but these

events have also resulted in a large number of stray archaeological finds many of them of late prehistoric date. Over forty sites of possible prehistoric date have been identified many of them by aerial photography. Some 46 actual or possible sites have been recorded (Fig. 163) and range from such substantial monuments as the enclosure known as Navan Fort to a number of more ephemeral crop marks.

There are two zones of prehistoric activity: one comprises the Navan enclosure (Fig. 163, 1) which contains a mound (2) placed just off centre, and a ring ditch (3). To the north are the sites of two mounds of possible 4th millennium BC date thought to have been passage tombs (9 and 10) and to the north-east is a small natural lake (shown on the plan at its original, larger extent) now called Loughnashade (4). The focus of a western zone is the multivallate hillfort now known as Haughey's Fort (6) and to its north-east is the artificial pond

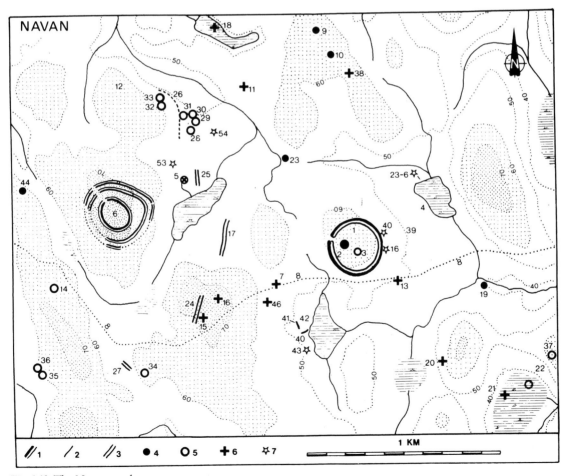

Fig. 163. The Navan complex.

traditionally called the King's Stables (5), already described in Chapter 6, with groups of ring ditches to the north and south. Several stretches of double linear ditch systems have been identified to the east and south, notably in Creeveroe townland (17 and 24). An eastern zone is represented by the ecclesiastical centre at Armagh 2.6km to the east.[16]

While the two possible passage tombs and a number of artefacts indicate early prehistoric activity, the Navan complex begins to develop around the 13th century BC with the construction of Haughey's Fort and the King's Stables. The excavations in the Navan enclosure in the central zone suggests that this became the focus of later activity perhaps coinciding with the abandonment of Haughey's Fort in or about the 10th century BC. Some activity did continue there; it will be recalled that one pit, which contained a small iron object possibly a strap handle, produced charcoal samples with radiocarbon dates which ranged from *c.* 400 to 200 BC.

THE NAVAN ENCLOSURE

Excavations were undertaken in the Navan enclosure by D. M. Waterman between 1963 and 1972. This large earthwork encloses the summit of a drumlin ridge and though only about 60m above sea level has commanding views in all directions, especially to the north-west. It is this site which, in the past, has been specifically identified as the legendary capital of Ulster, the *Emain Macha* of the tales of the Ulster Cycle.

The enclosure is six hectares in area and is a large circle surrounded by a wide deep ditch with a very substantial external earthen bank, with an overall diameter of approximately 286m (Fig. 164). There seems to have been an original entrance on the west. The enclosure itself has not been excavated so its date is uncertain. It has been suggested that it might be of 3rd millennium BC date (as is the case with some British 'henge monuments' with ditch and external bank) but a radiocarbon date from its ditch might indicate that it was constructed in later prehistoric times: a core from the ditch provided a date 766–398 BC but it is not known if the sample came from the very lowest levels of the ditch; the date simply indicates that the ditch was dug at some date before this time.

Waterman's excavations were conducted at two visible monuments in the interior: a ring ditch (site A), much ploughed over and surviving mainly as a wide shallow ditch with traces of an external bank,

50m in external diameter, south-south-east of the centre of the enclosure and at a large circular flat-topped mound (site B), 50m in diameter and 6m high, standing on the centre of the hill top about 55m west-north-west of the centre. Geophysical survey has demonstrated the presence of other features within the enclosure including a large double circle about 30m in diameter between sites A and B.

Site A was partially excavated in 1961 and consisted of a wide annular ditch 2m deep and 5.5m wide on average with a V-shaped profile. The average outer diameter of the ditch was 37m (Fig. 165). No entrance was found in the area excavated. The interior of the site appeared to be raised but this appearance seems to be mainly due to the selection of a slight pre-existing natural rise. There appeared to be a low, broad, external bank on the west.

The excavation of the interior of the monument revealed two main phases. Features of Phase A (which definitely pre-dated the digging of the ditch) included three concentric slots 65cm wide on average, the outer and inner averaging almost 1m in depth but the middle one averaged only about 50cm. The diameters were 16.6m, 18.8m and 20.3m respectively and they were cut away by the later surrounding ditch. A sequence was established showing that the middle slot was dug first, then the outer and finally the inner and it seemed that each slot was used in turn independently of the others. Entrances were not found in the area investigated. A series of post-pipes, 1m apart on average, was located in the inner slot indicating that some form of timber walling had been embedded it and it is suggested therefore that the three circles represent three successive timber structures. Sherds of plain coarse bucket-shaped pottery and two radiocarbon dates from charcoal found in the inner and outer slots indicate a date between the 4th century BC and the 1st century AD.

The date of Phase B is uncertain; this phase is represented by a pair of concentric ring slots with diameters of 12.2m and 16.3m with a wide space of 2m between them. The slots were about 30cm in width and in depth and had an entrance on the east flanked by large post-holes. The inner slot continued across the fill of the outer Phase A slot on the west but all slots disappeared at this point. The Phase B slots were not concentric with the ditch and their relationship is not clear, it may be that the two are not contemporary. There was a large post-hole,

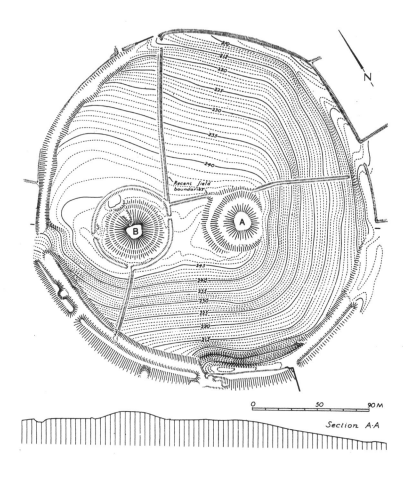

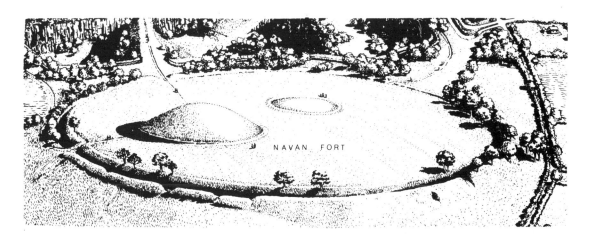

Fig. 164. Above. Contour plan of Navan Fort showing the large mound (B) and the ring ditch (A). Below. An artist's impression of Navan Fort today, the mound, site B, is on the left.

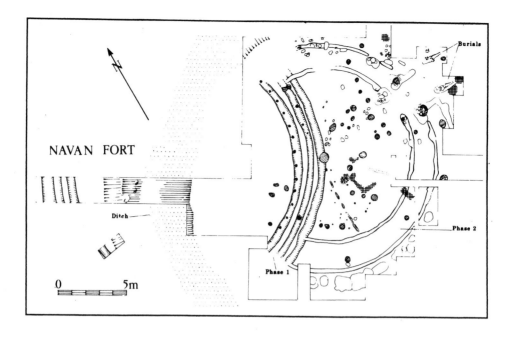

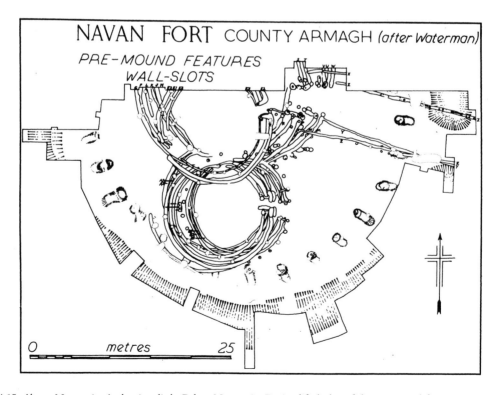

Fig. 165. Above. Navan site A: the ring ditch. Below. Navan site B: simplified plan of the pre-mound features.

70cm in diameter and 61cm deep, in the centre of this Phase B structure as well as a number of scattered post-holes and a hearth. No finds came from this phase and no radiocarbon samples were recovered but Waterman believed that the ring slots might represent a substantial house of the early Historic period because two east-facing extended unburnt burials (one of which had been in a nailed coffin) were found to the east of the entrance and more or less flanking the access. The only dating evidence for the ditched enclosure was provided by the terminal of a bronze brooch of early Historic or Viking Age found 90cm above the bottom of the ditch.

THE GREAT MOUND

The great mound (Site B) was excavated between 1963 and 1971. It is approximately 6m high and 50m in diameter at the base. About two thirds of the site were excavated and approximately one third of the lowest part of the mound, on the north, was left undisturbed for future investigation. After excavation the mound was restored to its original form.

Phases 1-2: there was some activity on the hill top in the 4th or 3rd millennia BC (Phase 1) marked by scatters of pottery and several hundred flaked flints, a number of flint implements (including a Bann flake) and three fragments of polished stone axes. The hilltop was ploughed sometime after this early activity as shown by faint shallow gullies filled with a thin fossil plough soil (Phase 2).

Phase 3 represents the major period of later prehistoric activity and is divided into three sub-phases (3i to 3iii). The earliest activity of this phase (3i), which probably began around the 9th century BC was the digging of a circular ditch about 5m wide and 1m deep enclosing a space approximately 45m in diameter (Fig. 165). Four or five metres inside this ditch, and apparently contemporary with it, was a ring of large pits a little over 4m apart centre to centre. The pits had been cut through the fossil soil and ranged in maximum diameter from 1.8m to 3.3m. They may have held the posts of a palisade standing within the ditch which was interrupted by a cobbled causeway 4.4m wide on the east. Although the circular structure and the ditch would seem to have been contemporary a radiocarbon date from one of the post-pits and two from the ditch do not overlap even at two standard deviations: the timber post date falls approximately into the period *c.* 1600 to 1200 BC while the ditch has yielded two dates in the range *c.* 900 to 550 BC.

Phase 3ii is represented by a complex sequence of circular timber structures (revealed as foundation trenches or ring slots) once thought to be of the Dowris Phase but now considered to date from after the mid 4th century BC to the late 2nd century BC.

A series of nine successive ring slots overlay the line of the presumed palisade of Phase 3i on the south (Figs 166-167). The earliest of these ring slots may have been dug while the palisade was standing but later examples cut the line of the palisade. A layer of dark soil *c.* 30 cm. deep, which would normally be interpreted as an occupation layer (called 'fossil soil' in the excavation report) accumulated during the period represented by the construction and use of the slots. The earliest slots were cut into subsoil but the latest examples barely reached subsoil and were filled with material identical to that into which they were cut. Apart from the earliest slot, the ring slots occurred in three groups of three more or less concentric slots (A–C) and the sequence in each group was middle, outer and inner (as in the group of larger early ring slots observed in the ring ditch). The diameters of the slots ranged from 13.5m to 10m and gaps on the east, 1m-2m wide, sometimes inturned and flanked by post-pits, were presumably entrances. Lumps of burnt clay were found in the loose fill of some slots which may have held vertical plank or post-and-wattle walls and some post-holes seemed to suggest the provision of additional support on occasion. Small burnt areas and groups of flat stones indicated the presence of hearths at the centres of the A–C structures.

Attached to or touching the northern side of the southern ring slots was a series of six further ring slots of greater diameter, *c.* 20m-25m. Their full extent was not revealed so that it is not possible to suggest exactly which of the five or six slots on the east (S–W) were linked with which of the six on the west (F–H, J–L).

It is clear that the individual elements of the northern and southern ring slot groups were attached and formed figure-of-eight units which communicated by means of narrow gaps on the northern sides of the southern ring slots. Which circle was connected with which is again not clear but it seems that the rebuilding of the northern structures did not follow the same sequence as those on the south. It is possible that the construction sequences of the two groups were to some extent independent or that some of the southern slots,

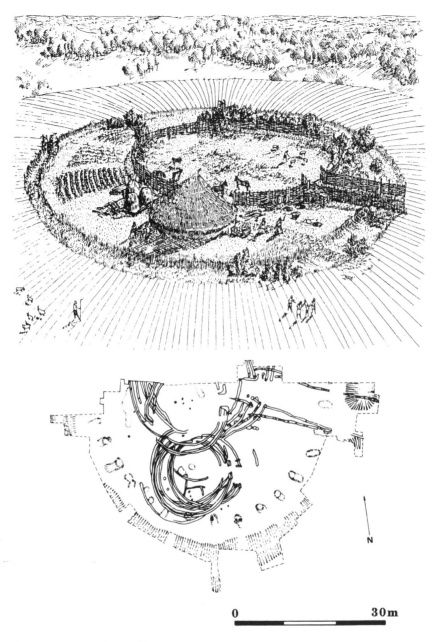

0   30m

Fig. 166. An artist's reconstruction of Navan Phase 3ii.

perhaps at the beginning, were not matched by northern ring slots. Chris Lynn has suggested that one reason for the consistent repositioning of the southern ring slots could be that each structure, or group of three structures, had to be placed so that it could be joined to a northern structure already in existence which was not renewed at the same time.

The northern ring slots had wide gaps on the east approached by parallel entrance palisade slots 5.5m apart, later replaced by a second pair 7.8m

apart. Some of the slots retained impressions of the sockets for stout upright posts *c.* 50cm apart.

It seems that the southern ring slots represented the wall trenches of eight or nine successive round houses with doors on the east, most of them communicating with open air enclosures on the north which may have been working areas, farmyards or stockyards, these in turn being approached by fenced avenues, perhaps droveways. Some ritual impulse is also possible, particularly

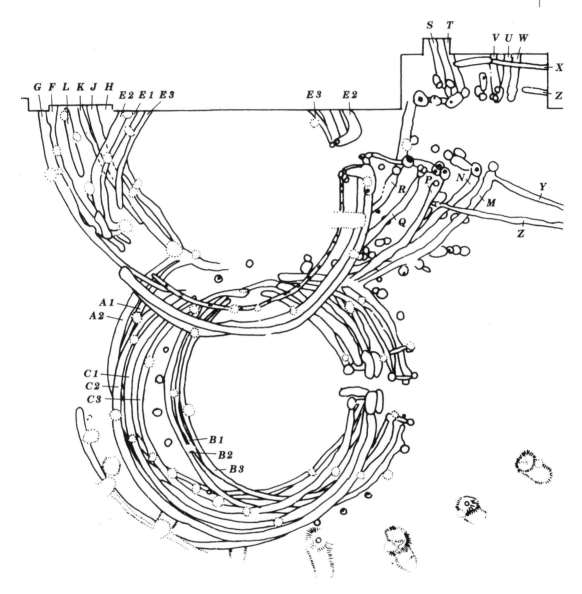

Fig. 167. Detail of successive ring-slots at Navan Phase 3ii.

given the extraordinary repetitive constructional sequence of middle and outer and inner ring slots observed in circles A–C although Lynn has suggested that this sequence could be due to careful wall replacement, a new wall being built while most of an earlier one was still standing.

In Phase 3iii, dated from the late 2nd century BC to not after 95 BC, another series of three ring slots (E1–3) replace the southern and northern structures and seemingly display the same construction sequence, middle, outer, inner. They range in diameter from about 11m to 13.5m but now have two opposed entrances on east and west. If they

were attached to larger enclosures these lie in the unexcavated area to the north. The latest ring slot, the inner one, is narrower than the others and it retained clear traces at intervals of the sockets of small elongated timbers (? stakes with timbering between them). This structure may have been removed to make way for the Phase 4 building.

A range of finds (several hundred sherds of coarse bucket shaped pots almost all from the fossil soil of Phase 3, shale armlets, glass beads, a bronze bar toggle, a fragment of a winged chape, part of a socketed bronze sickle, a tiny socketed bronze axe and a bronze pin with a spiral-ribbed head) indicates that occupation continued throughout the Dowris Phase and probably into the 4th century BC. Though a few small fragments of clay moulds (for a pin and a blade) were found, there was no evidence of metalworking on site. Some small iron objects and a ring headed pin presumably date to late in Phase 3. The discovery of a skull and jaw of a Barbary Ape (*Macaca sylvanus*) was an exceptional find. This animal must have been a prestigious import from North Africa and is an important indication that far flung contacts existed and included not just metalwork but perishable apes as well. The skull, which was found in ring slot C2 (Phase 3ii), has been radiocarbon dated to 390-20 BC. The bones of other animal species were present in unusual proportions; there were twice as many pigs as cattle and nine times as many pigs as sheep or goat. This and other anomalous features have prompted the suggestion that the bones might represent a ritual rather than domestic assemblage.

TRIBAL KINGS OR PRIESTLY KEEPERS?

Lynn believes that the hearths, animal bones, pottery and other finds of Phases 3ii and 3iii all indicate that circular houses were the domestic dwellings of an elite with attached enclosures to the north for livestock. In his discussion of the nature of the occupancy of the site at this time he considered the social position of the high-status inhabitants and posed the question were they 'kings or priestly keepers'? This phrase encapsulates the interpretative problems posed by the evidence and the argument as to a secular or ritual function. Again it is probably a mistake to consider the two roles as separate and distinct. As already noted when examining Haughey's Fort and Rathgall, domestic occupation and ritual activity are not mutually incompatible and their combination may actually be a mark of enhanced status. The subsequent history of the site, which was undoubtedly ceremonial in quite an exceptional way, would tend to confirm that there was already a significant ritual or religious dimension to the Phase 3ii and 3iii settlement.

THE 'FORTY METRE STRUCTURE'

Phase 4 is represented by the construction of a huge multi-ring timber structure (Fig. 168). The structure seems to have been positioned to fit neatly inside and concentric with the Phase 3i ditch. In many excavated areas the surface of the fossil soil, which

accumulated during Phase 3iii, remained the ground surface with no further deposition during Phase 4. The timber structure was circular and consisted of five major concentric rings of posts and a large central post, some 280 in all. The outer wall of the building (37.3m in diameter) comprised 34 large post-pits, 1.25m in diameter and depth and approximately 3.5m apart. Each pit originally contained a single post (in every case supplemented later by the insertion of a second, identical, contiguous post) linked by horizontal split timbers in a trench. Outside this was a narrow deeper discontinuous slot, 40.5m in diameter. This slot and the light walling it contained were quickly abandoned, being cut away by the sloping pits dug to insert the secondary posts in the main wall, suggesting that it may have served as a fence slot during the construction phase or even as some sort of external lean-to against the main wall. The post-pits of the internal rings measured about 36cm-46cm in diameter and were dug to an average depth of about 91cm through the fossil soil into the subsoil; the oak butts of many of these large posts were preserved in the damp ground. The entrance was on the west and here the internal post-ring system was interrupted by four roughly parallel rows of posts forming three aisles leading to the centre of the structure. At the centre was a timber post so large that it had to be dragged at an angle into its post-pit on a sloping ramp 6m long cut into subsoil. The axe-dressed stump of this great post, about 50cm in diameter, was found in the central pit which was 2.3m deep. This central post (perhaps a carved timber pillar) could have been 13m or more in height.

Large patches of the area inside this structure were covered with spreads of relatively clean clay, material which could not be packed back into the post-pits. This often sealed the packing around individual posts as well as undisturbed Phase 3iii fossil soil and was in turn directly covered by Phase 5 material. There were no hearths or other evidence for occupation in this Phase 4 structure. Furthermore, surplus clay spread out from the very large central post-pit sealed the clay spreads and packing of neighbouring posts showing that the central post was inserted later than these and perhaps last of all. This huge monument was carefully built to a predetermined radial plan and it may have been temporarily roofed. Dendrochronological analysis has determined that the large central post was felled

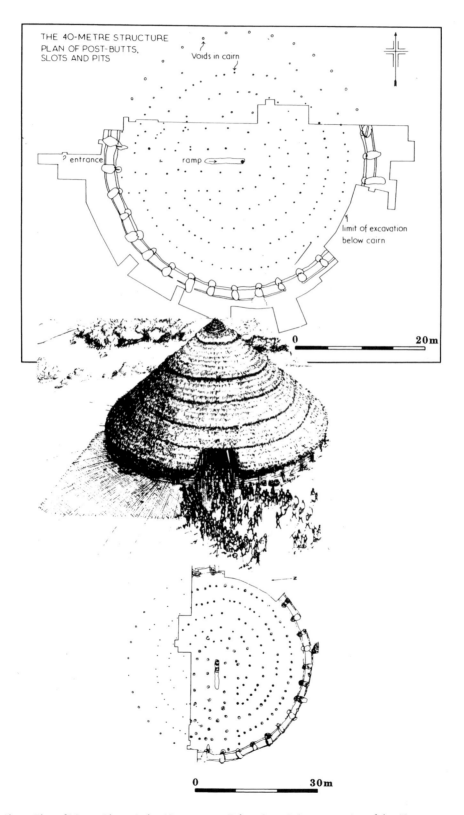

THE 40-METRE STRUCTURE
PLAN OF POST-BUTTS,
SLOTS AND PITS

Voids in cairn

? entrance

ramp

limit of excavation
below cairn

0   20m

0   30m

Fig. 168. Above. Plan of Navan Phase 4: the 40m structure. Below. An artist's reconstruction of the 40m structure.

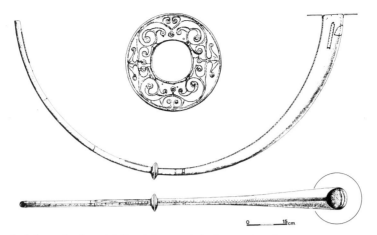

Fig. 169. The Loughnashade horn: the decorated disc at the mouth is shown enlarged.

in late 95 BC or early 94 BC and this dates the completion of the great timber structure.[17]

Phase 5 followed quickly and the multi-ring timber structure evidently had a relatively short period of use. While it was still standing its interior was filled with a cairn of limestone blocks. That the wooden structure still stood was demonstrated by the survival of roughly cylindrical vertical voids left by its rotted oak posts at a high level in the cairn (and continuing down into the post-pits) and by the fact that the wall of the structure also served as an external revetment for the cairn. The cairn was 37.5m in diameter with a maximum height of 2.8m at the centre. Its surface was divided into clearly-defined but somewhat irregular radial sectors by the use of different sizes of stones, by various arrangements of stones and by varying admixtures of soil, clay or turf in the sectors. The radial divisions visible in the top of the cairn did not apparently extend downwards through the cairn and they do not appear to be related in any significant way to the radial alignments in the timber structure which it entombed.

The next step, in what appears to have been a continuous process, was the burning of the outer wall of the forty metre structure. This burning, around and possibly over the cairn, was probably deliberate as plentiful remains of brush-wood survived as charred twigs around the excavated perimeter of the building against the base of the timber wall. The cairn was finally covered by a mound of turves, 2.5m high at the centre, and much of this material must have been obtained by stripping the turf and topsoil from a large area.

The great timber building of Phase 4 was not used for occupation and the size and plan of the

undertaking suggest that it may have been a communal effort under the supervision of a technically competent person or group. The free-standing post at the centre would seem to confirm the suggestion that it was used for a ritual or ceremonial purpose early in the 1st century BC and the construction of the building, its use, the building of the cairn, the burning and the addition of the sod mound may well have been planned from the start as parts of a more or less continuous series of ritual acts.[18]

During drainage works in nearby Loughnashade in or about the early 19th century four large bronze horns were found along with a number of human skulls and other bones. No precise details have been recorded and three of the horns have disappeared. One survives and is a great curving horn, about 1.86m in length, made of riveted sheet bronze with a decorative disc at the bell end bearing La Tène repoussé ornament (Fig. 169). The discovery of fine bronze work and human bones suggests that the site was the focus of ritual depositions some possibly contemporary with the ceremonial activity at the Navan enclosure.[19]

There is an interesting parallelism between the focal points of the two prehistoric zones of the general Navan complex – each consists of a large earthwork with a ritual body of water immediately below and to its north-east. This observation should not be pushed too far for the enclosures seem to be very different in form and function but it is interesting that a double linear ditch system (in Creeveroe townland) appears to separate Haughey's Fort and the King's Stables in one area and the Navan enclosure and Loughnashade in the other. A similar division of the landscape may be seen at Tara where a linear earthwork, 1.2km west of the complex on the hill, seems to separate an embanked enclosure in Riverstown townland and a hillfort in Ringlestown townland to the south of Tara itself.[20]

KNOCKAULIN, CO. KILDARE

Several interim reports on the excavations at Knockaulin, Co. Kildare, have appeared. Knockaulin is a rounded hill, rising to 180m above sea level, south-west of Kilcullen, Co. Kildare. Its summit is crowned by a great earthwork: an oval area of some 13 hectares is enclosed by a substantial rampart with internal ditch (Fig. 170). The monument has been identified since the 19th century as the *Dún Ailinne* of early Irish literature, the seat of the kings of Leinster. The only features in the enclosure were a small earthwork noted by John O'Donovan, a low mound on the summit of the hill (approximately circular with a diameter of about 20m and a height of some 80cm) and a well known as St John's Well.

From 1968 to 1975, apart from limited test excavation in the northern half of the enclosure and some trenches across the rampart and at the entrance on the east, excavation concentrated on the summit area. Geophysical prospection consisted of a magnetometer survey of the whole area within the enclosing bank and ditch with more intensive survey on the summit where resistivity survey was also undertaken: the only substantial anomalies detected were in the area of the low mound and correlated with areas of intense burning.

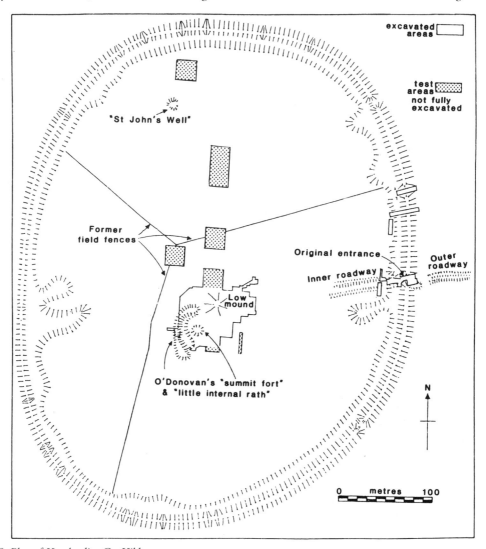

Fig. 170. Plan of Knockaulin, Co. Kildare.

The external bank and internal ditch are damaged in numerous places by small, recent quarries to extract bedrock. The ditch is interrupted by a causeway on the east and this seems to be the original entrance. Though this area had also been damaged by quarrying, excavation confirmed the existence of an 8m wide roadway with the remains of a low dry-stone revetment or kerb on either side; it did not have a prepared surface nor did it show any ruts. Its axis was aligned on the summit of the hill. This and the fact that the causeway proved to be undug bedrock confirmed the impression that this was an original entrance. The entrance appeared quite simple: the ends of the bank terminated without trace of revetting in either timber or stone and no evidence of a timber gate was found. The bank was of simple dump construction and the ditch was filled with natural silting. One radiocarbon date obtained from the humus beneath the rampart gives a terminal date for its construction – probably sometime after 700 BC.

Excavation revealed some slight traces of early prehistoric activity in the summit area. The earliest is attested by an irregular circular ditch (Fig. 171: 281) with a diameter of about 20m which contained a hollow scraper and part of a leaf-shaped flint arrowhead, a pit (293) which contained sherds of a decorated pot of the type found in Linkardstown burials of the 4th millennium BC, several hundred stray fragments of other pottery vessels as well as pieces of flint and chert and a cup-marked stone. Some sherds of a Bowl Tradition pot found in a pit (2790) are the only late 3rd millennium BC evidence.[21]

LATE PREHISTORIC STRUCTURES: FROM 390 BC

Three major phases of late prehistoric activity were identified on the summit in the area of the low mound: these were labelled the 'White', 'Rose' and 'Mauve' phases by the excavator. A thin and compressed ginger-coloured sod was identified where protected by undisturbed late prehistoric levels and a circular trench approximately 22m in diameter to support close-set timber uprights (a palisade or fence) was cut through this sod (Fig. 171: 512, 'White' phase). The entrance may have been on the north-east. There was no dating evidence in what remained of the primary fill of this trench but since the succeeding structure

('Rose' phase) appeared to have been built immediately or shortly after the extraction of the posts in trench 512, and since the 'Rose' phase is late, a similar late prehistoric date is inferred for the 'White' phase.

The remarkable structures of the 'Rose' phase were on a more ambitious scale. The three concentric trenches set about 1m apart (60, 513, 514) enclosed an inner area of 28.5m; the entrance to this circle was flanked by substantial fences (278, 314) forming a sort of 'funnel' which contained an avenue of posts, which in turn enclosed two short trenches (2231, 2232). On the southern side of the large 'Rose' enclosure were smaller conjoined timber circles (519, 520 etc.), with a narrow 1m wide entrance to the larger circles. No structures, or even isolated posts, could be shown to have stood within the main 'Rose' phase circle which was apparently an open space. Bernard Wailes believes that these concentric trenches and the timbers they contained supported some superstructure. The graded size of the posts in the three concentric trenches, the inner one (60) containing the smallest, the middle trench (513) containing timbers of middle size and the outer trench up to 1m deep (514) holding the largest timbers, suggests that this putative superstructure was raked, with the inner side being lower than the outer. According to Wailes this would be consistent with a two-tier standing (or seating) arrangement for persons viewing or participating in ceremonial events or displays conducted in the open interior space. However, there are obvious parallels with the structures at Navan 3ii which, of course, reflected a sequence of construction and which have been interpreted as circular houses with attached stockades but given the differences in scale it is debatable if this was the case at Knockaulin too (Fig. 172).[22]

The 'Rose' phase structures were dismantled (except for a few posts in trench 314 which were burnt in place) and a slightly larger but different structure built in the following 'Mauve' phase. Two concentric timber circles were constructed (515, 516) with an overall diameter of some 42m and with a substantial entrance to the east-north-east. A 25m diameter circle of large, free-standing, posts (1–30) was erected in the centre of this enclosure: where sufficient primary fill remained in place, it was estimated that these posts were about 50cm in diameter.

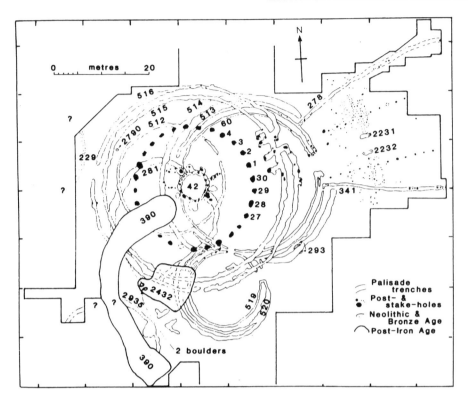

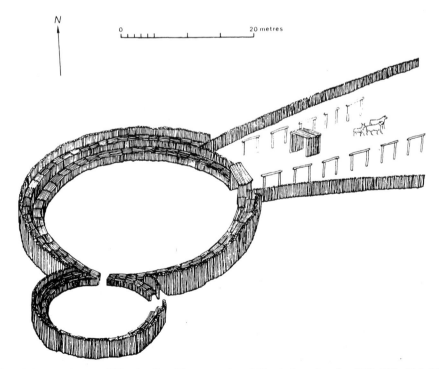

Fig. 171. Plan of the summit area of Knockaulin with construction of 'Rose' phase (trenches 519, 520, 514, 513, 60, 278, 341, etc.).

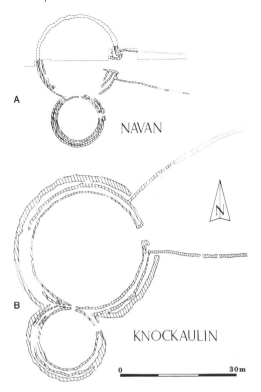

Fig. 172. A comparison of Navan Phase 3ii and Knockaulin 'Rose' phase.

In the centre of this circle was a circular trench 6m in diameter (42) in which several well-defined post-holes (most at least 25cm in diameter) could be identified. There was no obvious entrance. Around the perimeter of this structure were a series of holes of uncertain purpose – it was not possible to determine if they once held timbers. Wailes has tentatively reconstructed these features (Fig. 173) as a timber tower with supporting timber buttresses (rather than a hut, given the small diameter, the size of posts and absence of a hearth or entrance). The outermost timber circles (515 and 516) and the 25m circle of free-standing timbers were contemporary. While the presumed tower cannot be stratigraphically linked to the circles, given that they are all stratigraphically post-'Rose' and share the same geometric centre Wailes believes they all formed part of the same design and since the minimum distance between the outer wall (516) and the 25m timber circle, or between the latter and the tower, is 9m a roofed structure is considered implausible. A tentative reconstruction shows a buttressed central wooden tower 9m high surrounded by a circle of freestanding timber posts with the 42m diameter timber double palisade

around the outside. The latter may have supported a platform as in the 'Rose' phase circle. Again Chris Lynn has drawn attention to parallels with the Navan 40m structure: the dimensions are similar and both have a central timber feature, and if the four inturned entrance elements of trench 515 are extended inwards, they align with posts in the 25m circle and produce three aisles running from the entrance to the centre as at Navan (Fig. 173). He has also noted the possibility that the ring of large free-standing posts could conceivably have supported some sort of superstructure.

The 'Mauve' phase structure was dismantled in its turn, but not all at once. The posts in trenches 515 and 516 were extracted while the 25m timber circle remained standing, for some later material overlies the fill of 515 but not the fill of the post-holes of the circle. Eventually these were extracted and the tower dismantled though it is not certain if this all happened at the one time. Thus the 'White', 'Rose' and 'Mauve' structures were all deliberately dismantled. Wailes remarked that not one post had decayed in its socket but almost everywhere the packing of the post-holes had been disturbed by rocking the timbers in the course of extraction. The absence of any sterile humus may imply that the phases followed one another immediately, the whole sequence perhaps lasting only a few decades, at most a century or two.

Later material deliberately deposited on the site included redeposited glacial till with a small area of rough paving, followed by numerous thin lenses of humus containing animal bone, burnt stone, charcoal, and ash – perhaps the remains of periodic feasting. Cattle (54%) and pig (36%) make up the bulk of the animal bones with a little horse and sheep represented.[23] Many of the cattle were killed as very young calves in April or May shortly after birth, others were killed at about six months of age probably in late September or early October, possible evidence of feasting at two very different times of the year. This and the structural evidence would support the excavator's belief that late prehistoric Knockaulin was one very large ceremonial site. In this it seems to differ from Tara, Navan and Rathcroghan which are all concentrations of numbers of earthworks but it is possible that the ring barrows, enclosures and linear earthworks on the Curragh some 5km to the north-west should be considered part of a larger Knockaulin complex.[24]

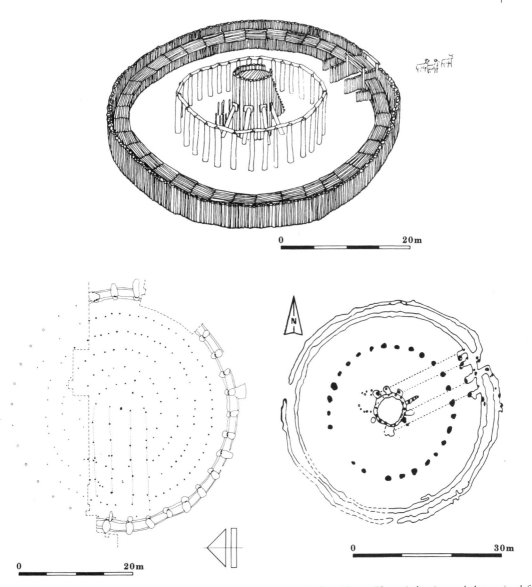

Fig. 173. Above. A reconstruction of Knockaulin 'Mauve' phase structure. Below. Navan Phase 4 showing ambulatory (on left) and (on right) Knockaulin 'Mauve' phase for comparison.

An irregular quarry ditch (390) cut through all the late prehistoric levels, its upcast forming the irregular earthwork noted by O'Donovan and clearly a feature much later than the abandonment of the site. A late prehistoric date for the ritual activity is indicated by a range of artefacts including an iron sword found in the fill of the 'Mauve' phase palisade trench 516 and possibly of the 2nd or 3rd centuries BC. Also found were an iron spear-head, several iron needles, fragments of bronze fibulae and glass beads. A series of radiocarbon dates do no more than confirm the general late prehistoric date which possibly extends from 390 BC to 320 AD.[25]

RATHCROGHAN, CO. ROSCOMMON

Rathcroghan is probably best known as the royal seat of the legendary Queen Maeve and her consort Ailill, King of Connacht, and the place where that great Cattle Raid of Cooley, the *Táin Bó Cúailgne*, was initiated. Known as *Cruachain* in early literature, it figures, like Navan and Tara, as a major royal settlement; it is also sometimes described as the location of a great cemetery where many warriors are buried, as well as the inauguration site of kings, and as a magic place with an entrance to the Otherworld.

Rathcroghan today is a complex of earthworks and other monuments about 5km north-west of the

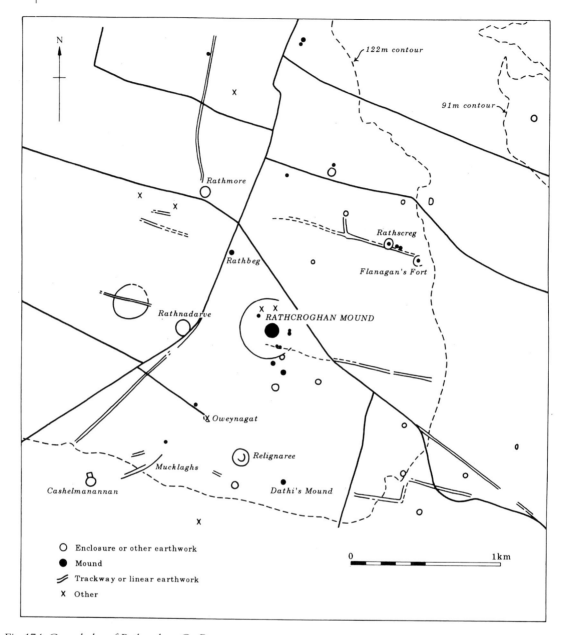

Fig. 174. General plan of Rathcroghan, Co. Roscommon.

village of Tulsk, in Co. Roscommon (Fig. 174). The monuments are scattered across the eastern end of a broad, elevated plateau with commanding views, particularly to the east and south, over part of the rolling pasture land of Mag nAí ('the plain of the sheep'). Most of them lie just above or just below the 120m contour. A little over 50 sites are known and no less than a dozen of them have been discovered in the last few years by means of aerial reconnaissance. They range greatly in date, at least from early prehistoric to Medieval times.[26]

This complex of monuments extends over an area of about 800 hectares and has the large mound known as Rathcroghan Mound at its approximate centre. The name *Cruachain* may derive from the noun *crúach*, a hill or mound, and may have meant 'the people of the mound(s)', possibly a tribal name. Circular mounds, many of them burial mounds including ring barrows (about 43%) and enclosures (about 23%) are the commonest monument types in the complex which also contains pillar stones, linear earthworks, platform earthworks and miscellaneous – if not unclassifiable – sites such as the cave known as Oweynagat fabled as that entrance to the Otherworld.

RATHCROGHAN MOUND

At the approximate centre of the complex stands the great circular mound called Rathcroghan Mound. It has been variously suggested that a royal residence once stood on top of it, that it was an inauguration or assembly mound or a burial mound used for ceremonial purposes, that it might contain a passage tomb or was a natural glacial hillock scarped to its present shape. The mound is broad, low and approximately circular with an average

diameter of some 85m. From its base it slopes fairly steeply at first and then more gently to an almost flat summit about 30m across. There is a low, irregular mound measuring about 4m across eccentrically placed on the flat summit; an 18th century watercolour shows this mound standing to a height about 1m at that time. Two sloping ramps occur on the west and east respectively (Fig. 175). A programme of geophysical analysis has demonstrated that this great mound is a complex multi-period monument. Its foundation may have been a low elongated glacial till ridge deliberately levelled to form a sort of platform; this has been detected by ground probing radar.[27] Ground

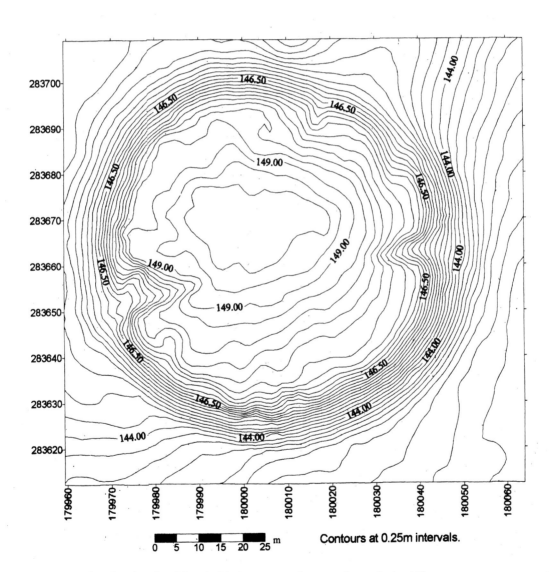

Fig. 175. Contour plan of Rathcroghan Mound with the ramps on the east and west clearly visible.

probing radar along with magnetic and resistivity survey have revealed that several large enclosures have been entombed within the mound: the largest is about 80m in diameter with another enclosure within it about 35m in diameter. Within this again and beneath the centre of the mound is a third enclosure 20m in diameter. If these are all contemporary – and this has not been established – the mound covers and is concentric with a large trivallate monument. The surface of the mound has also produced evidence of complex activity: both magnetic and resistivity survey have revealed a number of overlapping circular and linear features just below the surface: a pair of concentric circles at the centre are about 17m and 30m in diameter respectively and other circles and arcs are also visible. Oddly enough none of the geophysical surveys detected the small burial mound still just visible on the mound's summit. In addition to this, resistivity survey has shown what may be an encircling trench or ditch some 15m from the base of the mound and has confirmed the existence of a very large encircling trench or ditch, possibly a palisade trench, with a diameter of about 370m.

Other monuments encompassed by this great circle include an enclosure composed of a double circle about 30m across and a number of linear features revealed by magnetic gradiometry, several low and almost imperceptible ring barrows, two circular mounds, and a prostrate limestone pillar named Miosgan Meva (or Maeve's heap), a name also given to the huge cairn on Knocknarea near Sligo.

The monument variously called Dathi's stone or Dathi's mound has the appearance of an embanked burial mound; the encircling bank has opposed entrances on east and west and an overall diameter of about 40m; there is a prominent pillar stone on the summit of the mound. Dathi was, supposedly, the last pagan king of Ireland; according to legend he died about AD 429 and was buried at Rathcroghan. Limited excavation in 1981 confirmed that the circular mound was natural and carved out of a small gravel ridge.[28] A considerable amount of the mound's surface was exposed and no graves were found. The enclosing bank proved to be roughly built of small stones and earth and some charcoal from its base provided a series of radiocarbon dates which suggest it was built either in the last two centuries BC or the early centuries AD. While the radiocarbon determinations did not offer a more precise chronology, they did at least contradict the traditional 5th century AD date. Excavation demonstrated that there was a substantial ditch inside the bank which was filled with a fairly homogenous and possibly deliberate clay deposit. This internal ditch indicates that the site has affinities with the ring barrow type but the large pillar stone does set it apart from the rest of the mounds in the area and it could have had a ceremonial rather than a funerary purpose.

A number of other mounds seem to be variants on the ring barrow type too. Rathbeg near Rathcroghan crossroads is a prominent site. Despite its name it is not a rath or ringfort but a burial mound situated on a hillock. The mound is surrounded by two concentric banks situated on the steep sides of the hillock and there may be internal ditches. Flanagan's fort (which acquired its name from a man who lived nearby) seems to have consisted of a bank with internal ditch enclosing an area of rising ground with a low oval artificial mound on the summit. But not all mounds are ring barrows with mound, ditch and external bank, a number of simple circular mounds occur (and could well be of early prehistoric date). Rathscreg is round mound on a low hill apparently enclosed by two widely-spaced banks.

An interesting group of earthworks is situated on and just below the 120m contour about 600m west of Relignaree. Two linear earthworks known as the Mucklaghs are among the most imposing of the Rathcroghan monuments; they are so called because legend has it they are the results of the rootings of a magical boar. The northern example is the shorter and more massive of the two and consists of a relatively closely set pair of large earthen banks which curve very slightly and run roughly east to west down a gentle slope for a distance of about 100m; the banks, which are set 2.5m to 3m apart, average 3m in height and are 5m to 7m in width. The southern Mucklagh is a more or less straight pair of earthen banks some 200m long and set about 6m apart which measure up to 2m in height and up to 4m in width. At the north-eastern end, one bank with traces of a ditch on its north-western side continues on for over 150m. At the other end, the parallel banks terminate not far from a pool of water. Leaving porcine explanations aside, it is difficult to suggest anything other than a ceremonial purpose for these large embankments. They may be compared to the long parallel earthen banks known as the Knockans, which once stood at Teltown, Co. Meath.[29]

Enclosures include sites such as Cashelmanannan (Manannan's Fort), near the Mucklaghs, which is a much ruined monument with two small fields attached. Rathnadarve, to the north, is a fine circular enclosure with bank and external ditch. There are slight traces of an external bank and the monument has an overall diameter of about 110m (Fig. 176). Its builders decided to encompass a low, oval, natural hillock which means that much of the interior is higher than the enclosing rampart. This is somewhat unusual but the external ditch suggests that this site has some affinity with the typical ringfort or rath; it is not a ring barrow as has been claimed. There is a large enclosure, about 250m across, some 200m to the northwest. It is barely detectable on the ground but, for the most part, clearly visible from the air in the right conditions. Further to the north is the imposing monument called Rathmore which seems to be a sort of raised rath perhaps built on top of a natural hillock to give some additional height. The base of the steep-sided mound is surrounded by a broad ditch and traces of an outer rampart are visible some distance away. A substantial monument such as this could well have been a chieftain's residence and would normally be considered to date to the second half of the first millennium AD.

A small group of earthworks, called platform earthworks, are also probable settlements. These low, elevated monuments of sub-rectangular plan sometimes have traces of low banks at their edges; they may also date to the first millennium AD or even to the Medieval period.

The enclosure called Relignaree lies to the south of Rathcroghan Mound and is a large univallate monument of circular plan with an internal diameter of 100m; there is no visible external ditch for most of its circumference but on the northwest there is a segment of ditch some 6m wide and 50cm deep. The bank seems to be built of large stones and earth and is about 2.6m wide and 1m in height; there are over a dozen gaps in it, none certainly an entrance. In the interior there are traces of a smaller circular enclosure whose bank is concentric with the larger circle. In places this bank is 50cm to 1m high, it is clearly visible from the air for some four-fifths of its circumference and on the east shows traces of an external ditch. This small enclosure has an internal diameter of about 48m and it is difficult to say whether or not it is an earlier monument superseded by the larger one. Several field banks run across the large site and other internal features include a souterrain and traces of at least three rectangular houses (at least one which probably belongs to recent centuries). The site seems to have

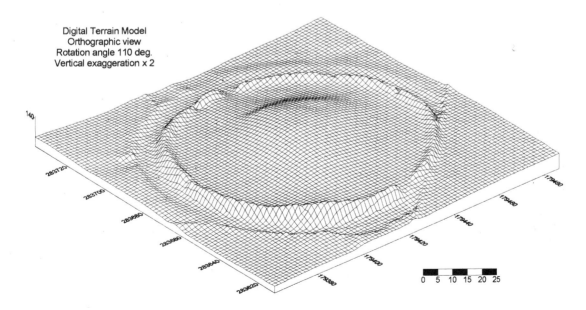

Digital Terrain Model
Orthographic view
Rotation angle 110 deg.
Vertical exaggeration x 2

Fig. 176. A digital terrain model of Rathnadarve clearly showing the rising ground in its interior and the external ditch. The enclosure has a maximum overall diameter of 110m and the vertical scale is exaggerated x 2.

had a long and complicated history from early Historic to Medieval times. The name, 'the cemetery of the kings', is a fanciful one and those references to a great cemetery in the early literature may well refer to the mounds of the Rathcroghan complex as a whole.

A noteworthy site is undoubtedly the cave of *Cruachain* ('the cave of the cats'), an entrance to the Otherworld and the focus of much magical activity in early legend. The Morrigan, an ancient war goddess, had temporary residence here and a host of fearsome animals, birds and monsters are associated with it. It is a long narrow natural limestone cave entered via part of a stone-built souterrain with ogham inscriptions on two roof stones one of which contains the name 'Maeve' and reads VRAICCI MAQI MEDVVI ('of Fraic son of Medf'). Aside even from the intriguing inscription, the mere presence of an ogham stone at Oweynagat is noteworthy: such stones are very rare in Connacht, the majority being found in the south of Ireland.

Various writers have commented on the absence of a large embanked enclosure with internal ditch at Rathcroghan but apart from this, the wealth of burial mounds and the presence of other large enclosures and linear earthworks demonstrate parallels with both Tara and Navan. It is evident that not one of these four 'royal sites' is exactly the same as any other but all display in one way or another a remarkable preoccupation with ritual expression in various guises and with the construction of imposing monuments of different sorts in later prehistoric times. Though situated at modest elevations, they also have commanding locations often with impressive views over surrounding territory.

The similarities they share might suggest that they served similar functions over a long period of time from early prehistoric times to the historic era. This usage may not have been continuous but was certainly prolonged in some instances, there is evidence of remarkable ritual persistence at Tara and Navan in particular. In Medieval sources they were perceived to have similar status and were portrayed in epic literature as royal settlements, the seats of kings, hence the term 'royal site'. Some of the descriptions are clearly variations on a stock storyteller's formula: the account in the 8th century *Táin Bó Fraich* of the house of Ailill and Medb in the rath of *Cruachain*: 'This was the arrangement of the house: seven partitions in it, seven beds from the fire to the wall in the house all around. There was a

fronting of bronze on each bed, carved red yew all covered with fair varied ornament ...' is very similar to other fanciful descriptions including that of Conchobar's house at *Emain Macha*.[30] Thus to what extent such literary descriptions are constructs of an imaginary past (perhaps with the aim of legitimizing royal status and political power) is now a matter of debate.

The wealth of literary references to *Emain Macha*, in epic tales, *Dindshenchas,* poetry and other sources, do reflect its importance during the period of their composition and transmission and have had a considerable influence on archaeological interpretation in the past, but – while it was undoubtedly a very important site in later prehistory and despite its later literary importance – it may not have been the most important site in Ulster at the end of the last millennium BC.

Archaeological excavation at Navan and Knockaulin has produced abundant evidence for later prehistoric cult and ritual, and possible evidence for permanent high-status domestic settlement at Navan. The large earthworks, with ditches inside the banks, far from having hillfort type ramparts with external ditches, have an obvious non-defensive symbolic character.[31]

While the structures from Navan Phase 3ii (the houses with attached stockades) present interpretative difficulties, the weight of present evidence suggests that this 'royal site' may have been both a settlement and a ritual site in a sacred enclosure. Thus it and Knockaulin may well have been assembly places – and the evidence for occasional feasting from the latter is pertinent here. It is possible that Knockaulin may differ from Navan in so far as it may have been a place for periodic but temporary settlement on such occasions.[32]

Both the ritual and the royal aspects are reflected in the association of some sites with inauguration rites and a goddess of sovereignty. For instance, in the epic *Táin Bó Cúailnge*, at *Cruachain*, Ailill was king of Connacht because of his marriage to Maeve or Medb who had previously been the wife of Conchobar, king of Ulster, and two other Connacht kings. The original Medb was not a historical person but a goddess and her name is cognate with words in Irish and other languages signifying drunkenness (like the English word 'mead'), her name means 'the drunken one' or 'she who intoxicates'. The reign of each Irish pagan king was inaugurated by a mystic marriage with a goddess and the marriage may have taken the form of a ceremonial drinking session which induced a 'divine' intoxication of the new king. To gain possession of Medb of *Cruachain* was to gain possession of the kingship, a fact which explains the unusual number of her husbands – she wed each king in turn. She had a counterpart in Medb Lethderg of Tara who, it is said, 'mated with nine of the kings of Ireland'. The kings of Tara, *Emain Macha* and *Cruachain* were inaugurated in an ancient fertility rite which took the form of a symbolical mating *(feis)* with the local earth-goddess. At Tara, this inauguration took place at *Feis Temro* (the *feis* or feast of Tara) held once in the reign of each king.[33]

There is a celebrated description in the *Annals of Connacht* of the inauguration of Feidhlim Ó Conchobhair as king of Connacht in 1310 AD. He was proclaimed king on a mound containing the bones of his O'Conor ancestors at Carnfree just over six kilometres to the south-south-east of Rathcroghan: '... in a style as royal, as lordly and as public as any of his race from the time of Brian son of Eochu Muigmedoin till that day. And when Fedlimid mac Aeda meic Eogain had married the Province of Connacht his foster-father waited upon

him during the night in the manner remembered by the old men and recorded in the old books; and this was the most splendid king-ship marriage ever celebrated in Connacht down to that day'. This was an extraordinary Medieval re-enactment of an archaic rite intended to ensure the fertility of man and beast and earth throughout the kingdom.

Carnfree is a reminder that smaller ceremonial sites of possible prehistoric date also exist and present some of the features of their larger and better known counterparts: notably mounds and enclosures located in prominent positions. Here, the prehistoric burial cairn known as *Carn Fraich* (Carnfree – the cairn of Fraich) stands at just over 120m above sea level on a broad ridge known as *Ard Chaoin* ('the smooth height') or *Cnoc na Dala* ('the hill of the assembly'). Nearby is a large circular tumulus traditionally called *Dumha Shelga* ('the mound of the hunt') with several ring barrows in the immediate vicinity. Other monuments on the ridge include other ring barrows, a tall pillar stone in an embanked circle, and a conjoined earthwork very similar to the Forradh and Teach Chormac at Tara (Fig. 177).

Excavations at Raffin, Co. Meath, at a large circular enclosure with internal ditch on a

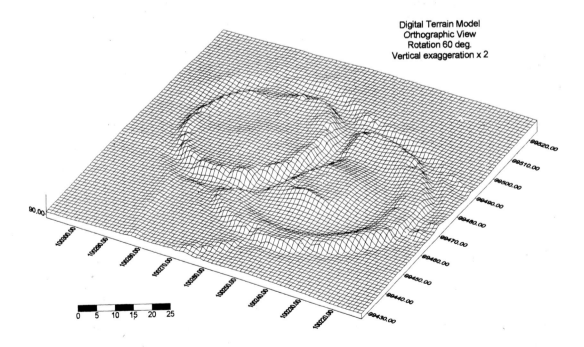

Fig. 177. A digital terrain model of a conjoined ring barrow and ringfort at Lismurtagh, Carnfree, Co. Roscommon. The ring barrow has an overall diameter of about 65m. The vertical scale is exaggerated x 2.

prominent drumlin, have revealed a complex multi-phase site which includes a circular timber ceremonial structure dating to the 1st or 2nd centuries AD. Another minor site is Cornashee, near Lisnaskea, Co. Fermanagh, where an enclosure, on top of a drumlin with extensive views, consists of a low bank with internal ditch and an overall diameter of some 120m. At the centre is a large mound with a small cairn on top. Traditionally this is the inauguration site of the Maguires.[34]

THE HILLFORT PROBLEM

As we have seen, when considering Haughey's Fort and other contemporary sites, the appearance of numbers of enclosed settlements, particularly those of large size occupying naturally defensible locations, may be considered as indicators of social change in later prehistory. These hillforts as they are often called lend support to the idea that society was becoming increasingly hierarchical and complex, and their emergence may even reflect tribal formation. If defence was a primary consideration, then they at the very least suggest the emergence of powerful local individuals and the adoption of heroic pastimes such as persistent raiding. The term hillfort, of course, implies a defensive capability and is widely used of large hilltop enclosures which seem to deliberately exploit the natural terrain for this purpose. Barry Raftery has noted that there are probably between sixty and eighty hilltop sites in Ireland which may be termed hillforts and he has identified three classes.

A common type is the univallate monument, with a single line of defence (Class 1). One of the largest known is Knocknashee, near Ballymote, in Co. Sligo, where the denuded remains of a rampart enclose an entire hilltop at a height of about 270m above sea level, an approximately oval area of some 22 hectares (Fig. 178, 1). A stretch of outer bank exists on the east. Two fairly intact prehistoric cairns lie within the enclosure towards its northern end. There are over 30 hut circles or small enclosures also visible within it mainly on the sheltered eastern side but their chronological relationship to the defences is unknown. Most univallate enclosures are much smaller, usually less than 3.5 hectares in extent. Carn Tigherna, near Fermoy, Co. Cork, is an irregular oval with large stone rampart – approximately 250m in maximum dimensions – enclosing a little over 2 hectares. In the centre is a cairn which produced one or two prehistoric

burials in the 19th century and a vase of early 2nd millennium BC date. The small hillfort at Freestone Hill, Co. Kilkenny, with a single stony bank and external ditch enclosing an area of about 2 hectares, was excavated in the late 1940s. As already mentioned, some coarse pottery, glass beads and a radiocarbon date now indicate Dowris Phase occupation on the site. Later activity there is attested by some provincial Roman bronzes, including bracelet fragments, and a coin of Constantine II of the middle of the 4th century AD. The latter was once believed to offer a central date for the occupation. Now it is clear that its prehistory was more complicated and the date of the defences is uncertain.[35]

The excavations on Freestone Hill also revealed that, at some stage, the occupants had partly destroyed a prehistoric cemetery mound of about 2000 BC. This destruction contrasts with the fact that a numbers of other sites a cairn seems to survive more or less intact. This is the case at Knocknashee and Carn Tigherna and at a number of other hillforts such as Mountfortescue, Co. Meath, Croaghan and Glasbolie, Co. Donegal, Knockacarrigeen, Co. Galway, Dunmurry Hill, Co. Kildare, and Kesh, Co. Sligo. Univallate examples with no trace of such mounds include Garrangrena Lower, Co. Tipperary (Fig. 178, 2), and Ballybuckley and Courthoyle New in Co. Wexford.[36]

Class 2 hillforts are multivallate, usually with two or three surrounding ramparts which may be closely or widely spaced. Haughey's Fort is an example with three more or less concentric ditches, widely spaced, which presumably once had associated earthen banks (Fig. 89). Its approximately oval outer ditch measured about 340 by 310m, the intervals between the ditches being 25m and 55m. Mooghaun, Co. Clare, is one of the largest known with its three stone ramparts encompassing a total area of almost 12 hectares (Fig. 127). All three ramparts were of broadly similar dump construction and a radiocarbon date of 1260-930 BC provided a terminal date after which the outer one was built.

There was a hilltop enclosure at Dún Aonghasa, on Aran, Co. Galway, which was occupied from about 1300 to 800 BC if not earlier but the date of the multivallate fort visible today is uncertain (Fig. 90). It, with its inner stone-built fort, two outer walls, the fragment of a third, the stone *chevaux-de-frise*. and a total area of 5.7 hectares, must date to some time after 800 BC, either to the last few

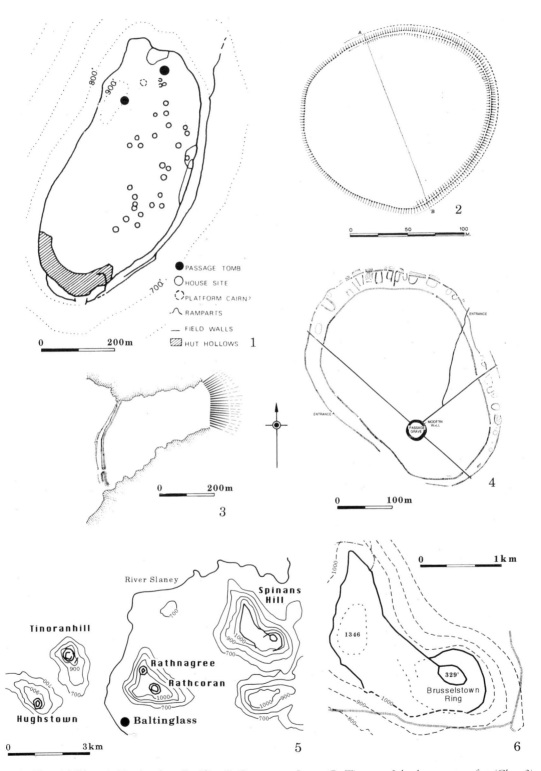

Fig. 178. Class 1 hillforts. 1. Knocknashee, Co. Sligo. 2. Garrangrena Lower, Co. Tipperary. Inland promontory fort (Class 3). 3. Knockdhu, Co. Antrim. Class 2 hillforts. 4. Rathcoran, Baltinglass Hill, Co. Wicklow. 5. General map of hillforts in the Baltinglass, Co. Wicklow, complex. 6. Spinan's Hill, Co. Wicklow.

centuries BC or even to the early Historic period. Rathgall Co. Wicklow (Fig. 128) has four more or less concentric ramparts enclosing an area of some 7.3 hectares but the innermost enclosure, with its stone rampart, may be a structure of Medieval or more recent date. The other ramparts have not been securely dated but may be contemporary with the late prehistoric, Dowris Phase, occupation on the hilltop which lay in part beneath the late stone enclosure.

Toormore, Co. Kilkenny, at 525m above sea level, has two ramparts enclosing about 12 hectares but much of it has been damaged by afforestation and land reclamation. Formoyle Hill, south-west of Killaloe, Co. Clare, is crowned by a very large trivallate hillfort, partly obscured by peat. The oval inner enclosure is about 210m across, the middle enclosure – with maximum dimensions of about 350m – lies 50m to 80m away and the outermost enclosure, only traceable in part, is about 100m from the middle one. Cashel, Co. Cork, in Clashanimud townland, is one of three or four hillforts in east Cork. It is an oval bivallate monument with widely spaced banks of earth and stone enclosing a commanding hilltop. Its maximum dimensions are about 370m and there is a distance some 48m between the two ramparts. The famous Grianán of Aileach, in Co. Donegal, overlooking both Lough Swilly and Lough Foyle, is a multivallate site with a long and complex history. A central stone fort, restored in the late 19th century, may be of early Historic date and is traditionally identified with the Uí Néill dynasty. Its relationship to the remains of three enclosing and very denuded earthen banks is uncertain; these are usually considered to be a prehistoric hillfort, though it has been suggested that they are no more than token ramparts contemporary with the inner stone fort. A low stony mound may be the remains of a supposed tumulus noted in the 19th century – this is situated between the inner and middle banks.[37]

Examples of hillforts with closely spaced multivallate defences include Belmont, north of Tuam, Co. Galway, which consists of a bank with external ditch, measuring about 160m by 135m, enclosing an area of about 1.5 hectares. There is a slight counterscarp bank (surmounted by a modern stone wall) outside this ditch with traces of another external ditch in places. The only visible feature in the interior is a small modern graveyard. Ballinkillen, Co. Carlow, with maximum dimensions of 267m by 225m is enclosed by a double bank with intervening ditch. The banks are close together with a maximum overall width of 13m. Laghtea, Co. Tipperary, also consists of a double bank with intervening ditch, of similar maximum width, surrounding three sides of a hilltop; on the east a series of crags and bluffs may have offered some natural protection. Ballymartin, Co. Mayo, situated on a low hilltop, is an oval monument approximately 100m across and consists of three earthen banks (and remains of a fourth) with intervening ditches.[38]

There is a remarkable concentration of multivallate hillforts in an area of some 30km² near Baltinglass, Co. Wicklow (Fig. 178, 4–6). Two occur on Baltinglass Hill itself: Rathcoran on the summit, at an elevation of about 360m, appears to be an unfinished bivallate monument with traces of quarry hollows between the two incomplete ramparts which enclose 10.5 hectares. A passage tomb surrounded by a modern wall lies on the highest point in its southern part. Rathnagree, on Tuckmill Hill, a lower ridge 500m to the north, is a small trivallate monument about 270m in diameter. Across the River Slaney, no more than 5km away, the 300m high hills at Tinoranhill, Co. Wicklow, and Hughstown, Co. Kildare, both have denuded enclosures on their summits. Tinoran is a bivallate or trivallate enclosure over 500m across and Hughstown is bivallate. Just over 3km north-east of Baltinglass Hill, on the long ridge of Spinan's Hill, at a height of about 400m, is a bivallate enclosure known as Brusselstown Ring. This monument has two widely spaced ramparts encompassing more than 17 hectares and occupies the south-eastern end of the ridge. Attached to it on the west and north-west is another huge outer enclosure of irregular plan formed for most of its visible length by a double rampart with intervening ditch averaging 15m in overall width. This rampart has been traced for about 4km and runs just above the 300m contour; it may originally have enclosed an area of 132 hectares. Several cairns, possibly a passage tomb cemetery, and another possible enclosure, have been traced on Spinan's Hill itself in the north-western section of the great enclosure. It is quite possible that the Spinan's Hill complex, and indeed various hillforts in the Blessington cluster as a whole, represent a sequence of activity over a long period of time. The huge enclosure, however, seems to have been conceived as a unit and may have been a major late prehistoric undertaking like the Dorsey enclosure in Co. Armagh.[39]

Class 3 hillforts are inland promontory forts and fewer than a dozen are recorded. Lurigethan, Co. Antrim, is a large and steep sided promontory of some 13 hectares defended by a series of closely set ramparts and ditches some 300m in length. The number of ditches and banks varies in places from three to six. Knockdhu, Co. Antrim (Fig. 178, 3) is about 8 hectares in extent and defended by two closely set banks and ditches. Other examples, like several in Counties Kerry, Louth and Meath, are generally much smaller. Castle Gale, Co. Limerick, has an enclosed area of only 1.4 hectares and is defended on its southern side by a pair of banks with an intervening ditch. An additional stretch of rampart defends part of the northern slope. A possible cairn crowns the summit of the hill.[40]

In the absence of excavation, the date and purpose of these hilltop enclosures can only be guessed at, and, at present, surface morphology – neither size nor rampart form – or elevation provide few clues. As we have seen, the evidence from a very small number of excavations, from Haughey's Fort, Dún Aonghasa and Mooghaun in particular, demonstrates the construction of multivallate enclosures in the late 2nd and 1st millennia BC. Sites such as Lyles Hill and Donegore, Co. Antrim, of course, show that hilltop palisaded enclosure may be as old as the 4th millennium BC and while most large hilltop enclosures may well belong to the later prehistoric period, it would be unwise to assume that all are of this date. Dún Aonghasa was evidently a multi-period monument and given the evidence from Haughey's Fort for some activity there around c. 400 BC to 200 BC and the evidence for iron working at Rathgall, Co. Wicklow, sometime in the period 180 AD to 540 AD, it is clear that some sites were the focus of later activity too. In general the practice of hilltop enclosure on a substantial scale may have spanned more than a millennium.

Though the term hillfort is commonly used, it is by no means certain that all these hilltop sites served the same function and not all may have been defensive sites. The widely spaced dump stone ramparts at Mooghaun, with no carefully con-structed vertical faces, seem a less than effective impediment to an attacking force and the defence of such a long perimeter here and at Spinan's Hill, for instance, in the face of a determined onslaught

would demand an impossibly large body of defenders. Closely spaced ramparts would have had a defensive capability and the denuded ramparts and the silted-up ditches at many sites may still prove, on excavation, to have been imposing defences perhaps with timber breastworks. It is unlikely that there is a single explanation for hilltop enclosures: it is possible that some were hillforts and built primarily as defended settlements or as intermittently occupied refuge places, but others may have been stock compounds, perhaps associated with seasonal upland grazing. Those multivallate sites with widely spaced ramparts, 10m to more than 50m apart, could well have served this purpose.[41]

The consistent association of a number of sites with prehistoric cairns may be more than just a coincidental preference for hilltop siting. Freestone Hill is an exception, but at many sites the burial monument seems not to have been disturbed and may have conferred a special status on the enclosure. It is possible that the cairns, or the social activities that were associated with them, legitimized the hilltop in some way.[42] If some enclosures were not defensive and used only for periodic communal gatherings or ceremonial with associated intermittent settlement, periodic refurbishment or aggrandizement of the ramparts may still have occurred. The scarcity of post-800 BC material at both Dún Aonghasa and Mooghaun raises the possibility that these enclosures had some purpose of this sort and their ramparts may have been more symbolic than defensive.

Whatever the uses of these large enclosures, their construction represented a considerable investment in time and labour and this alone is testimony of their importance; the total length of the stone ramparts at Mooghaun exceeds 2km and those of the great enclosure at Spinan's Hill may have been more than twice that length. The strategic role of large hilltop enclosures in the organization of the wider landscape, perhaps as focal points in a pattern of smaller dispersed and possibly undefended homesteads, remains unclear. Their distribution is puzzling too (Fig. 156, 3) with large multivallate enclosures more or less confined to the southern half of the island and a general scarcity of hillforts in the north. The contrast between this pattern and the distribution of supposedly contemporary artefacts such as beehive querns and metalwork has prompted the suggestion that the multivallate enclosures are unrelated and possibly earlier than this material.[43] Some caution is necessary here, survey will undoubtedly augment present distribution maps and, of course, the date of the great majority of hillforts is unknown. Comparisons with the loosely dated artefactual evidence, broadly assigned to the period 300 BC to 300 AD, are therefore premature and, in any event, beehive querns apart, this material is represented, albeit slightly, in the southern half of the island. Since much of it has been recovered from bogs, it is possible that the Munster scarcity could be due to the absence or to the limited commercial or agricultural exploitation of certain types of contexts such as lowland bogs.[44] There are many intriguing questions to be answered, of course, not least about the distribution of beehive querns and multivallate enclosures, but it is not certain that these questions are related.

LINEAR EARTHWORKS

The term linear earthwork is loosely applied to a varied group of bank or bank and ditch systems and includes such puzzling earthworks as the parallel pairs of banks at Tara, the so-called Banqueting Hall, the Mucklaghs at Rathcroghan, and much longer earthworks as well. Some pairs of parallel banks, like some of the other examples at Rathcroghan, may have been droveways for animals but others are on such a scale they probably had another purpose. As already mentioned, some may have served to demarcate sections of the landscape, as with the 700m long stretch of parallel banks in Riverstown townland to the west of Tara and the system of parallel ditches in Creeveroe townland in the Navan complex. Others may have been ceremonial roadways: the Friar's Walk, Kiltierney, Co. Fermanagh, is a long linear earthwork of L-shaped plan which has been traced for some 1100m in an area rich in prehistoric remains including a passage tomb and a stone circle. Excavation demonstrated that it consisted of a pair of parallel earthen banks 15m apart with internal rock-cut ditches with a strip of level ground between. No dating evidence was found but the association with a complex of ritual or burial monuments is noteworthy. This is the case at sites like Tara and Rathcroghan and on the Curragh in Co. Kildare where a long earthwork seemingly consisting of a pair of low banks with an intervening ditch is called 'the race of the Black Pig'.

While it must be stressed that both date and purpose remain matters of speculation, some particularly long linear systems may mark major territorial divisions and may be associated in some way with hilltop enclosures. At Shankill, Co. Kilkenny, a limited excavation at part of a 2km long stretch of low earthen bank with a ditch on its southern side failed to produce any clues as to its date; local information suggested that it was part of an earthwork known as the Rathduff dyke or trench recorded near Paulstown on the borders between Kilkenny and Carlow and about 8km north-east of Freestone Hill. Aerial photography has revealed a system of four parallel ditches, 14m apart, running for some 500m, at Grevine West, south of Kilkenny, and about 1.5km north-east of a probable hillfort. At Woodsgift, in north-western Co. Kilkenny, another system of two pairs of ditches with an overall width of 40m runs for over 800m about 3km south of Clomantagh Hill with a hillfort on its summit.[45]

The Claidh Dubh or Black Dyke is a well known earthwork in Co. Cork where it has been traced in several discontinuous sections for some 24km from the Limerick-Cork boundary, north-west of Charleville, to east Cork near Carrigtohill. The longest stretch, across the valley of the River Blackwater between the Ballyhoura Hills and the Nagles Mountains, is 22km long. Excavation of a section which forms the townland boundary between Castleblagh and Ballydague, near the village of Ballyhooley, revealed an earthen bank with a shallow ditch on either side and a well-made trackway running parallel to it. There may have been a palisade on top of the bank. No direct dating evidence was found but peat, which sealed the ditch and partly covered the bank, had apparently commenced to form about 100 AD and thus indicated a date sometime prior to this for this section of the earthwork.[46]

THE BLACK PIG'S DYKE

The best known linear earthwork is the Black Pig's Dyke in Ulster, so named after a folk tale about a magical black pig which − when chased across several counties − rooted up large tracts of land. It is just one of several northern linear earthworks with various names identified in Counties Leitrim, Cavan, Monaghan, Armagh and Down. The Black Pig's Dyke has been claimed by earlier writers to have been a single defensive earthwork stretching from Bundoran in the west to Dundalk in the east. In Co. Leitrim it is a discontinuous section of ditch some 2.5m wide traced for some 9km in the Kiltyclogher area between Lough Melvin and Lough Macnean Upper and variously called the Black Pig's Race or the Worm Ditch. Another ditch has been noted between Dowra and Lough Allen to the south. A 2km length of the earthwork occurs in Co. Cavan, east of Bellananagh. In Co. Monaghan similarly named discontinuous segments of one or two banks and ditches have been recorded in over a dozen townlands south of Scotshouse running from the Fermanagh lake system, north of Redhills, Co. Cavan, south-eastwards to Drumcor Lough, then eastwards to Ballinageeragh, near Drum, a total distance of some 9km.

A limited excavation of a section of the dyke in Aghareagh West, near Scotshouse, demonstrated that the monument there had consisted of a timber palisade and external ditch with a double bank with intervening ditch beyond. The overall width was about 24m, the ramparts were of dump construction, surviving to a maximum height of about 1.5m. The palisade trench contained the burnt remains of oak timbers which provided a radiocarbon determination of 390-70 BC.

A small section of linear earthwork occurs in east Monaghan, just west of Lough Ross, near Crossmaglen, in Co. Armagh. Sections of linear earthwork in Armagh include a stretch north-east of the village of Meigh running northwards towards Camlough west of Newry and, further north, a segment 6km south of Armagh city called the Dane's Cast. This is the name given to half a dozen lengths of earthwork in western Co. Down extending southwards for some 10km on the eastern side of the Newry Canal from north of Scarva to near Goraghwood Station. Survey has shown that the various sections of this earthwork are all located on land about 30m above sea level and link natural obstacles such as Lough Shark and areas of bogland. It consists mostly of a bank and ditch though in places there are two banks with an intervening ditch. In the early 19th century it was said to have continued southwards in the area of Bessbrook, Co. Armagh, but now cannot be traced. A short length of earthwork south of Goraghswood on the western side of the canal suggests that the dyke did run south-westwards into Co. Armagh.[47]

The Dorsey, in Co. Armagh, 5km north-east of Crossmaglen, is a series of earthworks and timber palisades which appear to form a large and irregularly rectangular enclosure of some 68 hectares (Fig. 179).[48] The name, from *dóirse*, the doors, reflects the tradition that this earthwork was believed to be a gateway to the north. On the south,

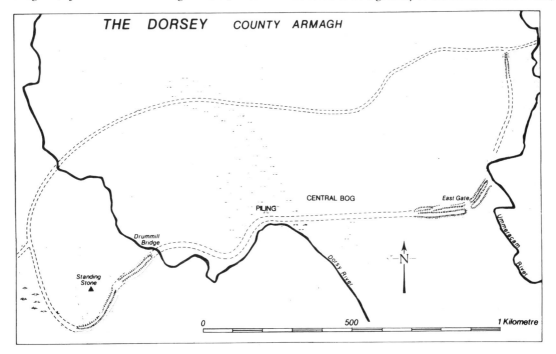

Fig. 179. The Dorsey earthworks, Co. Armagh.

facing north Louth, there are two separate lengths of earthworks to the west and to the east about 800m apart and separated from one another by an area of bogland along the Dorsy River. The discovery of oak timbers in this bog in the 19th century suggests the presence of a palisade at this point. Both southern earthworks consist of an impressive rampart, up to 6m high in places, between two large ditches with a second outer bank in places. The overall width is about 40m. On the west and east the ends of these earthworks turn northwards, the western element becoming a palisade of roughly squared oak posts, traced for over 70m, with external ditch on the edge of a bog, the eastern consisting of a substantial bank and ditch running northwards more or less parallel to the Ummeracam River. On the north discontinuous lengths of a smaller bank and ditch have been identified some of it only traceable from the air. Some oak timbers were unearthed on the north-west in 1988 and may have come from the ditch. The northern elements appear to continue to both west and east and this has led to suggestions that these extensions were part of the Black Pig's Dyke.

It is not certain if all the parts of the Dorsey complex are contemporary and it has been suggested that it is not an enclosure but two separate linear earthworks of different dates, the northernmost being possibly the earlier. It may have been a multi-phase monument, oak timbers from the south-western palisade were dendrochronologically dated to about 100-90 BC and the oak timbers found in 1988 at the northern rampart were felled around 140 BC; some radiocarbon determinations are consistent with these general dates.[49]

Various writers have interpreted the Dorsey as a stronghold on the Black Pig's Dyke and part of the boundary defences of late prehistoric Ulster, the discontinuous nature of the dyke being explained by the fact that it was mainly intended to augment the natural obstacles offered by high ground, lake or bog, and to be an impediment to cattle-raiders. Since the regeneration of woodland detected in pollen analyses from Loughnashade, Co. Armagh, and possible evidence for a period of climatic deterioration from about 200 BC could mean a reduction in the available winter grazing, it is possible that boundary markers or defences would become more important in such times of stress. If it is a single contemporary construction, the Black

Pig's Dyke is an impressive boundary marker. If it is not, it is equally significant that different communities may have felt the need to monumentally demarcate sections of their territories.

The theory of monumental frontier defences has been inspired in part by the supposed contemporaneity of the whole linear earthwork complex with Navan Fort and the perception, encouraged by the much later tales of the Ulster Cycle such as the *Táin Bó Cúailgne,* that cattle-raiding was a major preoccupation of a heroic society in the last few centuries BC. An alternative interpretation for the Dorsey earthworks has been offered by N. B. Aitchison who suggests that this monument was neither stronghold nor cattle compound but a focus of ritual activity with familiar wetland and watery associations. The location has no particular defensive advantage and much of the interior is bog with the Dorsy and Ummeracam Rivers on either side. A 1.5m high pillar stone stands in its south-western quarter. Its boundaries, which may have been redefined and even increased from time to time, may have served, like the circular boundary of Navan Fort, to restrict access, the impressive nature of the southern earthworks being an indication of status. Rather than a frontier defence of the people who built Navan Fort, the Dorsey may have been the ritual centre of a different socio-political group.

Another irregular enclosure, created by a huge earthen embankment, about 6m high and 30m wide, which cuts off a large promontory on the River Shannon at Drumsna, in north-east Roscommon, may have served a similar purpose. It too seems non-defensive in character with two out-turned entrance ways, one with a minimum width of no less than 16m.[50]

CULT AND BURIAL

Almost a thousand years after the roughly carved wooden idol was placed in a bog at Ralaghan, Co. Cavan (Fig. 97), the first clear evidence for anthropomorphic carving in stone is found. The most remarkable example of early iconic stone carving is probably the Corleck head found about 1855 some 7km to the south-east of Ralaghan, near Shercock (Fig. 180, 2). It is carved from a block of local sandstone and has three stylized faces each slightly different. All share closely set round eyes, a spatulate nose and a simply grooved mouth. A hole in the base of the head was probably a mortise for

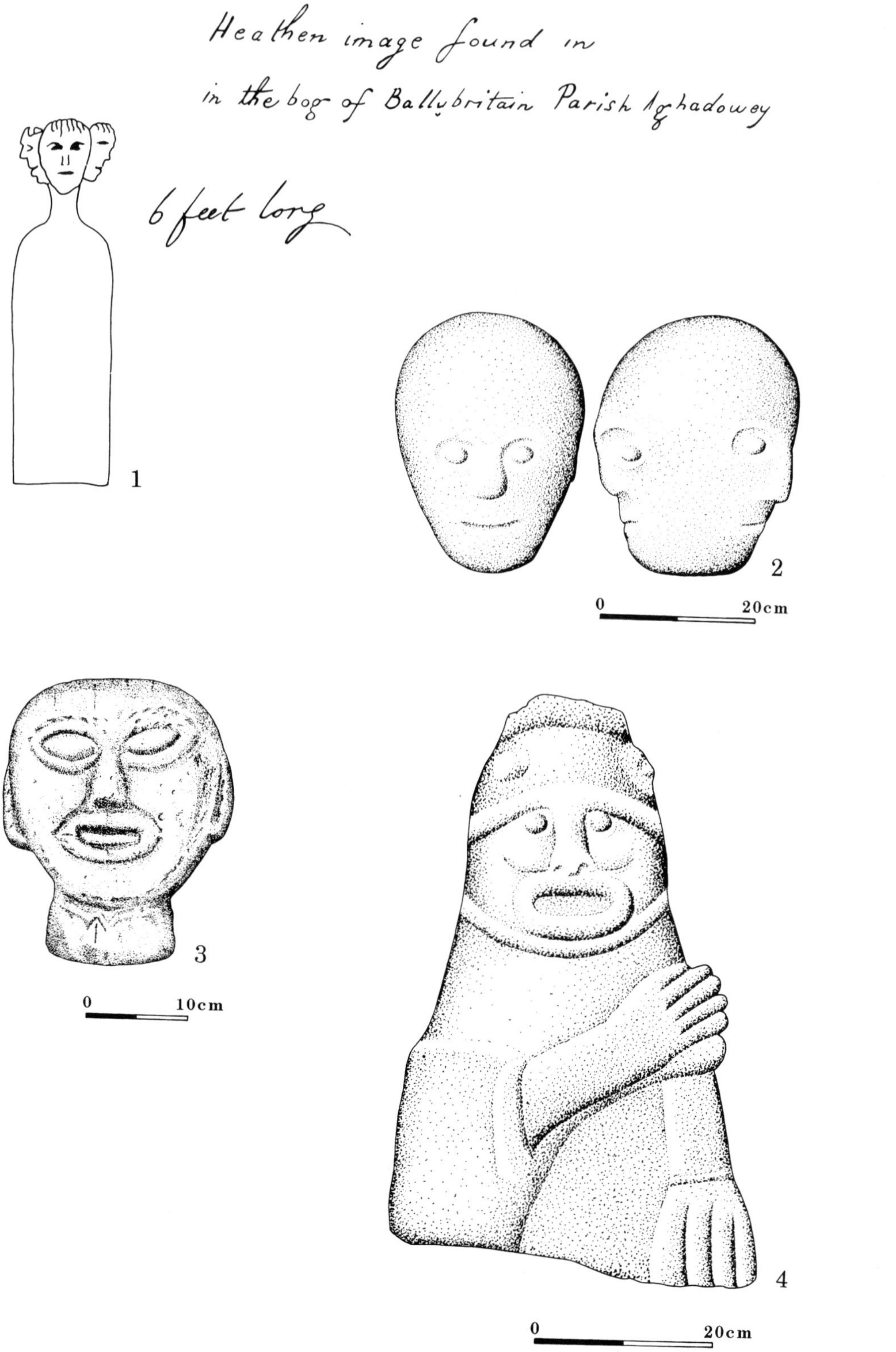
Heathen image found in
in the bog of Ballybritain Parish Aghadowey
6 feet long
1
2
0
20cm
3
0
10cm
4
0
20cm

Fig. 180. 1. A 19th century sketch of a wooden idol with four heads or faces found in a bog at Ballybritain, Co. Derry. 2. Stone three-faced head from Corleck, Co. Cavan. 3. Stone head said to come from Beltany, Co. Donegal. 4. The Tandragee idol, Co. Armagh.

attaching it to a base, possibly a timber pillar. If this was the case, it may be compared to a 1.8m high wooden carving found in the 1790s in a bog at Ballybritain, just north of Aghadowey, Co. Derry (Fig. 180, 1). Sadly this 'heathen image,' which was carved from a tree trunk and had four heads or faces with hair depicted, was allowed to fall to pieces and is only known from a minute sketch. These primitive carvings are very difficult to date but since three-faced or three-headed carvings are known in Roman Britain and Gallo-Roman France, the Irish examples may well be pre-Christian and belong to the early centuries AD; but since pagan practices are unlikely to have expired with the alacrity implied in early historical sources, a somewhat later date is quite possible too.

Numerous other stone heads of various sorts are also claimed to be pre-Christian and groups of them have been identified in Counties Donegal, Armagh, Cavan and Fermanagh, with scattered examples elsewhere. None are precisely dated, some may be prehistoric, others are probably of Medieval or post-Medieval date and some are probably folk art of the 17th or 18th centuries. A crude three-faced stone bust from Woodlands, near Raphoe, Co. Donegal, once believed to be pre-Christian, may have been carved in the 19th century. A stone head from Beltany, Co. Donegal (Fig. 180, 3), is a good illustration of the dating problems posed by carvings of this sort. The circumstances of its discovery are vague, it was reputedly found near a stone circle but, in effect, it is not known where it came from originally and its archaeological context is unknown. There are faint traces of what may be a collar on the neck and this has been compared to a torc; the eyes and mouth have been compared to these features on the two faces of a stone idol on Boa Island, Co. Fermanagh, itself of uncertain date but judging from other carvings in the region probably assignable to sometime in the 1st millennium AD. The Beltany head is also comparable to various human heads on other stone and metalwork of the early Historic period and attempts to date it are inevitably a subjective exercise.[51]

An intriguing group of stone carvings comes from the Armagh area but once again the picture is complicated by the presence of carvings and fragments of likely Medieval date and by the vigorous local production of primitive stone heads and possibly other sculpture in the 19th century. One carving which may be of early date is the striking Tandragee idol, as it is now called (Fig. 180, 4). This is a bust of a ferocious-looking human figure with a horned helmet and with its right arm in what is usually considered a ritual pose comparable to that of some prehistoric carvings of the later 1st millennium BC in Germany. There are few other points of comparison, however, and this unique piece, which may have been found near St Patrick's (Church of Ireland) Cathedral in Armagh, remains an enigma. Equally puzzling are stone carvings of three bears which may also have been found in the church precincts on Cathedral Hill during rebuilding work in the 19th century, these and some other undated carvings have led to the suggestion that the hill was the site of a pre-Christian cult centre.[52]

ANICONIC CARVINGS

It is possible that carvings like the Ballybritain pillar and the Corleck head once stood in small shrines or cult centres and the same may have been true of a number of more elaborate, non-representational, carved stones. Five are known but unfortunately, once again, nothing is recorded about their original archaeological context. The finest of these aniconic carvings is the Turoe stone, a pillar stone profusely decorated with a superbly executed La Tène design (Fig. 181, 1). It is a glacial erratic of fine-grained granite, 1.68m in maximum length, dressed to a cylindrical shape with a rounded top. The upper part of the stone, for some 68cm, is decorated with a finely carved curvilinear pattern delimited below by a rather irregularly executed step pattern. Set in the ground, it stands about 1.2m high and it may well have been painted originally. Its shape has led some commentators to suggest that it is a phallic symbol but it should be noted that rounded and elongated glacial erratics occur naturally in the locality.

At first glance, the free-hand curvilinear pattern appears to cover the stone in a seamless fashion but a detailed analysis by Michael Duignan revealed that the decorative scheme constituted four separate unitary compositions in two broad D-shaped and two narrower triangular panels, a quadripartite arrangement appropriate to a panelled or four-sided pillar. Any attempt to analyse the motifs employed demonstrates the imprecise and often ambiguous terminology common in La Tène art studies but such detailed examination is necessary if the art of the stone is to be placed in its proper context. Some motifs are readily recognizable and include

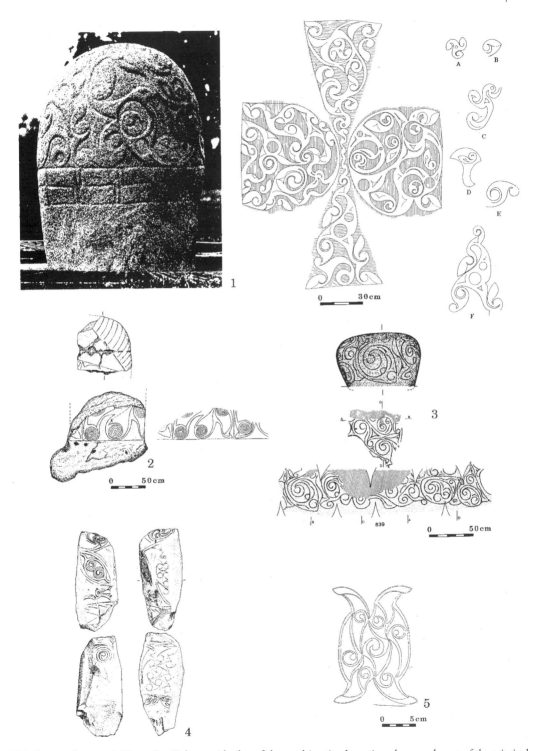

Fig. 181. Decorated stones. 1. Turoe, Co. Galway, with plan of the quadripartite decorative scheme and some of the principal motifs employed: A: symmetrical triskele, B: trumpet curve with comma leaf, C: bird's head and asymmetrical triskele, D: curving-sided triangular shape or void with floating comma leaf, E: pelta shape with spiral ends, F: complex triskele terminating in a pelta shape and comma leaves. 2. Killycluggin, Co. Cavan. 3. Castlestrange, Co. Roscommon. 4. Mullaghmast, Co. Kildare. 5. Derrykeighan, Co. Antrim.

roundels, a symmetrical triskele, a bird's head, trumpet curves and comma leaves, motifs already encountered on various pieces of metalwork. Comma leaf shapes and trumpet curves are placed at the bottom corners of each panel. Curving-sided triangular shapes are a feature of the background or negative pattern and in two prominent cases these triangular voids contain a floating comma leaf. More complex curvilinear forms include pelta shapes with one or two spiral ends, and asymmetrical triskeles or swirling shapes whose limbs sometimes terminate in other motifs such as pelta shapes or comma leaves and trumpet curves.[53]

Today the Turoe stone stands in the townland of Bullaun, near Loughrea, Co. Galway. It was discovered at the foot of a low hill in nearby Feerwore townland in the 1850s and taken as a garden ornament to Turoe House, now no more. It may have been displaced from the summit of the hill where it would have stood not far from the site of the ringfort of Feerwore which did have a number of other low rounded and undecorated boulders in its vicinity to the north and north-west. Unfortunately, in the excavation of the ringfort in 1938, no attempt was made to identify the former location of the decorated stone or to try and determine the relationship of the various stones to the earthwork or to one another.[54] The possibility that this stone once stood on a low hill along with some other undecorated stones is worth bearing in mind, because this was the case at Killycluggin.

The Killycluggin stone (Fig. 181, 2) once stood on a low drumlin near Ballyconnell, Co. Cavan, though where precisely is uncertain. It had been deliberately broken in the past and only two decorated fragments have been located; the larger had been partly buried on the upper slope of the hill, the smaller had found its way to the bottom of the drumlin. The larger fragment lay about 10m east of a small circle of at least 16 stones with a diameter of about 20m. While limited excavation determined that this large fragment was not in primary position, its original location was not identified but given its size it probably had not been moved very far. A small excavation in the stone circle was unproductive and the relationship between it and the decorated stone is not clear. The two fragments do not allow an accurate estimate of height to be made but it seems as if the stone was originally cylindrical in shape with a rounded top, the same general shape as the Turoe stone.[55] The carved

decoration on the lower part was seemingly in four rectangular panels framed by engraved lines and consisted of tightly coiled spirals linked by curving lines. The rounded top was partly covered by a zone of parallel lines.

The original location of the Castlestrange stone (Fig. 181, 3) is unknown. Like the Turoe stone, it too was moved to serve as an estate ornament and now lies near Athleague, Co. Roscommon. It is a squat granite boulder about 90cm high, oval in plan it has a more or less flat top, damaged in part, and straight but slightly sloping sides. The flat base is plain and the carved asymmetrical curvilinear decoration appears to cover the rest of the stone without a significant break. Motifs include two triskeles, loose spirals and shallow C-shaped curves.[56]

The Mullaghmast stone (Fig. 181, 4) is a fragment of a slender four-sided schist pillar with a sloping flat top; all surfaces have been damaged, the lower part is missing and what survives is about 90cm in length. It was found built into a castle wall on Mullaghmast hill, Co. Kildare. Decoration is either engraved or carved in relief. The principal motifs include, on the sloping top a triskele within a circle partly framed by a trumpet curve which springs from a large lentoid motif on one of the sides which in turn contains two plump spirals with lobed terminals. Another similar spiral survives on the much damaged opposing side. The two other opposing sides each have similar decoration consisting of a pattern of interlocking C-shaped curves. At least two narrow horizontal panels of mainly rectilinear ornament occurred on the lower parts of the stone. The pattern of interlocking C-shaped curves and the motif of two spirals in a lentoid field are designs found on some artwork of the 5th century AD and later and though the Mullaghmast stone is not precisely dated it is usually considered a late expression of La Tène art foreshadowing the more rigid and symmetrical representation of some of its motifs in the repertoire of artists of the early Historic period.[57]

The fifth decorated stone is a fragmentary piece of basalt of rectangular shape found incorporated as a quoin-stone a ruined church at Derrykeighan, Co. Antrim (Fig. 181, 5). One of two decorated faces has an engraved curvilinear design, based on a pattern of compass-drawn curves, which has been described as a 'pattern of recurved spirals and broken-back curves ... symmetrical about the diagonal axes' which finds a particularly good parallel on one of a number of decorated bone flakes from Loughcrew, Co. Meath. Curving-sided triangular voids, of course, are also a feature of the decorative scheme on the Turoe stone.[58]

Analysis of the decorative motifs on the Turoe stone indicated that its sculptor was familiar with late insular styles of La Tène art on decorated metalwork in Wales such as a plaque and a shield boss from the votive deposit at Llyn Cerrig Bach, Anglesea, and on several engraved bronze mirrors in southern England, such as Old Warden, Bedfordshire, and Great Chesterford, Essex, dating to the 1st centuries BC and AD.[59] The recognition that the Turoe stone represents an advanced stage of insular La Tène art was a significant conclusion because the stone was generally considered to have been inspired by some simpler decorated stones on the Continent, notably a number of pillar stones in Brittany, and since large decorated stones of this sort are unknown in Britain, a direct Irish connection with north-western France was a common assumption. It may be that the idea of decorating pillar stones was a Breton fashion, and in Ireland 'a foreign concept rendered in an entirely native form', as Barry Raftery has claimed, but it seems much more likely that the Turoe stone and various other decorated pillar stones wherever they occur are the scattered lithic survivors of a more widespread timber form. It is unlikely that the intricate symbolism of La Tène art, where some motifs must have been charged with magical meaning, was only expressed in stone and bronze. It is unfortunate so little is known about the original context of these stones but the fact that some of them were probably the targets of early Christian iconoclasts may be another indication of their former significance.[60]

RING BARROW, RING BANK, RING DITCH

Our limited understanding of the burial customs of late prehistory may be blamed, in part, on a lack of excavation but the scarcity of evidence may also be due to the fact, as in earlier times, that only a minority of the population were accorded the privilege of formal burial, the disposal of the majority leaving no archaeological trace. There is good evidence that quite a variety of burial customs were practised, some representing a continuity of funerary tradition from at least the 2nd millennium BC. It is possible to identify half a dozen different types of burial with various sorts of mound or other earthwork being used, earlier monuments occasionally re-used and both cremation and unburnt burial being practised.[61]

Ring barrows are circular mounds of earth surrounded by a ditch with an external bank. Mounds are usually quite low and frequently no higher than the surrounding bank. In many cases mounds are so slight as to be almost imperceptible, if there at all, and some monuments appear to consist of ditch and bank enclosing a level area. Here it is questionable if the term barrow is appropriate and a name such as ring bank, or embanked enclosure as they have been called, would be more accurate. The principal distinguishing feature of both ring barrow and ring bank is a bank and inner ditch, and in many cases these are annular. Some have an entrance through the bank and a corresponding causeway across the ditch, often on the eastern side; examples with two opposed entrances are also known. A small number of elaborate ring barrows have multiple banks and ditches (Fig. 182).

These monuments are widely distributed but both numbers and distribution are difficult to assess since classification is sometimes problematic and many ring ditches revealed by aerial photography may be ploughed-out ring barrows.

They vary in size: a few are very large exceeding 30m in overall diameter; both the northern and southern Claonfhearta or 'Sloping Trenches' on the western slopes of the Hill of Tara are exceptionally large examples 80m and 57m in diameter respectively, and the northern one is the largest mound in that celebrated complex. Most ring barrows seem to range in overall diameter from about 15m to 25m.

A number occur in groups or cemeteries, often along with other monuments, those at Tara, Rathcroghan, Carnfree and the Curragh have already been mentioned. Examples of other cemeteries are Slieve Breagh, on a hill north-west of Slane, Co. Meath, where an extensive series of earthworks includes at least a dozen ring barrows, a complex of some eight examples at Greatheath, north-east of Portlaoise, Co. Laois, a group of four at Knockbrandon Lower, Co. Wexford, three at Doonnagore, near Doolin, Co. Clare, and several near Nenagh, Co. Tipperary.[62]

Excavation of a relatively small number of ring barrows has revealed a complicated picture. Mounds

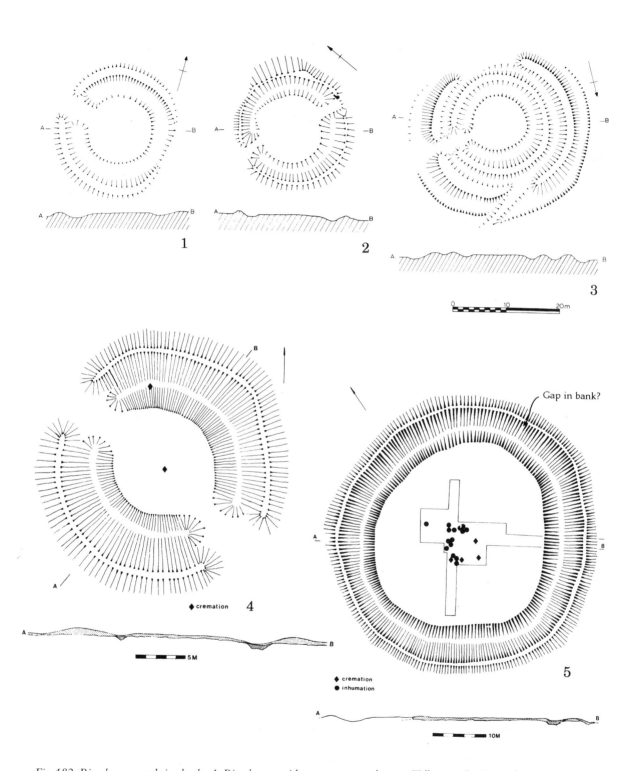

Fig. 182. Ring barrows and ring banks. 1. Ring barrow with an entrance on the west, Tullymore, Co. Donegal. 2. Ring barrow with opposed entrances, Coumgagh, Co. Kerry. 3. Multivallate ring barrow with three ditches and two banks, Creevy, Co. Donegal. 4-5. Ring banks on Carbury Hill, Co. Kildare.

with encircling banks and internal ditches are known from the second millennium BC if not earlier: Lissard, Co. Limerick, yielded a vase urn and cremation, Carrowlisdooaun, Co. Mayo, contained a cremation and a flat bronze axehead was found in the ditch, Lemonstown, Co. Wicklow, produced a vessel of the Bowl Tradition, and a pit filled with sand and turves contained a token cremation in a mound at Pubble, Co. Derry.[63] A complex ring barrow at Mullaghmore, Co. Down, contained a central burial consisting of the cremated bones of four persons accompanied by sherds of a number of coarse bucket-shaped pots and a blue glass bead (above a large pit filled with loose stones); sherds of a coarse bucket-shaped urn accompanied another cremation outside the ring barrow to the south-east and comparisons with the burials and pottery from Rathgall suggest a Dowris Phase date.

Some other excavated ring barrows probably date to the end of the 1st millennium BC or the early centuries AD. A small annular ring barrow, just over 15m in overall diameter, at Grannagh, near Ardrahan, Co. Galway, was partly investigated in 1916 and completely excavated in 1969. A scattered deposit of cremated human bone, a bead of green glass and the top of a small bone pin were found at the centre and the deep internal ditch contained several more pockets of cremated bone at various points. Finds included bronze fibulae, multi-coloured glass beads, a dumb-bell shaped glass bead, bone beads, bone pins, and iron fragments mostly from the ditch. A date in the 1st century BC or the 1st century AD seems probable. A smaller ring barrow at Oran Beg, near Oranmore, Co. Galway, measured 11m in overall diameter with a low bank and shallow internal ditch. A token deposit of cremated bone was found near the centre of the mound and an even smaller deposit of burnt bone was found in the ditch in the north-eastern quadrant. This was accompanied by over 80 tiny glass beads, mainly blue but some yellow, evidently fused together in the cremation pyre, a small fragmentary bronze ring and a small bronze toggle.

Excavation of a number of mounds in a barrow cemetery at Carrowjames, south-west of Balla, Co. Mayo, demonstrated that while several were of 2nd millennium BC date and contained pottery and other finds of the Cordoned Urn Tradition, two of the others, Tumuli 4 and 8, the largest in the cemetery, were later ring barrows. Tumulus 4 had an overall diameter of 21.35m and the very low

mound, a thin layer of material from the surrounding ditch covered three scattered cremations and two small pockets of cremated bone; an earlier burial, which consisted of a token cremation in a bucket-shaped urn, was found beneath the bank. Nothing was found to securely date the burials. Tumulus 8 was a smaller ring barrow of similar construction with an overall diameter of 15.5m. Some 25 small cremations were found and ten of them were accompanied by small objects such as glass beads, bronze dumb-bell shaped beads or toggles, and a small bronze ring. One cremation, a substantial deposit in a pit, was accompanied by two small bronze rings and three small bronze studs.[64]

In contrast to these few western ring barrows a majority of which produced multiple cremations accompanied by trinkets such as glass beads, excavations elsewhere have sometimes been less productive. A series of earthworks on the Curragh, in Co. Kildare, were excavated in 1944, and one of them, a small ring barrow 14m across, yielded no finds. At Dathi's Mound, Rathcroghan, Co. Roscommon, a small natural gravel ridge had been cut by a ditch to make a circular mound with opposed entrances on east and west through the surrounding bank. A large central pillar stone is the most prominent feature. Excavation of much of the surface of the natural mound revealed no burials. A substantial ditch inside the enclosing bank was filled with a fairly homogenous and possibly deliberate clay deposit. However, this ditch was sectioned at only three places and was not completely excavated. This was also the case at the Curragh where again just part of the ditch was investigated and obviously any deposits placed elsewhere in the ditch would not have been discovered.

One possible multivallate ring barrow was also excavated on the Curragh: a long pit containing the extended skeleton of an adult and covered by a small mound was surrounded by a pair of concentric ditches with diameters of about 12m and 18m respectively each possibly having an external bank. Unfortunately the burial is undated and the history of this partially excavated site was complicated by the presence of later unburnt burials which the excavator thought Medieval in date.[65]

A minimal mound, consisting of no more than a thin spread of redeposited material in the central area, is a feature of some ring barrows with low profiles such as Tumulus 8 at Carrowjames, Co.

Mayo, and this tendency finds its most extreme expression in the related ring banks or embanked enclosures which have internal ditches but no trace of a central raised area at all. Two were excavated on Carbury Hill, Co. Kildare (Fig. 182). One, 26m in overall diameter, had opposed entrances with causeways on the north-west and south-east. The central area and the ditch were fully excavated, a small pocket of cremated bone was found in the centre in a small hollow in the bedrock below the humus, a fragment of fused blue glass was found nearby, and a second deposit of burnt bone was found in the ditch on the north just 10cm above its base. A small handled spoon made of jet was an intriguing find on the site, though exactly where it was discovered is not recorded; it has been compared to late Roman silver spoons of about 400 AD. The second ring bank was exceptionally large with an overall diameter of over 51m. It was only partially excavated and a mix of burials revealed in the central area. Four cremations were found, two of them apparently disturbed by later unburnt burials. One of the cremated deposits was accompanied by two small iron rings and a pin-shaped fragment. There were also 15 unburnt burials, three disturbed by other later interments. All the undisturbed burials were extended with heads to the south-west and one, an adult male, was accompanied by an iron shears, an implement not easily dated.

Three ring banks were partly excavated on the Curragh: one, situated on the highest point in the area was about 45m in overall diameter with an entrance on the west, a second, about 35m in overall diameter with entrances on the east and west, enclosed the unburnt burial of an adult female in a central pit which S. P. Ó Ríordáin thought was an instance of burial alive, while the third, over 28m in diameter, had one entrance on the south-west. None produced any dating evidence.[66]

A number of ring ditches are late prehistoric in date and, whether they once had low external banks or not, they are evidently a related phenomenon. At the Rath of the Synods at Tara, the first phase of funerary activity included an oval ring ditch and a low ring barrow to the north-west, the latter contained five primary cremations and several more burials added later. A small cemetery of four ring ditches was recently excavated by Valerie Keeley during the construction of a by-pass at Ballydavis, near Portlaoise, Co. Laois. The largest (Site 1) was

16m in diameter with an entrance on the east. A central burial deposit consisted of a cremation, a small cylindrical bronze box with an iron mount on the lid decorated with red enamel, a bronze fibula of Nauheim type, bronze wire and over 80 stone and glass beads. The ditch produced an iron blade, nails, part of a bronze bracelet and pin, evidence of iron working and cremated bone, all of which seemed to represent several phases of activity. A smaller ring ditch (Site 2), some 40m to the east, measured 8m in diameter and had one entrance on the south-east; an iron blade and a fragment of bronze were found in the ditch and one of a number of shallow pits nearby contained a bronze fibula. Two further ring ditches (Sites 3 and 4) were each 6m in diameter, one was annular and its ditch contained charcoal, burnt bones, four glass beads and some decorated pieces of bone, the other had an entrance on the north-west and the ditch fill contained charcoal. The bronze box is a particularly interesting discovery because it recalls a small decorated bronze box found in a chariot grave at Wetwang Slack, Yorkshire, and since the burial of a dismantled chariot is a relatively rare indication of high status in north-eastern England, it suggests that a small cremation in a modest ring ditch might nonetheless be a high status burial.[67]

The evidence, limited though it is, from circular ring barrow and ring ditch, indicates one funerary pattern in the later centuries BC and early centuries AD that involved cremation and the occasional deposition of small or token deposits of bone sometimes accompanied by small but significant items of glass or bronze. As we have seen, unburnt burial was also practised, crouched burial is recorded and extended burials may also be a feature of the early centuries AD but dating evidence is still scarce.

It is believed that the reappearance of the rite of unburnt burial at this time reflects the influence of contacts with Roman Britain from the 1st century BC onwards. Crouched unburnt burial, at sites such as the Rath of the Synods and on Lambay Island, Co. Dublin, are amongst the earliest manifestations of this particular ritual. One of two crouched unburnt burials in a cemetery of extended burials at Betaghstown, Co. Meath, was accompanied by two iron penannular brooches of the 1st century BC or slightly later, an iron belt buckle and a bronze disc. A series of unburnt burials, most of them crouched or flexed, have been found in the vicinity of the great mound at Knowth, Co. Meath, and a number of them were accompanied by necklaces or armlets of glass beads. At Carrowbeg North, Co. Galway, a small mound of earth and stone covering a cremation and bronze razor of the early 2nd millennium was surrounded by a broad ditch about 1.2m deep. Four unburnt burials, of three adult females and one adult male, were inserted into the northern part of the ditch. Three were extended and one was flexed. One of the female burials, the flexed skeleton, was accompanied by 11 bone beads, a small bone toggle and a small bronze locket-like object, probably an amulet; none of these objects are precisely dateable but the excavator cited Roman parallels for the amulet.[68]

Few extended unburnt burials have been dated but some are probably early, emulating the custom in Roman Britain from the 2nd century AD. But many such interments, in both pit and slab-lined graves, belong to early Historic and later times. An extended burial at Ninch, Co. Meath, has been radiocarbon dated to 422-648 AD. Late prehistoric dates have also been claimed for others, though with little or no supporting evidence.[69]

Other forms of burial were practised too. The occasional use of earlier monuments occurs, and the burials at the passage tomb cemetery at Knowth have already been mentioned. The mound of a passage tomb at Kiltierney, Co. Fermanagh, was modified in the 1st century BC or the 1st century AD when a shallow ditch was dug around it, the mound was enlarged and 19 small mounds each about 3m in diameter and 1m high were built around the edge of the monument just outside the ditch forming, in effect, a discontinuous outer bank in ring barrow fashion. Some cremated burials were placed in shallow pits in the augmented original mound and one was accompanied by fine leaf-bow fibula (Fig. 152, 5) and four glass beads. Some

cremated bone was also found beneath some of the small satellite mounds and one produced a cremation, an iron fibula and burnt fragments of decorated bronze, possibly part of a mirror handle. This cremation, like the deposit of burnt bone found in a bronze bowl in a pit at Fore, Co. Westmeath, was presumably the burial of someone of importance. The presence of small deposits of cremated bone without grave goods at Kiltierney, for instance, also raises the question if such a simple ritual was a widespread fashion in later prehistory and hitherto unrecognized in the absence of radiocarbon dating.[70]

Other sorts of ritual deposits may have been common too. The 6th century BC deposits of three different kinds of cereals (barley, rye and oats) in the boulder circle at Carrowmore no. 26, Co. Sligo, of animal bones in the passage tomb at Carrowmore no. 3, dated to 230-520 AD, or the deposits of charcoal, shell fish and fish remains in the wedge tomb at Altar, Co. Cork, dated to the last few centuries BC and the early centuries AD, have all provided revealing evidence of organic offerings. The significance of the numerous bone flakes, some decorated with La Tène art, a number of finely made bone combs and other objects found in a passage tomb (Cairn H) at Loughcrew, Co. Meath, is uncertain but they could also have been votive offerings. A series of exotic objects including a hoard of five gold objects comprising two bracelets, two rings and a chain necklace, numerous Roman coins, two Roman disc brooches, a fragment of a torc with some inscribed Roman lettering, and glass beads all found in front of the passage tomb at Newgrange are not only evidence of contacts with Roman Britain but have also been considered 'offerings made to the gods of Newgrange' in the early centuries AD.[71]

NOTES

1 Feerwore, Co. Galway: J. Raftery 1944 thought the ringfort pre-Christian because what seemed to be a prehistoric cist burial had allegedly been inserted in its bank. The stratigraphical position of this cist is uncertain but it may have been below the bank, see Waddell 1975, 10, and Lynn 1983, 50. Dunsilly, Co. Antrim: McNeill 1992; Warner et al. 1990, 47. Lisdoo, Co. Fermanagh: Brannon 1982, 55; Warner et al. 1990, 48. Millockstown, Co. Louth: Manning 1986. Ballyhenry, Co. Antrim: Lynn 1983a. Lislackagh, Co. Mayo: G. Walsh 1995.

2 Banagher Glebe vitrified fort, Rallagh, near Dungiven, Co. Derry: Warner 1983, 176, fig. 79. Scrabo Hill, Co. Down: Owens 1971, 11; Jope et al. 1966, 179; Warner

et al. 1990, 48. Knocknarea, Co. Sligo: Burenhult 1984, 71: Settlement 2 in Grange West townland and Settlement 8 in Luffertan townland were excavated. Settlement 3 in Grange West was sampled.

3 Rathtinaun, Co. Sligo: Raftery 1994, 33; Warner et al. 1990, 49. Corlea, Co. Longford: Raftery 1996a, 7, 231; 1990.

4 Slaves are likely to leave only their chains behind: an iron slave fetter dredged from a river at Oldgrange, Co. Kildare, is stated to be of probable sub-Roman date: Lucas 1960, 33, fig. 23; see also Thompson 1993.

5 Glengarriff, Co. Cork: McCarthy 1986, 15. Ballymulholland, Co. Derry: Mallory and McCormick

1988. Some other coastal sites in the north are noted in Mallory and McNeill 1991, 150.

6 Raftery 1995.

7 Beehive querns: Heslop 1988. Anthropological evidence suggests that it may have taken an hour of hard labour on a saddle quern to prepare sufficient corn for the needs of one family whereas experimentation has shown that a little over half an hour on a rotary quern would produce 396g of wholewheat flour: Coles 1979, 122; also Hayes *et al.* 1980.

8 Caulfield 1977; the position of the handle socket is the basis of an imprecise three-fold subdivision: B1 with horizontal handle sockets, B2 with vertical sockets and B3 with sockets 'off the horizontal'. For illustrations of some beehive querns from Cavan and Monaghan: Barron 1976.

9 Warner 1991, 49, states 'the querns and the metalwork of La Tène tradition are not, therefore, part of the same artifactual culture' and suggests a distinction between pastoral and grain-growing communities. The general northern distribution of beehive querns is quite striking and Caulfield 1981 has suggested the existence of distinct northern and southern provinces in later prehistory, but see MacEoin 1986.

10 Weir 1995, 106. A hiatus in oak growth at 208 BC may be significant and reflect the onset of wetter conditions: Baillie 1992 and 1995, 143.

11 Scotland: Armit 1991.

12 Bronze and wooden vessels: Raftery 1984, 214. Trawsfyndd, Merioneth: Fox 1958, 109, pl. 65. Wooden bowls: Earwood 1989, Co. Armagh: 2070 ± 65 BP (213 BC - 61 AD, OxA-2417); Cloughmills, Co. Antrim: 1985 ± 70 BP (174 BC - 134 AD, OxA-2430); cauldron from Clogh, Co. Fermanagh: 2385 ± 70 BP (663-363 BC, OxA-2418). Drinking rituals: Vencl 1994.

13 Tara, Co. Meath: Newman 1993, 1995, 1997; Bhreathnach 1995, Bhreathnach and Newman 1995. Panoramic views from Tara: Fenwick 1997.

14 ApSimon 1986: 4260 ± 160 BP (3355-2465 BC, D-43).

15 Piggott 1975, 64.

16 The Navan complex: Mallory 1987, 1995; Warner 1994a and b. *Emain Macha*: Mallory in Lynn 1997, 197.

17 Excavations: Lynn 1997. Enclosure ditch: Simpson 1989; the radiocarbon date is 2420 ± 40 BP (UB-3091): Warner 1994a, 169; Weir 1989. Radiocarbon dates: Warner in Lynn 1997, 173; Barbary ape: 2150 ± 70 BP (390-20 BC, OxA-3321). For the tree-ring date of the central post see Baillie 1988. Geophysical surveys: Kvamme 1996; Ambos *et al.* 1996.

18 Navan Phases 4-5: Lynn 1992, 1993, 1994, 1996, has made a number of intriguing suggestions as to the possible religious and cosmological significance of this sequence of acts including the possibility that it all may have been an attempt to reconstruct an example of a mythical Otherworld hostel of the type then believed to exist underneath ancient mounds. The suggestion that some form of solar worship may have taken place there has been pursued by Warner 1996.

19 Loughnashade, Co. Armagh: Raftery 1983, 239; 1987a.

20 Warner 1994a. For Tara see Condit 1993.

21 Knockaulin, Co. Kildare: preliminary reports include Wailes 1970, 1971, 1973, 1974, 1974a, 1976, 1982, the most recent being Wailes 1990; also Johnston 1990. Early history: Grabowski 1990. For radiocarbon dates see Wailes 1976, 338; Warner *et al.* 1990, 48. The pre-rampart date is 2410 ± 60 BP (764-396 BC, P-2411): Wailes 1990, 20.

22 Lynn 1991.

23 Crabtree 1990. A minute quantity of barley seeds was also found: Raftery 1994, 123.

24 Aitchison 1994, 72; Evans 1966, 136; Ó Ríordáin 1950.

25 Iron sword: Raftery 1983, 90, figs 103-4, 1994, fig. 82f; iron spearhead: Wailes 1990, fig. 6, iron needles, fragments of bronze fibulae: Wailes 1990, figs 7-8.

26 Rathcroghan, Co. Roscommon: Waddell 1983, 1988, 1988a; Herity 1983 [published September 1984], 1984, 1987a, 1988, 1991, 1993. *Cruachain*: Ó hUiginn 1988.

27 Waddell and Barton 1995; Fenwick *et al.* 1996.

28 Waddell 1988.

29 Evans 1966, 177.

30 Literary accounts of royal sites: Aitchison 1994; Byrne and Dillon 1937; Mallory and Baillie 1988.

31 Other large hilltop enclosures with ramparts with internal ditches: Ballylin, Co. Limerick: Cody 1981; possibly Knockbrack, Co. Dublin: Keeling 1983. (See note 38.)

32 As Warner 1988, 57, has suggested for the early Historic period.

33 MacCana 1956, 76; Binchy 1958.

34 Carnfree, Co. Roscommon: Waddell 1988a, pls 15-16. Raffin, Co. Meath: Newman 1993a; 1994. Cornashee, Co. Fermanagh: Evans 1966, 115.

35 Hillforts: Raftery 1994, 38. Knocknashee, Co. Sligo: Condit *et al.* 1991, fig. 3, who note other hillforts in Sligo and Leitrim; also in Norman and St Joseph 1969, pl. 10. Carn Tigherna, Co. Cork: sketch plan in Raftery 1994, 40, fig. 23. Freestone Hill, Co. Kilkenny: Raftery 1969; 1976a; Raftery 1995. At least two other hillforts are known in Co. Kilkenny: Gibbons 1990.

36 Mountfortescue, Co. Meath: 164m in diameter with earthen bank and external ditch, with large tumulus in centre: Moore 1987, 126. Croaghan, Co. Donegal: 85m in internal diameter, cairn near centre: Lacy 1983, 115, fig. 55. Glasbolie, Co. Donegal: Lacy 1983, 115, fig. 56. Knockacarrigeen, Co. Galway, approximately 160m in diameter with cairn and later(?) enclosure: Byrne and Gosling 1988, pl. 1; Dunmurry Hill, Co. Kildare, with mound: Raftery 1976, pl. VII; Kesh, Co. Sligo: Condit *et al.* 1991, fig. 5. Also Kneigh and Ballincurra Hill, Tipperary: Raleigh 1985, 27. Garrangrena Lower, Co. Tipperary, with an average internal diameter of about 150m: Raftery 1968. Ballybuckley and Courthoyle New, Co. Wexford, with diameters of about 130m and 110m: Moore 1996, 25, pl. 1a and fig. 6 respectively.

37 Toormore, Co. Kilkenny: Raftery 1994, 43, fig. 28; Gibbons 1990, 18. Formoyle Hill, Co. Clare: Condit 1995. Cashel, Co. Cork: Power 1994, 66; Raftery 1976, pl. IX. Grianán of Aileach, Co. Donegal: Lacy 1983, 111; Colhoun 1995, 97; Wailes 1976, 334.

38 Belmont, Co. Galway: Raftery 1976b. Ballinkillen, Co. Carlow: Brindley and Kilfeather 1993, 19, fig. 7. Laghtea, Co. Tipperary: Condit 1995. Ballymartin, Co.

Mayo: Lavelle 1994, 19, pl. 5. Also Knockadigeen, Co. Tipperary (16 hectares): Raftery 1994, 43, fig. 25; Glenbane, Co. Kerry (12 hectares): Raftery 1994, 43, pl. 12; and possibly Knockbrack, Co. Dublin, an enclosure of 8.8 hectares possibly formed by two banks with intervening ditch or one bank with internal ditch(?) encompassing one of a cluster of burial mounds: Keeling 1983. However, the latter may be a site like Ballylin, Co. Limerick, a large bivallate enclosure of some 20.5 hectares with ditches inside the banks: Cody 1981. Other internally ditched enclosures are Carrownrush and Carrowgilhooly, Co. Sligo: Condit *et al.* 1991.

39 Rathcoran, Co. Wicklow: Norman and St Joseph 1969, fig. 3. Raftery 1994, pl. 11. Rathnagree, Co. Wicklow: Raftery 1972, pl. VI. Tinoranhill, Co. Wicklow: Stout 1994, 39. Spinan's Hill and Brusselstown Ring, Co. Wicklow: Condit 1992; Raftery 1994, 62.

40 Lurigethan, Co. Antrim: Raftery 1972, pl. V; Chart 1940, 20; Evans 1966, pl. 16. Co. Kerry: Cuppage 1986, 81. Co. Louth: Buckley and Sweetman 1991, 96. Co. Meath: Moore 1987, 48. Castle Gale, Co. Limerick: Doody *et al.* 1995.

41 The widely spaced ramparts of hillforts in south Wales and south-western England have long been interpreted as combining defensive and economic functions with the outer enclosures in particular constructed for the protection of livestock: Cunliffe 1991, 252; Fox 1961. See also Alcock 1965 and Bowden and McOmish 1989.

42 Raftery 1994, 41, notes that burial mounds are a feature of at least eleven Class 1 hillforts and apparently rare on Class 2 sites.

43 Raftery 1994, 60, is suitably cautious and emphasizes the preliminary nature of distribution maps of hillforts.

44 Woodman 1993, 15.

45 Linear earthworks: Kiltierney, Co. Fermanagh: Daniells and Williams 1977; see also ApSimon 1969, 60, and Hamlin and Lynn 1988, 24. Curragh, Co. Kildare: excavated section by Ó Ríordáin 1950, 270, who also notes another long earthwork known as the Black Ditch on the south-eastern part of the Curragh. Shankill/Rathduff: O'Flaherty 1987; Gibbons 1990, 21. Grevine West and Woodsgift, Co. Kilkenny: Gibbons 1990, 20.

46 Claidh Dubh, Co. Cork: Doody 1995; Power 1994, 67. A number of linear earthworks have been identified in neighbouring Co. Waterford, mainly from 18th and 19th century sources: Condit and Gibbons 1988. The Claidh Ruadh or Red Ditch in north Kerry is a discontinuous low bank with a lateral ditch; three separate sections, each several kilometres long, have been identified and it has been claimed that it continues into Co. Limerick: O'Donovan 1987; Toal 1995, 307.

47 The Black Pig's Dyke: General bibliography: Lynn 1989a. Leitrim and Armagh: Evans 1966, 58, 140. Cavan: O'Donovan 1995, 35. Monaghan: Brindley 1986, 94. Down: Jope *et al.* 1966, 144; Evans 1966, 96. Aghareagh West, Co. Monaghan: Walsh 1987: 2165 ± 55 BP (390-70 BC, UB-2600); a second similar radiocarbon date was obtained from another sample of charcoal from an accidental exposure of the dyke's palisade trench during construction work in the townland of Aghnaskew 1.6km to the west: 2190 ± 55 BP (390-100 BC, UB-2601).

48 The Dorsey: Aitchison 1993; Lynn 1982; 1989; 1989b; Lynn 1992a; Hamlin and Lynn 1988, 21. The spelling of the townland name and that of the Dorsy River is different from that of the monument.

49 Charcoal immediately pre-dating the construction of the bank on the north-east produced three radiocarbon dates, two of which had a range of 161 BC to 76 AD: 2020 ± 45 BP (161 BC to 73 AD, UB-2219) and 2015 ± 45 BP (157 BC to 76 AD, UB-2221), the third may come from heart-wood: 2240 ± 45 BP (387 BC to 191 BC, UB-2220): Lynn 1992a. South-western dendrochronological samples: 89 ± 9 BC (Q-4629), 96 ± 9 BC (Q-4633) and 95 ± 9 BC (Q-2888): Baillie 1988; Lynn 1992a. Northern dendrochronological samples: 150 ± 9 BC, 140 ± 9 BC and 135 ± 9 BC (Q-7598, Q-7604 and Q-7584): Baillie and Brown 1989; however the context of these northern timbers and their relationship to the rampart is unknown

50 Aitchison 1993. Drumsna, Co. Roscommon: Condit and Buckley 1989; Buckley *et al.* 1990; Lanting *et al.* 1991.

51 For Irish stone heads see Rynne 1972. Though often illustrated, the Corleck head has never been fully published; one face with slight brow ridges also has a small round hole in the centre of the mouth, a rare and curious feature found on a number of other carved heads of various dates from as far apart as Wales and Bohemia. The head was found either in Corleck townland or in the adjacent townland of Drumeague with, it has been claimed, another stone carving consisting of the head of a man with hair and beard set back-to-back in Janus fashion with a ram's head: Hickey 1976. Only the bearded head, provenanced Corraghy, Co. Cavan, survives: Rynne, *op. cit.* pl. IX, 1. For British and Continental material: Ross 1967, 74. Ballybritain, Co. Derry: the small sketch is preserved in the Ordnance Survey Memoranda: Waddell 1982; Day and McWilliams 1993, 30. Woodlands and Beltany, Co. Donegal: Rynne 1964; 1972; Lanigan Wood and Verling 1995.

52 Tandragee idol: not found in a bog near Newry but possibly found on Cathedral Hill and brought to Tandragee rectory along with other fragments according to Paterson and Davies 1940, 90; Ross 1967, 146; compare Megaw 1970, pls 12, 14, 142 and 285. For the three bears – one of which has absconded: Rynne 1972, pl. VII, 1; Ross *op. cit.*, 349, pl. 84a, b, 85a; Raftery 1994, pl. 76. Excavation has uncovered traces of a substantial ditch of possible late prehistoric date on Cathedral Hill; two radiocarbon dates provide a terminal date: 1660 ± 80 BP, 220-560 AD (UB-283: twigs from bottom of ditch) and 1845 ± 85 BP, 30 BC to 390 AD (UB-284: charcoal from ditch fill): Gaskell Brown and Harper 1984.

53 Turoe Stone, Co. Galway: Duignan 1976; in analysing the La Tène motifs on the Turoe stone, Duignan recognized the difficulties imposed by the absence of an

agreed English terminology and more or less followed the sometimes less than helpful terms used by Fox in his 1958 *Pattern and Purpose*. Thus the comma leaf shapes and trumpet curves at the bottom corners of each panel are called, after Fox, 'domed "trumpets" with one lateral coil or boss or roundel' and the curving-sided triangular shapes are 'three-sided, alias "Llyn Cerrig", voids' which have one convex and two concave sides. What are here called pelta shapes with one or two spiral ends are 'sub-triangular, curvilinear forms (otherwise "trumpets with two lateral coiled tendrils" ...)'. The triskeles or swirling shapes which sometimes terminate in pelta shapes or comma leaves and trumpet curves are called 'capped triskele-limbs'. For the step pattern see Waddell 1982.

54 Waddell 1986.

55 Killycluggin, Co. Cavan: Raftery 1978. The fragments are now in the National Museum of Ireland.

56 Castlestrange, Co. Roscommon: Raftery 1983, no. 839; the base is partly illustrated in Raftery 1984, pl. 103.

57 Raftery 1983, no. 838. Raftery 1993 excludes the Mullaghmast stone from the prehistoric group of decorated stones and places it in the early Historic period. For an illustration of the double spiral motif in a lentoid field on a brooch of the early Historic period, see Ryan 1983, 112.

58 The Derrykeighan stone has not been fully published; the description of the decoration is D. M. Waterman's; see Raftery 1984, 293, and 1994, 167.

59 Llyn Cerrig Bach: Savory 1976, fig. 27 (shield boss), pl. IV (plaque), also Megaw 1970, pl. 254. Great Chesterford mirror: Megaw 1970, no. 261; Old Warden: Fox 1958, 94, pl. 60, on which 'the voids are meant to please the eye as much as the pattern'.

60 For the alleged Breton connection see Waddell 1982 and Raftery 1984, 300. Given that the decoration on a pillar stone on Cape Clear, Co. Cork, is indecipherable its status must remain uncertain: O'Leary and Shee Twohig 1993.

61 Burials: Raftery 1981.

62 Slieve Breagh, Co. Meath: De Paor and Ó h-Eochaidhe 1956; Moore 1987, 25. Greatheath, Co. Laois: Sweetman *et al.* 1995, 9. Knockbrandon Lower, Co. Wexford: Moore 1996, 4. Doonnagore, Co. Clare: Rynne 1982a. Knockanpierce, Nenagh, Co. Tipperary: Farrelly 1995. Four ring barrows and an enclosure containing several more occur at Belpatrick, Co. Louth, but the enclosure may be a later monument: Buckley and Sweetman 1991, 44. Local studies of ring barrows are few: for example Dunkellin area, Co. Galway: McCaffrey 1955; Carrowmore, Co. Sligo: Timoney 1984; mid-Roscommon: Herity 1984, with confusing classification.

63 Summaries and references to second millennia sites in Waddell 1990, 29. Three ring barrows at Rathjordan, Co. Limerick, have produced Limerick style pottery of the third millennium BC: Ó Ríordáin 1947a and 1948.

64 Mullaghmore, Co. Down: Mogey 1949; Mogey and Thompson 1956; Raftery 1981, 176. Grannagh, Co. Galway: the 1969 excavation by Etienne Rynne is

unpublished: see Hawkes 1982; summarized in Raftery 1981; plan in Raftery 1994, fig. 112. Oran Beg, Co. Galway, unpublished: Rynne 1970. Other ring barrow excavations include Clogher, Co. Tyrone: Warner 1988a; Rathnarrow, Co. Westmeath: McCabe 1973; Knocknashammer, Co. Sligo: Timoney 1984, 324; Rathdooney Beg, Co. Sligo: Mount 1996; Haynestown, Co. Louth: O'Sullivan 1994, and Leckaneen, Co. Cork: O'Shaughnessy 1990. A ring barrow with an overall diameter of about 7.3m was 'trenched across' at Uisneach, Co. Westmeath, without result: Macalister and Praeger 1929. Carrowjames, Co. Mayo: J. Raftery 1941.

65 Curragh, Co. Kildare (Site 2): Ó Ríordáin 1950, 253. Dathi's Mound, Rathcroghan, Co. Roscommon: 2120 ± 25 BP (350-70 BC, GrN-11220), 1940 ± 70 BP (100 BC to 230 AD, GrN-11429), 1825 ± 30 BP (90 AD to 320 AD, GrN-11430): Waddell 1988. Possible multivallate ring barrow, Curragh, Co. Kildare (Site 6): Ó Ríordáin 1950, 259.

66 Carbury Hill, Co. Kildare: Willmot 1938 who mentions a gap or possible entrance in the bank of the larger ring bank on the north-east but does not show this on his published plan; Raftery 1984, 242. Ring banks, Curragh, Co. Kildare: Ó Ríordáin 1950, sites 1, 4 and 5. A ring bank at Reanascreena South, Co. Cork, surrounded a stone circle: Fahy 1962.

67 Ballydavis, Co. Laois: Keeley 1996. Wetwang Slack, Yorkshire: Dent 1985.

68 E. O'Brien 1990; 1992. Betaghstown, Co. Meath: Kelly 1988; E. O'Brien 1990; 39; 1992, 135. Knowth, Co. Meath: Eogan 1968, 365; 1974b, 68; Raftery 1994, 195, 230, notes late prehistoric radiocarbon dates for four unburnt burials including a double burial containing two decapitated males accompanied by bone dice and gaming pieces – gamblers according to Eogan – dated to 1960 ± 30 BP (40 BC - 108 AD, GrN-15371). Carrowbeg North, Co. Galway: Willmot 1939; Raftery 1984, 205. Child burial with glass bead and ear ring, Culleenamore, Co. Sligo: Burenhult 1984, 339.

69 Ninch, Co. Meath: from bone 1510 ± 65 BP (422-648 AD, GU-1453) and 1820 ± 115 BP (UB-2425) from nearby charcoal, Sweetman 1983. An early date for some extended unburnt burials at Kiltale, Co. Meath, has been claimed because some of them were disturbed by the ditch of a later but undated ringfort: Rynne 1974; the presence of a skull burial was one factor to prompt the suggestion of a pre-Christian date for some extended burials at Ballinlough, Co. Laois: Rynne 1975.

70 Kiltierney, Co. Fermanagh: Hamlin and Lynn 1988, 24; Raftery 1994, 193, figs. Fore, Co. Westmeath: Kelly 1993, 22, pl. 7; Raftery 1994, 196, fig. 123.

71 Carrowmore no. 26, Co. Sligo: Burenhult 1980, 40 and 1984, 60; Carrowmore no. 3: unburnt bones of cattle, sheep or goat and pig, 1690 ± 55 BP (LU-1811): Burenhult 1984, 64, 198. Altar, Co. Cork: W. O'Brien 1993. Loughcrew, Co. Meath: Raftery 1984, 210, 251. Newgrange, Co. Meath: Topp 1956; Carson and O'Kelly 1977.

10

Protohistory

'THE PEOPLE OF THE FERTILE EARTH'
The literate world encroaches slowly on late prehistoric Ireland. It would be agreeable if early historical sources added a new dimension to our understanding of the later centuries BC and the early 1st millennium AD, but this is not the case. The earliest references to places and people are tantalizingly brief. Fragments of an account of a voyage to the Atlantic from the Greek colony of Massilia are preserved. Known as the Massiliote Periplus, this was a sea journey from present day Marseilles, through the straits of Gibraltar into the 'Outer Sea' and along the coasts of western Europe; it may have been written shortly before 500 BC but survives only in part in the *Ora Maritima* of Festus Rufus Avienus of the late 4th century AD. This Periplus or manual for navigators recorded the existence of the islands of *Ierne* and *Albion*, Greek forms of the earliest known names of Ireland and Britain. The name *Ierne* (or *Iverni*) is an ethnic name meaning the 'people of the fertile earth'.

About 325 BC, another voyager, Pytheas of Massilia, whose account is also known only at second hand in later works, simply refers to both islands as the *Pretanic* islands, a name later rendered as Britanni and the earliest usage of the term 'the British isles'. Early in the 1st century AD, Philemon recorded from merchants that the length of the island of Ireland was twenty days' journey, a reasonably accurate estimation if an average daily journey of 21 miles (33km) is accepted. Philemon was probably one of the sources for Ptolemy's *Geography* compiled in Alexandria in the 2nd century AD. This is a list of placenames, including settlement, headland, island and river names, and tribal names given with their longitude and latitude. From this information it is possible to reconstruct Ptolemy's map which is the oldest documentary account of this island (Fig. 183). Some names are inaccurate, a few are readily identifiable and scholars disagree about many others. *Buvinda* is the River Boyne, *Senos* the Shannon, *Oboca* may be

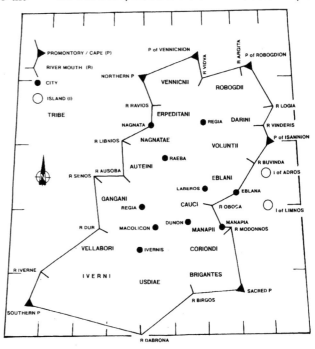

Fig. 183. A reconstruction of Ptolemy's map of Ireland of the 2nd century AD.

the River Liffey, *Limnos* may be Lambay Island, and the name *Regia* which occurs twice may refer to royal sites. It has been suggested that *Isamnion*, though shown as a promontory, may in fact be a reference to *Emain Macha* or Navan Fort and if this is so, the northern *Regia* may be Clogher, Co. Tyrone. Some tribal names, such as the *Manapii* and the *Brigantes*, are also found in Britain.[1]

References by Roman writers are for the most part less than helpful as they almost invariably reflect the common view of the barbarian world as a savage and inhospitable place. Tacitus is an exception, in the late 1st century AD he wrote: Ireland 'is small in comparison with Britain, but larger than the islands of the Mediterranean. In soil and climate, and in the character and civilization of its inhabitants, it is much like Britain; and its approaches and harbours have now become better known from merchants who trade there. An Irish prince, expelled from his home by a rebellion, was welcomed by Agricola, who detained him, nominally as a friend, in the hope of being able to make use of him. I have often heard Agricola say that Ireland could be reduced and held by a single legion with a fair-sized force of auxiliaries ...'.[2]

Though the 1st century AD references to merchants and traders are interesting, they are not very illuminating and the nature and degree of Ireland's contact with the Roman world are obscure and the subject of continuing debate. In the 19th and early 20th century it was claimed there may have been a Roman invasion of Ireland and various finds of Roman material seemed to lend some support to this hypothesis. The casual discovery in or about 1842 of a Roman oculist's stamp at Golden, on the River Suir, in Co. Tipperary, was considered particularly significant, these small engraved stones being usually associated with the Roman army.[3] However, the circumstances of discovery of this object are not well documented and it is clear that not all Roman finds are ancient imports. Coins are the commonest item reported and these and other finds have been reviewed by Donal Bateson who has concluded that most Roman coins found in Ireland (some 80%) were probably imported in relatively recent times, in the 18th or 19th centuries or even later.[4] A number of coin finds and other discoveries may be accepted as genuine when the circumstances of their discovery seem plausible or when they have been found with other objects or unearthed in an archaeological

excavation. This authentic material seems to fall into two major groups, one belonging to the 1st and 2nd centuries AD, the other mainly to the 4th and early 5th centuries AD.

Genuine finds of Roman date include the material excavated at Newgrange and at Freestone Hill, Co. Kilkenny. The acceptable numismatic evidence includes two large hoards of silver coins of the 2nd century AD. One found in 1827 at Flower Hill, near Bushmills, Co. Antrim, comprised 300 silver coins, the other found on Feigh Mountain, near the Giant's Causeway, may have contained 500 silver coins. The 2nd century date indicates that there is no connection with a large hoard of Roman silver found in 1854 west of Coleraine at Ballinrees, Co. Derry, which contained over 1500 coins and over 5kg of silver bars, ingots, fragments of plate, a bowl and two spoons. The coin evidence indicated that this hoard was probably deposited between 420 and 425 AD. A smaller hoard of broadly similar date was found at Balline, near Knocklong, Co. Limerick, in 1940, in a gravel pit; it comprised four silver ingots and three pieces of cut silver plate and was presumed to have been looted in Britain in the early 5th century. A hoard of five gold objects was found in 1842 at Newgrange, Co. Meath, and consisted of two finger rings, two spiral twisted bracelets and a gold chain. Because of its location, near the entrance to the passage tomb, this hoard and a significant number of other finds such as gold coins, two disc brooches and other objects have been considered votive offerings. What precipitated the concealment of the other deposits of Roman material elsewhere is not clear but most have usually been considered the property of traders or the booty of raiders or pirates hidden for safekeeping and never recovered.[5]

Stray finds are even more difficult to interpret: the Roman fibula found with the Annesborough, Co. Armagh, hoard of late 2nd millennium BC bronzes (Fig. 73) may be a casual loss and an accidental association with earlier material or it may be a late dedicatory offering when that find was re-buried. Small objects like this, though not common, are widely distributed. Roman fibulae have been found in sandhills at Ballyness and Dunfanaghy, Co. Donegal, 'near Galway' and near Bantry, Co. Cork. Toilet implements, such as nail cleaners and probes, also come from Ballyness and from Dooey, Co. Donegal, and a bronze patera or ladle has been found on Rathlin Island. Coastal finds of this sort could well denote the use of local landing or beaching spots as part of a network of coastal trading places. At first glance, this might also seem to be a reasonable explanation for a sherd of Samian ware excavated at a site in the Dundrum sandhills, Co. Down, but numerous fragments of souterrain pottery of the early Historic period were also found there and this Roman pot sherd, like a number of others from various locations in Ireland, may be imports of the late 1st millennium AD or later and acquired as relics, for grinding down for pigments, for medicinal usage or for some other purpose. Indeed the Dundrum fragment seemed to have been neatly squared as if it had been shaped as a decorative inlay.[6] However, Roman pottery fragments from demonstrably early archaeological contexts are probably genuine imports. Fragments of Roman pottery from Knowth, a bronze toilet implement or cosmetic spoon and the unburnt burials attributed to Roman influence may all be related. It is possible that a pair of substantial concentric ditches which ringed the great mound may have enclosed a contemporary settlement on its summit but since the surface of the mound had been destroyed this cannot now be verified. Clogher, Co. Tyrone, occupied in the Dowris Phase and a major royal settlement in the early Historic period, was also a defended enclosure at some time prior to 400 AD, this occupation perhaps associated with a 1st century AD Romano-British brooch and pot sherds. Some Roman material, including pottery, a lead seal, a glass inset for a ring or brooch and an iron barrel padlock, is also reported from the Rath of the Synods at Tara and bronze fibulae were found at Knockaulin, Co. Kildare.[7]

A small number of discoveries imply especially close contact with Roman Britain and the most important of these is a remarkable cremation found at Stonyford, Co. Kilkenny, in the 19th century. It was reportedly found in a 'rath' (a term which could have been applied at the time to either a ringfort or a mound) and protected by stones. It consisted of a cremation in a glass urn accompanied by a small bronze mirror and a glass phial perhaps for cosmetics (Fig. 184). This sort of burial was typical of the Roman middle-class in the 1st century AD and suggests the presence of a Roman individual, possibly a woman, or even a Roman community in the valley of the King's River, a tributary of the Nore, just west Thomastown. It may be noteworthy that the Nore was possibly navigable from Waterford

to this point. The identification of the remains of a wooden boat in Lough Lene, Co. Westmeath, is an important indication of the role inland waterways played in trade and communications (Fig. 184). This was a slender flat-bottomed craft over 8m long, in part constructed in a Roman technique in which each oak plank or strake is carvel built with timbers placed edge to edge, joined with mortise and tenon and held together with wooden pegs; the tenons were of yew and the oak parts of the 1m wide bottom portion were stitched together by wooden withies inserted into drilled holes. Fragments of two oar blades were also found.[8]

If the Stonyford burial was that of a woman, it must recall the possible female cremation and glass beads and other objects found at Loughey, near Donaghadee, Co. Down. The evidence here is less than satisfactory and whether possible Roman women mean possible Roman communities is difficult to know. A series of burials found in 1835 on Bray Head, Co. Wicklow, is also poorly documented but it has been suggested that they too could have been the remains of such a community; a small cemetery consisted of a number of extended unburnt skeletons, each with a stone at their head and feet; copper coins of Trajan (97-117 AD) and Hadrian (117-138 AD) were found and had perhaps been placed in the mouths of the corpses in the Roman manner as payment for the ferryman Charon on the final journey across the river Acheron to the land of the dead.

Finally, another group of burials was found on Lambay Island off the north Dublin coast in 1927 and, unfortunately, was equally poorly recorded. A number of crouched unburnt skeletons were apparently accompanied by a range of grave goods. Five Romano-British brooches of 1st and 2nd century AD date are preserved and one grave contained the remains of an iron sword and a cup-shaped bronze object of uncertain purpose, possibly a shield boss. Other objects include bronze scabbard mounts, a bronze bracelet, a bronze finger ring, an iron mirror, a beaded collar or torc, a decorated bronze disc and a triangular bronze mount. The collar is a well-known northern British type and the triangular mount has close parallels in Wales, and it is evident that the Lambay folk had close contacts with these parts of Britain. There is of course nothing to confirm the often expressed belief that these people were refugees. The Lambay material is part of a larger body of evidence testifying to a

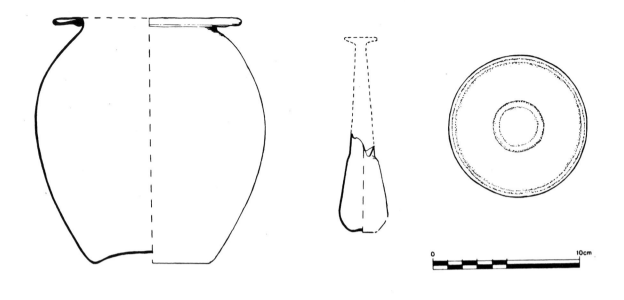

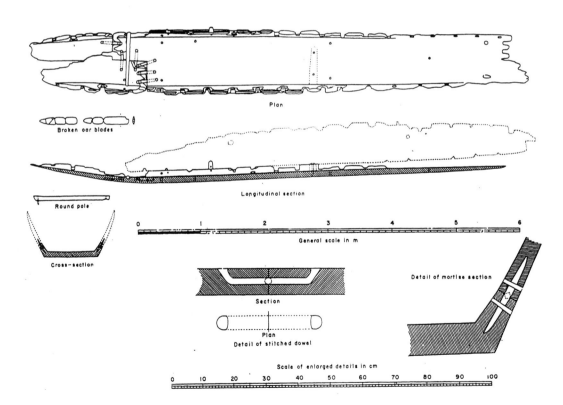

Fig. 184. Above. Objects from a Roman burial at Stonyford, Co. Kilkenny: a glass urn containing a cremation was accompanied by a circular bronze mirror and a small glass phial. Below. The remains of a carvel-built wooden boat from Lough Lene, Co. Westmeath.

pattern of significant contact across the Irish Sea in the 1st and 2nd centuries AD and the people buried there and at Bray may equally well have been members of settled coastal communities.[9]

The discovery of Roman pottery, coins and other material in a large coastal promontory fort at Drumanagh, near the village of Loughshinny, in north Co. Dublin, suggests that this site may have been an important settlement of the period and one which figured prominently in the trading networks of the time. But the economic significance of a site like this is impossible to gauge without excavation. A number of pollen analyses, notably from sites such as Loughnashade, Co. Armagh, and Whiterath Bog, Co. Louth, indicate that the centuries after 200 AD witnessed widespread land clearance and a resurgence of arable agriculture. The chronology and extent of these developments require further study but rye pollen suggests that this cereal may now have become an important arable component and oats, recognized in later early Historic contexts, may have been grown in greater quantity early in the 1st millennium AD too. Agricultural intensification may denote population growth but corresponding settlement evidence is scanty.[10]

Some of the finds from Lambay Island, just 6km south-east of Drumanagh, are a useful reminder that contacts across the Irish Sea were also contacts with native, non-Roman, communities in Britain who, in some instances, may have been intermediaries in the transmission of Roman goods. There may well have been Romano-British traders in Ireland and some Irish people may have travelled to late Roman Britain. Richard Warner has speculated that some of the Roman material found in Ireland may be best explained by one or more military intrusions, perhaps on occasion by mixed forces of Romanized Irish and Romano-British adventurers, in the 1st or 2nd centuries AD. This is by no means impossible. After all, there were Irish raids on Britain a century or two later.

The implications of Roman finds in Ireland will continue to be debated and they will, no doubt, be variously attributed to settlers, traders, invaders, refugees, free-booters and others. Indeed a single explanation is unlikely and many or all of these factors may have been involved. While some of the later material of the 4th and 5th centuries (such as the Balline hoard) may have been the ill-gotten gains of looters, some other finds may be attributable to early Christian missionaries, the precursors of other more profound and long-lasting changes which would reshape the millennia-old constants of agriculture and ritual in particular.[11]

NOTES

1 Tierney 1976; Killeen 1976; Freeman 1995. *Ierne*: Koch 1986. Ptolemy: O'Rahilly 1946; Byrne 1984; for a discussion of northern names: Mallory and McNeill 1991, 143.

2 Tacitus, *Agricola,* chapter 24.

3 Raftery 1994, fig. 142; chapter 9 is a comprehensive review of the evidence for contact with Roman Britain. See also Rankin 1996, 300.

4 Bateson 1973; 1976. Warner 1976. A significant quantity of Roman antiquities lies at the bottom of the sea off Killiney, Co. Dublin, when a shipload of objects acquired by Lord Cloncurry was lost in a storm in 1806: Stanford 1970, 69, notes 213-215.

5 Flower Hill and Feigh Mountain, Co. Antrim: Bateson 1971. Ballinrees, Co. Derry: Mattingly and Pearce 1937. Balline, Co. Limerick: Ó Ríordáin 1947, 43. Newgrange, Co. Meath: Topp 1956; Carson and O'Kelly 1965.

6 Warner 1976, 285; Rynne 1975a. Dundrum, Co. Down: Collins 1959.

7 Knowth, Co. Meath: Bateson 1973, 67, fig. 1; Eogan 1991, 118. Clogher, Co. Tyrone: preliminary excavation reports: Warner 1972; 1973; 1974a; 1974b; 1976a; 1988a; *Radiocarbon* 21. Romano-British brooch and pottery: Hawkes 1982, pl. 1, 2; Warner 1995, 28. Rath of the Synods, Tara: Bateson 1973, 71, fig. 1. Knockaulin, Co. Kildare: Wailes 1990, figs 7 and 8.

8 Stonyford, Co. Kilkenny: Bourke 1989. Lough Lene, Co. Westmeath: Brindley and Lanting 1990a; Ó hEailidhe 1992; a radiocarbon date of 2195 ± 25 BP (400-100 BC, GrN-17263) which may have been obtained from a sample of slow-growing yew thus still allowing an early Roman period date for the boat in the 1st century AD (Brindley and Lanting 1991).

9 Bray Head, Co. Wicklow: Bateson 1973, 45; the graves seem to have been pits with stones at either end, not long cists or slab-lined graves. Lambay Island, Co. Dublin: Rynne 1976; Raftery 1983, 288.

10 Weir 1993, 1995. Monk 1986. Drumanagh, Co. Dublin: Raftery 1996.

11 Ireland and the late Roman world: Swift 1996. 'Romanization': Laing 1985. Roman incursions: Warner 1995.

Bibliography

Addyman, P. V. 1965. Coney Island, Lough Neagh: prehistoric settlement, Anglo-Norman castle and Elizabethan fortress, *Ulster Journal of Archaeology* 28, 78-101.

Addyman, P. V. and Vernon, P. D. 1966. A beach pebble industry from Dunaff Bay, Inishowen, Co. Donegal, *Ulster Journal of Archaeology* 29, 6-15.

Aitchison, N. B. 1987. The Ulster Cycle: heroic image and historical reality, *Journal of Medieval History* 13, 87-116.

Aitchison, N. B. 1993. The Dorsey: a Reinterpretation of an Iron Age Enclosure in South Armagh, *Proceedings of the Prehistoric Society* 59, 285-301.

Aitchison, N. B. 1994. *Armagh and the Royal Centres in Early Medieval Ireland*. Woodbridge.

Alcock, L. 1965. Hillforts in Wales and the Marches, *Antiquity* 39, 184-195.

Allen, D. 1991. Hot water and plenty of it, *Archaeology Ireland* 8, no. 1, 8-9.

Allen, I. M., Britton, D. and Coghlan, H. H. 1970. *Metallurgical Reports on British and Irish Bronze Age Implements and Weapons in the Pitt Rivers Museum.* Oxford.

Almagro, M. 1958. Deposito de la Ria de Huelva, *Inventaria Archaeologica, España,* Fasc. 1-4. Madrid.

Almagro, M. 1966. *Las Estelas Decoradas del Suroeste Peninsular.* Madrid.

Almagro-Gorbea, M. 1995. Ireland and Spain in the Bronze Age, in J. Waddell and E. S. Twohig (eds), *Ireland in the Bronze Age. Proceedings of the Dublin Conference, April 1995,* 136-148. Dublin.

Ambos, E. L., Larson, D. O., Kvamme, K., Conway, M. and Cibbarelli, S. 1996. Remote Sensing Surveys of Navan Fort, *Emania* 15, 15-32.

Anderson, E. 1993. The Mesolithic: Fishing for Answers, in E. S. Twohig and M. Ronayne (eds), *Past Perceptions. The Prehistoric Archaeology of South-West Ireland,* 16-24. Cork.

Anderson, E. and Johnson, G. 1993. A Refitting and Use-wear Analysis of a Later Mesolithic Flint Assemblage from Bay Farm, County Antrim, *Archeomaterials* 7, 83-100.

Anderson, E. and Johnson, G. 1995. Irish Later Mesolithic Flint Technology: Further Developments, in E. Grogan and C. Mount (eds), *Annus Archaeologiae. Archaeological Research 1992,* 7-21. Dublin.

Anderson, R. 1989. Haughey's Fort: Analysis of an Insect Death Assemblage, *Emania* 6, 37-42.

ApSimon, A. 1969. The Earlier Bronze Age in the North of Ireland, *Ulster Journal of Archaeology* 32, 28-72.

ApSimon, A. 1969a. An Earlier Neolithic house in Co. Tyrone, *Journal of the Royal Society of Antiquaries of Ireland* 99, 165-168.

ApSimon, A. 1976. Ballynagilly and the beginning and end of the Irish Neolithic, in S. J. de Laet (ed.), *Acculturation and Continuity in Atlantic Europe mainly during the Neolithic period and the Bronze Age, Dissertationes Archaeologicae Gandensis,* 15-30. Bruges.

ApSimon, A. 1986. Chronological Contexts for Irish Megalithic Tombs, *The Journal of Irish Archaeology* 3, 5-15.

Armit, I. 1991. The Atlantic Scottish Iron Age: five levels of chronology, *Proceedings of the Society of Antiquaries of Scotland* 121, 181-214.

Armstrong, E. C. R. 1915. On the localities and distribution of the various types of bronze celts in the National Museum, Dublin, *Proceedings of the Royal Irish Academy* 27C, 253-259.

Armstrong, E. C. R. 1917. Some associated finds of bronze celts discovered in Ireland, *Proceedings of the Royal Irish Academy* 33C, 511-526.

Armstrong, E. C. R. 1917a. The Great Clare Find of 1854, *Journal of the Royal Society of Antiquaries of Ireland* 47, 21-36.

Armstrong, E. C. R. 1918. Associated Finds of Irish Neolithic Celts, *Proceedings of the Royal Irish Academy* 34C, 81-95.

Armstrong, E. C. R. 1924. The Early Iron Age, or Hallstatt Period in Ireland, *Journal of the Royal Society of Antiquaries of Ireland* 54, 109-127.

Armstrong, E. C. R. 1933. *Guide to the Collection of Irish Antiquities. Catalogue of Irish Gold Ornaments in the Collection of the Royal Irish Academy* (Second edition). Dublin.

Baillie, M. G. L. 1982. *Tree-Ring Dating and Archaeology.* Chicago.

Baillie, M. G. L. 1985. Irish Dendrochronology and Radiocarbon Dating, *Ulster Journal of Archaeology* 48, 11-23.

Baillie, M. G. L. 1988. The dating of the Timbers from Navan Fort and the Dorsey, Co. Armagh, *Emania* 4, 37-40.

Baillie, M. G. L. 1992. Dendrochronology and Past Environmental Change, *Proceedings of the British Academy* 77, 5-23.

Baillie, M. G. L. 1995. *A Slice through Time. Dendrochronology and precision dating.* London.

Baillie, M. G. L. and Brown, D. M. 1989. Further Dates from the Dorsey, *Emania* 6, 11.

Bamford, H. 1971. Tullywiggan Neolithic/Early Bronze Age Occupation, in T. G. Delaney (ed.), *Excavations 1971*, 24-25. Belfast.

Barber, J. 1973. The orientations of the recumbent-stone circles of the south-west of Ireland, *Journal of the Kerry Archaeological and Historical Society* 6, 26-39.

Barclay, G. J. and Russell-White, C. J. 1993. Excavations in the ceremonial complex of the fourth to second millennium BC at Balfarg/Balbirnie, Glenrothes, Fife, *Proceedings of the Society of Antiquaries of Scotland* 123, 43-210.

Barfield, L. and Hodder, M. 1987. Burnt mounds as saunas, and the prehistory of bathing, *Antiquity* 61, 370-379.

Barrett, J. C. and Needham, S. P. 1988. Production, Circulation and Exchange: Problems in the Interpretation of Bronze Age Bronzework, in J. C. Barrett and I. A. Kinnes (eds), *The Archaeology of Context in the Neolithic and Bronze Age: Recent Trends,* 127-140. Sheffield.

Barron, T. J. 1976. Some Beehive Quernstones from Counties Cavan and Monaghan, *Clogher Record* 9, 95-105.

Barry, T. B. 1981. Archaeological Excavations at Dunbeg Promontory Fort, County Kerry, *Proceedings of the Royal Irish Academy* 81C, 295-329.

Bateson, J. D. 1971. The Finding of Roman Silver Coins in the Vicinity of the Giant's Causeway, *Ulster Journal of Archaeology* 34, 50-57.

Bateson, J. D. 1973. Roman Material from Ireland: a re-consideration, *Proceedings of the Royal Irish Academy* 73C, 21-97.

Bateson, J. D. 1976. Further Finds of Roman Material from Ireland, in Colloquium on Hiberno-Roman Relations and Material Remains, *Proceedings of the Royal Irish Academy* 76C, 171-180.

Beck, C. and Shennan, S. 1991. *Amber in Prehistoric Britain.* Oxford.

Bengtsson, H. and Bergh, S. 1984. The Hut Sites at Knocknarea North, Co. Sligo, in G. Burenhult (ed.), *The Archaeology of Carrowmore*, 216-318. Stockholm.

Bergh, S. 1995. *Landscape of the Monuments. A study of the passage tombs in the Cúil Irra region, Co. Sligo, Ireland.* Stockholm.

Bhreathnach, E. 1995. *Tara. A Select Bibliography, Discovery Programme Reports* 3 [*Discovery Programme Monograph* 1]. Dublin.

Bhreathnach, E. and Newman, C. 1995. *Tara.* Dublin.

Bigger, F. J. 1917. Some recent archaeological discoveries in Ulster, *Proceedings of the Royal Irish Academy* 33C, 1-8.

Binchy, D. A. 1958. The Fair of Tailtiu and the Feast of Tara, *Eriu* 18, 113-138.

Boreland, D. 1996. Late Bronze Age Pottery from Haughey's Fort, *Emania* 14, 21-28.

Bourke, C. 1993. Antiquities from the River Blackwater II, Iron Age Metalwork, *Ulster Journal of Archaeology* 56, 109-113.

Bourke, E. 1989. Stoneyford: a first-century Roman burial from Ireland, *Archaeology Ireland* 3, no. 2, 56-57.

Bourke, L. 1996. A watery end – prehistoric metalwork in the Shannon, *Archaeology Ireland* 10, no. 4, 9-11.

Bouzek, J. 1968. Einige Bemerkungen zum Beginn der Nipperwiese-Schilde, *Germania* 46, 313-316.

Bowden, M. and McOmish, D. 1989. Little boxes: more about hillforts, *Scottish Archaeological Review* 6, 12-16.

Bowen, E. G. 1972. *Britain and the Western Seaways.* London.

Boyne, P. 1987. *John O'Donovan (1806-1861) a biography.* Kilkenny.

Bracken, G. G. and Wayman, P. A. 1992. A Neolithic or Bronze Age Alignment for Croagh Patrick, *Cathair na Mart. Journal of the Westport Historical Society* 12, 1-11.

Bradley, J. 1991. Excavations at Moynagh Lough, County Meath, *Journal of the Royal Society of Antiquaries of Ireland* 121, 5-26.

Bradley, J. 1997. Archaeological excavations at Moynagh Lough, County Meath, 1995-96, *Ríocht na Midhe* 9, no. 3, 50-61.

Bradley, R. 1979. The interpretation of later Bronze Age metalwork from British rivers, *The International Journal of Nautical Archaeology and Underwater Exploration* 8, 3-6.

Bradley, R. 1982. The destruction of wealth in later prehistory, *Man* 17, 108-122.

Bradley, R. 1984. *The social foundations of prehistoric Britain.* London.

Bradley, R. 1989. Deaths and Entrances: A Contextual Analysis of Megalithic Art, *Current Anthropology* 30, 68-75.

Bradley, R. 1990. *The Passage of Arms. An archaeological analysis of prehistoric hoards and votive deposits.* Cambridge.

Bradley, R. 1991. Rock Art and the Perception of Landscape, *Cambridge Archaeological Journal* 1, 77-101.

Bradley, R. 1993. Archaeology: the loss of nerve, in N. Yoffee and A. Sherratt (eds), *Archaeological theory: who sets the agenda?*, 131-133. Cambridge.

Bradley, R. 1995. After MacWhite: Irish Rock Art in its International Context, in J. Waddell and E. S. Twohig (eds), *Ireland in the Bronze Age. Proceedings of the Dublin Conference, April 1995,* 90-96. Dublin.

Bradley, R. 1997. *Rock Art and the Prehistory of Atlantic Europe.* London.

Bradley, R. and Edmonds, M. 1993. *Interpreting the Axe Trade. Production and Exchange in Neolithic Britain.* Cambridge.

Brailsford, J. 1975. *Early Celtic Masterpieces from Britain in the British Museum.* London.

Brannon, N. F. 1979. An Excavation at Bradley's Cairn, Beaghmore townland, County Tyrone, *Ulster Journal of Archaeology* 42, 20-22.

Brannon, N. F. 1982. A Rescue Excavation at Lisdoo Fort, Lisnaskea, County Fermanagh, *Ulster Journal of Archaeology* 44-45, 53-59.

Brannon, N. F. 1984. Examination of a Bronze Cauldron from Raffrey Bog, Co. Down, *The Journal of Irish Archaeology* 4, 51-57.

Brannon, N. F., Williams, B. B. and Wilkinson, J. L. 1990. The Salvage Excavation of Bronze Age Cists, Straid Townland, County Londonderry, *Ulster Journal of Archaeology* 53, 29-39.

Brennan, J., Briggs, C. S. and ApSimon, A. M. 1978. A giant beaker from Cluntyganny townland, County Tyrone, *Ulster Journal of Archaeology* 41, 33-36.

Brennan, M. L. 1973. Robert Alexander Stewart Macalister 1871-1950. A Bibliography of his published work, *Journal of the Royal Society of Antiquaries of Ireland* 103, 167-176.

Briggs, C. S. 1976. The indigenous minerals and metallurgy of the earliest Irish Bronze Age, *Irish Archaeological Research Forum* 3, no. 1, 9-15.

Briggs, C. S. 1984. Amber in Ireland: some geological notes, *Éile. Journal of the Roscrea Heritage Society* 2, 81-85.

Briggs, C. S. 1987. Buckets and Cauldrons in the Late Bronze Age of North-west Europe: a review, in J. C. Blanchet (ed.), *Les Relations entre le Continent et les Iles Britanniques à l'Age du Bronze*, 161-187. Amiens.

Briggs, C. S. 1988. Stone Resources and Implements in Prehistoric Ireland: a review, *Ulster Journal of Archaeology* 51, 5-20.

Briggs, C. S. 1997. The discovery and origins of some Bronze Age amber beads from Ballycurrin Demesne, Co. Mayo, *Journal of the Galway Archaeological and Historical Society* 49, 104-121.

Briggs, C. S. and Haworth, R. 1978. Dean Sankey Winter and the Bronze Trumpet from 'Manooth', *Journal of the Royal Society of Antiquaries of Ireland* 108, 111-115.

Briggs, C. S., Brennan, J. and Freeburn, G. 1973. Irish Prehistoric Gold-Working: some Geological and Metallurgical Considerations, *Bulletin of the Historical Metallurgy Group* 7, no. 2, 18-26.

Brindley, A. L. 1986. *Archaeological Inventory of County Monaghan*. Dublin.

Brindley, A. L. 1994. *Irish Prehistory. An Introduction*. Dublin.

Brindley, A. L. and Kilfeather, A. 1993. *Archaeological Inventory of County Carlow*. Dublin.

Brindley, A. L. and Lanting, J. N. 1990. Radiocarbon Dates for Neolithic Single Burials, *The Journal of Irish Archaeology* 5, 1-7.

Brindley, A. L. and Lanting, J. N. 1990a. A Roman boat in Ireland, *Archaeology Ireland* 4, no. 3, 10-11.

Brindley, A. L. and Lanting, J. N. 1991. A boat of the Mediterranean tradition in Ireland: preliminary note, *Nautical Archaeology* 20, 69-70.

Brindley, A. L. and Lanting, J. N. 1992. Radiocarbon Dates from Wedge Tombs, *The Journal of Irish Archaeology* 6, 19-26.

Brindley, A. L. and Lanting, J. N. 1992a. Radiocarbon Dates from the Cemetery at Poulawack, Co. Clare, *The Journal of Irish Archaeology* 6, 13-17.

Brindley, A. L. and Lanting, J. N. 1995. Irish Bog Bodies: the Radiocarbon Dates, in R. C. Turner and R. G. Scaife (eds), *Bog Bodies. New Discoveries and New Perspectives*, 133-136. London.

Brindley, A. L., Lanting, J. N. and Mook, W. G. 1983. Radiocarbon dates from the Neolithic burials at Ballintruer More, Co. Wicklow, and Ardcrony, Co. Tipperary, *The Journal of Irish Archaeology* 1, 1-9.

Brindley, A. L., Lanting, J. N. and Mook, W. G. 1988. Radiocarbon Dates from Moneen and Labbacallee, County Cork, *The Journal of Irish Archaeology* 4, 13-20.

Brindley, A. L., Lanting, J. N. and Mook, W. G. 1990. Radiocarbon Dates from Irish Fulachta Fiadh and Other Burnt Mounds, *The Journal of Irish Archaeology* 5, 25-33.

Britnell, W. J. 1976. Antler Cheekpieces of the British Late Bronze Age, *The Antiquaries Journal* 56, 24-34.

Brodie, N. 1994. *The Neolithic-Bronze Age Transition in Britain*, British Archaeological Reports 238. Oxford.

Buckley, L. and Ó Donnabháin, B. 1992. Trephination: early cranial surgery in Ireland, *Archaeology Ireland* 6, no. 4, 10-12.

Buckley, V. 1985. Curraghtarsna, *Current Archaeology* 98, 70-71.

Buckley, V. (ed.). 1990. *Burnt Offerings. International Contributions to Burnt Mound Archaeology*. Dublin.

Buckley, V. M. and Lawless, C. 1988. Two C14 Dates for Fulachta Fiadh at Turlough, near Castlebar, *Cathair na Mart. Journal of the Westport Historical Society* 8, 23-25.

Buckley, V. M. and Sweetman, P. D. 1991. *Archaeological Survey of County Louth*. Dublin.

Buckley, V. M., Condit, T., Haigh, J. G. B. and MacGarry, D. C. 1990. A Resistivity Survey of the Eastern Entrance at the 'Doon' of Drumsna, *Emania* 7, 51-53.

Burenhult, G. 1980. *The Archaeological Excavation at Carrowmore, Co. Sligo, Ireland. Excavation Seasons 1977-1979. Theses and Papers in North European Archaeology*, no. 9. Stockholm.

Burenhult, G. 1980a. *The Carrowmore Excavations. Excavation Season 1980, Stockholm Archaeological Reports*, no. 7. Stockholm.

Burenhult, G. 1984. *The Archaeology of Carrowmore. Environmental Archaeology and the Megalithic Tradition at Carrowmore, Co. Sligo, Ireland. Theses and Papers in North European Archaeology*, no. 14. Stockholm.

Burenhult, G. 1995. *The Illustrated Guide to the Megalithic Cemetery of Carrowmore, Co. Sligo*. Tjörnarp.

Burgess, C. B. 1968. The Later Bronze Age in the British Isles and North-western France, *The Archaeological Journal* 125, 1-45.

Burgess, C. B. 1968a. *Bronze Age Metalwork in Northern England c. 1000 to 700 BC*. Newcastle.

Burgess, C. B. 1969. Review of *Catalogue of Irish Bronze Swords* by George Eogan, *The Antiquaries Journal* 49, 152-153.

Burgess, C. B. 1974. The bronze age, in C. Renfrew (ed.), *British Prehistory. A New Outline*, 165-232. London.

Burgess, C. B. 1976. An Early Bronze Age Settlement at Kilellan Farm, Islay, Argyll, in C. B. Burgess and R.

Miket (eds), *Settlement and Economy in the Third and Second Millennia B.C, British Archaeological Reports* 33, 181-207. Oxford.

Burgess, C. B. 1976a. Burials with metalwork of the later Bronze Age in Wales and beyond, in G. C. Boon and J. M. Lewis (eds), *Welsh Antiquity, essays presented to H. N. Savory*, 81-104. Cardiff.

Burgess, C. B. 1979. The background of early metalworking in Ireland and Britain, in M. Ryan (ed.), *The Origins of Metallurgy in Atlantic Europe. Proceedings of the Fifth Atlantic Colloquium*, 207-214. Dublin.

Burgess, C. B. 1980. *The Age of Stonehenge*. London.

Burgess, C. B. 1982. The Cartington knife and the double-edged knives of the Late Bronze Age, *Northern Archaeology* 3, 32-45.

Burgess, C. B. 1985. Population, Climate and Upland Settlement, in D. Spratt and C. Burgess (eds), *Upland Settlement in Britain, British Archaeological Reports* 143, 195-230. Oxford.

Burgess, C. B. 1990. The Chronology of Cup- and Cup-and-ring Marks in Atlantic Europe, in *La Bretagne et l'Europe préhistoriques, mémoire en hommage à Pierre-Roland Giot, Revue archéologique de l'Ouest, Supplément* 2, 157-171.

Burgess, C. B. 1995. A Bronze Age rapier from Catterick Bridge, *Yorkshire Archaeological Journal* 67, 1-5.

Burgess, C. B. and Cowen, J. D. 1972. The Ebnal Hoard and Early Bronze Age Metalworking Traditions, in F. Lynch and C. B. Burgess (eds), *Prehistoric Man in Wales and the West: Essays in honour of Lily F. Chitty*, 167-182. Bath.

Burgess, C. B. and Gerloff, S. 1981. *The Dirks and Rapiers of Great Britain and Ireland. Prähistorische Bronzefunde* IV:7. Munich.

Burgess, C. B., Coombs, D. and Davies, D. G. 1972. The Broadward Complex and Barbed Spearheads, in F. Lynch and C. B. Burgess (eds), *Prehistoric Man in Wales and the West. Essays in honour of Lily F. Chitty*, 211-283. Bath.

Burl, A. 1976. *The Stone Circles of the British Isles*. New Haven and London.

Burl, A. 1993. *From Carnac to Callanish. The Prehistoric Stone Rows and Avenues of Britain, Ireland and Brittany*. New Haven and London.

Butler, J. J. 1963. Bronze Age Connections across the North Sea, *Palaeohistoria* 9, 1-286.

Butler, J. J. and van der Waals, J. D. 1966. Bell Beakers and Early Metalworking in the Netherlands, *Palaeohistoria* 12, 41-139.

Byrne, C. and Gosling, P. 1988. A Hilltop Enclosure on Knockacarrigeen, near Knockmaa, Co. Galway, *Journal of the Galway Archaeological and Historical Society* 41, 138-141.

Byrne, F. J. 1984. Ptolemy's Map of Ireland, *c.* 150 A. D., in T. W. Moody, F. X. Martin and F. J. Byrne (eds), *A New History of Ireland. Maps, Genealogies, Lists.* IX, 16, 98. Oxford.

Byrne, G. 1991. Rathlackan. Court tomb with associated pre-bog settlement, in I. Bennett (ed.), *Excavations 1990*, 46. Bray.

Byrne, G. 1994. Rathlackan. Court tomb with associated pre-bog settlement, in I. Bennett (ed.), *Excavations 1993*, 61-62. Bray.

Byrne, M. E. and Dillon, M. 1937. Táin Bó Fraich, *Etudes Celtiques* 2, 1-27.

Cahill, M. 1983. Irish Prehistoric Gold-working, in M. Ryan (ed.), *Treasures of Ireland. Irish Art 3000 B.C. – 1500 A.D.*, 18-23. Dublin.

Cahill, M. 1988. A preliminary account of a Later Bronze Age hoard from Kilbride, Co. Mayo, *Cathair na Mart. Journal of the Westport Historical Society* 8, 26-29.

Cahill, M. 1994. Boxes, Beads, Bobbins and ... Notions, *Archaeology Ireland* 8, no. 1, 21-23.

Cahill, M. 1994a. Some unrecorded Bronze Age gold objects from Co. Limerick, *North Munster Antiquarian Journal* 35, 5-23.

Cahill, M. 1994b. Mr Anthony's Bog Oak Case of Gold Antiquities, *Proceedings of the Royal Irish Academy* 94C, 53-109.

Cahill, M. 1995. Later Bronze Age Goldwork from Ireland – Form, Function and Formality, in J. Waddell and E. S. Twohig (eds), *Ireland in the Bronze Age. Proceedings of the Dublin Conference, April 1995*, 63-72. Dublin.

Carson, R. A. G. and O'Kelly, C. 1977. A catalogue of the Roman coins from Newgrange, Co. Meath, and notes on the coins and related finds, *Proceedings of the Royal Irish Academy* 77C, 35-55.

Case, H. 1961. Irish Neolithic pottery: distribution and sequence, *Proceedings of the Prehistoric Society* 27, 174-233.

Case, H. 1966. Were Beaker-people the First Metallurgists in Ireland?, *Palaeohistoria* 12, 140-177.

Case, H. 1969. Settlement Patterns in the North Irish Neolithic, *Ulster Journal of Archaeology* 32, 3-27.

Case, H. 1973. A Ritual Site in North-East Ireland, in G. Daniel and P. Kjaerum (eds), *Megalithic Graves and Ritual, Jutland Archaeological Society Publications*, 173-196. Copenhagen.

Case, H. 1977. An early accession to the Ashmolean Museum, in V. Markotic (ed.), *Ancient Europe and the Mediterranean*, 19-34. Warminster.

Case, H. 1993. Beakers: Deconstruction and After, *Proceedings of the Prehistoric Society* 59, 241-268.

Case, H. 1995. Irish Beakers in their European Context, in J. Waddell and E. S. Twohig (eds), *Ireland in the Bronze Age. Proceedings of the Dublin Conference, April 1995*, 14-29. Dublin.

Case, H. 1995a. Beakers: loosening a stereotype, in I. Kinnes and G. Varndell (eds), *'Unbaked Urns of Rudely Shape'. Essays on British and Irish Pottery for Ian Longworth*, 55-67. Oxford.

Caulfield, S. 1977. The Beehive Quern in Ireland, *Journal of the Royal Society of Antiquaries of Ireland* 107, 104-138.

Caulfield, S. 1978. Neolithic Fields: the Irish Evidence, in H. C. Bowen and P. J. Fowler (eds), *Early Land Allotment in the British Isles: a survey of recent work, British Archaeological Reports* 48, 137-143. Oxford.

Caulfield, S. 1981. Celtic Problems in the Irish Iron Age, in D. Ó Corráin (ed.), *Irish Antiquity. Essays and Studies presented to Professor M. J. O'Kelly*, 205-215. Cork.

Caulfield, S. 1983. The Neolithic Settlement of North Connaught, in T. Reeves-Smyth and F. Hamond (eds),

Landscape Archaeology in Ireland, British Archaeological Reports 116, 195-216. Oxford.

Caulfield, S. [1988]. *Céide Fields and Belderrig. A guide to two prehistoric farms in north Mayo*. Killala [pamphlet: no date].

Caulfield, S. [1992]. *Ceide Fields, Ballycastle, Co. Mayo* [15pp guidebook: no date or place of publication].

Champion, T. C. 1971. The End of the Irish Bronze Age, *North Munster Antiquarian Journal* 14, 17-24.

Champion, T. C. 1976. Britain in the European Iron Age, *Archaeologia Atlantica* 1, 127-145.

Champion, T. C. 1980. The early development of iron working, *Nature* 284, 513-514.

Champion, T. C. 1982. The Myth of Iron Age Invasions in Ireland, in B. G. Scott (ed.), *Studies on Early Ireland. Essays in honour of M. V. Duignan*, 39-44. Belfast.

Champion, T. C. 1987. The European Iron Age: assessing the state of the art, *Scottish Archaeological Review* 4, 98-107.

Champion, T. C. 1989. From Bronze Age to Iron Age in Ireland, in M. L. Stig Sørensen and R. Thomas (eds), *The Bronze Age-Iron Age Transition in Europe, British Archaeological Reports, International Series* 483, 287-303. Oxford.

Champion, T. C. 1995. Power, Politics and Status, in M. Green (ed.), *The Celtic World*, 85-94. London.

Champion, T. C. 1996. The Celt in Archaeology, in T. Brown (ed.), *Celticism*, 61-78. Amsterdam.

Channing, J. 1993. Aughrim wedge tomb, in I. Bennett (ed.), *Excavations 1992*, 4. Bray.

Chapman, M. 1992. *The Celts. The Construction of a Myth*. Basingstoke.

Chart, D. A. (ed.). 1940. *A Preliminary Survey of the Ancient Monuments of Northern Ireland*. Belfast.

Chippendale, C. 1988. The Invention of Words for the Idea of 'Prehistory', *Proceedings of the Prehistoric Society* 54, 303-314.

Clark, G. 1975. *The Earlier Stone Age Settlement of Scandinavia*. Cambridge.

Clarke, D. L. 1970. *Beaker Pottery of Great Britain and Ireland*. Cambridge.

Clarke, D. L. 1976. Mesolithic Europe: the economic basis, in G. de G. Sieveking, I. H. Longworth and K. E. Wilson (eds), *Problems in Economic and Social Archaeology*, 449-482. London.

Clarke, D. V., Cowie, T. G. and Foxon, A. 1985. *Symbols of Power at the Time of Stonehenge*. Edinburgh.

Clarke, R. R. 1954. The Early Iron Age Treasure from Snettisham, Norfolk, *Proceedings of the Prehistoric Society* 20, 27-86.

Clarke, R. R. and Hawkes, C. F. C. 1955. An Iron Anthropoid sword from Shouldham, Norfolk, with related Continental and British weapons, *Proceedings of the Prehistoric Society* 21, 198-227.

Cleary, R. M. 1993. The Later Bronze Age at Lough Gur: Filling in the Blanks, in E. S. Twohig and M. Ronayne (eds), *Past Perceptions. The Prehistoric Archaeology of South-West Ireland*, 114-120. Cork.

Cleary, R. M. 1995. Later Bronze Age Settlement and Prehistoric Burials, Lough Gur, Co. Limerick, *Proceedings of the Royal Irish Academy* 95C, 1-92.

Cleary, R. M. 1995a. Irish Later Bronze Age Pottery: a preliminary technological assessment, in A. Lindahl and O. Stilborg (eds), *The Aim of Laboratory Analyses of Ceramics in Archaeology*, 77-90. Stockholm.

Cleary, R. M., Hurley, M. F. and Twohig, E. A. (eds). 1987. *Archaeological Excavations on the Cork-Dublin Gas Pipeline (1981-82)*. Cork.

Clermont, N. and Smith, P. E. L. 1990. Prehistoric, prehistory, prehistorian ... who invented the term?, *Antiquity* 64, 97-102.

Cody, E. 1981. A Hill-fort at Ballylin, County Limerick, with a note on Mooghaun, County Clare, *Journal of the Royal Society of Antiquaries of Ireland* 111, 70-80.

Coffey, G. 1894. Notes on the Classification of Spearheads of the Bronze Age found in Ireland, *Proceedings of the Royal Irish Academy* 19, 486-510.

Coffey, G. 1906. Early iron sword found in Ireland, *Proceedings of the Royal Irish Academy* 26C, 42-43.

Coffey, G. 1909. The Distribution of Gold Lunulae in Ireland and North-western Europe, *Proceedings of the Royal Irish Academy* 27C, 251-258.

Coffey, G. 1911. Stone with cup-and-ring markings at Ryfad, County Fermanagh, *Journal of the Royal Society of Antiquaries of Ireland* 41, 25.

Coffey, G. 1913. Ornamented Bronze Spear-heads with apertures in the blades, *Proceedings of the Royal Irish Academy* 30C, 445-448.

Coffey, T. 1985. Field Notes, *The Other Clare* 9, 27-31.

Coghlan, H. H. and Raftery, J. 1961. Irish Prehistoric Casting Moulds, *Sibrium* 6, 223-244.

Coles, B. 1990. Anthropomorphic Wooden Figures from Britain and Ireland, *Proceedings of the Prehistoric Society* 56, 315-333.

Coles, J. M. 1959. Scottish Swan's-neck Sunflower Pins, *Proceedings of the Society of Antiquaries of Scotland* 92, 1-9.

Coles, J. M. 1960. Scottish Late Bronze Age Metalwork: Typology, Distributions and Chronology, *Proceedings of the Society of Antiquaries of Scotland* 93, 16-134.

Coles, J. M. 1962. European Bronze Age Shields, *Proceedings of the Prehistoric Society* 28, 156-190.

Coles, J. M. 1963. Irish Bronze Age Horns and their relations with Northern Europe, *Proceedings of the Prehistoric Society* 29, 326-356.

Coles, J. M. 1964. Scottish Middle Bronze Age Metalwork, *Proceedings of the Society of Antiquaries of Scotland* 97, 82-156.

Coles, J. M. 1965. The Archaeological Evidence for a 'Bull Cult' in Late Bronze Age Europe, *Antiquity* 39, 217-219.

Coles, J. M. 1967. Some Irish Horns of the Late Bronze Age, *Journal of the Royal Society of Antiquaries of Ireland* 97, 113-117.

Coles, J. M. 1969. Scottish Early Bronze Age Metalwork, *Proceedings of the Society of Antiquaries of Scotland* 101, 1-110.

Coles, J. M. 1971. The early settlement of Scotland: excavations at Morton, Fife, *Proceedings of the Prehistoric Society* 37, 284-366.

Coles, J. M. 1971a. Bronze Age Spearheads with Gold Decoration, *The Antiquaries Journal* 51, 94-95.

Coles, J. M. 1971b. Dowris and the Late Bronze Age of Ireland: a footnote, *Journal of the Royal Society of Antiquaries of Ireland* 101, 164-165.

Coles, J. M. 1975. The 1857 Law Farm Hoard: an addition, *The Antiquaries Journal* 55, 128.

Coles, J. M. 1979. *Experimental Archaeology*. London.

Coles, J. M. 1984. Review of *The Dirks and Rapiers of Great Britain and Ireland* by C. B. Burgess and S. Gerloff, *Proceedings of the Prehistoric Society* 50, 420-421.

Coles, J. M. and Trump, B. A. V. 1967. A Rapier and its Scabbard from West Row, Suffolk, *Proceedings of the Cambridge Antiquarian Society* 60, 1-5.

Coles, J. M., Coutts, H. and Ryder, M. L. 1964. A Late Bronze Age Find from Pyotdykes, Angus, *Proceedings of the Prehistoric Society* 30, 186-198.

Coles, J. M., Heal, S. V. E. and Orme, B. J. 1978. The Use and Character of Wood in Prehistoric Britain and Ireland, *Proceedings of the Prehistoric Society* 44, 1-45.

Colhoun, M. R. 1995. *The Heritage of Inishowen*. Coleraine.

Collins, A. E. P. 1952. Excavations in the sandhills at Dundrum, Co. Down, 1950-51, *Ulster Journal of Archaeology* 15, 2-26.

Collins, A. E. P. 1954. The Excavation of a Double Horned cairn at Audleystown, Co. Down, *Ulster Journal of Archaeology* 17, 7-56.

Collins, A. E. P. 1956. A Stone Circle on Castle Mahon Mountain, Co. Down, *Ulster Journal of Archaeology* 19, 1-10.

Collins, A. E. P. 1957. Trial excavations in a round cairn on Knockiveagh, Co. Down, *Ulster Journal of Archaeology* 20, 8-28.

Collins, A. E. P. 1957a. Excavations at the Giant's Ring, Ballynahatty, *Ulster Journal of Archaeology* 20, 44-50.

Collins, A. E. P. 1957b. Excavations at two Standing Stones in Co. Down, *Ulster Journal of Archaeology* 20, 37-42.

Collins, A. E. P. 1959. Further Investigations in the Dundrum Sandhills, *Ulster Journal of Archaeology* 22, 5-20.

Collins, A. E. P. 1959a. Further work at Audleystown long cairn, Co. Down, *Ulster Journal of Archaeology* 22, 21-27.

Collins, A. E. P. 1964. Further Finds of Bronze Axes with some Remarks on Winged Axes, *Ulster Journal of Archaeology* 27, 59-61.

Collins, A. E. P. 1965. Ballykeel Dolmen and Cairn, Co. Armagh, *Ulster Journal of Archaeology* 28, 47-70.

Collins, A. E. P. 1966. Barnes Lower Court Cairn, Co. Tyrone, *Ulster Journal of Archaeology* 29, 43-75.

Collins, A. E. P. 1970. Bronze Age Moulds in Ulster, *Ulster Journal of Archaeology* 33, 23-36.

Collins, A. E. P. 1973. A re-examination of the Clyde-Carlingford Tombs, in G. Daniel and P. Kjaerum (eds), *Megalithic Graves and Ritual. Jutland Archaeological Society Publications*, 93-103. Copenhagen.

Collins, A. E. P. 1976. Dooeys Cairn, Ballymacaldrack, County Antrim, *Ulster Journal of Archaeology* 39, 1-7.

Collins, A. E. P. 1977. A sand-dune site at the White Rocks, County Antrim, *Ulster Journal of Archaeology* 40, 21-26.

Collins, A. E. P. 1978. Excavations on Ballygalley Hill, County Antrim, *Ulster Journal of Archaeology* 41, 15-32.

Collins, A. E. P. 1981. Flint Javelin Heads, in D. Ó Corráin (ed.) *Irish Antiquity. Essays and Studies presented to Professor M. J. O'Kelly,* 111-133. Cork.

Collins, A. E. P. and Evans, E. E. 1968. A cist burial at Carrickinab, Co. Down, *Ulster Journal of Archaeology* 31, 16-24.

Collins, A. E. P. and Seaby, W. A. 1960. A crannog at Lough Eskragh, Co. Tyrone, *Ulster Journal of Archaeology* 23, 25-37.

Collins, A. E. P. and Waterman, D. M. 1955. *Millin Bay. A Late Neolithic Cairn in Co. Down*. Belfast.

Collins, A. E. P. and Wilson, B. 1963. The Slieve Gullion cairns, *Ulster Journal of Archaeology* 26, 19-40.

Collins, A. E. P. and Wilson, B. 1964. The Excavation of a court cairn at Ballymacdermot, Co. Armagh, *Ulster Journal of Archaeology* 27, 3-22.

Collis, J. 1997. Celtic Myths, *Antiquity* 71, 195-201.

Colquhoun, I. and Burgess, C. B. 1988. *The Swords of Britain. Prähistorische Bronzefunde* IV:5. Munich.

Condit, T. 1992. Ireland's Hillfort Capital – Baltinglass, Co. Wicklow, *Archaeology Ireland* 6, no. 3, 16-20.

Condit, T. 1993. Travelling earthwork arrives at Tara, *Archaeology Ireland* 7, no. 4, 10-14.

Condit, T. 1993a. Ritual enclosures near Boyle, Co. Roscommon, *Archaeology Ireland* 7, no. 1, 14-16.

Condit, T. 1995. Hillfort discoveries near Killaloe, Co. Clare, *Archaeology Ireland* 9, no. 1, 34-37.

Condit, T. 1996. Gold and fulachta fiadh – the Mooghaun find, 1854, *Archaeology Ireland* 10, no. 4, 20-23.

Condit, T. and Buckley, V. M. 1989. The 'Doon' of Drumsna – Gateways to Connacht, *Emania* 6, 12-28.

Condit, T. and Gibbons, M. 1988. Linear Earthworks in County Waterford, *Decies* 39, 19-28.

Condit, T. and Gibbons, M. 1991. A glimpse of Sligo's prehistory, *Archaeology Ireland* 5, no. 3, 7-10.

Condit, T., Gibbons, M. and Timoney, M. 1991. Hillforts in Sligo and Leitrim, *Emania* 9, 59-62.

Condit, T., Synnott, P. and Masterson, B. 1994. Planning the Prehistoric Past, *Archaeology Ireland* 8, no. 4, 20-23.

Connolly, A. 1994. Saddle Querns in Ireland, *Ulster Journal of Archaeology* 57, 26-36.

Connolly, M. 1991. A Prehistoric Decorated Pillar-Stone from Teeromoyle, Co. Kerry, *Journal of the Kerry Archaeological and Historical Society* 24, 32-39.

Connolly, M. 1996. The Passage Tomb of Tralee – a megalithic tomb at Ballycarty, Co. Kerry, *Archaeology Ireland* 10, no. 4, 15-17.

Coombs, D. 1975. Bronze Age Weapon Hoards in Britain, *Archaeologia Atlantica* 1, 49-81.

Cooney, G. 1979. Some Aspects of the Siting of Megalithic Tombs in County Leitrim, *Journal of the Royal Society of Antiquaries of Ireland* 109, 74-91.

Cooney, G. 1981. A Saddle Quern from Baltinglass Hill, County Wicklow, *Journal of the Royal Society of Antiquaries of Ireland* 111, 102-106.

Cooney, G. 1983. Megalithic Tombs in their Environmental Setting: a settlement perspective, in T. Reeves-Smyth and F. Hamond (eds), *Landscape Archaeology in Ireland, British Archaeological Reports* 116, 179-194. Oxford.

Cooney, G. 1985. Stone Axes of County Louth: a first report, *County Louth Archaeological and Historical Journal* 21, 78-97.

Cooney, G. 1987. Dermot and Grania's Bed, Melkagh, in I. Bennett (ed.), *Excavations 1986,* 30. Dublin.

Cooney, G. 1989. Stone Axes of North Leinster, *Oxford Journal of Archaeology* 8, 145-157.

Cooney, G. 1990. The place of megalithic tomb cemeteries in Ireland, *Antiquity* 64, 741-753.

Cooney, G. 1991. Irish Neolithic Landscapes and Land Use Systems: the Implications of Field Systems, *Rural History* 2, 123-139.

Cooney, G. 1992. Body Politics and Grave Messages: Irish Neolithic Mortuary Practices, in N. Sharples and A. Sheridan (eds), *Vessels for the Ancestors,* 128-142. Edinburgh.

Cooney, G. 1992a. Irish prehistoric mortuary practice: Baurnadomeeny reconsidered, *Tipperary Historical Journal* 1992, 223-229.

Cooney, G. 1993. Lambay: an island on the horizon, *Archaeology Ireland* 7, no. 4, 24-28.

Cooney, G. 1993a. A sense of place in Irish prehistory, *Antiquity* 67, 632-641.

Cooney, G. 1994. Sacred and secular neolithic landscapes in Ireland, in D. L. Carmichael, J. Hubert, B. Reeves and A. Schanche (eds), *Sacred Sites, Sacred Places,* 32-43. London.

Cooney, G. 1995. At the cutting edge, *Technology Ireland* 26, no. 9, 26-29.

Cooney, G. 1995a. Lambay Island, in I. Bennett (ed.), *Excavations 1994,* 34-35. Bray.

Cooney, G. 1995b. Theory and practice in Irish archaeology, in P. J. Ucko (ed.), *Theory in Archaeology. A world perspective,* 263-277. London.

Cooney, G. 1996. Building the future on the past: archaeology and the construction of national identity in Ireland, in M. Díaz-Andreu and T. Champion (eds), *Nationalism and archaeology in Europe,* 146-163. London.

Cooney, G. 1997. A tale of two mounds: monumental landscape design at Fourknocks, Co. Meath, *Archaeology Ireland* 11, no. 2, 17-19.

Cooney, G. and Grogan, E. 1991. An archaeological solution to the 'Irish' problem?, *Emania* 9, 32-43.

Cooney, G. and Grogan, E. 1994. *Irish Prehistory. A Social Perspective.* Dublin.

Cooney, G., Feehan, J., Grogan, E. and Stillman, C. 1990. An axe and an adze from Co. Tipperary with a preliminary list and distribution map of stone axes in Co. Tipperary, *Tipperary Historical Journal* 2, 197-203.

Cooney, G., Mandal, S. and O'Carroll, F. 1995. Stone axes as icons: approaches to the study of stone axes in Ireland, in E. Grogan and C. Mount (eds), *Annus Archaeologiae. Archaeological Research 1992,* 23-36. Dublin.

Cooney, G., O'Carroll, F., Grogan, E. and Mandal, S. 1990. Stone Axes of County Louth: a second report, *County Louth Archaeological and Historical Journal* 22, 178-186.

Corcoran, J. X. W. P. 1964. Excavation of two chambered cairns at Kilnagarns Lower, Co. Leitrim, *Journal of the Royal Society of Antiquaries of Ireland* 94, 177-98.

Corcoran, J. X. W. P. 1965. A Bronze Bucket in the Hunterian Museum, University of Glasgow, *The Antiquaries Journal* 45, 12-17.

Corcoran, J. X. W. P. 1972. Multi-Period Construction and the origins of the Chambered Long Cairn in Western Britain and Ireland, in F. Lynch and C. B. Burgess (eds), *Prehistoric Man in Wales and the West,* 31-63. Bath.

Cordier, G. 1969. Deux hallebardes du Bronze ancien de la vallée de la Loire, *Antiquités Nationales* 1, 47-51.

Corlett, C. 1997. The prehistoric archaeology of the parish of Kilgeever, south-west County Mayo, *Journal of the Galway Archaeological and Historical Society* 49, 65-103.

Costello, T. B. 1921. A Bronze Cauldron, *Journal of the Galway Archaeological and Historical Society* 11, 72-75.

Cotter, C. 1993. Western Stone Fort Project. Interim report, *Discovery Programme Reports* 1, 1-19.

Cotter, C. 1995. Western Stone Fort Project. Interim report, *Discovery Programme Reports* 2, 1-11.

Cotter, C. 1996. Western Stone Fort Project. Interim report, *Discovery Programme Reports* 4. 1-14.

Cotter, C. 1996a. Dún Aonghasa, Kilmurvey, Inis Mór, Cliff Fort, in I. Bennett (ed.), *Excavations 1995,* 36-37.

Cowen, J. D. 1967. The Hallstatt Sword of Bronze: on the Continent and in Britain, *Proceedings of the Prehistoric Society* 33, 377-454.

Coxon, P. 1993. Irish Pleistocene Biostratigraphy, *Irish Journal of Earth Sciences* 12, 83-105.

Crabtree, P. 1990. Subsistence and Ritual: the faunal remains from Dún Ailinne, Co. Kildare, Ireland, *Emania* 7, 22-25.

Craddock, P. 1979. Deliberate alloying in the Atlantic Bronze Age, in M. Ryan (ed.), *The Origins of Metallurgy in Atlantic Europe. Proceedings of the Fifth Atlantic Colloquium,* 369-385. Dublin.

Crone, B. A. 1993. Crannogs and chronologies, *Proceedings of the Society of Antiquaries of Scotland* 123, 245-254.

Cross, R. E. 1953. Lough Gara: a preliminary survey, *Journal of the Royal Society of Antiquaries of Ireland* 83, 93-96.

Cross, S. 1996. Identifying Complexity in the Record: a Case Study of the Irish and British Mesolithic, in D. A. Meyer, P. C. Dawson and D. T. Hanna (eds), *Debating Complexity. Proceedings of the Twenty-Sixth Annual Chacmool Conference,* 254-262. Calgary.

Cunliffe, B. 1991. *Iron Age Communities in Britain.* London.

Cuppage, J. 1986. *Archaeological Survey of the Dingle Peninsula.* Ballyferriter.

Curran-Mulligan, P. 1994. Yes, but it *is* Art!, *Archaeology Ireland* 8, no. 1, 14-15.

Daly, A. and Grogan, E. 1993. Excavation of Four Barrows in Mitchelstowndown West, Knocklong, County Limerick, *Discovery Programme Reports* 1, 44-60.

Daniells, M. J. and Williams, B. B. 1977. Excavations at Kiltierney Deerpark, County Fermanagh, *Ulster Journal of Archaeology* 40, 32-41.

Dark, K. R. 1995. *Theoretical Archaeology.* London.

Darvill, T. C. 1979. Court Cairns, Passage Graves and Social Change in Ireland, *Man* 14, 311-327.

Davies, D. G. 1967. The Guilsfield Hoard: a reconsideration, *The Antiquaries Journal* 47, 95-108.

Davies, O. 1937. Excavations at Ballyrenan, Co. Tyrone, *Journal of the Royal Society of Antiquaries of Ireland* 67, 89-100.

Davies, O. 1938. Castledamph Stone Circle, *Journal of the Royal Society of Antiquaries of Ireland* 68, 106-112.

Davies, O. 1939. Excavation of a Horned Cairn at Aghanaglack, Co. Fermanagh, *Journal of the Royal Society of Antiquaries of Ireland* 69, 21-38.

Davies, O. 1939a. Excavation at the Giant's Grave, Loughash, *Ulster Journal of Archaeology* 2, 254-68.

Davies, O. 1939b. Excavations at Clogherny, *Ulster Journal of Archaeology* 2, 36-43.

Davies, O. 1939c. Stone Circles in Northern Ireland, *Ulster Journal of Archaeology* 2, 2-14.

Davies, O. 1949. Excavations at the horned cairn of Ballymarlagh, Co. Antrim, *Ulster Journal of Archaeology* 12, 26-42.

Davies, O. and Evans, E. E. 1933. Excavations at Goward, near Hilltown, Co. Down, *Proceedings of the Belfast Natural History and Philosophical Society* 1932-1933, 90-105.

Davies, O. and Evans, E. E. 1962. Irish Court Cairns, *Ulster Journal of Archaeology* 24-5, 2-7.

Davies, O. and Mullin, J. B. 1940. Excavation of Cashelbane Cairn, Loughash, Co. Tyrone, *Journal of the Royal Society of Antiquaries of Ireland* 70, 143-163.

Davies, O. and Radford, C. A. R. 1936. Excavation of the Horned Cairn of Clady Halliday, *Proceedings of the Belfast Natural History and Philosophical Society* 1935-1936, 76-85.

Davis, M. 1993. The identification of various jet and jet-like materials used in the early Bronze Age in Scotland, *The Conservator* 17, 11-18.

Day, A. and McWilliams, P. 1993. *Ordnance Survey Memoirs of Ireland*, Vol. 22. Belfast.

Day, R. 1880. Find of Broken Things, including Fragment of Sword Scabbard, *Journal of the Royal Society of Antiquaries of Ireland* 15, 265-266.

De hÓir, S. 1990. A Letter from W. F. Wakeman to James Graves in 1882, *Journal of the Royal Society of Antiquaries of Ireland* 120, 112-119.

De hÓir, S. 1993. Additions to the Bibliography of R. A. S. Macalister ..., *Journal of the Royal Society of Antiquaries of Ireland* 123, 170.

De Paor, L. 1967. *Archaeology, an illustrated introduction*. Harmondsworth.

De Paor, L. and Ó h-Eochaidhe, M. 1956. Unusual Group of Earthworks at Slieve Breagh, Co. Meath, *Journal of the Royal Society of Antiquaries of Ireland* 86, 97-101.

De Valera, R. 1951. A Group of 'Horned Cairns' near Ballycastle, Co. Mayo, *Journal of the Royal Society of Antiquaries of Ireland* 81, 161-197.

De Valera, R. 1960. The Court Cairns of Ireland, *Proceedings of the Royal Irish Academy* 60C, 9-140.

De Valera, R. 1965. Transeptal Court Cairns, *Journal of the Royal Society of Antiquaries of Ireland* 35, 5-37.

De Valera, R. and Ó Nualláin, S. 1961. *Survey of the Megalithic Tombs of Ireland. Vol. I. Co. Clare*. Dublin.

De Valera, R. and Ó Nualláin, S. 1964. *Survey of the Megalithic Tombs of Ireland. Vol. II. Co. Mayo*. Dublin.

De Valera, R. and Ó Nualláin, S. 1972. *Survey of the Megalithic Tombs of Ireland. Vol. III. Cos Galway, Roscommon, Leitrim, Longford, Westmeath, Laoighis, Offaly, Kildare, Cavan*. Dublin.

De Valera, R. and Ó Nualláin, S. 1982. *Survey of the Megalithic Tombs of Ireland. Vol. IV. Cos Cork, Kerry, Limerick, Tipperary*. Dublin.

Devereux, P. and Jahn, R. G. 1996. Preliminary investigations and cognitive considerations of the acoustical resonances of selected archaeological sites, *Antiquity* 70, 665-666.

Devoy, R. J. 1984. Possible landbridges between Ireland and Britain: a geological appraisal, in D. P. Sleeman, R. J. Devoy and P. C. Woodman (eds), *Proceedings of the Postglacial Colonization Conference, University College, Cork, 15-16 October 1983, Occasional Publication of the Irish Biogeographical Society* 1, 15-26. Cork.

Devoy, R. J. 1985. The problems of a Late Quaternary landbridge between Britain and Ireland, *Quaternary Science Reviews* 4, 43-58.

De Wilde, M. L. 1982. Le 'Style de Cheshire Cat', un phénomène caractéristique de l'art celtique, in P-M. Duval and V. Kruta (eds), *L'Art Celtique de la Période d'Expansion*, 101-123. Geneva.

Dent, J. 1985. Three Cart Burials from Wetwang, Yorkshire, *Antiquity* 59, 85-92.

Dickins, J. 1996. A remote analogy?: from Central Australian *tjurunga* to Irish Early Bronze Age axes, *Antiquity* 70, 161-167.

Doody, M. G. 1987. Ballyveelish, Co. Tipperary, in R. M. Cleary, M. F. Hurley and E. A. Twohig (eds), *Archaeological Excavations on the Cork-Dublin Gas Pipeline (1981-82)*, 8-35. Cork.

Doody, M. G. 1987a. Late Bronze Age Huts at Curraghatoor, Co. Tipperary, in R. M. Cleary, M. F. Hurley and E. A. Twohig (eds), *Archaeological Excavations on the Cork-Dublin Gas Pipeline (1981-82)*, 36-42. Cork.

Doody, M. G. 1988-1992. Curraghatoor, in I. Bennett (ed.), *Excavations 1987-1991*. Dublin.

Doody, M. G. 1993. Bronze Age Settlement, in E. S. Twohig and M. Ronayne (eds), *Past Perceptions. The Prehistoric Archaeology of South-West Ireland*, 93-100. Cork.

Doody, M. G. 1993a. Ballyhoura Hills Project. Interim report, *Discovery Programme Reports* 1, 20-30.

Doody, M. G. 1995. Ballyhoura Hills Project. Interim report, *Discovery Programme Reports* 2, 12-44.

Doody, M. G. 1996. Ballyhoura Hills Project. Interim report, *Discovery Programme Reports* 4. 15-25.

Doody, M. G. 1997. Bronze Age Settlements in Co. Tipperary: fifteen years of research, *Tipperary Historical Journal* 1997, 94-106.

Doody, M. G., Synnott, P., Tobin, R. and Masterson, B. 1995. A topographic survey of the inland promontory fort at Castle Gale, Carrig Henry, Co. Limerick, *Discovery Programme Reports* 2, 39-44.

Doran, P. F. 1978. The Hunt Museum, *North Munster Antiquarian Journal* 20, 3-15.

Doran, P. F. 1993. *50 Treasures from the Hunt Collection*. Limerick.

Drewett, P. 1982. Later Bronze Age Downland Economy and Excavations at Black Patch, East Sussex, *Proceedings of the Prehistoric Society* 48, 321-400.

Dronfield, J. 1995. Subjective vision and the source of Irish megalithic art, *Antiquity* 69, 539-549.

Dronfield, J. 1995a. Migraine, light and hallucinogens: the neurocognitive basis of Irish megalithic art, *Oxford Journal of Archaeology* 14, 261-275.

Dronfield, J. 1996. Entering alternative realities: cognition, art and architecture in Irish passage-tombs, *Cambridge Archaeological Journal* 6, 37-72.

Duignan, M. 1976. The Turoe Stone: its place in insular La Tène art, in P-M. Duval and C. Hawkes (eds), *Celtic Art in Ancient Europe, Five Protohistoric Centuries,* 201-217. London.

Dunning, G. C. 1959. The Distribution of Socketed Axeheads of Breton Type, *Ulster Journal of Archaeology* 22, 53-55.

Duval, P-M. 1977. *Les Celtes.* Paris.

Earwood, C. 1989. Radiocarbon dating of late prehistoric wooden vessels, *The Journal of Irish Archaeology* 5, 37-44.

Earwood, C. 1992. A Radiocarbon Date for Early Bronze Age Wooden Polypod Bowls, *The Journal of Irish Archaeology* 6, 27-28.

Earwood, C. 1993. *Domestic Wooden Artefacts in Britain and Ireland from Neolithic to Viking Times.* Exeter.

Edmonds, M. 1995. *Stone Tools and Society. Working Stone in Neolithic and Bronze Age Britain.* London.

Edwards, K. J. 1985. The Anthropogenic Factor in Vegetational History, in K. J. Edwards and W. P. Warren, (eds), *The Quaternary History of Ireland,* 187-220. London.

Edwards, K. J. and Hirons, K. R. 1984. Cereal pollen grains in pre-elm decline deposits: implications for the earliest agriculture in Britain and Ireland, *Journal of Archaeological Science* 11, 71-80.

Ehrenberg, M. 1977. *Bronze Age Spearheads from Berkshire, Buckinghamshire and Oxfordshire, British Archaeological Reports* 144. Oxford.

Ehrenberg, M. 1981. The Anvils of Bronze Age Europe, *The Antiquaries Journal* 61, 14-28.

Ehrenberg, M. 1989. The interpretation of regional variability in British and Irish Bronze Age metalwork, in H-Å Nordström and A. Knape (eds), *Bronze Age Studies. Transactions of the British-Scandinavian Colloquium in Stockholm, May 10-11, 1985,* 77-88. Stockholm.

Ehrenberg, M. 1989a. *Women in Prehistory.* London.

Eluère, C. 1981. Réflexions à propos de 'boucles d'oreilles' torsadées en or de types connus à l'Age du Bronze, *Antiquités Nationales* 12-13, 34-39.

Eluère, C. 1982. *Les Ors Préhistoriques.* Paris.

Eluère, C. 1987. Celtic Gold Torcs, *Gold Bulletin* 20, 22-37.

Eogan, G. 1963. A Neolithic habitation-site and megalithic tomb in Townleyhall townland, Co. Louth, *Journal of the Royal Society of Antiquaries of Ireland* 93, 37-81.

Eogan, G. 1964. The Later Bronze Age in Ireland in the light of recent research, *Proceedings of the Prehistoric Society* 30, 268-351.

Eogan, G. 1965. *Catalogue of Irish Bronze Swords.* Dublin.

Eogan, G. 1966. Some notes on the origin and diffusion of the bronze socketed gouge, *Ulster Journal of Archaeology* 29, 97-102.

Eogan, G. 1967. Knowth (Co. Meath), excavations, *Antiquity* 41, 302-4.

Eogan, G. 1967a. The Associated Finds of Gold Bar Torcs, *Journal of the Royal Society of Antiquaries of Ireland* 97, 129-175.

Eogan, G. 1968. Excavations at Knowth, Co. Meath, *Proceedings of the Royal Irish Academy* 66C, 299-400.

Eogan, G. 1969. 'Lock-rings' of the Late Bronze Age, *Proceedings of the Royal Irish Academy* 67C, 93-148.

Eogan, G. 1969a. Excavations at Knowth, Co. Meath, 1968, *Antiquity* 43, 8-14.

Eogan, G. 1972. 'Sleeve-fasteners' of the Late Bronze Age, in F. Lynch and C. B. Burgess (eds), *Prehistoric Man in Wales and the West: Essays in honour of Lily F. Chitty,* 189-209. Bath.

Eogan, G. 1974. Regionale Gruppierungen in der Spätbronzezeit Irlands, *Archäologisches Korrespondenzblatt* 4, 319-327.

Eogan, G. 1974a. Pins of the Irish Late Bronze Age, *Journal of the Royal Society of Antiquaries of Ireland* 104, 74-119.

Eogan, G. 1974b. Report on the excavations of some passage graves, unprotected inhumation burials and a settlement at Knowth, Co. Meath, *Proceedings of the Royal Irish Academy* 74C, 11-112.

Eogan, G. 1981. The Gold Vessels of the Bronze Age in Ireland and Beyond, *Proceedings of the Royal Irish Academy* 81C, 345-382.

Eogan, G. 1981a. Gold Discs of the Irish Late Bronze Age, in D. Ó Corráin (ed.), *Irish Antiquity. Essays and Studies presented to Professor M. J. O'Kelly,* 147-162. Cork.

Eogan, G. 1983. *The Hoards of the Irish Later Bronze Age.* Dublin.

Eogan, G. 1983a. Ribbon Torcs in Britain and Ireland, in A. O'Connor and D.V. Clarke (eds), *From the Stone Age to the 'Forty-Five. Studies presented to R. B. K. Stevenson,* 87-126. Edinburgh.

Eogan, G. 1984. *Excavations at Knowth I.* Dublin.

Eogan, G. 1986. *Knowth and the Passage Tombs of Ireland.* London.

Eogan, G. 1990. Irish Megalithic Tombs and Iberia: Comparisons and Contrasts, in *Probleme der Megalithgräberforschung. Vorträge zum 100 Geburtstag von Vera Leisner,* 113-137. Berlin.

Eogan, G. 1990a. Possible Connections between Britain and Ireland and the East Mediterranean region during the Bronze Age, in *Orientalisch-Ägäische Einflüsse in der Europäischen Bronzezeit,* 155-163. Bonn.

Eogan, G. 1991. Prehistoric and Early Historic Cultural Change at Brugh na Bóinne, *Proceedings of the Royal Irish Academy* 91C, 105-132.

Eogan, G. 1993. The Late Bronze Age: Customs, Crafts and Cults, in E. S. Twohig and M. Ronayne (eds), *Past Perceptions. The Prehistoric Archaeology of South-West Ireland,* 121-133. Cork.

Eogan, G. 1993a. Aspects of metal production and manufacturing systems during the Irish Bronze Age, *Acta Praehistorica et Archaeologica* 25, 87-110.

Eogan, G. 1994. *The Accomplished Art. Gold and Gold-Working in Britain and Ireland during the Bronze Age (c. 2300-650 BC).* Oxford.

Eogan, G. 1995. Ideas, People and Things: Ireland and the External World during the Later Bronze Age, in J. Waddell and E. S. Twohig (eds), *Ireland in the Bronze Age. Proceedings of the Dublin Conference, April 1995*, 128-135. Dublin.

Eogan, G. 1997. 'Hair-rings' and European Late Bronze Age Society, *Antiquity* 71, 308-320.

Eogan, G. and Richardson, H. 1982. Two Maceheads from Knowth, County Meath, *Journal of the Royal Society of Antiquaries of Ireland* 112, 123-138.

Eogan, G. and Aboud, J. 1990. Diffuse Picking in Megalithic Art, in *La Bretagne et l'Europe préhistoriques, mémoire en hommage à Pierre-Roland Giot, Revue archéologique de l'Ouest, Supplément* 2, 121-140.

Eogan, G. and Roche, H. 1997. Pre-tomb Neolithic house discovered at Knowth, Co. Meath, *Archaeology Ireland* 11, no. 2, 31.

Eogan, G. and Roche, H. 1997a. *Excavations at Knowth 2.* Dublin.

Evans, E. E. 1933. The Bronze Age Spear-head in Great Britain and Ireland, *Archaeologia* 83, 187-202.

Evans, E. E. 1935. Excavations at Aghnaskeagh, Co. Louth, *County Louth Archaeological Journal* 8, 235-55.

Evans, E. E. 1938. Doeys Cairn, Dunloy, Co. Antrim, *Ulster Journal of Archaeology* 1, 59-78.

Evans, E. E. 1939. Excavations at Carnanbane, County Londonderry. A double horned cairn, *Proceedings of the Royal Irish Academy* 45C, 1-12.

Evans, E. E. 1941. A Sandhill site in Co. Donegal, *Ulster Journal of Archaeology* 4, 71-75.

Evans, E. E. 1953. *Lyles Hill. A Late Neolithic Site in Co. Antrim.* Belfast.

Evans, E. E. 1966. *Prehistoric and Early Christian Ireland. A Guide.* London.

Evans, E. E. and Davies, O. 1934. Excavation of a Chambered Horned Cairn at Ballyalton, Co. Down, *Proceedings of the Belfast Natural History and Philosophical Society* 1933-34, 79-103.

Evans, E. E. and Davies, O. 1935. Excavation of a Chambered Horned Cairn, Browndod, Co. Antrim, *Proceedings of the Belfast Natural History and Philosophical Society* 1934-35, 70-87.

Evans, E. E. and Mitchell, G. F. 1954. Three Bronze Spear-Heads from Tattenamona, near Brookborough, Co. Fermanagh, *Ulster Journal of Archaeology* 17, 57-61.

Evans, E. E. and Watson, E. 1942. The stone houses, Ticloy, Co. Antrim, *Ulster Journal of Archaeology* 5, 62-5.

Evans, J. 1881. *The Ancient Bronze Implements, Weapons and Ornaments of Great Britain and Ireland.* London.

Fahy, E. 1959. A Recumbent-stone circle at Drombeg, Co. Cork, *Journal of the Cork Historical and Archaeological Society* 64, 1-27.

Fahy, E. 1960. A Hut and Cooking-place at Drombeg, Co. Cork, *Journal of the Cork Historical and Archaeological Society* 65, 1-17.

Fahy, E. 1961. A stone circle, hut and dolmen at Bohonagh, Co. Cork, *Journal of the Cork Historical and Archaeological Society* 66, 93-104.

Fahy, E. 1962. A Recumbent stone circle at Reanascreena South, Co. Cork, *Journal of the Cork Historical and Archaeological Society* 67, 59-69.

Farrell, A. W. and Penny, S. 1975. The Broighter Boat: a reassessment, *Irish Archaeological Research Forum* 2, no. 2, 15-28.

Farrelly, J. 1995. A recently discovered barrow cemetery in Nenagh, *Tipperary Historical Journal* 1995, 178-180.

Fenton, A. 1972. Early Yoke Types in Britain, *Magyar Mezögazdasági Múzeum Közleményei [Proceedings of the Hungarian Agricultural Museum]* 1971-1972, 69-75.

Fenwick, J. 1995. The Manufacture of the Decorated Macehead from Knowth, County Meath, *Journal of the Royal Society of Antiquaries of Ireland* 125, 51-60.

Fenwick, J. 1997. A panoramic view from the Hill of Tara, Co. Meath, *Ríocht na Midhe* 9, no. 3, 1-11.

Fenwick, J., Brennan, Y. and Delaney, F. 1996. The Anatomy of a Mound: Geophysical Images of Rathcroghan, *Archaeology Ireland* 10, no. 3, 20-23.

Fitzpatrick, A. P. 1991. Celtic (Iron Age) Religion – Traditional and Timeless?, *Scottish Archaeological Review* 8, 123-129.

Flanagan, L. N. W. 1959. Department of Antiquities, Belfast Museum and Art Gallery Archaeological Acquisitions of Irish Origin for the Year 1958, *Ulster Journal of Archaeology* 22, 43-52.

Flanagan, L. N. W. 1961. Wessex and Ireland in the early and middle bronze ages, in G. Bersu (ed.), *Bericht über den V. Internationalen Kongress für Vor- und Frühgeschichte Hamburg vom 24. bis 30. August 1958*, 284-291. Berlin.

Flanagan, L. N. W. 1964. Necklace of Amber Beads, Kurin, Co. Derry, *Ulster Journal of Archaeology* 27, 92-93.

Flanagan, L. N. W. 1965. Flint Hollow Scrapers and the Irish Neolithic, in M. Pallottino *et al.* (eds), *Atti del VI Congresso Internazionale delle Scienze Preistoriche e Protostoriche, Roma, 29 Agosto-3 Settembre 1962*, Vol. 2, 323-328. Rome.

Flanagan, L. N. W. 1966. An unpublished flint hoard from the Braid Valley, Co. Antrim, *Ulster Journal of Archaeology* 29, 82-90.

Flanagan, L. N. W. 1966a. A Bronze Halberd from County Armagh, *Ulster Journal of Archaeology* 29, 95-96.

Flanagan, L. N. W. 1970. *Ulster.* London.

Flanagan, L. N. W. 1970a. The Petit Tranchet Derivative Arrowhead and the Irish Neolithic, in J. Filip (ed.), *Actes du VII Congrès International des Sciences Préhistoriques et Protohistoriques, Prague, 21-27 août 1966*, 523-527. Prague.

Flanagan, L. N. W. 1970b. A flint hoard from Ballyclare, Co. Antrim, *Ulster Journal of Archaeology* 33, 15-22.

Flanagan, L. N. W. 1974. Cloughskelt Bronze Age Cemetery, in T. G. Delaney (ed.), *Excavations 1973*, 10. Belfast.

Flanagan, L. N. W. 1976. The Composition of Irish Bronze Age Cemeteries, *Irish Archaeological Research Forum* 3, no. 2, 7-20.

Flanagan, L. N. W. 1977. Court Graves and Portal Graves, *Irish Archaeological Research Forum* 4, no. 1, 23-29.

Flanagan, L. N. W. 1979. Industrial resources, production and distribution in earlier Bronze Age Ireland, in M. Ryan (ed.), *The Origins of Metallurgy in Atlantic Europe. Proceedings of the Fifth Atlantic Colloquium*, 145-163. Dublin.

Flanagan, L. N. W. and Flanagan, D. E. 1966. The Excavation of a Court Cairn at Bavan, Co. Donegal, *Ulster Journal of Archaeology* 29, 16-38

Fleming, A. 1972. Vision and design: approaches to ceremonial monument typology, *Man* 7, 57-73.

Fleming, A. 1973. Tombs for the living, *Man* 8, 177-193.

Fleming, A. 1987. Coaxial field systems: some questions of time and space, *Antiquity* 61, 188-202.

Fleming, A. 1989. Coaxial field systems in later British prehistory, in H-Å Nordström and A. Knape (eds), *Bronze Age Studies. Transactions of the British-Scandinavian Colloquium in Stockholm, May 10-11, 1985,* 151-162. Stockholm.

Foley, C. 1983. A stone circle complex at Copney Hill, County Tyrone, *Ulster Journal of Archaeology* 46, 146-148.

Foley, C. 1985. A Cist Burial at Tremoge, Co. Tyrone, *Ulster Journal of Archaeology* 48, 63-68.

Foley, C. 1988. Only an old pile of stones. Creggandevesky Court Tomb, Co. Tyrone, in A. Hamlin and C. Lynn (eds), *Pieces of the Past*, 3-5. Belfast.

Fowler, P. J. 1981. Wildscape to landscape: 'enclosure' in prehistoric Britain, in R. J. Mercer (ed.), *Farming Practice in British Prehistory,* 9-54. Edinburgh.

Fowler, P. J. 1983. *The Farming of Prehistoric Britain.* Cambridge.

Fox, A. 1961. South-Western Hill-Forts, in S. S. Frere (ed.), *Problems of the Iron Age in Southern Britain,* 35-60. London.

Fox, C. 1939. The Socketed Bronze Sickles of the British Isles, *Proceedings of the Prehistoric Society* 5, 222-248.

Fox, C. 1958. *Pattern and Purpose. A Survey of Early Celtic Art in Britain.* Cardiff.

Freeman, P. M. 1995. Greek and Roman Views of Ireland: a Checklist, *Emania* 13, 11-13.

Frey, O-H. and Megaw, J. V. S. 1976. Palmette and Circle: Early Celtic Art in Britain and its Continental Background, *Proceedings of the Prehistoric Society* 42, 47-65.

Gaskell Brown, C. and Harper, A. E. T. 1984. Excavations on Cathedral Hill, Armagh, 1968, *Ulster Journal of Archaeology* 47, 109-161.

Gerloff, S. 1975. *The Early Bronze Age Daggers in Great Britain and a Reconsideration of the Wessex Culture. Prähistorische Bronzefunde* VI:2. Munich.

Gerloff, S. 1986. Bronze Age Class A Cauldrons: Typology, Origins and Chronology, *Journal of the Royal Society of Antiquaries of Ireland* 116, 84-115.

Gerloff, S. 1995. Bronzezeitliche Goldblechkronen aus Westeuropa, in A. Jockenhövel (ed.), *Festschrift für Hermann Müller-Karpe zum 70 Geburtstag,* 153-194. Bonn.

Gibbons, M. 1990. The archaeology of early settlement in County Kilkenny, in W. Nolan and K. Whelan (eds), *Kilkenny: History and Society. Interdisciplinary Essays on the History of an Irish County,* 1-32. Dublin.

Gibbons, M. and Higgins, J. 1988. Connemara's emerging prehistory, *Archaeology Ireland* 2, 63-66.

Gibson, A. M. 1982. *Beaker Domestic Sites: a study of the domestic pottery of the late third and early second millennia BC in the British Isles, British Archaeological Reports* 107. Oxford.

Gibson, A. M. and Simpson, D. D. A. 1987. Lyles Hill, Co. Antrim, *Archaeology Ireland* 1, no. 2, 72-75.

Glover, W. 1975. Segmented cist grave in Kinkit townland, County Tyrone, *Journal of the Royal Society of Antiquaries in Ireland* 105, 150-155.

Glover, W. 1979. A Prehistoric Bow Fragment from Drumwhinny Bog, Kesh, Co. Fermanagh, *Proceedings of the Prehistoric Society* 45, 323-327.

Gogan, L. S. 1931. The Ballycotton Gold Collar or 'Gorget', *Journal of the Cork Historical and Archaeological Society* 36, 87-100.

Goldmann, K. 1981. Guss in verlorener Sandform – das Hauptverfahren alteuropäischer Bronzegiesser?, *Archaeologisches Korrespondenzblatt* 11, 109-116.

Gosling, P. 1993. *Archaeological Inventory of County Galway. Vol. 1: West Galway.* Dublin.

Gosling, P. 1994. Prehistoric settlement on Clare Island, in P. Coxon and M. O'Connell (eds), *Clare Island and Inishbofin, Irish Association for Quaternary Studies Field Guide No. 17,* 39-53. Dublin.

Gowen, M. 1988. *Three Irish Gas Pipelines: New Archaeological Evidence in Munster.* Dublin.

Gowen, M. and Halpin, E. 1992. A Neolithic House at Newtown, *Archaeology Ireland* 6, no. 2, 25-27.

Gowen, M. and Tarbett, C. 1988. A third season at Tankardstown, *Archaeology Ireland* 2, no. 4, 156.

Gowen, M. and Tarbett, C. 1990. Tankardstown South Neolithic house sites, in I. Bennett (ed.), *Excavations 1989,* 38-39. Dublin.

Grabowski, K. 1990. The Historical Overview of Dún Ailinne, *Emania* 7, 32-36.

Grant, C. 1995. Mapping a Bronze Age Burren Landscape, *Archaeology Ireland* 9, no. 1, 31-33.

Gräslund, B. 1967. The Herzsprung Shield Type and its Origin, *Acta Archaeologica* 38, 58-71.

Gray, W. 1873. On some stone celts found near Belfast ..., *Journal of the Royal Society of Antiquaries of Ireland* 12, 138.

Green, H. S. 1978. Late Bronze Age wooden hafts from Llyn Fawr and Penwyllt and a review of the evidence for the selection of wood for tool and weapon handles in Neolithic and Bronze Age Britain and Ireland, *Bulletin of the Board of Celtic Studies* 28, 136-141.

Green, H. S. 1980. *The Flint Arrowheads of the British Isles, British Archaeological Reports* 75. Oxford.

Green, M. 1989. *Symbol and Image in Celtic Religious Art.* London.

Green, M. 1992. *Animals in Celtic Life and Myth.* London.

Green, M. 1992a. *Dictionary of Celtic Myth and Legend.* London.

Green, S. W. and Zvelebil. M. 1990. The Mesolithic Colonization and Agricultural Transition of South-east Ireland, *Proceedings of the Prehistoric Society* 56, 57-88.

Green, S. W. and Zvelebil. M. 1993. Interpreting Ireland's Prehistoric Landscape: the Bally Lough Archaeological Project, in P. Bogucki (ed.), *Case Studies in European Prehistory,* 1-29. Boca Raton, Florida.

Griffiths, R. 1843. A collection of antiquities discovered in the Shannon ..., *Proceedings of the Royal Irish Academy* 2, 312-316.

Groenman-van Waateringe, W. 1983. The Early Agricultural Utilisation of the Irish Landscape: the last word on the elm decline?, in T. Reeves-Smyth and F. Hamond (eds), *Landscape Archaeology in Ireland, British Archaeological Reports* 116, 217-232. Oxford.

Groenman-van Waateringe, W. and Butler, J. J. 1976. The Ballynoe Stone Circle. Excavations by A. E. van Giffin, 1937-1938, *Palaeohistoria* 18, 73-104.

Grogan, E. 1990. Bronze Age Cemetery at Carrig, Co. Wicklow, *Archaeology Ireland* 4, no. 4, 12-14.

Grogan, E. 1991. Neolithic Settlements, in M. Ryan (ed.), *The Illustrated Archaeology of Ireland,* 59-63. Dublin.

Grogan, E. 1993. North Munster Project. Interim Report, *Discovery Programme Reports* 1, 39-68.

Grogan, E. 1995. North Munster Project. Interim Report, *Discovery Programme Reports* 2, 45-61.

Grogan, E. 1996. North Munster Project. Interim Report, *Discovery Programme Reports* 4, 26-72.

Grogan, E. 1996a. Neolithic houses in Ireland, in T. Darvill and J. Thomas (eds), *Neolithic Houses in Northwest Europe and Beyond,* 41-60. Oxford.

Grogan, E. and Cooney, G. 1990. A preliminary distribution map of stone axes in Ireland, *Antiquity* 64, 559-561.

Grogan, E. and Eogan, G. 1987. Lough Gur Excavations by Seán P. Ó Ríordáin: Further Neolithic and Beaker Habitations on Knockadoon, *Proceedings of the Royal Irish Academy* 87C, 299-506.

Halpin, E. 1992. Newtown Neolithic House, in I. Bennett (ed.), *Excavations 1991,* 37-39. Dublin.

Halpin, E. 1995. Excavations at Newtown, Co. Meath, in Grogan, E. and Mount, C. (eds), *Annus Archaeologiae. Archaeological Research 1992,* 45-54. Dublin.

Hamlin, A. and Lynn, C. 1988. *Pieces of the Past. Archaeological Excavations by the Department of the Environment for Northern Ireland 1970-1986.* Belfast.

Harbison, P. 1967. Mediterranean and Atlantic Elements in the Early Bronze Age of Northern Portugal and Galicia, *Madrider Mitteilungen* 8, 100-122.

Harbison, P. 1967a. Some Minor Metal Products of the Early Bronze Age in Ireland, *Journal of the Cork Historical and Archaeological Society* 72, 93-100.

Harbison, P. 1968. Catalogue of Irish Early Bronze Age associated finds containing copper or bronze, *Proceedings of the Royal Irish Academy* 67C, 35-91.

Harbison, P. 1968a. Irish Early Bronze Age exports found on the Continent and their derivatives, *Palaeohistoria* 14, 175-186.

Harbison, P. 1969. *The Axes of the Early Bronze Age in Ireland. Prähistorische Bronzefunde* IX:1. Munich.

Harbison, P. 1969a. *The Daggers and Halberds of the Early Bronze Age in Ireland. Prähistorische Bronzefunde* VI:1. Munich.

Harbison, P. 1970. Two prehistoric bronze weapons from Ireland in the Hunt Collection, *Journal of the Royal Society of Antiquaries of Ireland* 100, 191-199.

Harbison, P. 1971. Wooden and Stone *Chevaux-de-frise* in Central and Western Europe, *Proceedings of the Prehistoric Society* 37, 195-225.

Harbison, P. 1973. The Earlier Bronze Age in Ireland, *Journal of the Royal Society of Antiquaries of Ireland* 103, 93-152.

Harbison, P. 1976. *Bracers and V-perforated Buttons in the Beaker and Food Vessel Cultures of Ireland. Archaeologia Atlantica Research Report I.* Bad Bramstedt.

Harbison, P. 1978. A Flat Tanged Dagger from Co. Tyrone now in the Monaghan County Museum, *Clogher Record* 9, 333-335.

Harbison, P. 1988. *Pre-Christian Ireland. From the First Settlers to the Early Celts.* London.

Harbison, P. and Laing, L. 1974. *Some Iron Age Mediterranean Imports in England, British Archaeological Reports* 5. Oxford.

Hardakar, R. 1974. *A Corpus of Early Bronze Age Dagger Pommels from Britain and Ireland, British Archaeological Reports* 3. Oxford.

Harding, A. F. 1976. Bronze agricultural implements in Bronze Age Europe, in G. de G. Sieveking (ed.), *Social and Economic Problems in Archaeology,* 513-522. London.

Harding, A. F. 1984. *The Mycenaeans and Europe.* London.

Harding, A. F. 1993. British Amber Spacer-plate Necklaces and their Relatives in Gold and Stone, in C. W. Beck and J. Bouzek (eds), *Amber in Archaeology. Proceedings of the Second International Conference on Amber in Archaeology, Liblice 1990,* 53-58. Prague.

Harding, A. F. and Young, R. 1979. Reconstruction of the hafting methods and function of stone implements, in T. H. McK. Clough and W. A. Cummins (eds), *Stone axe studies. Archaeological, petrological, experimental and ethnographic,* 102-105. London.

Harrison, R. J. 1974. Ireland and Spain in the Early Bronze Age, *Journal of the Royal Society of Antiquaries of Ireland* 104, 52-73.

Harrison, R. J. 1980. *The Beaker Folk. Copper Age archaeology in Western Europe.* London.

Hartnett, P. J. 1951. A Neolithic burial from Martinstown, Kiltale, Co. Meath, *Journal of the Royal Society of Antiquaries of Ireland* 81, 19-23.

Hartnett, P. J. 1957. Excavations of a Passage Grave at Fourknocks, Co. Meath, *Proceedings of the Royal Irish Academy* 58C, 197-277.

Hartnett, P. J. 1971. The Excavation of Two Tumuli at Fourknocks (Sites II and III), Co. Meath, *Proceedings of the Royal Irish Academy* 71C, 35-89.

Hartnett, P. J. and Eogan, G. 1964. Feltrim Hill, Co. Dublin; a Neolithic and Early Christian site, *Journal of the Royal Society of Antiquaries of Ireland* 94, 1-37.

Hartnett, P. J. and Prendergast, E. 1953. Bronze Age Burials in Co. Wexford, *Journal of the Royal Society of Antiquaries of Ireland* 83, 46-57.

Hartwell, B. 1991. Recent Air Survey Results from Navan, *Emania* 8, 5-9.

Hartwell, B. 1991a. Ballynahatty – A Prehistoric Ceremonial Centre, *Archaeology Ireland* 5, no. 4, 12-15.

Hartwell, B. 1994. Late Neolithic Ceremonies, *Archaeology Ireland* 8, no. 4, 10-13.

Hawkes, C. F. C. 1932. The Towednack Gold Hoard, *Man* 32, 177-186.

Hawkes, C. F. C. 1961. Gold Ear-rings of the Bronze Age, East and West, *Folklore* 72, 438-474.

Hawkes, C. F. C. 1971. The Sintra Gold Collar, in G. de G. Sieveking (ed.), *Prehistoric and Roman Studies,* 38-50. London. [*British Museum Quarterly* 35].

Hawkes, C. F. C. 1981. Alcoholic food vessels?, *Current Archaeology* 79, 255.

Hawkes, C. F. C. 1982. The wearing of the brooch: early Iron Age dress among the Irish, in B. G. Scott (ed.), *Studies on Early Ireland. Essays in honour of M. V. Duignan,* 51-73. Belfast.

Hawkes, C. F. C. and Clarke, R. R. 1963. Gahlstorf and Caister-on-Sea. Two finds of Late Bronze Age Irish Gold, in I. Ll. Foster and L. Alcock (eds), *Culture and Environment. Essays in honour of Sir Cyril Fox,* 193-250. London.

Hawkes, C. F. C. and Smith, M. A. 1957. On Some Buckets and Cauldrons of the Bronze and Early Iron Ages: the Nannau, Whigsborough, and Heathery Burn bronze buckets and the Colchester and London cauldrons, *The Antiquaries Journal* 37, 131-198.

Hawkes, J. 1941. Excavation of a Megalithic Tomb at Harristown, Co. Waterford, *Journal of the Royal Society of Antiquaries of Ireland* 71, 130-147.

Haworth, R. 1971. The Horse Harness of the Irish Early Iron Age, *Ulster Journal of Archaeology* 34, 26-49.

Haworth, R. 1975. Archaeological Field Survey in Ireland – Past, Present and Future, *Irish Archaeological Research Forum* 2, no. 1, 7-19 [corrections in 2, no. 2, ii].

Hawthorne, M. 1991. A Preliminary Analysis of Wood Remains from Haughey's Fort, *Emania* 8, 34-38.

Hayden, A. 1994. Coarha More, Valentia Island. Bronze Age settlement, in I. Bennett (ed.), *Excavations 1993,* 42-43.

Hayes, R. H., Hemingway, J. E. and Spratt, D. A. 1980. The Distribution and Lithology of Beehive Querns in Northeast Yorkshire, *Journal of Archaeological Science* 7, 297-324.

Hedges, R. E. M., Housley, R. A., Ramsey, C. B. and van Klinken, G. J. 1991. Radiocarbon dates from the Oxford AMS system: *Archaeometry* datelist 12, *Archaeometry* 33, 121-134.

Hedges, R. E. M., Housley, R. A., Ramsey, C. B. and van Klinken, G. J. 1993. Radiocarbon dates from the Oxford AMS system: *Archaeometry* datelist 17, *Archaeometry* 35, 305-326.

Hedges, R. E. M., Pettitt, P. B., Ramsey, C. B. and van Klinken, G. J. 1997. Radiocarbon dates from the Oxford AMS system: *Archaeometry* datelist 23, *Archaeometry* 39, 247-262.

Heggie, D. C. 1981. *Megalithic Science.* London.

Hencken, H. O'N. 1935. A Cairn at Poulawack, County Clare, *Journal of the Royal Society of Antiquaries of Ireland* 65, 191-222.

Hencken, H. O'N. 1939. A Long Cairn at Creevykeel, Co. Sligo, *Journal of the Royal Society of Antiquaries of Ireland* 69, 53-98.

Hencken, H. O'N. 1942. Ballinderry Crannog No. 2, *Proceedings of the Royal Irish Academy* 47C, 1-76.

Hencken, H. O'N. 1951. Palaeobotany and the Bronze Age, *Journal of the Royal Society of Antiquaries of Ireland* 81, 53-64.

Hencken, H. O'N. and Movius, H. L. 1934. The Cemetery-Cairn of Knockast, *Proceedings of the Royal Irish Academy* 41C, 232-284.

Henderson, J. 1987. The Iron Age of 'Loughey' and Meare: some inferences from glass analyses, *The Antiquaries Journal* 67, 29-42.

Henderson, J. 1988. Glass production and Bronze Age Europe, *Antiquity* 62, 435-451.

Henry, D. (ed.). 1995. *Viking Ireland. Jens Worsaae's accounts of his visit to Ireland 1846-47.* Balgavies, Angus.

Henry, M. 1992. Prehistoric Life in Co. Galway: a distributional analysis, *Journal of the Galway Archaeological and Historical Society* 44, 29-46.

Henshall, A. S. 1950. Textiles and Weaving Appliances in Prehistoric Britain, *Proceedings of the Prehistoric Society* 16, 130-162.

Henshall, A. S. 1972. *The Chambered Tombs of Scotland. Volume Two.* Edinburgh.

Herity, M. 1964. The Finds from the Irish Portal Dolmens, *Journal of the Royal Society of Antiquaries of Ireland* 94, 123-144.

Herity, M. 1969. Early Finds of Irish Antiquities, *The Antiquaries Journal* 49, 1-21.

Herity, M. 1974. *Irish Passage Graves.* Dublin.

Herity, M. 1981. Irish Decorated Neolithic Pottery and its Context, *Journal of Indo-European Studies* 9, 69-93.

Herity, M. 1981a. A Bronze Age farmstead at Glenree, Co. Mayo, *Popular Archaeology* 2, 258-265.

Herity, M. 1982. Irish Decorated Neolithic Pottery, *Proceedings of the Royal Irish Academy* 82C, 247-404.

Herity, M. 1983. A Survey of the Royal Site of Cruachain in Connacht I, *Journal of the Royal Society of Antiquaries of Ireland* 113 [published September 1984], 121-142.

Herity, M. 1984. A Survey of the Royal Site of Cruachain in Connacht II, *Journal of the Royal Society of Antiquaries of Ireland* 114, 125-138.

Herity, M. 1987. The Finds from Irish Court Tombs, *Proceedings of the Royal Irish Academy* 87C, 5-281.

Herity, M. 1987a. A Survey of the Royal Site of Cruachain in Connacht III, *Journal of the Royal Society of Antiquaries of Ireland* 117, 125-141.

Herity, M. 1988. A Survey of the Royal Site of Cruachain in Connacht IV, *Journal of the Royal Society of Antiquaries of Ireland* 118, 67-84.

Herity, M. 1991. *Rathcroghan and Carnfree. Celtic Royal Sites in Roscommon.* Dublin.

Herity, M. 1993. Moats and Mounds at Royal Sites in Ireland, *Journal of the Royal Society of Antiquaries of Ireland* 123, 127-151.

Herity, M. and Eogan, G. 1977. *Ireland in Prehistory.* London.

Herne, A. 1988. A Time and a Place for the Grimston Bowl, in J. C. Barrett and I. A. Kinnes (eds), *The Archaeology of Context in the Neolithic and Bronze Age. Recent Trends,* 9-29. Sheffield.

Herring, I. J. 1938. The Cairn Excavation at Well Glass Spring, Largantea, Co. Londonderry, *Ulster Journal of Archaeology* 1, 164-88.

Herring, I. J. and May, A. McL. 1937. The Giant's Grave, Kilhoyle, Co. Londonderry, *Proceedings of the Belfast Natural History and Philosophical Society* 1936-37, 34-48.

Herring, I. J. and May, A. McL. 1940. Cloghnagalla Cairn, Boviel, Co. Londonderry, *Ulster Journal of Archaeology* 3, 41-55.

Heslop, D. H. 1988. The Study of Beehive Querns, *Scottish Archaeological Review* 5, 59-65.

Hewson, L. M. 1938. Notes on Irish Sandhills, *Journal of the Royal Society of Antiquaries of Ireland* 68, 69-90.

Hickey, H. 1976. *Images of Stone.* Belfast.

Higgins, J. 1978. A Bann Flake from Oughterard, Co. Galway, *Journal of the Galway Archaeological and Historical Society* 36, 84-5.

Higgins, J. 1986. Some further Mesolithic finds from near Oughterard, Co. Galway, *Journal of the Galway Archaeological and Historical Society* 40, 144-145.

Higgins, J. 1991. A new group of Fulachta Fiadh in Co. Mayo, *Cathair na Mart. Journal of the Westport Historical Society* 11, 31-34.

Hillam, J. 1976. The Dating of Cullyhanna Hunting Lodge, *Irish Archaeological Research Forum* 3, no. 1, 7-20.

Hirons, K. R. and Edwards, K. J. 1986. Events at and around the first and second *Ulmus* declines: palaeoecological investigations in Co. Tyrone, Northern Ireland, *New Phytologist* 104, 131-153.

Hodder, I. 1984. Burials, houses, women and men in the European Neolithic, in D. Miller and C. Tilley (eds), *Ideology, power and prehistory,* 51-68. Cambridge.

Hodder, I. (ed.). 1991. *Archaeological Theory in Europe. The last three decades.* London.

Hodges, H. W. M. 1954. Studies in the Late Bronze Age in Ireland. 1. Stone and clay moulds and wooden models for bronze implements, *Ulster Journal of Archaeology* 17, 62-80.

Hodges, H. W. M. 1955. The Excavation of a Group of Cooking-Places at Ballycroghan, Co. Down. *Ulster Journal of Archaeology* 18, 17-28.

Hodges, H. W. M. 1956. Studies in the Late Bronze Age in Ireland. 2. The typology and distribution of bronze implements, *Ulster Journal of Archaeology* 19, 29-56.

Hodges, H. W. M. 1958. A Hunting Camp at Cullyhanna Lough, near Newtown Hamilton, County Armagh, *Ulster Journal of Archaeology* 21, 7-13.

Holmes, P. 1979. The Manufacturing Technology of the Irish Bronze Age Horns, in M. Ryan (ed.), *The Origins of Metallurgy in Atlantic Europe. Proceedings of the Fifth Atlantic Colloquium,* 165-188. Dublin.

Holmes, P. and Coles, J. M. 1981. Prehistoric brass instruments, *World Archaeology* 12, 280-286.

Hook, D. R. and Needham, S. P. 1990. A comparison of recent analyses of British Late Bronze Age goldwork with Irish parallels, *Jewellery Studies* 3, 15-24.

Hunt, J. 1967. Prehistoric Burials at Cahirguillamore, Co. Limerick, in E. Rynne (ed.), *North Munster Studies. Essays in commemoration of Monsignor Michael Moloney,* 20-42. Limerick.

Ireland, A. 1992. The finding of the 'Clonmacnoise' gold torcs, *Proceedings of the Royal Irish Academy* 92C, 123-146.

Ivens, R. J., Simpson, D. D. A. and Brown, D. 1986. Excavations at Island MacHugh 1985 – Interim Report, *Ulster Journal of Archaeology* 49, 99-103.

Jackson, J. S. 1979. Metallic Ores in Irish Prehistory: Copper and Tin, in M. Ryan (ed.), *The Origins of Metallurgy in Atlantic Europe. Proceedings of the Fifth Atlantic Colloquium,* 107-125. Dublin.

Jockenhövel, A. 1974. Fleischhaken von den Britischen Inseln, *Archäologisches Korrespondenzblatt* 4, 329-338.

Jockenhövel, A. 1980. *Die Rasiermesser in Westeuropa. Prähistorische Bronzefunde* VIII:3. Munich.

Jockenhövel, A. 1982. Zu den ältesten Tüllenhämmern aus Bronze, *Germania* 60, 459-467.

Johnston, S. 1990. The Neolithic and Bronze Age activity at Dún Ailinne, Co. Kildare, *Emania* 7, 26-31.

Johnston, S. 1991. Distributional Aspects of Prehistoric Irish Petroglyphs, in P. Bahn and A. Rosenfeld (eds), *Rock Art and Prehistory. Papers presented to symposium G of the AURA Congress, Darwin 1988,* 86-95. Oxford.

Johnston, S. 1993. The Relationship between Prehistoric Irish Rock Art and Irish Passage Tomb Art, *Oxford Journal of Archaeology* 12, 257-279.

Jones, C. 1996. Parknabinnia Habitation, in I. Bennett (ed.), *Excavations 1995,* 5. Bray.

Jones, V., Bishop, A. C. and Wooley, A. R. 1977. Third Supplement of the Catalogue of Jade Axes from Sites in the British Isles, *Proceedings of the Prehistoric Society* 43, 287-293.

Jope, E. M. 1951. A Late Bronze Age Shield Mould of Wood from County Antrim, *Ulster Journal of Archaeology* 14, 62-65.

Jope, E. M. 1951a. A Crescentic Jet Necklace from Rasharkin, Co. Antrim, *Ulster Journal of Archaeology* 14, 61.

Jope, E. M. 1952. Porcellanite Axes from Factories in North-east Ireland: Tievebulliagh and Rathlin, *Ulster Journal of Archaeology* 15, 31-60.

Jope, E. M. 1953. Three Late Bronze Age Swords from Ballycroghan, near Bangor, Co. Down, *Ulster Journal of Archaeology* 16, 37-40.

Jope, E. M. 1954. An Iron Age decorated sword-scabbard from the River Bann at Toome, *Ulster Journal of Archaeology* 17, 81-91.

Jope, E. M. 1955. Chariotry and Paired-draught in Ireland during the Early Iron Age: the evidence of some horse-bridle-bits, *Ulster Journal of Archaeology* 18, 37-44.

Jope, E. M. 1958. A heavy bronze ring of Italian type from Co. Derry, *Ulster Journal of Archaeology* 21, 14-16.

Jope, E. M. 1958a. The beginnings of La Tène ornamental style in the British Isles, in S. S. Frere (ed.), *Problems of the Iron Age in Southern Britain,* 69-83. London.

Jope, E. M. 1962. Iron Age brooches in Ireland: a summary, *Ulster Journal of Archaeology* 24-25, 25-38.

Jope, E. M. 1971. Review of J. V. S. Megaw, *Art of the European Iron Age. A study of the elusive image* (1970), *Ulster Journal of Archaeology* 34, 115-119.

Jope, E. M. 1975. The style of the Broighter collar and its significance, *Irish Archaeological Research Forum* 2, no. 2, 24-26.

Jope, E. M. and Wilson, B. C. S. 1957. A Burial Group of the First Century A.D. near Donaghadee, Co. Down, *Ulster Journal of Archaeology* 20, 73-95.

Jope, E. M. and Wilson, B. C. S. 1957a. The Decorated Cast Bronze Disc from the River Bann near Coleraine, *Ulster Journal of Archaeology* 20, 96-102.

Jope, E. M. et al. 1966. *An Archaeological Survey of County Down.* Belfast.

Jørgensen, L. B. 1992. *North European Textiles until AD 1000.* Aarhus.

Kaul, F. 1995. Ships on Bronzes, in O. Crumlin-Pedersen and B. M. Thye (eds), *The Ship as Symbol in Prehistoric and Medieval Scandinavia,* 59-70. Copenhagen.

Kavanagh, R. 1973. The Encrusted Urn in Ireland, *Proceedings of the Royal Irish Academy* 73C, 507-617.

Kavanagh, R. 1976. Collared and cordoned cinerary urns in Ireland, *Proceedings of the Royal Irish Academy* 76C, 293-403.

Kavanagh, R. 1977. Pygmy cups in Ireland, *Journal of the Royal Society of Antiquaries of Ireland* 107, 61-95.

Kavanagh, R. 1991. A Reconsideration of Razors in the Irish Earlier Bronze Age, *Journal of the Royal Society of Antiquaries of Ireland* 121, 77-104.

Kavanagh, R. 1992. Sir William Wilde, M.D., F.R.C.S.I. 1815-1876, *Co. Roscommon Historical and Archaeological Society Journal* 4, 34-38.

Keeley, V. 1996. Ballydavis Early Iron Age Complex, in I. Bennett (ed.), *Excavations 1995,* 51-52. Bray.

Keeling, D. 1983. A Group of Tumuli and a Hill-Fort near Naul, County Dublin, *Journal of the Royal Society of Antiquaries of Ireland* 113, 67-74.

Keeling, D. and Keeley, V. 1994. Excavation of a Flint Scatter on Paddy's Hill (Robswalls), Malahide, Co. Dublin, *Proceedings of the Royal Irish Academy* 94C, 1-23.

Kelly, D. 1985. A possible wrist-bracer from County Tyrone, *Journal of the Royal Society of Antiquaries in Ireland* 115, 162.

Kelly, E. P. 1974. Aughinish Island, in T. G. Delaney (ed.), *Excavations 1974,* 20-21. Belfast.

Kelly, E. P. 1984. A prehistoric amber find from Ballylin, Co. Offaly, *Éile. Journal of the Roscrea Heritage Society* 2, 67-86.

Kelly, E. P. 1985. A bronze bracelet from Grangeford, County Carlow, *Journal of the Royal Society of Antiquaries of Ireland* 115, 158-159.

Kelly, E. P. 1988. Betaghstown Iron Age Cemetery, in Excavations Bulletin 1977-1979, *The Journal of Irish Archaeology* 4, 75.

Kelly, E. P. 1991. Observations on Irish Lake Dwellings, in C. Karkov and R. Farrell (eds), *Studies in Insular Art and Archaeology, American Early Medieval Studies 1,* 81-98. Oxford, Ohio.

Kelly, E. P. 1993. *Early Celtic Art in Ireland.* Dublin.

Kelly, S. 1995. Artefact decomposition in peatlands, *Irish Archaeological Wetland Unit Transactions* 4, 141-154. Dublin.

Kilbride-Jones, H. E. 1939. The excavation of a composite tumulus at Drimnagh, Co. Dublin, *Journal of the Royal Society of Antiquaries of Ireland* 69, 190-220.

Kilbride-Jones, H. E. 1951. Double Horned Cairn at Cohaw, County Cavan, *Proceedings of the Royal Irish Academy* 54 C, 75-88.

Kilbride-Jones, H. E. 1954. The excavation of an unrecorded megalithic tomb on Kilmashogue Mountain, Co. Dublin, *Proceedings of the Royal Irish Academy* 56C, 461-79.

Killeen, J. F. 1976. Ireland in the Greek and Roman Writers, in Colloquium on Hiberno-Roman Relations and Material Remains, *Proceedings of the Royal Irish Academy* 76C, 207-215.

Kinnes, I. A. 1988. The Cattleship Potemkin: Reflections on the First Neolithic in Britain, in J. C. Barrett and I. A. Kinnes (eds), *The Archaeology of Context in the Neolithic and Bronze Age: Recent Trends,* 2-8. Sheffield.

Kirk, S. M. 1974. High altitude cereal growing in County Down, Northern Ireland? A note, *Ulster Journal of Archaeology* 36-37, 99-100.

Knight, R. W., Browne, C. and L. V. Grinsell. 1972. Prehistoric Skeletons from Tormarton, *Transactions of the Bristol and Gloucestershire Archaeological Society* 91, 14-17.

Knowles, W. J. 1886. A flint arrowhead with portion of shaft ..., *Journal of the Royal Society of Antiquaries of Ireland* 17, 126-128.

Knowles, W. J. 1909. On the mounting of leaf-shaped arrowheads of flint, *Proceedings of the Society of Antiquaries of Scotland* 43, 278-283.

Koch, J. T. 1986. New thoughts on *Albion, Ierne,* and the Pretanic Isles, *Proceedings of the Harvard Celtic Colloquium* 6, 1-28.

Koch, J. T. 1991. *Ériu, Alba* and *Letha:* When was a language ancestral to Gaelic first spoken in Ireland?, *Emania* 9, 17-27.

Koch, J. T. 1994. Windows on the Iron Age: 1964-1994, in J. P. Mallory and G. Stockman (eds), *Ulidia. Proceedings of the First International Conference on the Ulster Cycle of Tales,* 229-242. Belfast.

Kristiansen, K. 1984. Ideology and material culture: an archaeological perspective, in M. Spriggs (ed.), *Marxist Perspectives in Archaeology,* 72-100. Cambridge.

Kristiansen, K. 1987. From stone to bronze – the evolution of social complexity in Northern Europe 2300-1200 BC, in E. M. Brumfiel and T. K. Earle (eds), *Specialization, Exchange, and Complex Societies,* 30-51. Cambridge.

Kruta, V. and Lessing, E. 1978. *Les Celtes.* Paris.

Kvamme, K. L. 1996. A Proton Magnetometry Survey at Navan Fort, *Emania* 14, 83-88.

Lacy, B. 1983. *Archaeological Survey of County Donegal.* Lifford.

Laing, L. 1985. The Romanization of Ireland in the fifth century, *Peritia* 4, 261-278.

Lang, J., Meeks, N. D. and McIntyre, I. 1980. The metallurgical examination of a Bronze Age torc from Shropshire, *Historical Metallurgy* 14, 17-20.

Lanigan Wood, H. and Verling, E. 1995. Stone Sculpture in Donegal, in W. Nolan, L. Ronayne and M. Dunlevy (eds), *Donegal: History and Society. Interdisciplinary Essays on the History of an Irish County,* 51-83. Dublin.

Lanting, J. N. and Brindley, A. L. 1996. Irish Logboats and their European Context, *The Journal of Irish Archaeology* 7, 85-95.

Lanting, J. N. and Van der Waals, J. D. 1972. British Beakers as seen from the Continent: a review article, *Helinium* 12, 20-46.

Lanting, J. N., Brindley, A. L., Buckley, V. and Condit, T. 1991. Preliminary Carbon 14 Dates from the Doon of Drumsna, *Emania* 9, 66.

Lavelle, D. 1994. *An Archaeological Survey of Ballinrobe and district including Lough Mask and Lough Carra.* Castlebar.

Lawless, C. 1990. A Fulacht Fiadh Bronze Age Cooking Experiment at Turlough, Castlebar, *Cathair na Mart. Journal of the Westport Historical Society* 10, 1-10.

Lawlor, H. C. 1915. Investigation of the Cairne Grannia Cromlech near Mallusk, Co. Antrim, *Proceedings of the Royal Irish Academy* 32C, 239-48.

Leask, H. G. and Price, L. 1936. The Labbacallee Megalith, Co. Cork, *Proceedings of the Royal Irish Academy* 43C, 77-101.

Leeds, E. T. 1930. A Bronze Cauldron from the River Cherwell, Oxfordshire, with notes on cauldrons and other bronze vessels of allied types, *Archaeologia* 80, 1-36.

Leerssen, J. 1996. *Remembrance and Imagination. Patterns in the Historical and Literary Representation of Ireland in the Nineteenth Century.* Cork.

Lewis-Williams, J. D. and Dowson, T. A. 1993. On Vision and Power in the Neolithic: Evidence from the Decorated Monuments, *Current Anthropology* 34, 55-65.

Liversage, G. D. 1957. An Object of Giant Deer Antler, *Journal of the Royal Society of Antiquaries in Ireland* 87, 169-171.

Liversage, G. D. 1958. An Island Site at Lough Gur, *Journal of the Royal Society of Antiquaries of Ireland* 88, 67-81.

Liversage, G. D. 1960. A Neolithic Site at Townleyhall, Co. Louth, *Journal of the Royal Society of Antiquaries of Ireland* 90, 49-60.

Liversage, G. D. 1968. Excavations at Dalkey Island, Co. Dublin, 1956-1959, *Proceedings of the Royal Irish Academy* 60C, 53-233.

Lohan, M. 1993. Moytura Conga: A Mythical and Ritual Landscape, *Cathair na Mart. Journal of the Westport Historical Society* 13, 16-31.

Longworth, I. H. 1984. *Collared Urns of the Bronze Age in Great Britain and Ireland.* Cambridge.

Longworth, I. H. 1985. *Prehistoric Britain.* London.

Lowery, P. R., Savage, R. D. A. and Wilkins, R. L. 1971. Scriber, Graver, Scorper: notes on Experiments in Bronzeworking Technique, *Proceedings of the Prehistoric Society* 37, 167-182.

Lucas, A. T. 1950. Neolithic burial at Norrismount, Co. Wexford, *Journal of the Royal Society of Antiquaries of Ireland* 80, 155-157.

Lucas, A. T. 1960. National Museum of Ireland: Archaeological Acquisitions in the Year 1958, *Journal of the Royal Society of Antiquaries of Ireland* 90, 1-40.

Lucas, A. T. 1961. National Museum of Ireland: Archaeological Acquisitions in the Year 1959, *Journal of the Royal Society of Antiquaries of Ireland* 91, 43-107.

Lucas, A. T. 1964. COWA Survey, British Isles, *Council for Old World Archaeology, Surveys and Bibliographies,* Area 1, no. III, 1964.

Lucas, A. T. 1964a. National Museum of Ireland: Archaeological Acquisitions in the Year 1962, *Journal of the Royal Society of Antiquaries of Ireland* 94, 85-104.

Lucas, A. T. 1965. Washing and Bathing in Ancient Ireland, *Journal of the Royal Society of Antiquaries of Ireland* 95, 65-114.

Lucas, A. T. 1966. National Museum of Ireland: Archaeological Acquisitions in the Year 1963, *Journal of the Royal Society of Antiquaries of Ireland* 96, 7-27.

Lucas, A. T. 1967. National Museum of Ireland: Archaeological Acquisitions in the Year 1964, *Journal of the Royal Society of Antiquaries of Ireland* 97, 1-28.

Lucas, A. T. 1968. National Museum of Ireland: Archaeological Acquisitions in the Year 1965, *Journal of the Royal Society of Antiquaries of Ireland* 98, 93-159.

Lucas, A. T. 1970. National Museum of Ireland: Archaeological Acquisitions in the Year 1967, *Journal of the Royal Society of Antiquaries of Ireland* 100, 145-166.

Lucas, A. T. 1971. National Museum of Ireland: Archaeological Acquisitions in the Year 1968, *Journal of the Royal Society of Antiquaries of Ireland* 101, 184-244.

Lucas, A. T. 1972. Prehistoric block-wheels from Doogarymore, Co. Roscommon, and Timahoe East, Co. Kildare, *Journal of the Royal Society of Antiquaries of Ireland* 102, 19-48.

Lynch, A. 1981. *Man and Environment in South-West Ireland, British Archaeological Reports* 85. Oxford.

Lynch, A. 1981a. Astronomical Alignment or Megalithic Muddle?, in D. Ó Corráin (ed.) *Irish Antiquity. Essays and Studies presented to Professor M. J. O'Kelly,* 23-27. Cork.

Lynch, A. 1982. Astronomy and stone alignments in S. W. Ireland, in D. Heggie (ed.), *Archaeoastronomy in the Old World,* 205-213. Cambridge.

Lynch, A. 1988. Poulnabrone – a stone in time, *Archaeology Ireland* 2, 105-7.

Lynch, A. and Ó Donnabháin, B. 1994. Poulnabrone, Co. Clare, *The Other Clare* 18, 5-7.

Lynch, F. 1979. Ring Cairns in Britain and Ireland: their design and purpose, *Ulster Journal of Archaeology* 42, 1-19.

Lynch, F. 1991. *Prehistoric Anglesea.* Llangefni.

Lynn, C. J. 1974. The Excavation of a Ring-cairn in Carnkenny Townland, Co. Tyrone, *Ulster Journal of Archaeology* 36-37, 17-31.

Lynn, C. J. 1977. Trial Excavations at the King's Stables, Tray Townland, Co. Armagh, *Ulster Journal of Archaeology* 40, 42-62.

Lynn, C. J. 1982. The Dorsey and other linear earthworks, in B. G. Scott (ed.), *Studies on Early Ireland. Essays in honour of M. V. Duignan,* 121-128. Belfast.

Lynn, C. J. 1983. Some 'Early' Ring-forts and Crannogs, *The Journal of Irish Archaeology* 1, 47-58.

Lynn, C. J. 1983a. Two Raths at Ballyhenry, County Antrim, *Ulster Journal of Archaeology* 46, 67-91.

Lynn, C. J. 1986. Navan Fort: A Draft Summary of D. M. Waterman's Excavations, *Emania* 1, 11-19.

Lynn, C. J. 1988. Armagh in 3000 BC, in A. Hamlin and C. Lynn (eds), *Pieces of the Past,* 8-10. Belfast.

Lynn, C. J. 1989. An Interpretation of 'The Dorsey', *Emania* 6, 5-14.

Lynn, C. J. 1989a. A Bibliography of Northern Linear Earthworks, *Emania* 6, 18-21.

Lynn, C. J. 1989b. Linear Earthworks in Drumellier, Co. Down, and Goragh, Co. Armagh, *Emania* 6, 15-16.

Lynn, C. J. 1991. Knockaulin (Dún Ailinne) and Navan: Some Architectural Comparisons, *Emania* 8, 51-56.

Lynn, C. J. 1992. The Iron Age Mound in Navan Fort: A Physical Realization of Celtic Religious Beliefs?, *Emania* 10, 33-57.

Lynn, C. J. 1992a. Excavations at the Dorsey, County Armagh, 1977, *Ulster Journal of Archaeology* 54-55, 61-77.

Lynn, C. J. 1993. Navan Fort – home of gods and goddesses?, *Archaeology Ireland* 7, no. 1, 17-21.

Lynn, C. J. 1993a. House-urns in Ireland?, *Ulster Journal of Archaeology* 56, 70-77.

Lynn, C. J. 1994. Hostels, Heroes and Tales: Further Thoughts on the Navan Mound, *Emania* 12, 5-20.

Lynn, C. J. 1996. That Mound Again: the Navan Excavations Revisited, *Emania* 15, 5-10.

Lynn, C. J. 1997. *Excavations at Navan Fort 1961-71 by D. M. Waterman.* Belfast.

Macalister, R. A. S. 1928. *The Archaeology of Ireland* (First edition). Dublin.

Macalister, R. A. S. 1949. *The Archaeology of Ireland* (Second edition). Dublin.

Macalister, R. A. S. and Praeger, R. Ll. 1929. Report on the Excavation of Uisneach, *Proceedings of the Royal Irish Academy* 38C, 69-127.

Macalister, R. A. S., Armstrong, E. C. R. and Praeger, R. 1912. Report on the explorations of Bronze-Age Carns on Carrowkeel Mountain, Co. Sligo, *Proceedings of the Royal Irish Academy* 29C, 311-347.

Macalister, R. A. S., Armstrong, E. C. R. and Praeger, R. 1913. A Bronze Age Interment near Naas, *Proceedings of the Royal Irish Academy* 30C, 351-360.

MacCana, P. 1956. Aspects of the theme of king and goddess in Irish literature, *Etudes Celtiques* 7, 76ff.

MacDermott, M. 1949. Excavation of a Barrow in Cahercorney, Co. Limerick, *Journal of the Cork Historical and Archaeological Society* 54, 101-102.

MacDonagh, M. 1995. Copney stone circles, in I. Bennett (ed.), *Excavations 1994,* 81. Bray.

MacEoin, G. 1986. The Celticity of Celtic Ireland, in K. H. Schmidt (ed.), *Geschichte und Kultur der Kelten,* 161-174. Heidelberg.

MacLean, R. 1993. Eat your greens: an examination of the potential diet available in Ireland during the Mesolithic, *Ulster Journal of Archaeology* 56, 1-8.

Madden, A. C. 1968. Beaker pottery in Ireland, *Journal of the Kerry Archaeological and Historical Society* 1, 9-24.

Madden, A. C. 1969. The Beaker Wedge Tomb at Moytirra, Co. Sligo, *Journal of the Royal Society of Antiquaries of Ireland* 99, 151-159.

Magee, R. W. 1993. Faience Beads of the Irish Bronze Age, *Archeomaterials* 7, 115-125.

Mahr, A. 1930. A wooden idol from Ireland, *Antiquity* 4, 487.

Mahr, A. 1937. New Aspects and Problems in Irish Prehistory. Presidential Address for 1937, *Proceedings of the Prehistoric Society* 3, 261-436.

Mallory, J. P. 1982. The Sword of the Ulster Cycle, in B. G. Scott (ed.), *Studies on Early Ireland. Essays in honour of M. V. Duignan,* 99-114. Belfast.

Mallory, J. P. 1984. The Origins of the Irish, *The Journal of Irish Archaeology* 2, 65-69.

Mallory, J. P. 1984a. The Long Stone, Ballybeen, Dundonald, County Down, *Ulster Journal of Archaeology* 47, 1-4.

Mallory, J. P. [1985]. *Navan Fort. The Ancient Capital of Ulster.* Belfast.

Mallory, J. P. 1986. Donegore Hill, in C. Cotter (ed.), *Excavations 1985,* 11. Dublin.

Mallory, J. P. 1987. The Literary Topography of Emain Macha, *Emania* 2, 12-18.

Mallory, J. P. 1989. *In Search of the Indo-Europeans.* London.

Mallory, J. P. 1990. Trial Excavations at Tievebulliagh, Co. Antrim, *Ulster Journal of Archaeology* 53, 15-28.

Mallory, J. P. 1991. Excavations at Haughey's Fort: 1989-90, *Emania* 8, 10-26.

Mallory, J. P. 1991a. Two Perspectives on the Problem of Irish Origins, *Emania* 9, 53-58.

Mallory, J. P. 1992. Migration and Language Change, *Peregrinatio Gothica III. Universitetets Oldsaksamlings Skrifter, Ny rekke,* no. 14, 145-153.

Mallory, J. P. 1992a. The World of Cú Chulainn: the Archaeology of *Táin Bó Cúailnge,* in J. P. Mallory (ed.), *Aspects of the Táin,* 103-159. Belfast.

Mallory, J. P. 1992b. A Neolithic Settlement at Bay Farm II, Carnlough, Co. Antrim, *Ulster Journal of Archaeology* 54-55, 3-12.

Mallory, J. P. 1994. The Other Twin: Haughey's Fort, in J. P. Mallory and G. Stockman (eds), *Ulidia: Proceedings of the First International Conference on the Ulster Cycle of Tales,* 187-192. Belfast.

Mallory, J. P. 1995. Haughey's Fort and the Navan Complex in the Late Bronze Age, in J. Waddell and E. S. Twohig (eds), *Ireland in the Bronze Age. Proceedings of the Dublin Conference, April 1995,* 73-86. Dublin.

Mallory, J. P. and Baillie, M. G. L. 1988. *Tech ndaruch:* The Fall of the House of Oak, *Emania* 5, 27-33.

Mallory, J. P. and Hartwell, B. 1984. Donegore, *Current Archaeology* 92, 271-275.

Mallory, J. P. and McCormick, F. 1988. Excavations at Ballymulholland, Magilligan Foreland, Co. Londonderry, *Ulster Journal of Archaeology* 51, 103-114.

Mallory, J. P. and McNeill, T. E. 1991. *The Archaeology of Ulster from Colonization to Plantation.* Belfast.

Mallory, J. P., Moore, D. G. and Canning, L. J. 1996. Excavations at Haughey's Fort 1991 and 1995, *Emania* 14, 5-20.

Mallory, J. P. and Warner, R. B. 1988. The Date of Haughey's Fort, *Emania* 5, 36-40.

Mandal, S. 1996. Irish Stone Axes – rock and role of the petrologist, *Archaeology Ireland* 10, no. 4, 32-35.

Mandal, S. and Cooney, G. 1996. The Irish Stone Axe Project: a second petrological report, *The Journal of Irish Archaeology* 7, 41-64.

Mandal, S., Cooney, G., Grogan, E., O'Carroll, F. and Guinan, B. 1992. A review of the petrological techniques being utilised to identify, group and source Irish stone axes, *The Journal of Irish Archaeology* 6, 1-11.

Manning, C. 1984. Prehistoric sites in the neighbourhood of Ardcrony, *Éile. Journal of the Roscrea Heritage Society* 2, 43-55.

Manning, C. 1985. A Neolithic Burial Mound at Ashleypark, Co. Tipperary, *Proceedings of the Royal Irish Academy* 85C, 61-100.

Manning, C. 1986. Archaeological excavations of a succession of enclosures at Millockstown, Co. Louth, *Proceedings of the Royal Irish Academy* 86C, 135-181.

Manning, C. 1988. A Note on Sacred Trees, *Emania* 5, 34-35.

Manning, C. and Eogan, G. 1979. A Find of Gold Torcs from Coolmanagh, County Carlow, *Journal of the Royal Society of Antiquaries of Ireland* 109, 20-27.

Manning, W. and Saunders, C. 1972. A socketed axe from Maids Moreton, Bucks., with a note on the type, *The Antiquaries Journal* 52, 276-292.

Mattingly, H. and Pearce, J. 1937. The Coleraine Hoard, *Antiquity* 2, 39-45.

May, A. McL. 1942. Cornaclery Round Cairn, Townland of Ballydullaghan, County of Londonderry, *Journal of the Royal Society of Antiquaries of Ireland* 72, 81-97.

May, A. McL. 1953. Neolithic habitation site, stone circles and alignments at Beaghmore, Co. Tyrone, *Journal of the Royal Society of Antiquaries of Ireland* 83, 174-197.

May, A. McL. and Batty, J. 1948. The Sandhill Cultures of the River Bann Estuary, Co. Londonderry, *Journal of the Royal Society of Antiquaries of Ireland* 78, 130-156.

McCabe, J. 1973. Rathnarrow Barrow, in T. G. Delaney (ed.), *Excavations 1973*, 27. Belfast.

McCaffrey, P. 1955. The Dunkellin Barrow Group, *Journal of the Royal Society of Antiquaries of Ireland* 85, 218-225.

McCarthy, A. 1986. 'Poul Gorm', Glengarriff, in C. Cotter (ed.), *Excavations 1986*, 15. Dublin.

McCormick, F. 1986. Faunal Remains from Prehistoric Irish Burials, *The Journal of Irish Archaeology* 3, 37-48.

McCormick, F. 1991. The Dog in Prehistoric and Early Christian Ireland, *Archaeology Ireland* 5, no. 4, 7-9.

McCormick, F. 1992. Early Faunal Evidence for Dairying, *Oxford Journal of Archaeology* 11, 201-209.

McCormick, F. 1994. Faunal Remains from Navan and Other Late Prehistoric Sites in Ireland, in J. P. Mallory and G. Stockman (eds), *Ulidia: Proceedings of the First International Conference on the Ulster Cycle of Tales*, 181-186. Belfast.

McCormick, F. 1995. False Bay, Co. Galway, in the Bronze Age, *Archaeology Ireland* 9, no. 1, 12-13.

McCormick, F., Gibbons, M., McCormac, F. G. and Moore, J. 1996. Bronze Age to Medieval Shell Middens near Ballyconneely, Co. Galway, *The Journal of Irish Archaeology* 7, 77-84.

McDonald, M. 1986. Celtic Ethnic Kinship and the Problem of being English, *Current Anthropology* 27, 333-347.

McGrail, S. 1987. *Ancient Boats in North West Europe.* London.

McGrail, S. 1995. Celtic Seafaring and Transport, in M. Green (ed.), *The Celtic World*, 254-281. London.

McMann, J. 1993. *Loughcrew: The Cairns. A Guide to an Ancient Irish Landscape.* Oldcastle.

McMann, J. 1994. Forms of power: dimensions of an Irish megalithic landscape, *Antiquity* 68, 525-44.

McNeill, T. E. 1992. Excavations at Dunsilly, County Antrim, *Ulster Journal of Archaeology* 54-55, 78-112.

Meeks, N. D. and Varndell, G. L. 1994. Three Bronze Age torc fragments from Woodham Walter, Essex, *Essex Archaeology and History* 25, 1-2.

Megaw, B. R. S. and Hardy, E. M. 1938. British Decorated Axes and their Diffusion during the Earlier Part of the Bronze Age, *Proceedings of the Prehistoric Society* 4, 272-307.

Megaw, J. V. S. 1966. A 'Bull Cult' in Late Bronze Age Europe: a musical footnote, *Antiquity* 40, 56-58.

Megaw, J. V. S. 1970. *Art of the European Iron Age. A study of the elusive image.* Bath.

Megaw, J. V. S. and Megaw, M. R. 1995. The Prehistoric Celts: Identity and Contextuality, in M. Kuna and N. Venclová (eds), *Whither Archaeology? Papers in honour of Evȋen Neustupnȳ* , 230-245. Prague.

Megaw, J. V. S. and Megaw, M. R. 1996. Ancient Celts and modern ethnicity, *Antiquity* 70, 175-181.

Megaw, J. V. S., Megaw, M. R. and Trett, R. 1992. A Late Iron Age Cast Bronze Head probably from Chepstowe, *The Antiquaries Journal* 72, 54-75.

Megaw, R. and Megaw, V. 1989. *Celtic Art. From its beginnings to the Book of Kells.* London.

Meighan, I. G., Jamison, D. D., Logue, P. J. C., Mallory, J. P. and Simpson, D. D. A. 1993. Trace element and isotopic provenancing of North Antrim porcellanites: Portrush – Tievebulliagh – Brockley (Rathlin Island), *Ulster Journal of Archaeology* 56, 25-30.

Meinander, C. F. 1981. The concept of culture in European archaeological literature, in G. Daniel (ed.), *Towards a History of Archaeology*, 100-111. London.

Meyer, M. 1985. Hallstatt Imports in Britain, *University of London. Bulletin of the Institute of Archaeology* 21-22, 69-84.

Mitchell, G. F. 1947. An early kitchen-midden in County Louth, *County Louth Archaeological Journal* 11, 169-174.

Mitchell, G. F. 1949. Further early kitchen-middens in County Louth, *County Louth Archaeological Journal* 12, 14-20.

Mitchell, G. F. 1955. The Mesolithic site at Toome Bay, Co. Londonderry, *Ulster Journal of Archaeology* 18, 1-16.

Mitchell, G. F. 1956. Post-Boreal pollen diagrams from Irish raised bogs, *Proceedings of the Royal Irish Academy* 57B, 185-251.

Mitchell, G. F. 1956a. An early kitchen-midden at Sutton, Co. Dublin. *Journal of the Royal Society of Antiquaries of Ireland* 86, 1-26.

Mitchell, G. F. 1970. Some chronological implications of the Irish Mesolithic, *Ulster Journal of Archaeology* 33, 3-14.

Mitchell, G. F. 1971. The Larnian culture: a minimal view, *Proceedings of the Prehistoric Society* 37, 274-283.

Mitchell, G. F. 1972. Further excavation of the early kitchen-midden at Sutton, Co. Dublin, *Journal of the Royal Society of Antiquaries of Ireland* 102, 151-159.

Mitchell, G. F. 1972a. Some Ultimate Larnian sites at Lake Derravarragh, Co. Westmeath, *Journal of the Royal Society of Antiquaries of Ireland* 102, 160-173.

Mitchell, G. F. 1985. Antiquities, in T. Ó Raifeartaigh (ed.), *The Royal Irish Academy, a bicentennial history 1785-1985*, 93-165. Dublin.

Mitchell, G. F. 1989. *Man and Environment in Valencia Island.* Dublin.

Mitchell, G. F. 1990. *The way that I followed: a naturalist's journey around Ireland.* Dublin.

Mitchell, G. F. 1992. Notes on Some Non-Local Cobbles at the Entrance to the Passage-Graves at Newgrange and Knowth, County Meath, *Journal of the Royal Society of Antiquaries of Ireland* 122, 128-145.

Mitchell, G. F. and de G. Sieveking, G. 1972. Flint flake, probably of Palaeolithic age, from Mell townland, near Drogheda, Co. Louth, Ireland, *Journal of the Royal Society of Antiquaries of Ireland* 102, 174-177.

Mitchell, G. F. and Ó Ríordáin, S. P. 1942. Early Bronze Age pottery from Rockbarton Bog, Co. Limerick, *Proceedings of the Royal Irish Academy* 48C, 255-272.

Mitchell, G. F., O'Leary, M. and Raftery, J. 1941. On A Bronze Halberd from Co. Mayo and a Bronze Spearhead from Co. Westmeath, *Proceedings of the Royal Irish Academy* 46C, 287-298.

Mitchell, G. F. and Ryan, M. 1997. *Reading the Irish Landscape*. Dublin.

Mogey, J. M. 1941. The 'Druid Stone', Ballintoy, Co. Antrim, *Ulster Journal of Archaeology* 4, 49-56.

Mogey, J. M. 1949. Preliminary Report on Excavations in Mullaghmore td., Co. Down, *Ulster Journal of Archaeology* 12, 82-88.

Mogey, J. M. and Thompson, G. B. 1956. Excavation of Two Ring-Barrows in Mullaghmore Townland, Co. Down, *Ulster Journal of Archaeology* 19, 11-28.

Molleson, T. I. 1986. New radiocarbon dates for the occupation of Kilgreany Cave, County Waterford, *The Journal of Irish Archaeology* 3, 1-3.

Molloy, K. 1997. Prehistoric farming at Mooghaun – a new pollen diagram from Mooghaun Lough, *Archaeology Ireland* 11, no. 3, 22-26.

Molloy, K. and O'Connell, M. 1987. The nature of the vegetation changes at about 5000 B.P. with particular reference to the elm decline: fresh evidence from Connemara, western Ireland, *New Phytologist* 106, 203-220.

Molloy, K. and O'Connell, M. 1991. Palaeoecological investigations towards the reconstruction of woodland and land-use history at Lough Sheeauns, Connemara, western Ireland, *Review of Palaeobotany and Palynology* 67, 75-113.

Molloy, K. and O'Connell, M. 1993. Early land use and vegetation history at Derryinver Hill, Renvyle Peninsula, Co. Galway, Ireland, in F. M. Chambers (ed.), *Climate Change and Human Impact on the Landscape*, 185-283. London.

Molloy, K. and O'Connell, M. 1995. Palaeoecological investigations towards the reconstruction of environment and land-use changes during prehistory at Céide Fields, western Ireland, *Probleme der Küstenforschung im südlichen Nordseegebiet* 23, 187-225.

Moloney, A. 1993. *Excavations at Clonfinlough, Co. Offaly. Irish Archaeological Wetland Unit Transactions* 2. Dublin.

Monk, M. A. 1986. Evidence from macroscopic plant remains for crop husbandry in prehistoric and early historic Ireland: a review, *The Journal of Irish Archaeology* 3, 31-36.

Monk, M. A. 1993. People and Environment: In Search of the Farmers, in E. S. Twohig and M. Ronayne (eds), *Past Perceptions. The Prehistoric Archaeology of South-West Ireland*, 35-52. Cork.

Moore, M. J. 1987. *Archaeological Inventory of County Meath*. Dublin.

Moore, M. J. 1995. A Bronze Age settlement and ritual centre in the Monavullagh Mountains, County Waterford, Ireland, *Proceedings of the Prehistoric Society* 61, 191-243.

Moore, M. J. 1996. *Archaeological Inventory of County Wexford*. Dublin.

Mount, C. 1991. Early Bronze Age Burials – the Social Implications, *Archaeology Ireland* 5, no. 2, 21-23.

Mount, C. 1994. Aspects of Ritual Deposition in the Late Neolithic and Beaker Periods at Newgrange, Co. Meath, *Proceedings of the Prehistoric Society* 60, 433-443.

Mount, C. 1995. New Research on Irish Early Bronze Age Cemeteries, in J. Waddell and E. S. Twohig (eds), *Ireland in the Bronze Age. Proceedings of the Dublin Conference, April 1995*, 97-112. Dublin.

Mount, C. 1995a. The Environmental Siting of Early Bronze Age Burials in County Kildare, *Journal of the Co. Kildare Archaeological Society* 18, 117-128.

Mount, C. 1996. Rathdooney Beg Iron Age barrow cemetery, in I. Bennett (ed.), *Excavations 1995*, 78-79. Bray.

Mount, C. 1996a. The Environmental Siting of Neolithic and Bronze Age Monuments in the Bricklieve and Moytirra Uplands, Co. Sligo, *The Journal of Irish Archaeology* 7, 1-11.

Mount, C. 1997. Adolf Mahr's Excavations of an Early Bronze Age Cemetery at Keenoge, County Meath, *Proceedings of the Royal Irish Academy* 97C, 1-68.

Mount, C. and Hartnett, P. J. 1993. Early Bronze Age Cemetery at Edmondstown, County Dublin, *Proceedings of the Royal Irish Academy* 93C, 21-79.

Movius, H. L. 1935. Kilgreany Cave, Co. Waterford, *Journal of the Royal Society of Antiquaries of Ireland* 65, 254-296.

Movius, H. L. 1937. A Stone Age site at Glenarm, Co. Antrim, *Journal of the Royal Society of Antiquaries of Ireland* 67, 181-220.

Movius, H. L. 1940. An early postglacial archaeological site at Cushendun, Co. Antrim, *Proceedings of the Royal Irish Academy* 46C, 1-48.

Movius, H. L. 1940a. Report on a Stone Age excavation at Rough Island, Strangford Lough, Co. Down, *Journal of the Royal Society of Antiquaries of Ireland* 70, 111-142.

Movius, H. L. 1942. *The Irish Stone Age*. Cambridge.

Movius, H. L. 1953. Curran Point, Larne, Co. Antrim: the type-site of the Irish Mesolithic, *Proceedings of the Royal Irish Academy* 56C, 1-195.

Muckelroy, K. 1981. Middle Bronze Age trade between Britain and Europe: a maritime perspective, *Proceedings of the Prehistoric Society* 47, 275-297.

Müller-Karpe, H. 1956. Das Urnenfeldzeitliche Wagengrab von Hart a. d. Alz, *Bayerische Vorgeschichtsblätter* 21, 46-75.

Munro, R. 1890. *The Lake-Dwellings of Europe*. London.

Murphy, B. 1977. A handaxe from Dun Aenghus, Inishmore, Aran Islands, Co. Galway, *Proceedings of the Royal Irish Academy* 77C, 257-259.

Murphy, E. and McCormick, F. 1996. The Faunal Remains from the Inner Ditch of Haughey's Fort. Third Report: 1991 Excavation, *Emania* 14, 47-50.

Murray, J. 1994. Jade axes from Scotland: a commentary on the distribution and supplementary notes, *Proceedings of the Prehistoric Society* 60, 97-104.

Mytum, H. C. and Webster, C. J. 1989. A Survey of the Iron Age Enclosure and *Chevaux-de-Frise* at Carn Alw, Dyfed, *Proceedings of the Prehistoric Society* 55, 263-267.

Needham, S. 1979. The Extent of Foreign Influence on Early Bronze Age Axe Development in Southern Britain, in M. Ryan (ed.), *The Origins of Metallurgy in Atlantic Europe. Proceedings of the Fifth Atlantic Colloquium*, 265-293. Dublin.

Needham, S. 1979a. Two Recent Shield Finds and their Continental Parallels, *Proceedings of the Prehistoric Society* 45, 111-134.

Needham, S. 1979b. A Pair of Early Bronze Age Spearheads from Lightwater, Surrey, in C. B. Burgess and D. Coombs (eds), *Bronze Age Hoards, British Archaeological Reports* 67, 1-40. Oxford.

Needham, S. 1982. *The Ambleside Hoard. A discovery in the Royal Collections.* London.

Needham, S. 1988. Selective deposition in the British Early Bronze Age, *World Archaeology* 20, 229-248.

Needham, S. 1990. The Penard-Wilburton succession: new metalwork finds from Croxton (Norfolk) and Thirsk (Yorkshire), *The Antiquaries Journal* 70, 253-270.

Needham, S. 1993. A Bronze Age Goldworking Anvil from Lichfield, Staffordshire, *The Antiquaries Journal* 73, 125-132.

Needham, S. 1993a. The Beeston Castle Bronze Age metalwork and its significance, in P. Ellis (ed.), *Beeston Castle, Cheshire. A report on the excavations 1968-85 by Laurence Keen and Peter Hough*, 41-50. London.

Needham, S., Lawson, A. J. and Green, H. S. 1985. *British Bronze Age Metalwork. A1-6 Early Bronze Age Hoards.* London.

Neill, K. 1993. The Broighter Hoard, *Archaeology Ireland* 7, no. 2, 24-26.

Neill, M. 1996. Haughey's Fort Excavation 1991: Analysis of Wood Remains, *Emania* 14, 29-46.

Newman, C. 1993. The Tara Survey. Interim Report, *Discovery Programme Reports* 1, 69-89. Dublin.

Newman, C. 1993a. 'Sleeping in Elysium,' *Archaeology Ireland* 7, no. 3, 20-23.

Newman, C. 1994. Raffin Fort, in I. Bennett (ed.), *Excavations 1993,* 64-65. Bray.

Newman, C. 1995. The Tara Survey. Interim Report, *Discovery Programme Reports* 2, 62-67. Dublin.

Newman, C. 1997. *Tara, an archaeological survey, Discovery Programme Monograph* 2. Dublin.

Norman, E. R. and St Joseph, J. K. 1969. *The Early Development of Irish Society. The Evidence of Aerial Photography.* Cambridge.

Northover, J. P. 1980. The Analysis of Welsh Bronze Age Metalwork, in H. N. Savory, *Guide Catalogue of the Bronze Age Collections, National Museum of Wales*, 229-243. Cardiff.

Northover, J. P. 1982. The exploration of the long-distance movement of bronze in Bronze and Early Iron Age Europe, *Bulletin of the Institute of Archaeology* 19, 45-72.

Northover, J. P. 1989. The Gold Torc from Saint Helier, Jersey, *Annual Bulletin of the Société Jersiaise* 25, 112-137.

O'Brien, E. 1990. Iron Age Burial Practices in Leinster: Continuity and Change, *Emania* 7, 37-42.

O'Brien, E. 1992. Pagan and Christian Burial in Ireland during the first Millennium AD: Continuity and Change, in N. Edwards and A. Lane (eds), *The Early Church in Wales and the West*, 130-137. Oxford.

O'Brien, W. 1990. Prehistoric Copper Mining in South-West Ireland: The Mount Gabriel-Type Mines, *Proceedings of the Prehistoric Society* 56, 269-290.

O'Brien. W. 1992. Boulder-burials: a Later Bronze Age megalith tradition in south-west Ireland, *Journal of the Cork Historical and Archaeological Society* 97, 11-35.

O'Brien, W. 1993. Aspects of Wedge Tomb Chronology, in E. S. Twohig and M. Ronayne (eds), *Past Perceptions: The Prehistoric Archaeology of South-West Ireland*, 63-74. Cork.

O'Brien, W. 1993a. Altar Tomb and the Prehistory of Mizen, *Mizen Journal* 1, 19-26.

O'Brien, W. 1993b. Aspects of Wedge Tomb Chronology, in E. S. Twohig and M. Ronayne (eds), *Past Perceptions: The Prehistoric Archaeology of South-West Ireland*, 63-74. Cork.

O'Brien, W. 1994. *Mount Gabriel. Bronze Age Mining in Ireland.* Galway.

O'Brien, W. 1994a. Ross Island Bronze Age copper mines, in I. Bennett (ed.), *Excavations 1993,* 46. Bray.

O'Brien, W. 1995. Ross Island early copper mine, in I. Bennett (ed.), *Excavations 1994,* 47. Bray.

O'Brien, W. 1995a. Ross Island and the Origins of Irish-British Metallurgy, in J. Waddell and E. S. Twohig (eds), *Ireland in the Bronze Age. Proceedings of the Dublin Conference, April 1995,* 38-48. Dublin.

O'Brien, W. 1996. *Bronze Age Copper Mining in Britain and Ireland.* Princes Risborough.

O'Brien, W. 1996a. Ross Island Copper Mine, in I. Bennett (ed.), *Excavations 1995,* 42. Bray.

O'Brien, W, Northover, P. and Cameron, E. 1990. An Early Bronze Age Metal Hoard from a Wedge Tomb at Toormore, Co. Cork, *The Journal of Irish Archaeology* 5, 9-18.

O'Carroll, F. and Ryan, M. 1992. A Late Bronze Age Hoard from Enagh East, Co. Clare, *North Munster Antiquarian Journal* 34, 3-12.

O'Connell, M. 1980. Pollen analysis of fen peat from a Mesolithic site at Lough Boora, Co. Offaly, Ireland, *Journal of Life Sciences (Royal Dublin Society)* 2, 45-49.

O'Connell, M. 1986. Reconstruction of local landscape development in the post-Atlantic based on palaeoecological investigations at Carrownaglogh prehistoric field system, County Mayo, Ireland, *Review of Palaeobotany and Palynology* 49, 117-176.

O'Connell, M. 1987. Early cereal-type pollen records from Connemara, western Ireland and their possible significance, *Pollen et Spores* 29, 207-224.

O'Connell, M. 1990. Origins of Irish Lowland Blanket Bog, in G. J. Doyle (ed.), *Ecology and Conservation of Irish Peatlands,* 49-71. Dublin.

O'Connell, M. 1994. *Connemara. Vegetation and Land Use since the last Ice Age.* Dublin.

O'Connell, Martin. 1986. *Petters Sports Field Egham. Excavation of a Late Bronze Age/Early Iron Age Site.* Guildford.

O'Connor, B. 1975. Six prehistoric phalerae in the London Museum and a discussion of other phalerae from the British Isles, *The Antiquaries Journal* 55, 215-226.

O'Connor, B. 1980. *Cross-Channel Relations in the Late Bronze Age, British Archaeological Reports, International Series* 91. Oxford.

O'Curry, E. 1873. *On the Manners and Customs of the Ancient Irish. A Series of Lectures delivered by the late Eugene O'Curry, M.R.I.A. Edited with an introduction, appendixes, etc., by W. K. O'Sullivan, Ph.D.* Dublin.

Ó Donnabháin, B. and Brindley, A. L. 1990. The Status of Children in a Sample of Bronze Age Burials containing Pygmy Cups, *The Journal of Irish Archaeology* 5, 19-24.

O'Donovan, P. 1987. An Claidh Ruadh. A travelling earthwork from Kerry, *Emania* 3, 20-21.

O'Donovan, P. F. 1995. *Archaeological Inventory of County Cavan.* Dublin.

Ó Drisceoil, D. 1988. Burnt Mounds: cooking or bathing?, *Antiquity* 62, 671-680.

Ó Drisceoil, D. 1990. Fulachta fiadh: the value of early Irish literature, in V. Buckley (ed.), *Burnt Offerings. International Contributions to Burnt Mound Archaeology,* 157-164. Dublin.

Ó Drisceoil, D. 1991. Fulachta fiadh: a general statement, *North Munster Antiquarian Journal* 33, 3-6.

Ó Duibhir, S. 1988. Music of the Late Bronze Age in Ireland, *Archaeology Ireland* 2, 135-136.

Ó Duibhir, S. 1994. *Coirn na hÉireann. Horns of ancient Ireland.* [Text and a compact disc recorded in the National Museum of Ireland]. Dublin.

O'Flaherty, B. 1987. A Linear Earthwork at Shankill, Co. Kilkenny, in R. M. Cleary, M. F. Hurley and E. A. Twohig (eds), *Archaeological Excavations on the Cork-Dublin Gas Pipeline (1981-82),* 53-54. Cork.

O'Flaherty, R. 1995. An Analysis of Irish Early Bronze Age Hoards containing copper or bronze objects, *Journal of the Royal Society of Antiquaries of Ireland* 125, 10-45.

O'Flaherty, R. 1996. The Crane-Bag of the Fianna, *Archaeology Ireland* 10, no. 1, 27-29.

Ó Floinn, R. 1992. A Neolithic Cave Burial in Limerick, *Archaeology Ireland* 6, no. 2, 19-21.

Ó Floinn, R. 1993. Annagh Neolithic cave burial, in I. Bennett (ed.), *Excavations 1992,* 41-42. Bray.

Ó Floinn, R. 1995. Recent Research into Irish Bog Bodies, in R. C. Turner and R. G. Scaife (eds), *Bog Bodies. New Discoveries and New Perspectives,* 137-145. London.

O'Hara, B. 1991. *The Archaeological Heritage of Killasser, Co. Mayo.* Galway.

Ó hEailidhe, P. 1992. 'The Monk's Boat – a Roman-period relic from Lough Lene, Co. Westmeath, Eire, *The International Journal of Nautical Archaeology* 21, 185-190.

Ó h-Iceadha, G. 1946. The Moylisha Megalith, Co. Wicklow, *Journal of the Royal Society of Antiquaries of Ireland* 76, 119-128.

Ó hUiginn, R. 1988. Crúachu, Connachta, and the Ulster Cycle, *Emania* 5, 19-23.

O'Kelly, C. 1971. *Illustrated Guide to Newgrange.* Wexford.

O'Kelly, M. J. 1946. Excavation of a cist grave at Ballynahow, Fermoy, Co. Cork, *Journal of Cork Historical and Archaeological Society* 51, 78-84.

O'Kelly, M. J. 1951. An Early Bronze Age Ringfort at Carrigillihy, Co. Cork, *Journal of the Cork Historical and Archaeological Society* 56, 69-86.

O'Kelly, M. J. 1952. Excavation of a Cairn at Moneen, Co. Cork, *Proceedings of the Royal Irish Academy* 54C, 79-93.

O'Kelly, M. J. 1954. Excavations and Experiments in Ancient Irish Cooking-places, *Journal of the Royal Society of Antiquaries of Ireland* 84, 105-155.

O'Kelly, M. J. 1956. Review of E. E. Evans, *Lyles Hill. A Late Neolithic Site in Co. Antrim,* Belfast, 1953, *Journal of the Royal Society of Antiquaries of Ireland* 86, 113-115.

O'Kelly, M. J. 1958. A Horned Cairn at Shanballyedmond, Co. Tipperary, *Journal of the Cork Historical and Archaeological Society* 63, 37-72.

O'Kelly, M. J. 1958b. A Wedge-shaped Gallery Grave at Island, Co. Cork, *Journal of the Royal Society of Antiquaries of Ireland* 88, 1-23.

O'Kelly, M. J. 1960. A Wedge-shaped Gallery Grave at Baurnadomeeny, Co. Tipperary, *Journal of the Cork Historical and Archaeological Society* 65, 85-115.

O'Kelly, M. J. 1961. The Cork Horns, the Petrie Crown and the Bann Disc, *Journal of the Cork Historical and Archaeological Society* 66, 1-12.

O'Kelly, M. J. 1970. An Axe Mould from Lyre, Co. Cork, *Journal of Cork Historical and Archaeological Society* 75, 121-159.

O'Kelly, M. J. 1982. *Newgrange. Archaeology, Art and Legend.* London.

O'Kelly, M. J. 1983. The Megalithic Tombs of Ireland, in Renfrew, C. (ed.), *The Megalithic Monuments of Western Europe,* 113-126. London.

O'Kelly, M. J. 1989. *Early Ireland. An Introduction to Irish Prehistory.* Cambridge.

O'Kelly, M. J. and O'Kelly, C. 1983. The Tumulus of Dowth, County Meath, *Proceedings of the Royal Irish Academy* 83C, 135-190.

O'Kelly, M. J. and Shee, E. 1974. Bronze Age Burials at Coolnahane and Ballinvoher, Co. Cork, *Journal of Cork Historical and Archaeological Society* 80, 71-85.

O'Kelly, M. J. and Shell, C. A. 1979. Stone Objects and a Bronze Axe from Newgrange, Co. Meath, in M. Ryan (ed.), *The Origins of Metallurgy in Atlantic Europe. Proceedings of the Fifth Atlantic Colloquium,* 127-144. Dublin.

O'Kelly, M. J., Cleary, R. M. and Lehane, D. 1983. *Newgrange, Co. Meath, Ireland. The Late Neolithic/Beaker Period Settlement,* British Archaeological Reports International Series 190. Oxford.

O'Kelly, M. J., Lynch, F. and O'Kelly, C. 1978. Three Passage-Graves at Newgrange, Co. Meath, *Proceedings of the Royal Irish Academy* 78 C, 249-352.

O'Leary, E. 1902. Notes on the collection of Irish antiquities lately at Edenderry, *Journal of the Kildare Archaeological Society* 3, 325-333.

O'Leary, P. and Shee Twohig, E. 1993. A Possible Iron Age Pillar Stone on Cape Clear, Co. Cork, *Journal of the Cork Historical and Archaeological Society* 98, 133-140.

Ó Nualláin, S. 1968. A Ruined Megalithic Cemetery in Co. Donegal and its context in the Irish passage grave series, *Journal of the Royal Society of Antiquaries of Ireland* 98, 1-29.

Ó Nualláin, S. 1972. A Neolithic House at Ballyglass, near Ballycastle, Co. Mayo, *Journal of the Royal Society of Antiquaries of Ireland* 102, 49-57.

Ó Nualláin, S. 1972a. Ballyglass Neolithic settlement, in T. G. Delaney (ed.), *Excavations 1972*, 20-22. Belfast.

Ó Nualláin, S. 1975. The Stone Circle Complex of Cork and Kerry, *Journal of the Royal Society of Antiquaries of Ireland* 105, 83-131.

Ó Nualláin, S. 1976. The central court tombs of the north-west of Ireland, *Journal of the Royal Society of Antiquaries of Ireland* 106, 92-117.

Ó Nualláin, S. 1977. A Dual Court-tomb at Garran townland, County Monaghan, *Journal of the Royal Society of Antiquaries of Ireland* 107, 52-60.

Ó Nualláin, S. 1978. Boulder-burials, *Proceedings of the Royal Irish Academy* 78C, 75-114.

Ó Nualláin, S. 1983. Irish Portal Tombs: Topography, Siting and Distribution. *Journal of the Royal Society of Antiquaries of Ireland* 113, 75-105.

Ó Nualláin, S. 1984. A survey of stone circles in Cork and Kerry, *Proceedings of the Royal Irish Academy* 84C, 1-77.

Ó Nualláin, S. 1984a. Grouped Standing Stones, Radial-Stone Cairns and Enclosures in the South of Ireland, *Journal of the Royal Society of Antiquaries of Ireland* 114, 63-79.

Ó Nualláin, S. 1989. *Survey of the Megalithic Tombs of Ireland. Volume V. County Sligo*. Dublin.

Ó Nualláin, S. 1994. Stone rows in the south of Ireland, *Proceedings of the Royal Irish Academy* 88C, 179-256.

Ó Nualláin, S. 1995. *Stone Circles in Ireland*. Dublin.

Ó Nualláin, S. and Walsh, P. 1986. A Reconsideration of the Tramore Passage-Tombs, *Proceedings of the Prehistoric Society* 52, 25-29.

O'Rahilly, T. F. 1946. *Early Irish History and Mythology*. Dublin.

Ó Ríordáin, B. 1967. Cordoned Urn Burial at Laheen, Co. Donegal, *Journal of the Royal Society of Antiquaries of Ireland* 97, 39-44.

Ó Ríordáin, B. and Waddell, J. 1993. *The Funerary Bowls and Vases of the Irish Bronze Age*. Galway.

Ó Ríordáin, S. P. 1936. Excavations at Lissard, Co. Limerick, and other sites in the locality, *Journal of the Royal Society of Antiquaries of Ireland* 66, 173-185.

Ó Ríordáin, S. P. 1939. Excavation of a stone circle and cairn at Kealkil, Co. Cork, *Journal of the Cork Historical and Archaeological Society* 44, 46-49.

Ó Ríordáin, S. P. 1946. Prehistory in Ireland, 1937-46, *Proceedings of the Prehistoric Society* 12, 142-171.

Ó Ríordáin, S. P. 1947. Roman Material in Ireland, *Proceedings of the Royal Irish Academy* 51C, 35-82.

Ó Ríordáin, S. P. 1947a. Excavation of a Barrow at Rathjordan, Co. Limerick, *Journal of the Cork Historical and Archaeological Society* 52, 1-4.

Ó Ríordáin, S. P. 1948. Further Barrows at Rathjordan, Co. Limerick, *Journal of the Cork Historical and Archaeological Society* 53, 19-31.

Ó Ríordáin, S. P. 1950. Excavation of some earthworks on the Curragh, Co. Kildare, *Proceedings of the Royal Irish Academy* 53C, 249-277.

Ó Ríordáin, S. P. 1951. Lough Gur Excavations: the great stone circle (B) in Grange townland, *Proceedings of the Royal Irish Academy* 54C, 37-74.

Ó Ríordáin, S. P. 1954. Lough Gur Excavations: Neolithic and Bronze Age Houses on Knockadoon, *Proceedings of the Royal Irish Academy* 56C, 297-459.

Ó Ríordáin, S. P. 1955. A Burial with Faience Beads at Tara, *Proceedings of the Prehistoric Society* 21, 163-173.

Ó Ríordáin, S. P. and De Valera, R. 1952. Excavation of a megalithic tomb at Ballyedmonduff, Co. Dublin, *Proceedings of the Royal Irish Academy* 55C, 61-81.

Ó Ríordáin, S. P. and G. Ó h-Iceadha. 1955. Lough Gur Excavations: the megalithic tomb, *Journal of the Royal Society of Antiquaries of Ireland* 85, 34-50.

O'Shaughnessy, J. 1990. Leckaneen Ringbarrow, in I. Bennett (ed.), *Excavations 1990*, 17.

O'Sullivan, A. 1996. Later Bronze Age intertidal discoveries on North Munster estuaries, *Discovery Programme Reports* 4, 63-71.

O'Sullivan, A. 1996a. Neolithic, Bronze Age and Iron Age woodworking techniques, in B. Raftery, *Trackway Excavations in the Mountdillon Bogs, Co. Longford, 1985-1991. Irish Archaeological Wetland Unit Transactions* 3, 291-342. Dublin.

O'Sullivan, Ann, and Sheehan, J. 1993. Prospection and Outlook: Aspects of Rock Art on the Iveragh Peninsula, Co. Kerry, in E. S. Twohig and M. Ronayne (eds), *Past Perceptions. The Prehistoric Archaeology of South-West Ireland*, 75-84. Cork.

O'Sullivan, Ann, and Sheehan, J. 1996. *The Iveragh Peninsula. An Archaeological Survey of South Kerry*. Cork.

O'Sullivan, M. 1986. Approaches to Passage Tomb Art, *Journal of the Royal Society of Antiquaries of Ireland* 116, 68-83.

O'Sullivan, M. 1993. *Megalithic Art in Ireland*. Dublin.

O'Sullivan, M. 1993a. Recent Investigations at Knockroe Passage Tomb, *Journal of the Royal Society of Antiquaries of Ireland* 123, 5-18.

O'Sullivan, M. 1994. Haynestown Corn-drying kiln and ring barrow with other features, in I. Bennett (ed.), *Excavations 1993*, 57-58. Bray.

O'Sullivan, M. 1996. A platform to the past – Knockroe passage tomb, *Archaeology Ireland* 10, no. 2, 11-13.

Orme, B. 1981. *Anthropology for Archaeologists*. London.

Owens, M. 1971. Scrabo, in T. G. Delaney (ed.), *Excavations 1971*, 11. Belfast.

Palk, N. A. 1984. *Iron Age Bridle-bits from Britain*. Edinburgh.

Patay, P. 1990. *Die Bronzegefässe in Ungarn. Prähistorische Bronzefunde* II:10. Munich.

Paterson, T. G. F. and Davies, O. 1940. The Churches of Armagh, *Ulster Journal of Archaeology* 3, 82-103.

Pearce, S. 1977. Amber beads from the late bronze-age hoard from Glentanar, Aberdeenshire, *Proceedings of the Society of Antiquaries of Scotland* 108, 124-129.

Pearce, S. 1983. *The Bronze Age Metalwork of South Western Britain, British Archaeological Reports* 120. Oxford.

Peterson, J. D. 1990. Assessing Variability in Late Mesolithic Assemblages in Ireland, in P. M. Vermeersch and P. van Peer (eds), *Contributions to the Mesolithic in Europe*, 369-376. Leuven.

Peterson, J. D. 1990a. From Foraging to Food Production in South-east Ireland: Some Lithic Evidence, *Proceedings of the Prehistoric Society* 56, 89-99.

Piggott, S. 1949. An Iron Age Yoke from Ireland, *Proceedings of the Prehistoric Society* 15, 192-193.

Piggott, S. 1950. Swords and Scabbards of the British Early Iron Age, *Proceedings of the Prehistoric Society* 16, 1-28.

Piggott, S. 1954. *The Neolithic Cultures of the British Isles.* Cambridge.

Piggott, S. 1959. A Late Bronze Age Wine Trade?, *Antiquity* 33, 122-123.

Piggott, S. 1969. Early Iron Age 'Horn-Caps' and Yokes, *The Antiquaries Journal* 49, 378-381.

Piggott, S. 1975. *The Druids.* London.

Piggott, S. 1983. *The Earliest Wheeled Transport from the Atlantic Coast to the Caspian Sea.* London.

Piggott, S. and Daniel, G. E. 1951. *A Picture Book of Ancient British Art.* Cambridge.

Pilcher, J. R. 1969. Archaeology, Palaeoecology, and 14C Dating of the Beaghmore Stone Circle Site, *Ulster Journal of Archaeology* 32, 73-91.

Pilcher, J. R. 1975. Finds at Beaghmore Stone Circles, 1971 and 1972, *Ulster Journal of Archaeology* 38, 83-84.

Pilcher, J. R. and Smith, A. G. 1979. Palaeological Investigations at Ballynagilly, a Neolithic and Bronze Age Settlement in County Tyrone, Northern Ireland, *Philosophical Transactions of the Royal Society of London* 286, 345-369.

Pleiner, R. 1993. *The Celtic Sword.* Oxford.

Powell, T. G. E. 1941. Excavation of a Megalithic Tomb at Carriglong, Co. Waterford, *Journal of the Cork Historical and Archaeological Society* 46, 55-62.

Powell, T. G. E. 1966. *Prehistoric Art.* London.

Powell, T. G. E. 1972. The Problem of Iberian Affinities in Prehistoric Archaeology around the Irish Sea, in F. Lynch and C. B. Burgess (eds), *Prehistoric Man in Wales and the West. Essays in honour of Lily F. Chitty,* 93-106. Bath.

Powell, T. G. E. 1974. The Sintra Collar and the Shannongrove Gorget: aspects of Late Bronze Age goldwork in the west of Europe, *North Munster Antiquarian Journal* 16, 3-13.

Power, D. 1990. Fulachta fiadh in County Cork, in V. Buckley (ed.), *Burnt Offerings. International Contributions to Burnt Mound Archaeology,* 13-17. Dublin.

Power, D. 1992. *Archaeological Inventory of County Cork. Volume 1: West Cork.* Dublin.

Power, D. 1993. Archaeological Survey in the Republic of Ireland and the Cork Experience, in E. S. Twohig and M. Ronayne (eds), *Past Perceptions. The Prehistoric Archaeology of South-West Ireland,* 137-148. Cork.

Power, D. 1994. *Archaeological Inventory of County Cork. Volume 2: East and South Cork.* Dublin.

Pownall, T. 1775. An Account of some Irish Antiquities, *Archaeologia* 3, 355-370.

Preece, R. C., Coxon, P. and Robinson, J. E. 1986. New biostratigraphic evidence of the Post-glacial colonization of Ireland and for Mesolithic forest disturbance, *Journal of Biogeography* 13, 487-509.

Prendergast, E. 1959. Prehistoric burial at Rath, Co. Wicklow, *Journal of the Royal Society of Antiquaries of Ireland* 89, 17-29.

Prendergast, E. 1960. Amber Necklace from Co. Galway, *Journal of the Royal Society of Antiquaries of Ireland* 90, 61-66.

Proudfoot, V. B. 1955. *The Downpatrick Gold Find.* Belfast.

Proudfoot, V. B. 1956. Excavations at Cathedral Hill, Downpatrick, Co. Down, 1954, *Ulster Journal of Archaeology* 19, 57-72.

Proudfoot, V. B. 1957. A second gold find from Downpatrick, *Ulster Journal of Archaeology* 20, 70-72.

Pryor, F. 1980. *A Catalogue of British and Irish Prehistoric Bronzes in the Royal Ontario Museum.* Toronto.

Raftery, B. 1968. A Newly-discovered Hillfort at Garrangrena Lower, Co. Tipperary, *North Munster Antiquarian Journal* 11, 3-6.

Raftery, B. 1969. Freestone Hill, Co. Kilkenny: an Iron Age hillfort and Bronze Age cairn, *Proceedings of the Royal Irish Academy* 68C, 1-108.

Raftery, B. 1971. Rathgall, Co. Wicklow: 1970 excavations, *Antiquity* 45, 296-298.

Raftery, B. 1972. Irish Hill-forts, in C. Thomas (ed.), *The Iron Age in the Irish Sea Province,* 37-58. London.

Raftery, B. 1973. Rathgall: a Late Bronze Age burial in Ireland, *Antiquity* 47, 293-295.

Raftery, B. 1974. A prehistoric burial mound at Baunogenasraid, Co. Carlow, *Proceedings of the Royal Irish Academy* 74C, 277-312.

Raftery, B. 1974a. A Decorated Iron Age Horse-bit Fragment from Ireland, *Proceedings of the Royal Irish Academy* 74C, 1-10.

Raftery, B. 1974b. Rathgall, in T. G. Delaney (ed.), *Excavations 1973,* 28-29. Belfast.

Raftery, B. 1975. A Late Bronze Age Bar Toggle from Ireland, *Archaeologia Atlantica* 1, 83-89.

Raftery, B. 1976. Rathgall and Irish Hillfort Problems, in D. W. Harding (ed.), *Hillforts. Later Prehistoric Earthworks in Britain and Ireland,* 339-357. London.

Raftery, B. 1976a. Dowris, Hallstatt and La Tène in Ireland: problems of the transition from bronze to iron, in S. J. de Laet (ed.), *Acculturation and Continuity in Atlantic Europe mainly during the Neolithic period and the Bronze Age, Dissertationes Archaeologicae Gandensis,* 189-197. Bruges.

Raftery, B. 1976b. The Hillfort at Belmont in Co. Galway, *Journal of the Galway Archaeological and Historical Society* 35, 89-95.

Raftery, B. 1977. A much-repaired Horse-bit pair from Iron Age Ireland, in O-H. Frey (ed.), *Festschrift zum 50 jährigen Bestehen des Vorgeschichtlichen Seminars Marburg, Marburger Studien zu Vor- und Frühgeschichte,* 299-308. Marburg.

Raftery, B. 1978. Excavations at Killycluggin, County Cavan, *Ulster Journal of Archaeology* 41, 49-54.

Raftery, B. 1981. Iron Age Burials in Ireland, in D. Ó Corráin (ed.), *Irish Antiquity. Essays and Studies presented to Professor M. J. O'Kelly,* 173-204. Cork.

Raftery, B. 1982. Two Recently Discovered Bronze Shields from the Shannon Basin, *Journal of the Royal Society of Antiquaries of Ireland* 112, 5-17.

Raftery, B. 1982a. Knobbed Spearbutts of the Irish Iron Age, in B. G. Scott (ed.), *Studies on Early Ireland. Essays in honour of M. V. Duignan,* 75-92. Belfast.

Raftery, B. 1983. *A Catalogue of Irish Iron Age Antiquities.* Marburg.

Raftery, B. 1984. *La Tène in Ireland. Problems of Origin and Chronology.* Marburg.

Raftery, B. 1986. Three bronze rings of Continental La Tène type from Ireland, *Gedenkschrift für Gero von Merhart. Marburger Studien zur Vor- und Frühgeschichte 7,* 249-266. Marburg.

Raftery, B. 1987. Some glass beads of the Later Bronze Age in Ireland, in *Glasperlen der Vorrömischen Eisenzeit II, Marburger Studien zur Vor- und Frügeschichte 9,* 39-53. Marburg.

Raftery, B. 1987a. The Loughnashade Horns, *Emania 2,* 21-24.

Raftery, B. 1988. Hollow two-piece metal rings in La Tène Europe, *Marburger Studien zur Vor- und Frühgeschichte 11.* Marburg.

Raftery, B. 1990. *Trackways Through Time. Archaeological Investigations on Irish Bog Roads 1985-1989.* Dublin.

Raftery, B. 1992. Celtas, cultura y colonización: reflexions sobre la Edad del Hierro en Irlanda, in M. Almagro-Gorbea (ed.), *Los Celtas: Hispania y Europa,* 91-120. Madrid.

Raftery, B. 1993. La statuaire en bois et en pierre de l'Age du Fer irlandais, in J. Briard and A. Duval (eds), *Les représentations humaines du Néolithique à l'Âge du Fer,* 253-264. Paris.

Raftery, B. 1994. *Pagan Celtic Ireland.* London.

Raftery, B. 1994a. Reflections on the Irish Scabbard Style, in *Festschrift für Otto-Herman Frey zum 65. Geburtstag, Marburger Studien zur Vor- und Frühgeschichte 16,* 475-492. Marburg.

Raftery, B. 1995. The Conundrum of Irish Iron Age Pottery, in B. Raftery, V. Megaw and V. Rigby (eds), *Sites and Sights of the Iron Age. Essays on Fieldwork and Museum Research presented to Ian Matheson Stead,* 149-156. Oxford.

Raftery, B. 1996. Drumanagh and Roman Ireland, *Archaeology Ireland 10,* no. 1, 17-19.

Raftery, B. 1996a. *Trackway Excavations in the Mountdillon Bogs, Co. Longford, 1985-1991. Irish Archaeological Wetland Unit Transactions 3.* Dublin.

Raftery, B., Jennings, D. and Moloney, A. 1995. Annaghcorrib 1, Garryduff Bog, Co. Galway, *Irish Archaeological Wetland Unit Transactions 4,* 39-53.

Raftery, J. 1941. The Tumulus-Cemetery of Carrowjames, Co. Mayo, *Journal of the Galway Archaeological and Historical Society 19,* 16-85.

Raftery, J. 1942. Knocknalappa Crannóg, Co. Clare, *North Munster Antiquarian Journal 3,* 53-72.

Raftery, J. 1944. The Turoe Stone and the Rath of Feerwore, *Journal of the Royal Society of Antiquaries of Ireland 74,* 23-52.

Raftery, J. 1944a. A Neolithic burial in Co. Carlow, *Journal of the Royal Society of Antiquaries of Ireland 74,* 61-62.

Raftery, J. 1951. *Prehistoric Ireland.* London.

Raftery, J. 1960. A Bronze Age Tumulus at Corrower, Co. Mayo, *Proceedings of the Royal Irish Academy 61C,* 79-93.

Raftery, J. 1967. The Gorteenreagh Hoard, in E. Rynne (ed.), *North Munster Studies. Essays in commemoration of Monsignor Michael Moloney,* 61-71. Limerick.

Raftery, J. 1970. Prehistoric Coiled Basketry Bags, *Journal of the Royal Society of Antiquaries of Ireland 100,* 167-168.

Raftery, J. 1971. Irish Prehistoric Gold Objects: new light on the source of the metal, *Journal of the Royal Society of Antiquaries of Ireland 101,* 101-105.

Raftery, J. 1971a. A Bronze Age Hoard from Ballytegan, County Laois, *Journal of the Royal Society of Antiquaries of Ireland 101,* 85-100.

Raftery, J. 1972. George Petrie, 1789-1866: a reassessment, *Proceedings of the Royal Irish Academy 72C,* 153-163.

Raftery, J. 1973. A Neolithic burial mound at Ballintruer More, Co. Wicklow, *Journal of the Royal Society of Antiquaries of Ireland 103,* 214-219.

Raleigh, R. 1985. The archaeology of prehistoric Tipperary, in W. Nolan and T. G. McGrath (eds), *Tipperary: History and Society. Interdisciplinary Essays on the History of an Irish County,* 8-33. Dublin.

Ramsey, G. 1992. An Early Bronze Age Dagger from Duckingstool Point, County Tyrone, *Ulster Journal of Archaeology 54-55,* 161-162.

Ramsey, G. 1993. Damaged butts and torn rivet holes: the hafting and function of Middle Bronze Age 'Dirks' and 'Rapiers', *Archeomaterials 7,* 127-138.

Ramsey, G. 1995. Middle Bronze Age Metalwork: are artefact studies dead and buried?, in J. Waddell and E. S. Twohig (eds), *Ireland in the Bronze Age. Proceedings of the Dublin Conference, April 1995,* 49-62. Dublin.

Ramsey, G., Bourke, C. and Crone, D. 1992. Antiquities from the River Blackwater I, Bronze Age Metalwork, *Ulster Journal of Archaeology 54-55,* 138-149.

Rankin, D. 1996. *Celts and the Classical World* (Second edition). London.

Ray, K. 1990. Science and anomaly: burnt mounds in British prehistory, *Scottish Archaeological Review 9,* 7-14.

Ray, T. P. 1989. The Winter Solstice Phenomenon at Newgrange, Ireland: Accident or Design?, *Nature 337,* 343-5.

Read, S., Henig, M. and Cram, L. 1986. Three-horned Bull, *Brittania 17,* 346-347.

Renfrew, C. 1973. *Before Civilization.* London.

Renfrew, C. 1976. Megaliths, Territories and Populations, in S. J. de Laet (ed.), *Acculturation and Continuity in Atlantic Europe mainly during the Neolithic period and the Bronze Age, Dissertationes Archaeologicae Gandensis XVI,* 198-220.

Renfrew, C. 1987. *Archaeology and Language. The Puzzle of the Indo-Europeans.* London.

Renfrew, C. and Bahn, P. 1996. *Archaeology. Theory, Methods and Practice* (Second edition). London.

Ritchie, G. and Welfare, H. 1983. Excavations at Ardnave, Islay, *Proceedings of the Society of Antiquaries of Scotland 113,* 302-366.

Robb, J. 1993. A Social Prehistory of European Languages, *Antiquity 67,* 747-60.

Robinson, M., Shimwell, D. and G. Cribbin. 1996. Boating in the Bronze Age – two logboats from Co. Mayo, *Archaeology Ireland 10,* no. 1, 12-13.

Robinson, T. 1996. *Setting Foot on the Shores of Connemara and other writings.* Dublin.

Roche, H. 1989. Pre-tomb habitation found at Knowth, Co. Meath, Spring 1989, *Archaeology Ireland* 3, no. 3, 101-103.

Ross, A. 1967. *Pagan Celtic Britain. Studies in Iconography and Tradition*. London.

Rosse, A. 1984. The Dowris Hoard, *Éile. Journal of the Roscrea Heritage Society* 2, 57-66.

Roth, H. 1974. Ein Ledermesser der Atlantischen Bronzezeit aus Mittelfranken, *Archäologisches Korrespondenzblatt* 4, 37-47.

Rowlands, M. J. 1971. The archaeological interpretation of prehistoric metalworking, *World Archaeology* 3, 210-224.

Rowlands, M. J. 1976. *The Production and Distribution of Metalwork in the Middle Bronze Age in Southern England*, British Archaeological Reports 31. Oxford.

Rowlands, M. J. 1980. Kinship, alliance and exchange in the European Bronze Age, in J. Barrett and R. Bradley (eds), *Settlement and Society in the British Later Bronze Age*, British Archaeological Reports 83, 15-55. Oxford.

Rowley-Conwy, P. 1984. Slash and burn in the Temperate European Neolithic, in R. Mercer (ed.), *Farming Practice in British Prehistory*, 85-96. Edinburgh.

Ruggles, C. L. N. 1994. The stone rows of south-west Ireland: a first reconnaissance, *Archaeoastronomy* 19, 1-20 [*Journal for the History of Astronomy* 25, S1-S20].

Ruiz-Gálvez, M. 1991. Songs of a Wayfaring Lad. Late Bronze Age Atlantic Exchange and the building of the regional identity in the west Iberian Peninsula, *Oxford Journal of Archaeology* 10, 277-306.

Russel, A. D. 1990. Two Beaker Burials from Chilbolton, Hampshire, *Proceedings of the Prehistoric Society* 56, 153-172.

Ryan, M. 1973. The excavation of a Neolithic burial mound at Jerpoint West, Co. Kilkenny, *Proceedings of the Royal Irish Academy* 73C, 107-127.

Ryan, M. 1975. Urn Burial in Killeenaghmountain Townland, near Kilwatermoy, Tallow, County Waterford, *Journal of the Royal Society of Antiquaries of Ireland* 105, 147-149.

Ryan, M. 1980. An early Mesolithic site in the Irish midlands, *Antiquity* 54, 46-47.

Ryan, M. 1980a. Prehistoric burials at Clane, *Journal of the Kildare Archaeological Society* 16, 108-111.

Ryan, M. 1981. Poulawack, Co. Clare: the Affinities of the Central Burial Structure in D. Ó Corráin (ed.) *Irish Antiquity. Essays and Studies presented to Professor M. J. O'Kelly*, 134-46. Cork.

Ryan, M. 1983. (ed.). *Treasures of Ireland. Irish Art 3000 B.C. – 1500 A.D*. Dublin.

Rynne, E. 1962. Late Bronze Age rattle-pendants from Ireland, *Proceedings of the Prehistoric Society* 28, 383-385.

Rynne, E. 1963. Notes on some antiquities in Co. Kildare, *Journal of the Kildare Archaeological Society* 13, 458-462.

Rynne, E. 1964. The Three Stone Heads at Woodlands, near Raphoe, Co. Donegal, *Journal of the Royal Society of Antiquaries of Ireland* 94, 105-109.

Rynne, E. 1964a. Middle Bronze Age Burial at Knockboy, Co. Antrim, *Ulster Journal of Archaeology* 27, 62-66.

Rynne, E. 1967. The Bronze Bucket in the Hunterian Museum, *The Antiquaries Journal* 47, 109-110.

Rynne, E. 1970. Oran Beg Ring Barrow, in T. G. Delaney (ed.), *Excavations 1970*, 10. Belfast.

Rynne, E. 1972. Celtic Stone Idols in Ireland, in C. Thomas (ed.), *The Iron Age in the Irish Sea Province*, 79-98. London.

Rynne, E. 1972a. Tanged dagger from Derrynamanagh, Co. Galway, *Journal of the Royal Society of Antiquaries of Ireland* 102, 240-243.

Rynne, E. 1974. Excavations at 'Madden's Hill', Kiltale, Co. Meath, *Proceedings of the Royal Irish Academy* 74C, 267-275.

Rynne, E. 1975. Ancient Burials at Ballinlough, Co. Laois, *Journal of the Kildare Archaeological Society* 15, 430-433.

Rynne, E. 1975a. Some ancient finds from Boherduff, Co. Galway, *Journal of the Galway Archaeological and Historical Society* 34, 102-103.

Rynne, E. 1976. The La Tène and Roman Finds from Lambay, County Dublin: a re-assessment, in Colloquium on Hiberno-Roman Relations and Material Remains, *Proceedings of the Royal Irish Academy* 76C, 231-244.

Rynne, E. 1979. An Early Celtic Spanish-North Munster Connection, *North Munster Antiquarian Journal* 21, 7-10.

Rynne, E. 1982. A Classification of Pre-Viking Irish Iron Swords, in B. G. Scott (ed.), *Studies on Early Ireland. Essays in honour of M. V. Duignan*, 93-97. Belfast.

Rynne, E. 1982a. The Early Iron Age in County Clare, *North Munster Antiquarian Journal* 24, 5-18.

Rynne, E. 1983. Some Early Iron Age Sword-hilts from Ireland and Scotland, in A. O'Connor and D.V. Clarke (eds), *From the Stone Age to the 'Forty-Five. Studies presented to R. B. K. Stevenson*, 188-196. Edinburgh.

Rynne, E. 1984. Military and civilian swords from the River Corrib, *Journal of the Galway Archaeological and Historical Society* 39, 5-26.

Rynne, E. and Ó hÉailidhe, P. 1965. A Group of Prehistoric Sites at Piperstown, Co. Dublin, *Proceedings of the Royal Irish Academy* 64C, 61-84.

Rynne, E. and Timoney, M. A. 1975. Excavation of a Destroyed Wedge-tomb at Breeoge, Co. Sligo, *Journal of the Galway Archaeological and Historical Society* 34, 88-91.

Savage, R. J. G. 1966. Irish Pleistocene Mammals, *Irish Naturalists Journal* 15, 117-30.

Savory, H. N. 1968. *Spain and Portugal. The Prehistory of the Iberian Peninsula*. London.

Savory, H. N. 1971. A Welsh bronze age hillfort, *Antiquity* 45, 251-261.

Savory, H. N. 1976. *Guide Catalogue of the Early Iron Age Collections, National Museum of Wales*. Cardiff.

Savory, H. N. 1978. Some Iberian Influences on the Copper Age Pottery of the Irish Channel Area, *Boletin del Seminario de Estudios de Acte y Arqueología* 44, 5-13.

Savory, H. N. 1980. *Guide Catalogue of the Bronze Age Collections, National Museum of Wales*. Cardiff.

Schauer, P. 1971. *Die Schwerter in Süddeutschland, Österreich und der Schweiz I*, Prähistorische Bronzefunde IV:2. Munich.

Schauer, P. 1972. Zur Herkunft der bronzenen Hallstattschwerter, *Archäologisches Korrespondenzblatt* 2, 261-270.

Schauer, P. 1973. Kontinentaleneuropäische Bronzelanzenspitzen vom Typ Enfield, *Archaeologische Korrespondenzblatt* 3, 293-298.

Schmidt, P. K. 1979. Beile als Ritualobjekte in der Altbronzezeit der Britischen Inseln, *Jahresbericht des Instituts für Vorgeschichte der Universiteit Frankfurt-a-Main* 1978-79, 311-320.

Schmidt, P. K. and Burgess, C. B. 1981. *The Axes of Scotland and Northern England. Prähistorische Bronzefunde* IX:7. Munich.

Scott, B. G. 1974. Some notes on the transition from bronze to iron in Ireland, *Irish Archaeological Research Forum* 1, no. 1, 9-24.

Scott, B. G. 1977. Metallographic study of some early iron tools and weapons from Ireland, *Proceedings of the Royal Irish Academy* 77C, 301-317.

Scott, B. G. 1977a. Dancing, Drink or Drugs? Comments on the 'Beaker Cult-Package' Hypothesis, *Irish Archaeological Research Forum* 4, no. 2, 29-34.

Scott, B. G. 1990. *Early Irish Ironworking.* Belfast.

Scott, J. G. 1969. The Clyde Cairns of Scotland, in T. G. E. Powell (ed.), *Megalithic Enquiries in the West of Britain,* 175-222. Liverpool.

Scott, J. G. and Powell, T. G. E. 1969. A Bronze Horse Figurine found near Birkwood, Lesmahagow, Lanarkshire, *The Antiquaries Journal* 49, 118-126.

Shee, E. 1972. Three decorated stones from Loughcrew, Co. Meath, *Journal of the Royal Society of Antiquaries of Ireland* 102, 224-233.

Shee, E. and Evans, D. M. 1965. A Standing Stone in the townland of Newgrange, Co. Meath, *Journal of the Cork Historical and Archaeological Society* 70, 124-130.

Shennan, S. 1982. Ideology, change and the European Early Bronze Age, in I. Hodder (ed.), *Symbolic and Structural Archaeology,* 155-161. Cambridge.

Shennan, S. 1982a. Exchange and ranking: the role of amber in the earlier Bronze Age of Europe, in C. Renfrew and S. Shennan (eds), *Ranking, Resource and Exchange. Aspects of the Archaeology of Early European Society,* 33-45. Cambridge.

Sheridan, A. 1983. A Reconsideration of the Origins of Irish Metallurgy, *The Journal of Irish Archaeology* 1, 11-19.

Sheridan, A. 1986. Megaliths and Megalithomania: an account and interpretation of the development of Passage Tombs in Ireland, *The Journal of Irish Archaeology* 3, 17-30.

Sheridan, A. 1986a. Porcellanite Artifacts – a new survey, *Ulster Journal of Archaeology* 49, 19-32.

Sheridan, A. 1987. Nappan Neolithic site, in C. Cotter (ed.), *Excavations 1986,* 11. Dublin.

Sheridan, A. 1989. Pottery production in Neolithic Ireland: a petrological and chemical study, in J. Henderson (ed.), *Scientific Analysis in Archaeology and its interpretation,* 112-135. Oxford.

Sheridan, A. 1995. Irish Neolithic pottery: the story in 1995, in I. Kinnes and G. Varndell (eds), *'Unbaked Urns of Rudely Shape'. Essays on British and Irish Pottery for Ian Longworth,* 3-21. Oxford.

Sheridan, A. and Northover, P. 1993. A Beaker Period Copper Dagger Blade from the Sillees River near Ross Lough, Co. Fermanagh, *Ulster Journal of Archaeology* 56, 61-69.

Sheridan, A., Cooney, G. and Grogan, E. 1992. Stone Axe Studies in Ireland, *Proceedings of the Prehistoric Society* 58, 389-416.

Sherratt, A. 1991. Sacred and profane substances: the ritual use of narcotics in later Neolithic Europe, in P. Garwood, D. Jennings, R. Skeates and J. Toms (eds), *Sacred and Profane: Proceedings of a Conference on Archaeology, Ritual and Religion,* 50-64. Oxford.

Sherratt, A. 1995. Alcohol and its alternatives. Symbol and substance in pre-industrial cultures, in J. Goodman, P. E. Lovejoy and A. Sherratt (eds), *Consuming Habits. Drugs in History and Anthropology,* 11-46. London.

Shimwell, D. W., Robinson, M. E. and Cribbin, G. 1996. A Mortar-like Sealant Layer in a Bronze Age Burial Mound at Clogher Lower, Co. Roscommon, Ireland, *Journal of Archaeological Science* 23, 569-575.

Simpson, D. D. A. 1971. Beaker houses and settlements in Britain, in D. D. A. Simpson (ed.), *Economy and Settlement in Neolithic and Early Bronze Britain and Europe,* 131-152. Leicester.

Simpson, D. D. A. 1986. A Late Bronze Age Sword from Island MacHugh, Co. Tyrone, *Ulster Journal of Archaeology* 49, 103-104.

Simpson, D. D. A. 1988. The Stone Maceheads of Ireland, *Journal of the Royal Society of Antiquaries of Ireland* 118, 27-52.

Simpson, D. D. A. 1989. Neolithic Navan?, *Emania* 6, 31-33.

Simpson, D. D. A. 1989a. The Stone Maceheads of Ireland, Part II, *Journal of the Royal Society of Antiquaries of Ireland* 119, 113-126.

Simpson, D. D. A. 1990. The Stone Battle Axes of Ireland, *Journal of the Royal Society of Antiquaries in Ireland* 120, 5-40.

Simpson, D. D. A. 1990a. Irish Axe Hammers, *Ulster Journal of Archaeology* 53, 50-56.

Simpson, D. D. A. 1992. Excavations at Dun Ruadh, Crouck, Co. Tyrone, *Ulster Journal of Archaeology* 54, 36-47.

Simpson, D. D. A. 1993. Stone Artifacts from the Lower Bann Valley, *Ulster Journal of Archaeology* 56, 31-43.

Simpson, D. D. A. 1993a. Dún Ruadh – A Real Irish henge?, *Archaeology Ireland* 7, no. 2, 14-15.

Simpson, D. D. A. 1995. The Neolithic Settlement Site at Ballygalley, Co. Antrim, in E. Grogan and C. Mount (eds), *Annus Archaeologiae. Archaeological Research 1992,* 37-44. Dublin.

Simpson, D. D. A. 1996. The Ballygalley houses, Co. Antrim, Ireland, in T. Darvill and J. Thomas (eds), *Neolithic Houses in Northwest Europe and Beyond,* 123-132. Oxford.

Simpson, D. D. A. 1996a. Irish Perforated Stone Implements in Context, *The Journal of Irish Archaeology* 7, 65-76.

Simpson, D. D. A. and Gibson, A. 1989. Lyles Hill, *Current Archaeology* 114, 214-215.

Simpson, D. D. A., Conway, M. G. and Moore, D. G. 1990. The Neolithic Settlement Site at Ballygalley, Co. Antrim. Excavations 1989, Interim Report, *Ulster Journal of Archaeology* 53, 40-49.

Slater, L., Kulessa, B. and Barton, K. 1996. An Investigation of the Ability of Geophysical Methods to Detect and Define Fulachta Fia (Burnt Mounds) on Clare Island, Co. Mayo, *Archaeological Prospection* 3, 53-69.

Smith, A. G. 1975. Neolithic and Bronze Age landscape changes in northern Ireland, in J. G. Evans, S. Limbrey and H. Cleere (eds), *The Effect of Man on the Landscape: The Highland Zone,* 64-74. London.

Smith, A. G. 1984. Newferry and the Boreal-Atlantic transition, *New Phytologist* 98, 35-55.

Smith, A. G. and Willis, E. H. 1962. Radiocarbon Dating of the Fallahogy Landnam Phase, *Ulster Journal of Archaeology* 24-25, 16-24.

Smith, M. A. 1959. Some Somerset hoards and their place in the Bronze Age of southern Britain, *Proceedings of the Prehistoric Society* 25, 144-187.

Smith, R. A. 1920. *British Museum. A Guide to the Antiquities of the Bronze Age in the Department of British and Medieval Antiquities.* London.

Spratling, M. G. 1980. Weighing of gold in prehistoric Europe, in W. A. Oddy (ed.), *Aspects of Early Metallurgy,* 179-183. London.

Sprockhoff, E. 1955. Central European Urnfield Culture and Celtic La Tène: An Outline, *Proceedings of the Prehistoric Society* 21, 257-281.

Stanford, W. B. 1970. Towards a History of Classical Influences in Ireland, *Proceedings of the Royal Irish Academy* 70C, 13-91.

Stead, I. M. 1988. Chalk Figurines of the Parisi, *The Antiquaries Journal* 68, 9-29.

Stead, I. M. 1991. The Snettisham Treasure: excavations in 1990, *Antiquity* 65, 447-464.

Stead, I. M. 1991a. *Iron Age cemeteries in East Yorkshire.* London.

Stead, I. M. 1991b. Many more iron age shields from Britain, *The Antiquaries Journal* 71, 1-35.

Steensberg, A. 1943. *Ancient Harvesting Implements. A study in archaeology and human geography.* Copenhagen.

Stephens, N. and Collins, A. E. P. 1960. The quaternary deposits at Ringneill Quay and Ardmillan, Co. Down, *Proceedings of the Royal Irish Academy* 61C, 41-77.

Stokes, W. 1868. *The Life and Labours in Art and Archaeology of George Petrie, LL.D.* London.

Stout, G. 1991. Embanked Enclosures of the Boyne Region, *Proceedings of the Royal Irish Academy* 91C, 245-284.

Stout, G. 1994. Wicklow's Prehistoric Landscape, in K. Hannigan and W. Nolan (eds), *Wicklow: History and Society. Interdisciplinary Essays on the History of an Irish County,* 1-40. Dublin.

Stout, M. 1996. Emyr Estyn Evans and Northern Ireland: the archaeology and geography of a new state, in J. A. Atkinson, I. Banks and J. O'Sullivan (eds), *Nationalism and archaeology,* 111-127. Glasgow.

Sweetman, P. D. 1976. An Earthen Enclosure at Monknewtown, Slane, Co. Meath, *Proceedings of the Royal Irish Academy* 76C, 25-72.

Sweetman, P. D. 1983. Reconstruction and partial excavation of a burial mound at Ninch, Co. Meath, *Ríocht na Midhe* 7, no. 2, 58-68.

Sweetman, P. D. 1985. A Late Neolithic/Early Bronze Age Pit Circle at Newgrange, Co. Meath, *Proceedings of the Royal Irish Academy* 85C, 195-221.

Sweetman, P. D. 1987. Excavation of a Late Neolithic/Early Bronze Age Site at Newgrange, Co. Meath, *Proceedings of the Royal Irish Academy* 87C, 283-298.

Sweetman, P. D., Alcock, O. and Moran, B. 1995. *Archaeological Inventory of County Laois.* Dublin.

Swift, C. 1996. Pagan monuments and Christian legal centres in early Meath, *Ríocht na Midhe* 9, no. 2, 1-26.

Taylor, J. J. 1970. Lunulae Reconsidered, *Proceedings of the Prehistoric Society* 36, 38-81.

Taylor, J. J. 1979. The Relationship of British Early Bronze Age Goldwork to Atlantic Europe, in M. Ryan (ed.), *The Origins of Metallurgy in Atlantic Europe. Proceedings of the Fifth Atlantic Colloquium,* 229-250. Dublin.

Taylor, J. J. 1980. *Bronze Age Goldwork of the British Isles.* Cambridge.

Taylor, J. J. 1984. The Potterne Gold Bracelet and its Affinities, *Wiltshire Archaeological and Natural History Magazine* 78, 35-40.

Taylor, J. J. 1994. The first Golden Age of Europe was in Ireland and Britain (circa 2400-1400 B. C.), *Ulster Journal of Archaeology* 57, 37-60.

Taylor, T. 1991. Celtic Art, *Scottish Archaeological Review* 8, 129-132.

Teunissen, D. and Teunissen-Van Oorschot, H. G. C. M. 1980. The history of vegetation in S. W. Connemara (Ireland), *Acta Botanica Neerlandica* 29, 285-306.

Thom, A. S. 1980. The stone rings of Beaghmore: geometry and astronomy, *Ulster Journal of Archaeology* 43, 15-19.

Thomas, J. 1988. Neolithic Explanations Revisited: the Mesolithic-Neolithic Transition in Britain and South Scandinavia, *Proceedings of the Prehistoric Society* 54, 59-66.

Thomas, J. 1990. Monuments from the inside: the case of the Irish megalithic tombs, *World Archaeology* 22, 168-78.

Thomas, J. 1991. *Rethinking the Neolithic.* Cambridge.

Thomas, J. 1996. Neolithic houses in mainland Britain and Ireland – a sceptical view, in T. Darvill and J. Thomas (eds), *Neolithic Houses in Northwest Europe and Beyond,* 1-12. Oxford.

Thompson, H. 1993. Iron Age and Roman Slave-Shackles, *Archaeological Journal* 150, 57-168.

Thrane, H. 1995. Penultima Thule: the Bronze Age in the Western Baltic Region as an Analogy to the Irish Bronze Age, in J. Waddell and E. S. Twohig (eds), *Ireland in the Bronze Age. Proceedings of the Dublin Conference, April 1995,* 149-157. Dublin.

Tierney, J. J. 1976. The Greek Geographic Tradition and Ptolemy's Evidence for Irish Geography, in Colloquium on Hiberno-Roman Relations and Material Remains, *Proceedings of the Royal Irish Academy* 76C, 257-265.

Timoney, M. A. 1984. Earthen burial sites on the Carrowmore peninsula, Co. Sligo, in G. Burenhult, *The Archaeology of Carrowmore,* 319-325. Stockholm.

Tipping, R. 1994. 'Ritual' Floral Tributes in the Scottish Bronze Age – Palynological Evidence, *Journal of Archaeological Science* 21, 133-139.

Toal, C. 1995. *North Kerry Archaeological Survey.* Dingle.

Topp, C. 1956. The Gold Ornaments reputedly found near the entrance to New Grange in 1842, *University of London Institute of Archaeology, Twelfth Annual Report,* 53-62.

Topp, C. 1962. The Portal Dolmen of Drumanone, Co. Roscommon, *Bulletin of the University of London Institute of Archaeology* 3, 38-46.

Topping, P. 1996. Structure and ritual in the Neolithic house: some examples from Britain and Ireland, in T. Darvill and J. Thomas (eds), *Neolithic Houses in Northwest Europe and Beyond,* 157-170. Oxford.

Tratman, E. K. 1928. Excavations at Kilgreany Cave, Co. Waterford, *Proceedings of the Bristol Speleological Society* 3, 109-153.

Trigger, B. G. 1989. *A history of archaeological thought.* Cambridge.

Trump, B. A. V. 1968. Fenland rapiers, in J. M. Coles and D. D. A. Simpson (eds), *Studies in Ancient Europe. Essays presented to Stuart Piggott,* Leicester, 213-225.

Twohig, E. Shee and Doody, M. 1989. Standing Stone with Cremation from Killountain, Co. Cork, *Journal of the Cork Historical and Archaeological Society* 94, 52-55.

Twohig, E. Shee. 1981. *The Megalithic Art of Western Europe.* Oxford.

Twohig, E. Shee. 1990. *Irish Megalithic Tombs.* Princes Risborough.

Twohig, E. Shee. 1996. Context and Content of Irish Passage Tomb Art, in *Actes du 2ème Colloque Interrégional d'Art Mégalithique, Vannes, 1995, Revue archéologique de l'Ouest, Supplément* 8, 67-80.

Tylecote, R. F. 1973. Casting Copper and Bronze into Stone Moulds, *Bulletin of the Historical Metallurgy Group* 7, no. 1, 1-5.

Ucko, P. J. 1995. *Theory in Archaeology. A world perspective.* London.

Van Hoek, M. A. M. 1987. The Prehistoric Rock Art of County Donegal (Part I), *Ulster Journal of Archaeology* 50, 23-46.

Van Hoek, M. A. M. 1988. The Prehistoric Rock Art of Co. Donegal (Part II), *Ulster Journal of Archaeology* 51, 21-47.

Van Hoek, M. A. M. 1990. The Rosette in British and Irish Rock Art, *Glasgow Archaeological Journal* 16, 39-54.

Van Hoek, M. A. M. 1993. The Prehistoric Rock Art of the Boheh Stone, Co. Mayo, *Cathair na Mart. Journal of the Westport Historical Society* 13, 1-15.

Van Hoek, M. A. M. 1993a. Early Christian Rock Art at Clehagh, Co. Donegal, *Ulster Journal of Archaeology* 56, 139-147.

Van Hoek, M. A. M. 1993b. Addenda to the Prehistoric Rock Art of County Donegal, *Ulster Journal of Archaeology* 56, 179-180.

Van Hoek, M. A. M. 1993b. The Spiral in British and Irish Neolithic Rock Art, *Glasgow Archaeological Journal* 18, 11-32.

Van Hoek, M. A. M. 1995. The Keyhole-Pattern in the Prehistoric Rock Art of Ireland and Britain, *Cathair na Mart. Journal of the Westport Historical Society* 15, 15-25.

Van Hoek, M. A. M. and van Hoek, E. 1985. A new group of cup and ring rocks in Inishowen, Co. Donegal, *Ulster Journal of Archaeology* 48, 123-127.

Van Wijngaarden-Bakker, L. H. 1974. The Animal Remains from the Beaker Settlement at Newgrange, Co. Meath: first report, *Proceedings of the Royal Irish Academy* 74C, 313-383.

Van Wijngaarden-Bakker, L. H. 1985. Faunal Remains and the Irish Mesolithic, in C. Bonsall, C. (ed.), *The Mesolithic in Europe,* 125-33. Edinburgh.

Van Wijngaarden-Bakker, L. H. 1986. The colonisation of islands – the mammalian evidence, *Journal of the Irish Biogeographical Society, Occasional Publications* 1, 38-41.

Van Wijngaarden-Bakker, L. H. 1986a. The Animal Remains from the Beaker Settlement at Newgrange, Co. Meath: final report, *Proceedings of the Royal Irish Academy* 86C, 17-111.

Vencl, S. 1994. The archaeology of thirst, *Journal of European Archaeology* 2, 299-326.

Waddell, J. 1975. The Bronze Age Burials of County Galway, *Journal of the Galway Archaeological and Historical Society* 34, 5-20.

Waddell, J. 1975a. The Encrusted Urn in Ireland: some comments, *Irish Archaeological Research Forum* 2, no. 1, 21-28.

Waddell, J. 1976. Cultural interaction in the Insular Early Bronze Age: some ceramic evidence, in S. J. de Laet (ed.), *Acculturation and Continuity in Atlantic Europe, Dissertationes Archaeologicae Gandensis,* Vol. 16, 284-295. Bruges.

Waddell, J. 1978. The invasion hypothesis in Irish prehistory, *Antiquity* 52, 121-128.

Waddell, J. 1982. From Kermaria to Turoe?, in B. G. Scott (ed.), *Studies on Early Ireland. Essays in honour of M. V. Duignan,* 21-28. Belfast.

Waddell, J. 1983. Rathcroghan – A Royal Site in Connacht, *The Journal of Irish Archaeology* 1, 21-46.

Waddell, J. 1984. Bronzes and Bones, *The Journal of Irish Archaeology* 2, 71-72.

Waddell, J. 1986. Knocknagur, Turoe and local enquiry, *Journal of the Galway Archaeological and Historical Society* 40, 130-133.

Waddell, J. 1988. Excavation at 'Dathi's Mound', Rathcroghan, Co. Roscommon, *The Journal of Irish Archaeology* 4, 23-36.

Waddell, J. 1988a. Rathcroghan in Connacht, *Emania* 5, 5-18 [corrections in *Emania* 6, 42].

Waddell, J. 1990. *The Bronze Age Burials of Ireland.* Galway.

Waddell, J. 1991. The Celticization of the West: an Irish Perspective, in C. Chevillot and A. Coffyn (eds), *L'Age du Bronze Atlantique. Actes du Ier Colloque de Beynac,* 349-66. Beynac.

Waddell, J. 1991a. The Question of the Celticization of Ireland, *Emania* 9, 5-16.

Waddell, J. 1992. The Irish Sea in Prehistory, *The Journal of Irish Archaeology* 6, 29-40.

Waddell, J. 1995. Celts, Celticisation and the Irish Bronze Age, in J. Waddell and E. S. Twohig (eds), *Ireland in the Bronze Age. Proceedings of the Dublin Conference, April 1995,* 158-169. Dublin.

Waddell, J. 1995a. The Cordoned Urn tradition, in I. Kinnes and G. Varndell (eds), *'Unbaked Urns of Rudely Shape'. Essays on British and Irish Pottery for Ian Longworth,* 113-122. Oxford.

Waddell, J. and Barton, K. 1995. Seeing beneath Rathcroghan, *Archaeology Ireland* 9, no. 1, 38-41.

Wailes, B. 1970. Excavations at Dún Ailinne, Co. Kildare, *Journal of the Royal Society of Antiquaries of Ireland* 100, 79-90.

Wailes, B. 1971. Excavations at Dún Ailinne, near Kilcullen, 1971, *Journal of the Kildare Archaeological Society* 15, 5-11.

Wailes, B. 1973. Excavation at Dún Ailinne, near Kilcullen, 1973, *Journal of the Kildare Archaeological Society* 15, 234-41.

Wailes, B. 1974. Dún Ailinne, in T. G. Delaney (ed.), *Excavations 1973,* 13-14. Belfast.

Wailes, B. 1974a. Excavation at Dún Ailinne, near Kilcullen, 1974, *Journal of the Kildare Archaeological Society* 15, 345-58.

Wailes, B. 1976. Dún Ailinne: an interim report, in Harding, D. W. (ed.), *Hillforts: Later Prehistoric Earthworks in Britain and Ireland,* 319-38. London.

Wailes, B. 1982. The Irish 'Royal Sites' in History and Archaeology, *Cambridge Medieval Celtic Studies* 3, 1-29.

Wailes, B. 1990. Dún Ailinne: A Summary Excavation Report, *Emania* 7, 10-21.

Wakeman, W. F. 1884. On the *trouvaille* ... from the crannog at Lisnacroghera, near Broughshane, Co. Antrim, *Journal of the Royal Society of Antiquaries of Ireland* 16, 375-406.

Wakeman, W. F. 1888. On a cromleac-like altar, or monument, at Tumna, Co. Roscommon, *Journal of the Royal Society of Antiquaries of Ireland* 18, 107-111.

Wakeman, W. F. 1889. On the Crannog and Antiquities of Lisnacroghera, near Broughshane, Co. Antrim (Second Notice), *Journal of the Royal Society of Antiquaries of Ireland* 19, 96-106.

Wakeman, W. F. 1891. On the Crannog and Antiquities of Lisnacroghera, near Broughshane, Co. Antrim (3rd Notice), *Journal of the Royal Society of Antiquaries of Ireland* 21, 542-545 and (4th Notice) 673-675.

Wallace, P. 1977. A prehistoric burial cairn at Ardcrony, Nenagh, Co. Tipperary, *North Munster Antiquarian Journal* 19, 3-20.

Walsh, A. 1987. Excavating the Black Pig's Dyke, *Emania* 3, 5-11.

Walsh, G. 1995. Iron Age Settlement in Co. Mayo, *Archaeology Ireland* 9, no. 2, 7-8.

Walsh, P. 1995. Structure and Deposition in Irish Wedge Tombs: an open and shut case?, in J. Waddell and E. S. Twohig (eds), *Ireland in the Bronze Age. Proceedings of the Dublin Conference, April 1995,* 113-127. Dublin.

Walshe, P. T. 1941. The Excavation of a Burial Cairn on Baltinglass Hill, Co. Wicklow, *Proceedings of the Royal Irish Academy* 46C, 221-236.

Warner, R. B. 1972. Clogher Demesne, in T. G. Delaney (ed.), *Excavations 1972,* 27-28. Belfast.

Warner, R. B. 1973. The Excavations at Clogher and their Context, *Clogher Record* 8, 5-12.

Warner, R. B. 1974. The Irish Bronze-Iron Transition, *Irish Archaeological Research Forum* 1, no. 2, 45-47.

Warner, R. B. 1974a. Clogher Demesne, in T. G. Delaney (ed.), *Excavations 1973,* 25. Belfast.

Warner, R. B. 1974b. Clogher Demesne, in T. G. Delaney (ed.), *Excavations 1974,* 27. Belfast.

Warner, R. B. 1976. Some observations on the context and importation of exotic material in Ireland, from the first century B.C. to the second century A.D., in Colloquium on Hiberno-Roman Relations and Material Remains, *Proceedings of the Royal Irish Academy* 76C, 267-292.

Warner, R. B. 1976a. Clogher Demesne, in T. G. Delaney (ed.), *Excavations 1975-76,* 19. Belfast.

Warner, R. B. 1982. The Broighter Hoard: a reappraisal, and the iconography of the collar, in B. G. Scott (ed.), *Studies on Early Ireland. Essays in honour of M. V. Duignan,* 29-38. Belfast.

Warner, R. B. 1983. Ireland, Ulster and Scotland in the earlier Iron Age, in A. O'Connor and D. V. Clarke (eds), *From the Stone Age to the 'Forty-Five. Studies presented to R. B. K. Stevenson,* 160-187. Edinburgh.

Warner, R. B. 1988. The Archaeology of Early Historic Irish Kingship, in S. T. Driscoll and M. R. Nieke (eds), *Power and Politics in Early Medieval Britain and Ireland,* 47-68. Edinburgh.

Warner, R. B. 1988a. Clogher Demesne, in Excavations Bulletin 1977-1979, *The Journal of Irish Archaeology* 4, 78.

Warner, R. B. 1991. Cultural Intrusions in the Early Iron Age: some notes, *Emania* 9, 44-52.

Warner, R. B. 1993. Irish Prehistoric Goldwork: a provisional analysis, *Archeomaterials* 7, 101-113.

Warner, R. B. 1994. The Navan Complex: a new schedule of sites and finds, *Emania* 12, 39-44.

Warner, R. B. 1994a The Navan Archaeological Complex: a Summary, in J. P. Mallory and G. Stockman (eds), *Ulidia. Proceedings of the First International Conference on the Ulster Cycle of Tales,* 165-170. Belfast.

Warner, R. B. 1994b. *Emania Varia* I, *Emania* 12, 66-72.

Warner, R. B. 1995. Tuathal Techtmar: A Myth or Ancient Literary Evidence for a Roman Invasion?, *Emania* 13, 22-32.

Warner, R. B. 1996. Navan and Apollo, *Emania* 14, 77-81.

Warner, R. B., Mallory, J. P. and Baillie, M. G. L. 1990. Irish Early Iron Age Sites: a Provisional Map of Absolutely Dated Sites, *Emania* 7, 46-50.

Waterbolk, H. T. and van Zeist, W. 1981. A Bronze Age Sanctuary in the Raised Bog at Bargeroosterveld (DR.), *Helinium* 1, 5-19.

Waterman, D. M. 1963. A Neolithic and Dark Age site at Langford Lodge, Co. Antrim, *Ulster Journal of Archaeology* 26, 43-54.

Waterman, D. M. 1964. The Stone Circle, Cairn and Alignment at Drumskinny, Co. Fermanagh, *Ulster Journal of Archaeology* 27, 23-30.

Waterman, D. M. 1965. The Court Cairn at Annaghmare, Co. Armagh, *Ulster Journal of Archaeology* 28, 3-46.

Waterman, D. M. 1968. Cordoned Urn Burials and Ring-ditch at Urbalreagh, Co. Antrim, *Ulster Journal of Archaeology* 31, 25-32.

Waterman, D. M. 1975. A Bronze Age Habitation Site at Sheepland, Co. Down, *Ulster Journal of Archaeology* 38, 85-87.

Waterman, D. M. 1978. The Excavation of a Court Cairn at Tully, County Fermanagh, *Ulster Journal of Archaeology* 41, 3-14.

Weatherup, D. R. M. 1975. Armagh County Museum, Archaeological Acquisitions, 1960-1974, *Journal of the Royal Society of Antiquaries of Ireland* 105, 5-20.

Weir, D. A. 1987. Palynology and the Environmental History of the Navan Area, *Emania* 3, 34-43.

Weir, D. A. 1989. A Radiocarbon Date from the Navan Fort Ditch, *Emania* 6, 34-35.

Weir, D. A. 1993. Dark Ages and the pollen record, *Emania* 11, 21-30.

Weir, D. A. 1994. The Environment of Emain Macha, in J. P. Mallory and G. Stockman (eds), *Ulidia: Proceedings of the First International Conference on the Ulster Cycle of Tales*, 171-180. Belfast.

Weir, D. A. 1995. A palynological study of landscape and agricultural development in County Louth from the second millennium BC to the first millennium AD, *Discovery Programme Reports* 2, 77-126.

Weir, D. A. and Conway, M. 1988. Haughey's Fort: A Preliminary Palaeobotanical Analysis, *Emania* 4, 28-31.

Whelan, C. B. 1952. *A Bone Industry from the Lower Bann*. Belfast.

Whitfield, N. 1993. A massive marker for the Banagher Hoard, *Archaeology Ireland* 7, no. 2, 9-11.

Whittle, A. 1990. Prolegomena to the study of the Mesolithic-Neolithic transition in Britain and Ireland, in D. Cahen and M. Otte (eds), *Rubané et Cardial. Actes du Colloque de Liège, novembre 1988*, 209-227. Liège.

Wilde. W. R. 1850. *The Beauties of the Boyne and its Tributary the Blackwater* (Second edition). Dublin.

Wilde, W. R. 1857. *Catalogue of the Antiquities of Stone, Earthen, and Vegetable Materials in the Museum of the Royal Irish Academy*. Dublin.

Wilde, W. R. 1861. *Catalogue of the Antiquities of Animal Materials and Bronze in the Museum of the Royal Irish Academy*. Dublin.

Wilde, W. R. 1862. *Catalogue of the Antiquities of Gold in the Museum of the Royal Irish Academy*. Dublin.

Williams, B. B. 1978. Excavations at Lough Eskragh, County Tyrone, *Ulster Journal of Archaeology* 41, 37-48.

Williams, B. B. 1980. Bronze Age Stone Moulds from Sultan, County Tyrone, *Ulster Journal of Archaeology* 43, 102-103.

Williams, B. B. 1983. A wooden bucket found near Carrickmore, County Tyrone, *Ulster Journal of Archaeology* 46, 150-151.

Williams, B. B. 1984. Excavations at Kilsmullan, County Fermanagh, *Ulster Journal of Archaeology* 47, 5-8.

Williams, B. B. 1985. Excavations at Drumnakeel, County Antrim, *Ulster Journal of Archaeology* 48, 69-80.

Williams, B. B. 1986. Excavations at Altanagh, County Tyrone, *Ulster Journal of Archaeology* 49, 33-88.

Williams, B. B. 1987. A Passage Tomb at Craigs, Co. Antrim, *Ulster Journal of Archaeology* 50, 129-33.

Williams, B. B. and Wilkinson, J. L. 1988. Excavation of a Bronze Age Cist at Knockroe, County Tyrone, *Ulster Journal of Archaeology* 51, 85-90.

Williams, B. B., Wilkinson, J. L. and Magee, R. W. 1992. Bronze Age Burials at Kilcroagh, County Antrim, and Faience Beads in Ireland, *Ulster Journal of Archaeology* 54-55, 48-60.

Williams, E. 1989. Dating the introduction of food production into Britain and Ireland, *Antiquity* 63, 510-521.

Willmot, G. F. 1938. Three burials sites at Carbury, Co. Kildare, *Journal of the Royal Society of Antiquaries of Ireland* 68, 130-142.

Willmot, G. F. 1939. Two Bronze Age Burials at Carrowbeg North, Belclare, Co. Galway, *Journal of the Galway Archaeological and Historical Society* 18, 121-140.

Wilson, T. G. 1942. *Victorian Doctor. Being the Life of Sir William Wilde*. London.

Woodman, P. C. 1967. A flint hoard from Killybeg, *Ulster Journal of Archaeology* 30, 8-14.

Woodman, P. C. 1977. Recent excavations at Newferry, Co. Antrim, *Proceedings of the Prehistoric Society* 43, 155-199.

Woodman, P. C. 1978. The chronology and economy of the Irish Mesolithic: some working hypotheses, in P. Mellars (ed.), *The Early Postglacial Settlement of Northern Europe*, 333-369. London.

Woodman, P. C. 1978a. *The Mesolithic in Ireland*, British Archaeological Reports 58. Oxford.

Woodman, P. C. 1983. The Glencloy Project in Perspective, in T. Reeves-Smyth and F. Hamond (eds), *Landscape Archaeology in Ireland*, British Archaeological Reports 116, 25-34. Oxford.

Woodman, P. C. 1985. *Excavations at Mount Sandel 1973-77*. Belfast.

Woodman, P. C. 1985a. The Mesolithic in Munster; a preliminary assessment, in C. Bonsall (ed.), *The Mesolithic in Europe*, 116-24. Edinburgh.

Woodman, P. C. 1985b. Prehistoric Settlement and Environment, in K. J. Edwards and W. P. Warren (eds), *The Quaternary History of Ireland*, 251-278. London.

Woodman, P. C. 1985c. Mobility in the Mesolithic of Northwestern Europe: an alternative explanation, in T. Douglas Price and J. A. Brown (eds), *Prehistoric Hunter-Gatherers. The Emergence of Cultural Complexity*, 325-339. London.

Woodman, P. C. 1986. Why Not an Irish Upper Palaeolithic?, in D. A. Roe (ed.), *Studies in the Upper Palaeolithic of Britain and Northwest Europe*, British Archaeological Reports, International Series 296, 43-54. Oxford.

Woodman, P. C. 1987. The Impact of Resource Availability on Lithic Industrial Traditions in Prehistoric Ireland, in P. Rowley-Conwy, M. Zvelebil and H. P. Blankholm (eds), *Mesolithic Northwest Europe: Recent Trends*, 138-146. Sheffield.

Woodman, P. C. 1992. Excavations at Mad Man's Window, Glenarm, Co. Antrim: Problems of Flint Exploitation in East Antrim, *Proceedings of the Prehistoric Society* 58, 77-106.

Woodman, P. C. 1993. The Prehistory of South-West Ireland – An Archaeological Region or a State of Mind?, in E. S. Twohig and M. Ronayne (eds), *Past Perceptions. The Prehistoric Archaeology of South-West Ireland*, 6-15. Cork.

Woodman, P. C. 1995. Who possesses Tara? Politics in archaeology in Ireland, in P. J. Ucko (ed.), *Theory in Archaeology. A world perspective*, 278-297. London.

Woodman, P. C. 1996. Archaeology on the edge: learning to fend for ourselves, in T. Pollard and A. Morrison (eds), *The Early Prehistory of Scotland,* 152-161. Edinburgh.

Woodman, P. C. and Anderson, E. 1990. The Irish Later Mesolithic: a Partial Picture, in P. M. Vermeersch and P. van Peer (eds), *Contributions to the Mesolithic in Europe,* 377-387. Leuven.

Woodman, P. C. and Griffiths, D. A. 1988. The Archaeological Importance of Flint Sources in Munster, *Journal of the Cork Historical and Archaeological Society* 93, 66-72.

Woodman, P. C. and Johnson, G. 1996. Excavations at Bay Farm 1, Carnlough, Co. Antrim, and the Study of the 'Larnian' Technology, *Proceedings of the Royal Irish Academy* 96C, 137-235.

Woodman, P. C. and Monaghan, N. 1993. From Mice to Mammoths: Dating Ireland's Earliest Faunas, *Archaeology Ireland* 7, no. 3, 31-33.

Woodman, P. C. and O'Brien, M. 1993. Excavations at Ferriter's Cove, Co. Kerry: an interim statement, in E. S. Twohig and M. Ronayne (eds), *Past Perceptions. The Prehistoric Archaeology of South-West Ireland,* 25-34. Cork.

Woodman, P. C. and Scannell, M. 1993. A Context for the Lough Gur Lithics, in E. S. Twohig and M. Ronayne (eds), *Past Perceptions. The Prehistoric Archaeology of South-West Ireland,* 53-62. Cork.

Woodman, P. C., Doggart, R. and Mallory, J. P. 1992. Excavations at Windy Ridge, Co. Antrim, 1981-82, *Ulster Journal of Archaeology* 54-55, 18-35.

Woodman, P. C., McCarthy, M. and Monaghan, N. 1997. The Irish Quaternary Fauna Project, *Quaternary Science Reviews* 16, 129-159.

Wright, E. P. 1900. Notes on some Irish antiquities deposited with the Academy, *Proceedings of the Royal Irish Academy* 6, 283-288.

Yates, M. J. 1985. Restoration of the Cuilbane Stone Circle, Garvagh, County Londonderry, and the discovery of a cache of flints, *Ulster Journal of Archaeology* 48, 41-50.

Zvelebil, M. 1994. Plant Use in the Mesolithic and its Role in the Transition to Farming, *Proceedings of the Prehistoric Society* 60, 35-74.

Zvelebil, M. and Green, S. W. 1992. Looking at the Stone Age in south-east Ireland, *Archaeology Ireland* 6, no. 1, 20-23.

Zvelebil, M., Macklin, M. G., Passmore, D. G. and Ramsden, P. 1996. Alluvial Archaeology in the Barrow Valley, Southeast Ireland: the 'Riverford Culture' Revisited, *The Journal of Irish Archaeology* 7, 13-40.

Zvelebil, M., Moore, J. A., Green, S. W. and Henson, D. 1987. Regional Survey and the Analysis of Lithic Scatters: a case study from southeast Ireland, in P. Rowley-Conwy, M. Zvelebil and H. P. Blankholm (eds), *Mesolithic Northwest Europe: Recent Trends,* 9-32. Sheffield.

Index